S0-BPP-676

Essentials of Information Processing

SECOND EDITION

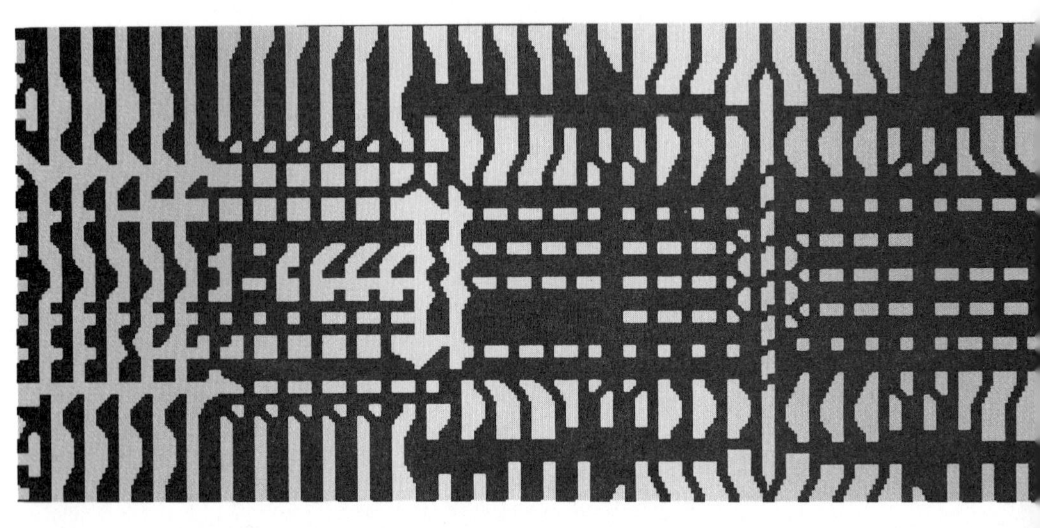

MARILYN BOHL

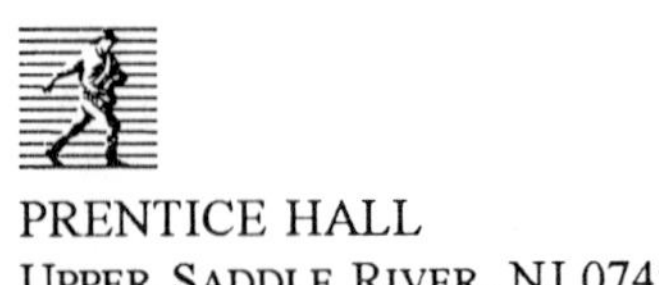

PRENTICE HALL
Upper Saddle River, NJ 07458

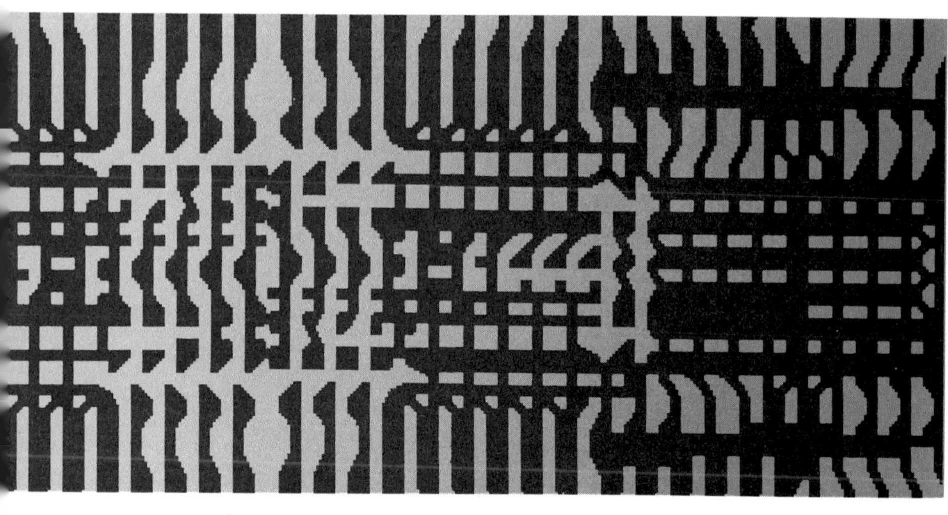

Essentials of Information Processing

SECOND EDITION

Library of Congress Cataloging-in-Publication Data

Bohl, Marilyn
Essentials of information processing / Marilyn Bohl.—2nd ed.
p. cm.
ISBN 0-02-311880-6
1. Electronic data processing. 2. Electronic digital computers.
I. Title.
QA76.B578 1990
004—dc20 89-13184
CIP

Editors: Charles E. Stewart, Jr., Johnna Barto, Mary Konstant
Production Service: York Production Services
Production Manager: Ann Berlin
Text Design: York Production Services
Chapter Opening Art: Kristin Nelson Design
Cover Design and Illustration: Brian Sheridan
Photo Researcher: Stuart Kenter
Illustrations: House of Graphics, York Production Services

This book was set in Simoncini Garamond by York Graphic Services.

© 1990 by Prentice-Hall, Inc.
A Simon & Schuster Company
Upper Saddle River New Jersey 07458

Earlier edition copyright © 1986 by Macmillan Publishing Company

All rights reserved. No part of this book may be reproduced, in any form or by any means, without permission in writing from the publisher.

Printed in the United States of America

10 9 8 7 6 5

ISBN 0-02-311880-6

Prentice-Hall International (UK) Limited, *London*
Prentice-Hall of Australia Pty. Limited, *Sydney*
Prentice-Hall Canada Inc., *Toronto*
Prentice-Hall Hispanoamericana, S.A., *Mexico*
Prentice-Hall of India Private Limited, *New Delhi*
Prentice-Hall of Japan, Inc., *Tokyo*
Simon & Schuster Asia Pte. Ltd., *Singapore*
Editora Prentice-Hall do Brasil, Ltda., *Rio de Janeiro*

Preface

This book, *Essentials of Information Processing,* second edition, is designed to help you learn more about computers. When you've completed the book, you'll know something about how computers work. You'll know a good deal more about how computers are being used—by individuals, in businesses and other organizations, throughout society.

Initially released in 1986, *Essentials of Information Processing* is used today in colleges, universities, and businesses in the United States and Canada. Throughout these areas, there are persons whose needs are best served by a book that adheres to the highest standards of technical accuracy and up-to-dateness with respect to computing technologies. These persons need a book that focuses more on where, why, and how computers are being used than on technical details. Ideally, the book should be user- and application-oriented. I wrote the first and second editions of this book, *Essentials of Information Processing,* with the needs of these persons in mind.

Many changes in computing and information systems have occurred during the four years since the first edition was published. Computers themselves are much smaller yet much more powerful. And they really are appearing everywhere. User-friendly graphic interfaces are encouraging more and more people to interact directly with computers in doing their jobs. Personal computers and workstations are as prevalent as typewriters in many businesses. Route salespeople use handheld computers to record their orders and deliveries at local supermarkets. Insurance agents bring lap-top computers into our homes. The computer systems of one organization employ techniques of electronic data interchange (EDI) to communicate directly with the computers of other organizations for order entry, billing, shipment, and payment purposes. These changes are reflected in the second edition of *Essentials of Information Processing.*

Productivity is a major issue in business environments, and it's a major issue in the use of computers in those environments. Organizations are applying computer-assisted software engineering (CASE) tools to plan their use of computers and then to develop the instructions needed to direct them. You'll learn about such tools, and you'll see how fourth generation languages (4GL's), natural languages, and object-oriented languages are making it easier and easier to use computers. Data, and information derived from that data, are being increasingly recognized as critical resources. This second edition is designed to help you understand why.

Because computers are so prevalent in our society, we may read about them in our daily newspapers. Concepts related to the "look and feel" of computers have become legal issues. Computer viruses have penetrated nationwide governmental and university communication networks. Concerns about the security and privacy of data about us that's stored in computer databases are being debated in our legislatures. As members of society, we need to understand these topics. Changes and enhancements throughout the second edition of *Essentials of Information Processing* will help you do so.

This book has unique features designed to make your study of computing both effective and enjoyable. Highlighted sentences alert you to key ideas; they serve either as prep notes for what you're about to read or as reinforcements for what you've just read and should remember. Short paragraphs in the margins complement the basic textual information. They provide additional insights and practical perspectives you might miss otherwise.

The mini-cases, or application briefs, were chosen carefully from a wealth of real-world application materials I've assembled over time. You'll read about computer uses in manufacturing, at fast-food restaurants, for city planning, in fire fighting, in sports, and so on. You'll gain some very practical career insights as you do so. The computing field is exciting, ever-changing, and expanding at an incredible rate. You'll share in that excitement as you study *Essentials of Information Processing.*

To make your studying easier, a topical outline of chapter content is included at the beginning of each chapter. A brief but complete summary of key points and discussion questions are included at the end of each chapter. A comprehensive glossary of terms is combined with the index at the back of the book.

Additional study helps are provided in the *Study Guide* to *Essentials of Information Processing,* which comes in two editions—one for those who are learning about computing in a traditional class setting and another for those who are using *Essentials* together with *The New Literacy,* a telecourse consisting of half-hour video lessons about computers and their uses. *The New Literacy* was produced under the leadership of the Southern California Consortium for Community College Television. It employs a full range of techniques to enhance learning—documentary sequences, on-location interviews, demonstration closeups, nationwide filming of real-world uses of computers, and computer animation, to name a few. Working with the Consortium staff was a stimulating and rewarding experience for me, and provided many opportunities to reinforce the textual materials by means of the video media.

For those of you who want to try your hand at program development, a BASIC appendix is included in *Essentials of Information Processing.* It guides you step-by-step in learning to use the computer as a tool in problems solving.

Instructors who are using this book will find general teaching guidelines in the *Instructor's Guide* to *Essentials of Information Processing.* A comprehensive set of transparency masters and a special, color set of ready-to-use transparencies are also provided. For students and instructors who want to supplement the study of *Essentials* with actual hands-on computing experiences using ready-to-run software, supporting software is available from the publisher. A testbank developed especially for *Essentials of Information Processing* is also available (in printed or machine-readable form) to qualified instructors.

Sincere thanks are due to the hundreds of students and teachers who have helped me to understand their wants and needs in computing instruction. A special note of appreciation is extended to those who served as reviewers of this manuscript as it was developed.

Stuart Kenter's photo research helped to build this book as a vibrant, living expression of computers in action. Mary Konstant coordinated the efforts of many of us throughout the multifaceted steps of development and production. Marilyn James managed the many details of the book's production. To these individuals and others whose names are unknown to me, I offer very sincere thanks.

Marilyn Bohl

About the Author

A list of Marilyn Bohl's professional activities might make one pause and wonder where she finds the time to pursue all her interests. Marilyn is an extremely dedicated and energetic person, with an impressive string of accomplishments to her credit.

Marilyn is an award-winning, 19-year IBM professional. Throughout the 1980s, she was responsible for advanced database development within IBM's General Products Division and product manager for IBM's relational database management system, DATABASE2 (DB2). Currently, Marilyn is vice president of engineering at INGRES Corporation, an Alameda, California-based firm that ranks among the "top 20" independent software vendors in terms of annual revenues. She is a member of the Technical Advisory Board of NUCLEUS International and serves on the Board of Directors of The Relational Institute.

Marilyn is experienced in software design, system and application programming, database concepts, and customer data-processing education and documentation. She is the author of nine books on data processing, programming, and related topics, which are widely used by colleges and universities throughout the world. A former teacher, Marilyn is sympathetic to the needs of educators and dedicated to helping students learn more about the use of computers and about computer-related careers. In her "spare" time, she is a jogger, a country music fan, and a pro football enthusiast.

Contents

Preface v

1 Computers and Their Uses 1

Data Processing 2
Computer-Aided Design 4
Computer-Aided Manufacturing 5
Computers and Space 11
Computers in Medicine 13
Computers and the Law 16
Computers and Finance 17
Computers in Education 20
Computers in Homes 22
Employment Opportunities 25
Chapter Summary 27
Discussion Questions 28

2 The Computer as a System 31

Basic Concepts 32
Stored Programs 35
Microcode 37
Functional Units 39
- The Processor Unit 41
- Secondary-Storage Devices 43
- Input and Output Devices 43

Communicating with the Computer 45
- Signing On 45
- Entering and Running the Program 47
- Signing Off 49

Chapter Summary 50
Discussion Questions 51

3 Entering Data 53

Punched Cards 55
Punched Paper Tape 57
Other Keyed Input 57
- Key-to-Tape Devices 57
- Key-to-Disk Devices 58
- Key-to-Diskette Devices 60

Magnetic-Ink Character Recognition 61
Optical Character Recognition 63
- Optical Marks 63
- Bar Codes 64
- Optical Characters 65
- Handwritten Data 66

Scanners 66
Voice-Input Units 68
Mice and Other Pointing Devices 71
Remote Terminals 72
- Special-Purpose Devices 73
- Data-Collection Devices 75
- Portable Terminals 75
- Handheld Terminals 77

Chapter Summary 80
Discussion Questions 81

4 Obtaining Information 83

Printed Output 84
- Impact Printers 87
- Nonimpact Printers 89
- PostScript 93

Plotters 94
Visual-Display Output 95
Voice Output 100
Micrographics 103
Chapter Summary 105
Discussion Questions 106

5 Storing Data 109

Primary Storage 110
Internal Data Representation 111
- Binary Components 112
- Binary Notation 112

EBCDIC 113
ASCII 113
Storage Capacity 114
Storage Addresses and Accessing 116
Access Times and Cycle Times 116
Storage Components 117
Types of Memory 120
Secondary Storage 123
Storage and Data-Processing Methods 124
- Sequential Processing 124
- Direct Processing 124

Magnetic Tape 126
- Data Representation 128
- Writing on and Reading from Magnetic Tape 129
- Tape Products 131

Magnetic Disk 132
- Data Representation 133
- Writing on and Reading from Magnetic Disk 133
- Floppy Disk Drives 135
- Winchester Disk Drives 136
- Conventional Disk Drives 137

Optical Storage 137
- CD ROM 138
- WORM 138
- Erasable Optical Storage 139

A Perspective 139
Chapter Summary 140
Discussion Questions 142

6 Processing Data 145

The Processor 147
The Control Section 148
The Arithmetic/Logic Unit 150
Registers 150
Instruction Counter 153
Adders 153
Stored-Program Instructions 154
Instruction Execution 158
- I-Time 158
- E-Time 160

Serial and Parallel Operations 160
Fixed-Length and Variable-Length Operations 162
Synchronous and Asynchronous Operations 164
Microprocessors 166
Reduced Instruction Set Computing (RISC) 169
Chapter Summary 173
Discussion Questions 174

7 Microcomputers in Use 177

What's Included in a Microcomputer System 178
Handheld Computers 180
Lap-Top Portables 180
Home Computers 184
Personal Computers 188
Tandy/Radio Shack 190
Apple Computer 191
IBM and Others 195
Workstations 198
Selecting a Microcomputer 201
Finding Out What's Available 203
Chapter Summary 205
Discussion Questions 206

8 System Analysis and Design 209

What Is a System? 210
The System Development Cycle 211
The Participants 213
Problems and Opportunities 214
Preliminary Investigation 215
Detailed Investigation 215
Fact-Finding 216
Data Analysis and Evaluation 218
Estimating Costs and Benefits 220
System Proposal 225
Using CASE Tools 225
System Design 226
The Chief Programmer Team 226
System Flowcharting 228
Output, Input, File Design 229
Top-Down Design 231
Structure Charts 233
Design Review 235
Project Review 235
Chapter Summary 236
Discussion Questions 237

9 Developing Programs 239

A First Problem 240
System Analysis and Design 240
System Implementation 241
More about Flowcharting 245
Coding the Solution 247
Top-Down Programming 250
Structured Programming 251
Pseudocode 255
Checking Out the Program 257
Top-Down Testing 260
Product Certification 260
Documentation 263
System Evaluation 264
Chapter Summary 268
Discussion Questions 269

10 Programming Languages and Application Development Tools 271

Machine Language 273
Assembler Languages 274
High-Level Programming Languages 276
FORTRAN 280
COBOL 283

PL/I 286
BASIC 288
Pascal 289
C 292
RPG 293
Fourth-Generation Languages 293
Natural Languages 296
Object-Oriented Languages 296
Selecting a Language 298
Chapter Summary 299
Discussion Questions 300

11 Application and System Software 303

System Software 304
Application Software 305
The Demand for Software 307
Early History of Software 308
Online Direct-Access Systems 311
Multitasking, or Multiprogramming 313
Integration and Windowing 315
Multiprocessing 317
Real-Time Systems 319
Time Sharing 320
- Types of Time-Sharing Systems 321
- Approaches to Time Sharing 322

Virtual Storage 324
Virtual Machines 326
Portable Operating Systems 327
Chapter Summary 332
Discussion Questions 333

12 Managing Data 335

File Systems 336
- Sequential 341
- Direct 341
- Indexed Sequential 341

Data Management Systems 342
The Database Approach 343
Database Design 344
Logical Data Structures 345
DBMS 350
SQL 354
Management Information Systems 354
- The Makeup of an MIS 355
- MIS Implementation 357

Decision Support Systems 358
Remote Databases 359
Distributed Databases 360
Chapter Summary 362
Discussion Questions 363

13 Data Communications and Office Automation 365

What It Takes to Communicate 367
Data Transmission Options 369
- Analog or Digital Transmission 369
- Start/Stop (Asynchronous) or Synchronous Transmission 371
- Simplex, Half-Duplex, or Full-Duplex Transmission 372

Communication Service Offerings 372
A Changing Telecommunications Industry 375

Distributed Processing; Cooperative Processing 380
Automating Office Functions 382
Workgroup Communications 384
Electronic Data Interchange 388
Teleconferencing 389
Computing Services 391
Chapter Summary 394
Discussion Questions 395

14 Computing Issues and Impacts 397

Computing and Organizations 398
Computing and Jobs 400
Telecommuting 402
Robotic Systems 404
Artificial Intelligence 407
Individualism and the Right of Privacy 411
Computer Crime 416
Organizational Protection Mechanisms 420
Legal Protection Mechanisms 422
- Trade Secrets 422
- Trademarks 422
- Copyrights 422
- Patents 424

Social Dependency and Vulnerability 424
Environmental Protection Mechanisms 427
A Perspective 429
Chapter Summary 430
Discussion Questions 431

BASIC Appendix: Using the Computer in Problem Solving 433

Glossary and Index 495

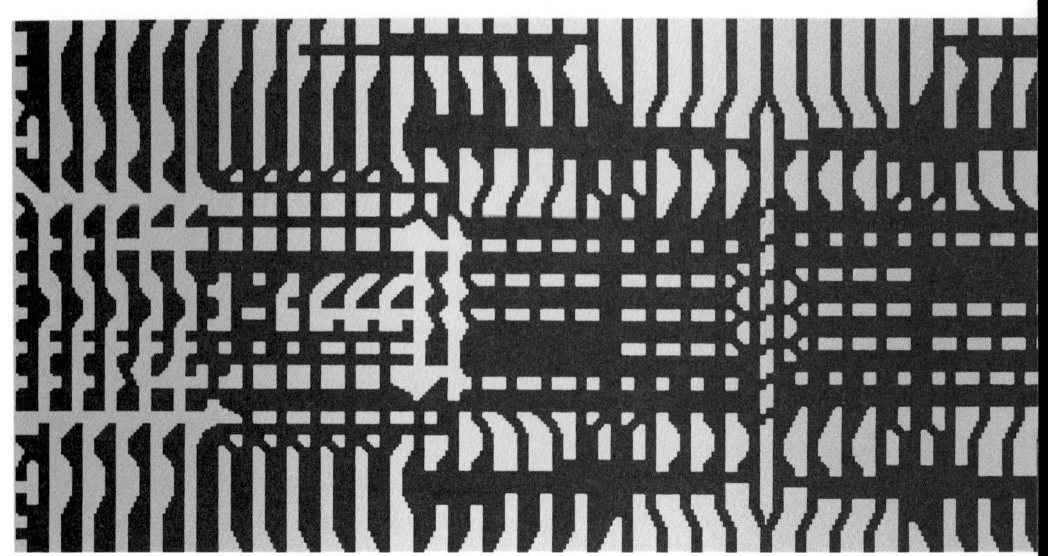

1 Computers and Their Uses

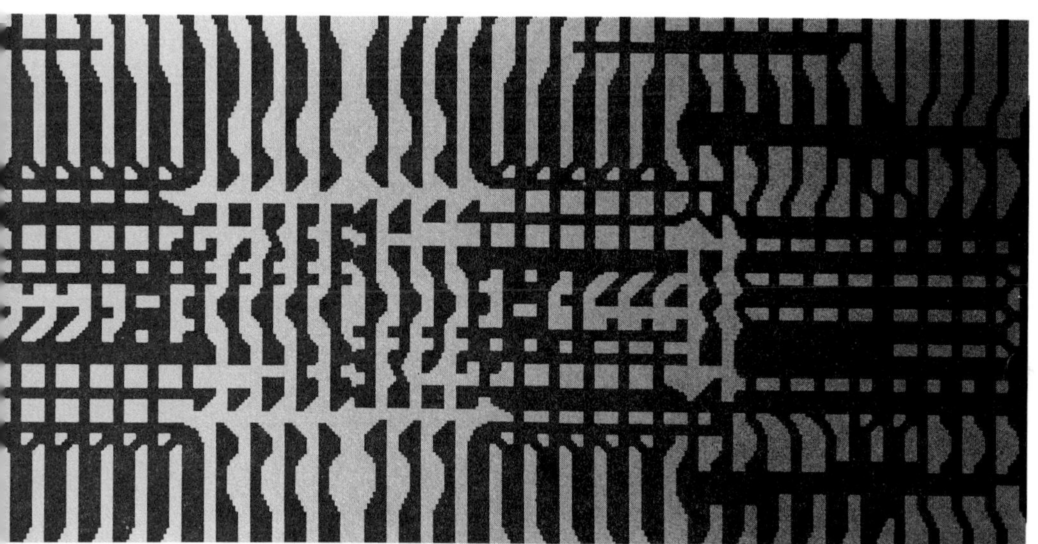

IN THIS CHAPTER

Data Processing
Computer-Aided Design
Computer-Aided Manufacturing
Computers and Space
Computers in Medicine
Computers and the Law
Computers and Finance
Computers in Education
Computers in Homes
Employment Opportunities

Every day you use tools. You need a certain key to unlock your bike padlock or your car door. A telephone puts you in contact with friends across town or across continents. Radio and television help you to learn about what's going on worldwide. This book is a tool to help you learn about computers. Computers may well be the most exciting, most powerful, most versatile tools yet developed.

Just as hammers, pulleys, cranes, and bulldozers extend our physical power, so computers extend our thinking power. Some of you may be "at home" (even literally) with computers; you use them as casually as you use pencil and paper. Others may be awed by computers—what are these fantastic machines everybody is talking about?

In fact, many of us use computers daily without even realizing we are doing so. Microprocessors—the "hearts" of today's smallest computers—are everywhere. Wristwatches, microwave ovens, automatic sprinkling systems, automobile carburetors, and electronic security systems contain them. Slide rules and pocket calculators are giving way to them. You may not be a grand master (or even an expert) at any computerized games, but you can probably learn to play most of them. Can you imagine blaming a hammer for hitting your thumb? Or an automobile for running a traffic light? Similarly, we can't blame a computer for mixing up class schedules, printing statements for bills that aren't owed, and so on. One purpose of this book is to help you understand why we must look beyond the computer to de-

termine who or what is responsible when things go right, or when things go wrong.

The phrase *computer literacy* has no single, universally accepted meaning. It means different things to different people. That should not surprise us since even the term *literacy* has several definitions. We may say that a literate person is one who can read and write, or one who demonstrates a basic ability to communicate. On the other hand, we may say a literate person is one who is especially knowledgeable, learned, or well read in a particular field or discipline.

In practice, scientific and technological literacy has come to mean the possession of (1) an in-depth knowledge in a chosen area of science or technology (say, botany, geology, or the electromagnetic spectrum), and (2) an understanding of the implications of that science or technology for individuals and for society. In keeping with this practice, we might choose to define *computer literacy* to be the knowledge and understanding one needs to function effectively within a given social role that directly or indirectly involves computers. With computers becoming so prevalent, the need to be computer literate confronts each and every one of us.

In this opening chapter, we look first at some simple examples of data processing. Then we look at some of the many, diverse ways computers are being used to process data. Finally, you're helped to think about job opportunities directly or indirectly involved with computers. The perspective you gain by studying this chapter will be useful in this course and in your daily exposure to computer applications.

Computer Literacy

"Computer science education now ranks with simple arithmetic, or literacy in the English language. A liberal education today requires computer literacy."

George Masiach, vice chancellor for research and former dean of engineering at the University of California, Berkeley (In: Irving, Carl, "The Hottest Course on Campus," *San Francisco Sunday Examiner and Chronicle,* November 8, 1981, p. A2)

DATA PROCESSING

Since very early times, we humans have searched continuously for efficient ways to obtain information. We want the facts. We want to manipulate those facts to obtain new facts, or results. Once we understand the results, we may decide we need other, related facts or results. We go after them. We manipulate them. Very soon, we become engulfed in a sea of paperwork.

Let's take a simple example. Suppose you're vacationing near Chicago. You wonder whether or not the Cubs are playing at home this weekend. If they are, you may want to find out when, where the ballpark is, and how to get there. Your quest for information may lead you to the TV sports news, area newspapers, phone books, maps, subway schedules, and so on. You calculate miles to be traveled and time to get there. You probably look up the opposing team's won/lost record and its current position in the league standings. A check of the weather forecast may be advisable.

Now let's consider a somewhat more formal situation involving paperwork. Doing so will increase our awareness of the manipulating of facts and figures that goes on in an ordinary business environment. Assume that Gray's Textiles is a rather large company that manufactures fabrics for the wholesale market. The research scientists in this company work daily to improve the quality of current materials; to develop new fabrics with greater resistance to wear, heat, and chemicals; to find easier ways to produce synthetic materials; and so on. These scientists record the data obtained from their experiments, use the data to make calculations, and summarize their findings in various recommendations and reports.

In the same company, the manufacturing department requires summarized data to control production. What items are needed? What raw materials must be purchased to produce the items? What people and machines are needed to meet current production goals?

The financial department of the company processes data to produce accurate records of the company's financial transactions. Accountants deal with vendors, invoices, purchase orders, shipping orders, customer statements, general ledgers, budgets, variance reports, annual reports, reports to stockholders . . . the list is endless. Together, these documents reflect the total worth and profitability of the company.

Data processing, the modern name for paperwork, is the collecting, processing, and distributing of facts and figures to achieve a desired result. The facts and figures are *data.* The equipment (devices) and procedures by which the result is achieved are part of a *data-processing system.* Today, many people think that all data-processing systems involve computers, but that's not true. In some data-processing systems, all work is done with pencil and paper; in others, the work is done by machines; in still others, people and machines work together. The machines may or may not be computers. (See Figure 1-1.)

***Data processing,* the modern name for paperwork, is the collecting, processing, and distributing of facts and figures to achieve a desired result.**

We can treat the terms *data* and *information* as synonyms, or we can distinguish between them by saying that data is raw material gathered from one or more sources, and that information is processed, or "finished," data. Generally, *information* implies data that is organized and meaningful to the person or group receiving it. Since knowledge and decision-making activities are important in many different areas, and at many different levels of detail, one person's information may be another person's data.

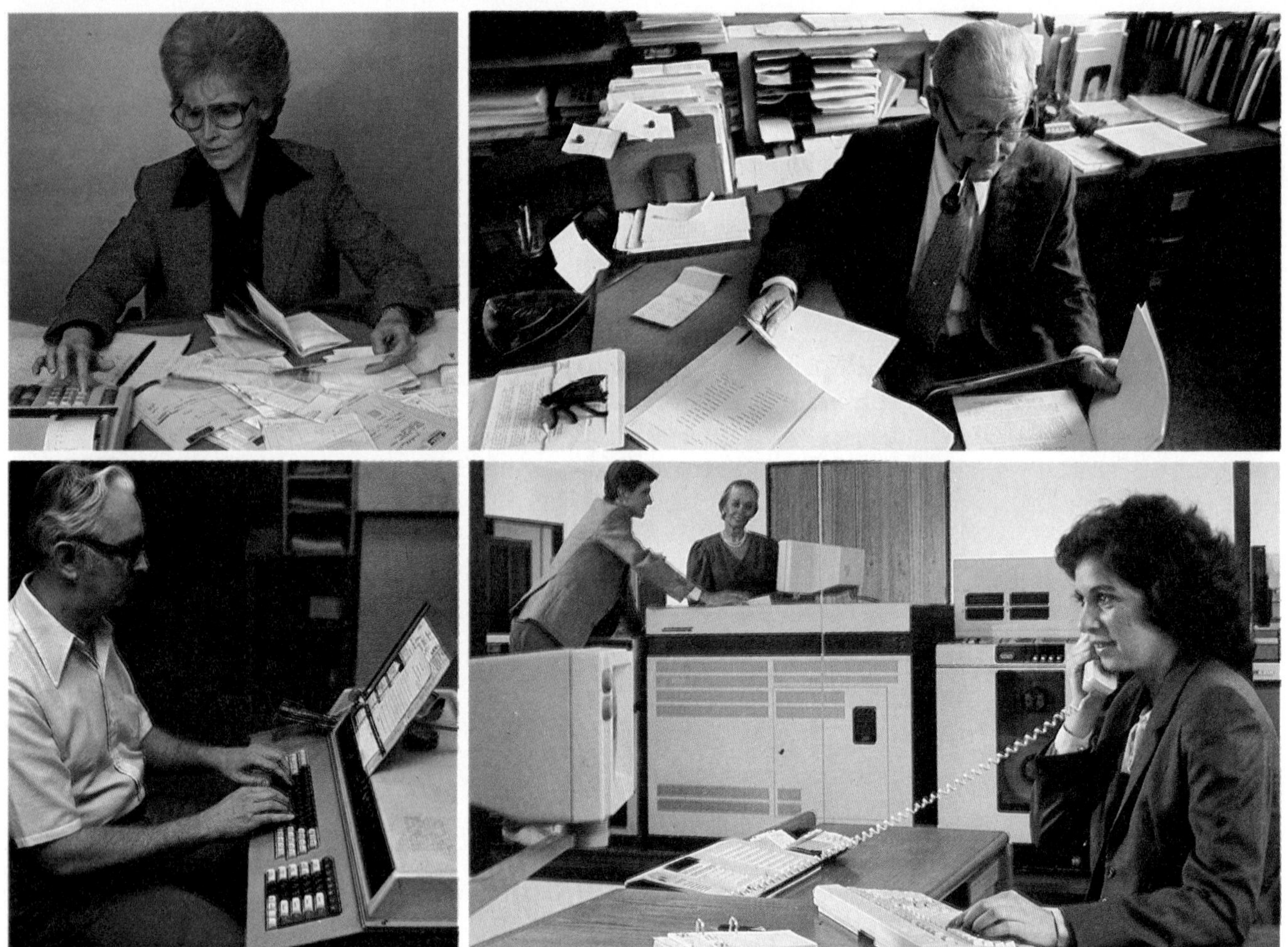

Figure 1-1 Data-processing systems vary widely, and may or may not include computers. (Courtesy [top left] Pick, Weber/Stock, Boston; [top right] Cary S. Wolinsky/Stock, Boston; [bottom left] Michael C. Hayman/Stock, Boston; [bottom right] Wang Laboratories, Inc.)

Computer-Aided Design

In today's business world, the pressure to beat one's competitors to the marketplace with new or improved products is intense. Both new firms and well-established ones are spending heavily on product research and development. *Computer-aided design (CAD)* techniques are being applied to cut the time required to conceive, design, and specify ("spec") a product in the first place—that is, to shorten the "front end" of the product development cycle. Engineers are using interactive CAD systems with high-resolution graphics capabilities to draw and analyze their designs for everything from children's toys to airplanes, from patio chairs to printed circuit boards containing the logic needed in today's most powerful computers. (See Figure 1-2.)

Both engineers and architects are using CAD systems to model ongoing, dynamic activities as well as static structures. For example, they often model traffic flow when designing large office complexes, shopping centers, and airports. Through interactive graphics, they develop detailed floor plans and create human-factored work centers (e.g., in kitchens or in office areas). The color schemes and interior decor for rooms can be chosen from a wide variety of alternatives. Then, both designers and clients can "walk through" the planned buildings and work centers. The computer generates graphics on the display screen from the perspectives of persons inside the buildings. When everyone is satisfied, architectural blueprints, contractual agreements, and orders for needed materials can be generated as printed output.

Computer-Aided Manufacturing

Product planning and control for even relatively simple items means dealing with raw material supply, inventory handling and storage, labor, work-center capacity, accounting, and many other factors. In the early 1960s, computers were first applied by manufacturing firms in the recording and processing of routine financial transactions. Employees received computer-generated paychecks; accounts-payable records were computerized; and so on. Shop foremen were still spending 50 to 75 percent of their time expediting, looking for materials, and in general, "putting out fires." Labor costs were on an ever-accelerating upward spiral.

In the 1970s, most if not all manufacturing firms faced the hard realities of increasing competition. Look what happened to audio equipment, cameras, calculators, and watches, they noted. How to increase *productivity* (the rate of finished output per unit of labor input) became, and remains, a major concern at all levels of business management.

How to increase productivity . . . became, and remains, a major concern at all levels of business management.

The acronym *MRP,* meaning *material requirements planning,* has received much attention since the late 1960s. Basically, MRP is a system that relates requirements for assembled products to an end product. It embraces a master production sched-

Figure 1-2 Computer-aided design systems allow engineers to specify design parameters of automobile components and test their designs before building physical prototypes. (Courtesy Chrysler Corporation)

6
IBM

COMPUTERIZED INVENTORY CONTROL

Manufacturers worldwide are using computers to determine and to maintain exactly the amount of supplies necessary for the manufacturing processes scheduled each day. Data on supplies received is entered into the computer. Supplies are then allocated and distributed, according to computer-generated instructions, to the plant and to production lines. This use of the computer minimizes the amount of storage space needed and the amount of capital tied up in inventory. It increases business flexibility and responsiveness to changing conditions. At some installations, computer-controlled inventory stocks have been cut as much as 75 percent with no loss of production or service, simply because the business operates with "just enough," and computers and personnel know what's on hand and where it's located. *(Photo courtesy Yasu Computer Plant/IBM Corporation)* ule for, say, a year, taking into account level of assembly and time requirements and making prompt adjustments when operations don't work out as planned. Various raw materials, components, and subassemblies from lower levels flow into the system and merge at higher and higher levels to become finished items.

On an automotive, TV, or typewriter assembly line, for example, hundreds of parts and subassemblies from all over the plant or elsewhere must converge in the final assembly area at the right time and place, and in the right sequence. Balancing the line for smooth, efficient production—that is, scheduling the manufacture, test, and movement of all parts and the assignments of workers—is a big job and a recurring one. It is a job that computers can do. They can also display or print reports that people on the shop floor need to manage the operation efficiently.

Today, some firms have moved beyond MRP to what's known as *MRP II,* or *manufacturing resource planning.* Here, all aspects of manufacturing (including not only production but also engineering, marketing, and finance) are tied together through one consistent set of numbers that can be analyzed by managers of all functions, for use in decision making. The numbers are financial numbers, expressed in dollars-and-cents terms, but they are derived directly from ongoing operations. This coordinated management was impossible before MRP II, when what was really happening on the plant floor bore little resemblance to the formal paperwork, or to what was supposed to be happening.

Computers can also take an active part in the physical control of manufacturing processes. *Numerical control (NC)* of machine tools was introduced in the late 1950s as a method of guiding a production machine through a complete manufacturing cycle by means of coded instructions recorded on a computer-generated NC tape. Once work has been placed in position on the machine, the coded instructions control the selection of the machine tools,

Contrary to what you might expect, robotic systems are not usually built to resemble humans. They are built to do work that might otherwise be done by humans, or not done at all.

feed rate, spindle speed, coolant setting, and the direction and distance of movements until the work is completed. A high-speed precision-drilling machine is a common example of a production machine often controlled by means of an NC tape. This is truly *computer-aided manufacturing (CAM).*

A step beyond the use of numerical control is the use of *robotic systems.* These are general-purpose machines that can do any of several tasks under the direction of stored sequences of instructions. The stored sequences of instructions are *computer programs.* Contrary to what you might expect, robotic systems are not usually built to resemble humans. They are built to do work that might otherwise be done by humans, or not done at all. Spray painting, spot welding, lifting, assembling, and packaging are some tasks that robots accomplish easily, without complaints, coffee breaks, sick days, or vacations. They can do fine work as

CAD/CAM

The aerospace industry pioneered in CAD because it had to: Planes became too big and too complicated to design with traditional tools and methods. At Chrysler, CAD/CAM played a key role in pulling the automaker back from the brink of bankruptcy. During the "farm crisis" of the 1980s, 150-year-old Deere & Co. saw its sales of farm equipment decrease from $4.7 billion in 1981 to $2.6 billion in 1986. The firm responded by simplifying and automating production processes. Inventory levels at its Ottumwa, Iowa, facility have been reduced by 58 percent, for example. The facility's break-even point is 22 percent less than it was in the early 1980s.

JUST IN TIME

Most of us have heard many stories about the excellence of Japan's manufacturing techniques. The quality of Japanese goods is said to be high. The price is right. One of the factors behind these achievements is the just-in-time (JIT) method of production. JIT was first implemented by Toyota in 1969 and is now used in one-third of plants in Japan. Its use is spreading.

In concept, JIT means that the components at various manufacturing stations in a production line proceed to the next stage of manufacturing just as they're needed. Hewlett-Packard's manufacturing site in Santa Clara, California, relies on JIT for most of its production. Employees at most stations on a line don't make parts until they check a display of red and green cards at the next station upstream. Most stations post one red card and one green card. The red card means that one additional part should be supplied for a safety margin. If the station posts two red cards, it's out of parts and needs a component immediately. Problems on the production line surface quickly. Management and/or workers are alerted to solve the problems, rather than to ignore or work around them.

JIT can increase product quality, improve material flow, and reduce work-in-process inventory. It allows rapid retooling for the production of new products because there is no built-in requirement to delay until surplus parts find their way through the production line into completed products. Many factories are seeking to improve their operations. The JIT concept and application software that supports it may help. *(Photo courtesy of Hewlett-Packard Company)*

200 mL
±5%
150
100
50

Figure 1-3 Computer-controlled robotic systems can do fine work as well as heavy work in plants and laboratories. (Courtesy Antonio Rosario/The Image Bank)

well as heavy work. (See Figure 1 3.) Given the decreasing costs of electronic components and circuitry, they are becoming less expensive rather than more costly. As we'll see, this means that small manufacturers as well as big auto, aerospace, and heavy-equipment companies can use them.

Today, major productivity gains are being achieved through combining the techniques of computer-aided design and computer-aided manufacturing in *CAD/CAM* applications. The data that a designer needs to specify the geometry of a part is also needed to determine how a cutting machine such as a lathe must be operated to shape the part. If all the data is stored in a computer-accessible database, engineering designs can be transferred directly to the manufacturing floor. By 1995, an estimated 190,000 CAD/CAM systems will be installed, doing mechanical design, civil engineering and architectural design, and electronic design and manufacture. (See Figure 1-4.)

The acronym *CIM* stands for *c*omputer-*i*ntegrated *m*anufacturing. It represents the tieing together of all of the tasks and systems of a manufacturing enterprise into an integrated whole. CAD, MRP II, NC, CAM, robotic systems, and other technologies are a part of it. So are word-processing, spreadsheets, and other office-automation applications. The ultimate objective of CIM is to transform the manufacturing enterprise into a modern, automated plant capable of producing superior products in a timely fashion at competitive prices. Many firms are positioning themselves to achieve this objective.

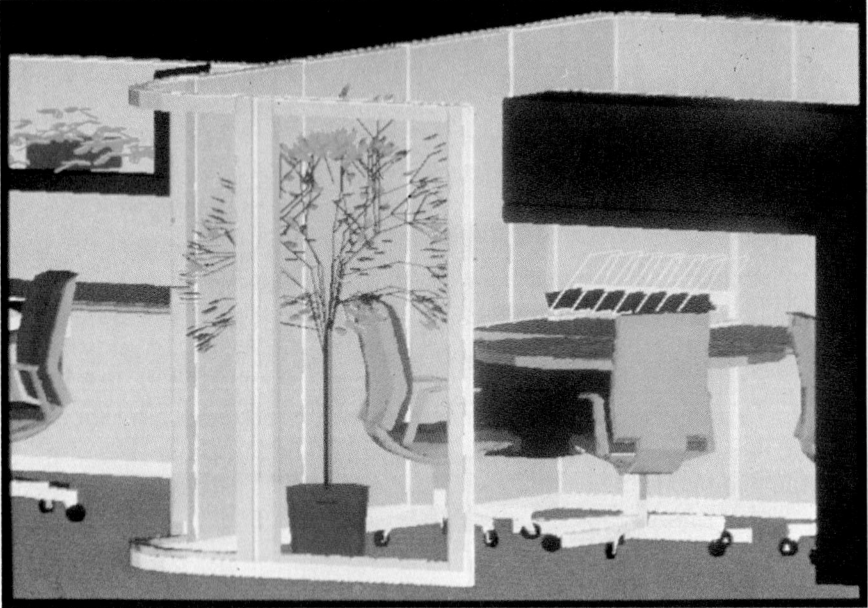

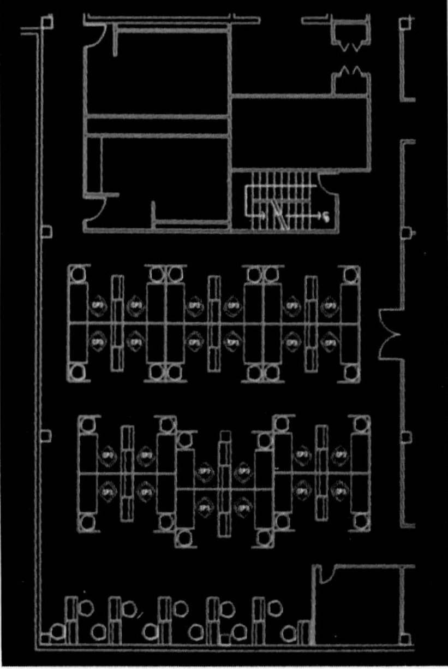

DESIGNING AN OFFICE

Computers are being used increasingly in architectural modeling. For example, a proposed model of an office can be viewed at many angles and from many distances with the aid of a computer. Space planning can also be done with computer help. Direct pathways, centrally located equipment centers and mail distribution points, ample space for each desk and for each chair, and so on—attention to every detail helps to insure that the normal flow of office activities will be carried out with speed and efficiency. Work can be fun in pleasant surroundings. *(Photos courtesy Intergraph Corporation)*

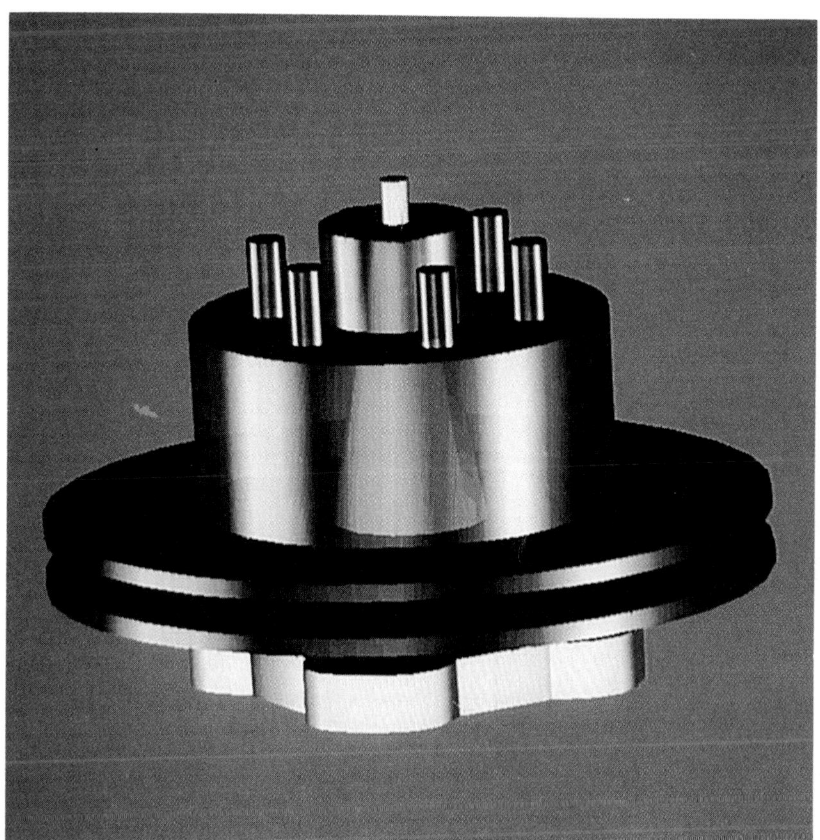

Figure 1-4 Solid modeling programs calculate physical properties, such as mass, volume, surface area, and center of gravity, of proposed products. They create models that can be displayed from many viewpoints during the design process. (Courtesy AUTODESK, Inc.)

Computers and Space

Without computers, the U.S. space program might never have come about. At the Kennedy Space Center, for example, a highly automated Launch Processing System (LPS) checked and rechecked thousands of bits of data, some as often as 100 times a second, during the 1981–82 space shuttle launching countdowns. Eight autonomous networks, each comprising up to 40 computers, participated. On board the Columbia orbiter were additional computers and associated display equipment. From prelaunch checkout through landing, these computers helped flight crews and controllers to monitor conditions, command and control the orbiter, and obtain status information.

Without computers, the U.S. space program might never have come about.

Practically speaking, there is no way an astronaut can take over a shuttle manually. The astronaut cannot assimilate and respond to the information needed to bring a heavy, powerless, 114-ton glider, traveling at 17,500 mph, out of orbit, then into a guided but blistering flight through the atmosphere, and into the turns that dissipate its speed. At 2500 feet, when the astronaut commander takes the stick for the orbiter's one-time-only chance to land, his or her every move is monitored by computers so

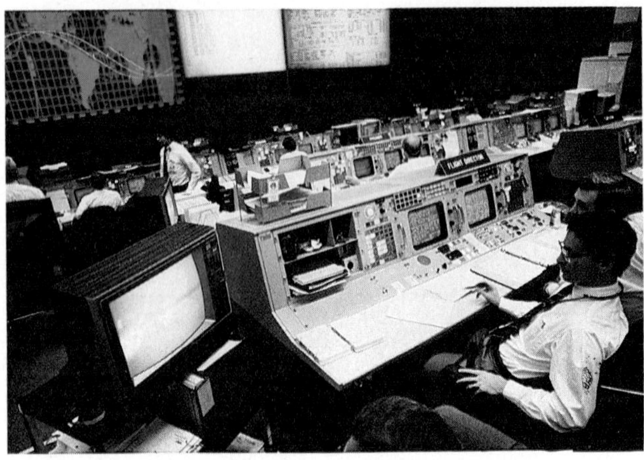

THE IMPOSSIBLE BECOMES ROUTINE

Few sights are as awesome or breathtaking to us as a space shuttle poised on its launching pad. Satellites and space shuttles may some day be commonplace, but they represent truly amazing engineering feats. Consider the vast amounts of data involved. During the design process, thousands of items of data are studied to reveal complex interrelationships of parts and functions. During each flight, myriad pieces of data must be collected and monitored. On the left above, the space shuttle orbiter Atlantis is launched from the Kennedy Space Center in Florida; on this May 1989 flight, Atlantis deployed the space probe Magellan on a 15-month journey to Venus to perform radar mapping operations. On the right above, an astronaut performs a space walk on an earlier space shuttle mission. Other astronauts and flight controllers at the Johnson Space Center in Houston (bottom) depend on computers throughout each launch countdown and in subsequent flight activities. *(Photos courtesy NASA)* that changes can be effected if required.

As awesome as these tasks are, the behind-the-scenes preparatory tasks that are basic to space flights are equally awesome. Before a spacecraft travels beyond Earth's gravity, goes into orbit, and even before it's built, computers are involved. Proposed characteristics of the spacecraft—shape, length, width, weight, exterior coating, power of thrust, and so on—are provided as input to a computer. Through simulation, the effects of gravity, thrust angles, weight loss with fuel burnup, and other environmental influences upon the proposed spacecraft are studied. If the spacecraft does not respond as desired, the characteristics can be changed and the simulation rerun. The computer completes within seconds or minutes intricate calculations that would take years to complete manually. *Computer-aided engineering (CAE),* which encompasses not only computer-aided design but also quality-control functions, process planning, and much more, has helped to make the U.S. space program a reality.

Computers in Medicine

In no area of human life is expert, personal service more essential than it is in medical care. Today, an electrocardiograph system containing a small computer can be wheeled to a patient's bedside. Within minutes, it can record and interpret an electrocardiogram (EKG). The EKG is a graph of the pulses that cause the patient's heart to beat. By interpreting the EKG, the computer helps the attending doctor to locate quickly any damaged or diseased heart areas. Proper treatment can then be prescribed.

At many hospitals, computers are being used to interpret medical X-rays. A CAT (computerized axial tomography) scanner takes many small X-ray views from slightly different positions about a patient's body. A computer combines all the X-ray pictures to form a cross-sectional view of the patient's body on a display screen.

Clinical laboratories that must deal with hundreds of chemical blood tests, tissue tests, urine tests, and so on, are putting computers to good use. In intensive care units, computers continuously monitor instruments and sensors attached to critically ill patients to detect and report any abnormalities.

Another machine containing a small computer, commonly known as a blood cell separator, can accept blood directly from donors or patients. The machine separates the blood into such major components as red cells, white cells, plasma, and platelets. Concentrates of the components are used in transfusions to control acute infections, plasma abnormalities, and other disorders. One pint of blood may go much further because the separated concentrates can be used exactly as needed. One patient may need only white blood cells; another may need only blood plasma.

Today's doctors, clinics, and hospitals could not get along without computers to help with administrative paperwork—insurance claims, patient billing, accounts receivable, payroll, inventory control, bed accounting, and the like. In hospital kitchens, menus are planned, food is ordered, and meals are cooked with computer help. From admission to discharge, data about a patient is added continually to the patient's history record. Doctors and nurses

PACEMAKERS KEEP THE BEAT

A normal heart has its own natural pacemaker. The pacemaker sends signals to the heart's four chambers, causing them to contract or beat. If a person's pacemaker no longer functions effectively, an artificial pacemaker can be implanted just below the skin, near the person's shoulder. A wire is routed from the pacemaker through a vein to the heart chamber. The pacemaker monitors the person's heart activity. If the natural pacemaker fails, the artificial pacemaker sends signals to cause the heart chambers to contract. Since 1958, artificial pacemakers have regulated the heartbeats of hundreds of thousands of people, allowing them to lead normal lives.

In the late 1970s, programmable pacemakers were developed. Cardiac physicians can now check a person's pacemaker and even make adjustments, such as changing the rate at which the heart beats, without having to surgically remove the device. One of the most advanced programmable pacemakers, developed by Cardiac Pacemakers, Inc. (CPI) of St.

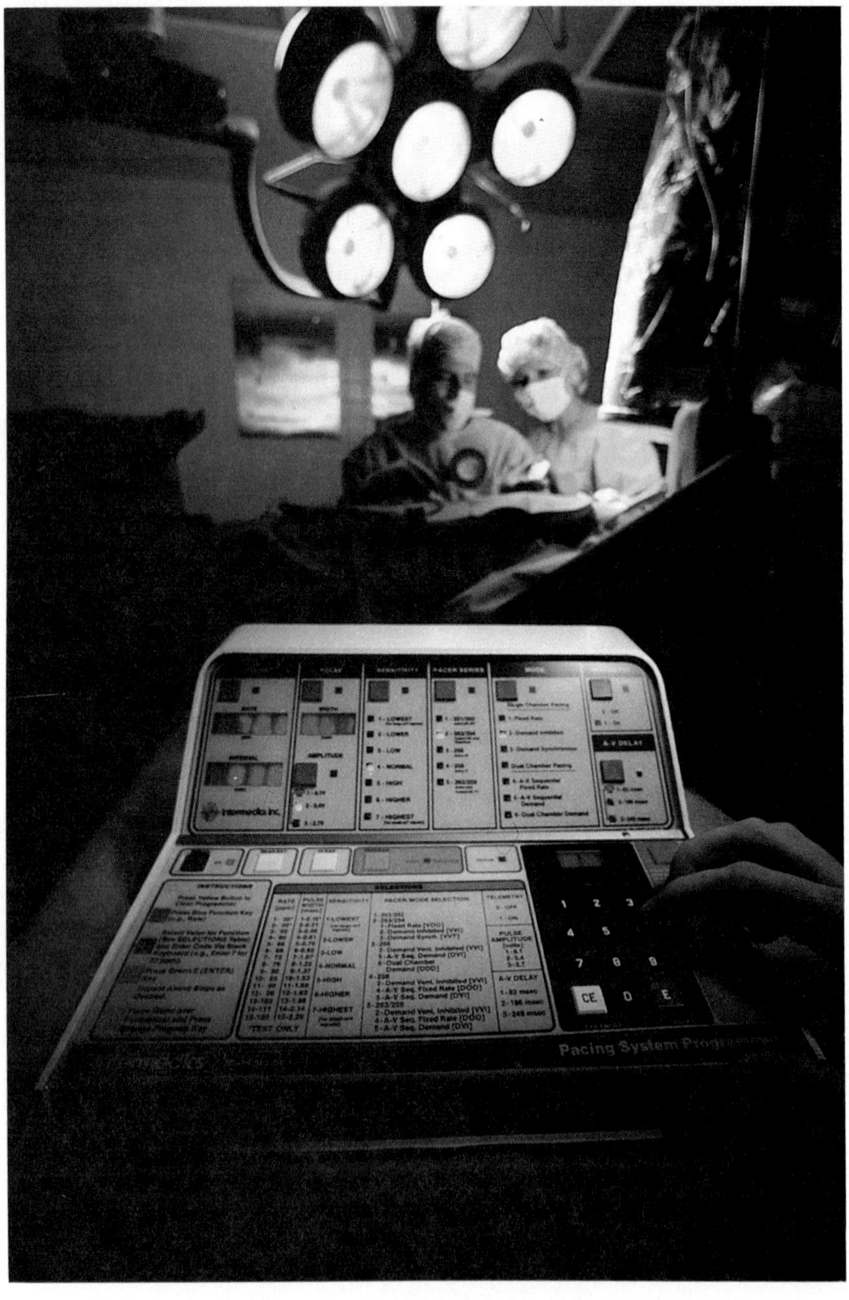
A-V DELAY
CE

Paul, Minnesota, uses a Hewlett-Packard personal computer coupled with a programmable wand reader to make adjustments.

To operate this system, the physician plugs the wand reader into the computer and holds the reader over a patient's chest where the pacemaker is implanted. The wand, in effect, asks the pacemaker how it's doing. The rate and sensitivity of the pacemaker are displayed on the visual-display screen of the computer system. If the physician decides that adjustments should be made, he or she need only enter the adjustments into the computer and press a button on the wand which then programs the pacemaker. The ultimate benefit belongs to the people with pacemakers: they are helped to lead busy, useful lives. *(Photo courtesy Gary Gladstone/The Image Bank)*

can access the patient's record to check the results of laboratory tests, to determine what drugs have been ordered from the pharmacy (or should be), and so on. By freeing doctors and nurses from routine clerical work, computers make it possible for them to give patients more personal attention. (See Figure 1-5.)

On an even broader scale, researchers are using computers to analyze thousands of medical records. They're studying the records to isolate causes of illnesses and to find relationships between people's habits or diets and certain diseases. For example, the link between cigarette smoking and lung cancer was proved with computer assistance.

A branch of the federal government charged with tracking cases of Acquired Immune Deficiency Syndrome (AIDS) is developing a national database of AIDS cases in cooperation with state and local health agencies. When a case occurs, the involved agency completes a 3-page questionnaire that serves as input to a central computer system. Microcomputer systems with database capabilities are being set up at the local agencies so that they can cross-check their data to be sure it's accurate, generate statistics for further analysis, and print summary reports.

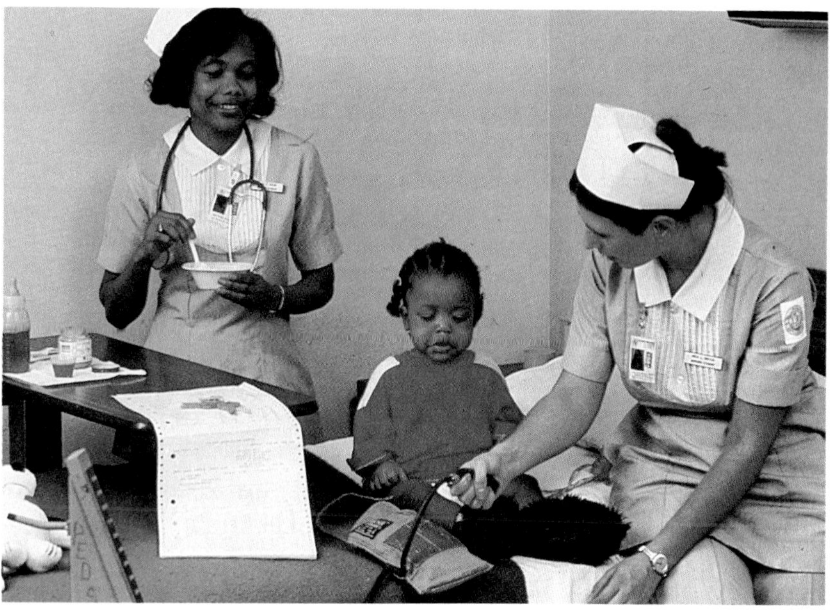

Figure 1-5 Hospital staff with ready access to current, complete information about their patients can give individual care and attention to each one of them. (Courtesy IBM Corporation)

Figure 1-6 Law enforcement officers at Houma, Louisiana, and similarly equipped facilities across the country obtain and share computerized information to help insure public safety. (Courtesy IBM Corporation)

Computers and the Law

In the late 1970s, the Bank of America building in Santa Barbara, California, was bombed. Evidence was collected, a suspect was identified, and the case was solved—with the help of a computer.

Among the collected evidence was a ceiling tile from the bank building containing bomb fragments and unburned explosives, a pipe from the suspect's garage, and soil from the suspect's shoes. These were taken to the Treasury Department's Bureau of Alcohol, Tobacco, and Firearms (ATF) Crime Laboratory. There, the material was chemically treated and exposed to radiation. The fragments embedded in the ceiling tile were made up of the same material as the pipe from the suspect's garage. The soil from the suspect's shoes matched the soil around the bank building. These findings were used as evidence in court.

In like manner, computers at the ATF Crime Lab are used frequently to analyze unidentified substances, check swabs from a suspect's hands for components of gunshot residue, determine the types of weapons used in misdeeds, and so on. The facilities are available to any law enforcement agency in the United States to aid in crimefighting. (See Figure 1-6.)

The FBI's computer system, known as the National Crime Information Center (NCIC), links 64,000 federal, state, and local law enforcement agencies. It contains millions of records about persons who have been officially accused of crimes. More than 300,000 queries are processed against the NCIC system daily. Local law enforcement officers may query the system for background information on persons they come in contact with, for example. If the persons have prior arrest records, the NCIC system will supply that background information.

In 1982, the New York City Police Department installed a new computer system to simplify and reduce the overwhelming burden of paperwork required to track each suspect, from time of arrest, through the judicial maze of district attorneys and city courts, to final disposition. Suspects are taken from any of the city's 73 precincts to a central booking station in lower Manhattan. Their arrests are entered immediately into the department's computer system. The current status and data of 300,000 arrest warrants and a list of 8000 so-called public enemies, or career criminals, are available at all times. This capability helps officers to more quickly identify suspects and alerts them when they're dealing with known offenders. Because attorneys can report back on the disposition of cases, police officers can follow up on bookings and create more effective crimefighting strategies.

Courtrooms, judges, juries, and cases are scheduled with computer help.

Our nation's court systems depend heavily on computers. Courtrooms, judges, juries, and cases are scheduled with computer help. Given the vast backlog of cases waiting to be heard at all levels of the judicial hierarchy, and the slow rate at which many of the cases move through that hierarchy, computerized tracking and record keeping are vital.

The rules we live by are an amalgamation of congressional laws and legal precedents established through court rulings. The texts of these laws and case histories are maintained in vast databases. Lawyers often need access to such data in preparing legal documents or advising clients. Without computers, the task of organizing and storing all this data, and then of finding the data relevant to a particular situation, would be difficult if not impossible. Often the data is transmitted quickly from where it's stored to awaiting lawyers via electronic mail facilities.

Computers and Finance

Banks, savings and loan associations, credit unions, brokerage firms, and other businesses heavily involved in financial transactions are large users of computers. Deposits and withdrawals, check processing, customer account updating, and loan processing are constantly needed. Accuracy and speed in processing are vital. Hence, these businesses are turning increasingly to office automation.

Many banking institutions have installed self-service *automated teller machines (ATM's)* in exterior walls of their buildings. Some have ATM's at other locations in their communities (for example, at local firms having many employees who do business with them). The ATM's enable customers to make deposits and withdrawals of funds at other than normal banking hours or without having to go to branch banking locations. (See Figure 1-7.)

Some banks have *electronic funds transfer (EFT) systems* that allow checking or savings account customers to make purchases at certain stores using special plastic debit

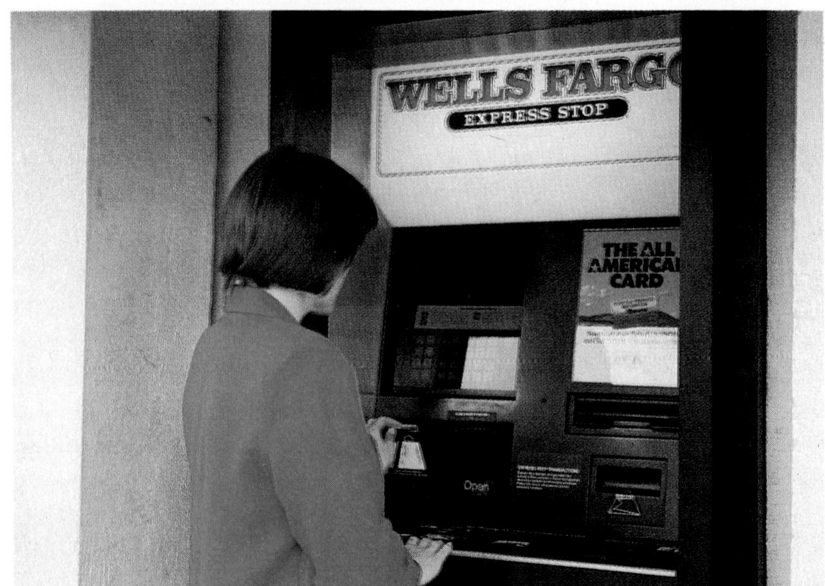
WELLS FARG
EXPRESS STOP
THE ALL
AMERICA
CARD
Open

Figure 1-7 Banks and other firms heavily involved in financial transactions now offer self-service facilities at their offices and at other consumer locations. (Courtesy Mark McKenna)

cards. A customer's debit card is inserted into a reading device when he or she makes a purchase at a participating store. This causes the transaction to be communicated to the bank, where it is credited to the store and debited to the account of the card owner. Such operations are designed for the convenience of both consumers and merchants. They also help to reduce the volume of clerical activities that must be performed by bank personnel.

Just a few years ago, a trading volume of 200 million shares per day was regarded as very heavy activity on the New York Stock Exchange. Today that's routine. On October 20, 1987, a record-setting 608 million shares changed hands. The day before, October 19, 1987, 604 million shares were traded. The Dow Jones Industrial Average fell 508 points, or 22.6 percent—a drop that far exceeded the 12.8 percent drop of October 28, 1929 (generally considered the start of the Great Depression).

The workload that must be handled by the computers supporting such activity is determined not so much by the number of shares traded as by the number of individual transactions. The average number of shares per trade is about 1800 today versus about half that number ten years ago. More and more "big players"—institutional investors that trade huge numbers of shares in one transaction—are participating.

In the days following October 20, 1987, many people first became aware of the practice of *program trading*. Under this practice, decisions to buy or sell stocks are made on the basis of ongoing analyses of trends, big buys or big sells on the stock floor, and so on. The analyses and decision making are done by computers as directed by computer programs, without humans having to be involved. Since that time, limits have been placed on the amount of trading that can be done in this manner. Clearly, extensive analyses can be done faster by computers than by humans. But, if programmed decisions are leading to large swings in the market, humans better become aware or involved.

THE MARKET WAITS FOR NO ONE

The New York Stock Exchange suggests situations that constantly call for current information. Transactions at the Exchange are monitored and recorded via computers. Overhead visual-display screens give last sale and quote information on stocks traded at the various stations. The underlying system comprises more than 150 networked Tandem NonStop fault-tolerant mainframes running an order-entry system known as Superdot 250. Microprocessors serve as device controllers on the trading floor and are used for administrative purposes.

Major exchanges such as the New York Stock Exchange, the Philadelphia Stock Exchange, and the Pacific Stock Exchange in Los Angeles allow brokerage firms to transmit orders directly from terminals in their offices to an exchange floor. In addition, most major exchanges belong to the computerized Intermarket Trading System (ITS), which links the exchanges and many over-the-counter dealers.

With large sums of money at stake, the timing of buy and sell decisions is often critical. An order received at an exchange booth is printed so that a floor broker can take the order to the station on the floor where the stock is traded and execute the order immediately. Although the broker may be able to negotiate a deal on a stock, the savings are not always greater than his or her commission, especially on small quantities. The Superdot 250 system routes any trade for less than 2000 shares directly to the station where the stock is traded. Floor brokers are freed to concentrate on larger trades, with potentially higher commission values.

Computers cannot insure that our decisions to buy or sell stock are good ones. They can provide information that forms the basis for good decisions. They can help to insure that our decisions are communicated and enacted with speed and accuracy. *(Photo courtesy of New York Stock Exchange)*

Growth of Microcomputers in U.S. Public Schools

School Year	% with Computers
1981–82	16.5%
1982–83	36.8%
1983–84	66.8%
1984–85	85.7%
1985–86	91.5%
1986–87	93.6%
1987–88	94.9%

Source: Quality Education Data, Inc. *USA TODAY,* January 17, 1989.

Computers in Education

"Speak and Spell," said Texas Instruments (TI) in the 1970s as it marketed its Speak and Spell handheld learning aid for youngsters. "An Apple computer and the computer language Logo can teach your child to think," said Apple Computer in about 1980.

"Try 'Writing to Read'," said IBM as it launched its "Writing to Read" program in the mid-1980s. The "Writing to Read" approach is based on the principle that children with oral vocabularies of from 4000 to 5000 words can learn to write anything they can say—and to read anything they can write. In a writing exercise, for example, a kite, boat, or similar object is shown on a display screen. A voice-output unit names the object and asks the child to spell the name. The computer then helps the child to find the right letters for the word by lighting areas in both phonetic and regular alphabets shown on the screen. The child learns to read the word through repeated exposure to it.

In fact, computer use in the classroom is expanding rapidly. In 1981, only 16 percent of U.S. public schools used some kind of personal computer for instruction. By 1988, 95 percent did. The U.S. average is one computer for every 32 public school students; 40 percent of the schools have a pupil-computer ratio that's less than 30-to-1. Some say that's not enough.

The computer's takeoff as a teaching tool has been fueled primarily by two developments: the widespread availability of personal computers, and the proliferation of educational programs *(courseware)* that fit into the schools' curricula. Apple focused early on the U.S. K–12 educational market. Its computers accounted for 60 percent of the installed base by the mid-1980s. In 1985, IBM formed an Educational Systems Division and hired teachers and top U.S. educators to consult with IBM staff about the most-needed software. Tandy's 1000 line of value-priced machines targeted at U.S. schools is backed by a nationwide distribution chain of company-owned Radio Shack stores. These stores help to insure that Tandy products are accessible to educators and stock courseware developed by other companies for use with Tandy machines. Commodore is another vendor focusing on the K–12 educational market; it has a large installed base of Commodore 64s and 128s and a new Amiga series offering.

According to a recent congressional report, more than 900 companies are developing courseware. About 800 of these companies were formed since 1985. The quality of the courseware is improving but "could be much better." Two-thirds of the courseware focuses on four subject areas: English, math, reading, and science. The most sophisticated programs are called *learning systems.* They provide a series of lessons that can be administered simultaneously to dozens of students. Each student's performance is monitored by an instructional management program within the system. It alerts the student and the teacher to areas in which the student may need additional help.

At college and university levels, computers may be the hottest thing on campus. According to a survey sponsored by the American Council of Education and the University of California at Los Angeles, in 1983, more than half the freshmen who entered state universities had written

EXAMS
HOMEWORK

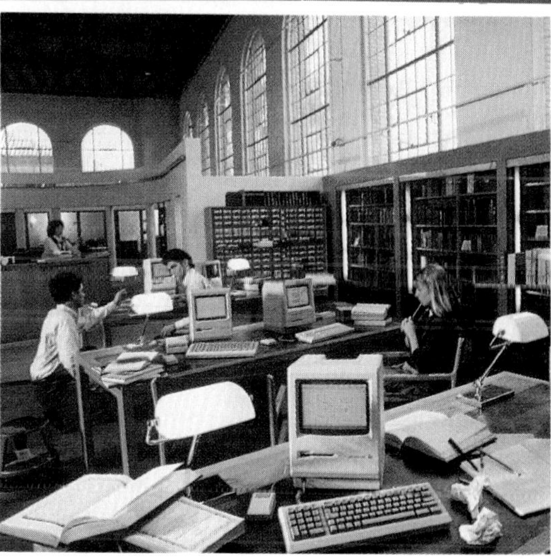

YOU'RE NEVER TOO YOUNG OR TOO OLD TO LEARN

Students of all ages are learning to use computers. In many instances the computers are being used by the students as tools to learn other concepts and skills. Writing a story can be lots of fun for a 9-year-old who has access to a computerized story board. At the high school level, students analyze and solve meaningful science problems with computer help. In many colleges and universities, computers have become an essential part of research and study in campus libraries. (Photos courtesy Apple Computer, Inc.)

Computers in Class

Student + Personal Computer = Early Brand-Name Loyalty

at least one computer program. About a third of the freshmen had taken at least one computer-assisted course in high school. A general introduction to computers or an introduction to business data processing was offered as a first-level course on most campuses.

As at the K–12 level, vendors are making their equipment available at large discounts to both students and instructors. However, while many colleges provide access to computers and some require students to own them, few colleges have integrated computers into their curricula. The students frequently use computers for electronic mail, spreadsheet calculations, and word-processing tasks. They do not use computers widely in other subject areas. The lack of courseware at the college level has been and remains a significant stumbling block. Computer program developers have tended to shy away from the higher-education market, viewing it as too narrow and without significant revenue potential. Hardware vendors such as IBM, Apple, and Digital Equipment Corporation are now promoting the development of such courseware. For example, IBM has allocated more than $200 million to the development of instructional programs at 19 universities.

The use of computers to simulate real-life experiences is an example of the unique contribution that computers can bring to the classroom. Students of French history who use a sophisticated computer game to play the role of a landowner in 17th century France gain an appreciation of how life revolved around the annual harvest that seldom comes across in textbooks. Students in another class can stage the plays of Shakespeare by manipulating figures on the screen of an Apple Macintosh computer. Medical students can perform simulated operations without endangering a patient's life. Chemical students can mix chemicals to their hearts' delight without the risk of an explosion. In such ways, computers supplement rather than replace textbooks and lectures. The learning experience is amplified.

By 1988, according to the Association for Computing Machinery's *Administrative Directory of College and University Computer Science/Data Processing Programs,* there were well over 800 academic programs in computer science or data processing at North American institutions of higher learning; about 500 of these had computer science departments. Students enrolled in these programs to prepare themselves for any of several careers requiring computer skills (see "Employment Opportunities" below). At many leading business schools—Columbia, Harvard, Stanford, and the University of Virginia, for example—computer literacy is a requirement. MBA students must demonstrate competency in the use of popular spreadsheet, word-processing, and data-management programs before receiving their diplomas. Corporations interviewing MBA candidates for jobs expect the candidates to be knowledgable of computers.

Computers in Homes

Initially, computers entered our homes under the guise of "smart machines"—as components of microwave ovens, dishwashers, washing machines, driers, cameras, and so on. In 1975, in a move largely unnoticed by the general public, the MITS Altair 8800 was offered to hobbyists who enjoyed assembling electronic

Figure 1-8 Computers are fun—not machines to be viewed with fear or awe—say youngsters of today. Their interactions with computers are happy, rewarding experiences. (Courtesy Commodore Electronics Ltd.)

gadgetry. A microcomputer in kit form, the Altair 8800 could be purchased for $395, then assembled in much the same way that high-fidelity music-system components and television sets had been assembled for years. Children clamored for the "smart toys" they saw on TV. Then came the video games: Pac-Man, Donkey Kong, and Space Invaders became household words. Parents reluctant to spend hundreds of dollars on a game machine could be persuaded if they saw "educational" value. (See Figure 1-8.)

From these humble beginnings have come the Tandy 1000, Apple II and Macintosh, Amstrad, Atari, Dell, and other computers now offered as off-the-shelf items. You'll find them at Radio Shacks, ComputerLands, Businesslands, and other specialty stores. You may choose one from the catalog of a mail-order house. Discount stores offer them. From KMart to Macy's, computers are in vogue.

Of course, the use of any of these computers requires computer programs as well as machines. Thousands of programs are available. They're marketed on cartridges, cassettes, and diskettes at widely varying prices. A user may also key a program into storage from the keyboard and save it on a diskette or hard disk for reuse. If you learn a programming language such as *BASIC,* you can write and enter your own programs.

We've already noted that computers can be used to play games and to provide individualized instruction to students of all ages. As a user's familiarity with a system increases, data on household budgets, taxes, car payments, transportation expenses, recipes and menus, tape or record collections, personal libraries, and so on, can be organized, indexed, stored, and retrieved at will. In fact, computers are used in many

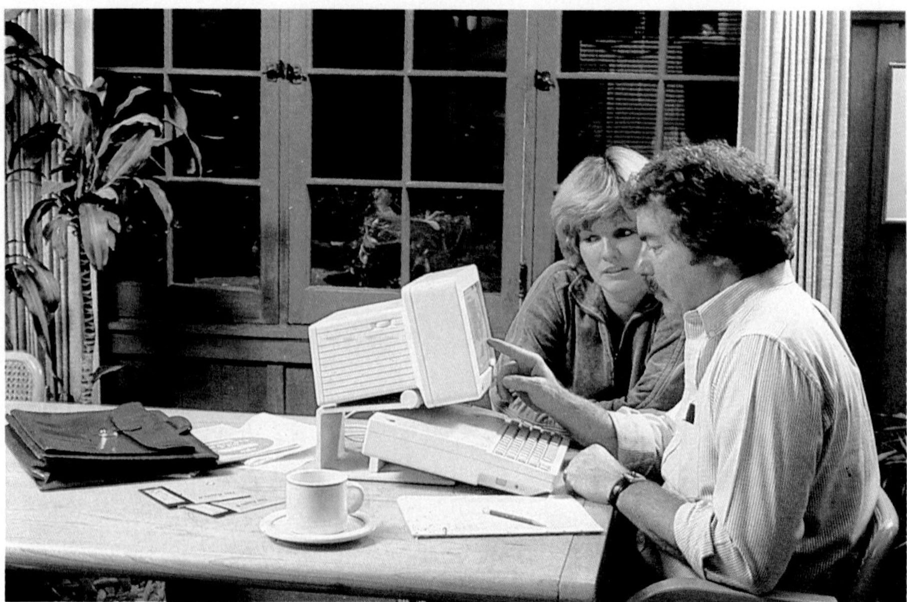

Figure 1-9 Families throughout the nation are finding home computers to be valuable tools for record keeping. (Courtesy of Apple Computer, Inc.)

homes in much the same ways they are used in businesses. The user acquires a word-processing program such as Microsoft Word, WordStar, or Word Perfect for use in writing letters, preparing bulletins for the local Cub Scouts or church youth group, and so on. A spreadsheet program such as Lotus 1-2-3 aids in financial planning. dBASE III Plus, DataEase, or a similar program helps the user to manage all of the data he or she collects. (See Figure 1-9.)

Corporate computing is generally a precursor to home use. Surveys show that more than 70 percent of users who have computers in offices in their homes also use computers in jobs outside their homes. These home-office users are likely to spend more for their systems than other home-nonbusiness users do. For example, in 1989, the initial investment of a typical home-office user was about $2000 whereas a typical home-nonbusiness user spent about $800 to get started. Furthermore, the home-office user invests more frequently in follow-on equipment and supplies than the home-nonbusiness user does—a higher-quality printer, more disks, and additional business or utility programs are likely purchases.

With the availability of low-cost communication interfaces to home computers has come a new, exciting dimension: the *home information system.* Both cable TV and telephone-based systems are currently testing the market for a wide array of consumer services. For example, armchair computerists who subscribe to The Source, an information utility owned by CompuServe, can access about 800 information services. You might choose to (1) get the latest news within minutes after it's filed by UPI correspondents; (2) scan current domestic and international airline schedules, book reservations on flights, rent a car, make hotel reservations, and then check the weather ahead and the best place to eat; or (3) obtain regularly updated reports on stocks, bonds, commodities, futures, options, gold and other precious metals, money markets, mutual funds, foreign exchanges, and U.S. Treasury rates. Subscribers can post classified ads, share ideas, sell or swap merchandise, and transmit simple messages or lengthy reports within minutes to other subscribers the world over—usually at lower costs than long-distance telephone or express mail.

Employment Opportunities

The image of a person replaced by a computer is a common one. We see an automated teller machine (ATM) on the outside of a bank, and we know that a computer is doing a job that was once done by a person. How many human employees would perform consistently, 24 hours a day, always smiling, always ready to respond to customers with prompt service? At $150 a month (the bank's operating cost for the ATM), how many of us would want the job?

Looking at computers from another point of view, we see that their use actually creates a wealth of new jobs. Well over 100 U.S. companies in the data-processing industry report annual revenues exceeding $100 million. These are the companies that develop and build computers and other equipment; prepare programs to instruct them; provide services such as processing time on a particular computer, use of a particular program, or expertise on how to design and implement a particular application; and sell products or services to other vendors and to end users. All these companies employ people.

System analysts work with users to understand their information needs. Business planners determine what products or services are required to respond to those needs. Engineers design computers and related equipment. System designers and programmers develop the programs needed to instruct computers. Operations personnel provide the computer system environments required to support product development efforts. Technical writers and other documentation specialists express product details in user-oriented terms. Sales personnel interact with potential customers, assisting them in acquiring and using computer capabilities. Customer-service personnel keep installed systems operating. Also needed are a manufacturing work force; quality-control personnel; order-processing, shipping, receiving, and inventory-control personnel; and managers to coordinate all these activities. Without computers, these jobs would not exist. The pay is good, and the number and kinds of opportunities are increasing daily. (See Figure 1-10.)

Thousands of government departments and agencies, businesses, educational institutions, and other organizations use computers. These organizations also need system analysts, system designers, and programmers. They need operations personnel to run their computers and related equipment; data-entry personnel to prepare computer-readable input; support personnel to maintain existing programs, respond to problems that arise, and so on; a database administration or library staff; output-distribution personnel; data-processing auditors; and managers for all these functions.

As one result of the reductions in computer size and cost, computers have entered small businesses and office environments. Here, firms may not have in-house system design and programming staffs. They do need

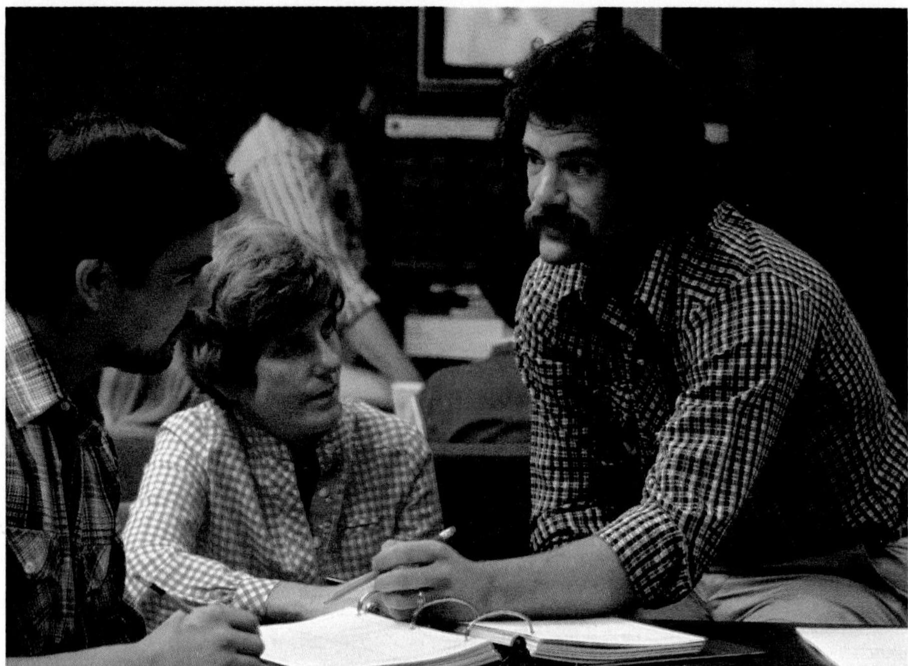

Figure 1-10 Many job opportunities exist for people who can analyze user information needs, design computer programs to meet those needs, and then write and test their programs on a computer. (Photo courtesy of Hewlett-Packard Company)

system analysts and operators. These same persons may also be the system users. Business professionals, administrative specialists, and office workers who understand data processing or know how to use a word-processing program often have "a foot in the door" when competing for jobs with persons who don't know about computers. Even the managers of fast-food stores and gas stations in your vicinity may prefer computer-knowledgeable employees.

There's room for the entrepreneur in the computing field. The freelance artists of the data-processing industry are the individuals who acquire the education and experience necessary to make it on their own. Some are consultants, specializing, for example, in how to use computers effectively in the insurance industry, or how to use computers to achieve inventory control, or how to design, develop, and install a management information system. Others are contract programmers who develop programs for specific clients on a per-job or per-hour basis.

With the advent of personal computers, self-employment opportunities in the data-processing industry have mushroomed.

With the advent of personal computers, self-employment opportunities in the data-processing industry have mushroomed. Some people act as consultants or contract programmers as noted above, but for individual user clients rather than for business, government, and other organizational users. Some, with about $100,000 of front money, have opened computer stores. Some are software publishers, offering computer-related newsletters, magazines, paperbacks, even complete programs as listings or on machine-readable media. Still others are software authors, writing and making available programs for which they receive royalties. People with a mechanical bent are designing, manufacturing, and marketing low-cost input/output units or circuitry to be used with computers, or handling equipment service calls for computer stores on a per-call basis.

As personal computers have become "big business," the chances of "making it big" on one's own have lessened. For every computer store that's successful, there's one that fails. Writing a really good business program may be a challenge, but getting attention in the distribution channels needed to sell it effectively is likely to be an even bigger challenge. Software publishing has become as competitive as textbook publishing. And so on.

It's been said that the 1960s were the decade of the technician, the 1970s the decade of the programmer, and the 1980s the decade of the end user. Most of us belong to at least one of these groups; some belong to all three. You may or may not decide to pursue a career in the computing field. Whatever you decide, you're sure to find an understanding of data processing helpful. Computers and their uses underlie the present and future in all aspects of our society.

CHAPTER SUMMARY

1. Computer literacy is the knowledge and understanding one needs to function effectively within a given role that directly or indirectly involves computers.

2. Data processing is the collecting, processing, and distributing of facts and figures to achieve a desired result.

3. Data consists of facts and figures gathered from one or more sources; information is processed, or "finished," data.

4. Engineers are using computer-aided design (CAD) systems with interactive graphics capabilities to draw and analyze designs for everything from children's toys to the logic of other computer systems.

5. Computers are aiding manufacturing in material requirements planning (MRP), manufacturing resource planning (MRP II), numerical control of machine tools, and robotic systems. Engineering designs are being transferred directly to the manufacturing floor in computer-aided design/computer-aided manufacturing (CAD/CAM) applications.

6. The ultimate objective of computer-integrated manufacturing, or CIM, is to transform the manufacturing enterprise into a modern, automated plant capable of producing superior products in a timely fashion at competitive prices.

7. Computers are involved in the design of spacecraft and in the planning of space flights long before the flights actually occur. Literally hundreds of computers assist in flight operations. Without computers, the U.S. space program might never have come about.

8. People in medical and legal professions are finding computers increasingly valuable. As individuals and as members of society, we benefit.

9. Businesses heavily involved in financial transactions are large users of computers. Self-service automated teller machines (ATM's) and electronic funds transfer (EFT) systems are among the direct benefits we as consumers can take advantage of.

10. Computer use in the classroom is expanding rapidly. This expansion is being fueled primarily by two developments: the widespread availability of personal computers and the proliferation of courseware that fits into the schools' curricula.

11. Many colleges provide access to computers and some require students to own them, but few colleges have integrated computers into their curricula. The lack of courseware at this level is a significant stumbling block.

12. A wide range of employment opportunities exists in the computing field. Companies in the data-processing industry, large computer-using organizations, and small businesses employ computer professionals. There are also opportunities for people to do freelance work as consultants or contract programmers, or to start their own businesses.

DISCUSSION QUESTIONS

1. What does the phrase *computer literacy* mean to you?

2. Justify the following statement: "The development of modern electrical power, machinery, and techniques of mass production created a need for computers."

3. Distinguish between *data* and *information.* In doing so, give several examples.

4. Select one modern business organization (such as a large construction firm, a telephone company, an automobile manufacturer, or a large discount store), and show how it uses data processing.

5. What benefits does MRP II offer that MRP fails to provide?

6. What is computer-integrated manufacturing?

7. In what ways do modern hospitals use computers?

8. Imagine that a long-delayed court case is being tried at a downtown municipal building. The defendant is charged with assault but has pleaded not guilty. Suggest various ways in which computers may be involved in court-related activities.

9. Argue for or against a bank's installation of automated teller machines (ATM's) from the point of view of an officer of the bank, a bank teller or other nonmanagement employee, or a depositor who has opened an account.

10. Show how the New York Stock Exchange depends on computers.

11. What factors are helping or hindering the use of computers in the U.S. public school systems? Are these same factors likely to affect the school systems in other countries? Why or why not?

12. Discuss some ways that computers are being used in homes.

13. What employment opportunities involving computers sound interesting to you, and why?

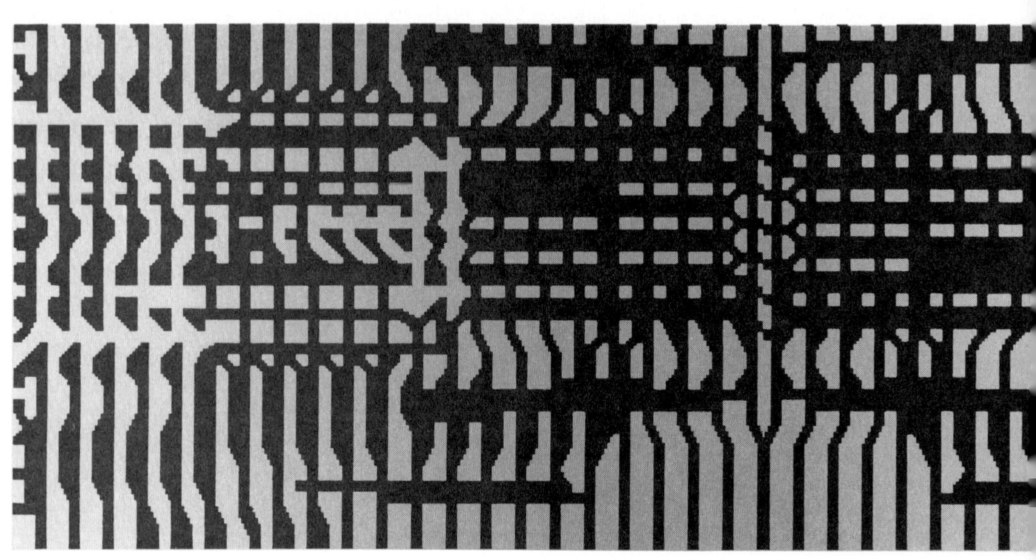

2 The Computer as a System

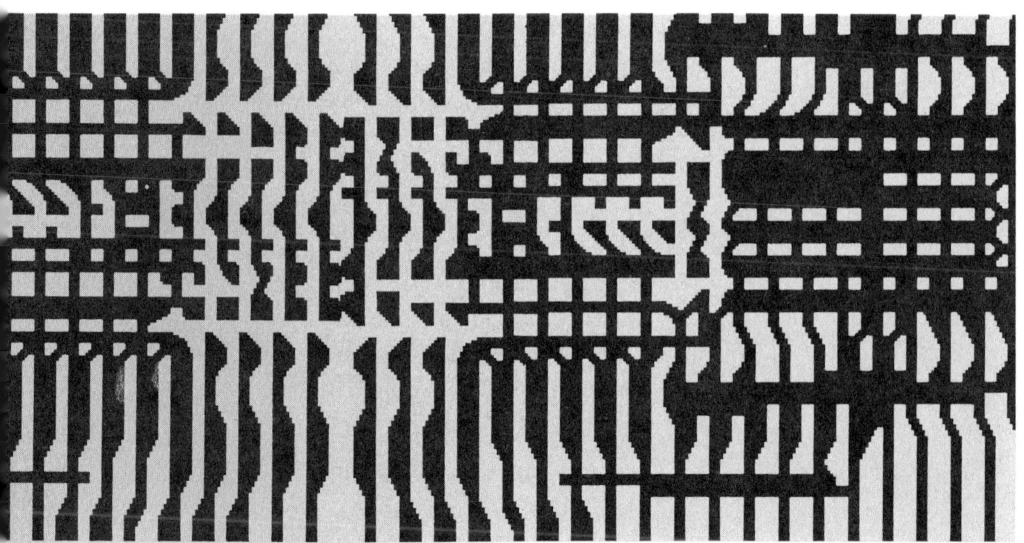

IN THIS CHAPTER

Basic Concepts
Stored Programs
Microcode
Functional Units
Communicating with the Computer

As we saw in Chapter 1, there are many types of data-processing systems. Each of them performs one or more operations on data by means of various devices. When a machine performs most of the required operations, the system is called an *automatic data-processing (ADP) system.* More particularly, when that machine is a computer, the system is called an *electronic data-processing (EDP) system* (or, sometimes, simply a *computer system*). If the system is designed and marketed especially for small businesses, it may be called a *small business system.* A computer intended for individual or home use may be called a *personal computer.*

In this chapter, we look first at three basic elements of data processing: input, processing, and output. We discuss how stored programs control operations during processing. Then we discuss the advantages of microcode. You're introduced to the functional units of an EDP system. (This introduction will be expanded in later chapters.) You will read about a typical interaction between a computer and a user. You will see how simple communicating with a computer really is. And you will use the computer to solve a problem.

Basic Concepts

EDP systems vary in cost, size, complexity, speed, and kinds of operations performed. Nonetheless, all data processing involves at least three basic elements:

- The source data, or *input,* entering the system
- The orderly, planned *processing* within the system
- The end result, or *output,* from the system

As a first example, let's consider a situation without a computer. Imagine that a utility company is preparing a customer's bill. First, a representative of the company reads the customer's meter. (See Figure 2-1.) The previous meter reading (from the end of the last billing period) is available in the company's records. This previous reading is subtracted from the current reading to determine the amount of electricity used during this billing period. An accountant uses established billing rates to calculate how much money the customer owes for this month's usage. Any outstanding balance is added to that total. Finally, the customer's bill is completed and mailed.

In this example, the *input* is the previous meter reading, the current reading, and the outstanding balance. The *processing* is the subtraction of one of these numbers from the other, the multiplication of measuring units by billing rates, and the addition of taxes and the outstanding balance to determine the total bill amount. The *output* is the customer's bill and the company's record of the amount owed. All together, then, these functions constitute a data-processing system.

Now suppose the same operations are performed with computer help. (See Figure 2-2.) The input values are the same. However, in this case, the customer's current meter reading may be keyed into the EDP system from a data-entry device that has a televisionlike screen and a typewriterlike keyboard. The previous meter reading and outstanding balance may be read into the computer from a magnetic tape or disk where it was stored the previous month. Then the calculations are carried out by the computer. The customer's bill is the output. The current meter reading and amount owed are stored on another magnetic tape or disk, to be used in next month's billing.

The processing is carried out as a pre-established sequence of instructions executed by the computer.

We can extend these ideas to EDP systems used today in many organizations. The input may consist of any type of data. It may be customer orders received by phone or by mail, the findings of scientific experiments in labs, sales figures from branch offices, atmospheric data for weather forecasting, and so on. Employees, suppliers, or customers may prepare the input as a by-product of other organizational functions or specifically for the job at hand in a separate data-preparation step. The processing is carried out as a pre-established sequence of instructions executed by the computer. The plan of processing is of human origin, though here too the computer may help. By sorting, classifying, calculating, and other operations, the computer determines results. The results may be used immediately for

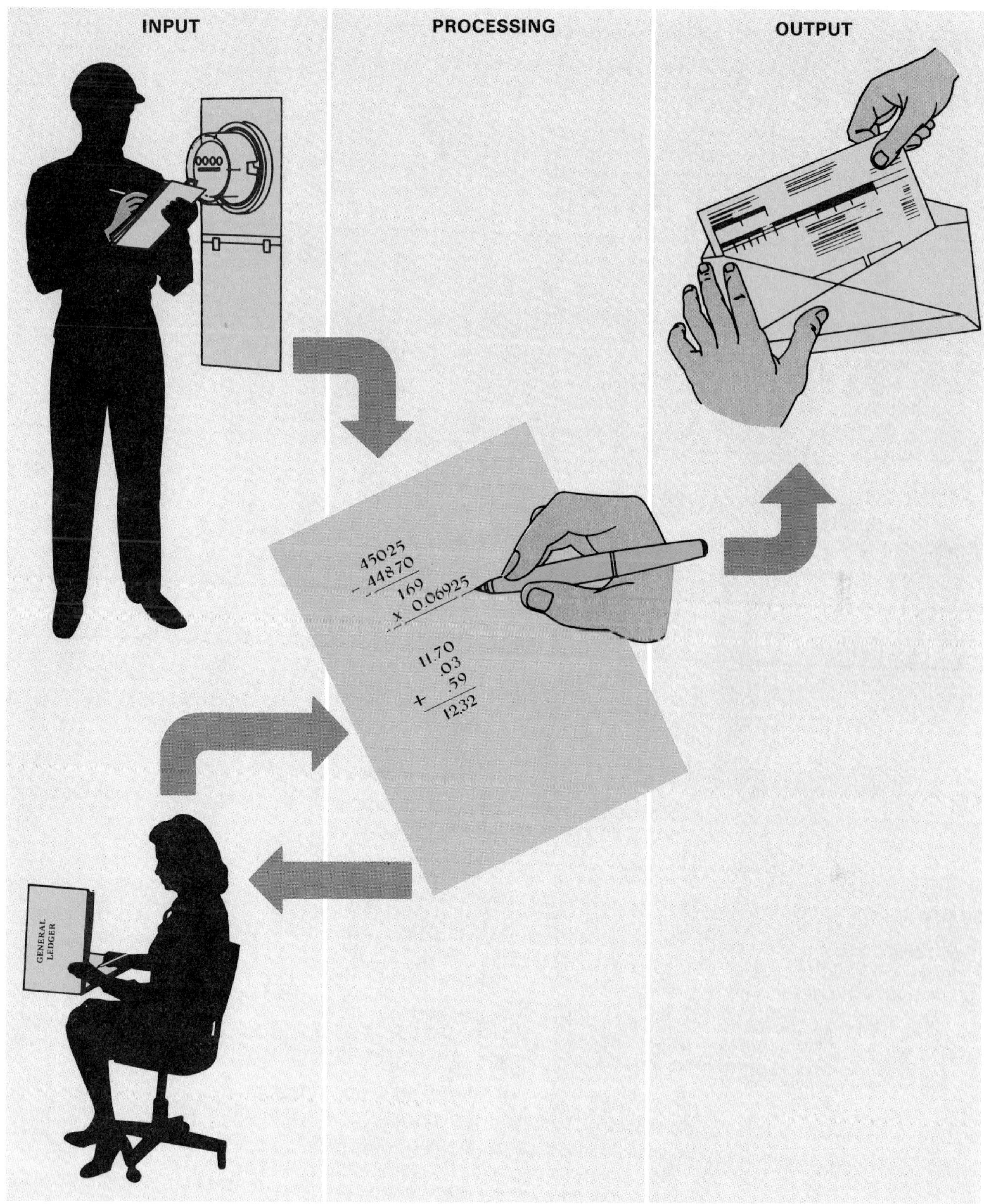
INPUT
PROCESSING
OUTPUT
45025
44870
169
x 0.06925
11.70
.03
+ .59
12.32
GENERAL LEDGER

Figure 2-1 A utility company may use a manual data-processing system (including input, processing, and output) for billing.

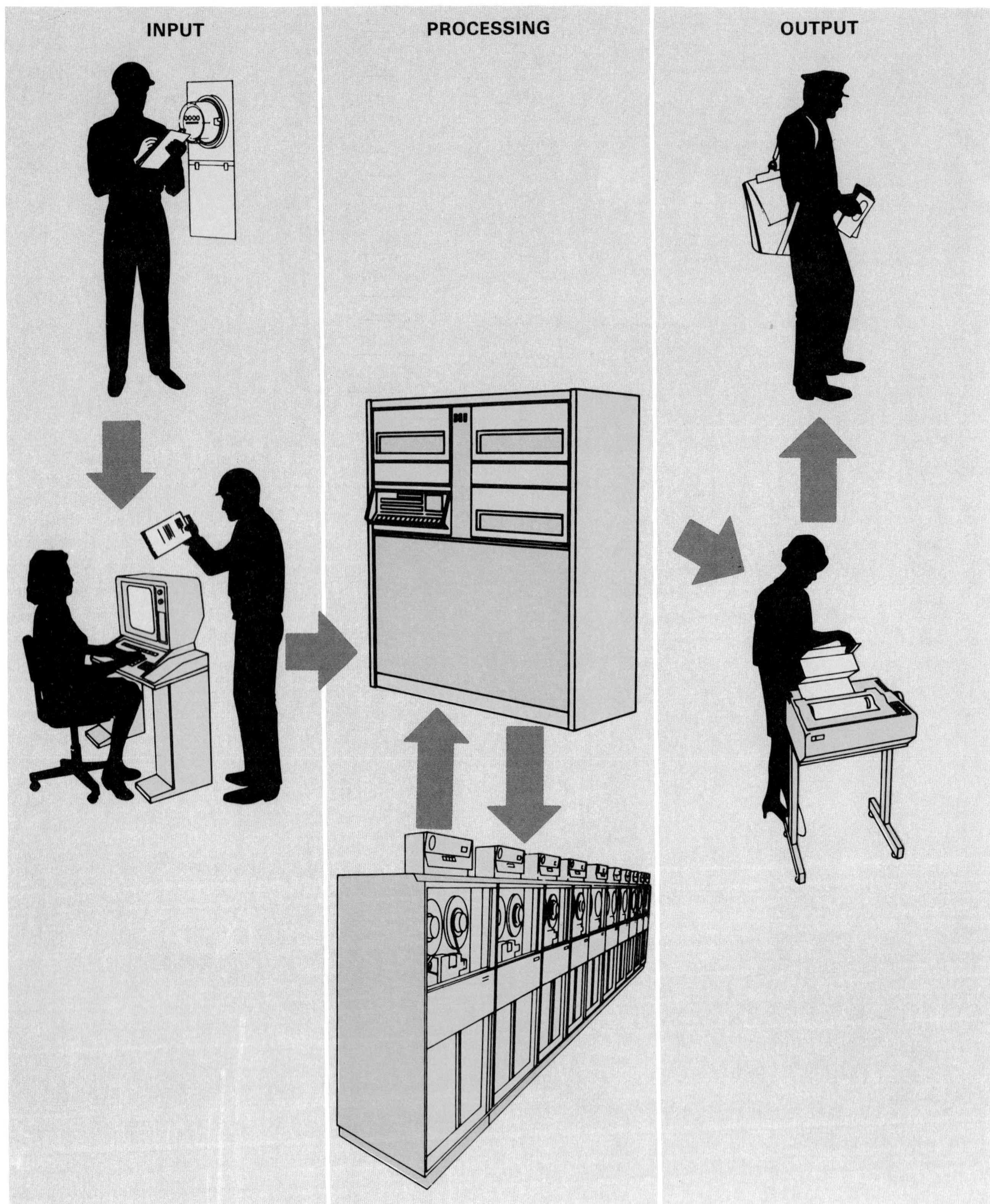
INPUT
PROCESSING
OUTPUT

Figure 2-2 An electronic data-processing system for billing also involves input, processing, and output.

further processing or provided as output in the form of printed reports, graphics on visual-display units, or spoken words.

Stored Programs

An EDP system is designed to perform specific kinds of operations. It is directed to perform each operation by an instruction that defines the operation and identifies the data or device needed to carry it out. As noted in Chapter 1, the entire series of instructions required to perform a given task is known as a *program.* Once a program is read (loaded) into the computer's internal storage unit, or *memory,* processing under its control can be initiated. It is the stored program that makes the computer "automatic." Because the stored-program instructions can be executed by the computer, one after another, little or no further human intervention is needed. The computer can operate at its own speed. It need not wait for step-by-step directions from a human operator.

MICRO-ASSISTED FIRE FIGHTING

A Hewlett-Packard desktop computer system is helping the U.S. Bureau of Land Management to detect and fight lightning-caused fires throughout most of California.

Sensors located at key points around the state scan constantly for positive electrical charges of the type emitted when lightning hits the ground. When a hit occurs, notification of the strike is transmitted—almost at the speed of lightning—to the Bureau's computer at headquarters. The time and location of the strike are determined and transmitted to fire agencies in the area of the strike. Latitude and longitude readings, accurate to a mile, are defined on a 10-inch-square map and are used to direct reconnaissance planes to the scene. The information is also used to direct ground fire-fighting forces if necessary.

Since over half of the fires that occur on Bureau-owned land are caused by lightning, the potential benefits of this system are enormous. The early detection capabilities of such a system and the immediate action that it makes possible are keys to effective fire fighting everywhere. Forests can be saved. Millions of dollars can be saved. Untold hardships can be avoided. *(Photos courtesy [left] John Running/Stock, Boston; [right] Don Landwehrle/The Image Bank)*

A computer can solve a seemingly infinite variety of problems. To solve a particular problem, we need only load a program designed to solve that type of problem into the computer's internal storage unit. Any of the common input devices can be used to do this, because instructions, like data, can be expressed in machine-readable form. After the data related to the problem has also been loaded into storage, operations can be performed on the data to solve the problem.

The task of writing instructions to direct the operations of a computer is called *programming*. The person who writes the instructions may be called a *programmer*. A simple program written in the BASIC programming language is shown in Figure 2-3. The program directs the computer to accept a set of five numbers as input. The processing performed under the direction of this program is to first add the five numbers and then divide their sum by 5 to find the average (see line 140). The quotient of the division operation (i.e., the average) is printed as output. The program user indicates whether or not there are more sets of numbers to process by typing "Y" (Yes) or "N" (No) in response to the prompt on line 160. Control is returned to line 120 to repeat the input-processing-output steps, or program execution is stopped.

A programmer or user of an EDP system does not have to write all of the instructions necessary to control the system. Computer manufacturers and other firms specializing in program development offer many ready-made programs. These programs are of two types: *system software* and *application software*. System software directs the computer in performing tasks that are basic to proper functioning of the system or are commonly needed by system users. For example, the major control program, also known as the *operating system, supervisor,* or *executive,* controls system resources; it allocates input devices, output devices, and internal storage to specific programs when they are executed. Application software directs the computer in performing specific user-related data-processing tasks. For example, accounts-payable programs, payroll-processing programs, and programs that help to control inventories are

The task of writing instructions to direct the operations of a computer is called *programming.*

Figure 2-3 This program tells the computer to find the average of a set of five numbers and print it as output.

```
100  REM AVERAGE
110  REM FIND THE AVERAGE OF A SET OF FIVE NUMBERS
120  PRINT "ENTER A SET OF 5 NUMBERS"
130  INPUT A, B, C, D, E
140  LET X=(A+B+C+D+E) / 5
150  PRINT "AVERAGE IS "; X
160  PRINT "ANY MORE SETS TO PROCESS? TYPE Y OR N"
170  INPUT R$
180  IF R$="Y" THEN 120
190  END
```

application software. Programs that direct the computer in controlling space flights or auto ignition systems, in helping students learn to spell or read, and in game playing are also in this category.

More than one program may be stored in the computer at any given time. The only limit is the number of storage locations available for both programs and data. Normally, after an application program has been loaded into storage and executed, control of the computer is released to the major control program (also in internal storage). The control program may, in turn, respond to commands entered by users at typewriterlike devices, direct any of a number of other input/output units to perform necessary operations, transfer control to another application program, and so forth. The capabilities of any one control program are, of course, determined by its human designers. We'll learn more about the programs available for microcomputers and for larger computer systems in later chapters.

Microcode

Since the mid-1940s, when computers were first introduced as huge, expensive, one-of-a-kind machines, designers have worked to develop machines that are ever faster and ever more powerful. Making a distinction between the *hardware* (physical components) of a computer system and the *software* (programs) that directs the hardware is no longer simple and straightforward. Although basic operations such as multiplication and division can be built into a computer in the form of permanently wired circuitry (called *hard-wired circuits*), more flexibility is possible if some of the basic operations are controlled by special stored-program instructions sometimes referred to as *firmware* or *microcode*.

Since the mid-1940s, when computers were first introduced as huge, expensive, one-of-a-kind machines, designers have worked to develop machines that are ever faster and ever more powerful.

Sequences of microcode instructions, called *microprograms,* are provided for some computers by their manufacturers. The microprograms are placed in *read-only memory (ROM),* where they can be interpreted by the computer during processing. Unlike other internal storage, the ROM cannot be occupied or altered by regular stored-program instructions or by data. Such a computer has certain standard features plus the optional capabilities that are wanted or needed. Through microprogramming, the basic operations of the computer can be tailored to meet the user's data-processing requirements.

Generally, it is to the user's advantage to have system functions controlled by microcode rather than by regular stored-program instructions. Because the microcode is in ROM, it cannot be altered accidentally. In effect, the user is protected from himself or herself. Instructions in ROM are ready to be executed when the power supply to the computer is turned on. No special step to load the instructions into internal storage from a diskette or other external storage medium is required.

THE ART AND SCIENCE OF WINE MAKING

Making wine is a simple task. With some grapes, a few chemicals, and a cask or jug, anybody can make wine. Making *good* wine, however, is quite another thing. And selling the wine complicates matters significantly. Because wine is viewed by the government as alcohol, its production, distribution, and sale are severely regulated.

The Napa Valley wine region is blessed with a variety of good soils. Mountain ranges protect the region, insuring hot days and few untimely storms. The nearby Pacific brings cool nights, lengthening the time available for vine growing and developing. The Napa Valley winemakers are complementing these natural advantages with computer technology—making it an integral part of the art and science of wine making.

At the Robert Mondavi winery, for example, an IBM System/36 computer handles accounting, order invoicing, general ledger, accounts payable, and accounts receivable. The system also assists in winemaking by producing reports on the wine crush, wine analysis, and wine blending.

Nearby, a Hewlett-Packard computer system regulates the temperature of 200 stainless steel tanks that range in size from 500 to 200,000 gallons. More than .5 million cases of premium wines and 1 million cases of table wine are produced annually at the facility.

Wine begins with grapes, and so do the models developed by Mondavi employees with the help of Lotus 1-2-3 spreadsheet programs running on IBM Personal Computers. For example, an advanced-planning model accepts sales projections as input and provides statistics of how many grapes will be needed to produce the desired amount of wine as output. Another model generates a grape delivery profile, telling when different varieties of grapes will arrive at the winery. For instance, 30 percent of the Chardonnay may

arrive in the second week of the 10-week harvest period, putting special demands on the winery facilities.

Winemakers are always trying to improve the quality of their wines. Their goal is to optimize the quality, given the constraints. A winemaker may tentatively decide to bring certain grapes in early to lower their sugar content. Doing so may mean that more barrels must be purchased or that currently aging wines must be moved through production. Bottlenecks must be avoided. A computer model captures the costs and implications of such actions on management of the winery facilities.

Even more than other businesses, winemakers must plan far into the future. A new vineyard may take 3 to 4 years to produce. Grape varieties such as Cabarnet may be 3 years in aging. That means the winemaker won't even begin to receive a return on investment (ROI) for 6 or 7 years. Since the various grapes (and wines) compete with each other for available winery resources, computerized models can help the winemaker to determine how different mixes of grapes may affect the firm's over-all rate of return.

Finally, computer programs help winemakers to determine wine availability—the proper time to sell their wines. The costs per ton of grapes, including growth, processing, and inventory costs, become the total cost by vintage (year) and variety. These figures are matched with the anticipated sales prices of the various wines to manage their profitability. *(Photo courtesy Peter Menzel)*

Another important advantage is speed of operation. Generally, a function controlled by microcode is executed much faster than it would be if it were controlled by regular stored-program instructions.

Usually, programs that are both stored in and executed from ROM must be written by programmers who know in advance that the programs will be executed from ROM. Certain programming guidelines apply. Some microcomputer system vendors are choosing to distribute certain programs stored in ROM as part of their product offerings, even though the programs are not designed to be executed from ROM. The programs are read into the computer's internal storage unit as soon as the electrical power supply for the unit is turned on (without any other special action by the user). This approach offers several benefits. It's straightforward and not subject to human errors in packaging or in distribution. Yet it's also simple for the user, who may not even know about ROM and doesn't have to.

Detailed knowledge of computer circuitry is required to write microcode instructions. In practical usage, only computer designers need be familiar with the techniques of microprogramming and of specific microcode. We shall not examine the makeup of any computer to the depth needed for microprogramming, but now you have some understanding of why certain programs are provided in ROM on some commonly available computers.

Functional Units

An EDP system typically consists of four types of functional units: the processor unit, secondary-storage devices, input devices, and output devices. The interrelationships of these units are shown schematically in Figure 2-4.

UNIVAC

EARLY HISTORY

Spurred by the U.S. Navy's need for faster ways to process data, Harvard graduate students and IBM engineers developed the world's first *electromechanical computer,* known as the *Mark I,* in the early 1940s. When completed, the Mark I was 51 feet long, 8 feet high, and weighed 5 tons (top). Shortly thereafter, working under a contract between the U.S. Army and the Moore School of Electrical Engineering at the University of Pennsylvania, John W. Mauchly and J. Presper Eckert developed the *ENIAC,* an *electronic digital computer.* The switching and control functions that had been performed by electromagnetic relays in the Mark I were handled by vacuum tubes in the ENIAC. The relatively slow movements of switches were replaced by the swift motions of electrons. Both Mauchly and Eckert were on hand when representatives of the U.S. Bureau of Census accepted delivery of a *UNIVAC I* electronic digital computer in 1951 (center). The UNIVAC I was the first commercially available (that is, other than one-of-a-kind) computer. The use of a UNIVAC I to predict the results of the 1952 presidential election was the first exposure of computers to the general public. *(Photos courtesy of [top] Craft Photo Lab, Harvard University. Photographer: Paul Donaldson; [center and bottom] Sperry Corp.)*

THE PROCESSOR UNIT

The *central processing unit (CPU)* is the computer part of an EDP system. It is the control center of the entire system. As such, it has two parts: an *arithmetic/logic unit* and a *control section.* As we'll see later, these two parts together are sometimes called the *processor* of the EDP system. If both parts are built on a single chip of silicon, we call that chip a *microprocessor.* The *internal storage unit* (also called *memory, primary storage,* or *main storage*) of the EDP system is often housed within the same physi-

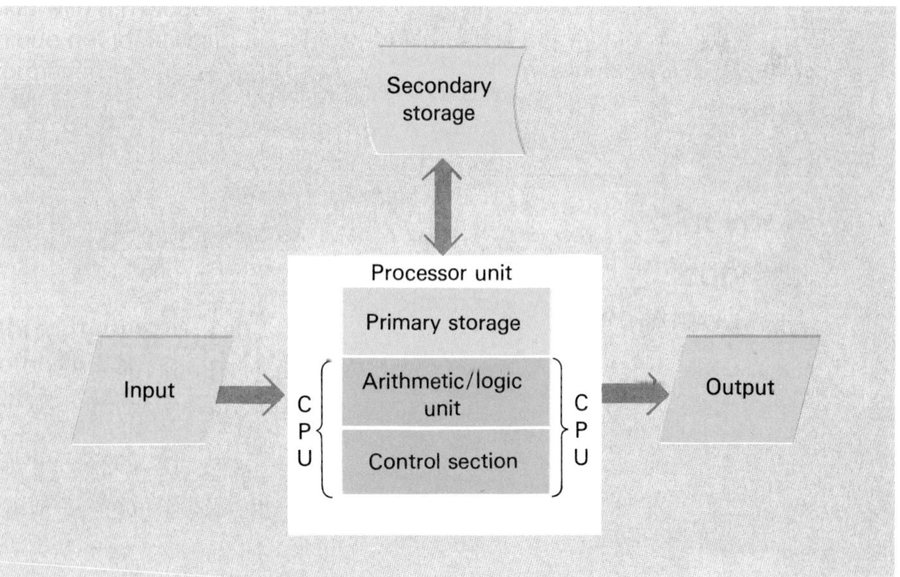

Secondary storage
Processor unit
Primary storage
Input
C P U
Arithmetic/logic unit
Control section
C P U
Output

Figure 2-4 The functional units of an EDP system interact during processing.

cal unit as the arithmetic/logic unit and the control section. All three of these units are integrally involved in the computer's internal processing operations. For this reason, the three of them are sometimes referred to collectively as "the CPU." Their physical housing is called the *processor unit.* A computer that is microprocessor-based is called a *microcomputer.*

The arithmetic/logic unit performs operations such as addition, subtraction, multiplication, and division, as well as moving and comparing data. This unit also has the ability to test conditions encountered during processing and to take action accordingly.

The control section of the CPU directs and coordinates all the operations of the computer system according to conditions set forth by stored programs. It fetches instructions from primary storage and interprets them. It then generates signals and commands that cause other system units to perform operations at appropriate times. That is, it controls the input/output units, the arithmetic/logic operations of the CPU, and the transfer of data and instructions to and from storage, within given design limits. It acts as a central nervous system but performs no actual processing operations on data. The processing must be carried out by other system components.

The internal storage unit, or primary storage, is somewhat like an electronic filing cabinet; each "bin," or location, can hold data or instructions. During normal system operation, this unit contains the following:

- All data being held for processing
- Data used in current processing
- The final result of processing until it is released as output
- Stored-program instructions that control the processing being carried out

Each position, or location, in storage is identified by a particular *address.* Using the addresses, the control section of the CPU can readily locate data and instructions as needed. The primary-storage capacity determines the amount of data and instructions that can be held within the system in a form directly accessible by the processor at any one time.

The primary-storage capacity determines the amount of data and instructions that can be held within the system in a form directly accessible by the processor at any one time.

Since primary storage is designed to permit very rapid storing and retrieving, systems that include large amounts of primary storage are often desirable. Because primary storage has been a relatively expensive part of an EDP system, however, the storage capacity in many computer systems has been limited. Furthermore, operating systems have not been designed to deal with large amounts of memory. For example, many users of systems operating under the control of the operating system called *MS-DOS* have been limited in what they could do because the version of MS-DOS installed on their systems could only access primary-storage locations with addresses less than or equal to 655,360 (known throughout the industry as 640K). Fortunately, this situation is changing. The cost of memory components has decreased; software and/or hardware "workarounds" have been devised to allow application programs (and therefore users) to take advantage of primary-storage locations above the 640K boundary if such physical storage is actually installed; and MS-DOS Version 4.0 (released by Microsoft in1988) has enhanced addressing capabilities. (We'll learn more about internal storage in Chapter 5.)

SECONDARY-STORAGE DEVICES

Frequently, the amount of data that a program must access exceeds the primary-storage capacity available. In such cases, the data is retained on *secondary,* or *auxiliary, storage devices.* The data can be retrieved as needed during system processing (albeit, more slowly than if it were in primary storage). Programs not currently in use are also kept in secondary storage. Various types of devices have been developed to provide storage space. The most common are magnetic-tape units and magnetic-disk units. (See Figure 2-5.)

Processing restrictions caused by limited primary-storage capacities have been alleviated in some systems by the development of *virtual-storage* techniques. In an EDP system with virtual-storage capabilities, the addresses within a program being executed can include secondary-storage locations as well as primary-storage locations. When data or instructions referenced during execution of the program are in secondary storage but not in primary storage, the portion of the program that contains them is moved to primary storage immediately. As we shall see, the capacity and design of the storage in a computer system affect the way data is handled and the speed of processing.

INPUT AND OUTPUT DEVICES

As part of its information-handling ability, the data-processing system requires devices that can introduce data into the system and devices that can accept data after it has been processed. These functions are performed by *input/output (I/O) de-*

Figure 2-5 Magnetic-tape units and magnetic-disk units are common secondary-storage devices. Those shown here are designed for use with large computer systems. Both tapes and disks are also available for use with microcomputers. (Courtesy [left] Hewlett-Packard Company; [right] Digital Equipment Corporation.)

87000-60469
NEW HAMPSHIRE
11501
Superior
clover
honey
OLD FASHIONED
SKIPPY
PEANUT BUTTER
SUPER CHUNK
KeyChart

Figure 2-6 Data enters, and information leaves, an EDP system by means of input/output devices. Left to right: portable laser scanner (OCR), courtesy MSI Data Corporation; QWERTY-style keyboard, courtesy Walter Bibikow/The Image Bank; magnetic-tape unit, courtesy of Memorex Corporation; portable terminal with wand reader, courtesy MSI Corporation; printer, courtesy Eastman Kodak Company; plotter, courtesy Houston Instrument.

Confucius says:

"I hear, and I forget.
I see, and I remember.
I do, and I understand."

Confucius (551–479 B.C.)

vices, or *terminals,* linked directly to the system. Some typical devices are shown in Figure 2-6.

Before data can be processed by the computer, it must be entered into the computer's storage. As EDP system users, we make the data available to it via an input device. The data may be recorded as punched holes on cards, as magnetized spots along a tape, as characters or drawings on paper, and so on. The data may also be keyed directly into the system (without first having been recorded on an input medium) by means of a direct-input device.

Output is data that has been processed. It may be in a form that humans can understand, or it may be in a form acceptable as input to another machine. For example, an output device such as a printer can display information in a form that is readily understandable to us. A magnetic tape unit used as an output device records information in a form that is useful only as input for further processing.

The number and types of I/O devices connected to a particular system depend on the design of the system and the kind of processing for which it is used. Some devices are used only for input, some only for output, and some for either. The variety of I/O devices available today seems almost unlimited. As you may have noticed, magnetic-tape units appear in both Figure 2-5 and Figure 2-6. A magnetic-tape unit may be regarded as both a secondary-storage device and an input or output device.

Communicating with the Computer

Now you have some idea of what a computer system is and what it does. Would you like to see how simple communicating with the computer (and even directing it) really is? In this section, we describe a user-computer interaction. If you have access to a microcomputer or to a terminal that is part of a larger computer system, you can interact with your system in much the same way as described here.

Most computer users today are not programmers. Today's users simply buy and load ready-made programs that run on their computer systems, or someone else configures their systems (installs both the hardware and the software) for them. For our purposes, we'll simply key in the BASIC program in Figure 2-3, which directs the computer in finding averages. We'll enter sets of data values as input and receive the results of processing as output. Where necessary, your instructor or lab assistant will provide information that is unique to your system. If you do not have access to a computer, you will still learn much about how to interact with a computer by reading this section.

Signing On

The first step in interacting with the computer is to establish contact with it. If you have access to a microcomputer, you may simply pull up a chair, sit down, and turn on the equipment. (If you can't find the power switch, just ask someone.) Apple II and IBM Personal Computer users must place a diskette containing certain system software in an available disk drive, from where the software is then loaded into storage. Commodore personal computer systems have some system software in ROM; they "come up" with BASIC ready for use.

I'M DREAMING OF A WHITE CHRISTMAS . . .

It's greeted enthusiastically by skiers and snowmobilers and welcomed by children who love to romp in it, build snowmen, and have snowball fights. It's painted or photographed for Christmas card scenes and calendars enjoyed by many of us. But it also brings delay, misery, and hard work to airplane travelers, people who have to drive through it, and people who have to shovel or otherwise get rid of it. What is "it"? Yes, "it" is snow.

To scientists at the Institute of Snow Research (ISR) in Houghton, Michigan, snow is a subject for investigation. Located on the Keweenaw Peninsula of upper Michigan, the ISR is an auxiliary unit of the Keweenaw Research Center (KRC). KRC is staffed by about 25 permanent employees and numerous academic staff members and graduate students from nearby Michigan Technological University. The site receives about 200 inches of heavy snowfall each year, so there's lots of "real stuff" for them to investigate. The scientists are supplementing their investigations with computer modeling, which allows them to conduct experiments all year round.

One example of a study using real snow and computer analyses is a civil-engineering-related project to examine the way snow bonds to pavements and airplane runways. ISR is working to determine how to dis-bond the snow. Track vehicles measure the amount of pressure exerted on snow in various situations and how much pressure is needed to collapse it. Statistics of the measurement situations—temperature, solar conditions, infrared data, and so on—are fed into the computer and analyzed to determine how bonding is affected.

In another study, scientists are using computer modeling to analyze how the intricate crystal shapes of ice and/or snow become round as they fall, then start to break up, and then bond together to form a snowpack. As additional layers fall, under certain conditions the bonding at the bottom of the snowpack weakens to form a sugarlike consistency. An avalanche may follow. Through the study, the scientists are learning what causes avalanches and therefore how to predict them. They're also learning how compacted snow can be used for environmental protection. What's safe and what's dangerous?

Research at KRC is supported entirely by external funding from both federal and state governments as well as from the private sector. Military research (for example, land mine performance in snow, detection and camouflage in snow) continues to be a strong part of their effort. Heavy emphasis is also placed on industrial concerns such as snow control, removal, and measurement. Not all studies are done in Michigan. In Antarctica, for example, ISR experiments are being conducted to devise methods of creating better snow roads and airstrips. Planes are landing directly on the snow, and, in some instances, sawdust is being mixed with the snow to create a stronger bond and hence firmer airstrips. *(Photo courtesy Institute of Snow Research, KRC, Michigan Technological University)*

If you intend to use a terminal to interact with a larger computer system, you may need to connect the terminal to the computer by using telephonelike dial-up facilities. To do this, you'll need to enter the computer's telephone number, listen for a high-pitched tone that tells you the computer is ready to receive input, and then place the telephone handset into the data set or acoustic coupler serving as a connection device. (See Figure 2-7.) After the connection has been established, you may have to enter an *account number* so that the computer knows which account to charge for your use. Most systems also require that you enter a unique *user identification* and *password.* Both are checked to insure that you have proper authorization before you are allowed access to the system. Assuming you pass the authorization checks, you type in a system command, such as BASIC, to tell the system that you intend to enter and run a BASIC program.

Entering and Running the Program

Most computer systems provide system messages as *prompts* to guide you. These messages help you decide what to do next. A representative interactive session is shown as an example in Figure 2-8. The messages generated by the system are differentiated by color in the example. After the user told the computer to load the Advanced BASIC system software into storage, the second screen header appeared. The user keyed in the BASIC program in Figure 2-3. As we know, the program directs the computer to find the average of five numbers keyed into the system by the user during processing.

Entering a BASIC program is really quite simple. You key in each statement, line by line, pressing the ENTER key or its equivalent after each statement. Whatever you key in will appear on the screen of your terminal or microcomputer as you enter

Figure 2-7 A user at a terminal may establish a connection to a distant computer by means of an acoustic coupler and ordinary telephone lines. (Courtesy National Semiconductor Corporation)

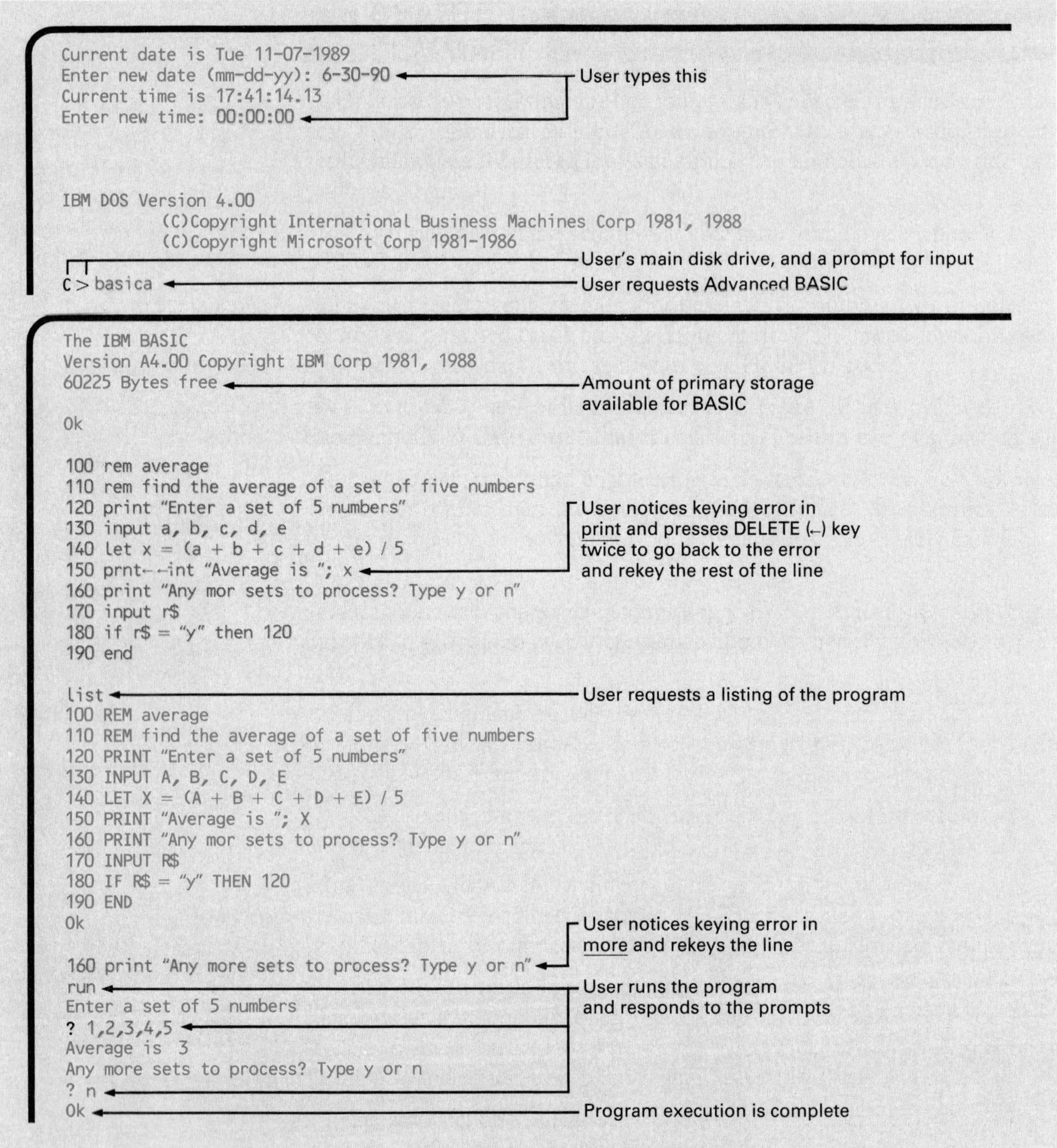
Current date is Tue 11-07-1989
Enter new date (mm-dd-yy): 6-30-90
Current time is 17:41:14.13
Enter new time: 00:00:00
User types this
IBM DOS Version 4.00
(C)Copyright International Business Machines Corp 1981, 1988
(C)Copyright Microsoft Corp 1981-1986
User's main disk drive, and a prompt for input
C> basica
User requests Advanced BASIC
The IBM BASIC
Version A4.00 Copyright IBM Corp 1981, 1988
60225 Bytes free
Amount of primary storage available for BASIC
Ok
100 rem average
110 rem find the average of a set of five numbers
120 print "Enter a set of 5 numbers"
130 input a, b, c, d, e
140 let x = (a + b + c + d + e) / 5
150 prnt←←int "Average is "; x
160 print "Any mor sets to process? Type y or n"
170 input r$
180 if r$ = "y" then 120
190 end
User notices keying error in print and presses DELETE (←) key twice to go back to the error and rekey the rest of the line
list
User requests a listing of the program
100 REM average
110 REM find the average of a set of five numbers
120 PRINT "Enter a set of 5 numbers"
130 INPUT A, B, C, D, E
140 LET X = (A + B + C + D + E) / 5
150 PRINT "Average is "; X
160 PRINT "Any mor sets to process? Type y or n"
170 INPUT R$
180 IF R$ = "y" THEN 120
190 END
Ok
160 print "Any more sets to process? Type y or n"
User notices keying error in more and rekeys the line
run
Enter a set of 5 numbers
? 1,2,3,4,5
Average is 3
Any more sets to process? Type y or n
? n
Ok
User runs the program and responds to the prompts
Program execution is complete

Figure 2-8 An interactive session between a user and a computer is documented by messages and responses that appear on the display screen as interactions occur.

Entering a BASIC program is really quite simple.

it. An underscore character called the *cursor* moves about on the screen to show your current position as you are keying. If you make a mistake while keying a line, most systems allow you to backspace to the point of the error and rekey the remainder of the line. (See line 150 in Figure 2-8.) If you see you've made an error after you've pressed the ENTER key, you can simply rekey the whole line,

line number and all. The computer will replace the erroneous line with the new line.

Of course, merely entering BASIC statements does not solve a problem. On most systems, you can enter a LIST command to tell the computer to print or display a list of the statements you've entered into storage. Doing this allows you to check the statements visually to make sure that what you think you entered is actually there. The statements will be listed in ascending line-number order. Remember, if any line is wrong, you can simply rekey it. (See the rekeying of line 160 after the program was listed, in Figure 2-8.) When you've done that, your next step is to tell the computer to execute the program.

Of course, merely entering BASIC statements does not solve a problem.

On most systems, a RUN command can be entered to tell the computer to execute a program in storage. Enter that command or its equivalent on your system now. You should see the prompt "Enter a set of 5 numbers" appear on your screen. A question mark should be displayed at the beginning of the next line. (Lines 120 and 130 of the program cause these actions to occur.) Now you must key in (on the same line) a set of five data values, separated by commas. For the first execution, enter the values 1, 2, 3, 4, 5 as shown in Figure 2-8. Then press the ENTER key again. You should see "Average is 3" appear on the screen as output. (The extra space between *is* and *3* would have been used for a minus sign if the value had been negative.)

Then line 160 of the BASIC program causes the computer to ask whether or not there are more sets of numbers to process. If you type "y" following the question mark that appears on the next line and then press the ENTER key, control will return to line 120 of the program. The process we've just described will be repeated, giving you an opportunity to enter another set of five values. If you type "n" following the question mark, control will pass to the END statement in line 190. Program execution will terminate, as in Figure 2-8.

If your interaction with the computer doesn't occur more or less as we've just described, you may have made a mistake—say, in procedure or in keying. The system may have printed a message on the screen to tell you about the mistake. Check the actions you've taken, or consult the system documentation. Correct your mistake and try again.

Next, choose another set of five data values. Calculate the average of the set of values manually. Then run the program again, enter the values as input, and see whether or not the computer's result agrees with the average you calculated. If not, you must find the error and try again. In computer jargon, errors are known as *bugs*. The process of finding errors and correcting them is known as *debugging*. If your program is error-free, there is no need for debugging.

Signing Off

When you're finished, it's time to sign off the computer system. On some systems, a command such as BYE or OFF is used to disconnect from the computer and terminate the session. In any case, your last step is to turn off your terminal or microcomputer.

Wasn't that simple? You've now entered a program into the storage of a computer system and caused that program to be executed. You've entered input values, which were processed as directed by statements of the program. You've received the results of execution as output. Programs to direct computers in processing payrolls, computing accounts receivable, scheduling airline flights, planning highways, playing chess, and so on, are longer and more complicated than the one we've shown here—but basic concepts are the same. This is what directing the computer is all about.

CHAPTER SUMMARY

1. All data processing (with or without computer help) involves input, processing, and output.

2. An EDP system is directed to perform operations by a series of instructions known as a *program.*

3. The task of writing instructions to direct the operations of a computer is called *programming.*

4. Programs are of two types: system software and application software. System software directs the computer in performing tasks that are basic to proper functioning of the system or are commonly needed by system users. Application software directs the computer in performing specific user-related tasks.

5. Special stored-program instructions known as *firmware,* or *microcode,* may be placed in read-only memory (ROM) to tailor a computer to the user's data-processing requirements.

6. The Mark I and the ENIAC were early one-of-a-kind computers developed in the 1940s. The UNIVAC I was the first commercially available computer.

7. An EDP system consists of four types of functional units: the processor unit, secondary-storage devices, input devices, and output devices.

8. The processor unit houses the central processing unit, or CPU, and the internal storage unit. The CPU has two parts: an arithmetic/logic unit and a control section. A one-chip CPU is called a *microprocessor.*

9. The internal storage unit, or primary storage, contains all data being held for processing, data being processed, the result of processing, and instructions that control the processing.

10. Using a computer may involve loading or keying in a program, causing that program to be executed, entering data values as input, and receiving output.

DISCUSSION QUESTIONS

1. What three factors are involved in any data-processing operation?

2. Consider a familiar situation that involves the processing of data (such as checking out at the counter of a supermarket, purchasing a roll of stamps at the post office, checking supplies in a company supply cabinet, or handling a concession stand at a school benefit).

(a) Explain how the factors given in your answer to Question 1 are involved in the situation.

(b) Explain how the steps you're describing can be carried out manually. Then suggest what might be done differently with the help of a computer.

3. (a) What are the functions of an instruction in an EDP system?

(b) What must be done with an instruction before it can do its job effectively?

4. (a) Distinguish between system software and application software.

(b) Give examples of functions directed by programs of each kind.

5. Notice that both the Mark I and the ENIAC were developed with the help of cooperative efforts of the U.S. government, education, and industry. What joint sponsorship of research or of training in the computing field are you aware of at your school or at other locations in your state or nation?

6. What is microcode and how is it used?

7. (a) List the four types of functional units of an EDP system.

(b) Explain each briefly.

8. (a) What are some typical input and output devices of modern computer systems?

(b) What devices can be used for either input or output?

9. Why is a magnetic-tape unit considered both a secondary-storage device and an input or output device?

10. If you have access to a computer system, describe how you establish contact with the computer and what you have used "your" computer to accomplish.

11. Refer to Figures 2-3 and 2-8. If you have access to a computer system that supports BASIC, enter the program into storage as suggested.

(a) What actions are caused by the statements on lines 120 and 130?

(b) If you provide the values 20, 30, 45, 30, and 25 as input, what information should the computer provide as output?

(c) How do you get the computer to stop?

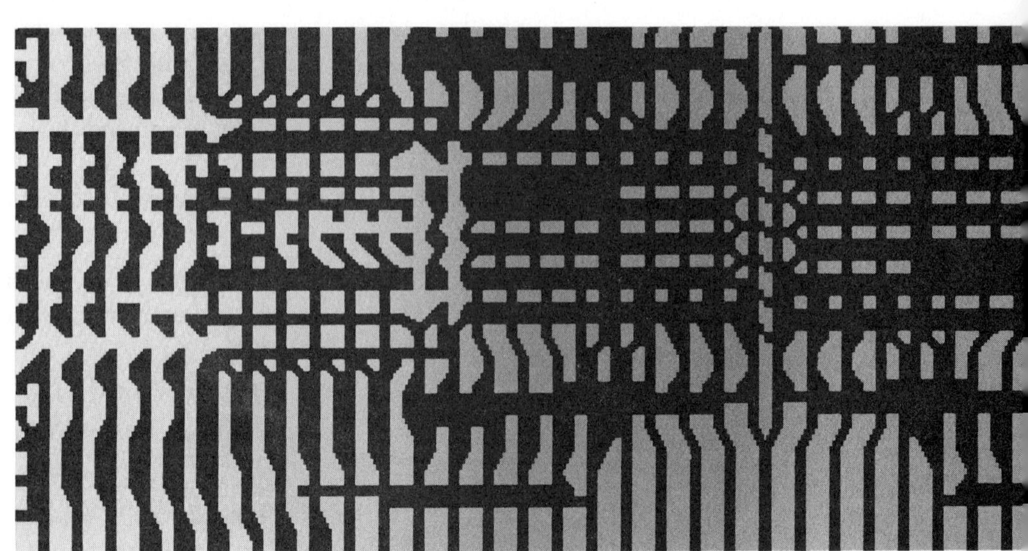

3 Entering Data

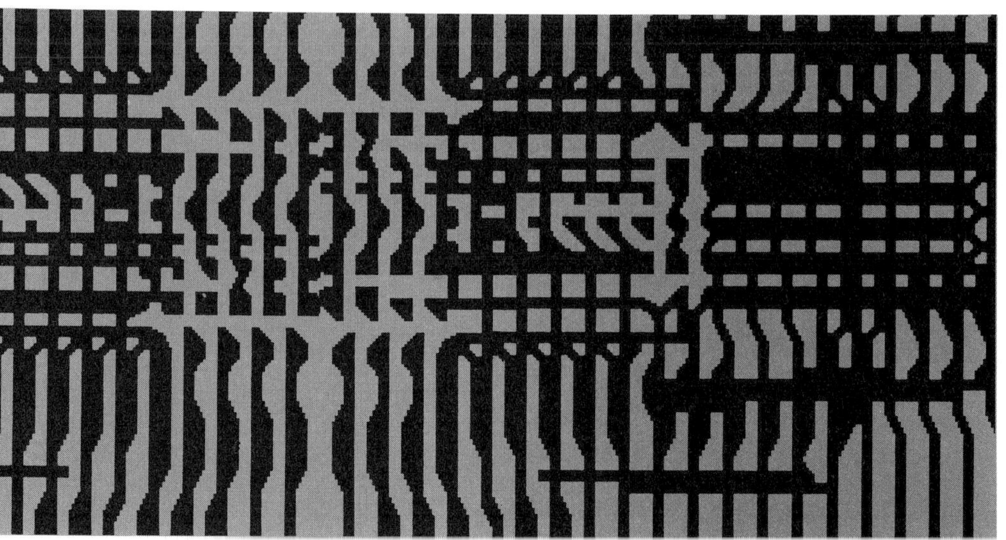

IN THIS CHAPTER

Punched Cards
Punched Paper Tape
Other Keyed Input
Magnetic-Ink Character Recognition
Optical Character Recognition
Scanners
Voice-Input Units
Mice and Other Pointing Devices
Remote Terminals

In simplest terms, the computer's primary job is to process data. It does so to provide useful information. Our first duty, as users who want to obtain that information, is to make the needed data available for processing.

Presenting data to a data-processing system is similar in many ways to writing a letter to a friend. The ideas and facts you want to convey must be expressed by *symbols* your friend can understand. In most cases, you use the letters of the English alphabet, numerals, and punctuation marks. You write these symbols in specific sequences to form words, sentences, and paragraphs. The letter is sent to your friend, who then reads and interprets the symbols. The symbols are your means of communication.

The first point you need to understand here is that symbols by themselves are not information. Rather, they represent information. The printed characters on this page are symbols that convey one meaning to some persons, a different meaning to others, and no meaning at all to persons who do not know how to interpret them. Look at the symbols in Figure 3-1. Which ones are meaningful to you?

Symbols that can be read and interpreted by data-processing machines often differ from those used by people. The nature and meaning of the symbols that can be read by a particular machine are determined by the designer of the machine. These symbols, once devised, become the language of the machine. If

30
48
STOP
ONE WAY

Figure 3-1 Many kinds of symbols are used to convey information.

the machine cannot understand the meaning of our human symbols, they must be converted from our language to the language that the machine is capable of understanding. That language becomes the means of communication between us and the machine.

Truly radical changes have occurred over the years in the methods, media, and devices used for data entry. Initially, all computer systems performed *batch processing.* In a batch-processing application, user data is collected in a group, or *batch,* before it is submitted as input to a computer system. For example, employee time cards may be collected by Friday noon from the employees in Building 28, grouped by department, and sent as a batch to the Payroll Department. Time cards from the employees in other locations of the firm may be collected, grouped, and forwarded similarly. The data from all the batches may be put together in one large batch that serves as input to weekly payroll processing.

Batch processing of input data usually involves gathering and transcribing data from *source documents* onto a data-recording medium that is acceptable as EDP-system input. The source documents may be invoices, sales slips, or simple listings on paper. The transcription step is usually a keying operation. For many years, the most common approach was to key the data onto punched cards.

Later, key-to-tape, key-to-disk, and key-to-diskette devices were used. As we'll see, magnetic-ink character-recognition devices and optical character-recognition devices reflect still further advances in the preparation of batch input. These devices help to ease the data-preparation task by capturing data in a machine-readable form at its source (the place where it is generated). This technique is known as *source data automation.* It is being used increasingly in business data processing.

In the mid-1950s and 1960s, as additional user applications were computerized, devices and techniques were developed to support *transaction processing.* In a transaction-processing application, data is not collected in batches. Instead, data is entered into the computer system for immediate processing whenever the activity that creates the data occurs. For example, customer requests for reservations on airline flights are *transactions* that generate one-by-one inputs to an airline reservations system. The requests may be submitted for any flight, at any time, via telephones or at airport service desks, and so on. Each request must be handled promptly. In many cases, an airline attendant keys in the transaction data (flight number, date, number of seats, and other information) from a visual-display terminal. The data is processed immediately. A confirmation that the reservation has been made, or a message indicating that it cannot be made, is sent back to the airline attendant. A transaction-processing system that not only allows users to enter transaction data as it is generated but also provides immediate feedback to those users supports *interactive,* or *conversational, processing.*

A device that has both a televisionlike screen and a typewriterlike keyboard is the most popular means of entering transaction data. As we'll see, alternatives to keyboard input are now appearing. And source data automation is "the name of the game" in transaction processing. Chances are you see examples of source data automation whenever you visit a local supermarket. Clerks responsible for stocking or inventory control commonly check shelves and record their findings on handheld terminals. Other clerks use optical scanners to enter sales data at checkout counters. If you've used an automated teller machine (ATM) to make a deposit or withdraw funds from a bank account, you've entered transaction data yourself.

The volume of data that users want to process with computer help is increasing. This means that the volume of data that must be entered into computers is increasing also. In this chapter, we look at the input options available to you and other users of computers. In the next chapter, we look at the options available for output.

Punched Cards

For years, *card readers* were the workhorses of data entry. They sensed data recorded as punched holes in the columns of cards, converted the data into electronic pulses, and forwarded the pulses to the computer as input.

The most common type of punched card was the Hollerith, or IBM, card. It contained 12 horizontal rows and 80 vertical columns. Data was represented (coded) by the presence or absence of small rectangular holes in specific locations in the columns. The method of data representation generally used with these cards was called *Hollerith code.* Each character in this code was represented by a unique combination of punched holes in one card column. The Hollerith code characters represented in the card columns in Figure 3-2 are printed directly above the appropriate columns at the top of the card.

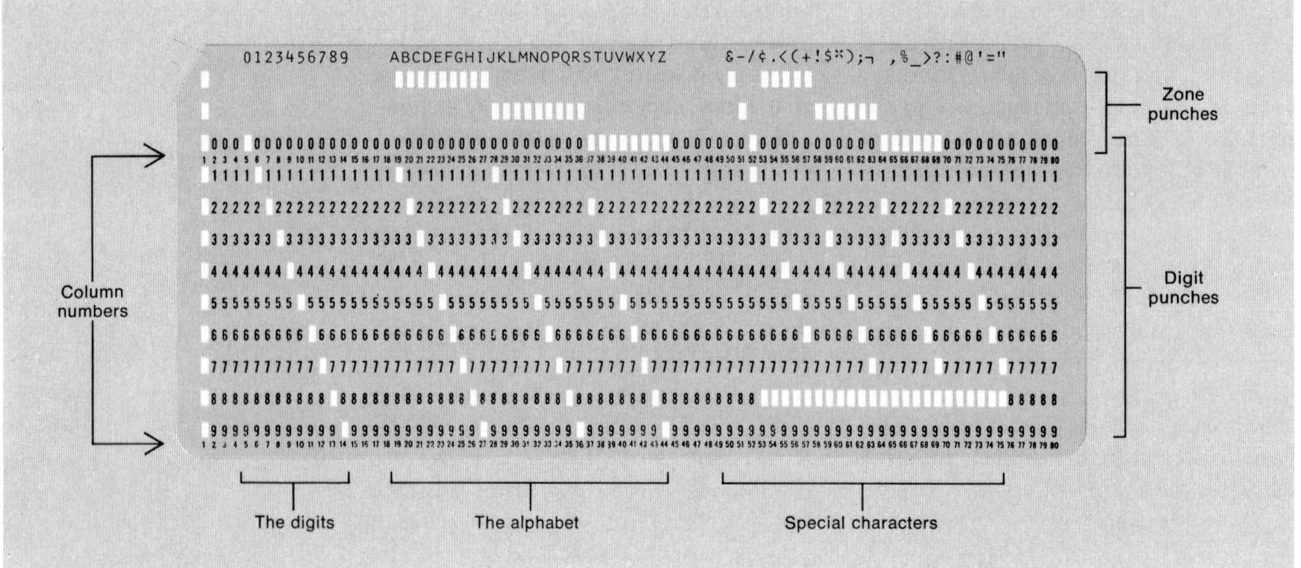
0123456789
ABCDEFGHIJKLMNOPQRSTUVWXYZ
&-/¢.<(+!$*);¬ ,%_>?:#@'="
Zone punches
Digit punches
Column numbers
The digits
The alphabet
Special characters

Figure 3-2 Hollerith code characters appear as unique combinations of holes in the columns of punched cards.

These characters are shown on the card for our convenience. They were not read by the card reader. It looked only at the combinations of holes.

Of course, before a card reader could read data from punched cards, the holes representing the data had to be punched into them. In common practice, the data was punched into cards in a separate data-preparation step using either of two approaches—*offline* or *online.* In the vast majority of offline operations, a human operator, using a machine called a *keypunch,* transcribed the data from source documents to the punched cards. (See Figure 3-3.) The keyboard of a keypunch was similar to that of a typewriter. The accuracy of the punched cards was then checked in a rekeying operation on another machine known as a *verifier.* Any incorrectly coded cards were removed from the batch of input. The data they were to contain was keypunched again into new cards.

Finally, the correctly punched cards were placed in the hopper of a card-reading machine attached (online) to the processor of the EDP system. The Hollerith code characters could be stored as 12-position characters in primary storage, but doing so would require a significant amount of storage. For this reason, input data in Hollerith code was converted to an internal data-representation scheme (ASCII or EBCDIC, which we'll learn about later). This conversion was performed by the control unit of the card reader as data was read from the card.

In an online data-preparation operation, the punching of holes into 80-column cards was controlled by the computer, rather than by a human operator. Electronic pulses were transmitted from the computer to a *card punch.* It interpreted the pulses and caused holes to be punched in specific locations on previously unpunched cards. These newly punched cards were then read by a card reader. Some vendors developed *card read-punch units* that operated online to perform both card-punching and card-reading operations. Such units may still be used today where much high-volume batch processing is required.

Punched Paper Tape

Initially, punched paper tape served as a primary input medium to message-sending devices (teletypewriters, for example). The data to be transmitted was punched into the tape, read by the message-sending device, and converted to electrical signals for transmission. At the message destination, a duplicate paper tape was produced by a message-receiving device. With the advent of computers and of devices that could read data punched into paper tape as input to a computer system, the data on tape could also be submitted to a computer for processing.

Not uncommonly, paper-tape input was produced as a byproduct of routine clerical procedures. For example, a paper tape was punched while an operator typed invoices to be mailed to customers. The paper tape containing the invoice data was used to update the company's accounting records.

A paper tape produced as output from a computer system was often used as input to machine tools used in production and manufacturing processes. The tape-driven tools were called *numerical control (NC) machines*. We discussed such machines under "Computers in Manufacturing" in Chapter 1. Today, more flexible robotic systems are replacing machines controlled by prepunched tapes in many user applications.

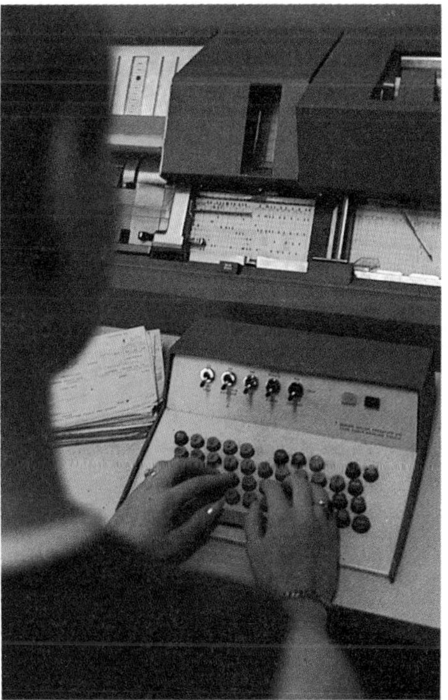

Figure 3-3 Keypunching is one "tried and true" way of preparing data to be read as input to a computer. (Courtesy Marvin Lazarus/Photo Researchers)

Other Keyed Input

Although punched cards gained widespread acceptance as a computer input medium, user organizations saw disadvantages—slow input rates, susceptibility to operator error, excessive card handling, large storage space requirements for cards, and so forth. Skyrocketing labor charges for data preparation, the need to keep pace with rapidly increasing amounts of data, and the requirements for fast system response (shorter *turnaround time*) led to searches for alternatives. Early alternatives still required keying operations, but they did not require the use of punched cards. These alternatives were suitable for creating batch input and are still used today where high-volume batch data-entry operations are required.

Key-to-Tape Devices

The concept of *key-to-tape* was introduced in 1965 when Mohawk Data Sciences Corporation marketed a data recorder as a single-unit replacement for the keypunch and the veri-

Doing It Right

Most of us know that making errors when keying is oh so easy. Procedures to check for errors and correct them must be an integral part of keyboard data entry. Correct output is possible only if correct input is provided.

fier. The data recorder consisted of a keyboard for entering data, a small memory to hold data while it was being checked for accuracy, and magnetic recording hardware to write data on tape. After data had been keyed on the tape, the tape was rewound and the same device was used to verify it.

In 1968 Honeywell became the first major computer manufacturer to compete with Mohawk Data Sciences for key-to-tape business. Soon many other companies entered the field. Two configurations were offered to users: standalone and key-to-central tape.

Standalone devices were initially the most common. Some had keypunchlike keyboards and were usually located in a centralized data-preparation area where they replaced keypunches on a one-for-one basis. Others had standard typewriterlike keyboards and were used where data was generated. In most cases, a typist without any special training simultaneously produced a printed document and recorded the data on tape. The contents of tapes created using these standalone devices were pooled onto a single, standard half-inch-wide magnetic tape. The tape was provided as batch input to a computer in subsequent processing.

Key-to-central-tape devices, or clustered key-to-tape devices, were introduced in 1968. Each cluster consisted of several keyboard workstations, a multiplexer device for control of the keyboards (accepting input from one, then another, and so on), and one or two magnetic-tape units. Such a configuration was especially useful for batch applications where large quantities of the same kind of data must be keyed. The pooling of the keyed data onto a single magnetic tape happened as part of the initial keying activity.

The early key-to-tape devices stored from 200 to 800 characters on one inch of tape. In contrast, to store 800 characters on punched cards, at least 10 cards were required. Data could be read from magnetic tape much faster than from cards. Whereas cards were bulky and difficult to store, magnetic tapes could be transported and stored easily. When the data stored on a tape was no longer needed, the tape could be reused to store other data.

Key-to-Disk Devices

The *key-to-disk,* or *shared processor,* concept was introduced by Computer Machine Corporation in 1968. It was a step toward direct input of data for processing. The data keyed by each operator entered a small computer system (usually a *minicomputer*) where it was edited and validated. If an error was detected, the responsible operator was notified so that the error could be corrected right away.

A typical key-to-disk configuration consisted of from 8 to 64 workstations linked to a minicomputer (the "shared processor"). It stored the keyed data temporarily on magnetic disk. Additional data stored previously could be combined with the keyed data under stored-program control. For example, operators keyed in customer numbers and amounts of orders. A stored program directed the minicomputer to read each customer number as it was entered, retrieve the corresponding customer name and address from a file on disk, and place that data following the customer number in the batch input that was being created. Less keying by operators and less verifying of newly keyed data was

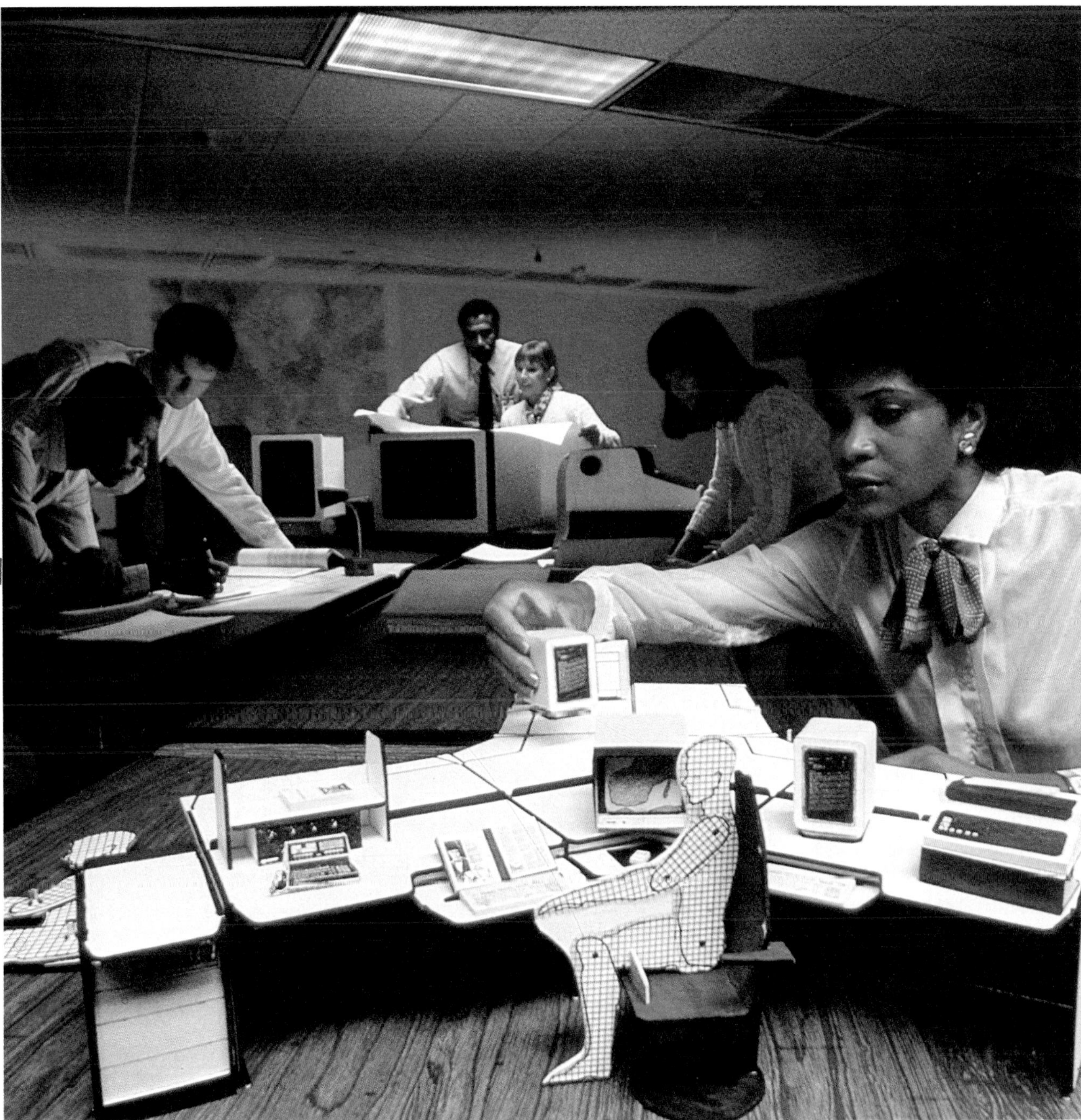

ERGONOMICS

The science that fits the workplace to the person, rather than the person to the workplace. Also referred to as *human engineering,* ergonomics involves taking body movements and body dimensions into account when designing and positioning chairs, work surfaces, keyboards, and displays. It is concerned with air, space, heat, light, and sound affecting workers' physical comfort. It advocates privacy without sacrifice of social and business communications. It seeks to promote feelings of well-being, security, and safety in work environments. *(Photo courtesy TRW Inc.)*

required. When the data entry was completed, the data on disk was written to a standard magnetic tape that could be used as batch input to a main computer. (See Figure 3-4.)

Key-to-Diskette Devices

In a key-to-diskette data-entry system, flexible (floppy) disks, or diskettes, are substituted for the single, conventional (hard) disk and tape of a key-to-disk system. Each operator inserts a diskette into a slot in the disk drive of his or her data-entry unit and then enters data via a keyboard that is also part of the device.

Today, some key-to-diskette units are treated much like typewriters. The recording of data on diskettes is a byproduct of routine office procedures. Operators are secretaries or administrative specialists rather than data-entry personnel. For example, the function being performed (from the operator's point of view) may be the preparation of a business letter. The format and content of the letter may be such that most of it can be copied from a general letter form already available. The operator need only modify that general letter form (in storage) to suit the particular business need. She or he then causes the modified letter to be printed on paper and written to diskette. The diskette copy of the letter is the company's record of the correspondence.

Today, some key-to-diskette units are treated much like typewriters.

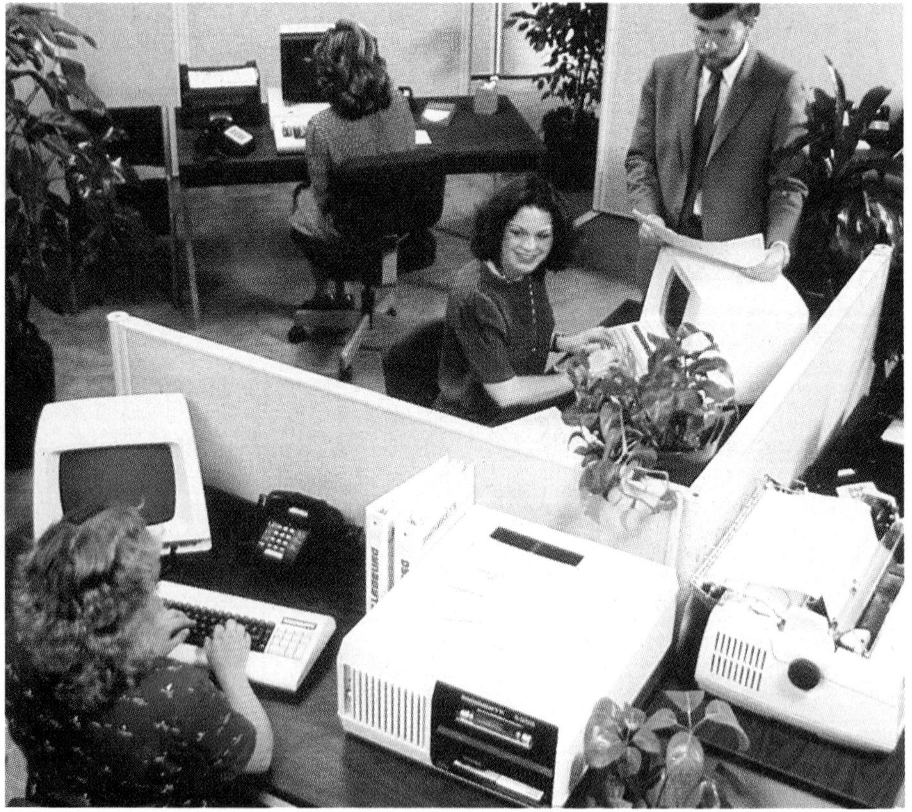

Figure 3-4 Operators work at devices with keyboards and visual-display screens in a key-to-disk data-entry environment. (Courtesy Dynabyte Business Computers)

The preparation of a business letter as just described is a typical *word-processing* activity. We'll say much more about word processing later. The important point to note here is that this kind of key-to-diskette device is a multifunction unit; it handles both word processing and data processing.

Users with large data-processing workloads may set up clustered key-to-diskette configurations. Like standalone key-to-diskette units, the role of clustered units often expands beyond that of data entry. Some are used for word-processing functions. Some are supported by system software that allows business application programs to be executed. Off-the-shelf software for common business operations such as accounts payable, accounts receivable, and payroll is available from well-known vendors.

In both the standalone and clustered key-to-diskette approaches, the initial medium of interchange between the key-to-diskette devices and the main computer was magnetic tape. The contents of diskettes were transcribed to tape for entry into the main computer. Then diskette input/output units that could read the contents of diskettes directly into large computers were developed. No special diskette-to-tape step was required.

Magnetic-Ink Character Recognition

Have you written a personal check recently? Or have you received your processed checks and a monthly statement showing which of the checks you've written found their way back to your bank during the past accounting period? Did you notice the stylized characters printed at the bottom of each check before you used it? Did you notice that the amount for which you wrote each check was also recorded in the same stylized characters at the bottom of the check when it was returned to you? The characters appear to be printed in ordinary black ink. The ink contains finely ground particles of iron oxide that can be magnetized and then sensed by *magnetic-ink character-recognition (MICR)* devices. (See Figure 3-5.)

MICR was adopted by the American Bankers Association (ABA) in the late 1950s as a way to meet an urgent need of the banking industry: the need to process an ever-increasing volume of checks with speed and accuracy. In common practice, a check may be written on an account at one bank (its home bank), cashed at another bank, and then handled by one or more Federal Reserve banks before it is finally returned to its home bank and then to its originator. Therefore, the need not only for speed but also for standardization in MICR processing soon became apparent. In 1960 the ABA agreed on the *E13B type font* as a MICR standard character set. You can see the four special symbols and most of the digits in this set in Figure 3-5.

When you order a supply of blank checks, the checks you receive contain certain information in MICR form: your account number and the bank number assigned to the firm that handles your account. When a check you have written is cashed or deposited at a bank, that bank's employees must insure that the amount for which the check was written is also encoded on the check in MICR characters. (See Figure 3-6.) A keyboard-type device is used to do this encoding. The characters on the check are then magnetized and read electronically. The bank numbers,

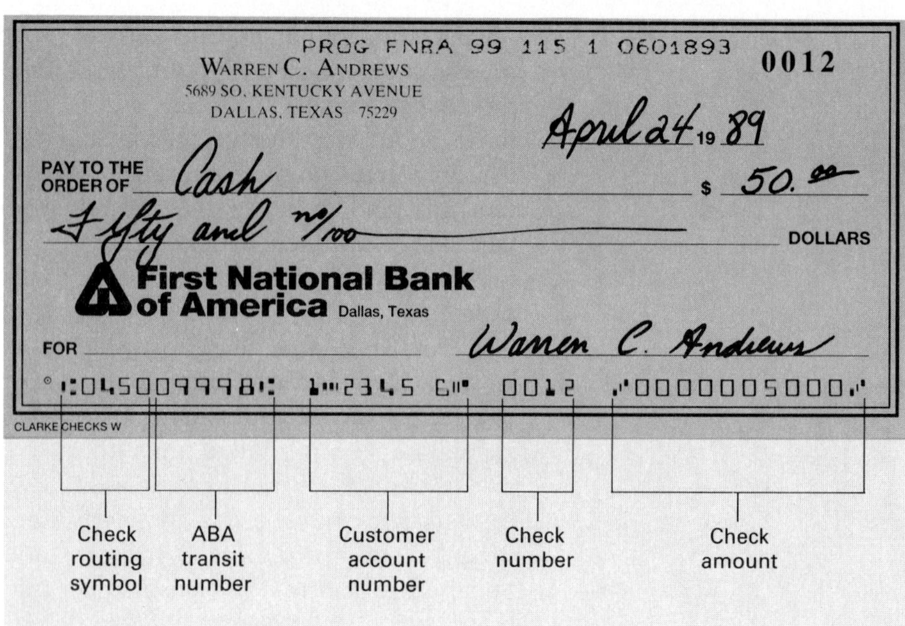
PROG FNRA 99 115 1 0601893
WARREN C. ANDREWS
5689 SO. KENTUCKY AVENUE
DALLAS, TEXAS 75229
0012
April 24, 19 89
PAY TO THE ORDER OF Cash
$ 50.00
Fifty and no/100
DOLLARS
First National Bank of America
Dallas, Texas
FOR
CLARKE CHECKS W
Check routing symbol
ABA transit number
Customer account number
Check number
Check amount

Figure 3-5 The magnetic-ink characters inscribed at the bottom of a personal check can be submitted as input to a computer system. (Courtesy Recognition Equipment Incorporated)

Figure 3-6 Banking personnel encode the amounts for which checks are written as MICR characters in preparation for further processing. (Courtesy NCR)

account numbers, and amounts of all the checks in a batch are converted to a machine-readable form acceptable as input to a computer system. This data may be used in preparing monthly banking statements or for control and auditing purposes.

Without MICR or similar automated data-entry and handling procedures, it is unlikely that the banking industry could process annually the more than 80 billion checks that it now handles.

An important labor-saving feature of the MICR approach is that data need not be transcribed from a source document to a special input form before it can be processed. The customer's check is the input form. A second point to notice is that only the amount of the check and whether it is to be debited or credited to a customer account must be recorded after the check is received at a bank.

The ability of the MICR unit to physically arrange the checks is another important labor-saving feature. The lengths, widths, and thicknesses of checks containing MICR characters can vary. MICR devices are also highly tolerant of smudges and wrinkles. Human involvement, which is both costly and error-prone (whether we like to admit it or not), is minimized. Without MICR or similar automated data-entry and handling procedures, it is unlikely that the banking industry could process annually the more than 80 billion checks that it now handles. Department stores, credit-card companies, government agencies, and data-processing centers are also taking advantage of MICR. The "bottom-line" benefit is increased productivity.

Computer Use Spreads

Pause to think a minute. In Chapter 2, we noted that the first commercially available computer, a UNIVAC I, was not installed until 1951. Yet the banking industry was heavily committed to electronic data processing before the 1950s were over. Today banks couldn't meet their customers' needs without computer help.

Optical Character Recognition

Data recorded on paper as optically readable symbols can be provided as input to some computer systems. The symbols can take any of a wide variety of forms: marks; bars; numbers, letters, and special characters of certain type fonts; and ordinary handwriting. You deal with many optically readable symbols daily without even realizing it. The letters and words you are reading now are "optically readable" by you and by some computer input devices.

You deal with many optically readable symbols daily without even realizing it.

Because *optical character recognition (OCR)* devices offer such a wide range of capabilities, the use of OCR devices to enter both batch and transaction data is increasing. Let's look at a few applications.

Optical Marks

Optical marks are the simplest form of optical data. An ordinary pencil or pen is used to make the marks in predetermined locations on source documents. An optical mark reader uses a light beam to scan the sheets and generates electrical signals to represent the data. The signals are forwarded to the computer for processing.

Multiple-choice test score sheets, forms used in surveys, and questionnaires are common examples of optical-mark source documents. Optical-mark data may also be used for order writing, inventory control, insurance policy rating, payroll, and so forth. (See Figure 3-7.) The source documents must be designed and manufactured carefully; unless they are people-proof (that is, can be understood and completed easily), users may not mark them correctly.

Because optical marks, like the magnetic-ink characters described earlier, do not have to be converted by an operator to a computer-acceptable form, they increase the speed with which data can be handled by an EDP system. Generally, the data is batch-processed. Nevertheless, in today's "hurry-up" world, speed is often a key requirement.

Bar Codes

Chances are good that you are already familiar with at least one kind of bar code: the *Universal Product Code (UPC)* that appears on many consumer products to facilitate checkout at retail stores. The code for each product is a unique combination of ten pairs of vertical bars. The bars are read, or sensed, by a handheld optical wand reader or a fixed optical scanner. This data is converted to electrical signals and forwarded to a computer for processing. Given only this data as input, the computer can determine what the product is, find its price from price lists in storage, and print out the name and the price of the product on a customer receipt. The computer also maintains inventory records of the products sold and thus helps store personnel keep merchandise in stock. The initial processing of the customer's purchase is an example of transaction processing. Maintaining inventory records may be done as a part of this processing. Alternatively, the inventory data may be accumulated for subsequent batch input to an inventory-control program that is run at a convenient time. Notice also that it's much easier to change the price of a product by changing one stored price in the computer than by restamping the price on a large, al-

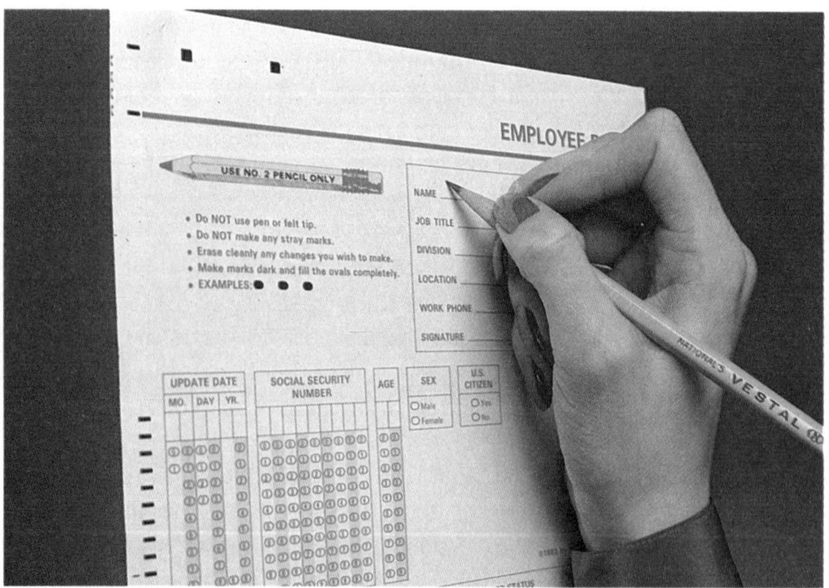
EMPLOYEE
USE NO. 2 PENCIL ONLY
• Do NOT use pen or felt tip.
• Do NOT make any stray marks.
• Erase cleanly any changes you wish to make.
• Make marks dark and fill the ovals completely.
• EXAMPLES:
NAME
JOB TITLE
DIVISION
LOCATION
WORK PHONE
SIGNATURE
UPDATE DATE
MO.
DAY
YR.
SOCIAL SECURITY NUMBER
AGE
SEX
U.S. CITIZEN
VESTAL

Figure 3-7 Employees who complete carefully designed employee fact sheets are creating optically readable data for use in subsequent processing. (Courtesy National Computer Systems)

0
35993 28031

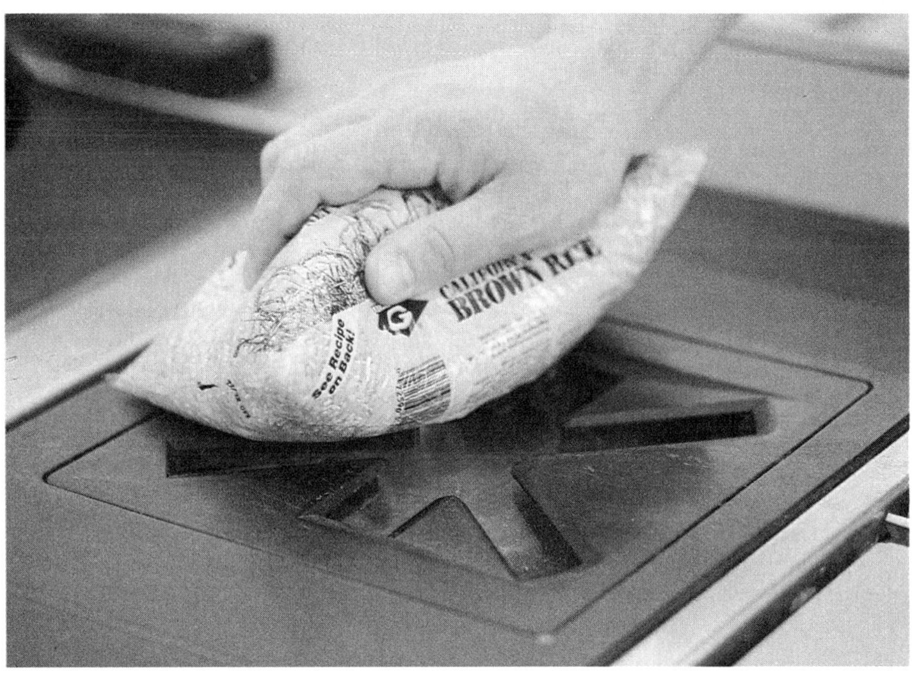
BROWN RICE
See Recipe on Back!

Figure 3-8 An optical scanner reads bar-code data at a supermarket checkout. Passing items over the scanner is simpler, faster, and more reliable than the cash-register keying operations required formerly. (Courtesy Mark McKenna)

ready-shelved supply of the product. (See Figure 3-8.)

Many organizations use bar-code tags to track items through an environment. The environment may be anything from a factory, to a loading dock or distribution center, to an office. The tagged items may be units of production or finished goods. Among the benefits are: higher people productivity, greater accuracy in record keeping, tighter control of inventories, and an ability to deliver the right items at the right time to customers.

Optical Characters

Consider the cents-off discount coupons included in the food section of your newspaper or in some of your magazines. Billions of these coupons are distributed annually. Consumers are hauling them back to supermarkets in record numbers. Have you ever wondered how the discounts are reconciled? One answer is: with the help of computers and OCR devices.

Large coupon clearinghouses are located in the United States and Mexico. Thanks to OCR reader/sorter capabilities, more than 35,000 of the coupons can be sorted, counted, and validated in one hour. Product manufacturers are achieving total coupon control. The OCR reader/sorters can also print a variety of related management, marketing, and accounting reports.

Some OCR scanners can read characters printed in any of a wide variety of type fonts. This capability has led to the use of OCR in word processing. The characters on each page of text are scanned, represented as electronic pulses, and stored in computer files. There is no need for typists to key in all the data. They can simply edit the stored text, make required content changes, and produce final documents. The initial data entry may be achieved 20 to 40 times faster than would be achieved with manual keying. Some users achieve

TYPEREADER 2
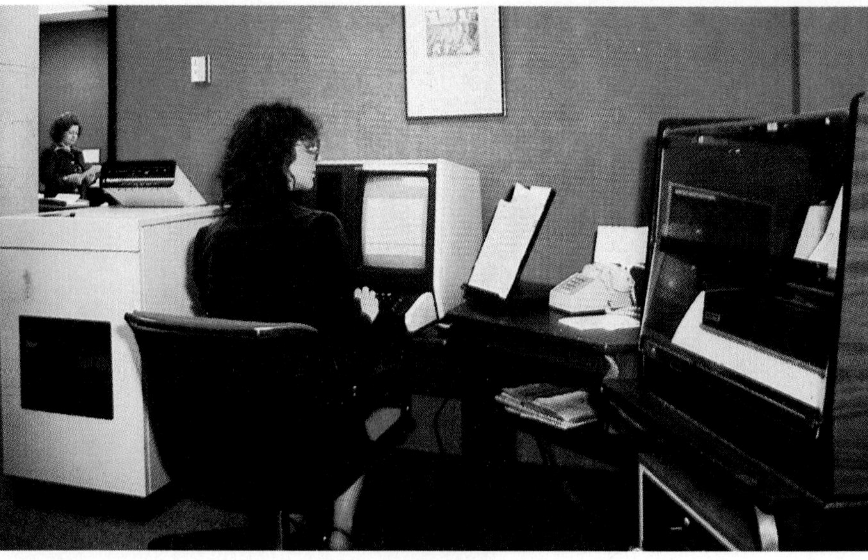

OCR IN THE OFFICE ASSISTS WORD PROCESSING

Word-processing systems with OCR input capabilities are helping many businesses to increase office productivity. For example, an attorney may create the first draft of a lease, purchase agreement, will, or pension plan, say, by dictation or handwriting. The draft is then typed in rough form and returned to the attorney for an initial review. At the same time, a second copy of the typed version is read by an optical scanner. It converts the data to a form that can be stored for word processing. Any corrections or changes to the document can be made with minimal rekeying. A final copy can be formatted and printed when desired. Existing, often lengthy, legal documents can also be read by the optical scanner. For these, scanning—not manual keying—is the initial means of data entry. Once the documents have been entered into storage, they can be changed, combined with portions of other documents, and printed with ease. High-quality final documents are provided to clients in a timely manner. *(Photos courtesy Hendrix Technologies, Inc.)*

an overall doubling or tripling of productivity.

In recent years, scanner prices have started to decline. Scanners have become increasingly popular as input devices in desktop computer systems. Some but not all of these scanners are OCR devices. Therefore, we discuss scanners again below.

Handwritten Data

Even greater versatility is available through the use of OCR devices that can read ordinary handwriting as well as machine-printed characters. For example, employee time cards may have employee names, numbers, and departments preprinted on them as OCR characters. Employees may use ordinary pencils to record working times each day on the cards. Both forms of data are read during payroll processing. As another example, credit-card receipts containing both OCR characters and handwritten data may be used as direct input to an accounts-receivable application.

Scanners

A *scanner* is an input device that reads data from paper and transmits

RULE	CORRECT	INCORRECT
1. Write big characters.	0 2 8 3 4	0 2 8 3 4
2. Close loops.	0 6 8 8 9	0 6 8 8 9
3. Use simple shapes.	0 2 3 7 5	0 2 3 7 5
4. Do not link characters.	0 0 8 8 1	0 0 8 8 1
5. Connect lines.	4 5 T	4 5 T
6. Block print.	C S T X Z	C S T X Z

WRITING FOR COMPUTERS

If you are writing data that is to be read as input to a computer system, you must write carefully. By following these few basic guidelines, you can help to insure that your data is machine-readable.

that data to a computer for processing. Today's scanners come in many shapes and sizes and range in price from about $200 to $50,000. Their capabilities are based on either of two technologies: optical character recognition (OCR), which we discussed above, or image scanning.

An OCR scanner, together with its associated software, can take pages of text and convert the text characters to ASCII code characters or to files formatted especially for use with a popular word-processing package (say, Microsoft Word, WordStar, or Word Perfect). Some OCR scanners are designed to recognize only a predefined set of typefaces. Others can recognize the shape of nearly any character through a set of recognition rules implemented as software algorithms. The scanning software typically marks a character that cannot be determined conclusively and allows the user to manually correct and enter it. The OCR software may have problems reading proportionally spaced text or text formatted in multiple columns. And OCR scanners cannot handle graphics. To scan company logos, charts, illustrations, and photographs, an image scanner is required.

The function of an image scanner is not to convert text characters to ASCII but rather to scan graphic elements and generate series of bits that correspond to the intensities of light reflected back from the graphics. The bit image generated by the scanner is converted to a usable form by software provided with the scanner. In data-processing terminology, we say that the graphics are *digitized.* The user can then retrieve and edit the graphics file much as he or she might edit a text file. (Indeed, photographs of planetary surfaces in outer space are read into computer storage and enhanced using similar technologies.)

Image scanners are used widely in *desktop publishing.* Assume, for example, that Ventura Publisher, a

Figure 3-9 Hewlett-Packard's ScanJet Plus desktop scanner enables personal-computer users to capture photos, line art, and text from a broad range of sources for use in desktop publishing applications. (Courtesy Hewlett-Packard Company)

popular desktop-publishing package, is being used to produce a company newsletter. Text for the lead article (initially entered into computer storage using a word-processing program or an OCR device) can be positioned anywhere on the opening page. An illustration read and stored as a graphics file with the help of an image scanner can also be positioned on the page and sized or cropped (trimmed at the edges) appropriately. The clarity of the illustration depends both on the resolution of the image scanner and the resolution of the output device. When the user is satisfied with the page layout as displayed on a visual-display screen, the page can be produced as printer output. (See Figure 3-9.)

Video digitizers are the latest scanning devices to hit the marketplace. They're designed to capture images from a live or recorded video source for analysis or touch up. A golfer's swing or a skater's dance movements can be captured and analyzed with computer help. A sales brochure showing a new car viewed from several angles can be created using this enhanced image technology.

Voice-Input Units

An increasing amount of work is being done to develop voice-input capabilities. Users of microcomputer systems are likely to appreciate such capabilities. They're also useful in large-system applications such as parts management and quality control, where users' hands and/or eyes are otherwise occupied. Assembly workers can speak the part numbers of components they're assembling. A quality-control inspector wearing a small microphone can follow a checklist on a televisionlike screen and orally describe the physical characteristics of components, subassemblies, or finished products. The voice input is transmitted directly to a computer. It can update stock status, determine the immediate disposition

Talking to Computers

Voice may well be the ultimate communication medium between people and machines. It's portable; most of us have it; and we can use it from any location—say, a phone at summer camp or a bus station in downtown Columbus.

of defective items, and provide timely, accurate reports for management. (See Figure 3-10.)

Most voice-input units can accept data (sounds) from locally connected microphones or from remote sources via telephones. Some are speaker-independent. They can understand any user. Others must be trained by each user to recognize his or her voice. The training involves repeating from 10 to 15 times each "word" (sound of 2 seconds or less duration) the system will be expected to recognize. At present, if you want speaker independence, you must be willing to accept a small vocabulary—perhaps "yes," "no," and the numbers 0 through 9.

Generally, voice-input units cannot as yet recognize continuous speech. Pauses of varying lengths are required between words. Computer recognition of human speech has not come easily. No one ever says a word exactly the same way twice. However, voice-recognition research is continuing. Recognition accuracies of better than 99 percent are being achieved. Increased worker productivity and significant cost savings are also being realized.

Computer recognition of human speech has not come easily.

CIT-101

Figure 3-10 An inspector whose hands are busy enters data by speaking into a voice-input device. (Voice Recognition Equipment by Interstate Voice Products)

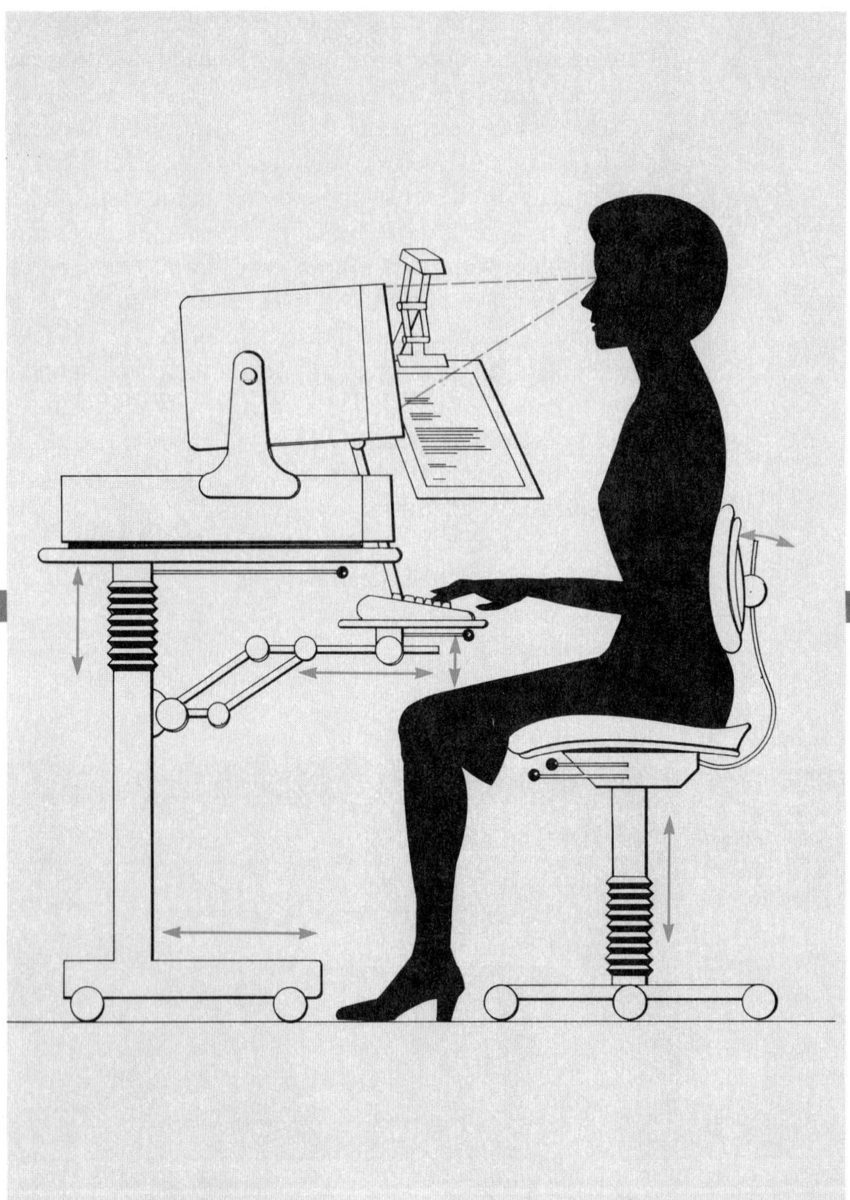

PRACTICAL TIPS FOR VISUAL-DISPLAY USERS

To work in comfort—

- Select a visual-display unit with a nonglare screen that can be tilted back about 10 to 20 degrees.
- The face of the screen should be about 18 inches from your eyes.
- The top of the screen should be no higher than your eye level.
- Select a chair with a seat that adjusts up or down and changes angles and a backrest that adjusts separately from the seat. When you're seated, the backrest should support the small of your back, and your feet should rest flat on the floor.
- Insure the keyboard is positioned at a comfortable working level (in general, that's lower than conventional tabletops). An adjustable work surface and/or a detachable keyboard provide maximum flexibility.
- Close nearby blinds or lower shades and avoid intense lighting from overhead fixtures. Use a small adjustable task light and position source documents for easy reading to avoid eye strain.
- Stretch occasionally. Look away from your work. Take a break once in awhile!

What's a Mouse?

To some, it's a rodent; to others, it's a pointing device.

Mice and Other Pointing Devices

Often, the user of a visual-display unit is obtaining information from a computer system rather than providing data to it. However, that's not always the case. Increasingly, the screens of terminals, workstations, and personal computer systems are being used interactively for input operations also. A special *cursor* character (usually, an underscore or an arrow) marks the current, or active, position on the screen. Menus from which selections can be made and forms with blanks to be filled in may be displayed to assist the user. The user may press special positioning keys on the keyboard or manipulate any of several pointing devices to move the cursor about on the screen; the current position on the screen is changed accordingly.

The *mouse* was introduced to the marketplace in 1983 when Apple Computer announced its Apple Lisa machine. The user-friendliness of its follow-on Apple Macintosh family, which also uses a mouse, is now widely recognized. (See Figure 3-11, left.) Instead of keying in a series of commands—which must be memorized or researched and then keyed correctly—the Macintosh user may simply (1) move the mouse to position the cursor atop a small on-screen graphic called an *icon,* and (2) click a button on the mouse to initiate action. For example, you might click while the cursor is on the icon of a pencil to start a word-processing program or you might click when the cursor's on a garbage can to delete a file. Mice are also used for data entry. You might choose the supplier from which to purchase a part by moving the cursor to the supplier's name on a menu list and then clicking the mouse button.

For some time, the mouse was viewed as simply a gimmick, a conversation piece that "computer nuts" could show to their friends. That's no longer true.

For some time, the mouse was viewed as simply a gimmick, a conversation piece that "computer nuts" could show to their friends. That's no longer true. The growing popularity of graphics interfaces among soft-

Figure 3-11 Cursor-positioning tools such as the palm-sized mouse used with Apple's Macintosh computer (left) and touch-sensitive screens (right) are helping to make it easy for almost anyone to interact with a computer system and submit data to it for processing. (Courtesy [left] Apple Computer, Inc.; [right] Hewlett-Packard Company)

ware developers and users is leading to increased use of mice. All Macintosh users have mice even though they may not use them 100% of the time. Mice are used extensively with engineering workstations in CAD/CAM applications. About 10% of the installed base of IBM and IBM-compatible personal computers have mice attached. As additional applications become available for use with graphics interface software such as Microsoft Windows and the OS/2 Presentation Manager, an increasing number of mice are likely to find homes in corporate America.

An electronic pen commonly known as a *light pen* allows the user to make fast, accurate menu selections by simply pointing to them on the screen rather than by moving a mouse. The lack of moving parts in the device helps to assure reliability, and training is as easy as teaching someone to point. Like mice, light pens are relatively inexpensive—from $100 to $200.

Touch-sensitive screens take the concept of pointing one step further by allowing the user to simply touch the screen with a finger to make a selection. (See Figure 3-11, right.) Our fingers are familiar to us; they don't require installation; and they are relatively maintenance-free. The touch screens themselves are surprisingly durable. You'll find one at an information booth in Disney World, where it withstands continual interaction with the general public. This technology is still relatively expensive, but its cost may be justified if users who are not trained in the use of a system must interact with it. Vendors commonly identify sports, retailing, automotive repair and other service firms, and government as target markets.

The user of a *digitizer* manipulates a penlike device known as a *stylus* over a paperlike pad on a flat surface. For someone with an art or drafting background, holding a stylus may seem more natural than holding a mouse. Using a *graphics tablet* (another common name for a digitizer) to create a drawing with computer help may not seem like a major step. Historically, the big advantage of digitizers has been that they offer more precise cursor placement than other pointing devices. You're likely to find them where many fine, detailed drawings are needed. At present, even low-end digitizers are priced two to four times higher than mice. However, digitizer advocates point out that mice wear out and have to be replaced again and again. Digitizers "last a lifetime" and require no maintenance.

Remote Terminals

Suppose you want to provide data to a computer, or to get information from it, but you're not near the computer. You may be in a different part of the building, across the state, or across oceans and continents. You may be at a nurses' station in a large hospital, a school library, the shop floor of an automobile plant, or an office in midtown Manhattan. A computer system that has both data-communication and data-processing capabilities, with attached remote terminals, allows you to interact with the computer any way.

A wide variety of remote terminals are available. Their number, types, and uses are increasing daily. In this section, we direct most of our attention to remote terminals used for data entry. As you'll see, many of

Your Lost
Dog's
Ticket

FINDING LOST PETS

Many public and private animal shelters across the United States and Canada are getting computerized—or rather, animals adopted from the shelters are. Thanks to the Infopet pet identification system, lost cats, dogs, rabbits, and even birds are being identified and reunited with their owners. Happy people and happy pets result.

Activities at the Marin Humane Society in the California Bay Area demonstrate how the system works. Before a dog or cat is adopted from the shelter, a microchip about the size of a grain of rice is implanted between the shoulder blades of the animal by a staff veterinarian. No surgery is required; the chip is simply injected below the surface of the skin with a hypodermic needle. Each chip carries a unique pet identification number. That number and information about the owner of the pet are entered into the society's computer system and forwarded to the Infonet Corporation in southern California, which maintains a nationwide toll-free hotline for tracking stray animals.

As the number of pets having these unique identification numbers increases, finding the owner of a stray pet will be as simple as (1) passing a wand reader over the surface of the pet where the chip has been implanted; (2) matching the scanned pet identification number against lists of such numbers stored in computerized files; and (3) contacting the owner so identified.

Initially, all scanning by the Marin Humane Society is being done at the shelter. Someday animal control officers may carry pocket-sized terminals or microcomputers with them so that the computer-matching process can be initiated from the field. Since lost pets usually belong to families who live near the areas where they're found, in most cases the pets will be back home with their owners promptly. *(Photo courtesy Mark McKenna)*

these terminals can also perform other functions.

Special-Purpose Devices

Many remote terminals are special-purpose devices. That is, they are designed to meet particular needs. For example, in retail operations, devices known as *point-of-sale (POS) terminals* are used to capture data at the point of sale. (See Figure 3-12, top.) *Teller terminals* like the one in Figure 3-12, center, are designed for

Plumbing
Carpenter Tools
Audio Visual
Exercise
Home and Office

BUNKER
RAMO

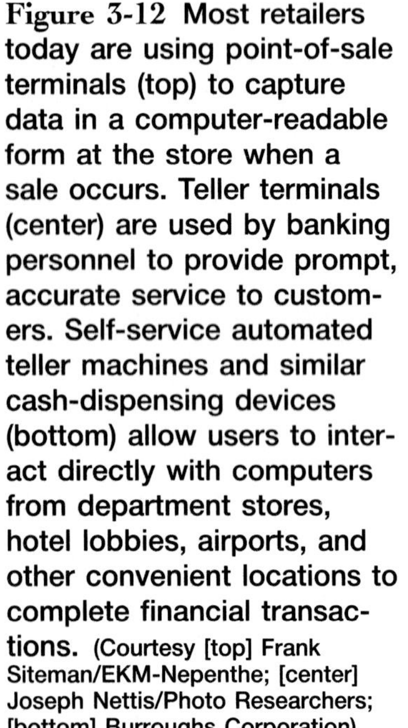

Figure 3-12 Most retailers today are using point-of-sale terminals (top) to capture data in a computer-readable form at the store when a sale occurs. Teller terminals (center) are used by banking personnel to provide prompt, accurate service to customers. Self-service automated teller machines and similar cash-dispensing devices (bottom) allow users to interact directly with computers from department stores, hotel lobbies, airports, and other convenient locations to complete financial transactions. (Courtesy [top] Frank Siteman/EKM-Nepenthe; [center] Joseph Nettis/Photo Researchers; [bottom] Burroughs Corporation)

ATM's

By the late 1980s, 97 of the top 100 banks in the United States were using automated teller machines (ATM's). More than 80% of all banks had installed them. The average operating cost of one ATM transaction was said to be about 65¢, whereas the cost of a teller-assisted transaction ranged from 90¢ to $1.20.

use by tellers in banks, savings and loans, and other financial institutions. The tellers can process deposit and withdrawal transactions, post passbooks, and print checks or receipts at their individual locations. *Automated teller machines (ATM's)* like the one in Figure 3-12, bottom, enable customers to withdraw cash from personal accounts, inquire about account balances, and take care of other business without teller assistance. (We discussed these terminals earlier under "Computers and Finance" in Chapter 1.)

Data-Collection Devices

In manufacturing and in distribution, remote terminals are often used as data-collection devices. The terminals must be sturdy—able to withstand the dust, temperature, humidity, and vibrations of shop floors, factory production lines, or warehouses. They must be accessible and easy to use. Many are wall-mounted. Desktop data-collection devices that accept keyed input are also common. As the term *data-collection device* implies, most remote terminals of this type are used to gather data for input to batch-processing applications. (See Figure 3-13.)

Portable Terminals

Computer power at your fingertips, anytime, anywhere—sound attractive? Whether you're on the road and want access to the latest home-office competitive sales data, or at home and want to avoid the early morning rush-hour commute, that computer power can be an important productivity booster. It's available through *portable terminals,* which we discuss here, and through *portable microcomputers,* which we'll discuss in Chapter 7. What's the difference between the two? A portable terminal is used to collect input or to receive output, but most of the processing is done after the input has been transmitted to a main computer elsewhere. In contrast, a portable microcomputer may do the whole job. For example, Lotus 1-2-3 may be installed and run on a portable microcomputer to calculate spreadsheet values.

Today the most popular portable terminals have typewriterlike keyboards. Some have small TV-like displays. Most have built-in acoustic couplers that can be used to establish computer connections via ordinary

Figure 3-13 At Chrysler assembly plants, workers enter a wide variety of data into online terminals positioned throughout the plants. Chrysler's automated systems feed back information to the workers and help keep track of work in process. (Courtesy Chrysler Corporation)

Computer power at your fingertips, anytime, anywhere—sound attractive?

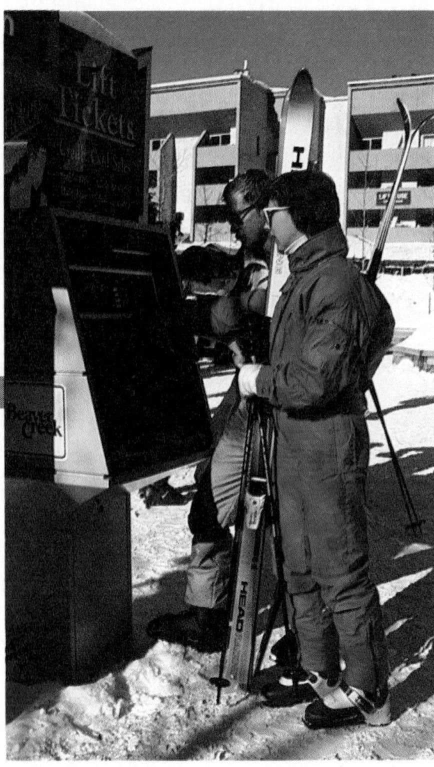
Lift Tickets
HEAD

COMPUTERS AT WORK ON THE SLOPES

There's nothing like a ski vacation, or even a quick weekend ski trip, to help you "get away from it all," you say. You'll find, however, that computers are involved there too—handling lodge reservations, monitoring and forecasting weather, making snow, and so on. If you make it to the slopes and want to get ski-lift tickets, you may even encounter an automated ski-lift ticketing terminal.

At Vail and Beaver Creek, Colorado, for example, several ticketing terminals have been installed. They run under the control of an online, automated ski-lift ticketing program. The program causes directions to skiers to be displayed on the screens of the ticketing terminals. Holders of American Express, Master Card, and VISA cards can purchase their ski-lift tickets electronically. A skier need only insert his or her card into a terminal, key in his or her personal identification number, and select a ticket type—adult or child, full-day or half-day.

The skier's authorization is checked and (if it's okay) the purchase request is processed. Ski-lift tickets dispensed from the terminal are adhesive-backed and can be applied to ski wickets just as conventional ski-lift tickets can. Because the automated verification and processing is completed in less than a minute, skiers are less likely to wait in long ticket lines. The firm operating the ski lift saves on personnel costs. The system installed at Vail and Beaver Creek is called MAX, a name that stands for *max*imum skiing pleasure. *(Photo courtesy Vail Associates, Inc. Photographer: David Lokey)* telephone lines. The terminals range in weight from about 12 to 20 pounds. (See Figure 3-14.)

Portable terminals equipped with internal storage units capable of holding several thousand characters of text are especially useful to persons whose jobs involve data gathering—poll takers, meter readers, news reporters, and the like. Those with nonvolatile internal storage units do not lose their stored data when shut off. A user of one of these terminals can enter data throughout the day, then dial the central computer location via an ordinary telephone to transmit that data during evening hours.

Handheld Terminals

Even more portable than the portables are handheld terminals. These units may weigh from 4 ounces to 3 pounds. Many resemble electronic calculators. Some are Touch-Tone devices that permit remote data entry from a telephone. (See Figure 3-15.)

We mentioned earlier that optically readable bar-code data is often entered into a computer system with the help of an optical wand reader. Wand readers with small internal storage units can function as handheld terminals. They're used to monitor shelf inventories, keep track of work in process, and the like. Many retailers and manufacturing firms

Figure 3-14 As a sales executive gathers facts pertinent to a client's needs, the facts can be keyed into a portable terminal and forwarded as input to a home-office computer. In minutes, or even seconds, a solution tailored to the client's needs will be returned as output. (Courtesy of Texas Instruments)

Meter Reading
Stockroom Control
Salesman Order Entry
Route Accounting

Figure 3-15 In meter reading, stockroom control, route accounting, and remote order-entry applications (clockwise from top left), handheld terminals are being used to enter data for processing. (Courtesy MSI Data Corporation)

could no longer get along without them.

At some hospitals, nurses use handheld terminals as electronic scratch pads. They "download" small amounts of patient-related data from a central computer to the terminals before making their rounds to patient bedsides. During the rounds, they use, update, or add to this data. When a nurse completes her rounds, she transmits the data in her terminal back to the central computer. It gets re-included in the hospital's patient database, and can be referred to by doctors caring for the patients and by other hospital personnel.

Some day, many of us may consider handheld terminals to be indispensable parts of our daily lives. We've become accustomed to checks, credit cards, and pocket calculators. We'd be lost without telephones. Handheld terminals put computing power at our fingertips and will go wherever we want to take them.

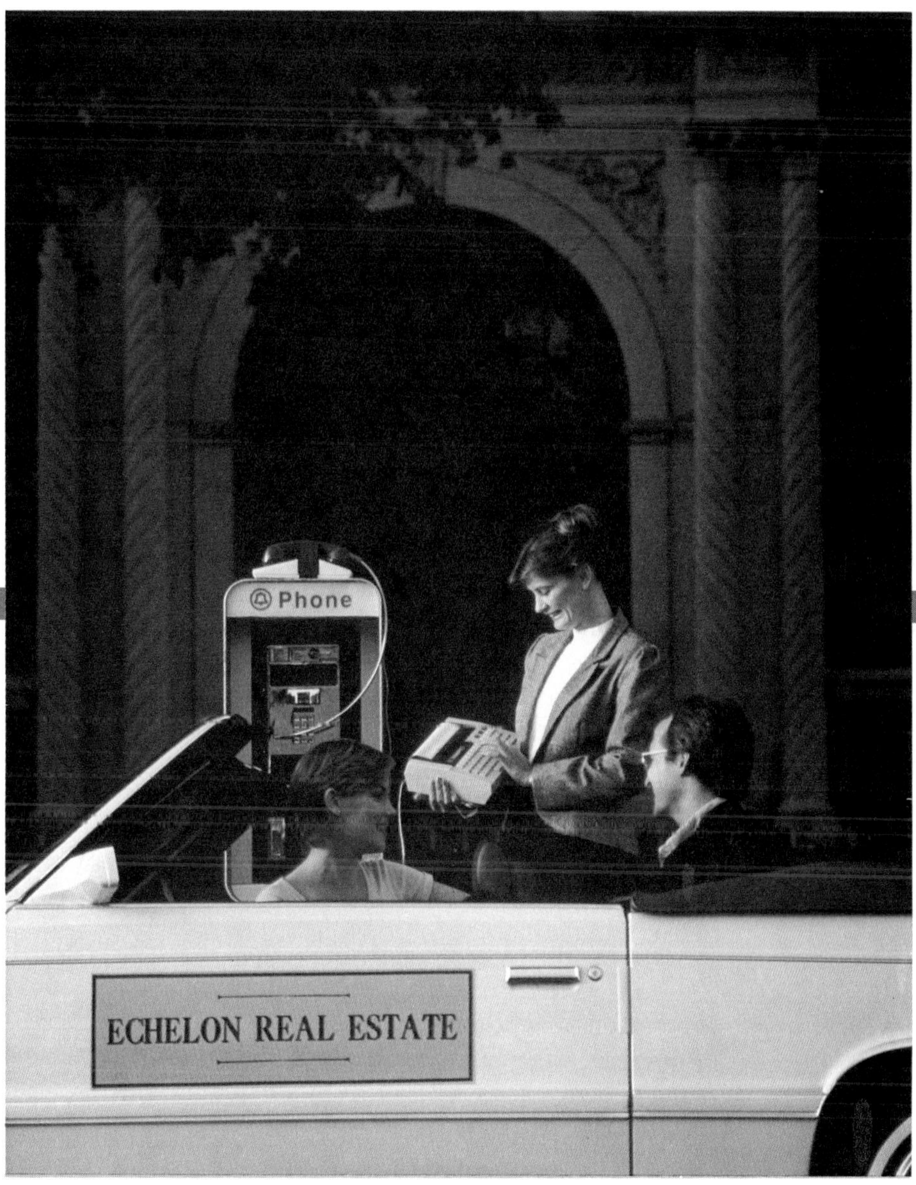
Phone
ECHELON REAL ESTATE

SELLING THE RIGHT PLACE FROM ANYPLACE

Take your office with you on your next sales call. You can fit a Texas Instruments Portable Data Terminal in just half of your briefcase. Yet it has a full-size typewriterlike keyboard and a silent, 80- or 132-characters-per-line printer.

If you're selling real estate, chances are good that you're a subscriber to one or more computerized multiple-listing real estate services. You'll want an acoustic coupler option that enables you to access these services or your firm's computer from the nearest phone. If a client shows interest in a property for which you don't have information, you can simply call a multiple-listing service and print out all the facts you need to close the deal. With just a few keystrokes, you can get the computer to help you write sales contracts, work out terms for mortgages and leases, and, best of all, calculate your commissions. *(Photo courtesy of Texas Instruments)*

CHAPTER SUMMARY

1. In a batch-processing application, data is collected in a group, or batch, before it is submitted as input to a computer. In a transaction-processing application, data is entered into a computer for immediate processing as user activities occur.

2. Capturing data in a machine-readable form at the place where it is generated is called *source data automation.*

3. A card reader converted data represented as combinations of holes in the columns of punched cards into electronic pulses. The most common method of punched-card data representation was Hollerith code.

4. Key-to-tape, key-to-disk, and key-to-diskette devices provided alternative methods of data input that did not require the use of punched cards.

5. *Ergonomics,* or human engineering, is a science that fits the workplace to the person (rather than the person to the workplace). It takes into account factors such as body movements, body dimensions, air, space, heat, light, and sound.

6. Magnetic-ink character-recognition (MICR) devices help the banking industry to process an ever-increasing volume of checks with speed and accuracy.

7. Optical character-recognition (OCR) devices can read data in many forms. The optically readable symbols may be marks; bars; numbers, letters, and special characters of certain type fonts; or ordinary handwriting.

8. Voice-input units are especially useful in applications where users' hands and/or eyes are otherwise occupied.

9. A mouse, light pen, or finger touch against a touch-sensitive screen may be used in screen-assisted data entry. The user may move a stylus over a graphics tablet, or digitizer, when more precise cursor placement is required.

10. Remote terminals allow users to enter data or retrieve information to locations away from the computer. Some are special-purpose devices designed to meet particular user needs. Point-of-sale (POS) terminals, teller terminals, and automated teller machines (ATM's) are examples.

11. Data-collection devices in a wide variety of user environments gather data for input to batch-processing applications.

12. Portable terminals resembling office typewriters with memories are especially useful to persons whose jobs involve data gathering. Even more portable are handheld terminals weighing from 4 ounces to 3 pounds. Data entry in meter reading, stockroom control, route accounting, and remote sales order-entry applications may be accomplished using these devices.

DISCUSSION QUESTIONS

1. Distinguish between batch-processing systems and transaction-processing systems. In doing so, give one or more examples of each.

2. What is source data automation, and what advantages does it offer?

3. Assume that data is to be entered into an EDP system on punched cards. Show how the Hollerith coding system can be used to represent the following data in the appropriate fields (card columns) on one 80-column card. Alphabetic or alphanumeric fields (combinations of alphabetic, numeric, and/or special characters) are punched left-justified; that is, with the leftmost characters filled and any unused positions at the right. Fields containing only numeric data are punched right-justified.

Card columns	Data
1–5	1742A
6–20	Dolan, Jane
70–73	40.0
74–76	0.05

4. (a) Why is data in Hollerith code converted to another code before being placed in storage?
   (b) When and how does the conversion take place?

5. What advantages did key-to-tape, disk, and diskette devices offer over punched-card data-entry devices?

6. What data-representation scheme was developed primarily to aid the banking industry, and how does it do so?

7. Describe some common business situations in which optical recognition of symbols is useful.

8. List some guidelines for preparing handwritten computer input.

9. Distinguish between OCR scanners and image scanners. In doing so, explain how either or both are being used in desktop publishing.

10. Describe some user applications for which voice-input capabilities are especially suitable.

11. What input options are available to users who prefer screen-assisted data-entry techniques?

12. Why is the popularity of mice increasing in corporate America?

13. Identify four types of remote terminals and describe applications for which each type is useful.

14. Explain how a portable terminal differs from a portable microcomputer, and show when and why their differences are likely to be important.

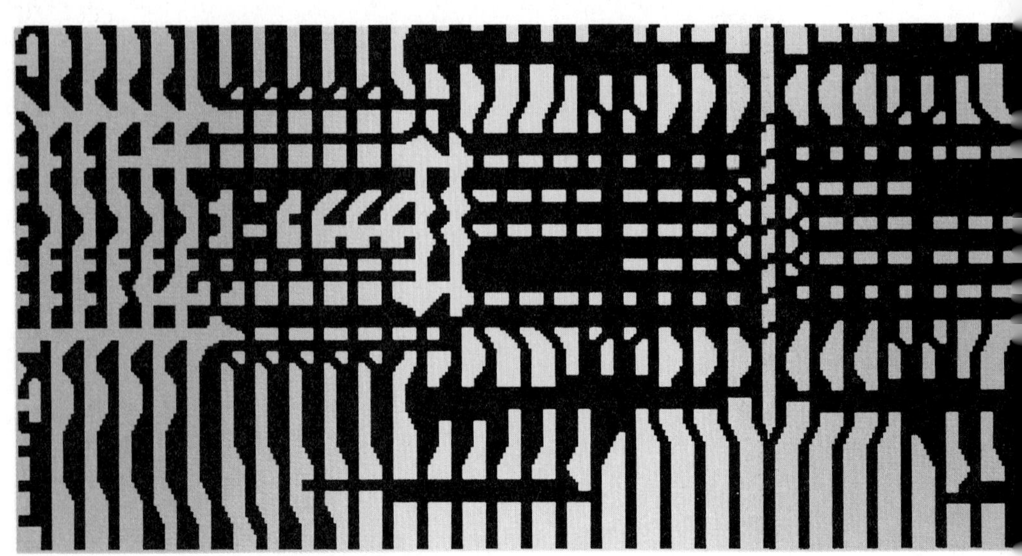

4 Obtaining Information

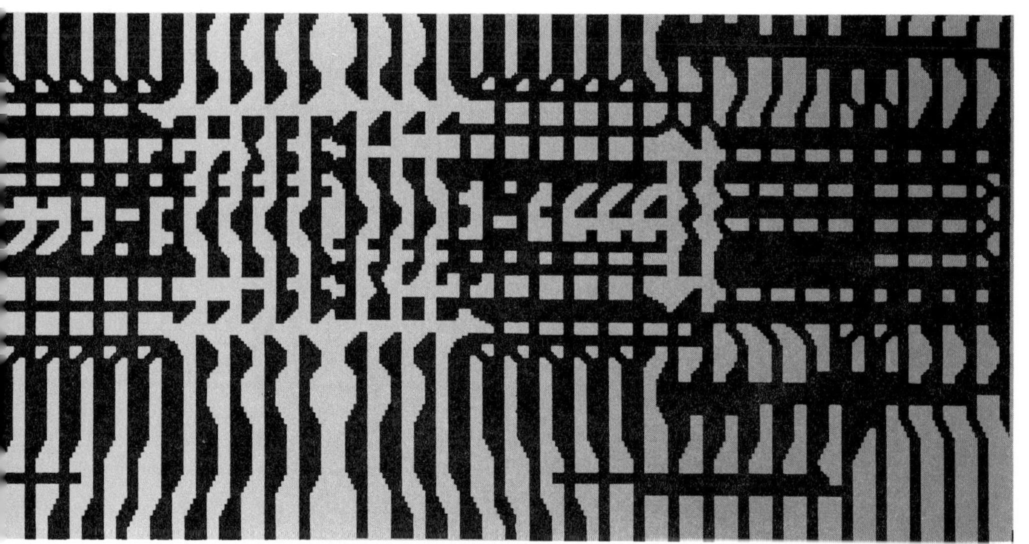

IN THIS CHAPTER

Printed Output
Plotters
Visual-Display Output
Voice Output
Micrographics

We know that data in a wide variety of forms can be provided as input to a computer system. The data is then processed. The results of processing—information—are usually written as output. From a user's point of view, the computer system itself is only as good as the output it provides.

Initially, all computer-system output was printed or displayed on devices connected directly to the processor unit and positioned next to it in a computer room. Users knew which reports were computer-generated because the reports were printed on continuous, $14\frac{7}{8}$-inch-wide, fan-fold paper striped horizontally with light green bars. The characters on the report were printed in black or green. Not very exciting. Today that's no longer the case.

Look at Figure 4-1. It shows examples of computer output. Computers can produce printed reports. They can also produce paychecks, invoices, and sales slips. They can print memos and letters addressed to named recipients. Some can produce bar graphs, line drawings, and pictures. Newsletters, manuals, and even complete books, including illustrations, are prepared and printed with the help of desktop publishing software. Because printed forms of output are relatively permanent, we call them *hard copy.*

On the other hand, *soft-copy* forms of output are temporary in nature. For example, if the user's information needs are best satisfied by a quick look at the results of computations displayed on a televisionlike screen, the computer can

Information Quality

Information is useful if it is accurate, timely, available, concise, complete, and relevant. Information that has these qualities can be studied, compared, shared, and communicated to other people within an organization.

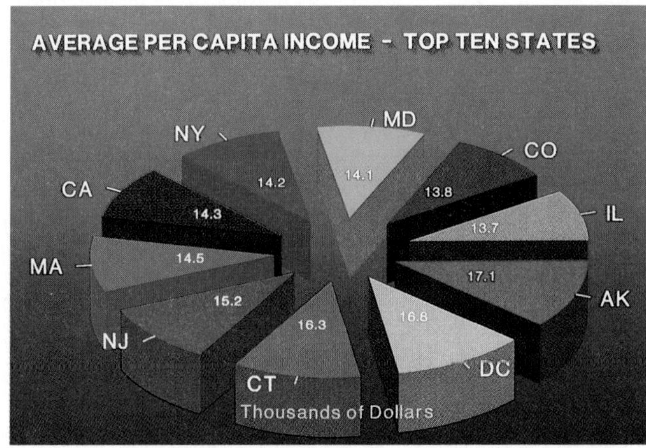
AVERAGE PER CAPITA INCOME - TOP TEN STATES
MD
14.1
CO
13.8
IL
13.7
AK
17.1
DC
16.8
CT
16.3
NJ
15.2
MA
14.5
CA
14.3
NY
14.2
Thousands of Dollars

Figure 4-1 Output in an amazing variety of forms and colors is being produced with computer help. It's meeting a wide range of user information needs. (Courtesy [left] Aldus Corporation; [right] MagiCorp)

be directed to write its output on a visual-display unit. Some units can display graphs and line drawings in a wide variety of colors. Some can generate sequences of images at very fast rates; we perceive the sequences as animated cartoons, filmstrips of natural phenomena, and so on. Even personal computers can be programmed to speak verbal responses, to "beep," or to play the latest hit tunes. If programmed to converse in a foreign language, their French or Spanish (for example) may be better than ours.

The output capabilities of a particular computer system are determined in large part by the software that directs it, and also by the types and features of its output devices. This chapter is about output devices. Since printed output has been and remains the most common form of output, we look first at printers. Then we discuss plotters. Visual-display units are especially popular where ongoing direct interaction with computers is required. Next, we consider voice output. Finally, we look at the unique advantages of computer output microfilm (COM) media and devices.

Printed Output

In the 1960s and 1970s, throughout organizations, more and more data was processed with computer help. Desktop computer systems and visual-display terminals connected to large computers elsewhere appeared increasingly—on shop floors and on secretaries' desks; in accounting, engineering, order processing, and shipping and receiving; at corporate headquarters, R&D labs, remote warehouses, and branch sales offices. Some computer enthusiasts began to predict that the paperless office was near at hand. In fact, a paperless office is about as practical as a paperless bathroom. People like paper—it's paperwork they want to avoid.

In fact, a paperless office is about as practical as a paperless bathroom. People like paper—it's paperwork they want to avoid.

Computers are taking over many of the burdensome chores of paperwork. They add, subtract, move, compare, store, and retrieve data, 24 hours a day, without complaining. Usually, when the data processing, or paperwork, is completed, we want them to print out the final results of that processing. We want to see the results in a tangible form that we can make notes on, show to a co-worker or client, or carry with us.

Printing devices provide the permanent, human-readable records that we desire. A printer receives information in the form of electronic pulses from a computer system. It converts the pulses to a form that we can understand. Even an inexperienced user of a desktop microcomputer system is likely to find a printed copy of output highly desirable. (You can't see what's on the display screen of a microcomputer system when the system is off. Indeed, nothing is—as those of you who are microcomputer users know.)

Obviously, a printer that meets the needs of a large brokerage firm or an insurance company is not suitable for a college student who simply wants to print out hard copies of homework assignments. Is $1000 (or $200,000) the price you should expect to pay for a printer? Or will a much less expensive printer do?

To answer such questions, you need to know more about the printing devices available. You also need to be aware of factors to consider when choosing from among them.

One way in which printers differ relates to how much information is printed:

- *Serial printers* print one character of information at a time. Their speeds are measured in terms of *characters per second (cps)* or *characters per minute (cpm).* Speeds up to 900 cps are possible with some models, but speeds of 20 to 240 cps are far more common.
- *Line printers* print one line of information at a time. Their speeds are measured in terms of *lines per minute (lpm).* Speeds of 300 to 1200 lpm are common, though up to 5000 lpm can be printed with some models.
- *Page printers* print complete pages, one-up or two-up (side-by-side) across the printer paper. Their speeds are measured in terms of lines per minute or *pages per minute (ppm).* Speeds up to 45,000 lpm are possible with some models.

The great differences in possible speeds of these devices are in large part due to the technology that is used in printing. Comparing speeds expressed in different units of measure can be difficult. A typical line on $8\frac{1}{2}$-inch-wide paper holds about ten 5-character words. Allowing for spacing and carriage returns, we might say that a 60-cps printer creates 1 line per second, or 60 lines per minute. Assuming 50 lines per page, a 60-lpm printer creates only a little

"Letter Quality"

When used in connection with word processing, the term *letter-quality* does not mean character-quality, A-quality, B-quality, etc. Instead, it means high-quality—suitable for use in preparing letters rather than only for in-house memos or draft-quality output.

more than one page per minute. In contrast, a 45,000-lpm printer creates 900 ppm as output. Of course, such speeds are rated maximums. In actual practice, speeds vary depending on the amount of blank space on the printout, the number of lines per inch, and other factors.

A second way of distinguishing between printers is based on the way that information is printed:

- *Impact printers* form images when electronic pulses activate printing elements that are pressed against an inked ribbon and form an image on paper.
- *Nonimpact printers* use thermal (heat), chemical, electrical, and/or optical techniques to form images.

In general, nonimpact printers are much faster than impact printers, primarily because there is less physical movement of parts. From a user's perspective, other common differences between impact and nonimpact printers are likely to be important also. We discuss them below.

A third way of distinguishing between printers is based on the way they form characters:

- *Fully-formed character printers* provide complete images of all printed characters.
- *Dot-matrix-character printers* form images as patterns of spots, or dots.

The characters you see in this book are fully-formed characters. Indeed, the reproduction masters for many books are created as computer output. In contrast, Figure 4-2 shows examples of dot-matrix characters printed at various densities. In general, the more dots used to form characters, the better the character resolution (and hence the better the print quality). Impact printers use either fully-formed characters or dot-matrix characters. Nonimpact printers use only matrix techniques.

Figure 4-2 Some printers can print dot-matrix characters at various densities, allowing users to trade over-all printing speed for higher quality for selected types of output.

Draft quality

other ticketing systems used in
prior Olympics games, at method
used by various sporting organi
zations now, and at general bus
ness applications before decidi
on the IBM system.
"We also felt it necessary to
be able to print tickets to ord

Memo quality

other ticketing systems used in
prior Olympics games, at method
used by various sporting organi
zations now, and at general bus
ness applications before decidi
on the IBM system.
"We also felt it necessary to
be able to print tickets to ord

Letter (also called near-letter) quality

other ticketing systems used in
prior Olympics games, at method
used by various sporting organi
zations now, and at general bus
ness applications before decidi
on the IBM system.
"We also felt it necessary to
be able to print tickets to ord

Graphics

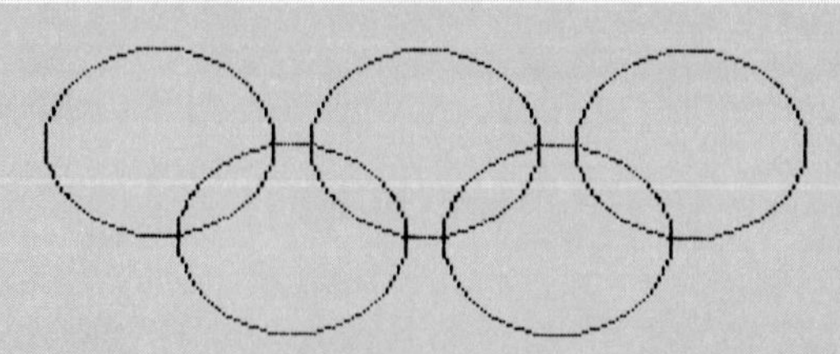

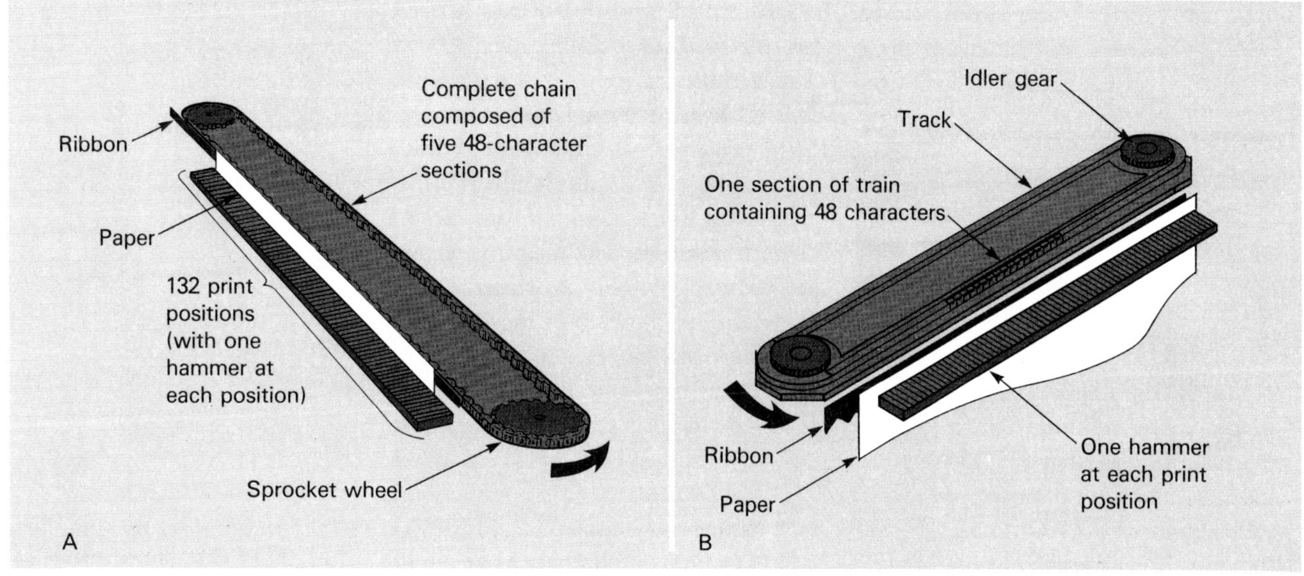
Ribbon
Paper
Complete chain composed of five 48-character sections
132 print positions (with one hammer at each position)
Sprocket wheel
A
Idler gear
Track
One section of train containing 48 characters
Ribbon
Paper
One hammer at each print position
B

Figure 4-3 A chain printer uses an interchangeable print chain (A) composed of linked character slugs. A train printer uses a track (B) containing individual character slugs of a user-selected character set.

Impact Printers

The earliest impact printers were the slow-speed fully-formed character printing devices. Their primary use was for system-to-operator communications in computer rooms. Then remote terminals with hard-copy output capabilities were developed. Known as *teleprinters,* they could be linked to a central computer facility from distant locations via established communication networks (say, installed telephone facilities).

Wire-matrix (today called *dot-matrix*) *printers* were developed to overcome the speed limitations of these early fully-formed-character printers. One line of dots was printed at a time as the vertical set of wires of the printing mechanism moved across the print line. Some users willingly traded print quality for greater speed and lower costs. Other users demanded letter-quality output because they wanted to use their printers in word-processing applications. Serial fully-formed-character printers known as *daisywheel printers* were developed to meet this user need. In these printers, a flat disk with petal-like projections holding raised fully-formed characters that could be pressed against a ribbon served as the printing mechanism. Printing could be done in either direction. Paper could be fed up or down. Character and line spacings were variable. Today, print speeds of 30 to 60 cps are typical of these typewriter-like devices.

Some users willingly traded print quality for greater speed and lower costs.

Impact line-at-a-time printers have been available since the 1950s. Initially, alphabetic, numeric, and special characters of engraved type were assembled in interchangeable *print chains* used as the printing mechanism. (See Figure 4-3A.) The chain moved horizontally in front of fixed hammers at the printing positions on a line. Whenever a character

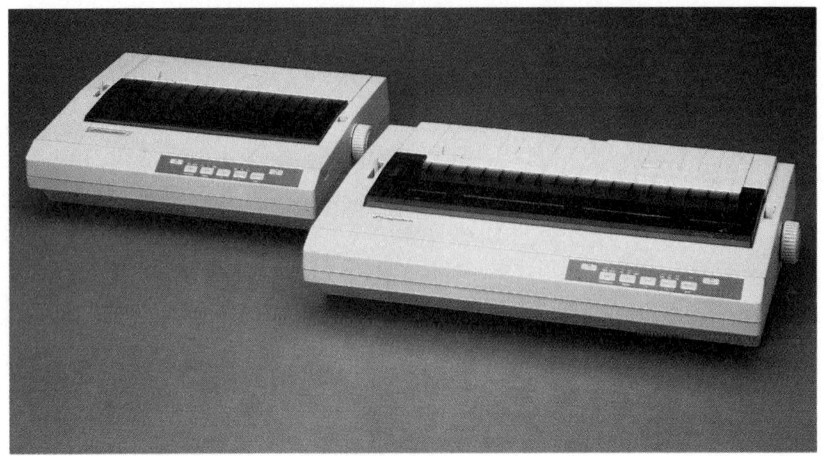

Figure 4-4 Serial dot-matrix printers in both narrow and wide carriage versions are meeting many users' printing needs. (Courtesy Data Products Corporation)

passed a position at which it was needed, the hammer at that position forced the paper and ribbon against the engraved type, thus printing the character. *Print trains* were similar to print chains but offered an additional advantage: Individual characters in the train as well as the entire train could be changed. (See Figure 4-3B.) Chain and train printers developed in recent years are capable of printing 2000, 3000, or even 3800 132-character lpm when a standard 48-character set is used.

Drum, belt, and band printers are other line-at-a-time fully-formed-character printers based on impact technologies. *Print drums* are inherently more reliable than chains or trains because they have fewer independently movable parts. From a user's point of view, however, a drum printer is inflexible. The character set engraved on the surface of the drum cannot be changed. *Belt printers* are similar to chain/train printers but slower. Many users of medium-sized and small computers are willing to accept a print speed of 300 to 400 lpm if that speed meets their output needs—especially if it's available at much less cost. The technology of *band printers* is progressing steadily. A band printer operating at 900 lpm used to be considered speedy; now band printers operating at 5000 lpm are available. Their stainless steel alloy bands are resistant to wear or damage and as easy to change as the interchangeable print elements of office typewriters.

Today, nonimpact printers based on laser technology are making the headlines (see below). Nevertheless, 9-, 18-, and 24-pin serial dot-matrix impact printers lead the field in terms of number of units sold annually. They are known for their versatility—the capability to handle everything in the office, from multiple-part forms to labels to letterheads; from business graphics to letter-quality text to spreadsheets. They are the clear favorite for bar-code label printing because they can produce sequentially numbered bar codes, print most if not all symbologies, print on any location on a label, and work with almost any kind of label stock. (See Figure 4-4.)

Most of these printers can operate in either draft-quality or near-letter-quality (NLQ) mode. Speeds of 200 to 400 cps are typical of the former; speeds of 40 to 60 cps are typical of the latter. These printers also meet user requirements in terms of purchase price, reliability, and software support. Line-at-a-time dot-matrix printers are also improving in print quality and reliability. They're competing with line-at-a-time fully-formed-character printers at conventional data-center environments.

Nonimpact Printers

Throughout the computer industry, one trend is unmistakable: User demands for nonimpact printers are increasing. Whereas nonimpact printers accounted for about 10 percent of total printer shipments in 1984, they may well account for 50 percent by 1994.

User demands for nonimpact printers are increasing.

As noted earlier, nonimpact printers tend to be faster than impact printers because they have fewer moving parts. For the same reason, they tend to be more reliable and quieter in operation. To managers whose basic business operations are dependent on computer-generated hard copy (invoices, paychecks, scheduling reports, and the like), reliable printers are essential. To users who work near their small business computer systems or remote printers (say, in office environments), quiet printers are essential.

Several nonimpact printing technologies have been developed. Because these technologies differ significantly, the nonimpact printers also differ. Nonimpact serial, line, and page printers ranging in price from $300 to more than $300,000 are available.

At the slow-speed serial end of the nonimpact group, *thermal printers* are common. Dot-matrix characters are formed by heating selected elements of a print head as it moves across a special heat-sensitive paper. Usually silver coated, the paper turns black wherever heat is applied. The print quality of the dot-matrix characters is generally acceptable for low-volume, routine business applications. You'll find these printers attached to microcomputers as well as on larger systems. Many lightweight terminals include thermal printers that produce hard copy at 12 to 30 cps rates. (See Figure 4-5.)

Serial and line printers using *ink-jet technology* shoot a stream of charged ink from a nozzle; the ink is deflected by plates to produce dot-matrix characters. Print quality is achieved through use of many dots—500 per character cell as opposed to 35, 63, or thereabouts in comparable thermal printers. Other advantages of ink-jet printers are their abilities to print with multiple type fonts (changeable electronically), to intermix graphics and text on the same page without sacrificing resolution, and to use ordinary paper. In 1988 Hewlett-Packard attracted the attention of microcomputer users who wanted to achieve letter-quality output at minimal cost when it offered its Deskjet ink-jet printer for $995. (See Figure 4-6.) Ink-jet printers that provide multiple-color output are also available.

At the other end of the user spectrum, ink-jet printing is well-suited for industrial uses because it is completely noncontact. Images can be formed on almost any receiving material of almost any contour, shape, or composition. Hence, industrial ink-jet printers are used widely for product coding on textiles and car-

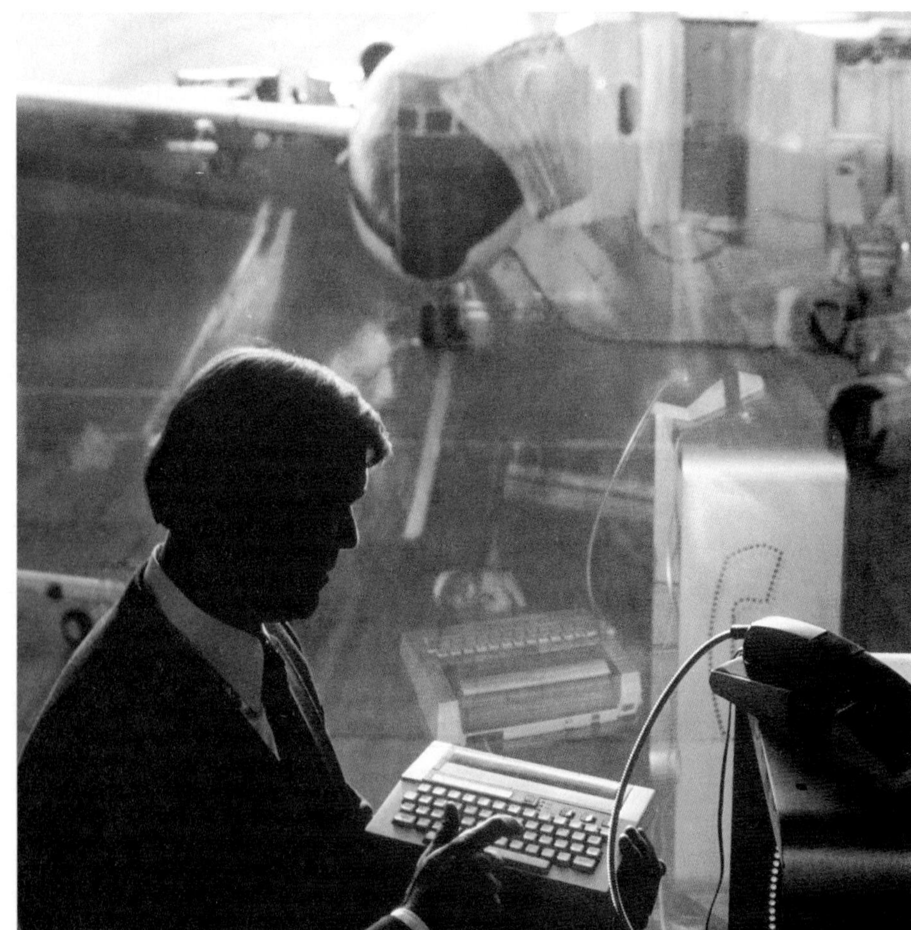

Figure 4-5 Low-cost thermal printers are common on portable terminals. Instead of searching an unfamiliar newspaper for the latest weather forecast or market quotations, a busy traveler can dial one of the popular remote database services and have the information listed out on his terminal. (Courtesy of Texas Instruments)

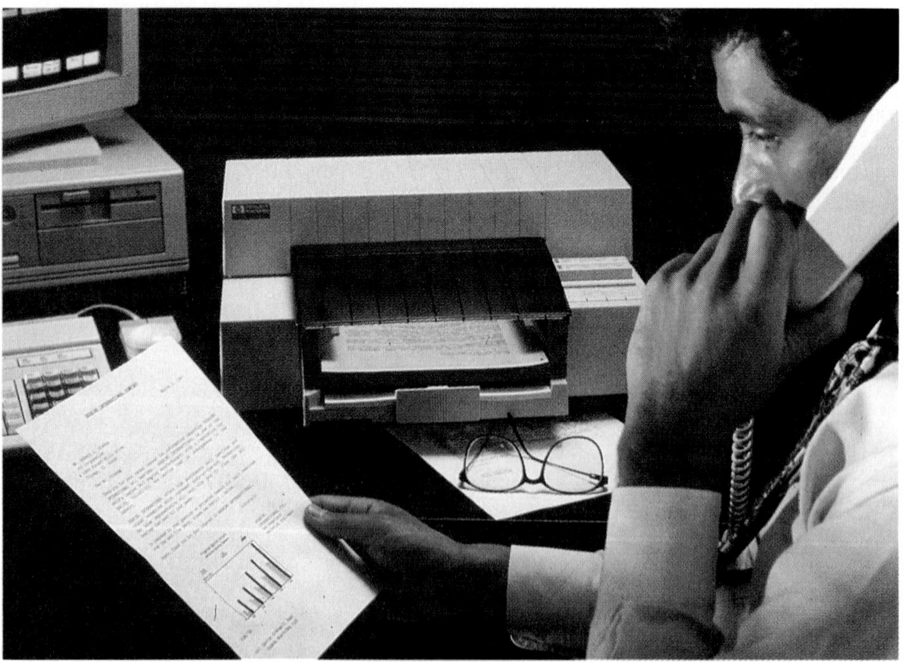

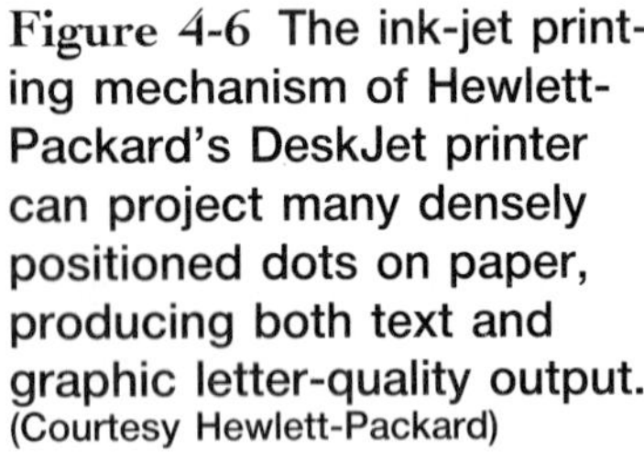

Figure 4-6 The ink-jet printing mechanism of Hewlett-Packard's DeskJet printer can project many densely positioned dots on paper, producing both text and graphic letter-quality output. (Courtesy Hewlett-Packard)

How Much?

The duty cycles—recommended number of pages to be printed each month—of high-speed laser printers vary from 60,000 to 2 million pages.

At What Cost?

The estimated cost per page of high-speed laser printing ranges from less than 1 cent to 3.7 cents. Some manufacturers include amortization of the printer, maintenance, and supplies in figuring costs, but others do not.

pet fabrics. Mass mail addressing is another common ink-jet printer application.

An *electrostatic printer* forms an image by means of charged pins or wires that supply a charge in the desired pattern to a nonconducting paper. The paper passes through a solution ("toner") containing ink particles of opposite charge. The particles adhere to the charged area of the paper and melt when exposed to high heat, thus forming the image. Graphic images as well as characters can be produced since the dots can be positioned to form pictures. Typical print speeds range up to 3600 lpm. Models capable of printing 18,000 or more lpm are available.

The Xerox 1200, introduced in 1973, was the world's first *xerographic* (also called *electrophotographic*) *page printer*. It used a process similar to the one first used in Xerox office copiers to print at a rate of 4000 lpm. Users soon learned to appreciate the distinct character images produced on letter-sized ($8\frac{1}{2}$ inch × 11 inch) paper rather than as traditional (11 inch × $14\frac{7}{8}$ inch) computer printouts.

In 1977, Xerox announced the first of its follow-on products: the 9700 Electronic Printing System. In the 9700, a *laser* (rather than an ordinary directed light and lens) forms character images with pinpoint accuracy on a rotating, coated drum. Xerox has expanded this product family to meet a wide range of departmental and data-center printing needs. Other vendors have developed products for this market sector. But it was in 1984 that the use of laser technology for printing first gained the attention of the vast majority of computer users. In that year, Hewlett-Packard introduced its LaserJet, the first desktop laser printer. The LaserJet could be used with Hewlett-Packard, IBM PC, and IBM PC-compatible microcomputers and was priced at just under $2500. (See Figure 4-7.)

The growth of the laser-printer industry has been phenomenal. Today laser printers account for 70 percent or more of nonimpact printer sales and motivate predictions that nonimpact printer sales will exceed those of impact printers by the mid-1990s. Low-end machines such as Hewlett-Packard's LaserJet Series II and Apple Computer's LaserWriter family print about 8 ppm and cost from $1500 to $5000. High-end laser printers generate 90 or more ppm and cost $100,000 and up. In-house desktop publishing services and firms whose business is publishing depend on the speed, versatility, and print quality of these devices.

The growth of the laser-printer industry has been phenomenal.

The two-sided printing capability of laser printers is especially useful for inventory listings, catalogs, directories, manuals, and the like. Forms, including company logos, signatures, vertical and horizontal lines for tables and charts, and so on, can be stored and then imaged electronically together with variable data. This feature eliminates the need for forms overlays or preprinted forms. Credit-card and utility statements, insurance policies, brokerage portfolio information, newsletters, and direct-mail sales and campaign literature, as well as business, governmental, and stockholder reports, are other examples of common output.

ON MAKING CHOICES

Now, what could make selecting a printer a difficult job—a printer is a printer is a printer. Or is it? In fact, the variety of printers available today seems almost as widespread as their use. A user or user organization can spend $300, $3000, $30,000, or even $300,000 for a printer. Which one should be chosen?

The *first* rule of all computer-related shopping applies here: Look *first* at your current and anticipated application requirements. Is a large volume of printing to be done, say, to satisfy governmental reporting requirements or to meet the information needs of department managers? Is the print quality acceptable if the output is merely readable? Or is letter-quality printing required for, say, final copies of user manuals to be distributed to customers? Are multiple copies required? Must output be provided as cut forms, or are continuous forms acceptable? Are specialized type fonts needed, and must they be readily interchangeable? Are graphic capabilities needed? Is color highly desirable, or does it belong in the "bells and whistles" category, so far as your applications are concerned?

Answers to questions such as these will help you to narrow your search. You can use the general overviews of the capabilities of various types of printers given in this chapter to help you.

Printer manufacturers are enhancing the ease-of-use characteristics of their machines by improving their print-handling capabilities. Examples are alternate input paths (bottom, front, and rear feeding); built-in sheet feeders, perforators, slitters, stuffers, and binders; multiple input bins so that printers can run unattended for long periods; and paper parking, which is the ability to stop printing on one type of paper and begin printing on another without physically changing the paper. Check the completeness and understandability of user documentation.

If you're selecting a laser printer, be sure to consider its random-access memory (RAM). Just as the amount of RAM available in a personal computer determines what application programs can do, so the amount of RAM available in a laser printer determines how much graphics can be done. You'll need at least 1.5 million bytes of RAM to print a full-page, 300-dpi (dots per inch) graphic illustration. The number of type fonts resident in the printer or available on plug-in modules is likely to be important to you if you're intending to create newsletters, brochures, and the like.

Whatever printer you buy must attach to your computer through an available interface. Make certain any printers you consider support an interface that works with your computer. If you don't have a software driver you need, verify that it's readily available.

Printer reliability can be expressed in either of two ways: mean time between failures (MTBF) and mean time to repair (MTTR). The cost of maintenance charges has to be figured for the life of the printer. A printer costing $400 more than the least expensive model but having a $10 per month lower maintenance fee may be a better buy in the long run.

Historically, the life expectancies of nonimpact fully-formed-character printers have exceeded those of comparable dot-matrix printers. That situation may be changing. The life expectancies of dot-matrix printers are usually stated in terms of number of characters. Currently, 9-pin print heads are typically rated at 100 million characters. Most 24-pin printers have print heads that are projected to last for 200 million characters; some are rated as high as 400 million characters. If you're shopping for a laser printer for use with your personal computer or workstation, life expectancies of 300,000 pages are typical. You probably shouldn't settle for less.

Check the *duty cycle,* or manufacturer's recommended usage, of the printers you're considering. For example, Hewlett-Packard's LaserJet 2000 operates at 20 ppm with a duty cycle of 30,000 pages per month. Its LaserJet Series II operates at 8 ppm with a duty cycle of 5000 pages per month. Saving $15,000 on the price of a printer is no bargain if the machine you purchase can't meet your needs.

The total cost of supplies, including paper, ribbons, ink, etc., over an anticipated usage period should be determined for each printer you consider. Many users don't realize that the total amount they may eventually spend on the operation of a printer is likely to be greater than the cost of the machine. As examples, the cost per page of toner and other consumables for the LaserJet 2000 mentioned above is .64 cents. For the LaserJet Series II, it's 3.13 cents—about five times as much.

How does the physical size of the printer compare with the amount of space you're willing (or able) to allow for one? You can't be squeezed and still enjoy using it. Finally, remember to listen as well as look. A printer that's to be installed in a central computer room or in a room at the back of a store can be noisy. But for a printer that's to be positioned on the table next to you or amid office staff, "mum's the word."

PostScript

Most printers, like other input/output devices, are controlled by commands sent to the printers from computers during processing. The commands are expressed in a *printer control language (PCL).* The PCL designed for a particular model and type of printer is tied very closely to that machine and is specific to it. To use an Epson LQ series printer with a particular microcomputer, for example, the user must insure that a software routine (commonly known as a *driver*) that can be used to control the Epson LQ exists for that microcomputer. Similarly, a printer manufacturer that wants to make sure its printers can be used with a wide variety of microcomputers must make sure that printer drivers are developed for those microcomputers and that the drivers are readily available to potential users. Some manufacturers include within their printers the ability to *emulate* (imitate) several popular printers for which drivers already exist. For example, Mannesmann Tally's MT222 can emulate the Epson LQ and the IBM Proprinter. But all of these approaches are expensive, time-consuming, and error prone.

Now that microprocessors are being included in printers themselves, a degree of device independence can be provided.

Now that microprocessors are being included in printers themselves, a degree of device independence can be provided. Use of a *page*

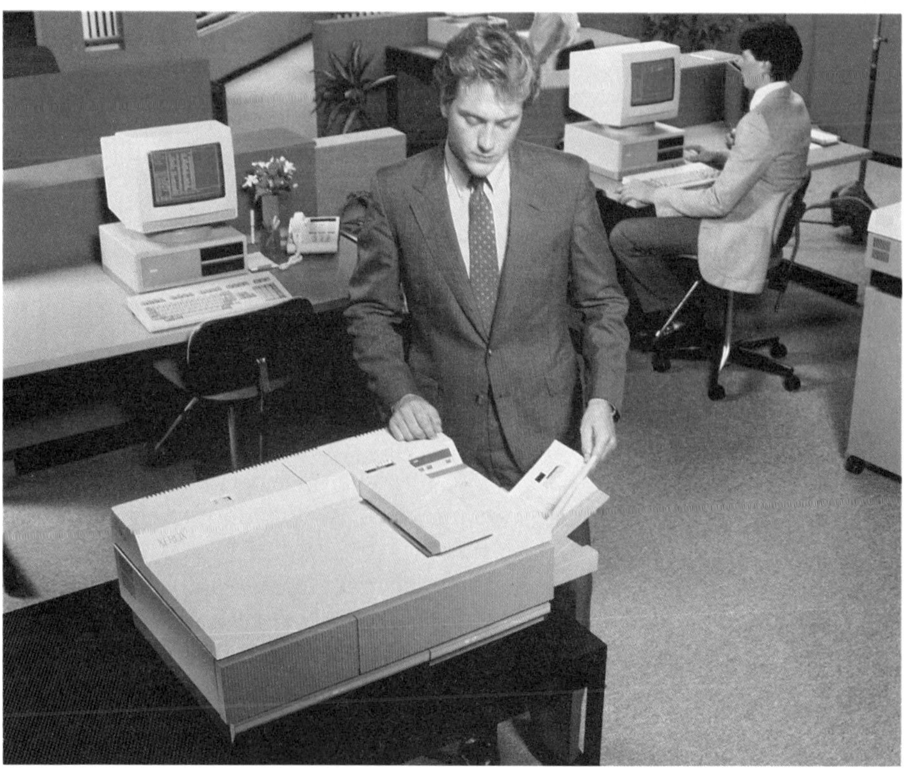

Figure 4-7 A laser printer that plugs into a standard electrical outlet, operates quietly, and can be shared by several personal computer users is an essential part of many automated office environments. (Photo courtesy of Xerox Corp.)

Paper Is Here to Stay

Not long ago, some computer-industry watchers were predicting that a terminal or workstation on every desktop would signal the arrival of the paperless office. But senior management likes tangible documents. The laser printer falls right in line with the desires of the business world; it has postponed the arrival of the paperless office indefinitely.

description language (PDL) rather than a PCL to direct a printer is analogous to using COBOL or BASIC rather than an assembler language or a machine language to direct a computer. If you're a microcomputer user, you've probably heard references to PostScript. *PostScript* is the PDL that is most widely used today. It was developed by Adobe Systems of Palo Alto, California, as part of its desktop publishing system.

An application running in a microcomputer sends PostScript generalized page-description commands that tell what is to be printed and where on a page to a language translator program known as an *interpreter* running in the printer. The interpreter converts the generalized commands into sequences of machine instructions needed to create the desired image on a page. Characters of a particular type font—for example, Courier or Times Roman—are treated like graphic elements, which means they can be scaled and rotated at will.

Because PostScript commands do not operate at the bit-image level, they are independent of the resolution of the device that's being controlled. The same PostScript commands can take optimal advantage of 300-, 600-, 1270-, or 2540-dpi device resolutions. Device independence, application portability, and high-quality output are among the benefits to users, vendors writing application software, and printer manufacturers.

A printer manufacturer who wants to support PostScript pays a license to Adobe for use of its code and for developing the interpreter code for its particular printer. Other PDL's exist and may increase in popularity over time. You can assume that a similar approach is used with these PDL's and that similar benefits are provided.

Plotters

"One picture is worth a thousand words" is a common saying—and one that many of us agree with daily as we attempt to understand what's going on around us. It should not surprise us, then, that users welcome graphic forms of computer output. A *plotter* is an output device that converts tabulated numerical data into graphic form. Bar charts and line graphs, work-flow charts of manufacturing projects, organization charts, engineering drawings, and maps are some of the many forms of data that can be displayed on a plotter. Most offer gray-scale halftones, which we might commonly refer to as *shading*. With some plotters, color output is provided.

"One picture is worth a thousand words" is a common saying . . .

Color plotting is fundamentally different from color printing. In color plotting, an image is created as lines of color ink placed on the output medium. The color of the ink is the same as the color that users see in the image that the ink creates. Most color printing is bit-image-oriented. An image is created by positioning hundreds, thousands, or millions of dots (picture elements, or *pixels*) on the output medium. Only four colors of ink—the three primary colors (red, yellow, and blue) and black—are used. Colors other than these are created by overprinting the dots repetitively.

Like printers, plotters are getting faster, smaller, less expensive, and smarter. The popularity of Autocad and other personal computer and workstation-based CAD/CAM (computer-aided design/computer-aided manufacturing) software has encouraged vendors to market complete CAD/CAM systems with plotters as basic components. These systems are widely used in computer printed-circuit-board design, tool design, and end-user product design. In fact, plotters are nothing new to engineers, scientists, and architects. They are also being used increasingly for routine business purposes. For example, product forecasts computed with the help of an electronic spreadsheet program may be displayed as plotter output.

Plotters are of two basic types: pen and electrostatic. Pen plotters were first to arrive on the scene; they may be drum, flatbed, or beltbed devices. In a *drum plotter,* recording is achieved by incremental movements of a pen on a paper surface (y-axis) and/or movements of the paper under the pen (x-axis). (See Figure 4-8.) A *flatbed plotter* is basically an electromechanical drafting table. Computer-controlled motors move a pen along x and y axes to produce a graph or schematic on stationary paper. (See Figure 4-9.) Some flatbed plotters produce $8\frac{1}{2}$-inch × 11-inch output. Large flatbed plotters can produce drawings up to 5 or 6 feet in width. A *beltbed plotter* has a vertical plotting surface. It operates much like a drum, but provides the flat plotting surface of a flatbed plotter. Like a drum, it moves the paper under the pen as well as the pen over the paper. Like a flatbed plotter, however, it plots on cut sheets of paper rather than on a continuous roll.

Electrostatic plotters work the same way as electrostatic printers. In fact, some vendors refer to their products as *printer/plotters.* These plotters are much faster than pen-type plotters because their speed is limited only by the speed of paper movement. Furthermore, they have a simultaneous print/plot capability that permits the overlay of plot data and characters on the same print area. In contrast, additional time is required if any characters are to be included in pen-type plotter output. A disadvantage of electrostatic plotters is their high cost when compared to pen plotters.

Visual-Display Output

No matter where you look these days—engineering lab, accountant's office, stock room, or shop floor—you're apt to see a device that looks much like an ordinary television set. The data-recording medium in most of these devices is a *cathode-ray tube (CRT),* similar in design and function to a television picture tube. We call the devices *CRT's, visual-display units (VDU's),* or *monitors.* They're used to provide input to computer systems (as we saw in Chapter 3) and to receive output.

The way a computer-system display screen *looks* to the user when entering commands and the way the system *feels* to the user when it responds are emerging as key considerations throughout the computer industry. System designers and users

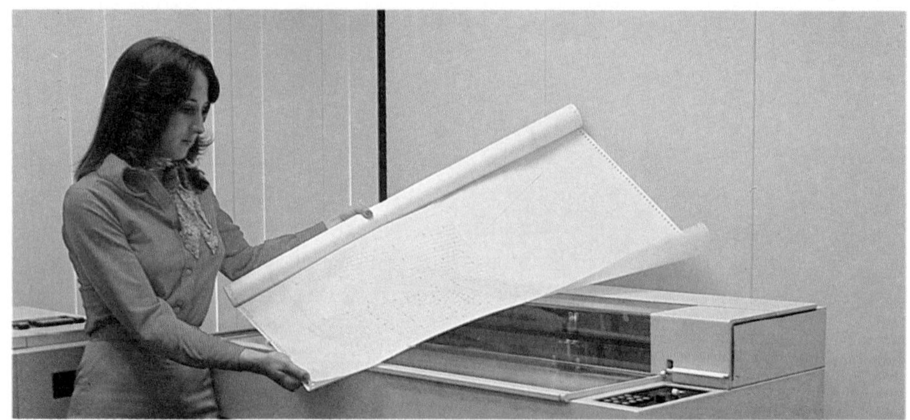

Figure 4-8 Calcomp's top-of-the-line drum plotter features a 6-foot wide plot area, .0005-inch resolution, and a 30-inches-per-second drawing speed. Such plotters can produce aircraft, automotive, and other designs; engineering drawings; architectural layouts; topological maps; and other large graphic output items. (Courtesy of Calcomp)

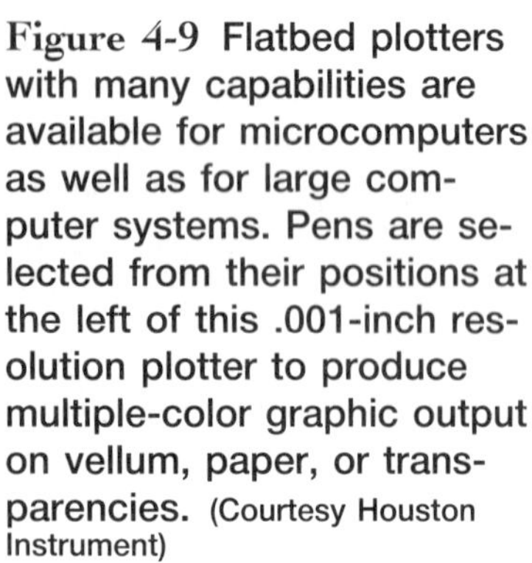

Figure 4-9 Flatbed plotters with many capabilities are available for microcomputers as well as for large computer systems. Pens are selected from their positions at the left of this .001-inch resolution plotter to produce multiple-color graphic output on vellum, paper, or transparencies. (Courtesy Houston Instrument)

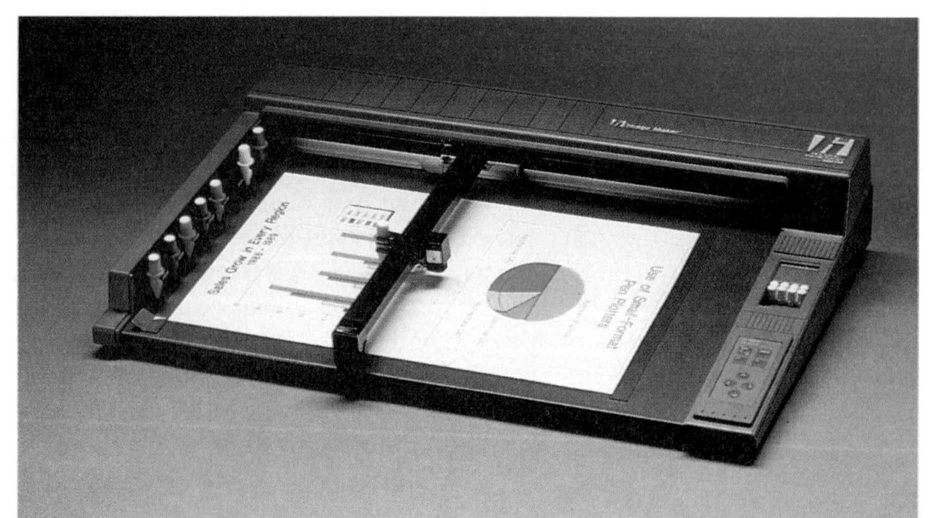
Sales Grow in Every Region
Use of Small-Format
Pen Plotters

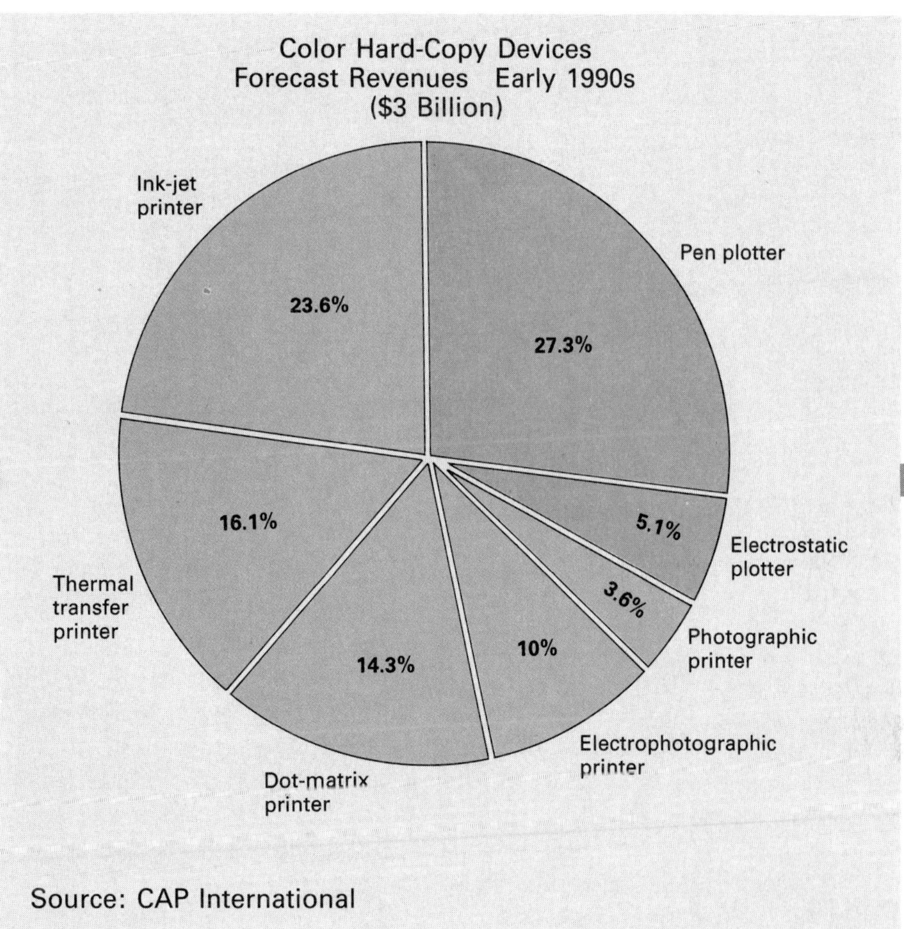
Color Hard-Copy Devices
Forecast Revenues Early 1990s
($3 Billion)
Ink-jet printer
23.6%
Pen plotter
27.3%
16.1%
5.1%
Electrostatic plotter
Thermal transfer printer
3.6%
Photographic printer
10%
14.3%
Electrophotographic printer
Dot-matrix printer
Source: CAP International

COLOR HARD-COPY DEVICES

Color hard-copy devices are expected to gain an increasing share of the computer graphics market. Among these devices, pen plotters are characterized by exceptional line quality, a large base of existing software, and reasonable price tags. More than 20 major pen plotter manufacturers are in business today, and more than 100 models of pen plotters are offered.

are increasingly focusing on the computer's graphical user interface, its "look and feel."

The time needed to analyze information displayed graphically is likely to be much less than would be required to analyze the same information in a multiple-column statistical report. The response to a management inquiry or the plot of a complex mathematical relation can be shown on the screen in a readily understandable way. Furthermore, many applications today are designed to offer "HELP" screens. If the user

System designers and users are increasingly focusing on the computer's graphical user interface, its "look and feel."

Figure 4-10 Output displayed on the screen of a monochrome visual-display unit is suitable for many applications (left). Colors can be put to functional use when the visual-display unit has color and graphic capabilities (right). (Courtesy [left] Control Data Corporation; [right] AST Research)

does not understand what is displayed on an initial screen, or wants additional detail, pressing a specified key or positioning the cursor at the word HELP on the screen causes a backup (nested) screen containing additional information to be displayed.

Initially, all CRT's were monochrome displays. They showed light characters on a dark background or dark characters on a light background. (See Figure 4-10, left). Today that's changed. CRT's that display output in 16, 64, or even 256 colors are available. (See Figure 4-10, right.) Ask yourself: "Do I learn more from material printed in several colors than from conventional black-and-white printing?" Your answer is probably "Yes." Now ask yourself: "Would I pay several dollars to have a telephone directory printed in eight colors?" Your answer is probably "No." For many applications, color enhances output; for others, it is not needed. As yet, color displays cost much more than comparable monochrome displays. Whether or not that cost should be incurred is a tradeoff that organizations, departments, and individuals must make on the basis of their requirements.

When a visual-display unit is used as a remote terminal, an entire record or even a page of information can be displayed almost instantly. If the visual-display unit has graphic capabilities, then charts, graphs, and line drawings as well as character data can be displayed. Such terminals are especially appreciated in areas where computer-generated statistical reports were previously analyzed and plotted manually.

In this book, we often use the acronym *CRT* interchangeably with the term *visual-display unit.* Most persons in industry do also. Be aware, however, that not all visual-display units use cathode-ray tubes as the data-recording medium. Non-CRT displays use plasma (gaseous displays), or light-emitting diodes (LED's), or liquid crystals (liquid-crystal displays, or LCD's). Of these, plasma displays have received the greatest attention. Because these dis-

Color, Anyone?

Some vendors insist that monochrome monitors are satisfactory, cost-effective viewing devices for word-processing, spreadsheet, and data-management applications. Others claim that users will migrate from monochrome to color monitors the way that consumers have switched from black-and-white to color television sets.

HIDING A TANK

How can our armed forces make military vehicles—say huge tanks—invisible so that enemy aircraft or heat-seeking missiles can't find and destroy them?

This question is one of many that researchers at the Keweenah Research Center of Michigan Technological University are using computers to answer. They're testing the performance of different kinds of military vehicles on various types of terrain. For example, the researchers may run a test to predict the temperature of a tank under certain conditions on a given day in a given location. The researchers provide data items such as the vehicle description, surrounding topography, expected temperature, air pressure, and general location data in terms of longitude, latitude, and altitude as input to the computer. Through techniques of infrared (IR) imaging, a thermal image of the tank is computed and displayed as output. The researchers may also photograph the actual tank under conditions that match those specified as input to the IR modeling program. The photographed image can then be displayed and analyzed. Next the researchers compare the results of their IR modeling with actual real-world results and so continue to improve the accuracy of their work. Tanks may be redesigned, modified in manufacture or in the field, and positioned or deployed in military situations accordingly. *(Photo courtesy Keweenah Research Center, Michigan Technological University)*

Bits or Objects?

Bit-mapped, or *raster,* graphics systems manipulate data presented as binary digits, or bits, and position the data in terms of specific addressable bit locations on a display screen. Object-oriented, or *vector,* graphic systems manipulate data represented as objects—lines, circles, arcs, and the like—without having to position each bit individually.

plays are not subject to flickering, they need not be backed by elaborate circuitry. Relatively flat panels mean smaller desktop computers and portable computers with displays large enough to show more than just five or seven lines of output.

More recently, the popularity of desktop publishing applications has created a demand for *WYSIWYG* (what-you-see-is-what-you-get) capabilities.

An early objection to visual-display output was that no permanent record of the data displayed on the screen was produced. More recently, the popularity of desktop publishing applications has created a demand for *WYSIWYG* (what-you-see-is-what-you-get) capabilities. Users want to plan the layout of a page on the screen and then print out a copy of the page that looks exactly the same.

Voice Output

Next time you put a coin into a pay phone and dial a long-distance call, listen carefully. The voice that tells you how much more money to deposit for the call may belong to a computer. The computer may also keep track of the coins you deposit and the time you talk. If a problem develops with the phone equipment, the computer may alert technicians that the phone is in need of repair.

As another example, suppose you enter an elevator. A voice says, "Second floor; this elevator will leave soon." You see no one. Again, the voice may belong to a computer.

An intelligible voicelike signal, or *audio response,* is a suitable form of output for limited-volume, formalized messages in many EDP systems. (See Figure 4-11.) In the banking industry, a talking computer may inform tellers or customers of account balances. Stock quotations, airline flight schedules, the current time, and weather conditions may be provided by computers as spoken output. A sales representative may sub-

Figure 4-11 Intelligible voicelike responses formed by a speech synthesizer can help persons who are blind to use computers effectively. (Courtesy The Picture Cube)

Stock quotations, airline flight schedules, the current time, and weather conditions may be provided by computers as spoken output.

mit a product order by calling the computer and then entering order data from a Touch-Tone telephone. The computer at the other end of the phone line may restate the order for instant verification. It may prompt the representative to enter additional data. It may then verify price and availability.

The data-recording medium, the output device, and even the computer system may not be obvious to voice-output users. In some systems, each word or phrase that may be spoken by the computer is prerecorded on a series of sound tracks. Digital output from the computer acts as a selector of the sounds to be played. The sounds then go through an amplifier and telephone or loudspeaker arrangement. Played in a controlled order, the recordings form the "spoken" responses. In other systems, the

HOW WOMEN SEE THEMSELVES

Elizabeth Arden Cosmetic Company uses computers in select New York department stores to help sell its products. A skilled beautician analyzes the customer's face for makeup possibilities. Color shades, blends, and positioning are then digitized with computer help. Color printouts of the proposed makeup combinations are given to the customer for review. Thus, women can see "their" faces in a variety of makeup patterns before making choices. *(Photo courtesy Hank Morgan/Photo Researchers)*

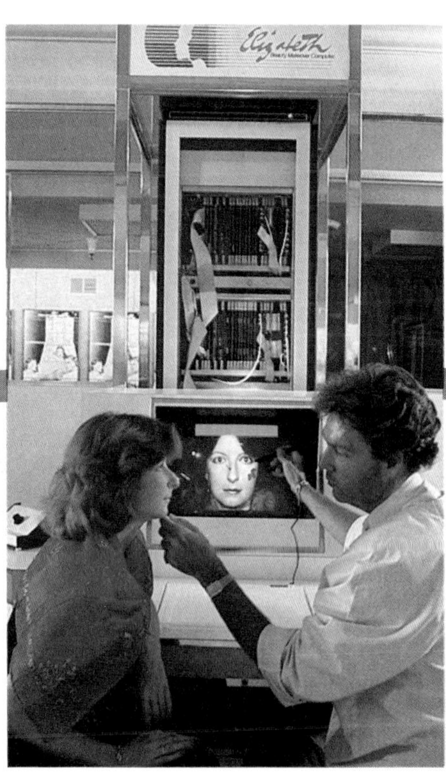
Elizabeth

voice-output devices are speech synthesizers. A mathematical model of the human throat formulates the spoken output.

The techniques of voice processing are software-intensive. They involve lots of processing and lots of data. The computer instructions are often stored and executed as microcode, provided on a silicon chip by the vendor. The data (vocabulary or library of sounds) may be stored in the computer or in a voice-output terminal. The prices of these systems may range from as low as $2000 to more than $50,000.

Research and development efforts in voice output are continuing.

KNOWING WHERE TO GO

If you're a vendor or a driver in the pickup and delivery business, even if you're not lost you may be losing money. In such businesses, time is money in many respects. Finding the most efficient route over a maze of city streets may take several minutes or the major part of an hour if you try to read an intricate city map. If you decide on a trial-and-error approach, it's likely to take even longer.

On a nationwide scale, suppose a fleet of 500 tractor-trailer trucks must be dispatched to hundreds of fast-food outlets from 30 distribution centers. Delivery routes for individual trucks may vary from 10 miles to 3000 miles. How many trucks are needed today? Which trucks should go where?

Fortunately, automated routing systems are coming to the aid of both individual truck drivers and transportation managers for large firms. Some of the systems run on microcomputers. Screen images showing computer-generated routes traced over actual street maps are likely to be much easier to follow than printed directions. The maps may show interstate highways or metropolitan downtown areas. They're stored in the computer beforehand and used by the computer in the routing process.

To build a map database for its use, a pickup and delivery firm may acquire a disk that has video maps stored on it. Alternatively, the firm may digitize its own maps by moving a mouse over streets and highways on paper copies of the maps and clicking the mouse at each potential stop, thus causing the latitude and longitude at that stop to be entered into the computer.

In computing a particular route or dispatching a fleet of trucks, the computer applies algorithms to the digitized information to compute possible routes from each source to required destinations. It takes factors such as delivery time commitments, speed limits, distances, order sizes, and types and availability of trucks into account. The system then generates the best routes and indicates what size truck is needed, the time it will take to make the deliveries, and the transportation costs for each run.

The benefits to users of these automated routing systems include improved customer service, reduced mileage, reduced overtime, fewer vehicles required, and increased efficiency in both driver and vehicle utilization. *(Photos courtesy Mark McKenna)*

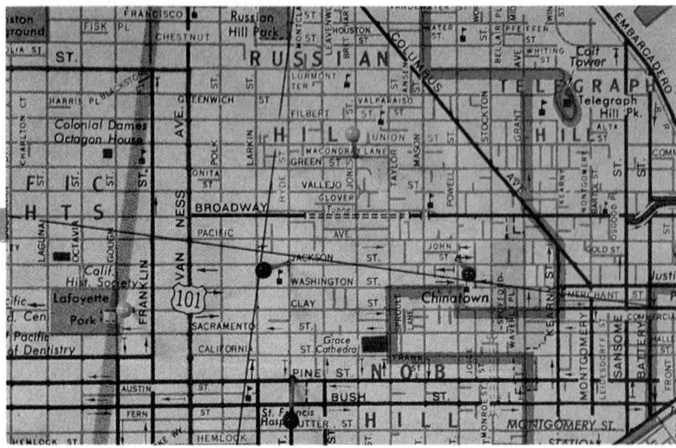
BROADWAY
PACIFIC
WASHINGTON
CLAY
SACRAMENTO
CALIFORNIA
PINE
BUSH
Chinatown
Lafayette Park
Telegraph Hill Pk.
Coit Tower
Grace Cathedral
VAN NESS
FRANKLIN
POLK
LARKIN
HYDE
MONTGOMERY
SANSOME
BATTERY
KEARNY
COLUMBUS

United Parcel Service

These efforts are directed primarily at increasing the practical limits of computer vocabularies and the quality of voice output. A computer that tells the time of day may need to say only "The time is . . . ," followed by a couple of numbers. A computer that trains pilots via simulated airplane flights may need to speak many words, in many sequences. Similarly, a voice coming from an EDP-system console that says, "Printer number four is jammed," need not speak eloquently. On an assembly line where the computer system reads bar codes on parts moving down the line and directs workers accordingly, a pleasant voice is essential; otherwise, fatigue and frustration are likely. The ultimate test of voice quality is transparency: Do at least 80 percent of uncued listeners fail to detect the voice as that of a computer?

MICROGRAPHICS

A *microfilm* is a photographic image, on a reduced scale, of information that might otherwise be handled in a printed form. Generally, it appears as a continuous roll, containing about 2000 frames—each of which may hold the equivalent of one printed page. A *microfiche* is a cardlike film medium. One 4-inch × 6-inch microfiche at 48× reduction can hold the equivalent of 270 pages of printed matter. The weight of 100 microfiches is 14 ounces; printed pages of the same data weigh about 200 pounds.

Computer output microfilm (COM) consists of photographic images produced in miniature with the aid of a computer. This term is also used to refer in general to the techniques and equipment used to combine micrographic technologies with work done by computers. We use the term in an inclusive way here to mean both products and processes.

Consider the volume of printed matter generated in our society—both with the computer's help and without it. COM is a satisfactory substitute in many cases. For example, a firm may print a letter acknowledging a customer's order. This letter is mailed to the customer. The file copy of this letter and other details relevant to the same order are stored on microfiche. These microfiches are distributed to the credit department, accounting, inventory, scheduling, manufacturing, distant branch warehouses, and shipping.

COM was proposed as a cost-saving alternative to printed reports for a number of years before it gained much acceptance. The need to process the film chemically (usually through an outside service organization) tended to limit its use. To overcome this drawback, printers employing a laser-imaging system to print computer output directly onto dry, heat-processed microfilm were developed. With them the need for a darkroom, a special processing machine, plumbing, and processing chemicals is eliminated. In-house micrographic systems are a reasonable alternative. (See Figure 4-12.)

Today, the main use of COM is archival storage. COM media can hold vast amounts of data (including graphics) compactly and safely. A 200-foot roll of 16-mm microfilm can store 10,000 standard document pages for about $15. With laser imaging, not only 48× reductions but also 60×, 72×, and 96× reductions are possible. *Optical disk* technology offers yet an additional measure of data compaction. More than 80,000 pages of information or about 1.3 million pages of keyboard input may be

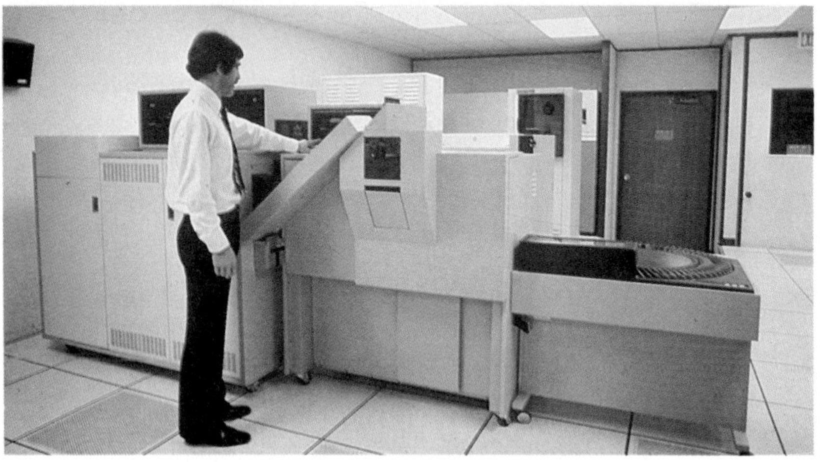

Figure 4-12 A full-function computer output microfilm (COM) recorder is designed for online or offline operation in a variety of data-processing environments. In some COM configurations, an interlink transport option eliminates the need for manual involvement in the fiche production process. (Courtesy Datagraphix Inc.)

may be stored on a single disk. (We'll learn more about optical disks in Chapter 5.)

When using COM, not only media costs but also storage costs are lower. Some users find that the cost of storing microfilm is about $\frac{1}{45}$th the cost of storing an equivalent volume of paper. Experienced COM users often state that COM printouts re-

THE COMPUTER AS ARTIST

Sometimes computer imagery can be used to restore things to their "ordinary" states. The U.S. Capitol dome in Washington is one of many buildings being restored with the help of computers. The computers are being used not only in project management of materials and labor, but also in reconstructing the original appearance of the buildings. *(Photo courtesy Bruce Hayes/Photo Researchers)*

quire only 2 percent of the space otherwise required for paper reports.

Because microfilm is compact and lightweight, distributing a report on microfilm is faster and less expensive than distributing computer printouts. Microfiches can be sent in envelopes to users through regular mail channels. Assume six copies of a 1000-page report weighing about 70 pounds are to be sent to other locations. Further assume United Parcel Service (UPS) is used. The delivery cost is about $9. Equivalent microfilm can be sent for about $1.50. A 200-page report may cost $4 to $5 to mail first class within the continental United States. The same report contained on one microfiche can be mailed at the cost of a single stamp.

An early disadvantage of microfilm was the inability to use a computer to retrieve microfilmed data. Now *computer input microfilm (CIM)* technologies are gaining recognition.

Computers and attached micrographic terminals are being used in both batch- and transaction-processing applications. At the Internal Revenue Service, a micrographic terminal can in seconds find a single wage report stored on microfilm, bypassing millions of others. Personnel at Warren County, Ohio, use online retrieval of microfilmed deeds and other documents to speed land transfers and to conduct title searches. Many organizations are finding COM to be a major aid in office automation.

Corporate users are also excited about another area of micrographics: the capability to create 35-mm slides, within minutes or hours, for use in high-quality business presentations.

Corporate users are also excited about another area of micrographics: the capability to create 35-mm slides, within minutes or hours, for use in high-quality business presentations. Business graphics software such as GEM Presentation Team and Harvard Business Graphics enables personal-computer users to produce bar graphs, pie charts, and other graphics as display output or in a file format that can be recorded on files. A file may be sent electronically to an outside service organization that produces slides within 24 hours at a cost of $10 or $15 per slide. Microprocessor-based *desktop film recorders* that can be used to produce such slides in-house range in price from $3000 to $10,000.

CHAPTER SUMMARY

1. Computer systems with attached printing devices can produce many printed, hard-copy forms of output. Those with output devices such as visual-display units and voice-output units can produce less permanent, soft-copy output. A system may include either or both kinds of devices.

2. Printers may be classified as serial (character), line, and page printers, according to how much information is printed in one output operation.

3. Printers may also be classified as either impact or nonimpact. The former are dependent on the physical movement of print elements; the latter print by thermal (heat), chemical, electrical, and/or optical techniques.

4. Some printers print fully-formed characters. Others print dot-matrix characters.

5. Low-cost dot-matrix printers were developed to overcome the speed limitations of early fully-formed-character printers. Today 9-, 18-, and 24-pin dot-matrix printers are known for their versatility.

6. Early impact line printers had chains, trains, and drums as printing mechanisms. Whereas a print chain or train can be changed, allowing different character sets to be used, a drum provides only one fixed character set. Belt and band printers are used on medium-sized and small computer systems.

7. Thermal printers and some ink-jet printers are at the low end of the nonimpact printer category. Very fast nonimpact printers using electrostatic, electrophotographic, and laser technologies are meeting business users' needs for high-volume output. Laser printers for use with microcomputer systems are an exciting, more recent development.

8. PostScript is a page description language used to tell what's to be printed on a page and where. Device independence, application portability, and high-quality output are among the benefits provided.

9. Plotters convert tabulated data into graphic form. Pen plotters of drum, flatbed, or beltbed types were first to arrive on the scene. Very fast electrostatic plotters are gaining in popularity.

10. Visual-display units record output on cathode-ray tubes (CRT's) in monochrome or multiple colors. Units with graphic capabilities can display charts, graphs, and line drawings as well as character data.

11. Audio responses are suitable where limited-volume, formalized messages are required as output.

12. Major technological advances are occurring in computer output microfilm (COM) products and processes. Users are achieving significant savings in media, storage, and distribution costs.

DISCUSSION QUESTIONS

1. What outputs of computer systems do you use in your daily life?
2. (a) What is meant by the term *hard copy?*
   (b) When might this kind of copy be desirable?
3. Distinguish between serial, line, and page printers.

4. (a) What are the two broad categories of printing methods?
   (b) What are some advantages of each of the methods that you named?
   (c) Describe some printers that use each of these methods.

5. Discuss some of the tradeoffs that printer-shopping users may make. In doing so, suggest situations where the various tradeoffs may be good ones from the users' points of view.

6. What is PostScript and why is it used?

7. Distinguish among the kinds of plotters available, showing how users may choose among them.

8. Select one type of plotter and build an argument to convince the manager of a particular business (also of your choice) to buy it.

9. Suggest some user applications for which visual-display output is appropriate.

10. Discuss the advantages of WYSIWYG capabilities.

11. (a) Suggest some applications for which audio output is especially suited.
    (b) What are its advantages and limitations?

12. Assume that you are the manager of a large discount store with access to a centralized EDP system. Give arguments to justify the use of microfilm at your facility.

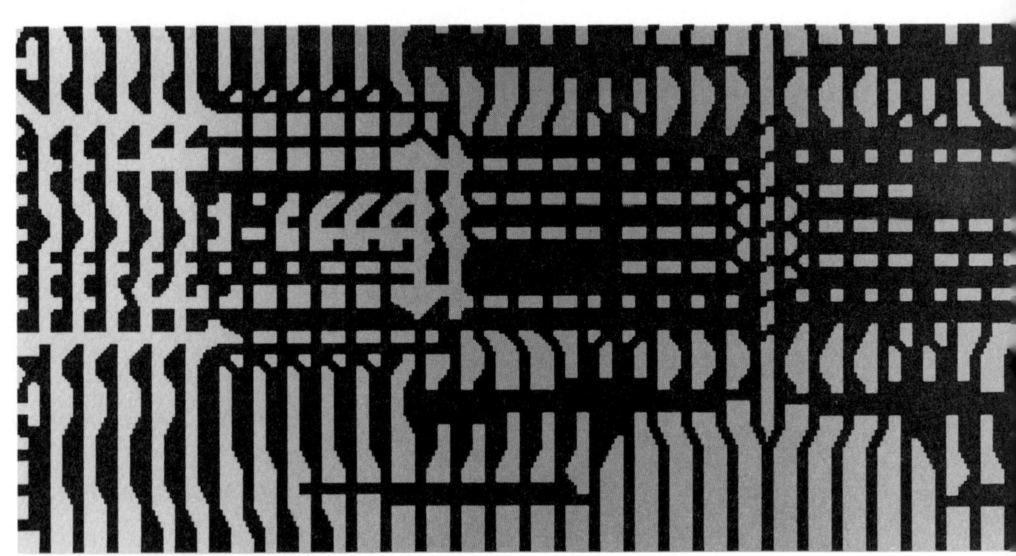

5 Storing Data

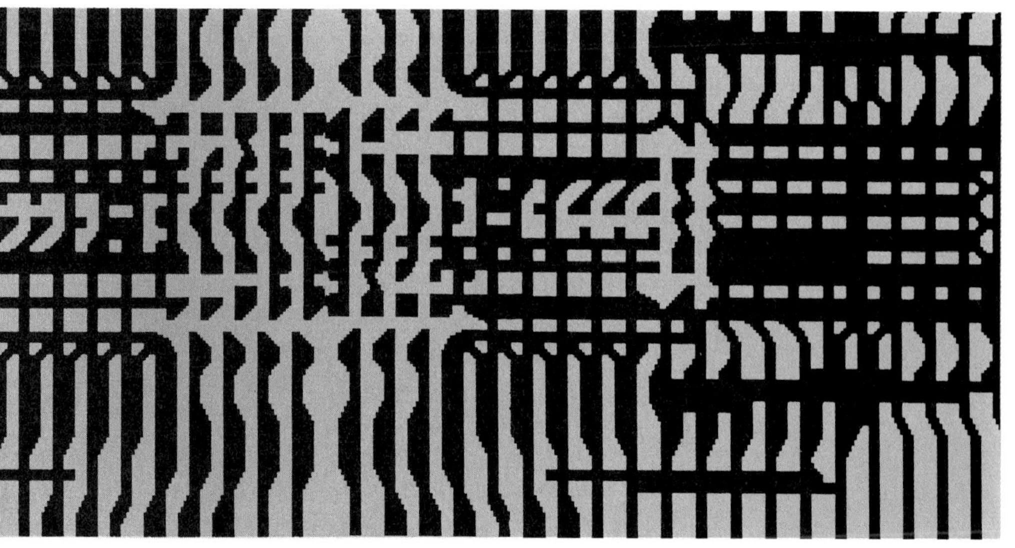

IN THIS CHAPTER

Primary Storage
Internal Data Representation
EBCDIC
ASCII
Storage Capacity
Storage Addresses and Accessing
Access Times and Cycle Times
Storage Components
Types of Memory
Secondary Storage
Storage and Data-Processing Methods
Magnetic Tape
Magnetic Disk
Optical Storage
A Perspective

When we make notes to ourselves on the backs of envelopes, we are storing data. Check stubs, sales slips, and duplicate tax forms are common data-storage devices. Businesses store large volumes of valuable data in customer account records, general ledgers, and filing cabinets. When a business elects to use a computer system, most of this data is stored in a form that is accessible to the computer.

Today's computers operate at "breakneck speeds." Even personal computers have very powerful processors. We can think of the processors as "data-processing engines." Like racing cars with engines that gulp gallons of fuel each second, today's computers accept data and perform operations on the data at unprecedented rates.

To match the performance of these data-processing engines, mechanisms and devices to store many programs and vast amounts of data *within* computer systems have been developed. The mechanisms also make the programs and data instantly available to the engines during processing. The speed and capacity of storage devices have increased dramatically over the past 10 years. Moreover, they're now available at much less cost. We look at many of the mechanisms and devices in this chapter.

When you've completed this chapter, you'll understand how large amounts of programs and data can be stored in a computer system. You'll also understand how we can access the programs and data, once they're stored. We look first at primary-storage concepts and technologies. Then we discuss secondary-storage concepts and devices.

Primary Storage

We learned in Chapter 2 that storage in an EDP system may be either of two types:

- *Primary storage,* the *internal storage unit,* also called *main storage* or *memory*
- *Secondary storage,* also called *auxiliary storage*

Primary storage is sometimes considered to be part of the central processing unit (CPU) of a computer system. It is always positioned near or with the computer's control section and arithmetic/logic unit. Secondary storage is often provided by tape or disk storage devices connected by cabling to the processor unit. (See Figure 5-1.) In a microcomputer system, secondary storage may be provided via diskettes that can be inserted in disk drives packaged neatly in a desktop configuration. (See Figure 5-2.)

During processing, primary storage accepts data from an input device, exchanges data with and supplies instructions to the CPU, and sends the results of processing to an output device. Its capacity must be sufficient to retain both a usable amount of data and the instructions needed to process it. Both the data and the instructions must be stored in a machine-readable form.

If you've used or read about microcomputer systems, you've probably come across phrases such as "up to 640K of RAM" and "4K of ROM." The *RAM,* or *random-access memory,* is primary data storage. It can hold user programs and data.

secondary storage
primary storage

Figure 5-1 An EDP system includes both primary and secondary storage. (Courtesy Hewlett-Packard Company)

primary
storage
secondary
storage

Figure 5-2 The amount of primary storage typically available in a microcomputer system is increasing rapidly as the physical sizes and costs of primary storage go down. Tape, disk, or removable diskettes may be used for secondary storage of programs and data. (Photo courtesy 3M)

The programs and data actually stored in RAM may change many times during processing. The *ROM*, or *read-only memory*, is control storage. It holds programs and data supplied by a vendor. They are essential to proper functioning of the system and cannot be changed by users. (As you may recall, we discussed the advantages of ROM earlier. See "Microcode" in Chapter 2.) The letter *K* is a common shorthand; here it means 1024 storage locations.

Internal Data Representation

It is easy to understand that there must be some method of representing data on employee time cards, credit-card receipts, and customer sales orders. There must also be a way to represent data inside a computer. When the data on a time card is read, for example, each data character is converted to a sequence of electronic pulses. The sequence of pulses is sent over a transmission medium (usually a wire or cable) to the computer. The sequence of pulses is one way of representing the character. Similarly, if you press, say, the key for the letter *M* on the keyboard of an input device, you cause a sequence of electronic pulses representing the letter *M* to be sent to the computer. (See Figure 5-3.) What happens when the pulses arrive?

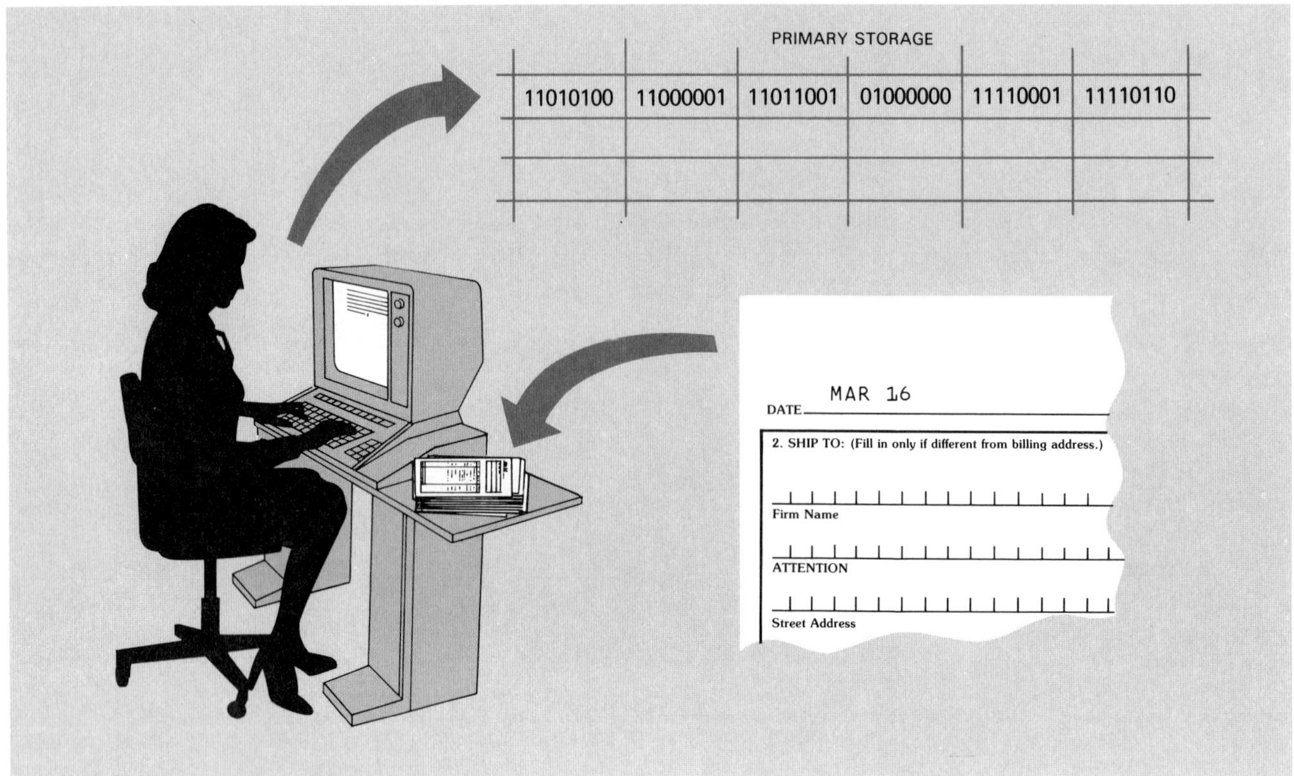
PRIMARY STORAGE
11010100
11000001
11011001
01000000
11110001
11110110
DATE
MAR 16
2. SHIP TO: (Fill in only if different from billing address.)
Firm Name
ATTENTION
Street Address

Figure 5-3 Data keyed in at a terminal may be converted to electronic pulses and stored internally in Extended Binary Coded Decimal Interchange Code (EBCDIC) form. (Courtesy TRW Inc.)

Binary Components

Consider an ordinary light bulb. At any one time, the light bulb is either on or off. It can be in only one of these two possible conditions. We say, therefore, that it operates in a *binary* or *two-state mode.* We refer to the two possible conditions, or settings, as *binary states.*

Computer components operate in the same way. Each component can be in only one of two possible conditions at any given time. We know that electronic pulses are either present or absent. Similarly, magnetic materials used in internal storage units are magnetized in one direction or the opposite. Logic gates planned by the computer designer to act as switches are either open or closed.

Binary Notation

In general, the sequence of electronic pulses representing a specific character or a specific numeric value causes a sequence of binary components making up storage to be set to certain states representing the same character or value. Since each component can be in only one of two possible states, we can use a *binary notation* to describe the pattern that the states of the components form. As we might expect from the term *binary,* this method of notation includes only two symbols. The symbols are the *binary digits,* or *bits,* 0 and 1. A 0 bit represents the absence of a value, and a 1 bit represents the presence of a value. A sequence of 0 bits and 1 bits (say, 0101 or 11010100) forms a *bit pattern.* The designers of a particular data-representation scheme, or *code,* decide how many bits should be included in a bit pattern. Then they assign a specific meaning to each unique combination of bits. The bit pattern 0101 might stand for the letter *A* in a particular code, for example. In Figure 5-3, the bit pattern 11010100 stands for the letter *M.*

The designers of a particular data-representation scheme, or *code,* decide how many bits should be included in a bit pattern.

EBCDIC

The *Extended Binary Coded Decimal Interchange Code,* or *EBCDIC* (pronounced eb′-si-dick), was developed by IBM. It is used extensively in medium and large computer systems produced by IBM and other manufacturers.

As Figure 5-4 suggests, each EBCDIC character is represented by a unique 8-bit code pattern. Since there are 2^8, or 256, possible combinations of eight bits, up to 256 different characters can be represented. This allows for the digits 0 through 9, both uppercase and lowercase letters, and a wide range of punctuation marks and other special characters. It also allows for control characters that are meaningful to certain input/output devices. In Figure 5-4, NUL means null (all zeros), SOH means Start of Heading, STX means Start of Text, and so on. Some bit patterns currently have no assigned meanings; they are available for future assignments.

There is no need for you, system analysts, programmers, or any other users of computers to memorize the EBCDIC bit patterns. However, persons who deal often with EBCDIC learn to recognize quickly the values represented. Each 8-bit pattern is simply divided into two parts. The leftmost four bits are the zone portion. The remaining (rightmost) four bits are the digit portion. Notice, for example, a zone portion of 1111 is a sure clue to a numeric character in the vast majority of cases.

ASCII

Another widely used data-representation scheme is the *American Standard Code for Information Interchange,* or *ASCII* (pronounced as′-key). This code was developed jointly by several equipment manufacturers and users. Their objective was to simplify and standardize machine-to-machine and system-to-system communication. They hoped to allow data to be passed freely between computers and devices produced by the same manufacturer or by different manufacturers.

ASCII may be treated as either a 7-bit code or an 8-bit code. The meanings of 128 of the bit patterns have been standardized by the International Standards Organization and the American National Standards Institute. (See Figure 5-5.) In an 8-bit representation scheme, the leftmost bit of bit patterns representing these characters is set to 0. As a convenience to users, a decimal number is often associated with each character in user documentation. (It's easier to look for the ASCII character corresponding to decimal 78 than to search for 1001110 in an ASCII table.)

The use of ASCII is especially common in data communication systems, where data is transmitted long

A Disappearing Act

Storage technologies have come a long way since the mid-1940s. Twenty-five years ago, one million characters of data could be stored on magnetic surfaces that together equaled the size of a double bed. Five years ago, one million characters fit on a surface the size of a postage stamp. Soon, they may fit on a point the size of a grain of salt. No single storage medium satisfies all EDP-system storage requirements. There are fast, expensive internal memories for calculations. There are slower, less expensive secondary-storage devices for large-volume storage. There is a significant gap between them in terms of speed and cost.

distances over telephone lines, microwaves, or other media. Input/output devices supporting the ASCII character set are often referred to as *ASCII terminals.* If the computer at the receiving end of the transmission stores data in EBCDIC, the ASCII bit patterns must be converted to EBCDIC bit patterns before they are placed in primary storage. Most microcomputer systems accept, store, process, and write out data in ASCII form.

STORAGE CAPACITY

In daily conversation, we often speak of the capacity of an object—say, a shopping cart, a swimming pool, or a football stadium. We express that capacity in terms of number of items, cubic feet, gallons, people, or whatever unit is appropriate. In each case, the capacity is a measure of how much the object can hold.

In like manner, we speak of the capacity of a computer's internal storage unit. The capacity is a mea-

EBCDIC	BIT PATTERN	EBCDIC	BIT PATTERN	EBCDIC	BIT PATTERN	EBCDIC	BIT PATTERN
	Zone Digit		Zone Digit		Zone Digit		Zone Digit
NUL	0000 0000	SP	0100 0000		1000 0000	PZ 7/11	1100 0000
SOH	0000 0001		0100 0001	a	1000 0001	A	1100 0001
STX	0000 0010		0100 0010	b	1000 0010	B	1100 0010
ETX	0000 0011		0100 0011	c	1000 0011	C	1100 0011
PF	0000 0100		0100 0100	d	1000 0100	D	1100 0100
HT	0000 0101		0100 0101	e	1000 0101	E	1100 0101
LC	0000 0110		0100 0110	f	1000 0110	F	1100 0110
DEL	0000 0111		0100 0111	g	1000 0111	G	1100 0111
	0000 1000		0100 1000	h	1000 1000	H	1100 1000
RLF	0000 1001		0100 1001	i	1000 1001	I	1100 1001
SMM	0000 1010	¢ [	0100 1010		1000 1010		1100 1010
VT	0000 1011	.	0100 1011		1000 1011		1100 1011
FF	0000 1100	<	0100 1100		1000 1100	⑀	1100 1100
CR	0000 1101	(	0100 1101		1000 1101		1100 1101
SO	0000 1110	+	0100 1110		1000 1110	⑂	1100 1110
SI	0000 1111	|	0100 1111		1000 1111		1100 1111
DLE	0001 0000	&	0101 0000		1001 0000	MZ 7/13	1101 0000
DC1	0001 0001		0101 0001	j	1001 0001	J	1101 0001
DC2	0001 0010		0101 0010	k	1001 0010	K	1101 0010
TM	0001 0011		0101 0011	l	1001 0011	L	1101 0011
RES	0001 0100		0101 0100	m	1001 0100	M	1101 0100
NL	0001 0101		0101 0101	n	1001 0101	N	1101 0101
BS	0001 0110		0101 0110	o	1001 0110	O	1101 0110
IL	0001 0111		0101 0111	p	1001 0111	P	1101 0111
CAN	0001 1000		0101 1000	q	1001 1000	Q	1101 1000
EM	0001 1001		0101 1001	r	1001 1001	R	1101 1001
CC	0001 1010	!]	0101 1010		1001 1010		1101 1010
CU1	0001 1011	$	0101 1011		1001 1011		1101 1011
IFS	0001 1100	*	0101 1100		1001 1100		1101 1100
IGS	0001 1101	)	0101 1101		1001 1101		1101 1101
IRS	0001 1110	;	0101 1110		1001 1110		1101 1110
IUS	0001 1111	¬	0101 1111		1001 1111		1101 1111
DS	0010 0000	—	0110 0000		1010 0000	RM 5/12	1110 0000
SOS	0010 0001	/	0110 0001	—	1010 0001		1110 0001
FS	0010 0010		0110 0010	s	1010 0010	S	1110 0010
	0010 0011		0110 0011	t	1010 0011	T	1110 0011
BYP	0010 0100		0110 0100	u	1010 0100	U	1110 0100
LF	0010 0101		0110 0101	v	1010 0101	V	1110 0101
ETB	0010 0110		0110 0110	w	1010 0110	W	1110 0110
ESC	0010 0111		0110 0111	x	1010 0111	X	1110 0111
	0010 1000		0110 1000	y	1010 1000	Y	1110 1000
	0010 1001		0110 1001	z	1010 1001	Z	1110 1001
SM	0010 1010	7/12	0110 1010		1010 1010		1110 1010
CU2	0010 1011	,	0110 1011		1010 1011		1110 1011
	0010 1100	%	0110 1100		1010 1100	H	1110 1100
ENQ	0010 1101	—	0110 1101		1010 1101		1110 1101
ACK	0010 1110	>	0110 1110		1010 1110		1110 1110
BEL	0010 1111	?	0110 1111		1010 1111		1110 1111
	0011 0000		0111 0000		1011 0000	0	1111 0000
	0011 0001		0111 0001		1011 0001	1	1111 0001
SYN	0011 0010		0111 0010		1011 0010	2	1111 0010
	0011 0011		0111 0011		1011 0011	3	1111 0011
PN	0011 0100		0111 0100		1011 0100	4	1111 0100
RS	0011 0101		0111 0101		1011 0101	5	1111 0101
UC	0011 0110		0111 0110		1011 0110	6	1111 0110
EOT	0011 0111		0111 0111		1011 0111	7	1111 0111
	0011 1000		0111 1000		1011 1000	8	1111 1000
	0011 1001	6/0	0111 1001		1011 1001	9	1111 1001
	0011 1010	:	0111 1010		1011 1010	≉	1111 1010
CU3	0011 1011	#	0111 1011		1011 1011		1111 1011
DC4	0011 1100	@	0111 1100		1011 1100		1111 1100
NAK	0011 1101	'	0111 1101		1011 1101		1111 1101
	0011 1110	=	0111 1110		1011 1110		1111 1110
SUB	0011 1111	"	0111 1111		1011 1111	EO	1111 1111

Figure 5-4 EBCDIC character representation.

ASCII	BIT PATTERN	DECIMAL	ASCII	BIT PATTERN	DECIMAL	ASCII	BIT PATTERN	DECIMAL
NUL	0000000	0	+	0101011	43	V	1010110	86
SOH	0000001	1	,	0101100	44	W	1010111	87
STX	0000010	2	-	0101101	45	X	1011000	88
ETX	0000011	3	.	0101110	46	Y	1011001	89
EOT	0000100	4	/	0101111	47	Z	1011010	90
ENQ	0000101	5	0	0110000	48	[	1011011	91
ACK	0000110	6	1	0110001	49	\	1011100	92
Bel	0000111	7	2	0110010	50	]	1011101	93
BS	0001000	8	3	0110011	51	^	1011110	94
HT	0001001	9	4	0110100	52	—	1011111	95
LF	0001010	10	5	0110101	53	'	1100000	96
VT	0001011	11	6	0110110	54	a	1100001	97
FF	0001100	12	7	0110111	55	b	1100010	98
CR	0001101	13	8	0111000	56	c	1100011	99
SO	0001110	14	9	0111001	57	d	1100100	100
SI	0001111	15	:	0111010	58	e	1100101	101
DLE	0010000	16	;	0111011	59	f	1100110	102
DC1	0010001	17	<	0111100	60	g	1100111	103
DC2	0010010	18	=	0111101	61	h	1101000	104
DC3	0010011	19	>	0111110	62	i	1101001	105
DC4	0010100	20	?	0111111	63	j	1101010	106
NCK	0010101	21	@	1000000	64	k	1101011	107
SYN	0010110	22	A	1000001	65	l	1101100	108
ETB	0010111	23	B	1000010	66	m	1101101	109
CAN	0011000	24	C	1000011	67	n	1101110	110
EM	0011001	25	D	1000100	68	o	1101111	111
SUB	0011010	26	E	1000101	69	p	1110000	112
ESC	0011011	27	F	1000110	70	q	1110001	113
FS	0011100	28	G	1000111	71	r	1110010	114
GS	0011101	29	H	1001000	72	s	1110011	115
RS	0011110	30	I	1001001	73	t	1110100	116
US	0011111	31	J	1001010	74	u	1110101	117
SP	0100000	32	K	1001011	75	v	1110110	118
!	0100001	33	L	1001100	76	w	1110111	119
"	0100010	34	M	1001101	77	x	1111000	120
#	0100011	35	N	1001110	78	y	1111001	121
$	0100100	36	O	1001111	79	z	1111010	122
%	0100101	37	P	1010000	80	{	1111011	123
&	0100110	38	Q	1010001	81	|	1111100	124
'	0100111	39	R	1010010	82	}	1111101	125
(	0101000	40	S	1010011	83	~	1111110	126
)	0101001	41	T	1010100	84	DEL	1111111	127
*	0101010	42	U	1010101	85			

Figure 5-5 ASCII character representation.

sure of the amount of programs and data the unit can hold. We may express that capacity in terms of *K*. One K may mean 1024 bits, 1024 8-bit *bytes,* or 1024 *words* of lengths 8, 16, 32, or 60 bits, and so on. As suggested earlier, each bit, byte, or word is an addressable storage location, as determined by the system architecture.

The capacity of some large internal storage units may also be described in terms of *M* or *MB*. Here, 1M means 1 megabyte, 2M means 2 megabytes, and so on. Each *megabyte* is equal to 1024 × 1024 8-bit bytes, or 1,048,576 storage locations. (That is, 1M = 1024K, where 1K = 1 *kilobyte*, or 1024 bytes.) Similarly, 1G (or 1 GB) means 1 gigabyte, 2G means 2 gigabytes, and so on. Each *gigabyte* is equal to 1024 × 1024 × 1024 8-bit bytes, or 1,073,941,824 storage locations.

Some computers use one byte as the basic unit of storage. Each byte holds one character of data. During processing, each character is operated on independently, one at a time. Other computers use one word as a basic unit of storage. Each word may hold one or several characters, depending on the number of bits required for each bit pattern and the number of bit positions in each word. When discussing amounts of storage, we must understand the unit of measure that applies.

Storage Addresses and Accessing

In Chapter 2, we pointed out that the internal storage unit of a computer resembles an electronic filing cabinet. The internal storage unit can also be compared to a group of numbered mailboxes. (See Figure 5-6.) Each mailbox is identified and located by a number. In the same way, storage is divided into locations, each of which has an assigned address and holds a specific unit of data. Depending on the system architecture, the unit of data may be a character, digit, the contents of a byte, or a word. To write data to a location or to read data from it, the address of the location must be known.

When data is written to a particular location, it replaces the previous contents of that location. The previous contents are no longer available to us. Thus, the "write" operation is a *destructive* operation.

When data is read from a location, the contents of the location are not altered. In contrast to the mailboxes discussed above, which are empty after their contents are removed, storage locations from which data has been retrieved (read) are not empty. Once written into storage, data may be read many times. Thus, the "read" operation is *nondestructive.* In effect, a duplicate copy of the stored data is made available each time a read occurs.

Once written into storage, data may be read many times.

To appreciate the nondestructive read capability, imagine that you are adding individual test scores for many students. As you do so, you write the total score for each student on a scratch pad for subsequent grand totaling, analysis, and computing of averages. Now suppose each total is erased the first time you read it from the scratch pad. You may be able to complete one calculation using the totals. Any subsequent calculations using the (erased) totals will be difficult!

Access Times and Cycle Times

The time the computer takes to locate and transfer data to or from storage is called *access time.* It varies for different storage media and devices. The time the computer takes to

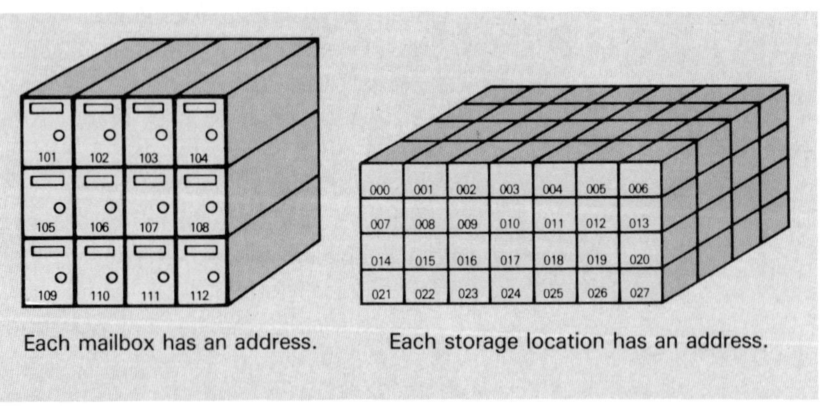
101
102
103
104
105
106
107
108
109
110
111
112
000
001
002
003
004
005
006
007
008
009
010
011
012
013
014
015
016
017
018
019
020
021
022
023
024
025
026
027
Each mailbox has an address.
Each storage location has an address.

Figure 5-6 When writing data to or reading data from a primary-storage location, the address of that location must be specified.

get ready to process the next request is called *cycle time.* It is uniform for each computer but varies from one kind of computer to another.

Because several storage media and devices are used within a computer system, we must be concerned about the access times of all of them. How fast can data be located and transferred? It does little good to have a very-high-speed internal storage unit if the over-all system spends much of its time waiting for data transfers to and from slower-speed tape or disk storage devices.

Internal data transfers are accomplished by electronic circuitry. Therefore, they are fast. The access times of the internal storage units of microcomputers are measured in millionths of a second, or *microseconds.* The access times of the internal storage units of large computers are measured in billionths of a second, or *nanoseconds.* So are cycle times. To appreciate how short such intervals of time are, consider a spaceship traveling at 100,000 miles per hour. In one microsecond, the spaceship would travel about $1\frac{3}{4}$ inches. In one nanosecond, it would travel about 1/1000th of $1\frac{3}{4}$ inches.

To increase the over-all speed of internal data transfers, computer system designers are continually trying to decrease the distances that data must travel.

To increase the over-all speed of internal data transfers, computer system designers are continually trying to decrease the distances that data must travel. That's why miniaturization is such an important consideration in memory development.

Storage Components

The internal storage units of the first electronic digital computers were made of *vacuum tubes.* Each tube was a two-state device through which an electronic current could flow. But each tube also took up much space, tended to overheat, and lasted only about 3000 hours.

In the 1960s and 1970s, *magnetic-core storage units* were common. Each core was a tiny ring of ferromagnetic material, a few hundredths of an inch in diameter. It could be magnetized in a few microseconds, and it retained that magnetism indefinitely (unless deliberately changed).

In core storage, the two possible magnetic states of a core were used to represent 0 and 1, positive and negative, on and off—conditions that are basic to a binary method of storing data. Because any specified location in storage had to be instantly accessible, the cores were arranged on wires so that any combination of 1s and 0s representing a character could be written magnetically or read back when needed. (See Figure 5-7.)

To provide for the selection of a specific core in storage for reading or writing, two wires were run through each core at right angles. When half the current needed to magnetize a core was sent through each wire, the core—and only that core—was magnetized. Generally, many cores were strung on one screen, or plane, of wires. Nevertheless, any one core in the screen could be selected for writing or reading without affecting any other core.

Through technological advancements, the diameters of both the cores and the wires were reduced to a few thousandths of an inch. Each reduction meant that reading and

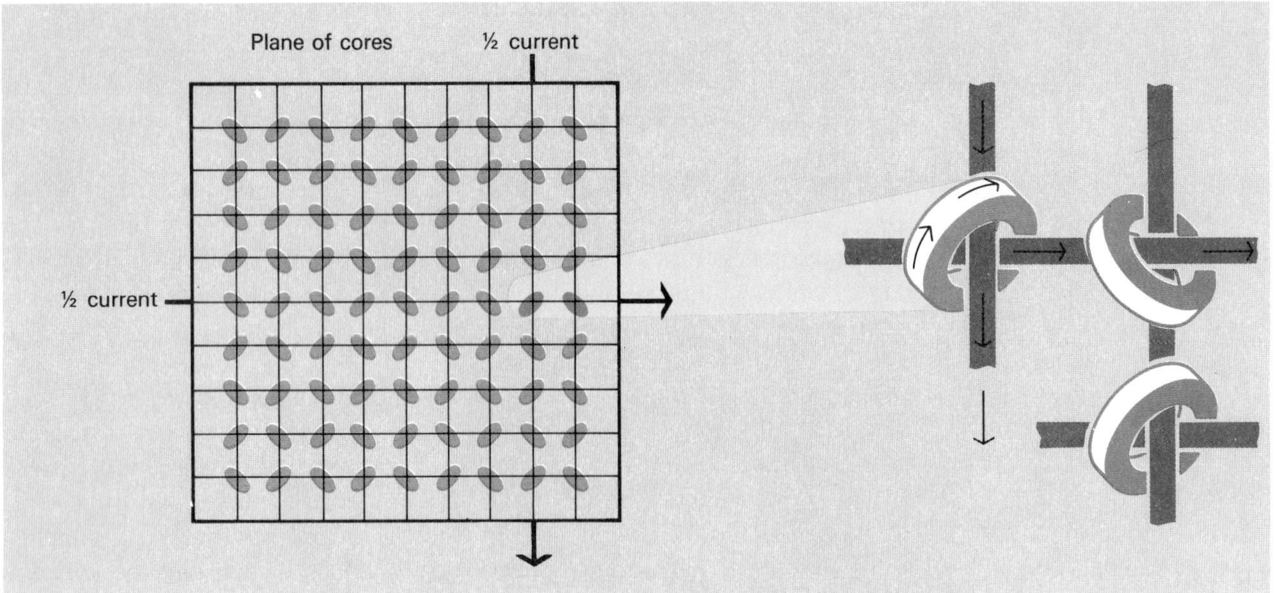
Plane of cores
½ current
½ current

Figure 5-7 In magnetic-core storage units, cores threaded on wires were magnetized to represent and store data.

COMPUTERS AT THE ZOO

Veterinarians at the San Diego Zoo are collecting vital statistics on this young orangutan and other zoo inhabitants. The statistics are placed in a computerized database aimed at maintaining healthy, self-sustaining animal populations worldwide. The detailed clinical and pathological data within the database is available not only to San Diego Zoo personnel but also to other zoological institutions, veterinary colleges, and medical schools. All benefit. *(Photo courtesy IBM Corporation)*

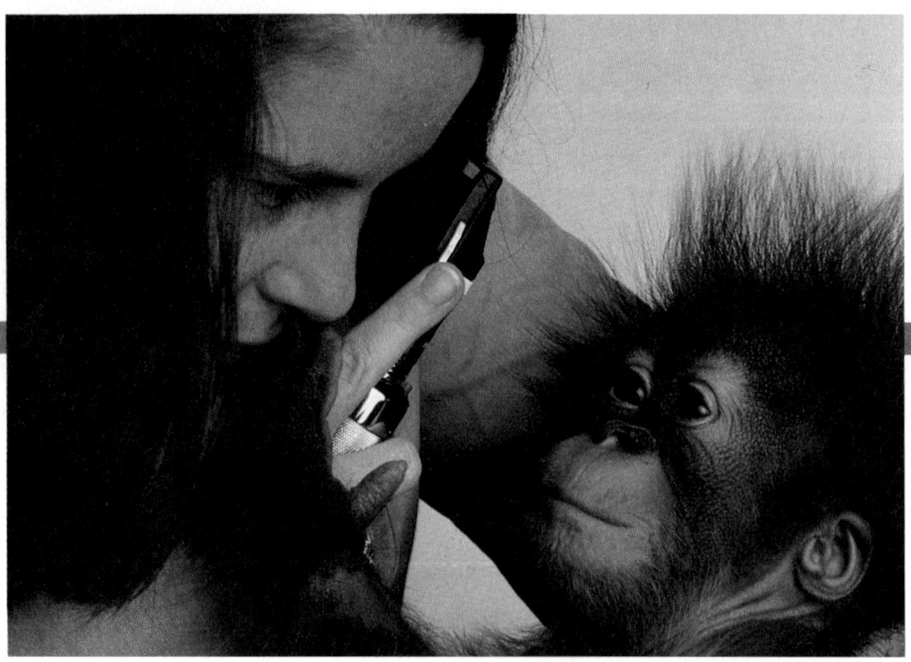

writing could be done faster. But to achieve even faster speeds and to create even more compact internal storage units, designers turned to *integrated circuit (IC)* technologies.

IC's are complete, complex electronic circuits made up of many electrical components (storage capacitors, transistors, resistors, and so on). In a complicated manufacturing process, all of these electrical components are built into a single chip of semiconductor material. Each chip forms an indivisible building block—hence, the name *semiconductor monolithic storage.* The electrical components are capable of being in either of two states: conducting a current or not conducting a current. Therefore, they can be used to represent 0 and 1, positive and negative, on and off—just as magnetic cores can. Even though the earliest chips, built on the semiconductor silicon, were only a little bigger than one magnetic core, they could hold not just one but thousands of bit settings. Like cores, the bit cells on a chip are arranged so that any combination of 1s and 0s representing a character can be written into or read from storage when needed. The acronym *RAM* is commonly understood today to mean semiconductor random-access memory. (See Figure 5-8.)

Each chip forms an indivisible building block—hence, the name *semiconductor monolithic storage.*

Besides increased speed and reduced size, semiconductor monolithic storage offers other advantages. It is easy to maintain because established techniques for circuit analysis can be applied to diagnose what's wrong if an equipment malfunction occurs. The manufacturers of semiconductor chips are continuing to perfect and automate their production processes. As a result, the cost of semiconductor storage is continuing to come down. However, most semiconductor storage does have one disadvantage. To understand this disadvantage, we need only remember that the components of semiconductor storage are circuits. An electrical current, or pulse, must be present to retain their bit settings. A loss of electrical power is a loss of stored data and instructions. We say that such storage is *volatile.* In contrast, magnetic-core storage, magnetic-tape storage, and magnetic-disk storage are *nonvolatile.*

LIBERTY
IN GOD
WE TRUST

Figure 5-8 How small is small? AT&T's megabit chip, which can hold over one million bits of data, is compared with a dime in this photograph. (Courtesy of AT&T Bell Labs)

Types of Memory

Since computers were introduced, the amount of primary storage that can be made available in a system has increased to meet users' application needs. Fortunately, vendors have decreased physical storage sizes and costs by factors of 100 or more at the same time they have increased storage capacities.

Since computers were introduced, the amount of primary storage that can be made available in a system has increased to meet users' application needs.

Twenty-five years ago, a large computer system may have had 32K, 64K, or 128K of primary storage. Today, microcomputer users need at least 512K. Just five years ago, 8 megabytes was considered to be a lot of memory. Today 64- or 128-megabyte memories are not uncommon.

Today, the amount of primary storage available to user application programs is determined by several factors. One is the amount of physical primary storage actually installed on the system. Another is the addressing capability of the system and application software. A third factor is whether or not the system supports some kind of switching technique that can make any of several blocks of instructions and data accessible during processing.

The constraints of limited storage are perhaps best known to users of personal computer systems running under control of the MS-DOS operating system. The user of a personal computer system based on an Intel 80286 microprocessor (say, an IBM PC/AT or PC/AT-compatible microcomputer) may have multiple types of memory on the system. (See Figure 5-9.) *Conventional memory* is primary storage that MS-DOS manages and in which application programs normally run. It's limited to 640K, or 640 × 1024 bytes. The memory from 640K up to 1000K, or 1 megabyte, is reserved for visual-display buffers, the ROM BIOS (basic input/output system), and other system functions. If a memory board that supports the Lotus/Intel/Microsoft Expanded Memory Specification (EMS) is installed in the system, a 64K "window" in this storage space may provide access to (be "mapped into") four 16K areas selected from up to 8 megabytes of storage space actually located on the EMS board. The window is called *expanded memory.* A leading application that's been modified to store and access data in expanded memory (if it's available) is the Lotus 1-2-3 electronic spreadsheet program.

The constraints of limited storage are perhaps best known to users of personal computer systems running under control of the MS-DOS operating system.

A second specification called the Enhanced EMS (EEMS) specification was developed later to increase the potential size and usability of expanded memory. Both of the specifications were then subsumed by an upgraded EMS referred to EMS 4.0 or LIM 4.0. Up to 1 megabyte of expanded memory may be active,

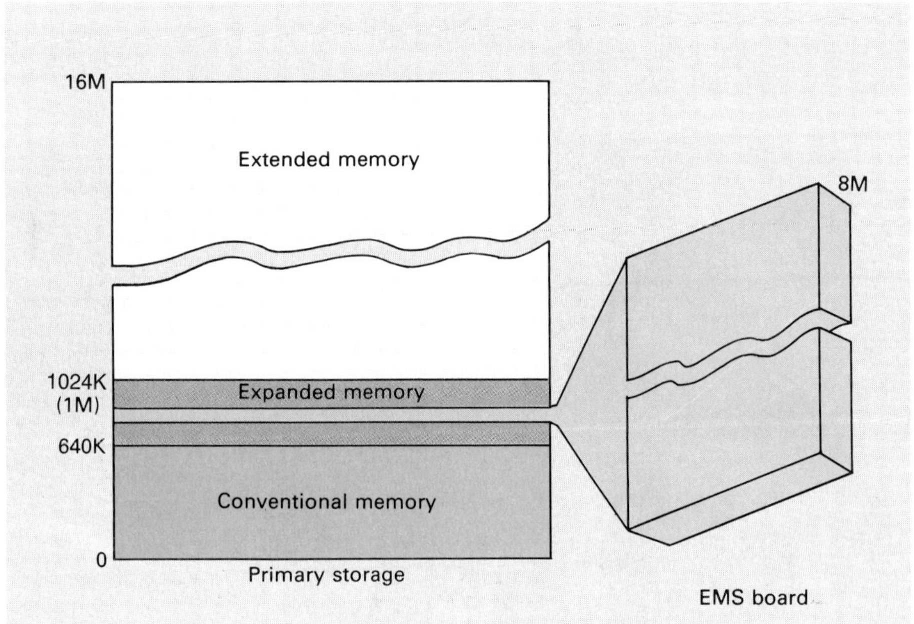
16M
Extended memory
8M
1024K
(1M)
Expanded memory
640K
Conventional memory
0
Primary storage
EMS board

Figure 5-9 Users of Intel 80286-based microcomputer systems may have multiple types of memory installed on their systems to increase the amount of work that can be accomplished.

mapped on up to 32 megabytes of storage space on an EMS board. Multiple windows may exist above or below the 640K boundary. It's feasible to store data and to store and run multiple application programs from this expanded memory. More work can be accomplished in a given amount of time than would be possible otherwise.

Extended memory starts at the 1-megabyte boundary and extends up to 16 megabytes. Programs must be written to run in what's called *protected mode* to take advantage of this storage space. The major characteristic of protected mode is that primary storage addresses are 24 bits in length (as opposed to 20 bits in *real mode,* the MS-DOS environment).

The OS/2 operating system was designed by Microsoft and IBM to run in protected mode. It can support larger applications than its predecessor, MS-DOS, and several of the applications can run concurrently. (We'll study operating systems in greater detail in Chapter 11.)

Even users of large computer systems may need expanded memory. Incredible as it may seem, for example, the 64 or 128 megabytes of primary storage (conventional memory) that can be installed on IBM 3090 computer systems is not enough to satisfy some user requirements. In 1985, IBM introduced *expanded storage* to or from which programs and data can be moved (from or to 3090 conventional memory) during processing. The 75-microsecond transfer time of the expanded storage is much slower than the 80- or 100-nanosecond cycle time of 3090 conventional memory, but much faster than the access times of disk or tape input/output operations that otherwise would be required.

Large automotive manufacturers, airlines, and insurance firms are examples of firms that depend heavily on systems with expanded storage. On some systems, up to 512 megabytes of expanded storage may be installed.

SELECTING GIFTS WITH COMPUTER HELP

Marriage by computer? Well, not exactly. But happy couples, friends, and relatives are enthusiastic advocates of the computerized gift list services available at Frederick & Nelson department stores.

The gift selection process begins when a couple receives a catalog containing more than 12,000 gift items available through Frederick & Nelson. The couple creates a "wish list," which is then entered into a microcomputer. The complete wish-list database is updated nightly and transferred to participating stores. Each store has access to the latest gift selection information.

When a friend or relative visits one of the stores and asks whether the couple has registered a preferred china pattern, silverware, or household appliances, a Frederick & Nelson attendant simply signs on to the microcomputer at the store and keys in the bride's or groom's name and the date of the wedding. The system produces a report showing the couple's preferred gift items, those that have been purchased by others, and those still needed. The friend or relative can then purchase a gift item accordingly.

In addition to helping Frederick & Nelson offer enhanced, personalized service to its customers, the system at Frederick & Nelson generates valuable management information. Store buyers can track the most popular patterns and gift items. Anniversaries can be tracked and serve as triggers for additional marketing opportunities. *(Photo courtesy of Cosmos, Inc. Photographer: Tim Hart, DHY Studios)*

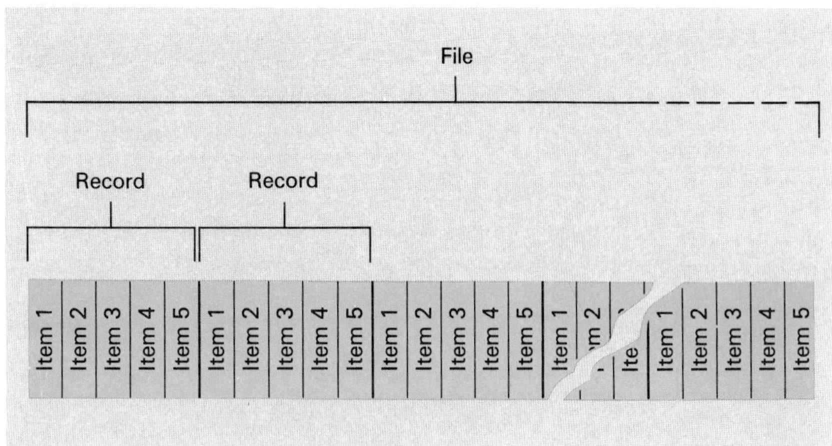
File
Record
Record
Item 1
Item 2
Item 3
Item 4
Item 5
Item 1
Item 2
Item 3
Item 4
Item 5
Item 1
Item 2
Item 3
Item 4
Item 5
Item 1
Item 1
Item 2
Item 3
Item 4
Item 5

Figure 5-10 Data is commonly organized by grouping related items into a record and related records into a file.

Secondary Storage

Some data-processing operations require more instructions and data than can be held in the available primary storage at one time. In such cases, primary storage is augmented by secondary, or auxiliary, storage.

For example, assume an automotive parts distributor maintains records for a warehouse inventory of 25,000 parts. Each part is identified by a 10-character number. Each part is stocked at one or more of 15 warehouse locations. At any time, some quantity of each part may (or may not) be available at each location. Other important facts about each part are the wholesale price per unit, whether volume discounts are available, the lead time required for reordering, and so on. Each of these facts about the part is an *item.* The complete set of items about one part is a *record.* The complete set of records for all parts is a *file.* (See Figure 5-10.)

Obviously, we don't want to keep the whole file in primary storage just so we can answer one dealer's inquiry about the closest warehouse with at least 20 fan belts of a particular type. Nor do we want to worry about whether or not the whole file will fit in primary storage each time the firm decides to stock a new type of part. So we create a machine-readable file, but we keep it on a secondary-storage device. Then, whenever an inquiry is received from a dealer, a stored program can access the file in secondary storage, read in the record for the part to be dealt with, and supply the needed information as output. When a new part is stocked, another stored program can add a new record to the file.

In like manner, data files and programs not in use are kept in secondary storage. From there, they can be transferred to primary storage when needed. The secondary storage may be either of two types:

- *Sequential:* punched-card, magnetic-tape, and other devices that hold files which must be read in sequence from the beginning in order to read or write a desired record.
- *Direct:* magnetic-disk units and other direct-access storage devices (DASD's) that give immediate access to individual records; there is no need to read from the beginning of a file to find a desired record.

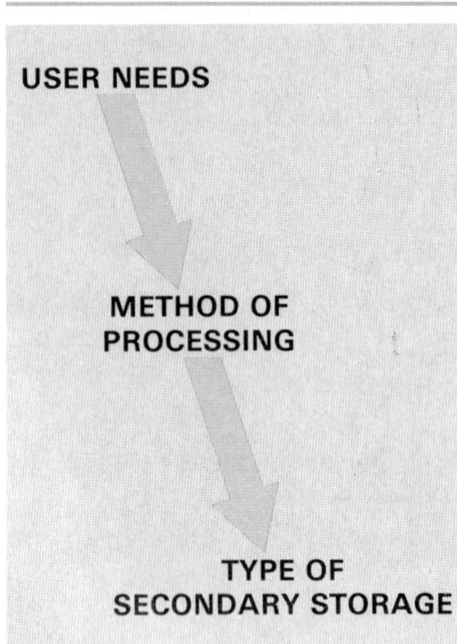
USER NEEDS
METHOD OF PROCESSING
TYPE OF SECONDARY STORAGE

Secondary-storage devices extend the storage capability of a computer system beyond that of primary storage by providing large-capacity, lower-cost, slower-speed, but accessible storage. A computer system may include both sequential and direct-access storage devices.

Storage and Data-Processing Methods

The two types of secondary storage—sequential and direct—correspond directly to the two primary methods of handling data: *sequential,* or *batch, processing* and *direct processing.* The user's needs determine which method of processing should be used. The method of processing, in turn, determines the type of secondary storage required.

Sequential Processing

In sequential processing, data is collected and stored in batches before being forwarded to the computer as input. Examples of data that may be handled in this manner are issues and receipts from inventory, accounts receivable, accounts payable, and employee work hours for payroll. These data records are called *transaction,* or *detail, records.* They form a *transaction* (or *detail*) *file.* The records in the file are arranged sequentially (sorted) according to part number, account number, or a similar entry that is common to all of them. The portion of a record containing the entry or entries that determine the record's position in the file is called its *control field,* or *key.*

For most applications, certain calculations must be performed on data items recorded in other fields of the transaction records. Additionally, most application processing also involves the updating of items within the company's *master records* (records of previous business activities) stored sequentially in *master files.* Therefore, both transaction and master records must be provided as input to a particular processing run. Furthermore, the sequence of the transaction records and the sequence of the master records must be the same. (See Figure 5-11.)

The outputs of a sequential processing run may include customer statements, employee paychecks, printed reports, or similar hard-copy information to be routed to users. A revised (updated, or new) master file is also part of the output; it will be used as input the next time the application is scheduled for processing. We call it a *turnaround file.* The old master file is generally kept for a fixed period as a *backup file.*

Sequential master files may be stored on magnetic tapes. They may also be stored on magnetic disks. As we'll soon see, there are many kinds of tape and disk devices.

Direct Processing

To appreciate the advantages of direct processing, think about searching for an entry in a large unabridged dictionary. Suppose you wanted to look up a particular word in that dictionary. How long would it take you to find it?

If you had to start reading from the beginning of the dictionary to find the word, you could expect to read, on the average, half the dictionary before you found it. Obviously, a much quicker approach is to look at the first letter of the word, go to that portion of the dictionary, look at succeeding letters of the word, and so on, until the exact word is found.

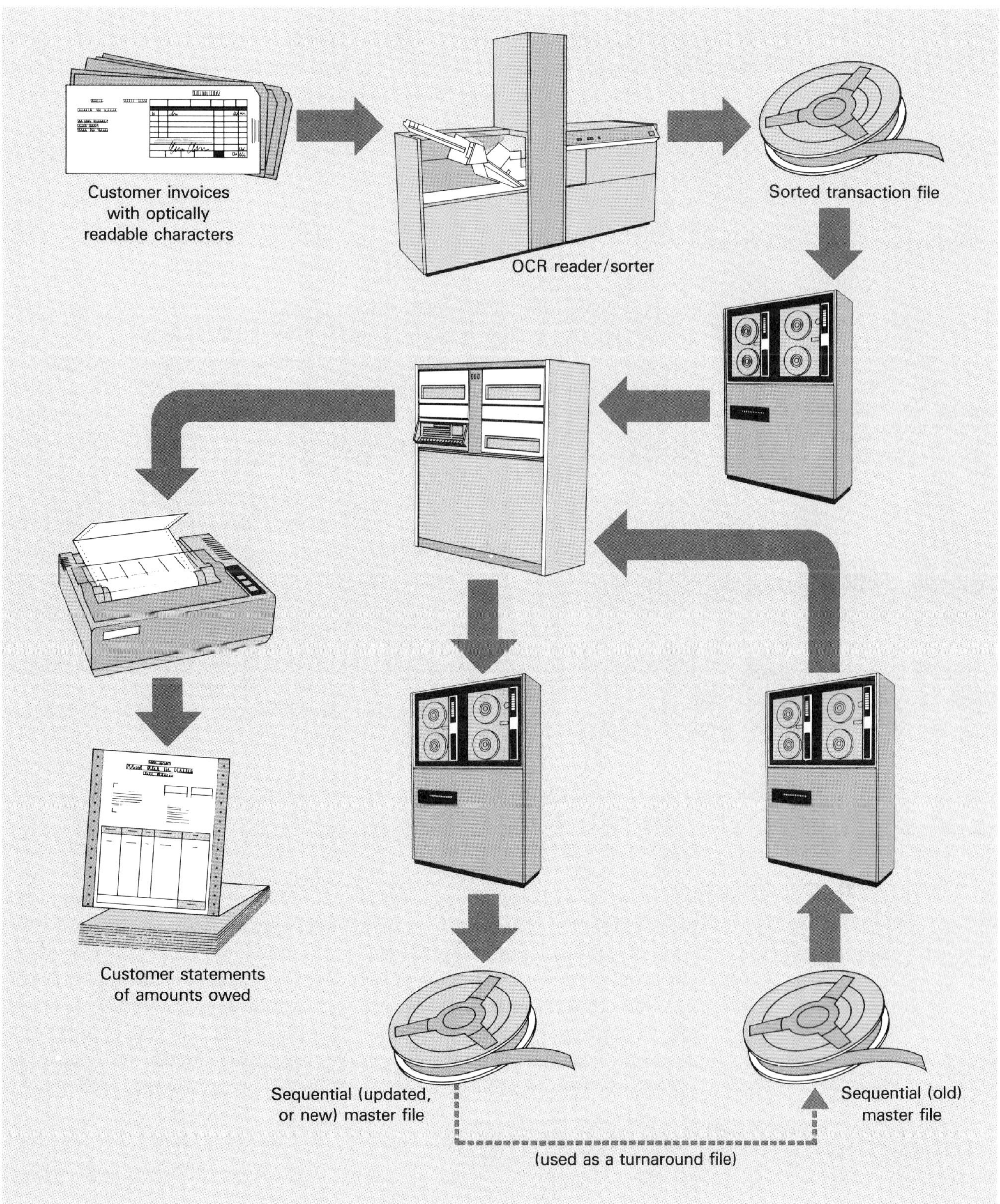
Customer invoices
with optically
readable characters
OCR reader/sorter
Sorted transaction file
Customer statements
of amounts owed
Sequential (updated,
or new) master file
Sequential (old)
master file
(used as a turnaround file)

Figure 5-11 Sorted customer invoices and customer master records serve as input to this sequential-processing application.

On Making Searches

Few (if any) of us would try to locate a doctor's name and phone number, or the number of a local hospital or fire department, in our area phone book by means of sequential processing.

Actually, it takes most people about 12 seconds to find a word in such a dictionary.

If the dictionary were stored on magnetic tape, which can only be read sequentially, the complete dictionary could be read in less than one minute. Note, however, that about half that time would be required to find any one word. (Even 30 seconds is a long time in electronic data processing.) In contrast, if the dictionary were stored using a direct method of organization on magnetic disk, the address of the location in which the desired word was stored would be available in the system. The word could be found instantaneously.

In direct processing, data need not be collected in batches before it is forwarded to the computer. It need not be placed in a particular order for processing. Usually, transaction records (transactions, for short) are forwarded to the computer as they occur. (See Figure 5-12.) Only the master records needed to supply data for, or receive data from, the transactions are actually read into primary storage. Each of these records is located directly by means of its storage address. There is no need to read the other records in the master file.

Direct processing, like sequential processing, may produce several types of output. Frequently, one output is in the form of responses to the users entering transactions. Another may be a printed summary report of situations needing attention, such as stock that must be recorded or bills that are due. Another output is the updated records of the master file. In updating records, the complete master file is not rewritten. Unchanged records remain as they were; updated records are rewritten in their original locations in the master file. When new records are added, they are either positioned appropriately between existing records or placed in an overflow area set aside for that purpose. An activity log showing before and after images of changed records may be written for backup purposes. The master file is current as of the last transaction and ready for subsequent processing.

Magnetic Tape

Magnetic tape is an important secondary-storage medium in many computer systems. It was introduced in the late 1940s and used extensively to store both program and data files for the next three decades. For example, a tape of daily sales totals was written as output by one program, then read as input by another program that arranged the sales in order by region, calculated average sales per region, checked for large discrepancies between actuals and quotas, and printed management-oriented sales reports.

When magnetic tape is initially manufactured, it is wound on individual reels or packaged in dust-resistant cartridges or cassettes. The cartridges and cassettes help to protect the tape from dust, humidity, temperature fluctuations, and other environmental factors that could destroy the tape contents or cause read or write errors during processing.

As users' direct-processing requirements increased, their need for direct-access storage devices increased also. Manufacturers focused their attention on techniques to increase the speeds and capacities of disk storage units. Some industry watchers predicted "tape is on the way out." That's not likely. Sales of tape storage units and media continue to increase. Let's see why.

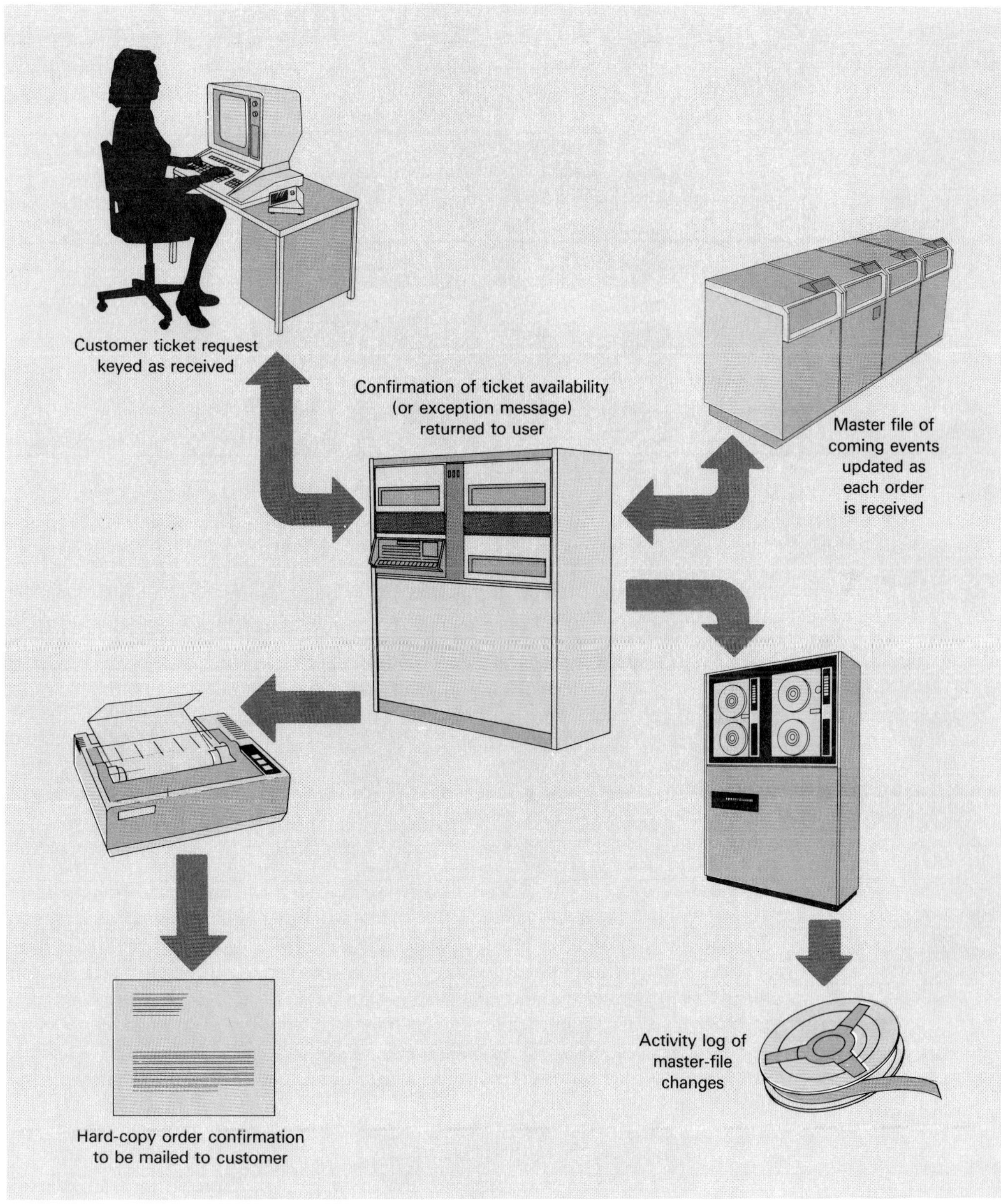
Customer ticket request
keyed as received
Confirmation of ticket availability
(or exception message)
returned to user
Master file of
coming events
updated as
each order
is received
Activity log of
master-file
changes
Hard-copy order confirmation
to be mailed to customer

Figure 5-12 Customer ticket requests cause master records to be accessed as needed in this direct-processing application.

SEEING IS BELIEVING

How good is our eyesight? Through its sensing and recording mechanisms, a computer typically "sees" (that is, obtains) more information about a subject than we do but interprets it less well. Image processing is the art of extracting information from photographs and other images for our use. Complex mathematical algorithms are applied to convert the computer's recorded version of an image into a form that's more useful to us. Expert systems embodying techniques of artificial intelligence (AI) may also be applied to aid in the interpretation process.

Starting at the upper left of the photograph and moving counterclockwise, we see a face as it originally appeared in a crude photograph and as it was progressively enhanced by sharpening its edges and creating more tones of gray than our eyes can normally see. The person shown in the photo was caught in the act of allegedly extorting money from a victim later found murdered. With the help of such images, the police and others are better equipped to recognize and identify suspects. If a suspect is brought to trial, the enhanced image of the suspect may serve as evidence linking the suspect to the crime of which he or she is accused. *(Photo courtesy, Philip Borden/PhotoEdit)*

Data Representation

Data is recorded on magnetic tape as magnetized spots called *bits.* The bits are positioned in parallel channels, or *tracks,* that run the length of the tape. The bits representing a particular character are aligned vertically in rows across the tracks. (See Figure 5-13.) The spacing between the rows is generated automatically during the write operation. It varies with the *tape density,* that is, the number of bits written per inch.

IBM introduced the first reel-to-reel tape unit using $\frac{1}{2}$-inch tape in 1953. It held 100 bits per inch (bpi). Today the IBM Model 3420, a follow-on reel-to-reel tape unit using $\frac{1}{2}$-inch tape, holds 6250 bpi. More than a 60-fold increase in data-recording density has been achieved. The format used by IBM in recording data on $\frac{1}{2}$-inch tape has been accepted widely as an industry standard. And it's this standardization that has led to one of the major uses of magnetic tape today: It is the favored means of *data interchange*—that is, of transferring data from one computer system to another.

As Figure 5-13 suggests, most ½-inch tapes in use today are 9-track tapes. Data is written on these tapes using any one of several coding schemes. Usually, EBCDIC or ASCII is used. In any row on the tape, eight of the nine tracks are reserved for the bit combinations that represent a particular letter, number, or special character. The ninth track is used for error-checking purposes.

Writing on and Reading from Magnetic Tape

Data is written to or read from magnetic tape by a magnetic-tape unit. The unit may be from 3 to 6 feet high. It houses one or two tape drives. Reading or writing occurs as the tape moves past the read/write head of a drive. The tape moves at a speed of, say, 50, 120, or 200 inches per second. It can be rewound, backspaced, or skipped ahead under stored-program control.

As with primary storage, writing to magnetic tape is a *destructive* operation: when new data is written, old data is destroyed. Also like primary storage, reading from tape is *nondestructive:* the same data can be read again and again. If the application needs warrant, the data recorded on a tape can be retained indefinitely. The data can also be erased by the magnetic-tape unit and the tape reused for other data.

An application program cannot cause a record to be written to a tape, then read from that tape, then read again, then written to it, and so on (repetitively and at random) during a single processing run. At any given time, a tape is "opened" either for input or for output (but not both). Remember, records can only be written or read sequentially from magnetic tape. Each record (except the first one) is written or read after the one before it.

Remember, records can only be written or read sequentially from magnetic tape.

For magnetic-tape units, the major performance considerations are the speed at which tape is moved past the read/write head and the tape

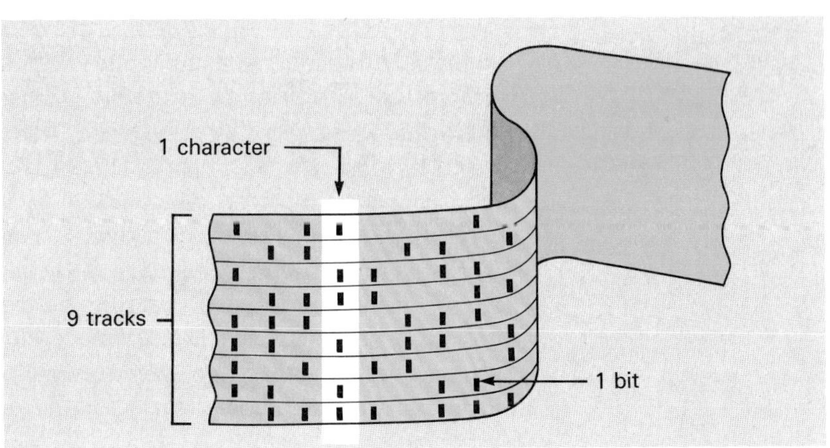
1 character
9 tracks
1 bit

Figure 5-13 Individual data characters are stored as magnetized areas (bits) across parallel tracks on 9-track tape.

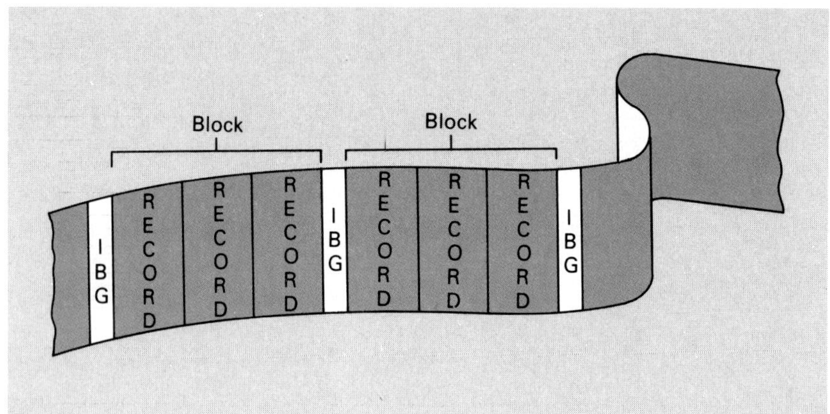
Block
Block
IBG
RECORD
RECORD
RECORD
IBG
RECORD
RECORD
RECORD
IBG

Figure 5-14 During processing, blocks of three records each are read from this employee master file into primary storage by a start/stop tape drive.

density (bpi). Both considerations affect the rate at which characters can be written or read. If a tape moves at 200 inches per second, and data is written on the tape at 6250 bpi, then up to 200 × 6250, or 1.25 million, characters can be transferred from the tape in one second. In common usage, however, the theoretical maximum and the effective maximum are not the same. We cannot assume that the records in a file are simply read from the tape into primary storage as fast as possible.

Initially , all magnetic tape units were designed to operate in a start/stop fashion.

Initially, all magnetic tape units were designed to operate in a start/stop fashion. Assume an employee master file was stored on magnetic tape, for example. Individual *blocks* containing one or more employee records were read into primary storage as needed during processing. Short areas of blank space (*interblock gaps,* or *IBG's*) between consecutive blocks on the tape allowed time for the tape to get up to the speed required for reading (or writing) or to come to a stop after reading (or writing). (See Figure 5-14.) Tape drives that operate in this manner are called *start/stop tape drives.*

Look again at Figures 5-11 and 5-12. As we discussed, one output of a sequential-processing application is a new master file. But the old master file still exists as well. It can be saved as a backup file and used to re-create the new master file if necessary. In a direct-processing application, that's not the case. When updating records, the complete master file on disk is not rewritten. Therefore, to insure that the data in the master file is not lost if the disk becomes damaged, if the disk storage drive malfunctions, or if a program or procedural error causes data to be overwritten unintentionally, the user must make a backup copy of the file. To store the data a second time on another disk is likely to be prohibitively expensive. Herein arises the second major use of magnetic tape today: The backup copy of data on a magnetic-disk file is often stored on tape. The writing (copying) of the data to tape and the subsequent reading (if necessary) are usually done by a *streaming tape drive*. As the word *streaming* suggests, this type of drive does not write or read data as blocks of records. The program that directs the computer to read or write the data does not deal with the data in a meaningful way. Instead, the data is simply written to tape as a continuous stream, or flow. It can be read back into storage and rewritten (restored) to disk in like manner. Users of personal computer systems as well as organizations using large computers with hundreds or even thousands of disk storage units are using magnetic tape for backup purposes.

Tape Products

So far, we've mentioned one type of tape storage product: reel-to-reel tape units using standard ½-inch tapes. An estimated 400 million reels of ½-inch tape are in use. NASA alone is said to record data on approximately 100,000 reels each day.

To meet users' needs to store increasingly large volumes of data for historical or archive purposes (as well as for backup), additional tape products are being developed. (See Figure 5-15.) Today's ¼-inch tape cartridge is about the size of a paperback book and holds up to 320 megabytes of data. Next-generation products that can hold up to 1 gigabyte of data are predicted for the 1990s. Similarly, the tape used in IBM 3480 ½-inch tape cartridges holds 38,000 bpi today but it has the potential to support over eight times as much.

More than 95% of today's largest companies have a mix of tape reel-to-reel and cartridge products installed. Only a few firms are shipping reel-to-reel tape drives today, but cartridge products represent less than 40% of the tape drives in use on medium and large computer systems. A tremendous installed base of reel-to-reel machines has built up over the past 30 years.

Digital audio tape (DAT) appeared first as a consumer electronics product, used to store music free of

Figure 5-15 A variety of tape products are available and still being enhanced to meet the diverse needs of both microcomputer and large computer system users.

TECHNOLOGY	TAPE WIDTH	TRACKS	DENSITY (bpi)	CAPACITY	TRANSFER RATE	TAPE SPEED (inch/second)
Reel-to-reel	½ inch	9	6250	165MB	1.25Mbits/second	200
Tape cartridge	¼ inch	26	16,000	320MB	240Kbits/second	120
Tape cartridge	½ inch	18	38,000	200MB	3Mbits/second	120
Digital audio tape (DAT)	3.81 mm	1869 stripes/inch	61,000	1.3GB	183Kbits/second	122

hiss and distortion in a digitized form. The ability of DAT machines to record digital signals suggests that they are a natural means of storing computerized data. One DAT cassette about the size of a credit card and $\frac{3}{8}$-inch thick can hold 1.3 gigabytes of data—the equivalent of two sets of encyclopedias. To promote the acceptance and use of DAT machines, designers at Hewlett-Packard and Sony Corporation have proposed a standard recording format. Other vendors have announced support for their proposal. The widespread use of DAT depends on such standardization and on competitive pricing, which in turn depends on volume. DAT products are expected to be used most as backup units on personal computers and workstations with hard-disk drives.

Magnetic Disk

A magnetic-disk storage unit looks simple enough. It's a box or a group of boxes. Inside each box is at least one disk storage drive. A certain number of read/write heads are part of the drive. One of the heads writes data to, or reads data from, a magnetic disk that spins beneath it. This means that one or more magnetic disks are also inside the box. They resemble phonograph records, but they are really storehouses for programs and data. Because there are so many kinds of disk storage units, we're going to discuss them from a user's point of view: What kinds of storage needs does each satisfy? Before doing so, we look briefly at how data is represented on disk. We also look at how reading and writing are accomplished.

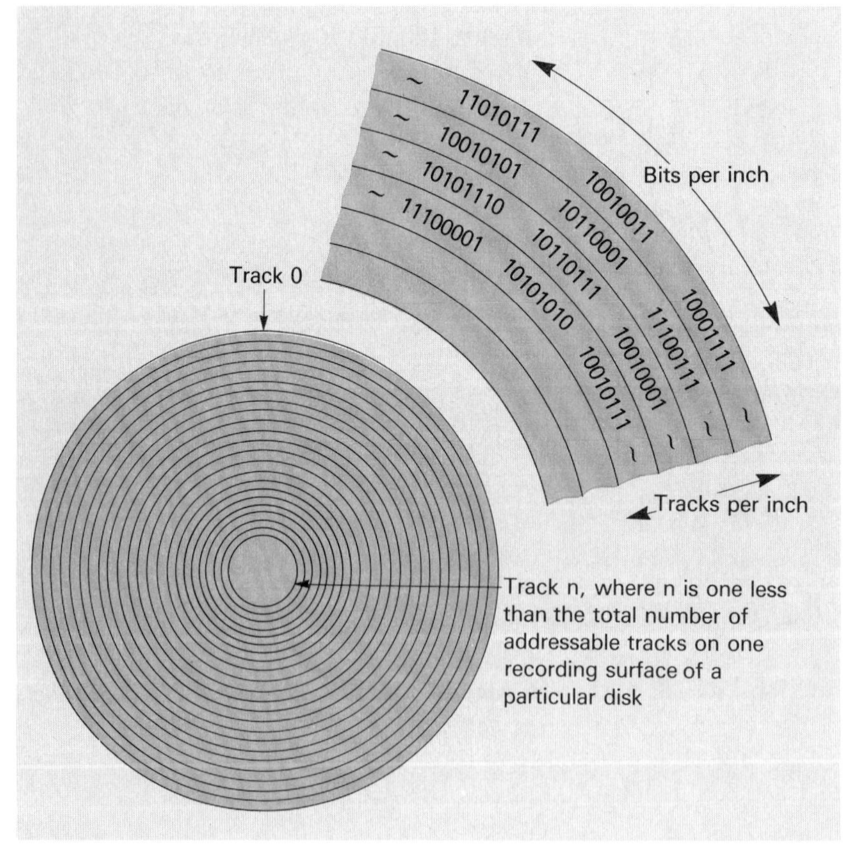

11010111
10010101
10101110
11100001
10010011
10110001
10110111
10101010
10001111
11100111
10010001
10010111
Bits per inch
Track 0
Tracks per inch
Track n, where n is one less than the total number of addressable tracks on one recording surface of a particular disk

Figure 5-16 Data is stored as adjacent magnetized areas (bits) in concentric circles, or tracks, on the surface of a magnetic disk. The tracks are independent, not a continuous spiral like the groove in a phonograph record. In many disk units, the same amount of data can be recorded on each track—the bits on the smaller, inner tracks are simply packed more closely.

Figure 5-17 Many disk drives have comb-type access mechanisms with read/write heads that move above the recording surfaces of disks to read or write data. (Courtesy of Sperry Corp.)

Data Representation

As with magnetic tape, any of several coding schemes may be used when storing data on disk. Again, EBCDIC and ASCII are common. The data is stored as magnetized areas in tracks that form concentric circles on the surface of the disk. (See Figure 5-16.) The combination of bits that represents a particular character is not spread across several tracks (as is the case with magnetic tape). Instead, all the bits representing one character are written serially, one after another, on a selected track. The bits representing the next character (assuming there is another one in the data record) are written immediately following it, on the same track. Remember, however, that data records are not necessarily stored sequentially on a disk. They may be, but they don't have to be. Individual storage locations on the disk surface have assigned storage addresses. An individual record can be written to, or read from, these storage locations directly—without writing or reading any records that immediately precede or follow it.

Writing on and Reading from Magnetic Disk

When data is to be written to or read from a disk, the disk storage drive must be powered on. The disk (or disks) in the unit must be rotating at the speed required for writing or reading. Data can be read from a disk repeatedly. When data is written on a disk, it replaces any data previously recorded on the same area of the disk surface.

Figure 5-17 shows the comb-type access mechanism and disk pack of a common disk storage unit. To operate on a particular track of a recording surface, the access mechanism is moved horizontally on a line to or from the center of the disk pack. All the read/write heads are moved at once, even though only one is used at a time. The access mechanism may, for example, be positioned over the 70th track on each recording surface.

REGENCY
CLUB

SERVICE WITH A SMILE

Guests phoning for reservations, registering, enjoying their stay, or checking out at one of about 150 Hyatt Regency Hotels worldwide may be largely unaware of computers at work. Yet reservations, room assignments, phone calls, laundry service, restaurant charges, and the like are all handled with computer help. Guests at the Regency Club—a special Hyatt feature known as "a hotel within a hotel"—receive a daily continental breakfast, afternoon honor bar and hot hors d'oeuvres, and additional room amenities such as vanity tables, hair dryers, and a television speaker in the bathroom. Here, a Regency Club concierge at the Hyatt Regency San Francisco uses an American Telephone & Telegraph terminal to access information ranging from guest profiles to area restaurants to airline services. Such data is kept in online disk storage units and updated frequently to insure that guests receive complete, accurate, up-to-date responses to their requests for information. In the future, Regency Club guests will be able to check in at the main-lobby registration desk or go directly to the Regency Club level for check in if they prefer to do so. *(Photos courtesy Mark McKenna)*

Together, all the tracks below the read/write heads at that position make up the 70th *cylinder* of the disk pack. Each track may be subdivided into segments known as *sectors* for addressing purposes.

Now suppose that data has to be read from another track on one of the recording surfaces. The access mechanism must be moved to position the read/write heads above that track. This movement is called *head positioning.* Naturally, the time required to move the access mechanism depends upon the distance it must be moved.

After the access mechanism has been positioned, the head that is going to read or write data is switched on. This *head switching* is simply activating an electrical current, so the time required is negligible. It need not be taken into account when calculating how much time is required to read or write data.

Finally, the disk-pack rotation positions the particular data to be read beneath the activated read/write head. The time required for this movement is called *rotational delay,* or *latency.* How long it takes is determined in part by the rotational speed of the disk. An average of one-half revolution is used in estimating the time required for rotational delay. In reality, one complete rotation, part of a rotation, or no rotation (if the activated read/write head is positioned directly over the desired data) may be required.

After rotational delay, the record can be read or written. The time required for data transfer (reading or writing data) is based on the length of the record transferred and the transfer rate of the disk storage drive.

Actually, it is difficult for humans to comprehend the speed at which reading or writing from disks takes place. All the actions we have just mentioned—access-mechanism movement, head switching, rotational delay, and data transfer—may be required to read data. The total time required for all these actions is referred to as the *access time* of the disk storage unit. Access times range widely—say, from 90 to 275 thousandths of a second (*milliseconds*) on floppy disk drives and from 12 to 175 milliseconds on other drives.

Floppy Disk Drives

In Chapter 3, we discussed the use of floppy disks (diskettes) in key-to-diskette data-entry systems. Today, diskettes are used in desktop computer systems as well. Each diskette is made of a soft Mylar plastic. The surface of the disk is coated with iron oxide. The coated disk is then packaged in a paper or plastic envelope. When the disk is to be used, the entire envelope is inserted into a disk storage unit. The disk rotates inside the protective covering. The read/write head of the disk drive reads or writes the data when the disk surface is exposed to it through the slot in the covering.

The early diskettes, which were 8 inches in diameter, could hold 242,000 data characters—the equivalent of more than 3000 punched cards. Today there are also $5\frac{1}{4}$-inch and $3\frac{1}{2}$-inch diskettes. Data can be stored on both sides of *double-sided diskettes.* Data can be recorded at twice the density per track on *double-density diskettes.* The most commonly used diskettes can hold about 1.44 megabytes of data, the rough equivalent of 700 typed pages.

The most commonly used diskettes can hold about 1.44 megabytes of data, the rough equivalent of 700 typed pages.

The advantages of flexible disks include ease of handling, ease of storage, and portability. The disks are often used on distributed computer systems—in offices, laboratories, shop rooms, and the like. Since the drives are standardized, the disks are readily available from numerous vendors. Furthermore, the disks are relatively inexpensive and reusable.

The limitations of floppy disk drives are inherent in the technology on which they are based. As with magnetic tape, the head that reads or writes data on the disk actually rides on the recording surface during reading or writing. This causes friction and wear and limits the disk's rotation speed to about 300 revolutions per minute. The Mylar plastic disk itself expands and contracts with changes in temperature and humidity. Therefore, the tracks on the disk must be far enough apart to allow for changes in dimension. This limits the amount of data that can be stored.

Looking at things from an operational point of view, flexible disks can become a user nightmare. Up to a dozen flexible disks may be needed to store the records of, say, 500 customers in an accounts-receivable master file. Most businesses also have inventory records, sales records, vendor records, employee records, and so forth. (See Figure 5-18.) Handy-dandy dust-tight storage cabinets for flexible disks are sold by many vendors. But what does the user do when there are no more desktops or floor space to put them on?

From 25 to 30 million flexible disk drives are being shipped annually. Shipments at this level are expected to continue through the early 1990s. Shipments of $3\frac{1}{2}$-inch drives will soon outnumber those of $5\frac{1}{4}$-inch drives. They're used in IBM's Personal System/2, Apple's product lines, Hewlett-Packard machines, and many others. The three largest areas of use are: business and professional microcomputers, consumer and hobby market, and dedicated-application office systems and workstations. Their low-cost, direct-access features, and media removability continue to be significant advantages.

Winchester Disk Drives

Does the term *Winchester* bring a picture to your mind? Strangely enough, the term does indeed refer to the Old West's famous Winchester 30-30 rifle. An early prototype disk storage unit contained two drives. Each drive could hold 30 megabytes of data. The product code name "Winchester" was a natural consequence.

In 1973, IBM introduced the first Winchester drive, known as the IBM 3340 Direct-Access Storage Facility, for use on its large computer systems. Not only the 14-inch aluminum disks but also the vertical shaft, access mechanism, and read/write heads of the disk storage drive were enclosed in a removable sealed cartridge. This approach eliminated head-to-disk alignment problems and reduced the exposure of recording surfaces to airborne contaminants. It also satisfied a primary objective of the design—high reliability. More bits could be written on a track and less space was required between tracks than on the conventional disks or on diskettes.

Figure 5-18 Diskettes are great, but if the user's needs for program and data storage expand, keeping track of what's where can be a major undertaking. (Courtesy Corona Data Systems, Inc.)

Per Megabyte Prices Falling

Users can buy an 80-megabyte disk drive today at a cost comparable to that of a 5-megabyte drive in 1980.

A Good Match

Users of 80286, 68020, or faster microprocessor-based systems should look for hard-disk drives with less than 30-millisecond access times.

About Permanency

The pencil has not totally supplanted the pen, although it offers one valuable feature the pen lacks—erasability. The pen survives not in spite of, but because of, ink's permanence. Both pen and pencil persist today because each has its own area of strength. A similar situation exists with optical storage media.

Shugart Associates announced the first *mini-Winchester,* using 8-inch disks, in 1979. Disk storage units of this type were best suited for use with small and medium-sized computers. The first *micro-Winchester,* which used 5¼-inch disks, was introduced by Seagate Technology in late 1980. In 1984, the 3½-inch micro-Winchester arrived. Here at last were disk storage units that addressed the online data storage needs of business users of microcomputers.

The initial micro-Winchester drives offered from 2.5 to 5 megabytes of storage. Today's small-business and home users typically rely on 40- to 80-megabyte drives. Advanced 3½-inch Winchesters can hold from 200 to 300 megabytes of data; advanced 5¼-inch Winchesters can hold from 700 to 800 megabytes. One reason users need additional disk space is that application programs for use on micros are getting larger. Another is that users' data volumes are increasing. The use of more powerful machines (based on Intel 80286 or 80386, or Motorola 68020 or 68030, microprocessors) is also driving the demand; users expect to do more complex tasks and to do them faster.

Some vendors use the term *Winchester* when describing their drives. Other vendors and industry analysts simply refer to all disks other than flexible disk as *hard,* or *rigid, disks.* These more general terms may also be used to describe conventional disks (below). In the mid-1980s, only one of every four microcomputers shipped had a hard-disk drive already installed. Now that's changed. For example, IBM has announced that 90% of its Personal System/2 machines are being shipped with hard-disk drives. Users may also purchase hard-disk drives as add-in or add-on devices.

Conventional Disk Drives

In 1956, just 10 years after the invention of the stored-program computer, IBM introduced the magnetic-disk technology that helped to spin the world rapidly into the Computer Age. Its 305 RAMAC system housed the first conventional disk drive, as we are using the term here. Fifty 24-inch disks were permanently mounted on the drive; all together they held 5 megabytes of data.

Today conventional disk storage drives with disks ranging from 8 to 14 inches in diameter are commonplace. IBM's top-of-the-line IBM 3380 Direct-Access Storage Device can hold up to 10.4 gigabytes of data. Digital Equipment Corporation offers a 9.4-gigabyte disk storage unit for use with its high-end systems. Many other vendors are marketing disk units to one or both of these customer bases as well as to users of other medium and large computer systems.

Disks are second only to processors in terms of importance to overall system performance in this marketplace. For high-volume, transaction-processing applications, high-speed disk storage units are required.

Optical Storage

In Chapter 4, we discussed the rapidly increasing use of laser printers. In this arena, laser-beam technology is being applied to provide high-speed, high-quality printer output. Laser-beam technology is also being applied in the data-storage arena. In recent years, users have been introduced to the acronyms *CD ROM, WORM,* and *EOS.* Each acronym refers to a type of optical storage having unique characteristics and especially suitable for certain applications.

CD ROM

Most music enthusiasts today are the owners of high-quality home stereo systems. In the past few years, audio compact disks capable of holding complete classical works or popular record albums and compact-disk players providing unmatched musical quality have become available. *Compact disk read-only memory (CD ROM) devices* now being used with computers are based on similar technologies.

Data is written, or pressed, onto a compact disk once as part of a special disk-mastering process. Once written, the contents of the disk cannot be changed. However, the disk can be duplicated quickly and inexpensively. A single 5¼-inch compact disk may hold 600 megabytes of data—the equivalent of 300,000 pages of text, or from 400 to 800 floppies.

From a user application point of view, CD ROM offers a means of distributing vast amounts of data at low cost.

From a user application point of view, CD ROM offers a means of distributing vast amounts of data at low cost. Databases are available in a wide variety of subject areas. Among them are financial, library/education, scientific/medical, law, government, and even consumer. For example, Computer Library, a joint venture of Lotus Development and Ziff Communications, provides full text and abstracts of more than 100 computer-related publications. Digital Equipment Corporation now offers the documentation for its system software—which in paper form spans 15 feet of shelf space—on one compact disk. Large corporations such as General Motors, Chrysler, and Dunn & Bradstreet are producing CD ROM disks holding parts catalogs, corporate financial data, and the like for internal distribution.

CD ROM drives are sold or leased to database subscribers by the publishers of the databases. CD ROM drives for use with microcomputers are also available at consumer outlets such as Radio Shack and Egghead Software. They range in price from $500 to $1500.

WORM

Write once, read many (WORM) devices are commonly marketed as components of integrated information management systems. A single WORM disk typically holds from 1 to 3 gigabytes of data. Jukebox-like devices with access mechanisms somewhat like the one shown in Figure 5-17 may hold from 2 to 20 or more of these disks. They're available for computers of all sizes. WORM systems are especially suitable for applications where large volumes of data in conventional character and graphic image forms must be dealt with and where storage permanency is an asset. The insurance industry is a natural. Other commercial application areas include: the pharmaceutical industry (new drug applications), banking (loan application processing), law and contract administration (vital records), and general industry (personnel and accounting records). The Internal Revenue Service and U.S. Patents and Trademarks Office are examples of government usage.

The access times of WORM devices are much slower than those of comparable Winchester drives, so they're not yet competitive with these devices for use as frequently referenced direct storage. However, they are gaining in popularity as a means of backup and archival storage where disk, tape, microfilm, or microfiche may otherwise have been used. They're also used as replacements for filing cabinets—complete documents are scanned and stored on disks rather than filed in paper form.

Erasable Optical Storage

Erasable optical storage (EOS) devices are in the early stages of product development. EOS drives first became commercially available in 1988. As yet, their data transfer rates are from three to five times slower than those of comparable hard-disk units. However, the EOS disk media are more reliable. Their capacities are comparable to those of WORM drives. Furthermore, most EOS units are designed so that individual disks can be removed from the drives and other disks mounted. In a sense, then, the storage capacities of the units are unlimited.

Today's EOS devices are gaining acceptance in application areas where vast amounts of storage are needed but immediate access and subsecond response are not mandatory.

Today's EOS devices are gaining acceptance in application areas where vast amounts of storage are needed but immediate access and subsecond response times are not mandatory. A classic example is inventory control. A major drawback of current voice-mail systems is the large amount of disk space needed for even the briefest message. EOS voice-mail systems are overcoming this objection. Company-specific libraries of images are being stored on EOS disks for CAD/CAM and other graphics-intensive applications. Like WORM drives, EOS devices are also used for backup and archival storage. They are cost competitive in this arena.

A Perspective

Surveys of medium-sized and large computer users show that their requirements for online storage are growing at rates of 45 percent to 60 percent per year. It's safe to say their requirements for backup storage are growing similarly. As our discussions show, manufacturers of tape and disk storage units are investing much time and money in responding to these requirements. Their objectives are to allow more data to be stored in less space and to help users get at that data faster. A statement made early in the chapter about the speed of internal data transfer applies here also: The shorter the distance that data must travel, the faster the data transfer can be accomplished. Access times of tape and disk storage units are measured in milliseconds rather than in microseconds or nanoseconds (as is the case with internal storage units). That's because the movement of physical parts is involved.

Care is needed in the selection and use of storage to avoid learning the hard way that the over-all efficiency of a computer system depends on the performance characteristics and frequency of interactions of all its parts.

ALL ABOARD

When resources such as coal and ores are found, they must be transported to where they can be used. The products that result from their use must also be transported to their buyers and users. Varying shipping schedules and load demands on railroads require precise routing of trains and knowledge of available equipment. Computers can keep track of the data involved and help make the thousands of decisions that are needed daily. Computers can also perform the actual switching that routes trains to the right tracks at the right times. All these processes require direct access to data stored on high-speed, large-capacity disk storage devices. *(Photo courtesy of Sperry Corp.)*

CHAPTER SUMMARY

1. A computer system has both primary and secondary storage.

2. Data in electronic pulse form is forwarded to the computer for processing. The pulses cause the binary components of the computer's internal storage unit to be set to either of two possible conditions, or states. A binary notation involving only the two binary digits, or bits, 0 and 1 can be used to describe these states.

3. Unique combinations of binary digits form bit patterns to which meanings can be assigned. A set of patterns forms a data-representation scheme, or code. Two of the most widely used codes are the Extended Binary Coded Decimal Interchange Code (EBCDIC) and the American Standard Code for Information Interchange (ASCII).

4. The capacity of a computer's internal storage unit is a measure of the amount of programs and data the unit can hold. Reading data from storage is a nondestructive operation, but writing is destructive. The amount of time required to locate and transfer data from and to storage is referred to as the access time of the computer.

5. Initially, computers had vacuum-tube memories. Then magnetic-core storage was developed. Today most computers have semiconductor monolithic memories consisting of integrated circuit (IC) chips. Microminiature bit cells on the chips contain electrical components whose conducting and nonconducting states are used to represent data.

6. Since computers were introduced, the amount of primary storage that can be made available in a system has increased to meet users' application needs. Expanded memory techniques alleviate the 640K conventional memory limitation of MS-DOS. OS/2 and other programs designed to run in protected mode can access extended memory, which begins at the 1 megabyte boundary of expanded memory and may range up to 16 megabytes.

7. Secondary storage may be either sequential or direct. Sequential, or batch, processing and direct processing, respectively, are used to process the stored data.

8. Magnetic tape is an important secondary-storage medium. Data is recorded (written) as magnetized spots on the tape and read sequentially as many times as needed by start/stop or streaming tape drives.

9. Magnetic disks can provide either sequential or direct storage. The data is recorded in concentric circles, or tracks, on the surface of a disk by a read/write head of the disk drive.

10. Flexible, or floppy, disks may be 8, $5\frac{1}{4}$, or $3\frac{1}{2}$ inches in diameter. Their speeds and capacities are limited, but they offer ease of handling, ease of storage, and portability.

11. Not only the disks but also the vertical shaft, access mechanism, and read/write heads of a Winchester drive are enclosed in a sealed cartridge. A Winchester drive offers greater storage capacity than floppy disks do and high reliability.

12. Conventional, or hard, disk storage units satisfy medium-size and large computer users' ever-growing requirements for online storage. Over time, the storage capacities of these units have been improved dramatically.

13. Compact disk read-only memory (CD ROM), write once, read many (WORM), and erasable optical storage (EOS) products are similar in that all offer high-capacity storage. Each has unique characteristics that make it especially suitable for certain applications.

DISCUSSION QUESTIONS

1. Distinguish between primary storage and secondary storage.

2. Why is storage capacity so important in a computer system?

3. Why is binary notation a likely choice for expressing values stored in a computer system?

4. Show how the following data items can be represented in EBCDIC:
(a) 632
(b) A. J. Rose

5. Show how the following data items can be represented in ASCII:
(a) #2 CLAMPS
(b) 995

6. Develop a 3-bit code to represent the vowels *a, e, i, o,* and *u*. What things must you consider in setting up the code?

7. Distinguish between destructive and nondestructive operations. Give examples of each.

8. Compare the capabilities and structure of semiconductor monolithic circuitry with magnetic-core technology.

9. What can an MS-DOS user do to increase the amount of work his or her system can accomplish?

10. Describe how the data of a restaurant, public library, or educational facility might be organized into items, records, and files.

11. Would you use sequential or direct processing for the following data-processing applications? Justify your answers.
(a) Printing of employee payroll checks
(b) Maintaining up-to-date control of inventory
(c) Preparing a monthly budget report
(d) Responding to a management inquiry about current costs vs budgeted expenses
(e) Solving a mathematical equation submitted from a terminal
(f) Calculating and printing customer statements
(g) Updating an accounts-receivable file

12. Discuss three major uses of magnetic tape in today's computing environments.

13. Why might a user installation have both magnetic-tape and magnetic-disk drives?

14. What actions that occur during reading and writing of data on a magnetic disk have a bearing on access time?

15. Compare the storage capacity of a 40-megabyte Winchester disk with that of a 1.44-megabyte floppy. For what types of use is each appropriate?

16. For what type of use is CD ROM especially well suited?

17. Some industry analysts suggest that EOS devices are likely to eliminate the need for WORM devices. Other analysts disagree. What do you think?

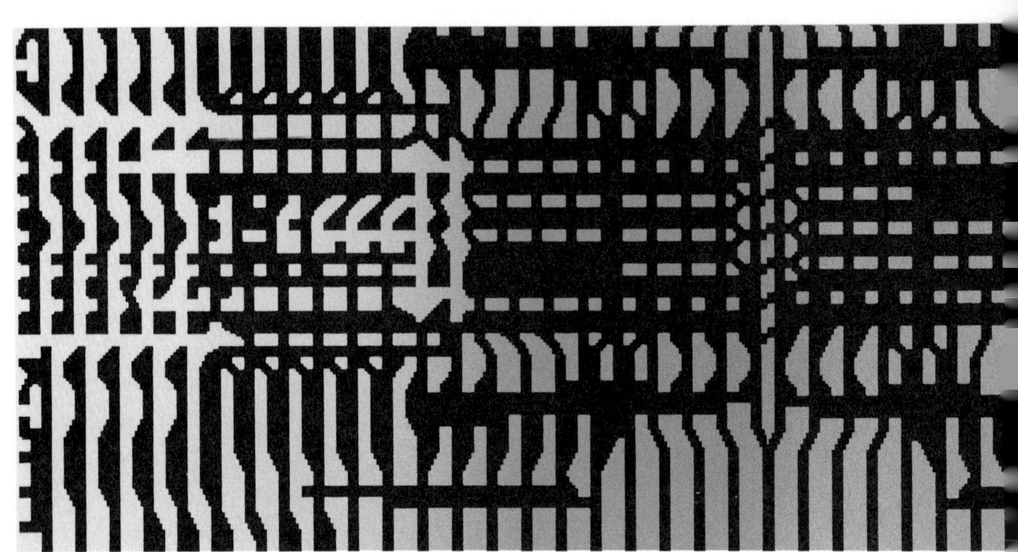

6 Processing Data

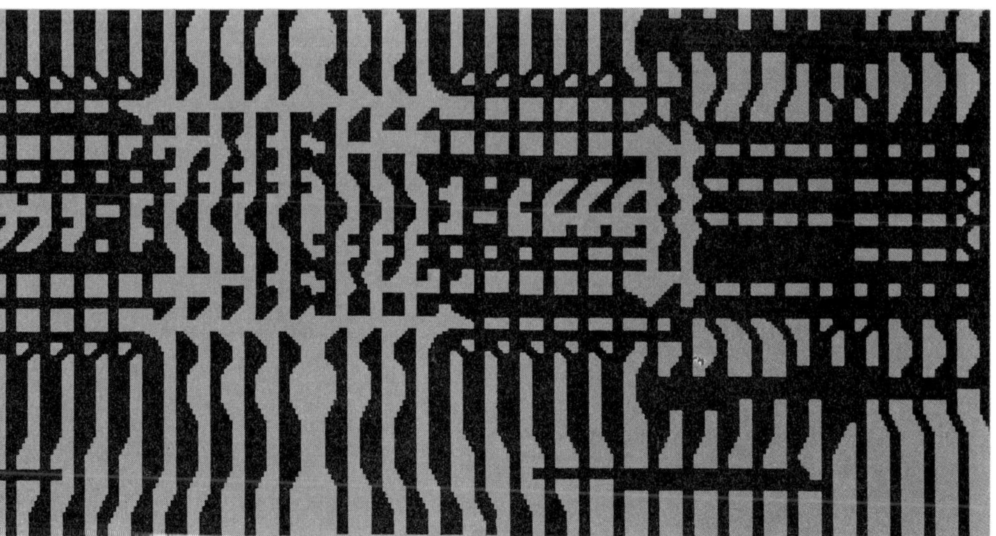

IN THIS CHAPTER

The Processor
The Control Section
The Arithmetic/Logic Unit
Registers
Instruction Counter
Adders
Stored-Program Instructions
Instruction Execution
Serial and Parallel Operations
Fixed-Length and Variable-Length Operations
Synchronous and Asynchronous Operations
Microprocessors
Reduced Instruction Set Computing (RISC)

The computer is the most significant new product of the twentieth century. It is not a luxury; it is a necessity. By the year 2001, nearly everyone will have not just one, but several. There may be only one comparable product—the automobile.

In its early years, the automobile was a technological mystery to most people. Carburetors, fuel pumps, distributors, and the like were magical components of that mystery. Starting a car, changing gears, and steering were remarkable feats attempted only by the daring! Yet, today, in many countries, nearly everyone of high school age or above knows how to drive a car. Many know how to fix or rebuild one.

So it is with computers. In their early years, the mid-1940s through the mid-1960s, computers were a rarity, known only to a few researchers, scientists, and educators. In the 1970s, as people became more aware of them, they were greeted, not with joy, but with doubt, fear, and resentment. Even while some people were trying to decide whether or not computers should be allowed to impact society, computers became an indispensable part of society. About 1978, when computers such as Radio Shack's TRS-80 and the Apple II arrived on the scene, they moved into our homes, schoolrooms, and offices.

> If you haven't learned yet how to use a computer or how to communicate with one, you can easily do so.

The computer is a tool. You need not be afraid of it. You need not even be in awe of it. If you haven't learned yet how to use a computer or how to communicate with one, you can easily do so.

How much do you need to know about an automobile in order to drive it? Well, you need to know where to get the key to the car. You need to know where the ignition is. You need to know how to steer the car, where the brakes are and how to use them, and how to stop the car's engine at the end of your trip. If you drive at night, you need to know how to turn the lights on, when and how to switch them to low beam (or high beam), and how to turn them off. You'd better learn how to use the windshield wipers, in case of rain or snow.

Do you have to know about mufflers, tailpipes, crankshafts, and fuel pumps? Are you an expert on intake manifolds, cooling systems, and engine blocks? Probably not.

On the other hand, suppose the car you are driving just doesn't have any pickup. Or suppose it starts to sputter when you're driving 55 miles per hour along a four-lane highway. It may help you to know that the car runs on unleaded gas (not regular, not diesel). There are times when you need to know what grade of oil should be used. You can probably avoid a labor bill if you know how to change the oil yourself. If you know something about how the car works, and about its parts, you may save yourself some unneeded repair costs. You need not panic at the first sign of a problem.

So it is with computers. As was pointed out in Chapter 1, many who are reading this book have probably used computers without even realizing it. You may know how to key in simple requests for information from a typewriterlike keyboard and receive that information back on a televisionlike screen. You may even know how to write or run computer programs.

Now, suppose you are keying in simple requests for information and the computer fails to respond to your requests. (It just "sits there.") Or suppose the computer prints out a message that you can't understand. Or suppose the computer responds, but only after you've had time to read the paper or go to the refrigerator for a snack.

Suppose you've got a job to do and you're wondering whether or not the computer can help you. Or you've decided to buy a computer but you don't know whether to buy one that costs \$500, or \$5000, or \$50,000. Or your boss thinks his firm should make more use of computers and he asks your advice. In the very near future, such situations will be commonplace. For some, they are already.

So far, we've taken a look at what computers can do. We know how data is entered into the computer and how information is obtained from it. We know about both primary and secondary storage. Now we're ready to learn about processors. In this book, you'll *not* learn about AND gates, OR gates, combinatorial logic, gate arrays, and so forth. That level of detail is best left to computer designers (just as we leave some details of our cars to engineers and other specialists at GM or Chrysler). When you've completed this chapter, you'll know something about how a computer works. And you'll understand how stored-program instructions are acted on by a computer.

The Processor

The processor (central processing unit, or CPU) of a computer system controls and supervises the entire system. It also performs arithmetic and logic operations on data. It has two major parts: a control section and an arithmetic/logic unit. As explained in Chapter 2, the computer's internal storage unit, or memory, is often packaged together with these components in a physical housing called the *processor unit.* You do not generally see the processor, but you do see the processor unit. (See Figure 6-1).

The processor of a large computer may be built as several circuit boards grouped within a boxlike structure, or frame (hence, the nickname *mainframe*). In a minicomputer, the processor may be constructed on a single processor circuit board. In a microcomputer, the processor is a microprocessor, contained on a single chip of silicon. This chip may be mounted together with memory, input, and output chips on a single circuit board. There may be other boards in the system, or the one board may hold all the chips required.

To increase the performance of their systems, some computer manufacturers are including not just one processor but several processors

In a microcomputer, the processor is a microprocessor, contained on a single chip of silicon.

Figure 6-1 Engineers at a Zenith Electronics plant in St. Joseph, Missouri, are applying microcomputer-based CAD techniques to produce Zenith Super Sport lap-top portable computers. (Courtesy Zenith Electronics Corp.)

within a single computer system. Such a system may include two, four, or more identical processors that operate independently; the processors may or may not communicate during processing. Alternatively, a system may include one main processor that controls and performs most operations and one or more specialized processors that perform specific functions. For example, Compaq's Deskpro 386/33 desktop computer system has an Intel 80386 microprocessor as its main processor. Users with compute-intensive applications may include one or two math coprocessors designed to perform arithmetic operations very quickly. For simplicity, we assume a single processor is controlling operations in our discussions here. The concepts we discuss apply to *multiprocessor systems* as well. (We'll say more about multiprocessor systems in Chapter 11.)

As we might expect, the processor of even a very small computer system is made up of many hardware components. Some of them are shown schematically in Figure 6-2. Each component has a specific function. It carries out that function during the execution of stored-program instructions. We cannot describe all the interrelationships of these components in this book, nor do we want to. The architectural details of one computer may differ in many ways from those of another. A general discussion will help us understand how any computer works. This will in turn remove some of the mystery that often seems to surround them.

Microprocessors are like other processors in some ways. They have many of the same types of components, carry out many of the same operations, and so on. They also share a common ancestry with other processors. What we say here is general and applies in large part to all processors. Some specific details for microprocessors are given later in the chapter.

The Control Section

Perhaps the best way to describe the control section of a processor is with a simple analogy. In many ways, the control section of a processor can be compared to a telephone exchange system. The telephone exchange contains all the equipment necessary to connect the telephones it services. The control section contains all the mechanisms necessary to transfer data from one part of the system to another.

In many ways, the control section of a processor can be compared to a telephone exchange system.

The telephone exchange controls the instruments that carry sound pulses from one phone to another, ring the phones, connect and disconnect circuits, and so on. The electronic path that permits calls between one telephone and another is set up by controls in the exchange itself.

The processor control section directs and coordinates all EDP-system operations. It governs input/output devices, entry and retrieval of data from storage, and routing of data between storage and the arithmetic/logic unit. For example, the control section may start or stop an

I/O device, turn a binary component on or off, or initiate a calculation. In some computers, a part of the control section consists of read-only memory that contains microcode to control circuits that perform operations designated by stored-program instructions. (Recall "Microcode" in Chapter 2.) Sometimes the control section also contains *emulator circuits*. These circuits enable the computer to execute stored-program instructions initially designed for another computer. In effect, one computer is directed to emulate another.

Figure 6-2 The processor unit of a computer system contains many components that perform specific functions during processing.

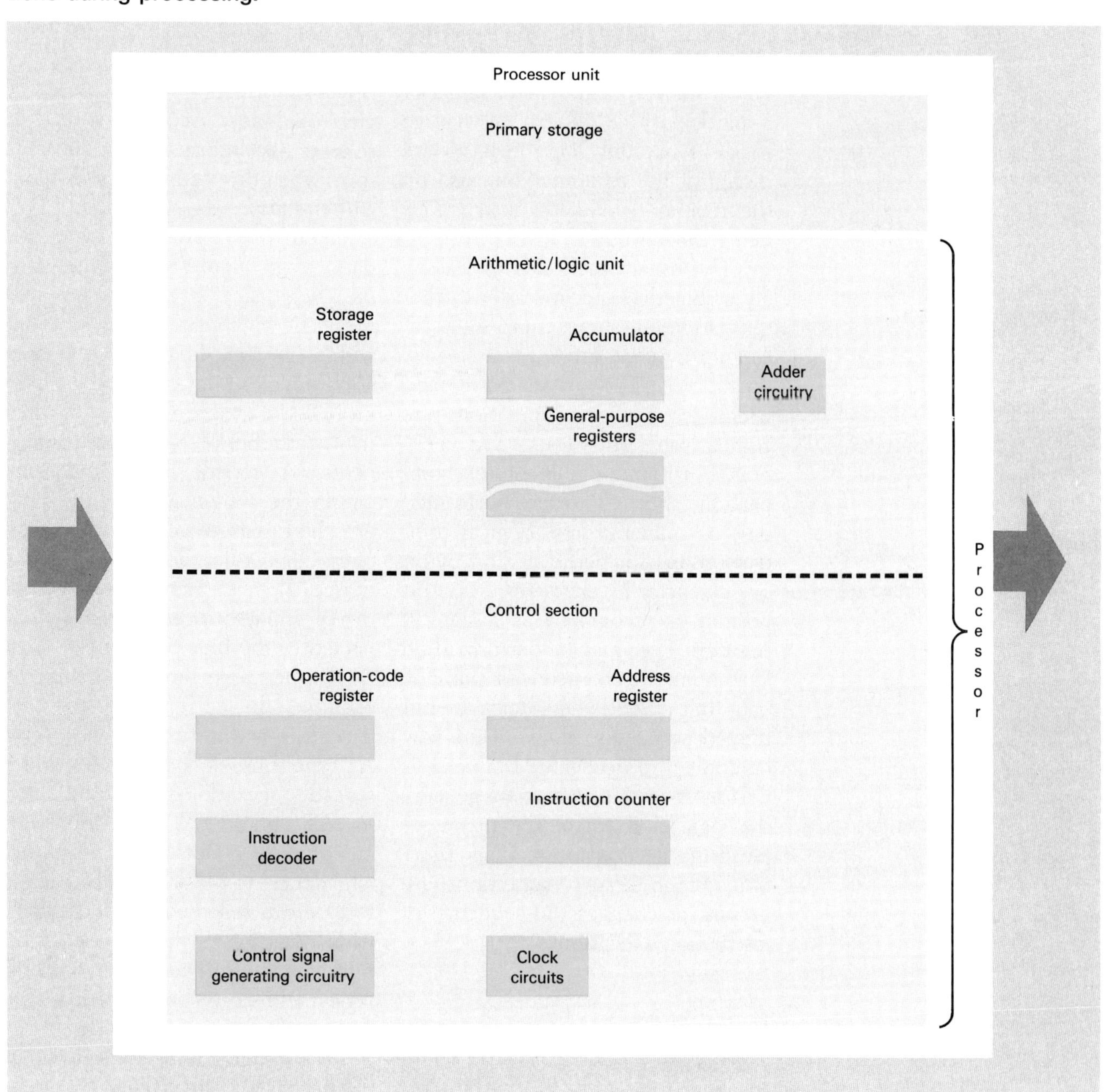

Processor unit
Primary storage
Arithmetic/logic unit
Storage register
Accumulator
Adder circuitry
General-purpose registers
Control section
Operation-code register
Address register
Instruction counter
Instruction decoder
Control signal generating circuitry
Clock circuits
Processor

The Arithmetic/Logic Unit

The arithmetic/logic unit contains the circuitry necessary to perform arithmetic and logical operations. The arithmetic circuitry calculates and sets the algebraic signs of results (0 for + or positive; 1 for − or negative). This circuitry also shifts numbers, rounds numbers, compares algebraically (taking the sign of each compared value into account), and so on. In some systems, the meaning of a particular bit pattern in storage depends not only on the hardware design of the computer but also on the type of arithmetic instructions being carried out.

The usual practice is to classify all arithmetic/logic operations other than addition, subtraction, multiplication, division, and shifts as logical operations. The most basic and widely used logical operations are comparisons and tests. We mentioned arithmetic (algebraic) comparisons above. They are performed only on numeric data. Logical comparisons may be performed bit-by-bit or character-by-character; no bit position is recognized as a sign-bit position. They may be performed on alphanumeric, character, or numeric data (but numeric data items are not treated as signed values). Tests may be applied to determine if a value is positive, negative, or zero. In general, the logic circuitry of the processor performs a decision-making function. When certain conditions are present, it changes the sequence of instruction execution.

Registers

Registers are devices capable of receiving information, holding it, and transferring it very quickly. (See Figure 6-3.) They are designed primarily for temporary storage. (The term *temporary storage* is used here to designate information that is stored only for the length of time required to execute one instruction.) As Figure 6-3 suggests, registers have bit positions just as primary-storage locations have. They are a part of the processor, but they are not considered a part of primary storage and are not included when discussing storage capacity. Each register receives information in the form of electronic-pulse representations. It releases that information in the same form when directed to do so by control circuitry.

Note the references to a 32-bit data bus in Figure 6-3. As the word *bus* suggests, a *data bus* is simply a means by which data can travel about within the computer system. It consists of a set of wires, or lines, grouped in a particular way to form a data path between system components. A set of rules (*protocols*) within the system architecture governs how data travels over the data path. Other rules dictate how add-on devices such as memory cards, disk drives, and co-processors can be connected to the bus.

In the microcomputer arena, for example, the current industry-standard bus architecture is the 16-bit AT-type bus; it has gained widespread acceptance within IBM PC/AT and PC/AT-compatible microcomputers. Device manufacturers who adhere to the AT-type bus architecture can sell their products for a wide range of machines. Users who purchase a microcomputer with an AT-type bus can choose from a wide variety of add-on devices.

If a system has 32-bit registers, it usually has a 32-bit data bus. This allows all the bits that are to be stored

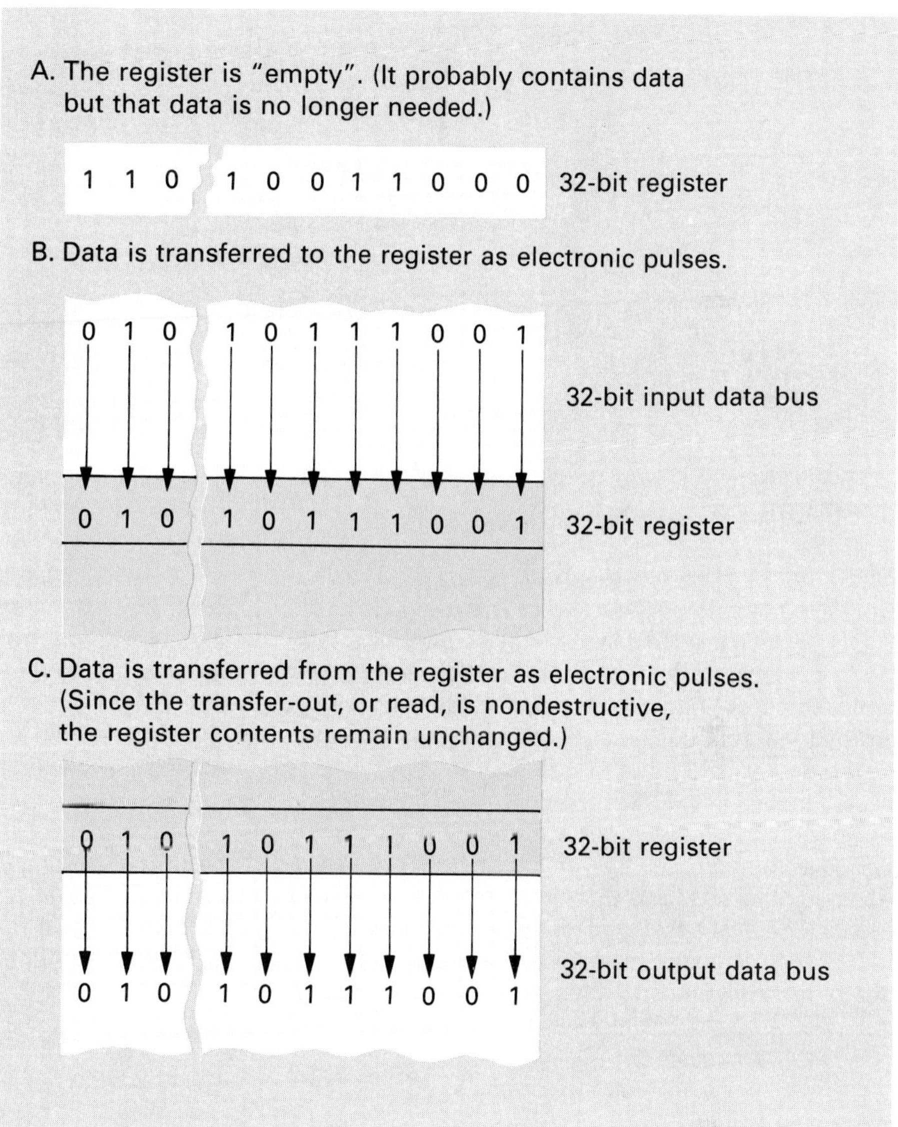
A. The register is "empty". (It probably contains data but that data is no longer needed.)
1 1 0 1 0 0 1 1 0 0 0
32-bit register
B. Data is transferred to the register as electronic pulses.
0 1 0 1 0 1 1 1 0 0 1
32-bit input data bus
0 1 0 1 0 1 1 1 0 0 1
32-bit register
C. Data is transferred from the register as electronic pulses. (Since the transfer-out, or read, is nondestructive, the register contents remain unchanged.)
0 1 0 1 0 1 1 1 0 0 1
32-bit register
32-bit output data bus
0 1 0 1 0 1 1 1 0 0 1

Figure 6-3 Data in the form of electronic pulses is transferred to and from registers very quickly during processing.

in a particular register to travel together to that register and arrive at the same time. The bit width of the data bus of a particular computer is an indicator of the amount of information immediately accessible to the processor in one instruction execution. It is a very concrete measure of the machine's power.

Certain registers perform very specific functions. An *accumulator* accumulates results. A *storage register* contains information taken from or being sent to storage. An *address register* holds the address of a location in storage or the address of a device. An *operation-code register* holds the operation-code portion of an instruction being executed.

If you read about processors in other literature, it may help you to know some synonyms. Storage registers are sometimes called *input/output buffers* or *data registers.* Address registers are sometimes called *address buffers* or *data counters.* Op-

COMPUTERS AT WORK IN THE FAST-FOOD BUSINESS

Who among us hasn't lunched at a fast-food restaurant? Who among us hasn't seen ads touting "the Big Mac"? To be successful in the highly competitive fast-food business, personnel at McDonald's and similar establishments know they must consistently excell in two major areas: customer service and product quality. Computers help them to do so.

Consider just one example: the cooking of McDonald's world-famous french fries. Since McDonald's personnel fry varying amounts of french fries and other products at various temperatures, they need a means of sensing the temperature of the shortening on an ongoing basis and compensating for detected heat variances. The McDonald's computer/timer was developed to insure that consistent, high-quality french fries are served to customers at all times.

One essential step in the effective use of the computer/timer is the establishment of a cooking profile for each product. The profile reflects a specific product temperature and time relationship that is correlated in the computer/timer. If the shortening temperature drops, the computer slows down the time function to extend the cooking time. Conversely, if the temperature rises, the computer speeds up the time function to increase the cooking rate. Clearly, McDonald's depends on its computer/timer. Whenever we ask for an order of fries at McDonald's, we're depending on it too, whether we realize it or not. (*Photos courtesy of* [*left*] *Mark McKenna*; [*right*] *McDonald's Corporation*)

eration-code registers are sometimes called *instruction registers.*

Some registers are *general-purpose registers,* or simply *general registers.* As their name implies, they can be used for any of several functions. Processors in common use contain 1, 2, 4, 8, or 16 of these registers. Remember that an important advantage of registers is that they provide for very fast access to data. Therefore, they also provide the potential for getting work done quickly. For this reason, most computers are designed so that at least some of these registers are available for use by programmers. The registers have assigned numbers. Programs that are part of the system software developed for a particular computer system often contain instructions that refer directly to the registers, either by their assigned numbers or by symbolic labels that have been equated to the assigned numbers. Because there are a limited number of these registers, and because their correct use is vital to proper functioning of the system, great care is required on the part of programmers who write instructions referring to them. Users who do not have in-depth knowledge of the internal architecture of their systems normally do not write such instructions.

On some systems, no registers serve strictly as accumulators. Any of the general-purpose registers can be used to perform accumulation functions.

How big is a register? Each register is designed to hold one unit of information at a time. If the computer's internal storage unit is constructed to deal with 8-bit bytes or words, then the processor registers used in data transfers are also constructed to hold 8-bit units of data. If the computer's internal storage unit holds 16-bit words, then its registers are constructed to hold 16-bit words; and so on.

During most processing, operations involving registers are completed quickly and effectively.

During most processing, operations involving registers are completed quickly and effectively. Data moves in and out of registers, and between registers, at nanosecond or microsecond speeds (depending on the processor). In some situations the data to be stored in a register will not fit in that register. A negative value that's too small (that is, too large negatively) causes an *underflow*. A positive value that's too large causes an *overflow*. If the user application or system processing that is being done cannot tolerate or recover from the underflow or overflow condition, the processing may be terminated.

Instruction Counter

A fundamental assumption of computer architecture is that the instructions of any program being executed are stored in consecutive memory locations. This assumption allows the use of a very simple mechanism to keep track of the next instruction to be executed. The mechanism is a special register known as the *instruction counter*. (In other literature, it may be referred to as the *instruction address register, program counter, control register,* or *sequence control register*.) Every processor has one.

When a stored program is to be executed, the instruction counter holds the primary-storage address of the first instruction of that program. While the first instruction is being executed, the instruction counter is automatically set to the address of the next instruction. This process continues throughout execution of the program.

Adders

The adder circuitry of a processor receives data from two or more sources, performs addition, and places the result in a location that can be referred to by stored-program instructions. Adder circuitry varies in complexity, depending upon how the data is represented internally and upon the way the arithmetic operations are carried out.

In many computer systems, numeric values that are to be used in arithmetic operations are not represented internally in EBCDIC or ASCII. Instead they are represented as *binary numerals*—multidigit symbols of a *binary number system* that is similar in many ways to the decimal number system we use every day. The digits in a binary numeral have position values based on a right-to-left progression of powers of 2 (2^0 or 1, 2^1 or 2, 2^2 or 4, etc.), just as the digits in a decimal numeral have position values based on powers of 10 (the 1s place, the 10s place, the 100s place, etc.). We need not study binary numerals or binary arithmetic in detail to understand something about how computers work. The binary numerals equivalent to the decimal numerals 0 through 15 are shown as examples in Figure 6-4.

With this background, we're ready to look at adder circuitry. Figure 6-5A shows a serial, or 1-digit, adder. In a computer having this type of adder, the two digits in the rightmost positions of the numbers to be added are added first and the rightmost digit of the result is stored. If there is a carry in this result, it is held by a delay device and then added to the result of the addition of the next-rightmost (next-higher-order) digits in the numbers being added. The process continues from right to left until all the digits in the numbers have been summed.

Figure 6-5B shows two positions of a parallel adder. It involves a more complex type of adder circuitry. The number of adder positions varies. The circuitry at all adder positions operates simultaneously, forming tentative sums and then sending carries (if any) forward to the next positions to the left. If additional carries result from adding these carries, they are forwarded, and so on. (We say more about serial and parallel operations later in this chapter.)

Stored-Program Instructions

Before we discuss how registers, the instruction counter, and adder circuitry perform their functions, we need to say more about stored-program instructions. Each instruction is a unit of information that is loaded into primary storage. This

Figure 6-4 Four-digit binary numerals and their decimal equivalents are shown on the left. You can use expanded notation to determine the equivalent values yourself as shown on the right.

DECIMAL NUMBER SYSTEM	BINARY NUMBER SYSTEM
0	0000
1	0001
2	0010
3	0011
4	0100
5	0101
6	0110
7	0111
8	1000
9	1001
10	1010
11	1011
12	1100
13	1101
14	1110
15	1111

HOW TO USE EXPANDED NOTATION TO DETERMINE EQUIVALENT VALUES:

$$0111 = (0 \times 2^3) + (1 \times 2^2) + (1 \times 2^1) + (1 \times 2^0) = 0 + 4 + 2 + 1 = 7$$

$$1101 = (1 \times 2^3) + (1 \times 2^2) + (0 \times 2^1) + (1 \times 2^0) = 8 + 4 + 0 + 1 = 13$$

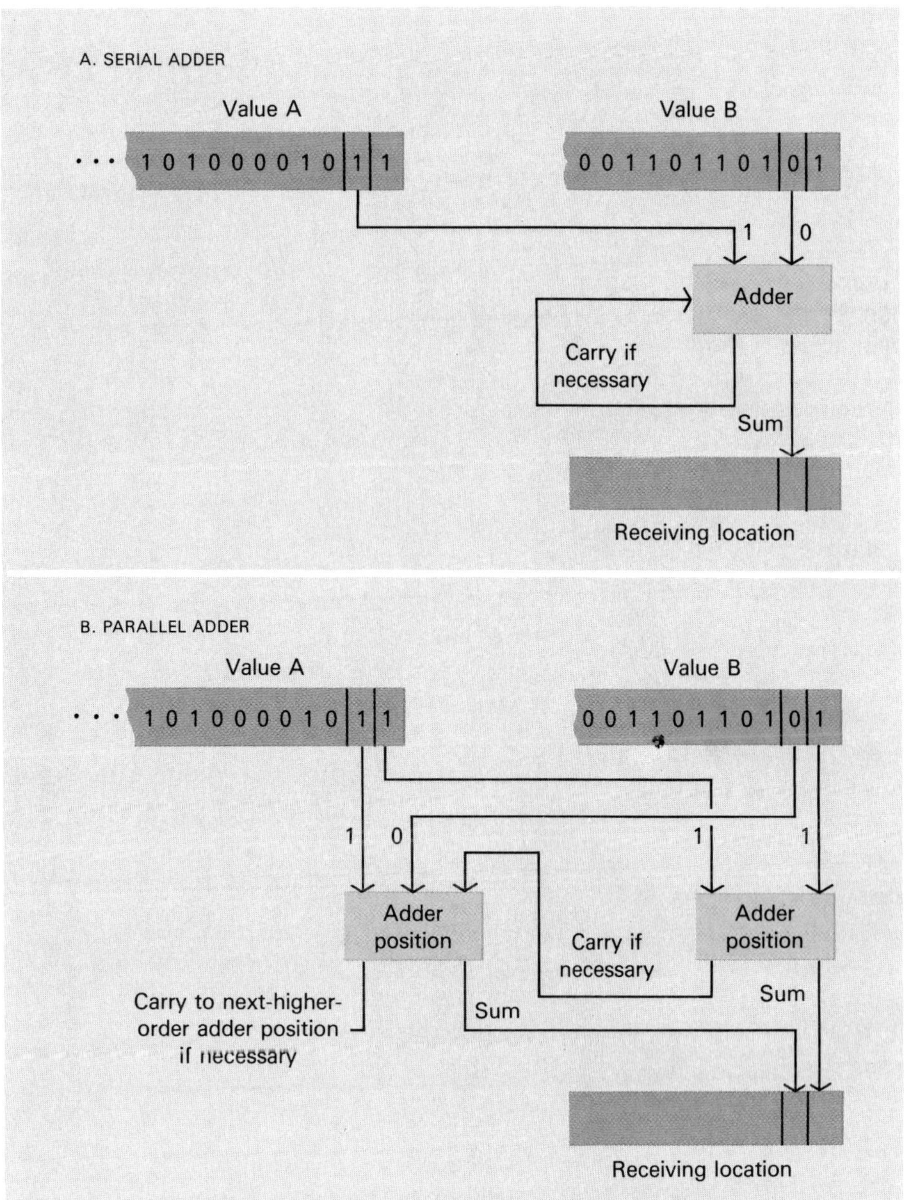
A. SERIAL ADDER
Value A
Value B
• • • 1 0 1 0 0 0 0 1 0 1 1
0 0 1 1 0 1 1 0 1 0 1
1
0
Adder
Carry if necessary
Sum
Receiving location
B. PARALLEL ADDER
Value A
Value B
• • • 1 0 1 0 0 0 0 1 0 1 1
0 0 1 1 0 1 1 0 1 0 1
1
0
1
1
Adder position
Adder position
Carry if necessary
Carry to next-higher-order adder position if necessary
Sum
Sum
Receiving location

Figure 6-5 A computer may have either serial or parallel adder circuitry, and performs arithmetic operations serially (A) or in parallel (B) accordingly.

unit of information is interpreted by the control section of the processor as an operation to be performed. If data is involved, the instruction directs the computer to the data. If some device (for example, a printer) is to be controlled, the instruction specifies the device and the required operation.

Instructions may copy data from one location in storage into another, add 1 to the contents of an accumulator, and so on. In some cases, an instruction specifies the address of the next instruction to be executed. The specification may be predetermined and unalterable, or it may depend on the result of some comparison or test. With such an instruction, it is possible to alter the sequence in which other instructions or blocks of instructions are executed.

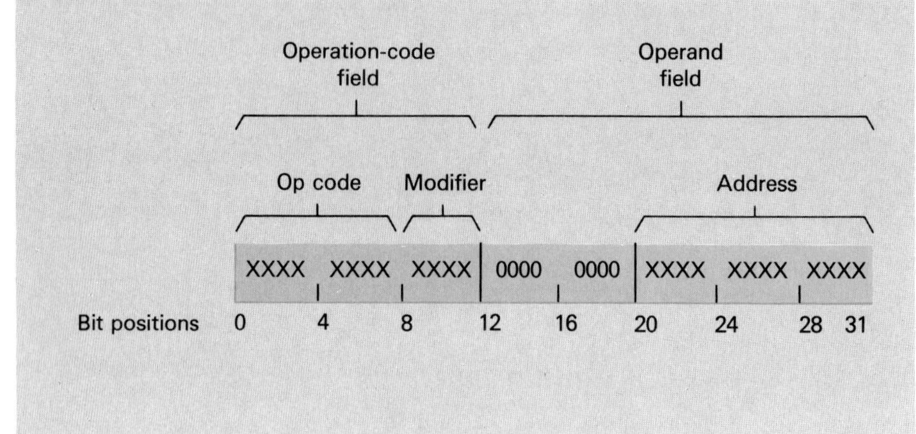
Operation-code field
Operand field
Op code
Modifier
Address
XXXX XXXX XXXX 0000 0000 XXXX XXXX XXXX
Bit positions 0 4 8 12 16 20 24 28 31

Figure 6-6 **A 32-bit instruction format allows many details about a required operation to be specified in a single machine-language instruction.**

All stored-program instructions must, of course, be represented in a machine-readable form. The machine-readable form is the *machine language* of the computer. In some computers, instructions are fixed in length. Each instruction is one word long. That means each instruction is 8 bits, or 16 bits, or whatever, in length (depending on the computer's architecture). In other computers, instructions are made of a variable number of characters; their lengths vary. In still other computers, instructions may be any of several fixed lengths. For example, each instruction may be one halfword, one full word, or one full word plus one halfword in length, depending upon what information has to be given about the operation it describes.

All stored-program instructions must, of course, be represented in a machine-readable form.

For our current purposes, let us assume that each instruction is 32 bits in length. (See Figure 6-6.) The 12 leftmost bits of the instruction make up the *operation-code field.* The remaining 20 bits make up the *operand field.*

The 8 leftmost bits of the operation-code field contain the *operation code,* or *op code.* These bits tell the computer what operation is to be performed. The computer may be directed to add, subtract, compare, move data, and so on. The remaining 4 bits of the operation-code field contain a *modifier.* For example, a bit setting of 0010 in positions 8 through 11 of an add instruction may tell the computer to place the result of the add operation in register 2.

The operand field of a stored-program instruction tells the computer where to find or store data to be processed, the address of the device needed for the specified operation, or where to find the next instruction to be executed when that instruction is not simply the next sequential instruction. For our current purposes, the rightmost 12 bits of this field contain a *primary-storage address.* The remaining positions of the word are assumed to contain zeros.

BINARY	HEXADECIMAL
0000	0
0001	1
0010	2
0011	3
0100	4
0101	5
0110	6
0111	7
1000	8
1001	9
1010	A
1011	B
1100	C
1101	D
1110	E
1111	F

HOW TO USE HEXADECIMAL NOTATION:

00010101111110101000111101010 0111

0001 0101 1111 0101 0001 1110 1010 0111

1 5 F 5 1 E A 7

1 5 F 5 1 E A 7

Figure 6-7 Equivalent binary and hexadecimal values are shown on the left. You can use hexadecimal notation as a shorthand for binary notation as shown on the right.

Writing a string of 32 1s and 0s to express an instruction in a particular machine-language is an error-prone activity at best. Therefore, a common practice is to use *hexadecimal notation* as a convenient shorthand for binary notation. One hexadecimal digit can stand for a sequence of four binary digits. (See Figure 6-7.)

Figure 6-8 shows a 32-bit machine-language instruction represented in this hexadecimal notation. The op code of the instruction (5A) tells the computer to add an amount to a value in an accumulator. The modifier (2) indicates that the accumulator—already containing one of the values to be added and into which the sum will be placed automatically—is register 2. The address (628) tells the computer that the second value to be added is in primary-storage location 628. Now let's see how the computer executes such an instruction.

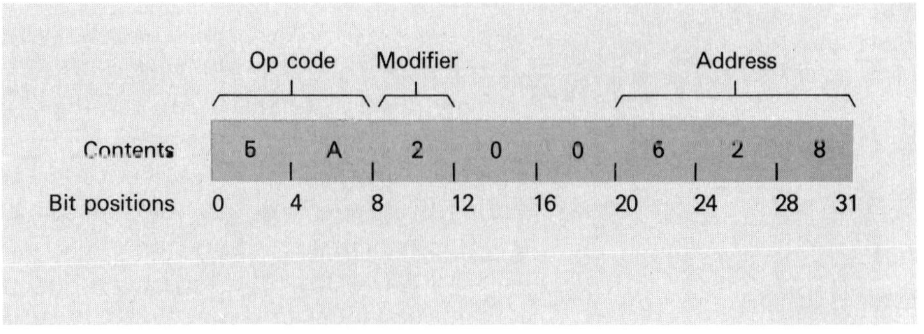

Op code
Modifier
Address
Contents
5 A 2 0 0 6 2 8
Bit positions
0 4 8 12 16 20 24 28 31

Figure 6-8 This 32-bit instruction tells the computer what to do (add) and where to find the data values to add (in primary-storage location 628 and in register 2).

Instruction Execution

The computer time required to perform one specific machine operation is called a *machine cycle*. The number of machine cycles required to execute one stored-program instruction depends on the kind of instruction. Sometimes several machine operations must take place.

All computer operations take place in fixed intervals of time. These intervals are measured by regular pulses of an electronic clock. In some computers, the pulses occur at frequencies as high as 100 million per second. As we've explained elsewhere, computer time measurements are expressed in terms of milliseconds, microseconds, and nanoseconds. It is difficult to imagine how infinitesimally short these intervals of time are. For example, the blink of an eye takes about one-tenth of a second, or 100 milliseconds. A microsecond is one-thousandth of a millisecond. A nanosecond is one-thousandth of a microsecond. Incredible as it may seem, the world's fastest computers may soon operate at speeds measured in *picoseconds*. One picosecond is one-trillionth of a second, or one-thousandth of a nanosecond.

Units of Time

There are as many *nanoseconds* in *one* second as there are seconds in 30 years.

I-Time

The first machine cycle involved in executing an instruction is called an *instruction cycle*. The time required to complete this cycle is called *instruction time*, or *I-time*. I-time is not under the control of the stored-program instruction. The actions during I-time are built into the control section circuitry. They are the same for each instruction and require a uniform amount of time.

I-time begins when the instruction to be executed is moved from primary storage to the storage register. The instruction is located and "moved" in the following manner. Control circuits decode the address in the instruction counter and send electronic pulses to storage to "read" (fetch) the instruction. The bit settings that make up the instruction are then converted to pulses to accomplish the move. The operation-code field of the instruction is routed to the operation-code register. The address portion of the operand field is routed to the address register. An *instruction decoder* interprets the op code and sets the circuit paths necessary to execute the instruction. The circuits may, for example, activate the "reading" of relevant bit cells in the primary-storage location pointed to by the address register and the bringing of the data (in the form of pulses) into the arithmetic/logic unit. The data flow that occurs during I-time is highlighted in Figure 6-9.

The location of the next instruction to be executed is also determined at this time. The instruction counter is set automatically to the address of this instruction.

Although instructions are stored in consecutive locations, they do not *have* to be executed in the sequence in which they are stored.

Although instructions are stored in consecutive locations, they do not *have* to be executed in the sequence in which they are stored. Certain instructions cause the computer to branch to another instruction. The op code of an instruction of this type indicates that the next instruction in sequence is not to be executed; the address in the operand field identifies the location of the instruction to be executed instead. The instruction counter is set to this address.

Some instructions cause the computer to *branch unconditionally;* that is, it must go to the instruction that is specified by the address in the operand field. Other instructions cause the computer to *branch conditionally;* that is, the computer must examine conditions elsewhere in the system

Figure 6-9 An instruction is fetched from primary storage and decoded during I-time.

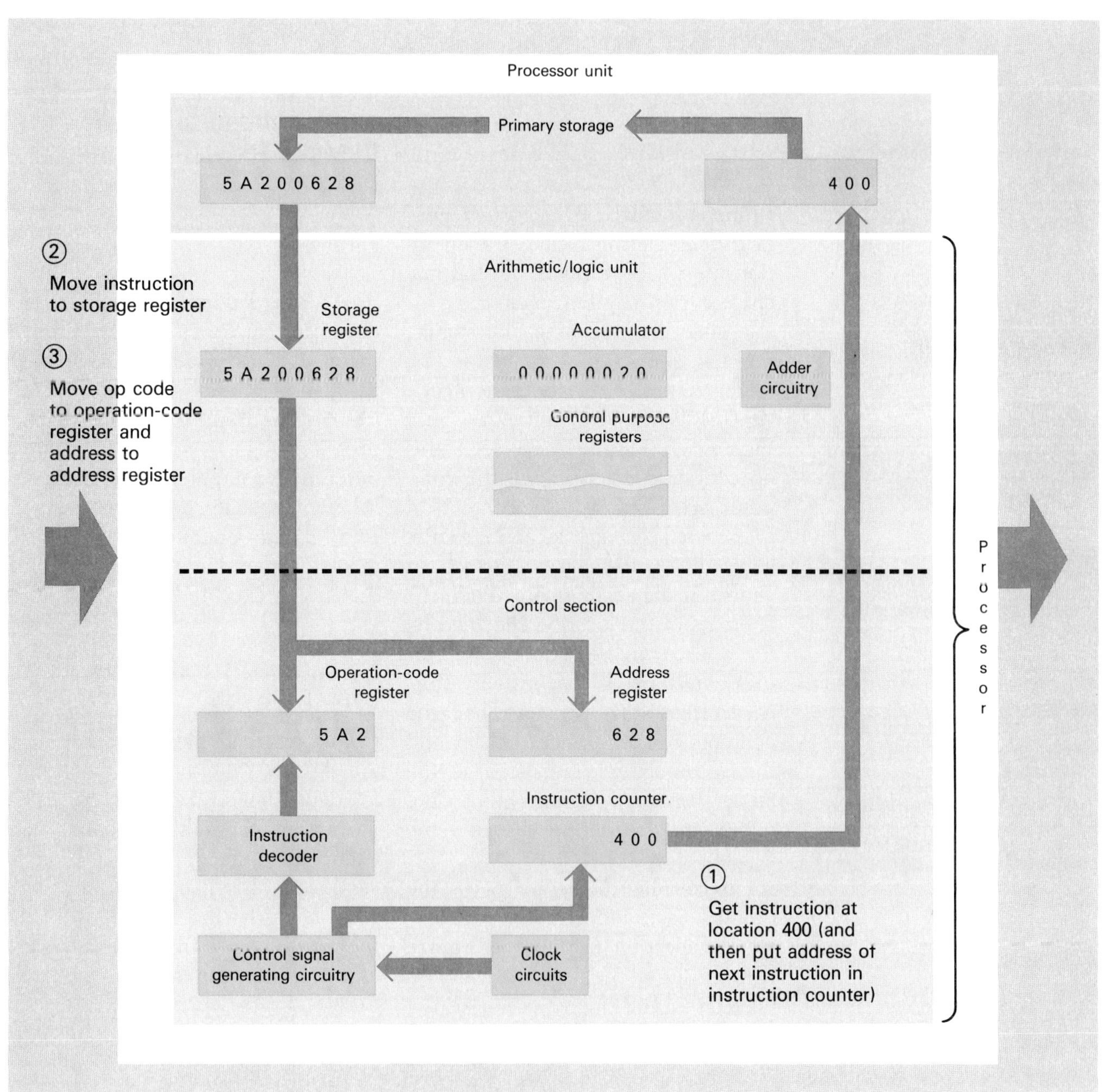
Processor unit
Primary storage
5 A 2 0 0 6 2 8
4 0 0
② Move instruction to storage register
Arithmetic/logic unit
Storage register
Accumulator
③ Move op code to operation-code register and address to address register
5 A 2 0 0 6 2 8
0 0 0 0 0 0 2 0
Adder circuitry
General purpose registers
Processor
Control section
Operation-code register
Address register
5 A 2
6 2 8
Instruction counter
Instruction decoder
4 0 0
① Get instruction at location 400 (and then put address of next instruction in instruction counter)
Control signal generating circuitry
Clock circuits

and select the address of the next instruction to be executed accordingly. An instruction may say, in effect: "Look at the sign of the quantity in the accumulator. If the sign is minus, execute the instruction at location 5000; if the sign is plus, proceed to the next instruction in sequence." The sign is checked by circuitry when this instruction is executed. The instruction counter is then set automatically either to location 5000 or to the address of the next instruction.

E-TIME

I-time is followed by *execution time,* or *E-time.* During E-time, the operation itself is performed. Several machine cycles may be required.

Since this is E-time, the storage register and the accumulator are under control of the operation-code register, which contains 5A2. (See Figure 6-10.) As we have seen, this op code and modifier tell the computer circuitry to add the contents of a specified storage location to the value already in register 2, which, of course, is the accumulator. First, the contents of the location specified by the address in the address register (628) are moved from primary storage to the storage register. Then, the contents of the storage register and the accumulator are placed in the adder circuitry, their values are added, and the sum is returned to the accumulator.

According to Figure 6-10, the original value moved from primary-storage location 628 to the storage register during the depicted E-time is 00003364. The original value in the accumulator is 00000020. These values are combined in the adder. Their sum, 00003384, will be in the accumulator at the end of E-time.

The only distinction between instructions and data in storage is related to the time they are forwarded to the processor. If machine-readable code is brought to the processor during an instruction cycle, it is interpreted as an instruction. If it is brought in during any other cycle, it is assumed to be data.

The only distinction between instructions and data in storage is related to the time they are forwarded to the processor.

If instructions are supplied as data, the computer can operate on them. As we'll see in Chapters 9 through 11, this capability is extremely important to persons writing programs to be executed by the computer. The computer cannot execute BASIC-language statements. However, it can operate on the statements, converting them to a form that it can execute.

SERIAL AND PARALLEL OPERATIONS

Computers and parts of computers are classified as either serial or parallel, depending on whether only a single action or multiple actions can occur at a time. This distinction is significant. It's like having a 1-lane road versus having a 2-, 4-, or 8-lane highway on which many cars, trucks, and campers can travel simultaneously.

Let's see how this applies in arithmetic operations. Essentially, all arithmetic is performed by addition. In a serial processor, numerals are

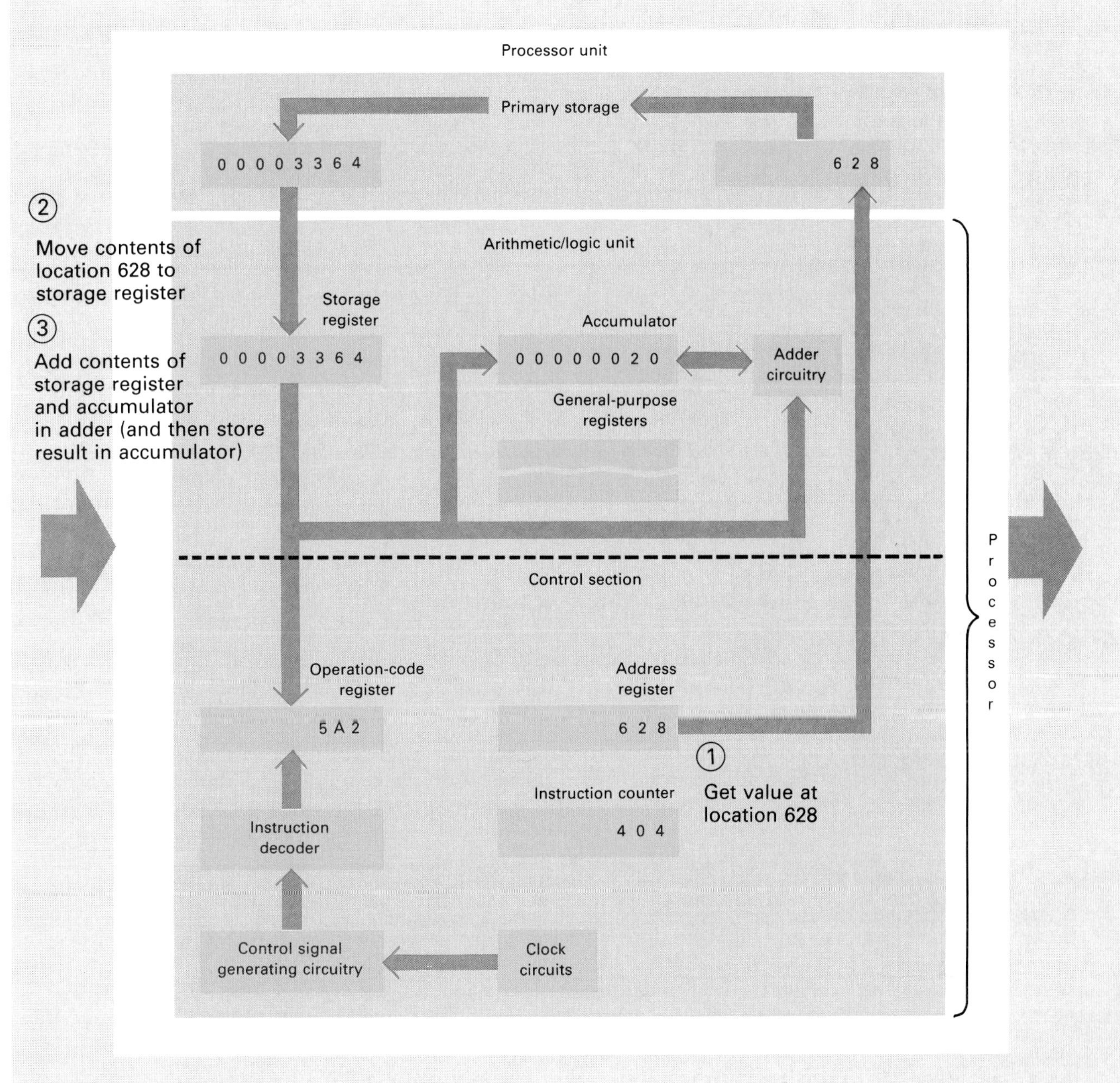
Processor unit
Primary storage
0 0 0 0 3 3 6 4
6 2 8
②
Move contents of location 628 to storage register
③
Add contents of storage register and accumulator in adder (and then store result in accumulator)
Arithmetic/logic unit
Storage register
Accumulator
0 0 0 0 3 3 6 4
0 0 0 0 0 0 2 0
Adder circuitry
General-purpose registers
Control section
Operation-code register
Address register
5 A 2
6 2 8
①
Get value at location 628
Instruction counter
4 0 4
Instruction decoder
Control signal generating circuitry
Clock circuits
Processor

Figure 6-10 During E-time, the operation specified in an instruction is carried out.

added one position at a time. (This is the way we add numbers when using pencil and paper.) Whenever a number must be carried, it is retained temporarily and then added to the sum of the next-higher-order position. The time required for the operation depends on the number of digits to be added. Serial addition of two numerals is shown in Figure 6-11. (Recall also the serial adder shown in Figure 6-5A.)

In a parallel processor, all positions of the numerals to be processed, including carries, are added in one step. The number of digits to be added does not significantly affect the amount of time required to do

	1ST STEP	2ND STEP	3RD STEP	4TH STEP
Addend	1234	1234	1234	1234
Augend	2459	2459	2459	2459
Carry	1	1		
Sum	3	93	693	3693

Figure 6-11 Serial addition occurs as a multiple-step operation. Step 1 must be completed before Step 2, and so on.

Addend	00564213
Augend	00000824
Carry	1
Sum	00565037

Figure 6-12 Parallel addition is a one-step operation in which the bits in all positions of a value are added simultaneously.

the addition. Figure 6-12 shows parallel addition. (We looked at parallel adder circuitry in Figure 6-5B.) Refer again to our highway analogy. Clearly, a multiple-lane highway is more expensive to construct than a single-lane road, but if lots of traffic must be handled daily, parallelism helps.

In these days, when computers are becoming smaller and smaller, it's easy to overlook the fact that computers are also becoming more powerful. Capabilities for parallel operation are behind much of this power. In Figure 6-3, we saw a data bus that is 32 bits wide. That means 32 bits can move in parallel along the bus. Some computers have data buses that are eight 8-bit bytes in width. That means 8 bytes, or 64 bits, of data can move in parallel. Still others can move 128 bits or more. Increased circuitry tends to mean increased costs.

As mentioned earlier, some systems have not just one processor, but several processors. That means not just one parallel operation, but several, distinct, parallel operations can be carried out in parallel (simultaneously). The ability of a system to do *parallel processing* in this manner can be increased by increasing the number of processors within the system. Such parallel processing is used in today's fastest computers.

Fixed-Length and Variable-Length Operations

We have learned that data is stored as binary digits, or bits. A certain number of binary digits, usually 8, can represent a character; the character may be a letter, a digit, or a special symbol such as the ampersand (&) or the dollar sign ($). Alternatively, the binary digits can be interpreted as a binary number.

In some computers, a single character can be referred to by stating the address of the location in which it is stored. Machines whose circuitry is designed to process data serially as single characters are said to be *character-addressable.* When a character-addressable computer is instructed to read from a specific location, it reads any number of succeeding locations or characters, depending on the particular instruction or on a code that is provided. In effect, the computer operates on *variable-length words.*

In other computers, each address refers to a fixed number of locations containing a fixed number of binary digits. Each group of digits is treated

WEATHER FORECASTING

Many of us know well an often-quoted saying: "Everybody talks about the weather, but nobody does anything about it." In fact, that's no longer the case. Some of today's most powerful supercomputers are dedicated to the task of creating atmospheric models and producing hundreds of maps of global high- and low-pressure areas.

Automated sensing devices and skilled meteorologists are observing and analyzing current weather conditions and trends at stratetgic points throughout the world. Often, a personal computer serves as the meteorologist's initial data-entry and analysis tool. It may also serve as a remote terminal whereby the results of observations are forwarded over telephone lines to a meteorological center. The observations collected at periodic intervals in this manner serve as inputs to one of the computerized atmospheric modules running on a supercomputer. The outputs of the model are in turn used by meteorologists to forecast temperatures, rainfall, barometric pressure, and humidity.

Not even the meteorologists themselves claim that their forecasts are always accurate. Nonetheless, for example, commercial airline flight paths are often planned or modified on the basis of forecasted weather conditions. How often do you listen to a local TV meteorologist to find out if you're likely to need an umbrella by nightfall or what the weather is likely to be at the "big game" tomorrow?

While a 20-minute downpour during a weekend campout may be annoying, truely severe thunderstorms and attendant phenomena (hail, damaging winds, flash floods, lightning) are much more serious. For this reason, the National Severe Storms Laboratory (NSSL) was established as a research facility by the National Oceanic and Atmospheric Adminstration, U.S. Department of Commerce, in 1964. NSSL is located at the University of Oklahoma in Norman, which lies within an area judged to have frequent severe storm phenomena. Visiting scientists from around the world work to understand these phenomena. By gaining an understanding of the structure and evolution of severe thunderstorms, the scientists are able to form criteria for more accurate and timely warnings of tornadoes and other storms. Computerized techniques for predicting where and when such storms will occur are under development.

How do we benefit? Improved guidelines for commercial aircraft safety in thunderstorm environments have been established. Improved methods for detection and prediction of tornadoes and other storms are already available. To help insure the health and safety of people throughout the world, another well-known saying applies here: "No surprises." (*Photos courtesy* [*left*] *L. L. T. Rhodes/Taurus Photos*; [*right*] *National Severe Storms Laboratory*, *National Oceanic and Atmospheric Administration*) as a single unit of data—a *fixed-length word.* The choice of word size is one aspect of the computer's architecture. That choice is designed into the computer. Internal processing operations are performed in parallel, as we've just described. Storage locations, accumulators, and other registers are designed to accommodate words. Such computers are said to be *word-addressable* and operate on fixed-length words.

Variable-length operations offer advantages in data-handling flexibility. Fixed-length operations usually offer greater speed. Some computers are designed to perform either kind of operation. In such computers, the type of operation performed depends upon the stored-program instruction controlling the operation.

Synchronous and Asynchronous Operations

As explained earlier, all computer operations take place in fixed intervals of time measured by regular pulses of an electronic clock. The execution (E-time) of one instruction may still be going on when the fetch (I-time) of the next instruction is initiated. Over-all, however, internal processing operations are carried out in a methodical, step-by-step fashion.

This design is fine, as far as it goes. However, it fails to provide for the fact that *before* data can be processed internally it must be read as input. Similarly, results that have been computed are only useful to us *after* they've been written as output. We know that input/output operations are slower than internal processing operations, but that doesn't mean we can choose to get along without them. A computer has to be designed to accept input and to provide output. Either of two basic design approaches may be followed.

Under one approach, the actions of I/O devices are permitted to occur only at fixed points in a program and only in a sequence established by the program. Such a system is said to support *synchronous operations.* As an example, assume a user wants to key in data from a visual-display unit. The keying activity may cause an indicator to be set automatically by hardware. Let's suppose a particular bit in storage is set to 1. The setting of the bit does not cause a read operation to occur immediately, however. At fixed intervals, the processor is directed to test that bit position. It also tests the bit positions reserved for other I/O devices on the system. This technique is called *polling.* When the visual-display unit's turn comes, and its bit is found to be set, the input operation is allowed to occur. Since internal processing operations occur very rapidly, the user may think the data keyed in is read immediately. That is not the case. All activities within the system are rigidly controlled by the hardware and/or by stored programs.

Other EDP systems perform *asynchronous operations.* Such systems are designed to permit the automatic interruption of processing whenever the need for I/O activity arises. The input or output device signals the processor by means of an *interrupt* when it is ready to read or to write. The interrupt means, in effect: "My particular job is done. As soon as convenient, use the data I have given you [if it was an input operation] or give me any additional information you have [if it was an output operation]." The signal may be the setting of a bit as above, but in this case, the bit has an immediate

Restrooms
Elevator

UNITED

TRAVEL BY COMPUTER

An arena where computer use continues to increase and expand into new areas is the airline industry. One part of the picture we usually see is the ticket counter. A terminal at the ticket counter tells the airline representative what flights are going to our destination and which seats are available on each flight. Similarly, computerized displays throughout the airport tell us departures and arrivals. What we usually don't see is the system of computerized baggage handling. Considering the millions of pieces of luggage handled every year, it's a technological miracle that most of them reach their intended destination at all—a miracle that's possible with computers. Obviously, scheduling, ticketing, and baggage routing existed before computers, but computers have enabled the airlines to accomplish such tasks with improved speed and efficiency. *(Photos courtesy Mark McKenna)*

effect. As soon as the processor finishes whatever instruction it is executing, it accepts the data as input or transmits the information as output.

Ideally, the configuration and speeds of the various I/O devices included in a computer system should be such that the processor can work at full capacity whenever the user workload dictates. Again because of the slower speeds of I/O devices, this means that the over-all system efficiency depends heavily on the extent to which input, internal processing, and output operations can be *overlapped,* or allowed to occur at the same time.

The effect of overlapped reading, processing, and writing can be achieved with either synchronous or asynchronous operations. Generally, synchronous operation requires greater attention to timing considerations on the part of persons who write programs to run on the system. Asynchronous operation is possible only when certain features are present in the system hardware. The system must be adapted, or *tuned,* to match the characteristics of the users' processing workload to take full advantage of the overlap that's possible.

Microprocessors

Even though microprocessors are just small processors, it's appropriate to spend some time looking at them specifically. They are being used not only in microcomputers but also in other machines, educational tools, household equipment, toys, and so on. Their potential is tremendous.

The first microprocessor, unveiled in 1971, contained 2250 transistors in an area barely $\frac{1}{6}$ inch × $\frac{1}{8}$ inch in size. In computational power, it almost matched the monstrous 1500-square-foot ENIAC completed just 25 years earlier. Known as the Intel 4004, the microprocessor was designed to handle 4 binary digits, or bits, at a time. It was followed a few months later by an 8-bit microprocessor, the Intel 8008. Other common early designs were the Intel 8080, Zilog Z80, and MOS Technology 6502. The Intel 8086 and Motorola MC68000 are faster, more powerful, 16-bit microprocessor chips. The Intel 80386 and Motorola 68020 are among the leading 32-bit microprocessors. (See Figure 6-13.) They're used, for example, in high-end IBM Personal System/2 and Apple Macintosh personal computers, respectively. Follow-on Intel 80486 and Motorola 68030 32-bit chips are now on the market.

Like the processor of a large computer system, a microprocessor performs certain well-defined functions. Its tasks are to

- Receive data in the form of binary digits from an input mechanism
- Store data for later processing
- Perform arithmetic and logical operations on data in accord with previously stored instructions
- Deliver results through an output mechanism

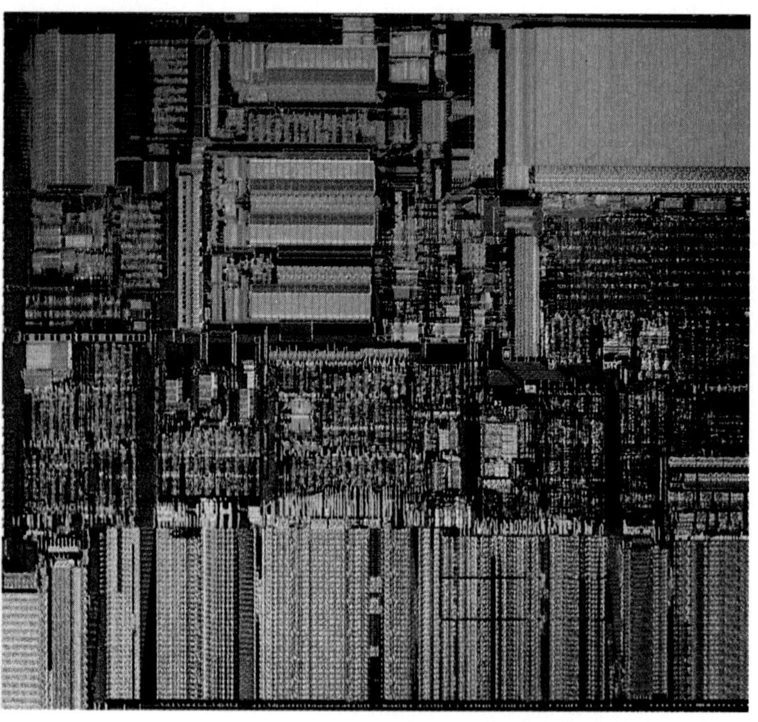

Figure 6-13 The Intel 80386 microprocessor provides a rich, generalized instruction set and a complete 32-bit architecture for addresses and data. (Courtesy Intel)

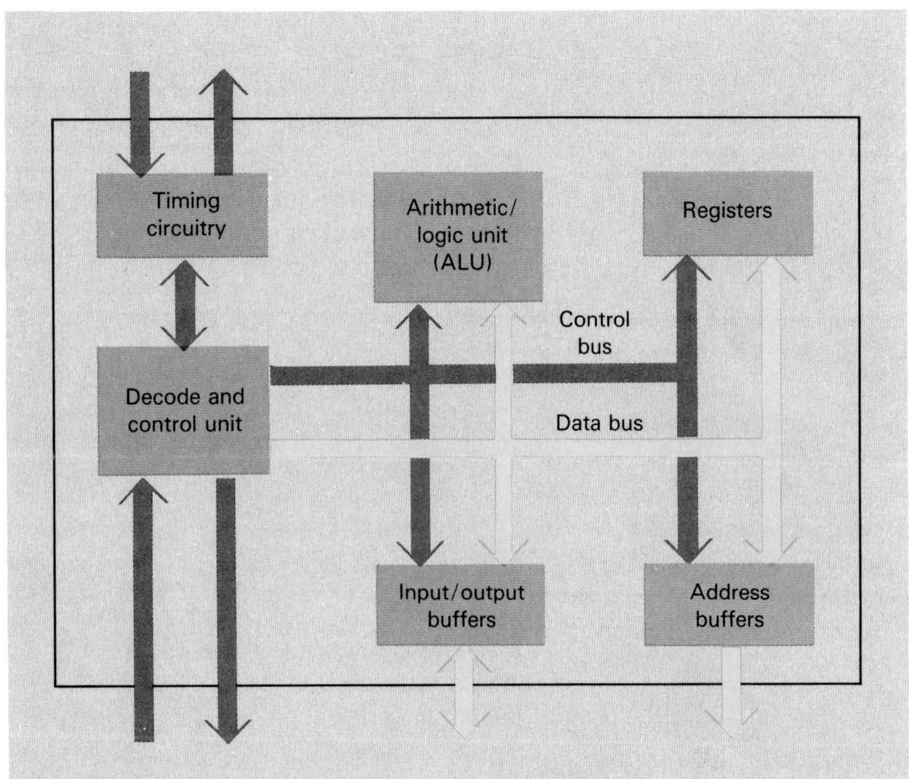
Timing
circuitry
Arithmetic/
logic unit
(ALU)
Registers
Control
bus
Decode and
control unit
Data bus
Input/output
buffers
Address
buffers

Figure 6-14 **The bus architecture of a microprocessor allows data, instructions, and control signals to move among its internal components during processing.**

Figure 6-14 shows the basic components of a typical microprocessor. The *decode and control unit* interprets the instructions of the stored program. The *arithmetic/logic unit (ALU)* performs arithmetic and logical operations. The *registers* provide readily accessible storage for data that is being manipulated. One of these, the *accumulator,* is one source of data for arithmetic and logical operations performed by the ALU and the immediate destination of all its results. The *address buffers* supply the address of the location from which the next instruction is to be fetched, and the address of the location from which a data item is to be read or in which it is to be written. The *input/output buffers* are used in reading instructions or data into the microprocessor and in writing them out. The data and instructions travel along the *data bus.* Control signals are carried by the *control bus.* The *timing circuitry* synchronizes the operations of all components.

Thus we see a basic similarity between the components of this microprocessor and those of the processor described earlier in this chapter. We did not label or even show many specific buses in Figures 6-9 and 6-10 because we wanted to avoid unnecessary complexity. However, you can assume that on most mainframe processors, the functional components that have to interact are connected point-to-point by separate buses. They don't have to share buses as shown here. This freedom allows several bit patterns in the form of electronic pulses—representing data, addresses, operation codes, and so on—to move simultaneously within the system. The over-all-speed

About Speed

What do we mean when we say that a processor operates at 33 megahertz, or millions of cycles per second? We mean that 33 million times a second, the processor is ready to move to the next step in processing.

What do we mean when we say that a particular computer is a 5-MIP machine? We mean that the computer can carry out 5 million instructions per second.

There is no direct correlation between megahertz and MIPS. The instruction set of one processor may differ significantly from that of another. Furthermore, remember that the over-all speed of a system depends on more than just the speed of the processor. Some representative pairings from one computer manufacturer follow:

Processor Type/ Megahertz	MIPS
Intel 286/12	2.45
Intel 286/16	3.27
Intel 386/20	4.91
Intel 386/33	6.13

In the late 1960s, large mainframes were 5-MIP machines. Today, many personal computers and workstations are that fast. Mainframes are typically 15- to 50-MIP machines. Those with multiple processors may be even faster.

of the system is faster than it would be otherwise.

Over time, the designers of large computer systems have applied numerous techniques to increase the over-all speed and efficiency of their systems. Now that microprocessor speeds have increased from the 4.77 *megahertz* (millions of cycles per second) rate of the initial IBM PC introduced in 1981 and other early machines to 20, 25, and 33 megahertz, designers of microcomputer systems face similar challenges. In general, memory chips are slower than processor chips. Input/output devices are slower yet. It does little good, for example, if the microprocessor may ask for data every two machine cycles, but the memory chip can never deliver data that fast: The microprocessor must wait.

One way designers are attacking this problem is to include a small amount of high-speed memory, known as a *cache,* as a kind of staging area between the microprocessor and conventional memory. Their objective is to avoid system delays, known as *wait states,* during processing. A microprocessor system that incurs no wait (i.e., "has a zero wait state") 95% of the time is likely to perform significantly faster than a system that incurs a wait whenever data is moved to or from the microprocessor. A user who's trying to complete spreadsheet calculations or to do computer-aided design will notice the difference.

Today, several computer manufacturers and a number of semiconductor chip manufacturers are producing microprocessor chips. The inventor of a particular chip design may produce the chip and license to others the right to produce it. Manufacturers may—and often do—incorporate the chips into products they produce and market. Alternatively, they may sell the chips to other firms known as *original equipment manufacturers (OEM's),* who in turn incorporate the chips into their own products. The microprocessor chips serve as standard building blocks of the electronics industry. By taking advantge of existing, proven chip designs, companies can achieve significant increases in the efficiency of their engineering and manufacturing efforts. (Consider, for example, the inefficiency that would exist in the housing industry if each contractor had to design individually every nail or plank instead of using standard 6-penny nails and 2-by-4 boards.)

Because a microprocessor is so small and relatively inexpensive, it can be incorporated into almost any device whose usability is improved by some "intelligence" (thinking power). Early examples included handheld calculators, video games, pinball machines, vending machines, sewing machines, and microwave ovens. Today microprocessors are also used widely in offices and other business environments. For example, a microprocessor within an electronic typewriter interprets signals from the keyboard and sends pulses to electromagnets that control printing. Sophisticated visual-display units, printers, and plotters also con-

Because a microprocessor is so small and relatively inexpensive, it can be incorporated into almost any device whose usability is improved by some "intelligence" (thinking power).

Figure 6-15 Microprocessor-based systems convert sounds of the human voice to a digital form for transmission purposes and then reconvert the digitized message to voice form later at the receiving locations. (Courtesy Lanier Corp.)

tain microprocessors. (See Figure 6-15.)

Through programming, a standard microprocessor chip can be tailored to initiate and control many of the functions of the device within which it is incorporated. When that device is a microcomputer with attached input/output devices, the user can simply change the program that's directing the microprocessor to use the microcomputer for any of a wide variety of purposes—game playing one minute, financial planning the next, and letter writing a few minutes after that.

Reduced Instruction Set Computing (RISC)

Today's computers are many times faster and yet much smaller than their predecessors. Electronic circuit designers have worked hard to increase the amount of circuitry that can be packed onto a single board or chip. They have also worked hard to decrease the distances that electronic pulses must travel. The results of their efforts are faster, more compact, more complex boards and chips. Computers have been applied to design follow-on computers.

Within the same time frame, however, another design philosophy has been emerging. Researchers in corporate laboratories and at large universities have pointed to yet another case where the "80/20 rule" often quoted in our society applies: About 20 percent of a computer's instruction set is used to do 80 percent of the work in a typical processing workload. It follows, then, that if the performance of that 20 percent of the instructions is optimized, significant over-all performance gains are likely. This design philosophy is referred to as *RISC,* or *reduced instruction set computing.*

About 20 percent of a computer's instruction set is used to do 80 percent of the work in a typical processing workload.

A RISC processor differs significantly from a typical processor of the past decade or so—now termed a *CISC (complex instruction set computing)* machine, for differentiation purposes. The RISC processor supports fewer instructions. The instruc-

NOW TAKING SIGN-UPS For
SUMMER Leagues
INQUIRE AT DESK
688
683

QUICK DEFROST
STAGE 1 2
CLOCK TIME POWER
CLOCK
CLEAR
START
WARM
LOW
SIMMER
MED. LOW
DEFROST
MEDIUM
ROAST
MED. HIGH
HIGH
TIMER

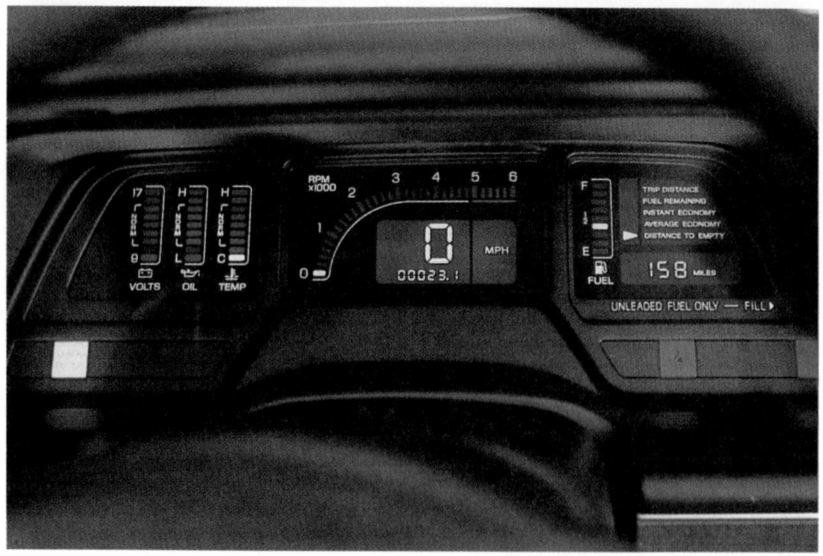
RPM x1000
VOLTS
OIL
TEMP
MPH
TRIP DISTANCE
FUEL REMAINING
INSTANT ECONOMY
AVERAGE ECONOMY
DISTANCE TO EMPTY
MILES
FUEL
UNLEADED FUEL ONLY — FILL

MICROPROCESSORS ALL AROUND US

Some of the most unsuspected or unnoticed uses of microprocessors occur around us in everyday life. Many bowling alleys, for instance, have electronic game-monitoring devices that allow everyone to follow the action without having to do scorekeeping duty. Some home appliances, such as microwave ovens, contain microprocessors to control temperature and cooking times . . . maybe allowing for an extra game at the bowling alley!

Microprocessors also control the traffic lights at busy intersections and provide timely, accurate indicators of car performance as we drive to and from daily activities. Most new cars have microprocessors that adjust their timings, mix air and fuel, and fine-tune their emission-control equipment. Digital speedometers, bar-chart fuel gauges, and illuminated message centers are interfaced with microprocessors throughout the car. Some models are equipped with voice synthesizers that tell us when fuel is low or parts are malfunctioning. (*Photos courtesy Mark McKenna*)

tions that remain are simple—each is designed to do only one thing, not several. Microprograms stored in ROM are often used to implement complex instructions in CISC processors, but there is little or no microcode in RISC machines. RISC designers opt for simplicity rather than complexity.

A goal of RISC designers is to use as few machine cycles as possible for each instruction. For example, the R3000 RISC chip from MIPS Computer Systems averages 1.2 machine cycles per instruction. In contrast, a single complex math instruction within the Intel 80386 instruction set may take 43 machine cycles.

Instead of putting complex functions into hardware, the RISC philosophy emphasizes efficient software. You won't find RISC computers that directly execute DOS or OS/2 programs. Sun Microsystems, a pioneer in RISC computing with its SPARC (Scalable Processor Architecture) chip, established a relationship with AT&T to create a version of the UNIX operating system that could be optimized for the SPARC architecture. UNIX is today the preferred operating system for most RISC machines. Efficient language-processor programs, or *compilers*, are also needed to convert user application programs written in COBOL, FORTRAN, or C to machine language. In addition to translating user-written statements into machine language, the compilers insure that the resultant machine code makes optimal use of the computer's registers and other hardware components.

Instead of putting complex functions into hardware, the RISC philosophy emphasizes efficient software.

Hewlett-Packard was perhaps first among the leading computer vendors to make a significant market impact with its RISC technology. Its RISC-based family of medium-sized computers, code named the Spectrum series during development, was delayed repeatedly for lack of soft-

Figure 6-16 RISC-based workstations with high-resolution graphic display capabilities are rapidly gaining acceptance in the marketplace. (Courtesy IBM Corporation)

ware. It is now gaining acceptance. SUN-4 SPARC-based workstations are widely used in computer-aided design/computer-aided manufacturing and other compute-intensive applications. IBM's RT PC is a RISC-based machine. (RT stands for RISC technology.) DEC has announced RISC-based workstations. Motorola has developed a RISC chip, the Motorola 88000. The 88Open Consortium comprises hardware and software developers who are creating products to take advantage of this technology. (See Figure 6-16.)

It's premature to suggest that RISC technology will someday replace CISC technology. However, the influence of RISC thinking is spreading. Intel's 80486 microprocessor chip introduced in 1989 is described as a CISC/RISC hybrid by some industry analysis. Simplicity in design and production offers potential benefits to vendors. Shorter market lead times and higher manufacturing yields are examples. Users are also experiencing benefits. Among them are faster, higher-quality products that meet the users' processing requirements.

CHAPTER SUMMARY

1. The processor of an EDP system consists of a control section and an arithmetic/logic unit. It may be housed in a boxlike structure, constructed on a single circuit board, or contained on a single silicon chip (in which case it's called a *microprocessor*).

2. The control section of a processor directs and coordinates all EDP-system operations; the arithmetic/logic unit contains the circuitry needed to perform arithmetic and logical operations.

3. Registers are small internal devices that receive information as electronic pulses, hold that information, and then release it very quickly when directed to do so. Registers such as the accumulator, storage register, address register, and operation-code register perform specific functions; general-purpose registers may be used for any of several functions.

4. An instruction counter keeps track of the next instruction to be executed. That instruction is normally the next instruction in primary storage.

5. A stored-program instruction may have any of several formats. The common 32-bit format includes a 12-bit operation-code field and a 20-bit operand field.

6. During I-time, an instruction is fetched from primary storage and interpreted to set up the circuit paths necessary to execute it.

7. During E-time, the operation specified in an instruction is performed.

8. Computer operations may be carried out serially or in parallel, depending on the architecture of the computer.

9. Some computers have character-addressable storage and operate on variable-length words. Others have word-addressable storage and operate on fixed-length words.

10. A synchronous computer system allows I/O operations to occur only at fixed points in a program and only in a sequence determined by the program. An asynchronous computer system responds to automatic interrupts whenever read or write operations are to occur.

11. Standard microprocessor chip designs allow microprocessors to serve as basic building blocks in a wide variety of products. The chips are tailored through programming to initiate and control many of the functions of the products within which they are incorporated.

12. Reduced instruction set computing (RISC) is a design philosophy that emphasizes the optimized performance of simple instructions. Efficient compilers translate user-written statements into machine-language instructions that make optimal use of the computer's registers and other hardware components.

DISCUSSION QUESTIONS

1. Distinguish between the processor and the processor unit of a computer system.

2. (a) Identify the two major parts of a processor.
(b) Discuss the functions of each major part.

3. (a) How are registers and primary-storage locations similar?
(b) How do they differ?

4. Use the binary number system to represent the following values:
(a) the number of days in a week
(b) the number of ounces in a pound
(c) the number of inches in a yard

5. Write the decimal numeral that is equivalent to each binary numeral below.
(a) 0101
(b) 00011110
(c) 00110011

6. (a) Name the two parts of a stored-program instruction.
(b) What is the function of each part?

7. Assume that the following operation codes are available for use with a particular computer:

Operation code	Meaning
58	Load accumulator
5A	Add to accumulator
5B	Subtract from accumulator
50	Store
47	Branch

Further assume that this computer is directed by 32-bit instructions like the one in Figure 6-8. Using binary notation, show how an instruction causing the computer to add the contents of location 34A to the accumulator, which is register 2, would be stored in one computer word.

8. Refer to Question 7. Write the same instruction in hexadecimal notation.

9. Using the same 32-bit instruction set, write a sequence of three instructions directing the computer to load the contents of storage location 608 in the accumulator, subtract the contents of storage location C44 from this value, and store the result, automatically placed in the accumulator, in location FB4. Use either binary or hexadecimal notation.

10. Distinguish between I-time and E-time.

11. Support or refute the following statement: "Parallel operations are apt to be faster than serial operations."

12. Compare variable-length operations with fixed-length operations. Discuss differences in execution and in effect.

13. Explain how synchronous operations differ from asynchronous operations.

14. (a) What is a microprocessor?
(b) Compare it with the processor of a large computer system.

15. What are some uses of microprocessors?

16. (a) Why is reduced instruction set computing (RISC) referred to as a design philosophy?
(b) Why are both hardware and software changes needed to implement RISC in today's environments?

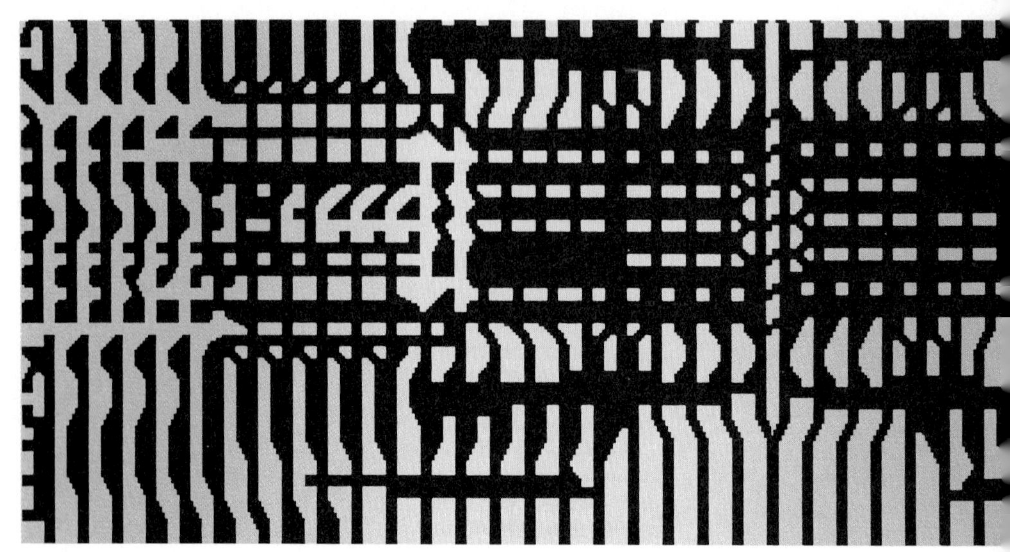

7 Microcomputers in Use

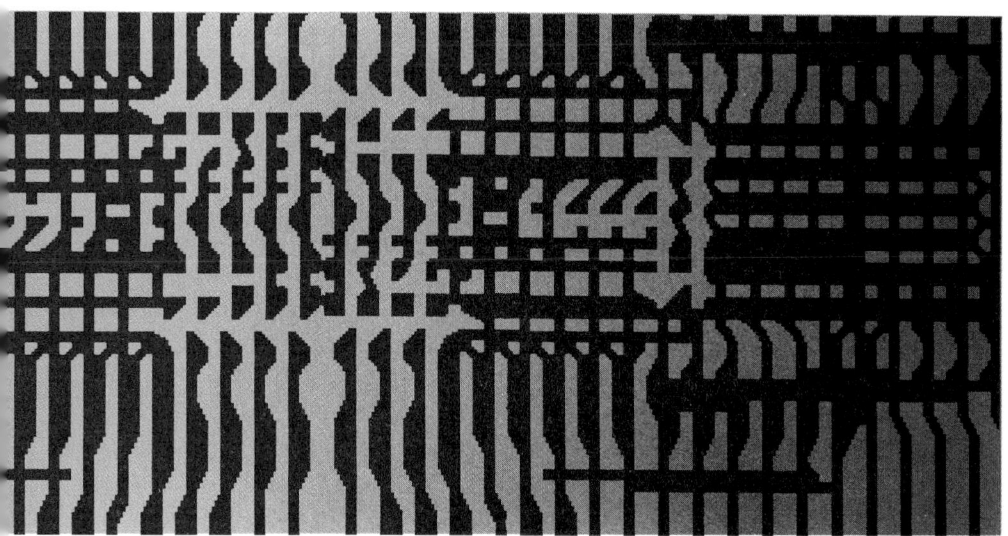

IN THIS CHAPTER

What's Included in a Microcomputer System
Handheld Computers
Lap-Top Portables
Home Computers
Personal Computers
Workstations
Selecting a Microcomputer
Finding Out What's Available

Just a few short years ago, computers were a total unknown. Many people alive today were born before computers had even been invented.

Yet, today computers are everywhere. You read about them in your local newspaper. You see ads for them on TV. You can order a computer by mail or carry one home in a shopping bag. You can hold a computer in your hand or put it in your pocket.

Of course, there are some very fast, very powerful, large computers that cost thousands of dollars to rent and millions of dollars to buy. There may always be. There are some very demanding user needs—structural, chemical, and mechanical analyses, control of electric power systems, reservoir modeling, nuclear research, and the like—that only these large supercomputers can satisfy.

There are also computers that cost $100 or less. These computers can be used for many of the tasks for which calculators have been used for years: simple arithmetic, adding up bills, figuring taxes, solving scientific equations, and the like. They can operate on letters, words, and paragraphs of text as well as on numbers. They can be directed by stored-program instructions instead of by keying. They can play games, make music, and talk. Indeed, their potential may be limited only by our human imagination.

Given such a wide range of computers, how can we talk about them? Historically, a common approach has been to group computers into three broad cate gories: *microcomputers, minicomputers,* and *mainframes.* Some people say, for example, that a micro is any computer that sells for $5000 or less, that a mini sells for $50,000 or less in a common configuration, and that a mainframe is any computer more costly than those. Supercomputers mentioned above may be grouped with mainframes or discussed separately. You can buy a lot more computer hardware for $5000 now than you could buy a year (or maybe even a month) ago. Thus, even if we accept cost as a classifier, the boundaries are moving.

Some people suggest that technology provides the best way to classify computers. They consider word sizes, processing speeds, or storage capacities. Initially, micros were 8-bit machines and minis were 16-bit machines. Now there are both micros and minis that process 32 bits at a time. The speeds of today's minis exceed the speeds of mainframes of a few years ago. So do the speeds of some 32-bit micros. A memory size that was typical of mainframes only a few years ago is now prevalent on minis and micros in business environments. Again, the boundaries are moving.

What many users really want to know are answers to questions such as: "Can I use the computer to keep track of who owes what?" "If I buy a computer, will it help me do my taxes?" "If our firm buys or leases a computer, how much faster can we get our bills out?" "How can a computer help us manage our inventory?" "What's the best word-processing program for micros?" "Do I really need to have a hard-disk drive?"

In earlier chapters, we referred often to microprocessors, microcomputers, and applications involving them. In this chapter, we focus our attention directly on these topics. We'll see that microcomputers differ widely in costs and capabilities. For convenience, we can group micros into several categories—say, handheld, lap-top, home, personal, and workstations. As noted earlier about the full range of computers, such classifications are not rigid. Nonetheless, they are useful for discussion purposes. Finally, we identify factors to consider when selecting a microcomputer system. We discuss microcomputer hardware and software distribution channels and how you can find out what's available.

What's Included in a Microcomputer System

As we saw in earlier chapters, a microprocessor is the central processing unit of a computer scaled down to fit on one silicon chip. Suppose we add chips to provide timing, control memory for instructions, read/write memory for use as temporary storage, and interfaces for input and output. In so doing, we assemble a complete computer on a single circuit board. We call the assembly a *microcomputer.*

Microcomputers are usually classified according to the word size of their processor. You may choose an 8-bit, 16-bit, or 32-bit machine. Their performance is judged by the richness of their instruction set and the speed with which they execute their programs. A computer that's suitable for home use may seem intolerably slow to an office worker who must enter a 15-page report at the keyboard, format, and print before the close of the business day.

Microcomputer memories are generally made of semiconductor chips, fabricated by the same technology that is used to make microprocessor chips. The control memory that holds instructions and fixed (unchanging, or permanent) data such as rate tables is *read-only memory (ROM).* Its contents cannot be altered during processing. Furthermore, ROM is nonvolatile; the retention of its contents is not dependent on a constant power supply. The read/write memory that provides for temporary storage of data while the microcomputer is operating is called *random-access memory (RAM).* As we learned in Chapter 5, most semiconductor RAM is volatile. Its contents are lost when the power supply is shut off. Microcomputers for specialized applications may use only ROM (if the registers of the microprocessor provide all the temporary storage needed). Other microcomputers may have only RAM, with a battery backup to maintain memory contents if required.

Microcomputer systems have I/O devices, just as larger systems do. At a minimum, there's a keyboard for data entry. A palm-sized mouse, graphics tablet, or voice input unit may be present. Some systems have visual-display units. A wide range of printers and plotters for micros is available. (See Figure 7-1.)

In some microcomputer systems, cassette tapes serve as secondary storage. Other systems allow programs and data to be read from, and written to, flexible disks. Some systems support Winchester or hard-disk drives. Cartridge tapes may be used for backup or archival purposes.

FIGURE 7-1 **Today's business executives work daily with an ever-increasing volume of facts and figures, memos, reports. Many are using personal computers to organize and analyze the data thereby converting it to useful information.** (Photo courtesy of Hewlett-Packard Packard Company)

A Decade of Personal Computing

The microcomputer has been accepted into society at about 10 times the rate of the automobile; the microcomputer industry has grown faster in its first 10 years than the mainframe industry grew in 20.

The software components of a microcomputer system are the programs that direct its operations. There would be far fewer users of microcomputers if each user had to write all the programs needed to make his or her machine work. Even game-playing is possible only if a program to direct the computer in playing its part is available in ROM or can be loaded into RAM. Fortunately, a wide variety of both system software and application software has been developed. Many of the programs sell for $50 or less. Some cost several hundred dollars.

There would be far fewer users of microcomputers if each user had to write all the programs needed to make his or her machine work.

The operating procedures for one microcomputer system differ from those for another. We described some simple procedures in Chapter 2 when we discussed how to enter and run a BASIC program. The procedures to be used with a particular system are generally described in the accompanying system documentation. Before using a system that's new to you, you'll need to read the system documentation.

Handheld Computers

The smallest microcomputers for individual use are *handheld,* or *pocket, computers.* They range in weight from about 6 ounces to 4 pounds. At first glance, many resemble handheld electronic calculators. A closer look may reveal a typewriter-like arrangement of alphabetic keys; another section of keys for numeric input, arithmetic functions, and editing; and a small display screen.

The first handheld computer marketed in the United States was Radio Shack's TRS-80 PC-1 Pocket Computer. It had a 1.9K RAM and sold initially for $249. By 1985—just five years later—pocket computers with up to 4K of RAM were selling for less than $100. By 1989, pocket computers to help with many day-to-day tasks were available. (See Figure 7-2.)

Users can key BASIC statements into pocket computers with only a few keystrokes. Most manufacturers offer an optional cassette interface that allows users to load and save their programs and data on ordinary cassette tapes. Ready-to-run game programs, financial programs, educational software, and other consumer-oriented application packages are available from many sources. Credit-card-sized integrated circuit (IC) cards containing popular software in ROM or providing RAM for storage of user programs and data are offered for some pocket computers. Users who need instant printouts of computed results at home, at the office, or in the field can buy a printer interface and a small thermal dot-matrix printer for about $100.

Lap-Top Portables

Some users want the go-anywhere, work-anywhere convenience of a calculator or pocket computer, but they also want more functions than these tools can provide. Osborne Computer addressed such wants in 1981 when it introduced the Osborne 1, the first briefcase portable computer. Its compact carrying case housed

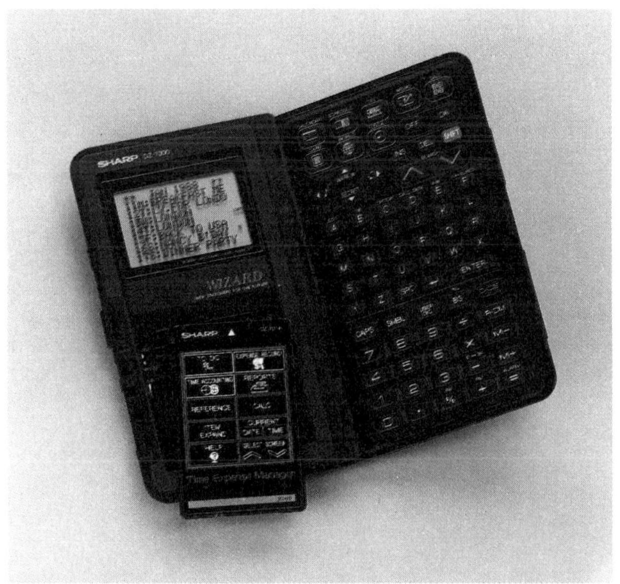

Figure 7-2 **Sharp's 8-ounce Wizard pocket computer includes calendar, scheduler, phonebook, searchable memo pad, local time, world time, and calculator functions. Credit-card-sized software cards offer additional capabilities.** (Courtesy [left] Sharp Electronics Corporation; [right] Mark McKenna)

64K of RAM, two flexible-disk drives (space for about 60 pages of typed, double-spaced text), and a 5-inch (diagonal measure) display that could hold up to 24 52-character lines.

In 1983 *InfoWorld,* a widely read weekly computing magazine, presented its Hardware Product of the Year award to Radio Shack's TRS-80 Model 100, a notebook-sized portable computer for consumers. The Model 100 weighed about 4 pounds and fit in a book bag. Nevertheless, it had up to 32K of RAM, a full-sized typewriterlike keyboard, a display that held up to eight 40-character lines, and interfaces to other I/O devices.

Today a wide range of machines popularly known as *lap-top portables* are available. At the low end are notebook-sized portables like the 4.4-pound NEC UltraLite. At the high end are 15- to 25-pound portables based on the Intel 80286 or 80386 microprocessor. Some vendors and industry watchers use the term *luggable* or *transportable* when referring to the larger portables to distinguish them from their lightweight counterparts. But the term *lap-top portable* is commonly used in trade publications as an inclusive term referring to all such machines. We shall use the term in this manner.

Though early lap-tops sparked user interest, they did not gain the widespread acceptance forecast for them. When asked why, prospective buyers often pointed to their limited screen sizes and poor screen quality. Lack of compatibility with a favored micro and limited disk storage space were sometimes named as concerns. Furthermore, the battery power of early lap-tops was short-lived. Users were unwilling to lug the relatively heavy units a long way, yet be able to use them only a short while even if they did so.

Over time, the situation is changing. Vendors convinced of the potential of this marketplace have continued to develop and exploit evolving technologies. Today's portables are lighter and more compact. Their screens are larger and more readable. Some include hard disks; some have floppies; and some have both. Some, like the Intel 80286-based Toshiba

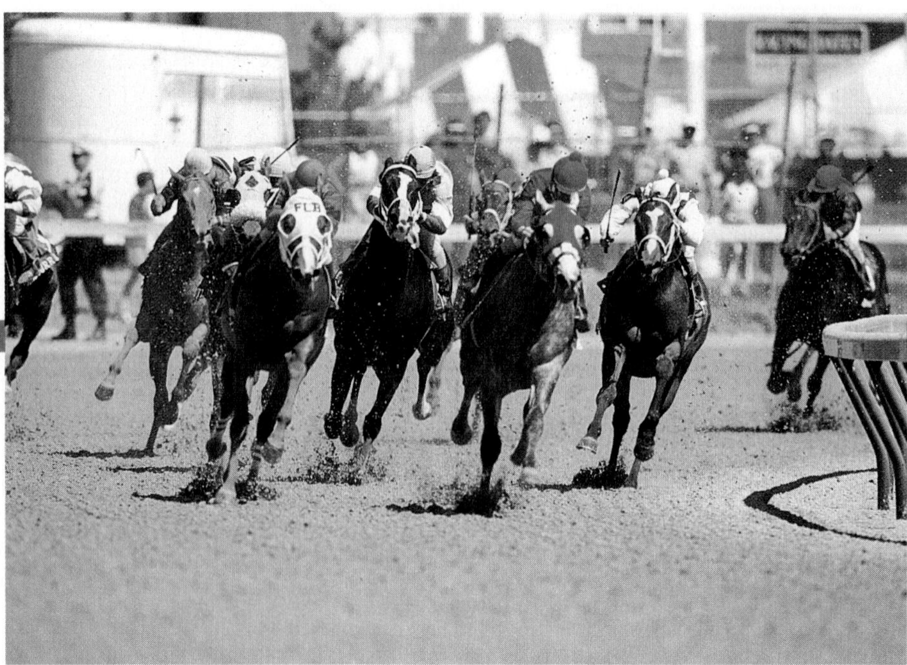

OFF TO THE RACES

Lap-top portables are going to the dogs, and to the horses—races, that is. Racing enthusiasts are using sports handicap software that runs on lap-top portables to guide them to winners. Versions of the software for greyhound, thoroughbred, harness, and quarter-horse races are among those available.

When using the greyhound version of the software, for example, the user is initially prompted for input. The program asks for each dog's post position, odds, time in its last race, and positions at the stretch and the finish line for the last three races. Given this data as input, the program then rates the dogs and designates the top four bets.

At prices ranging from $50 to $250, depending on the system type and the number of versions wanted, the sports handicap software may be a good investment for users. Of course, there's no guarantee of successful results. Users are "on their own" when it comes to accountability. *(Photo courtesy Focus on Sports)*

1600, have a resume feature that makes it convenient for users to save the work they are doing and shut off the machine when it won't be used for a few minutes (or longer), knowing that they can turn the machine on again and resume work right where they left off. (See Figure 7-3.)

Most of today's portables are IBM PC compatible. They run under the control of the MS-DOS, UNIX, or OS/2 operating system. Memory sizes of one megabyte or more are sufficient to run word-processing programs, electronic spreadsheets, and other popular user applications. Intel 80386-based portables offer the performance of desktop machines in compact, or "small-footprint," configurations. (See Figure 7-4.)

In practice, the two broadest categories of lap-top use are sales force automation and off-site auditing and accounting. On-the-road insurance agents can use their lap-tops to calculate the payments and benefits of a wide range of insurance plans to meet clients' needs. Traveling con-

Figure 7-3 Busy people whose jobs keep them on the go are choosing lightweight portables with ready-to-run software. (Courtesy Toshiba, Inc.)

sumer goods sales personnel can carry electronic catalogs rather than numerous loose-leaf volumes and spiral notebooks.

Pillsbury's consumer food sales personnel are using Zenith SuperSport 286 lap-tops when stocking flour, cake and cookie mixes, frozen foods, and canned vegetables in supermarkets. Chrysler salespeople use GridCase 3 lap-tops equipped with internal modems to access data stored in mainframes in Detroit from dealers' offices.

Figure 7-4 Hospitals, governmental research centers, and corporations are purchasing small-footprint, 80386-based portables for use in lab environments. (Courtesy Zenith Electronics Corp.)

The U.S. Internal Revenue Service has armed 18,000 examiners with Zenith lap-tops. Price Waterhouse accountants use Compaq portables equipped with 20-megabyte hard disks to complete tax and audit forms, financial schedules, memo writing, and other office tasks.

In practice, the two broadest categories of lap-top use are sales force automation and off-site auditing and accounting.

Lap-top portables also come in handy in rugged environments where computer help might otherwise not be accessible. Product durability, reliability, and ability to run for several hours away from a power source are key requirements for such uses. (See Figure 7-5.)

Today's lap-tops may cost as much as 30 to 40 percent more than desktop microcomputers having similar processors and storage. Nevertheless, about a million lap-tops were sold in 1988. Growth rates exceeding 30 percent per year are forecast into the 1990s.

Home? Office? or Both?

About 15 million U.S. households have home offices. Nearly 40 percent of the offices have microcomputer systems. The typical home office user spends from $2000 to $4000 for the micro and from $5000 to $10,000 for the complete system, including software and communication facilities.

Home Computers

What can entertain you, point out spelling errors in your letter to Mom, and show you how you're spending your money, all within 20 minutes or less? A home computer, of course.

When directed by appropriate software, your home computer can be a teammate in sports, an adventurer, a teacher, a financial planner, or a tax consultant. It can help you keep track of the phone numbers and addresses you're always misplacing. It can remind you of your next dental appointment the day *before* you're supposed to go. Thousands of programs for entertainment, education in a seemingly unlimited variety of subjects, home budgeting, financial planning, word processing, time management, and so on are readily available. (See Figure 7-6.)

In broadest terms, a *home computer* is any computer used in a home. Initially, analysts defined home computers as computers that had more capabilities than user-oriented handheld computers but sold for under $1000 in a basic configuration. The early leader here was Warner Communications' Atari Division, which capitalized on its strength in video games to develop and market Atari micros. (Few people today have not tried their hands at Pac-Man, Asteroids, Space Invaders, or Video Checkers.) IBM, Tandy, Apple, Commodore, and several East Asian manufacturers also produce home computers. Some of the machines are targeted for home users and used almost exclusively in home environments. (See Figure 7-7.) Others, like the Apple II, are used widely in homes and also in businesses. (We say more about the latter in the next section of this chapter.)

"What can I get for $1000 or less?" That's a question you and many others may be asking. One answer is: "With respect to home computers, usually more than you could a year ago." The least expensive models have limited typewriterlike keyboards, 128K of RAM, cartridge slots that allow the use of ready-to-run programs, and 8-bit microprocessors. Users willing to pay more can acquire more memory, add a couple of flexible-disk drives for secondary

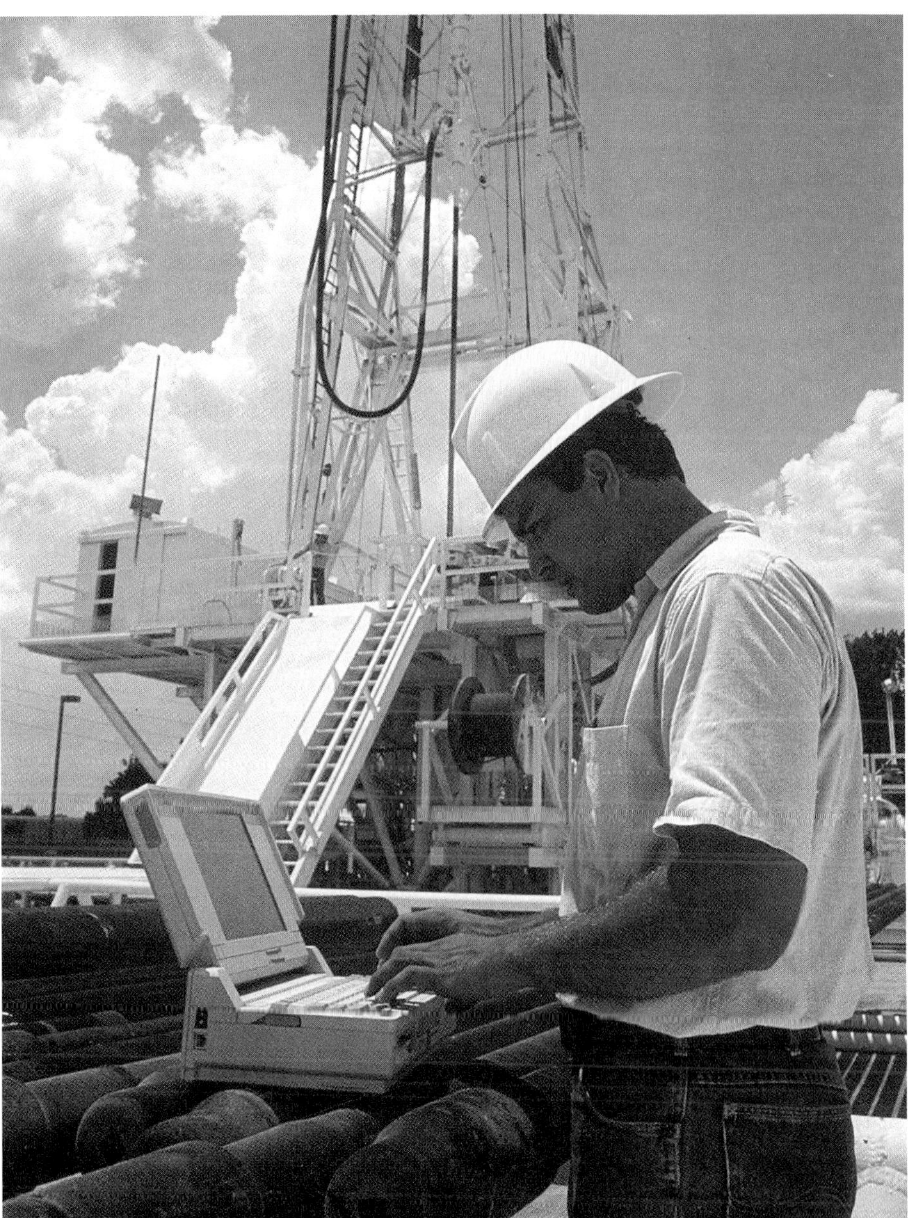

Figure 7-5 Field engineers, scientists, and researchers are using 80286-based laptops designed to work for several hours away from a power source to perform complex calculations and monitor ongoing activities. (Courtesy Compaq Computer Corp.)

storage, and attach a sound unit, line printer, plotter, or visual-display device.

In fact, most microcomputers going into homes today are not less expensive than those purchased for home use a few years ago. That's because most home computers are more powerful. Users want to do more with them. As an example, a 1988 survey of 15,000 computer-using households showed the primary applications for home computers purchased in 1988 break down as follows:

- 24 percent—office work brought home
- 23 percent—a business in the home
- 22 percent—personal or household business
- 17 percent—education
- 14 percent—entertainment

HOME	BUSINESS
Playing games Composing or playing music Drawing Learning math, spelling, other subjects Solving problems (calculations of all kinds) Indexing manually maintained files (phonograph records, hobbies, etc.)	Accounts receivable Accounts payable General ledger Payroll Personnel Benefits
Budgeting/financial planning Keeping track of expenses (actuals) Record-keeping for tax purposes Completing tax returns Playing the stock market Accessing commercial databases	Order processing Billing/invoicing Sales analysis
Mailing lists, address labels Personal correspondence Form letters Filling out forms Writing, editing, filing, and printing reports, other text materials Creating illustrations/artwork	Inventory control Material requirements planning Project costing Human resource planning Purchasing Receiving Computer-aided design/computer-aided manufacturing (CAD/CAM)
Receiving and placing phone calls Security (alarm systems) Controlling lights, appliances	Financial planning Capital budgeting Fixed-assets accounting Depreciation Completing quarterly government, stockholder reports Completing tax returns Forecasting Management reporting
Planning vacations, trips Catalog of daily activities Maintaining a "tickler" file Shopping lists Recipes and meal planning Buying/sales analysis	Electronic filing Electronic mail Word processing Desktop publishing
• • •	• • •

Figure 7-6 "What can I do with a computer?" (Starter lists—add your own ideas.)

A similar survey conducted in 1984 showed only 30% of home computers purchased for either office work brought home or home businesses.

How many U.S. homes today are without telephones? Some market enthusiasts insist that what the telephone is to home communications, the home computer may someday be to home information. Throughout the 1980s, vendors established pilot projects to offer *videotex* services—the delivery of information from computerized files and databases over cable or telephone lines for display on screens in homes and offices. The projects aroused user interest but were not wildly successful. Key market inhibitors were lack of an installed base of required access devices, high costs, unfriendly user interfaces, and lack of service diversity.

None of these early market inhibitors were insurmountable. The first—lack of an installed base—seems to be mostly a matter of timing; that is, there may now be a sufficient base of home computers to provide an attractive target market for advertisers. If advertisers are willing to sign up—as they do for TV slots—then user subscription costs can be lower. Not surprisingly, then, "second-generation" videotex services are arriving. For example, IBM and Sears, through Prodigy Services, Co., offer more than 500 services or features, including stock quotes, airline reservations, weather forecasts, home shopping, and weekly readers for kids. By mid-1989, over 50,000 households had subscribed and 170 advertisers were participating. Even skeptics are now admitting: If anybody can do it, IBM and Sears can.

Some market enthusiasts insist that what the telephone is to home communications, the home computer may someday be to home information.

Developing and marketing computers for home use has proved to be a challenge to both vendors and distributors. The demand for home computers has been brisk at times, but over-all, it's been below expectations. Many industry observers insist that today's consumers want tools they can use "right out of the box." They view themselves as appliance users. Only when the components of a home computer system work together in a near-transparent fashion that allows users to focus on *what* they want to do—not *how*—will the mass market for home computers really materialize.

The demand for home computers has been brisk at times, but over-all, it's been below expectations.

Nevertheless, the business uses of computers in homes have helped

Figure 7-7 Kids of all ages are playing computer games in many home environments. (Courtesy Commodore Electronics Ltd.)

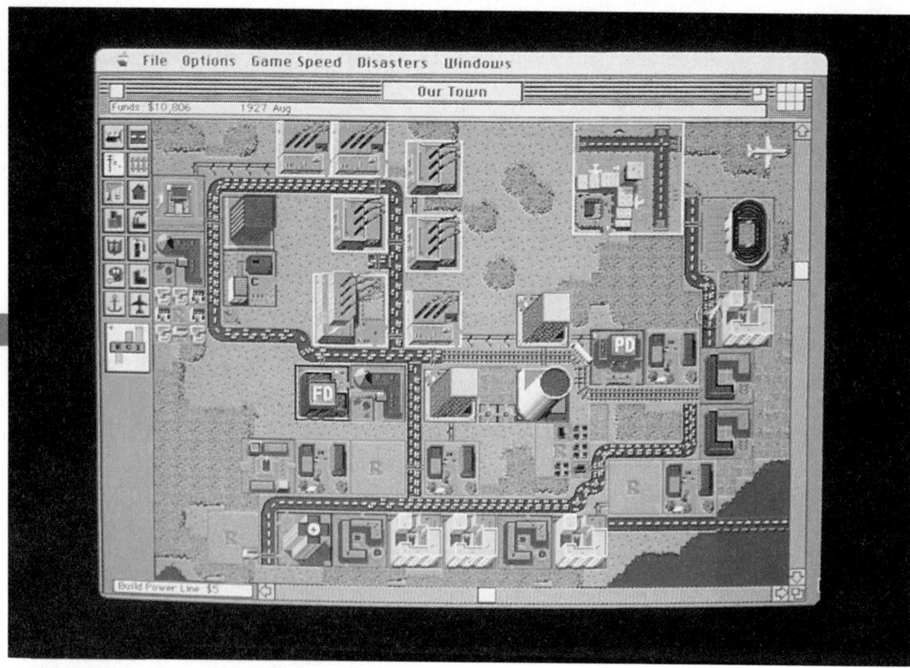
File Options Game Speed Disasters Windows
Our Town
PD
FD

PLANNING THE CITY OF YOUR DREAMS

Call it a game. Call it educational software. Sim City lets you design and plan your own city from the ground up. Start with undeveloped land. Decide where you want residential areas, position the cursor, and click a mouse button. Houses appear. Build commercial and industrial areas the same way. Add roads to connect them, and cars pop up. Game time is clocked in months and years. Single-family homes give way to high-rises; light industries are replaced by smoke-belching factories; and blocks of storefronts are overwhelmed by gleaming office towers.

If you develop rationally and manage resources carefully, your city will continue to thrive. If you develop too fast, you'll go bankrupt, thriving neighborhoods will become vacant lots, and your city will die—ghost town.

Sim City is marketed as a computer game by its owner, Maxis Software of Lafayette, California. Initial versions of the software ran on Macintosh, Commodore, and Amiga microcomputers. Additional versions are under development or already available. Some users are playing for hours. They're debating road systems versus mass transit, comparing zoning philosophies, and so on. Instructors of urban planning classes are also expressing interest. Clearly, the software has many uses. *(Photo courtesy Woodfin Camp)*

to foster a steady growth in the number of computer-using households. Numerous surveys show that computers were installed in about 14 percent of U.S. households by year-end 1986. Their penetration had increased to 16 percent by year-end 1987 and to 19 percent by year-end 1988. Some researchers predict that computers will be used in 30 percent of U.S. households by the early 1990s. That's a much lower number than some microcomputer enthusiasts predicted initially. Still, home computers are an ever-increasing reality.

Personal Computers

A handheld computer is a personal computer. A home computer is a personal computer. However, much more powerful, much more expandable computer systems are also included in the personal computer category. What, then, is a personal computer? It's a tool for a person. It's a computer so simple and easy to operate that you can learn to use it by yourself. You can use it at home or away from home, at work, at school, and at play.

Two primary questions are facing vendors of these computers:

- Which user-oriented capabilities can and should we package in a personal computer system, and yet price that system in a range that individual users can afford?
- Which user-oriented capabilities can and should we package in

AUTOMATING MEDICAL PAPERWORK

Like many other industry areas today, insurance is a paper-driven industry. Nowhere is the paperwork more evident or time-consuming than it is in medical claims processing.

A typical physician today may have to keep records on from 2000 to 5000 patients. An ever-increasing array of payment plans—Medicare, Medicaid, multiple third-party coverages, employee copayment policies, prepayment arrangements, and many other health insurance alternatives—has made patient record keeping and claims processing a complex, never-ending task. We all know that medical care and health insurance are expensive. How much of the expense is due to the paperwork involved?

Blue Cross and Blue Shield (BC/BS) offices throughout the country have developed a microcomputer-based application system to help physicians address the paperwork problem. A participating physician or office acquires a microcomputer, streaming tape drive backup unit, printer, and modem plus the application software. The software helps physicians and office staffs prepare forms for third-party billing through hard-copy printouts, bill primary and secondary insurance carriers, bill patients directly, and rebill carriers and patients if necessary. BC/BS and Medicare B claims can be transmitted directly from an office's microcomputer to the BC/BS claims-processing facility.

From a patient's point of view, the ever-increasing upward spiral of medical and health insurance costs may be alleviated, at least a bit. Repayments for claims may be received sooner because 3 to 5 days of mail time and several manual processing steps have been eliminated. From a physician's point of view, the computerized office procedures provide many opportunities for improved account control, better cash management, increased efficiency in the non-clinical aspects of medical practice, and improved service to patients (the physician's "customers"). *(Photo courtesy of Blue Shield of California)*

BLUE
SHIELD

a system that can be marketed as a productivity tool for the individual user, and yet price that system in a range acceptable to both large and small businesses and other organizations?

A potential buyer of a personal computer system—whether for personal use or for an organization—faces another dilemma:

- How can I choose one system from among the vast array of systems and options available?

The initial vendors of personal computers were not the established computer manufacturers. In 1975, the first personal computers were marketed as ready-to-assemble kits for hobbyists. Resistors, capacitors, RAM, ROM, and microprocessor chips, a teletype interface, timing crystal, and voltage regulator had to be soldered onto a small printed circuit board. I/O units had to be acquired or assembled similarly. Then came the rather awesome task of writing programs in a machine-oriented programming language to make the system work.

The initial vendors of personal computers were not the established computer manufacturers.

We've come a long way in a short time! In 1976, Commodore Business Machines announced the first ready-to-use, fully assembled microcomputer. Known as the PET (Personal Electronic Transactor), it had a 9-inch black-and-white display screen, a 73-key calculator-style keyboard, from 4K to 32K of RAM, and a built-in tape cassette recorder/storage unit for programs and data. This PET computer was Commodore's first entry into the computer field. Tandy's Radio Shack division and Apple Computer soon followed.

What's in a Name?

Tandy Corporation is a multibillion-dollar company—a firm that has even more retail outlets than hamburger-famous McDonald's. The firm has one division, managed somewhat as an entity. That division is Radio Shack. Many consumers heard the term *TRS-80* (pronounced T-R-S-eighty) long before they knew much about computers. The letters *TRS* stand, of course, for Tandy/Radio Shack. The *80* refers to the Z80 microprocessor used in the firm's first microcomputer. In 1984, Tandy began using the term *Tandy* rather than *TRS* in identifying its computers. Tandy's rationale: Many of us think of Radio Shack when we're looking for radios, stereos, or other electronics. However, organizations looking for business computer systems may fail to recognize that Radio Shack offers such systems as well. Today, many organizations know Tandy does.

Tandy/Radio Shack

Tandy Corporation's first venture into the microcomputer field surfaced in 1977. The TRS-80 Level I, a 4K RAM machine with an 8-bit Z80 microprocessor, could be programmed in minimal BASIC. The machine was soon renamed the Model I and enhanced with add-on memory kits and a (confusingly named) Level II BASIC. In 1980, Tandy announced the TRS-80 Model III as a replacement for the TRS-80 Model I. In 1983, it announced a further upgrade of this line of computers, the TRS-80 Model 4. These machines ran under the control of Radio Shack's TRS-DOS operating system or under the industry-standard operating system for 8-bit micros at that time, CP/M from Digital Research, Inc. The machines were targeted primarily at home and educational users.

Meanwhile, the TRS-80 Model II introduced in 1979 and subsequent models known as the TRS-80 Model 12 and Model 16 were marketed as another line of computers intended primarily for business. Organizations could acquire the TRS-XENIX operating system—a specially designed version of UNIX III—to use the Model 16 in a multiple-user environment.

In 1984, Tandy introduced the first products resulting from a major strategic decision within the firm—a decision to produce IBM-compatible computers. Its first MS-DOS-based machine, the Model 1000, was an immediate hit. It's often credited with turning the firm's computer business around. Tandy's DeskMate application software, an easy-to-use graphical interface, was packaged with the machine. Both MS-DOS and DeskMate (which provides support for filing, word processing, spreadsheet analysis, a spell checker, address book, etc.) are provided in ROM in subsequent 8088- and 80286-based machines of this series. (See Figure 7-8.)

Tandy also offers more powerful machines, often grouped within the workstation category we discuss below. The Tandy 4000 line comprises 80386-based IBM PC/AT-compatible micros marketed as high-performance low-cost workstations ideal for use as standalone business systems or in a connectivity environment. The Tandy 5000 line comprises 80386-based micros with the IBM Personal System/2 Micro Channel type of architecture.

Tandy products are marketed through about 7000 Radio Shack Computer Centers and Radio Shack retail outlets. In 1986, it mobilized a sales force of about 1500 to focus on the corporate computer marketplace. In 1988, it acquired GRiD Systems Corporation, a firm best known for its lap-top portables marketed primarily to large businesses and governmental users. Tandy's goal is to become "America's premier electronics company."

Apple Computer

Before 1977–78, an *apple* was something to eat—a fruit, red or green in

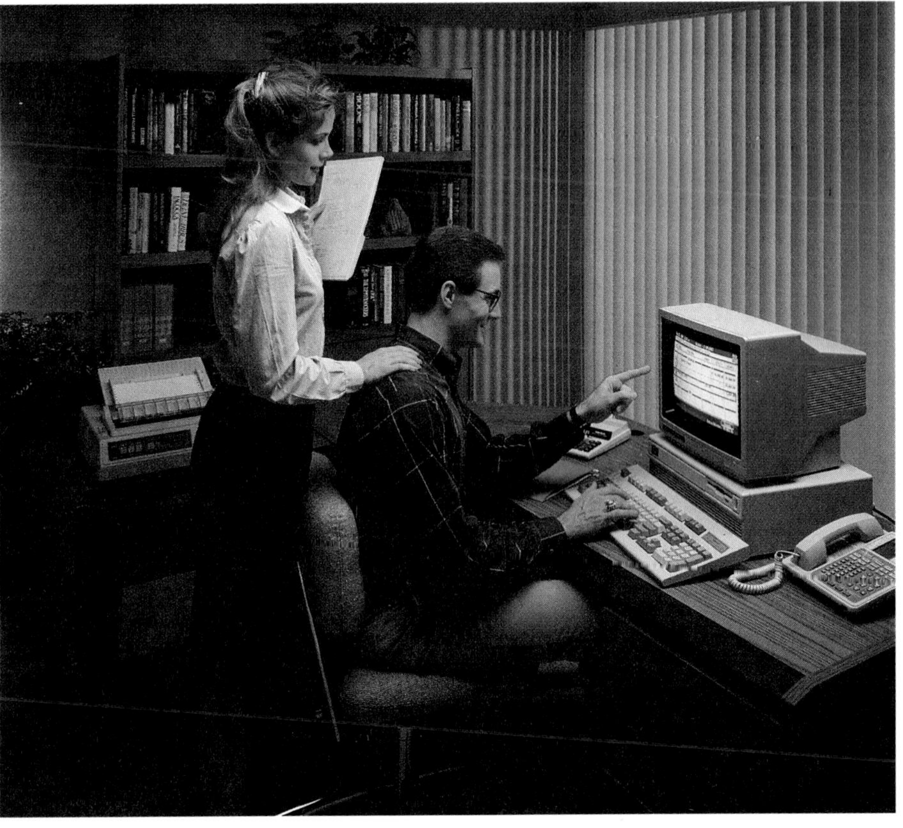

Figure 7-8 Tandy's PC-compatible 80286-based microcomputer systems are marketed for home, classroom, workgroup, and business use. (Courtesy Radio Shack, a Division of Tandy Corporation)

color, produced on a tree. Today there are still apples—but there are also Apples. An *Apple* is a personal computer—a machine, usually beige in color, produced by Apple Computer, Inc.

The first Apple, strangely called the *Apple II,* was a 12-pound desktop unit. It had a standard 52-key typewriterlike keyboard, a game I/O connector that allowed the use of paddles (joysticks) for interactive control, a speaker, and expansion slots for up to eight I/O devices. A built-in video interface allowed the attachment of a visual-display unit. The screen could be programmed to display (1) 24 lines of up to 40 uppercase characters each, (2) color graphics (40 horizontal by 48 vertical dots per location, 15 colors), or (3) high-resolution graphics (280 horizontal by 192 vertical dots, 4 colors: black, white, violet, and green). This versatility made the Apple II suitable for a wide range of applications. Thanks to a strong product and aggressive, timely marketing, Apple sales mushroomed. Apples appeared in homes, education environments, and business offices.

Before 1977–78, an *apple* was something to eat—a fruit, red or green in color, produced on a tree. Today there are still apples—but there are also Apples.

Apple's first machine targeted at business users was the Apple III, introduced in September 1980. Its second attempt to reach the business market, the Apple Lisa (local integrated software architecture), was a revolutionary machine. As mentioned in Chapter 3, the Lisa featured a palm-sized *mouse* that the user simply moved across the desk or table top to control an arrow (the *cursor*) on the screen. By positioning the cursor at the word *Print* and then pressing a button on the mouse, for example, an executive caused a copy of a memo to be printed (without ever touching the keyboard). The screen could be divided into four parts, or *windows,* allowing the user to look at a memo while writing a response to it, compare budgeted amounts in one file with year-to-date expenses just calculated by a program in storage, and so on. Though this user-friendliness was attractive, the $10,000 price of the machine was more than many individuals and organizations were willing to pay. The Lisa also lacked the software library and brand name recognition that the less-sophisticated IBM PC introduced about eight months earlier (April 1981) already enjoyed.

Apple fortified its presence in the home and education market over the next two years with the successful introduction of two new Apple II models: the Apple IIe and the smaller, 7-pound Apple IIc. (See Figure 7-9, top.) In January 1984, its much-anticipated Macintosh computer arrived. (See Figure 7-9, bottom.) The Macintosh featured not only user-friendliness but also a 32-bit architecture—the potential for increased processing speed, faster system response times, and more user work completed within a given amount of time. The suggested retail price of a system with 64K of ROM, 128K of RAM, one built-in $3\frac{1}{2}$-inch 400K flexible-disk drive, a high-resolution 9-inch black-and-white display, and Apple's proprietary system software was $2495.

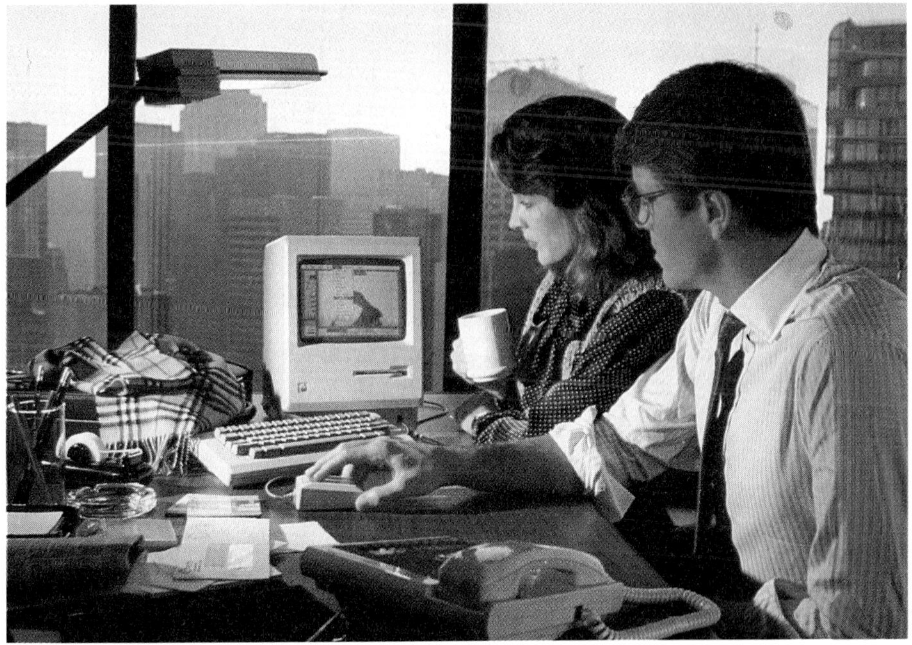

Figure 7-9 In homes and classrooms, you're likely to see Apple IIs (top). The Apple Macintosh is intended primarily for office environments (bottom). (Courtesy Apple Computer, Inc.)

Behind the scenes at Apple, other events were occurring. In 1983, John Sculley, former president of Pepsico, was brought to Apple by its young, charismatic chairman Steve Jobs. Sculley worked hard to overturn Apple's renegade, antiestablishment image. His logic: If Apple wanted to sell to corporate America, Apple had to become a company that corporate America would consider doing business with. In 1985 Sculley wrested control of Apple from Jobs, who subsequently left to form NeXT, Inc.

Apple has penetrated the business world with its Macintosh line primarily through an application that takes advantage of the Macintosh's advanced graphics, namely, *desktop publishing*. (See Figure 7-10.) Newsletters, brochures, even stockholder reports that formerly took months, thousands of dollars, and numerous outside services to prepare, can now be produced in-house. So can multicolor overhead transparencies, slides, and other presentation graphics. Microsoft's Excel electronic spreadsheet program and other applications written for the Macintosh are gaining widespread acceptance. Apple itself

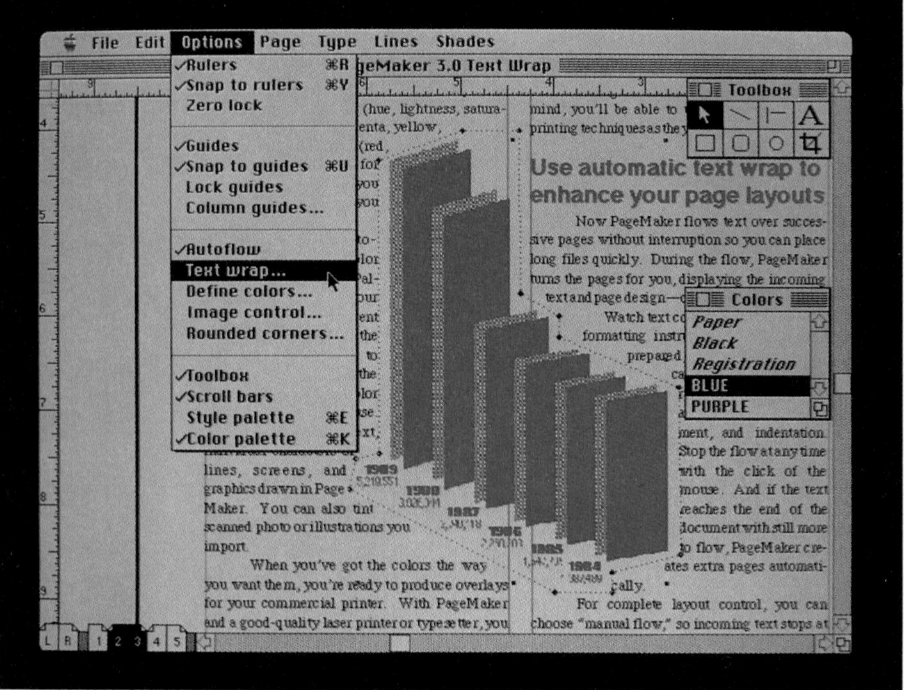

File Edit Options Page Type Lines Shades
✓Rulers ⌘R
✓Snap to rulers ⌘Y
Zero lock
✓Guides
✓Snap to guides ⌘U
Lock guides
Column guides...
✓Autoflow
Text wrap...
Define colors...
Image control...
Rounded corners...
✓Toolbox
✓Scroll bars
Style palette ⌘E
✓Color palette ⌘K
geMaker 3.0 Text Wrap
Toolbox
Use automatic text wrap to enhance your page layouts
Colors
Paper
Black
Registration
BLUE
PURPLE

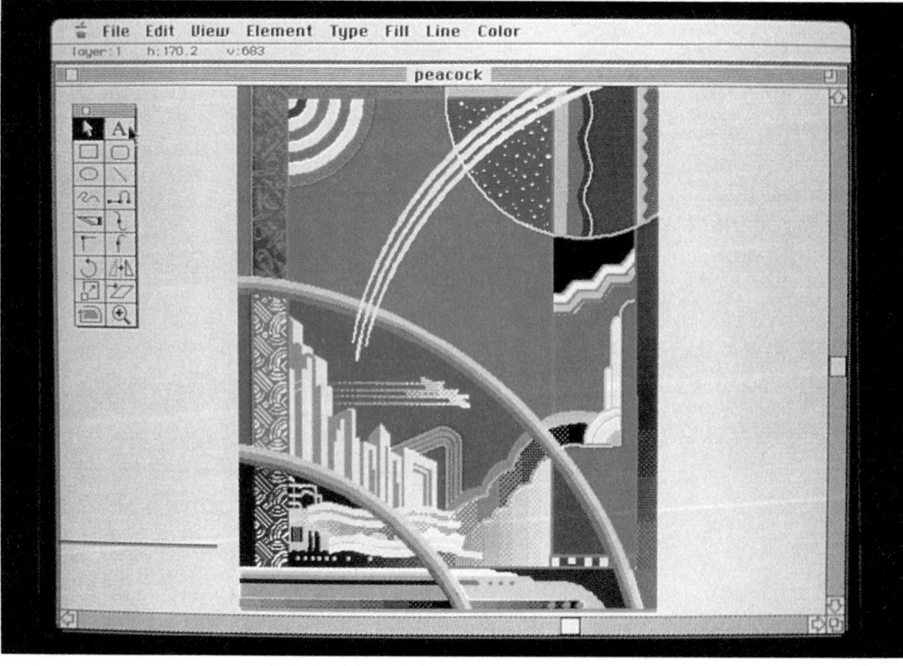

File Edit View Element Type Fill Line Color
peacock

Figure 7-10 Aldus' Pagemaker program for desktop publishing (top) and its Freehand program (bottom), which facilitates the creation of artwork, allow users to take advantage of Macintosh output capabilities. (Courtesy Aldus)

Ease of Use

The typical IBM PC or IBM PC-compatible microcomputer user in a large company uses the microcomputer less than an hour a day and works with only one or two applications. The typical Macintosh user commonly uses five or six applications. Why the difference? Because the former find it too difficult and time-consuming to learn additional applications. A consistent graphical user interface does make a difference.

offers Multifinder (a proprietary operating system that allows multiple application programs to be resident in memory and active), A/UX (a version of UNIX), HyperCard (a toolkit that helps users to create, customize, and use information using text, graphics, video, music, voice, and animation), and other system software. Claris, a wholly owned subsidiary of Apple, was established in 1987 to develop, market, and publish application software for Macintosh and Apple II microcomputers.

Apple's recent progress in corporate environments is attributable mainly to its Macintosh II and Macintosh SE lines of computers introduced in March 1987—just one month before IBM announced its PS/2 family. Like earlier Apple machines, these lines are based on the Motorola 68000 family of microprocessors. Full-size (13-inch) color monitors having the same high resolution as earlier monochrome screens are now available.

A 1988 survey of 10,000 leading U.S. corporations showed that 20 percent of them owned Apple computers, 90 percent of which were Macintoshes. Only IBM and Compaq Computer Corporation, with 89 percent and 30 percent respectively, had higher penetration rates. While education and home uses of microcomputers continue to be key to Apple, business uses now predominate.

IBM and Others

IBM, Digital Equipment Corporation (DEC), Hewlett-Packard, Honeywell, NCR, and other well-established computer manufacturers had developed desktop business computer systems in the 1970s. However, they had not marketed those systems primarily through consumer- and small-business-oriented retail dealerships. They were not promoting their products through ads in daily newspapers and multimillion-dollar prime-time TV commercials. Today that's changed.

IBM announced its first entry into this field, the IBM Personal Computer, or PC, in 1981. Based on the 16-bit Intel 8088 microprocessor, it had 40K of ROM, from 16K to 256K of RAM, and up to two built-in $5\frac{1}{4}$-inch floppy-disk drives. The system ran under the control of *PC-DOS,* an operating system developed for IBM and the IBM PC by Microsoft. Microsoft retained the right to market similar software for other machines—the result is *MS-DOS,* often referred to as the industry-standard operating system for 16-bit microcomputers.

IBM announced its first entry into this field, the IBM Personal Computer, or PC, in 1981.

In 1983, IBM announced the IBM PC XT, an expanded version of the PC having 128K of RAM, one 320K $5\frac{1}{4}$-inch flexible-disk drive, and one 10-megabyte $5\frac{1}{4}$-inch hard-disk drive in a basic configuration. Next came the IBM PC AT, based on the 32-bit Intel 80286 microprocessor. These systems were aimed primarily at small and medium-sized businesses or business units, and at professionals. (See Figure 7-11.)

The widespread acceptance of the IBM PC family stimulated the development of literally thousands of application programs, system utilities, and other software that runs in

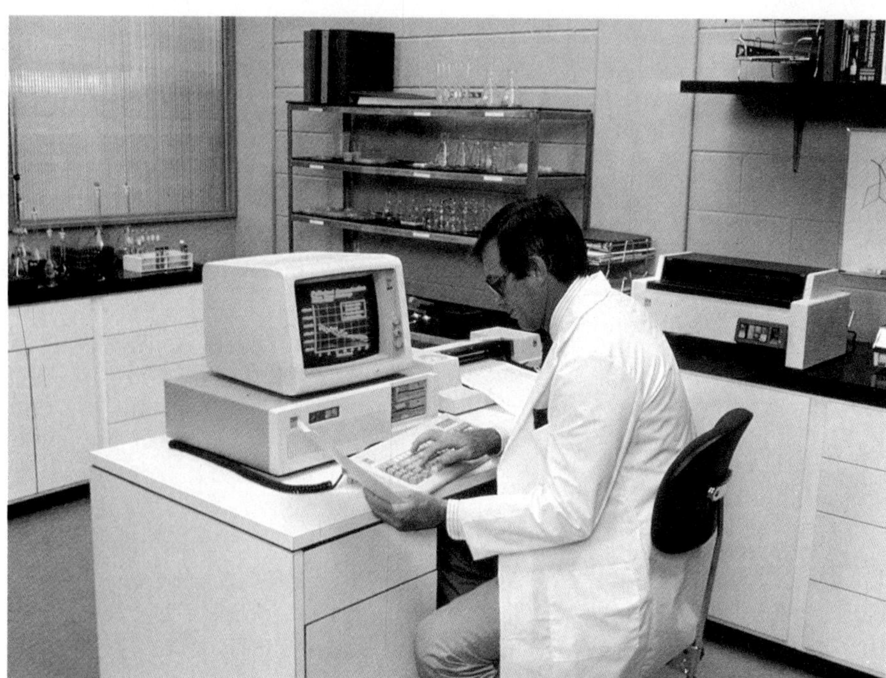

Figure 7-11 **The IBM PC AT and numerous AT-compatible machines are used in offices, plants, and laboratories worldwide.** (Courtesy IBM Corporation)

PC-DOS and MS-DOS environments. Numerous vendors are marketing memory boards, disk drives, printers, and other hardware for use with IBM PC's. Still other vendors are marketing IBM PC-compatible systems commonly known as *clones.* In 1981 Rod Canion, a Texas Instruments engineer, joined with two associates to form Compaq Computer Corporation. He led the company to quick success by producing compact, high-performing, IBM PC-compatible micros at competitive prices and by establishing a loyal dealer network. (See Figure 7-12.) As we saw earlier, Compaq ranks second only to IBM in placing its micros in U.S. corporations.

In April 1987, IBM gained worldwide attention when it announced its new line of personal computers, the IBM Personal System/2 (PS/2). Included were: two low-end models (replacements for the IBM PC and IBM PC XT); two heavier-duty 80286-based models (replacements for the IBM PC AT); and a high-end 80386-based Model 80. All machines used $3\frac{1}{2}$-inch disks rather than the $5\frac{1}{4}$-inch disks in common use. All but the low-end machines had a new internal bus architecture, referred to as the Micro Channel. DOS 3.3, a new release of the PC-DOS operating system announced at the time, can be run on the machines so application programs written for earlier IBM PC's can be used (but they must be transferred first to $3\frac{1}{2}$-inch disks). However, existing expansion circuit boards supporting additional memory, hard-disk drives, high-resolution displays, printer controllers, modems, and local area network (LAN) connections to IBM PC's and PC-compatibles cannot be used with PS/2 machines that have the Micro Channel architecture. Operating System/2 (OS/2), a complex operating system developed jointly by IBM and Microsoft, was to be available later. (See Figure 7-13.)

Figure 7-12 Powerful Intel 80386-based micros such as the Compaq Deskpro/386 are meeting user's computing needs within small and medium-sized businesses and within the world's largest corporations. (Courtesy Compaq Computer Corp.)

Meanwhile, AT&T, Data General, DEC, Hewlett-Packard, Honeywell, NCR, Unisys, Wang, Xerox, Zenith, and a host of additional U.S., European, and East Asian firms have introduced personal computers. Indeed, the list of firms now marketing microcomputers seems almost endless. Like Compaq's high-end machines and IBM's high-end PS/2s, many of these microcomputers are relatively powerful 32-bit machines aimed primarily at professionals in business, as discussed below.

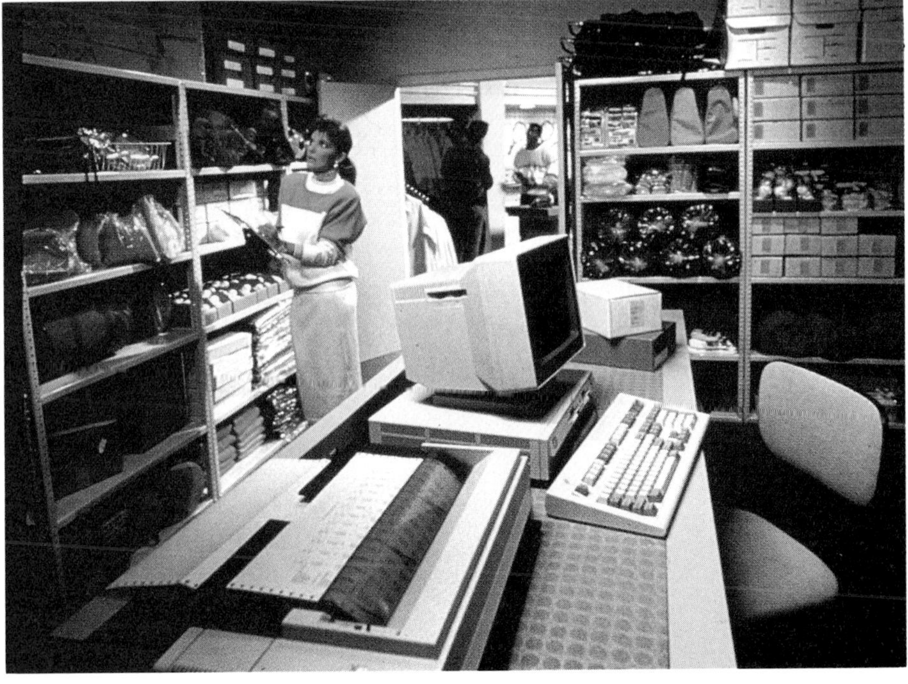

Figure 7-13 Desktop computers with capabilities that match or exceed those of early mainframes are handling the day-to-day business operations of many companies. (Courtesy IBM Corporation)

WORKSTATIONS

Many microcomputer systems are developed *for use by* individuals, but they are not *marketed to* individuals. Instead, they are marketed to persons acting on behalf of a business or other organization. The organization pays the bill. The microcomputer is used in the Tampa office, at a desk in the Shipping Department, and so on. Of course, the "personal computers" we discussed above are also used in these ways, but the computers we are talking about here are marketed primarily as *office computers, desktop computers,* or *workstations.*

Some of these microcomputer systems operate as standalone units for small businesses or for specific user departments within larger organizations. The systems are capable of handling payroll, inventory control, accounts receivable, billing, and other common business applications. (Look again at Figure 7-13.)

An attorney who has access to an office computer can file extensive data on completed cases, and then retrieve that data in seconds if needed. A doctor or dentist can keep patient and supply records up-to-date. Small contractors and instant-printing shops can quickly compile bids for jobs. Financial analysts are using electronic spreadsheet programs to do financial analysis and to obtain answers to "what if" questions on which company product development and marketing strategies are based. (See Figure 7-14.)

Before 1987, desktop computers were different from workstations. The former were used by millions to do word processing, spreadsheet analysis, and business management. The latter were used by a relatively small number of engineers and scientists to do "real work" like seismic analyses, computer-aided design, and three-dimensional modeling. Now that's changing.

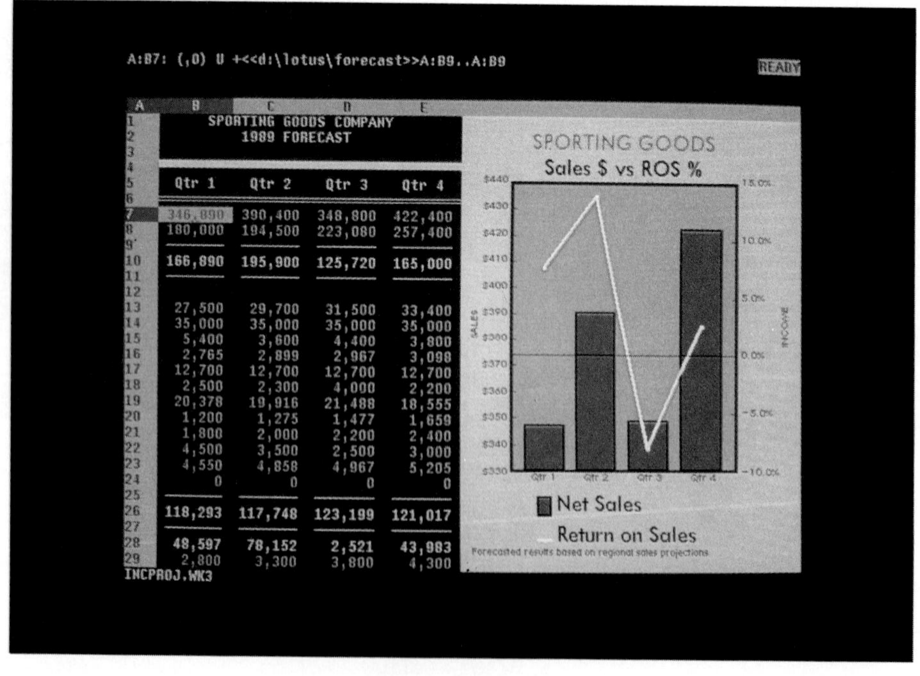
A:B7: (,0) U +<<d:\lotus\forecast>>A:B9..A:B9
READY
SPORTING GOODS COMPANY
1989 FORECAST
Qtr 1 Qtr 2 Qtr 3 Qtr 4
346,890 390,400 348,800 422,400
180,000 194,500 223,080 257,400
166,890 195,900 125,720 165,000
27,500 29,700 31,500 33,400
35,000 35,000 35,000 35,000
5,400 3,600 4,400 3,800
2,765 2,899 2,967 3,098
12,700 12,700 12,700 12,700
2,500 2,300 4,000 2,200
20,378 19,916 21,488 18,555
1,200 1,275 1,477 1,659
1,800 2,000 2,200 2,400
4,500 3,500 2,500 3,000
4,550 4,858 4,967 5,205
0 0 0 0
118,293 117,748 123,199 121,017
48,597 78,152 2,521 43,983
2,800 3,300 3,800 4,300
INCPROJ.WK3
SPORTING GOODS
Sales $ vs ROS %
Net Sales
Return on Sales

Figure 7-14 A desire to take advantage of the capabilities of the Lotus 1-2-3 electronic spreadsheet program has led to the purchase of desktop computers in many companies. (Courtesy Lotus Development Corporation)

The microprocessors in many desktop computers are as powerful as those used in many workstations. The graphic capabilities of desktop computers are nearing those of workstations. The fundamental distinctions between operating systems and other software that runs on the machines has started to blur. UNIX—and the scientific and engineering applications written for it—used to be found only on workstations. Now versions of UNIX are used widely on desktop computers. Techniques that alleviate the memory constraints of MS-DOS, and that allow multiple programs to run concurrently even in MS-DOS environments, are gaining acceptance. Perhaps most important, the prices of workstations have decreased significantly. For example, Sun Microsystems, an aggressive leader in this area, offered its RISC-based SPARCstation 1, rated at 12.5 MIPS (millions of instructions per second), with 8 megabytes of RAM, in April 1989 for $12,995. Twenty-one months earlier, the Sun-4 Model 200, a less powerful, 10-MIP, RISC-based workstation, with 8 megabytes of RAM, had been introduced at $39,900. (See Figure 7-15.)

Before 1987, desktop computers were different from workstations. . . . Now that's changing.

As impressive as having one's own workstation may be, at first use, many users of standalone systems soon experience a strong desire to access data that isn't available on their systems. For example, an engineer may know that the results of certain motion studies conducted last month are available in a mainframe database, if only he could access that database from his workstation. As another example, installed desktop computers can serve as nodes in a

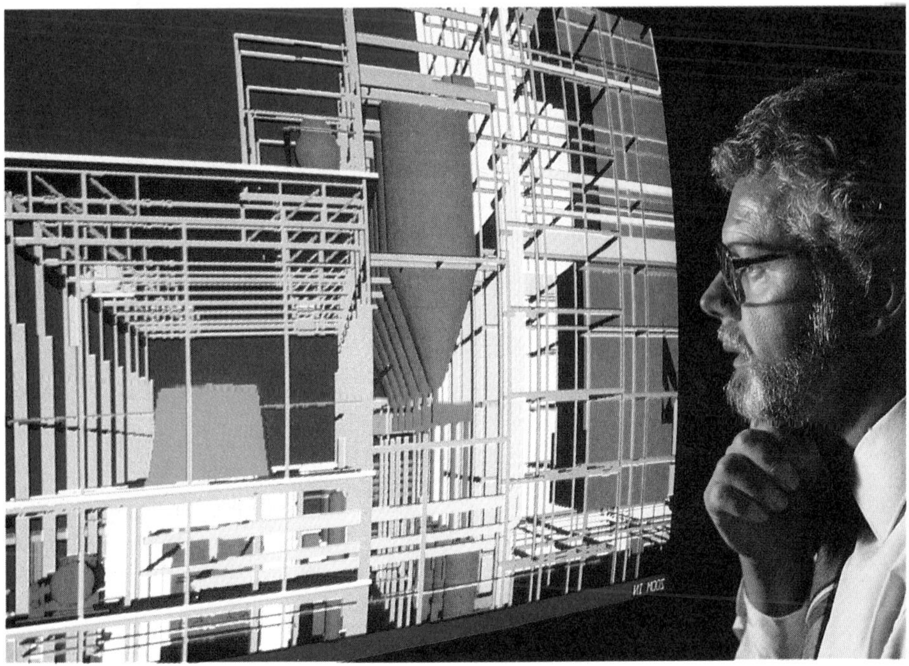

Figure 7-15 RISC-based workstations with high-resolution three-dimensional graphic capabilities are assisting in projects such as the design of environmentally clean fossil-fuel power plants. The benefits are better products in less time at less cost. (Courtesy Bechtel Corporation)

PLAY BALL!

Lap-top portables, IBM Personal System/2 (PS/2) microcomputers at all 26 American League and National League ballparks, and IBM medium-sized computers at Major League headquarters in New York's midtown Manhattan—together, these machines form the backbone of a Major League Baseball Information System that's used daily, all season long.

During each game, a home-team employee records every at-bat on a lap-top portable. The data is stored on floppy disks and transferred to an IBM PS/2.

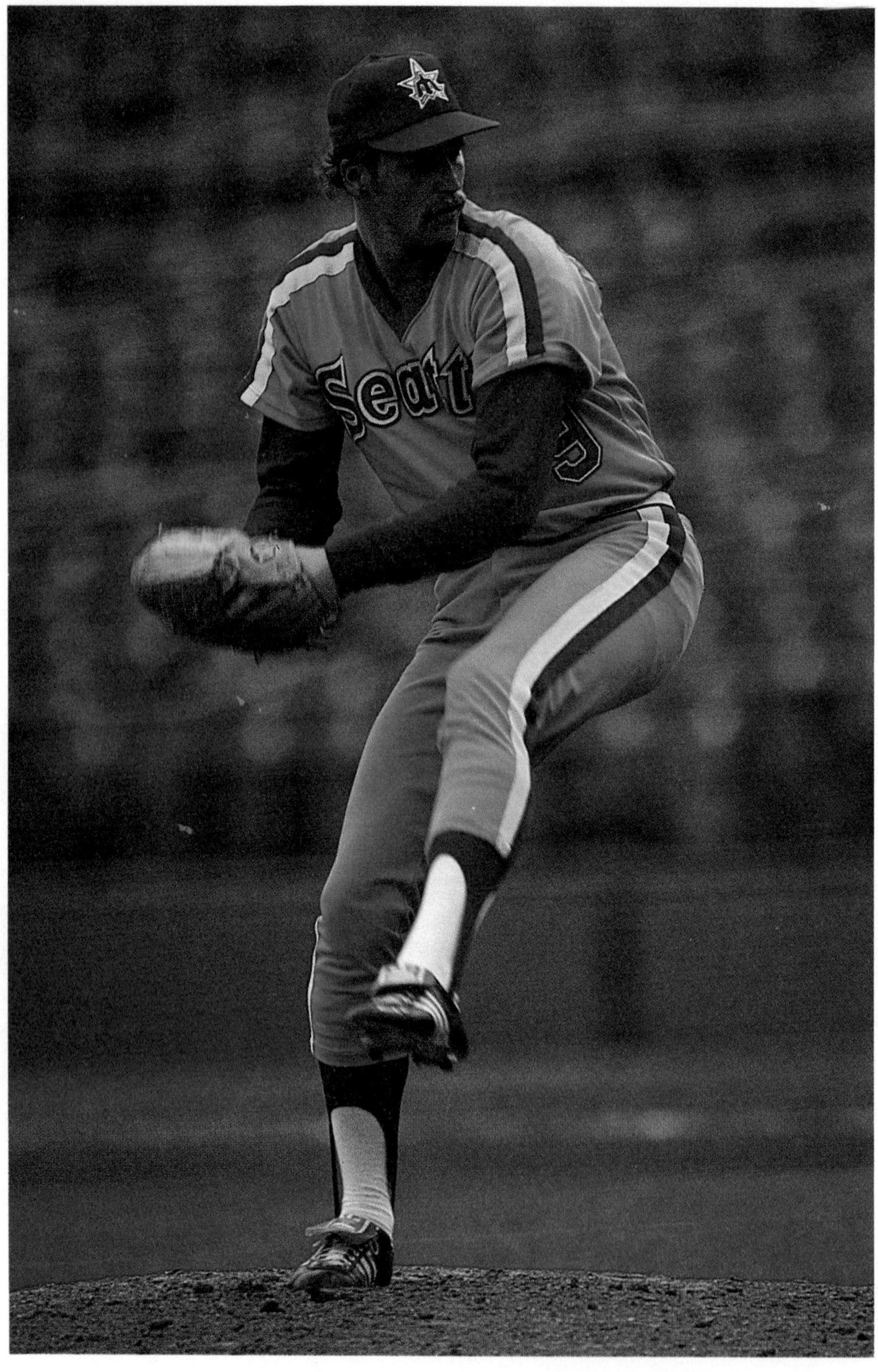

The PS/2 then transmits the data via communication lines to Major League headquarters.

The next morning, each team receives updated data in 320 different statistical categories, ranging from the Mets' record in night games on artificial turf to the Giants' team batting average against lefthanders.

The software produces an inning-by-inning, batter-by-batter summary of each game from the data transmitted. It provides a detailed box score with fielding totals and pinch-hitting results. This information is available to the media as well as the teams from opening day through the World Series in October. *(Photo courtesy Focus on Sports)*

vast intracompany communication system, or *local area network (LAN)*. Executives, administrative staffs, and field personnel can use the network to exchange up-to-the-minute business information via electronic mail facilities.

Vendors and in-house information system organizations are responding to these user needs in various ways. Firms such as Novell and 3Com offer local area networks that allow hundreds of micros from different manufacturers to be interconnected. Other communication vendors offer micro-to-mainframe links. Even Apple, DEC, and IBM are emphasizing techniques that allow users to integrate their micros together with mainframes in corporatewide information systems. (We'll say more about communications in Chapter 13.) Careful analyses of the user requirements to be satisfied and well-thought-out plans are essential in such environments.

A Word to the Wise:

DON'T TAKE ON ANOTHER SMALL COMPUTER WITHOUT LOOKING AT THE BIG PICTURE.

Selecting A Microcomputer

At some time you may shop for a microcomputer. You may want it for yourself, for your home or your own business, or for a large organization by whom you're employed. We've mentioned several factors you should consider as you shop.

One is cost. From just what's been said here, it should be clear that you can spend from less than a hundred dollars to several thousand for a micro. Furthermore, vendors' list prices and current "street prices" are never the same. What do you really need?

Hardware is a second factor. Again, we noted earlier, that microcomputers differ in word size, processing speed, and storage capacity. Perhaps more important is the fact that you're not just buying a microcomputer—you're buying a microcomputer system. You must consider not just the processor but also I/O and secondary-storage devices. If you just want to keep track of inventory, a low-cost dot-matrix printer that can produce reports for internal use may be adequate. If you want to prepare memos or newsletters, a laser printer may be a better choice. If you are buying a microcomputer for home tasks only, two flexible-disk drives may provide the secondary storage you need. For business use (even at home), you're likely to find that a hard-disk drive is required.

That leads us to another point: When shopping for a computer, you can't just think of the present. You must also think of the future. A system with 640K of RAM may meet your current data-processing needs. Can you attach additional memory modules later, when you want to do more?

When shopping for a computer, you can't just think of the present. You must also think of the future.

Never underestimate the importance of software. Many enthusiastic owners of computers have received rude awakenings: "I bought this computer to handle the weekly payroll and customer billings. I can't make it do either!" A first step here is to find out what programs are available for use with the systems you're considering. Will they accept your data as input? Will they produce the kind of output you want? If the system supports MS-DOS or UNIX, a number of application programs that run in that environment may be available. Compare the price, performance, and functions of the programs you're considering. Investigate the track record of each developer or supplier with respect to product, quality, product updates, and customer support. Be sure the developer of the software you select is well-financed and likely to be around for awhile.

A second step concerning software may be to find out how easy (or hard) it is to write new programs for the systems you're considering. What programming languages can be used on each system? Equally important, how easy (or hard) is each system to use?

Often the main factor determining how easy it is to use a system is not the system itself, but rather the documentation available for it. As mentioned earlier, some systems provide a programmed HELP facility. The printed documentation that tells how to use the system must be understandable and complete as well as accurate.

Finally, for the system as a whole, as well as for specific programs as noted above, don't overlook reliability and maintenance considerations. If you are buying a computer for home use, you want it to work. A "problem" may be a hardware error, a software bug, or a procedural mistake on your part. You need someone who can assist you. It's frustrating to wait minutes or hours for the answer to a question. It's frustrating to have to put the whole system back in your car and return it to the store. It's even more frustrating to have to mail an apparently failing part across the country and wait weeks to learn what's wrong or even to hear whether or not the part arrived at its destination.

Today's organizations depend on their information systems to carry out basic business operations. Many of the information systems include terminals, personal computers, and workstations. Today's organizations can't afford to have their systems inoperable ("down") for even short periods of time. Today's users won't tolerate being unable to use their personal computers and workstations. When a failure occurs, service personnel must be readily available to find the cause of the failure. Repairs or replacement parts must be readily obtainable.

What'll You Have?

There are microcomputers for different kinds of people having different kinds of needs. We don't think everyone should drive the same kind of car or wear the same kind of running shoes. Why should everyone use the same kind of computer?

Finding Out What's Available

As a prospective buyer or user of a microcomputer system, how can you find out more about them? Today, you and other prospective buyers can shop for and purchase complete systems or system components in any of several ways. The existing distribution channels for these products can be grouped as follows:

- Direct sales forces
- Retail outlets
- Mail-order houses
- Value-added resellers (VAR's)

Firms such as IBM, DEC, Apple, and Tandy are selling their microcomputers through direct sales forces. Some, like Tandy with its Radio Shack Computer Centers and consumer electronics stores, also use retail outlets. You may find what you want at Computerland, Businessland, Egghead, or at any of a wide variety of computer specialty stores. Such stores provide a nonthreatening environment in which anyone can learn about computers. (See Figure 7-16.) They not only stock hardware and/or software for immediate purchase, but also demonstrate systems, assist in configuration planning (so that you can be sure the pieces you select will work together as a system), and give application assistance. The only "dumb" question is the one you want the answer to, but don't ask.

Most of the stores carry a wide variety of personal computing magazines. *InfoWorld, PC Week, PC World,* and *Personal Computing* are popular. Some stores carry introductory books on computing, microprocessors, programming, and the like. Many product vendors provide both tutorial and reference materials. The materials may be in soft-copy or hard-copy form.

The first computer trade mart opened in Chicago in January 1981. Others, such as the Dallas Infomart, have followed. (See Figure 7-17.)

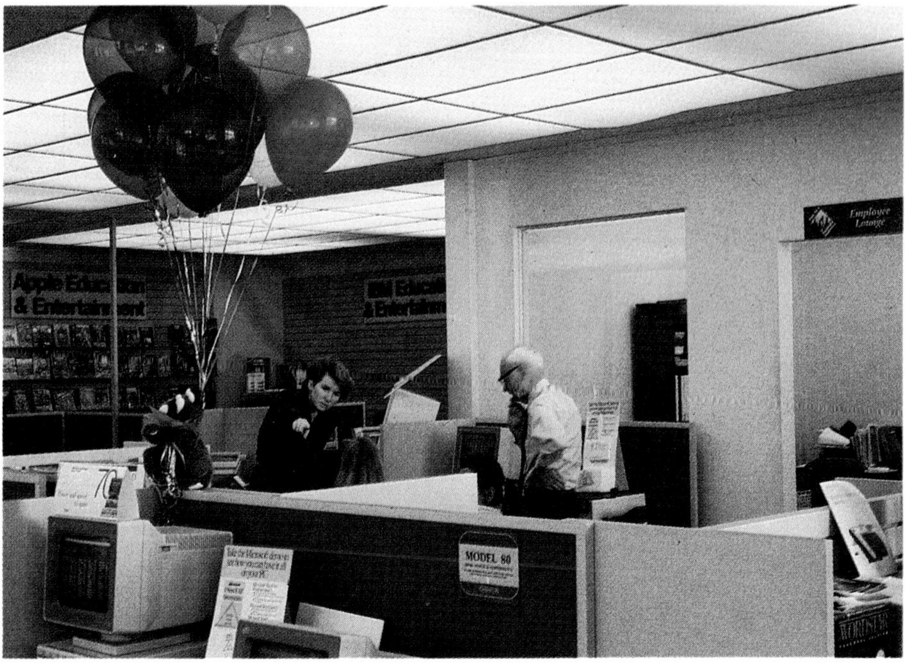
MODEL 80

Figure 7-16 Computer browsers and serious shoppers gain insights and product information from store employees, in-store materials, and other customers at retail and in-house corporate computer stores. (Courtesy Mark McKenna)

Figure 7-17 **Modeled after London's Crystal Palace (the most successful exhibition hall during the Industrial Revolution), the Dallas Infomart offers one-stop shopping to buyers and sellers of microcomputers.** (Courtesy Infomart, Dallas, Texas)

Some industry watchers liken these marts to year-round trade shows. To vendors they offer the potential for increased visibility of products, qualified leads, and cost effectiveness that's not achievable with a direct sales force because of the vast number and geographic scattering of potential buyers. To buyers they offer the opportunity to see many vendors' products, ask questions about the products, view demonstrations, and even get "hands-on" experience. Buying decisions can be made after all the facts have been gathered with relative ease in a relatively short time frame.

Mail-order houses such as 800 Software or 47th Street Photo offer microcomputers, other hardware, and software at bargain prices. Because they avoid the overhead of a direct sales force or of store fronts, their operating costs are lower. You may learn of them by reading their ads in magazines or daily newspapers or by talking with other potential buyers and users.

Value-added resellers (VAR's) are increasing in importance as microcomputer systems increase in capability and in perceived complexity. Some VAR's focus on specific vertical application markets such as pharmacists or corporate legal counsels; the VAR's put together comprehensive application solutions for their target markets. Other VAR's develop proprietary software for use with existing machines or system software from other vendors. Still others provide customized application development or support services.

Computer clubs and user groups are springing up everywhere. Some have been formed under the sponsorship of specific vendors or computer stores. Others are just neighborhood enthusiasts who have computer interests in common. Electronic bulletin boards are a source of practical information for many home computer users. You can find out about them through your friends or through people you meet while computer shopping.

Today, there are microcomputer shows just as there are national computer conferences for vendors and users of mainframes. At these shows, you can see the latest equipment in action, talk to the vendors, and obtain a wealth of product-related literature. The schedules for these shows are published widely. Attend one. You'll meet many interesting people and learn a lot about computers.

CHAPTER SUMMARY

1. A wide range of computers exists. They can be grouped into the categories of microcomputers, minicomputers, and mainframes. The boundary lines between these groups are not clear and are continually moving.

2. A microcomputer consists of a microprocessor together with chips to provide timing circuitry, control memory for instructions, read/write memory for use as temporary storage, and interfaces for input and output.

3. The smallest microcomputers for individual use are handheld, or pocket, computers. Many ready-to-run programs are available for them. Ordinary cassette tapes serve as storage media on some models.

4. Above the handheld micros in size are lap-top portables. Some are notebook-sized but others are larger. Like handheld micros, they are powered by batteries. They have many uses.

5. In broadest terms, a *home computer* is any computer used in a home. About 70 percent of computer use in the home relates to office work brought home, a business that's run out of the home, and personal or household business. The remaining use is for education and entertainment.

6. The first personal computers were marketed in 1975 as ready-to-assemble kits for hobbyists. In 1976, Commodore Business Machines announced its PET, the first ready-to-use, fully assembled microcomputer.

7. Tandy Corporation and Apple Computer were early vendors of personal computers. Both have continued to expand their product lines, offering personal computers that can be used in businesses as well as in home and education environments.

8. IBM, DEC, Hewlett-Packard, Honeywell, NCR, and other well-established computer manufacturers now also market machines they call *personal computers.* Some are used in homes. Others are used by individuals in businesses. Compaq ranks second only to IBM in placing its micros in U.S. corporations.

9. Some microcomputers are developed for use by individuals but they are not marketed to individuals. Instead they are marketed as office computers, desktop computers, or workstations to persons acting on behalf of a business or other organization. Some operate as standalone units. Others operate as nodes in local area networks or are connected via micro-to-mainframe links within corporatewide information systems.

10. When shopping for a microcomputer, not only cost but also hardware, software, documentation, reliability, and maintenance should be considered. Users' present and future needs must be taken into account.

11. Prospective buyers may shop for, and purchase, microcomputer systems and system components from vendors' direct sales forces, retail outlets, mail-order houses, and value-added resellers (VAR's).

12. Microcomputer product information is available from a wide variety of sources. Among them are computer stores, personal computing magazines, books, vendor publications, computer clubs, user groups, and microcomputer shows.

DISCUSSION QUESTIONS

1. Support or refute the following statement: "An electronic calculator is really a small computer."

2. (a) What are some factors we can use to categorize computers?
(b) What makes classification difficult?

3. Describe the hardware components of a microcomputer system.

4. Support or refute the following statement: "Software is less necessary on a microcomputer system than on a large computer."

5. Show how the terms *handheld computer, home computer,* and *personal computer,* as used in this chapter, are related.

6. Discuss the advantages and disadvantages of today's lap-top portables from a potential business user's point of view.

7. For what types of applications are lap-top portables likely to be especially suitable?

8. Discuss potential business and nonbusiness uses of computers in your home environment.

9. Trace computer developments at either Radio Shack or Apple Computer. Attempt to show what user needs are being taken into account as you do so.

10. What influence has IBM had on the personal computing industry?

11. Discuss how microcomputers are being used in today's office environments.

12. Show how the workstation market is evolving.

13. Suggest factors that either a college student or a business executive should consider when shopping for a microcomputer.

14. What are some ways that persons in your locality can find out about microcomputers?

15. Discuss, in detail, one application of microcomputers with which you have come in contact. What's good or bad about it? How might it be improved?

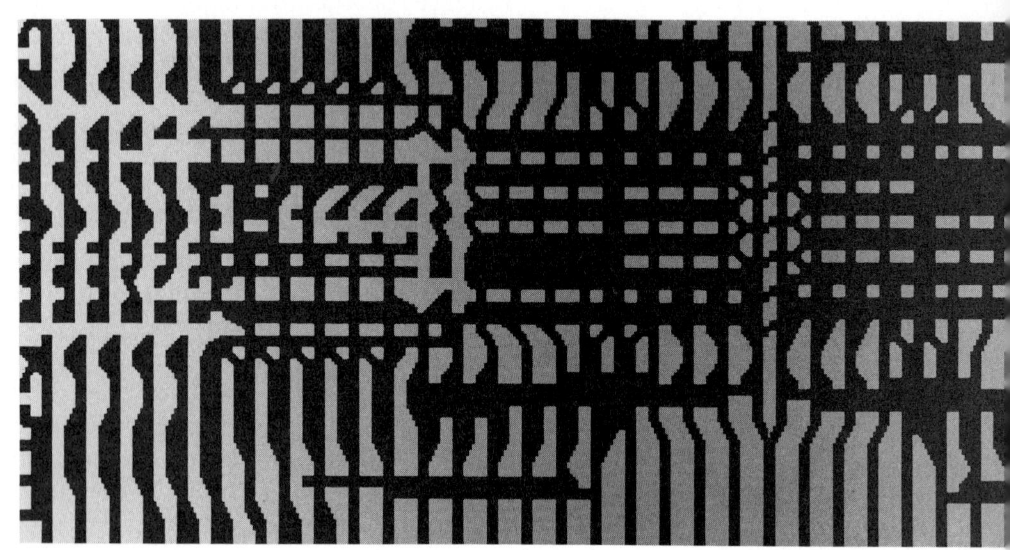

8 System Analysis and Design

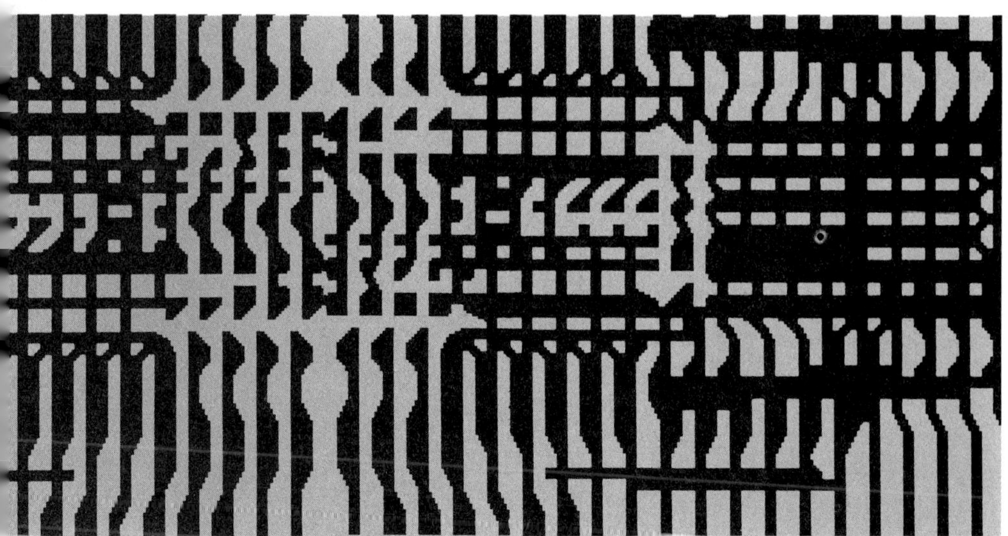

IN THIS CHAPTER

What Is a System?
The System Development Cycle
The Participants
Problems and Opportunities
Preliminary Investigation
Detailed Investigation
Using CASE Tools
System Design
Design Review
Project Review

Suppose you're driving a car in downtown Chicago. You're not quite sure how you got there, but that's not where you want to be. You have tickets to a Chicago Bears game at Soldier Field, or you're due at your aunt's home in Evanston in an hour. How do you get there? Aha—there's a map in the glove compartment. But it's a map of Detroit. It won't help you decide whether to go straight, turn left, or turn right when the traffic signal changes.

Take another example. You've been searching some time for new floor mats for your car. Now you come upon some quite accidentally while shopping for a bike light. The mats look acceptable. "How much are they?" you ask. The salesclerk tells you they come in brown, red, and beige. "How much are they?" you ask. The salesclerk tells you they stay in place well. "How much are they?" you ask. The salesclerk tells you they resist heat, tar, oil, and even strong chemicals. The mats may be great, but you leave the store without them.

Now consider a third example. You've just received an attractive, colorful brochure. There's a photo of Spanish dancers on the front. Inside, there are photos of old missions. You see the words *Mexico* and *Old Mexico.* Looks interesting! Unfortunately, the major portion of the brochure is written in Spanish, and you can read only English.

What can we conclude from these examples? For starters:

- Information is of little or no value if it doesn't meet the user's need.
- An answer is likely to be ignored if it fails to address the question it's supposed to answer.
- Information that is not understandable to the user is not usable information.

Notice that none of these examples involves a computer. However, the observations we've just made apply to computerized situations as well as to noncomputerized ones.

A computer is useful only if it's put to work on the right task. It may do a job in 10 microseconds, but if nobody wants the job done, who cares? It may be ready to accept sales data as input, but if the data-entry procedures aren't understandable, or don't exist, how can anyone provide the data to it? It may produce a 20-page inventory report, but if the report doesn't tell stock clerks, shipping personnel, or managers what they need to know, who gains? If the needed information is there, but it's buried on page 17, who finds it?

A computer is more expensive than many of the tools that an individual or organization acquires, but it is a general-purpose one. Many users can benefit from its help. The major objectives of system analysis and design are to understand fully user problems or information needs, and to plan how the computer can be used in addressing them (if, indeed, the computer can or should be used). An individual or an organization cannot afford to fail in meeting these objectives. The tasks of system analysis and design are crucial to the successful use of computers. And the successful use of computers is increasingly vital to success in today's fast-moving, competitive business environment.

System analysis and system design are discussed in this chapter. The use of ***computer-assisted software engineering (CASE) tools*** in system development is described. The purpose of the chapter is not to teach you to be a system analyst or system designer. Its purpose is not even to teach you how to do system analysis or system design. You can't learn those skills by reading one chapter of a book. The purpose of this chapter is to help you understand what system analysis and design are, and why they are important. Many people can benefit by learning some of the tools and techniques used by system analysts. Administrators, accountants, auditors, and users of computer-based systems need to understand how their roles relate to that of the analyst. Managers need to understand the steps involved in determining how to make the best use of computers within their organizations.

What Is a System?

The term *system* is not an unusual one; you probably hear or speak the term daily. Each of us depends directly on one continuously functioning system; it's a biological system: our human body. Our cars have ignition systems. When we attend classes, teach courses, or work in the dean's office, we're part of an educational system. To talk to friends across town, in a nearby state, or across continents, we use a telephone system. Businesses have accounting systems, payroll systems, inventory-control systems, and so on. Again, notice that some of these systems do not involve computers at all. Others may or may not. A *system* is simply a group of interrelated elements that work together to perform a specific task or function.

In Chapter 1, we looked at several examples of data-processing systems. In Chapter 2, we looked more closely at systems that involve computers. The business systems we just mentioned are, of course, data-processing systems. Increasingly, these systems are computer-based. A single computer or many computers are involved. Again, it's important to understand:

1. Each system consists of *interrelated elements.*
2. The elements *work together.*
3. The elements share a common objective: *to perform a specific task or function.*

The System Development Cycle

In this chapter, we direct our attention first to the over-all task of system development. You can assume that the system is a data-processing system. The steps of system development are referred to collectively by various names: the system development cycle, the system life cycle, the system development life cycle, and so on.

Figure 8-1 shows one way we can group the steps of the system development cycle into phases. No hard-and-fast rules determine how many phases there are, or how many steps make up each phase. Some development groups establish four phases, as shown here. Others define 10 or 20 phases. Some define 10, 20, or more steps in each of the phases. We view system development in this way to set up a general framework within which we can proceed. Our ultimate objec-

Figure 8-1 The steps of system development can be grouped into phases, each of which is followed by a checkpoint; together they form a system development cycle.

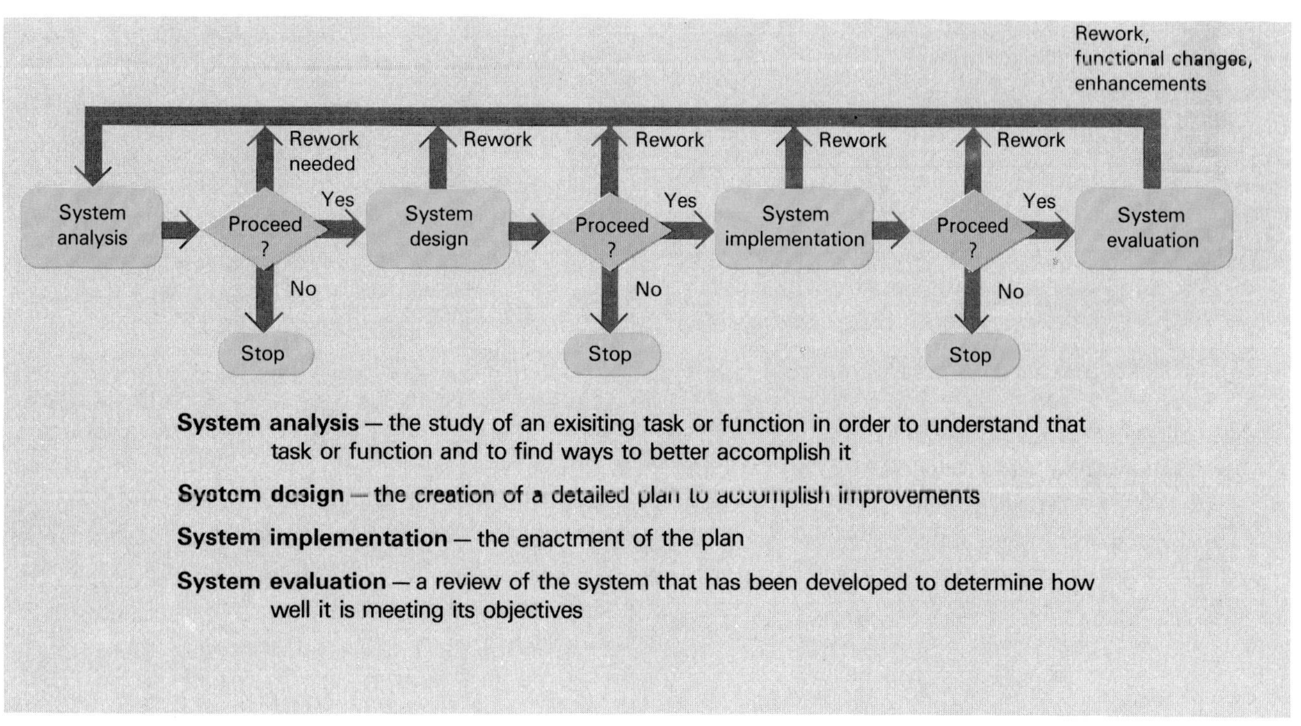
Rework, functional changes, enhancements
Rework needed
Rework
Rework
Rework
Rework
System analysis
Proceed ?
Yes
No
Stop
System design
Proceed ?
Yes
No
Stop
System implementation
Proceed ?
Yes
No
Stop
System evaluation
System analysis — the study of an exisiting task or function in order to understand that task or function and to find ways to better accomplish it
System design — the creation of a detailed plan to accomplish improvements
System implementation — the enactment of the plan
System evaluation — a review of the system that has been developed to determine how well it is meeting its objectives

Please
RETURN

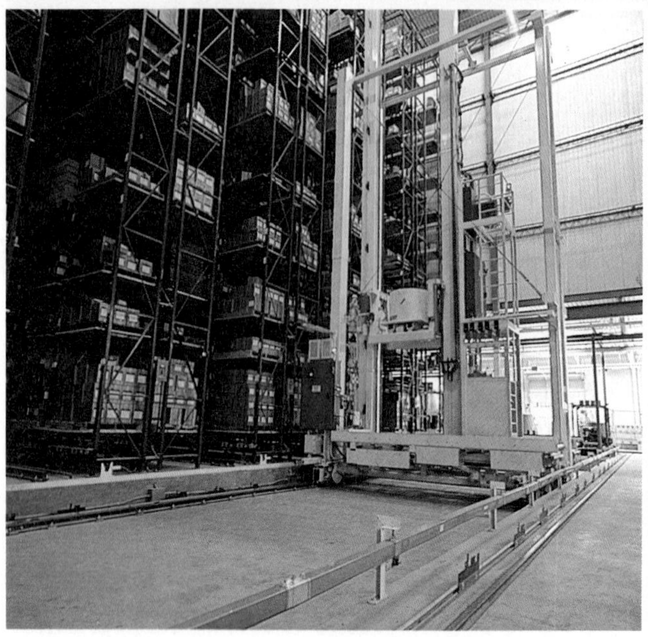

SYSTEMS IN OUR EVERYDAY WORLD

Systems differ widely, but they all have one characteristic in common: Each system involves a group of interrelated elements working together to perform a specific task or function. Our human body, a library card catalog, an automated materials storage and retrieval system, and the vast telephone network we use daily are not as dissimilar as we might think. Some systems—but not all systems—involve computers. *(Photos courtesy [top left] Ray Hunold/Photo Researchers; [top right] George E. Jones III/Photo Researchers; [bottom left] Burroughs Corporation; [bottom right] AT&T Information Systems)*

Following the Rules

There is no single set of rules to be followed by all analysts when approaching a problem, any more than there is a single set of rules for, say, writing a research paper or report. There are, however, valuable procedures that most analysts follow much of the time.

tive is project control. As a part of our plan, we can agree upon the amount of time to be allocated to each phase. At the completion of each phase, we can check our progress.

Even if we plan very carefully, we may gain additional insights during system development. For example, at the checkpoint following system design, a plant manager may see that he needs quarterly reports of absence and overtime by product or by function as well as by department. While doing the detailed design of department variance reports, a programmer may discover that travel data not currently being collected must be recorded in each department's operating expense file. Making even minor changes without considering what has been done previously can cause errors or have unanticipated effects elsewhere. Therefore, as Figure 8-1 shows, a return to the system analysis phase may occur at any point in the system development cycle.

The last phase in the system development cycle—system evaluation—often leads to follow-up actions. Few if any systems are "finished" when this phase is completed. The need for corrections, a desire for improvements, and new requirements often lead to another round of system development.

The Participants

Several persons or groups may take part in system development. The *user* may be an individual, manufacturing plant, distribution center, small business, or whatever, that has a problem or an opportunity to be investigated. Putting this another way, the *user* is the client for whom system development is done. User personnel are the only ones who know what they (and the systems of which they are a part) really do. They are the only ones who really know their requirements. Therefore, they must participate in system development. They can best perform the quality-control function because they have a self-serving interest that things be done right. After all, if a new or changed system results, they are the ones who will live with it.

Information system personnel are consultants or contractors to the user in system development. They may be members of an in-house information system staff. They may be hired from outside the organization. Sometimes the initial steps of system development are done by in-house analysts but products or services needed later are obtained from outside sources. In any case, the information system personnel apply their specialized knowledge to the system development effort. They also make recommendations. Final decision making is the user's responsibility.

Final decision making is the user's responsibility.

Usually, the information system personnel who participate in system analysis and design are called system analysts, system designers, or programmer/analysts. A *system analyst* works with the user to understand the problem or opportunity being investigated. He or she documents findings and develops alternatives. If some or all of a system is developed in-house, a *system designer* creates a detailed plan, or specification, for the system. This specification translates the *what* of the system into the *how*. Not uncommonly, system analysts do both system analysis and system design. There may be no one who holds a position specifically designated as that of system designer.

Small firms often employ one or more *programmer/analysts*. They may be full-time employees of the firm, or they may be hired on a contract basis. These persons have system analysis, system design, and programming responsibilities.

As the system development activity proceeds, outside groups, such as vendors of hardware and software being considered, may be contacted. In-house system support groups, such as data-processing operations personnel or financial analysts and accountants, may become involved. User and information system management must be kept fully informed of progress and problems.

Finally, we should consider the one-person situation, the individual who has purchased or is contemplating purchasing a microcomputer for business, home, or personal use. Obviously, this individual is the user. Such a user may seek analysis and design help. Usually, the software needed to address the user's problem or opportunity can be purchased. Alternatively, a contract programmer or software firm may be paid to develop it. A few brave, data-processing-knowledgeable, or optimistic individuals may tackle system development alone.

On Using Tools

Give a child a hammer and everything's a nail. Treating a computer as a solution-in-search-of-a-problem (instead of a tool to solve an already-identified problem) can only lead to similar mistakes.

Problems and Opportunities

Usually, the impetus for system development comes from the user community. The manager of a large supermarket may be concerned because the lines of customers awaiting checkout are too long (how can we speed up the checkout process?) or too short (how can we attract more customers on weekdays?). A regional sales manager may complain that the sales-by-salesperson reports she receives are incomplete or too slow in coming. A large wholesale distributor may perceive that additional revenues could be generated through short hauls if only better records of scheduled long hauls and of truck repair and maintenance activities were available.

Usually, the impetus for system development comes from the user community.

Sometimes the impetus for system development comes from the data-processing or information system staff. For example, a system analyst may learn of an optical scanner that appears to offer major opportunities for productivity increases in sales-order entry. Do the potential benefits of the productivity increases outweigh the equipment and training costs that would be incurred? If a laser printer were acquired, how much faster could customer bills be produced and readied for mailing? What effect would the faster billing capabilities have on the length of time before payments were received? How would these changes affect the cash position of the company?

In today's environments, individuals and organizations alike are faced with increasing costs and limited resources. Both problems and opportunities must be ranked by priority. If you're a personal computer user,

How Important Is Planning? (Or, What Do System Development and Chess Have in Common?)

You have to think ahead a few moves to win the game.

you may decide to pursue an idea further or to forget about it (at least for awhile). In a more formal environment, some requests for system development will be rejected. Others will be deferred. Still others will be assigned to system analysts for preliminary investigation.

Preliminary Investigation

The next step in system analysis is the preliminary investigation. If the term *preliminary investigation* seems awesome, replace it with the simple phrase *initial look.* That's what we're talking about here. The analyst decides whether the problem or opportunity that has been identified warrants further analysis. In effect, the analyst conducts a brief *feasibility study* of the proposed project.

In taking this initial look, most analysts work primarily through interviews. Managers should not speak for subordinates, and subordinates should not speak for managers. In talking with managers, for example, the analyst may find that not just the sales-by-salesperson report but rather all the sales reports are incomplete and late. In talking with sales personnel in the field, the analyst may learn that the results of daily sales activities are to be phoned in by 10 each night. Maybe that's not happening. Maybe the calls are being made, but at times when the sales data is not complete. In talking with the home-office staff, the analyst may find that the data recorded during the calls is hard to understand later. The volume of data to be keyed into the computer may exceed that which the staff can handle. Programmed input validation procedures may be inadequate or totally lacking.

One outcome of the feasibility study should be a determination of the scope of the problem. For example, the investigation may show a weak link between the sales force and the home office. If the problem is a broad one, all user activities and procedures associated with providing input may need to be addressed. Selected programs within the sales reporting system may need to be reviewed (and then rewritten or changed). If the scope of the problem is even broader, it may require an analysis of all managers' requirements for sales information, and of all existing or new systems that may be needed to provide this information.

In most cases, the analyst supplements interview findings by simple observations of how user activities are currently being done. He or she may also examine existing user documents. Both techniques will be applied in greater depth later if a decision is made to proceed to the next step of analysis, a detailed investigation.

At the conclusion of the initial look, the analyst usually prepares a 1- or 2-page *feasibility report.* The report documents the time period of the investigation and the persons or groups consulted. It describes the true nature and scope of the problem as determined by the analyst's findings. It also contains a recommendation as to whether or not the project should be pursued and, if so, how best to proceed.

Detailed Investigation

The information gathered during the preliminary investigation is the jumping-off point for the detailed investigation. Unless the scope of the problem or opportunity is very small, a project team consisting of both information system personnel and users is formed. The temptation to plunge immediately into fact-finding will be strong, but this temptation must be resisted. Specific objectives for the detailed investigation must be formulated, agreed upon, and documented. The specific tasks needed to achieve the objectives must be identified. A timetable reflecting all tasks should be charted in a form visible to all team members. (See, for example, Figure 8-2.) In a large project, several levels of detailed planning (and several levels of charts) may be required.

The existence of a problem or an opportunity indicates that there is at least a perceived difference between what is and what ought to be. To fully understand this difference, most project teams conduct the detailed investigation as a four-part process:

- Fact-finding
- Data analysis and evaluation
- Estimating costs and benefits
- Preparation of a system proposal

Fact-Finding

During fact-finding, analysts direct their attention to users and to all aspects of the activities within the scope of the matter being investigated. How many people key in order data? How long does keying an order take? Are there peak order periods during the day, week, or month? Is work checked? If so, how? Is the keying activity centralized or done at various locations? What are the working conditions (temperature, light, noise, furniture, and so on)?

Notice that these questions are alike in one very important way: They get at the facts. An analyst may gain valuable insights during fact-finding, but objectivity should be maintained throughout the investigating and recording processes. By maintaining objectivity, the analyst is better able to separate what's being done in what way because of habit or tradition from what's being done in what way because of actual requirements.

By maintaining objectivity, the analyst is better able to separate what's being done in what way because of habit or tradition from what's being done in what way because of actual requirements.

The methods commonly used in fact-finding are interviews, questionnaires, observations of work, and studies of user documents. As you might expect, each method has its advantages and disadvantages.

Interviews must be well planned in advance. Each of the participants should know the objectives of the interview beforehand and prepare for it. Persons are sometimes willing or eager to express orally information that they are unwilling to put in writing. The interviews provide opportunities for information system personnel to meet and establish rapport with users. Users learn of their own role in system development activity.

A questionnaire is a useful technique for obtaining the same kind of information from a large number of users. It may be the only practical method of obtaining information from users at several locations within a large organization. For best results, both the questionnaire and the questions on it should be short. Users

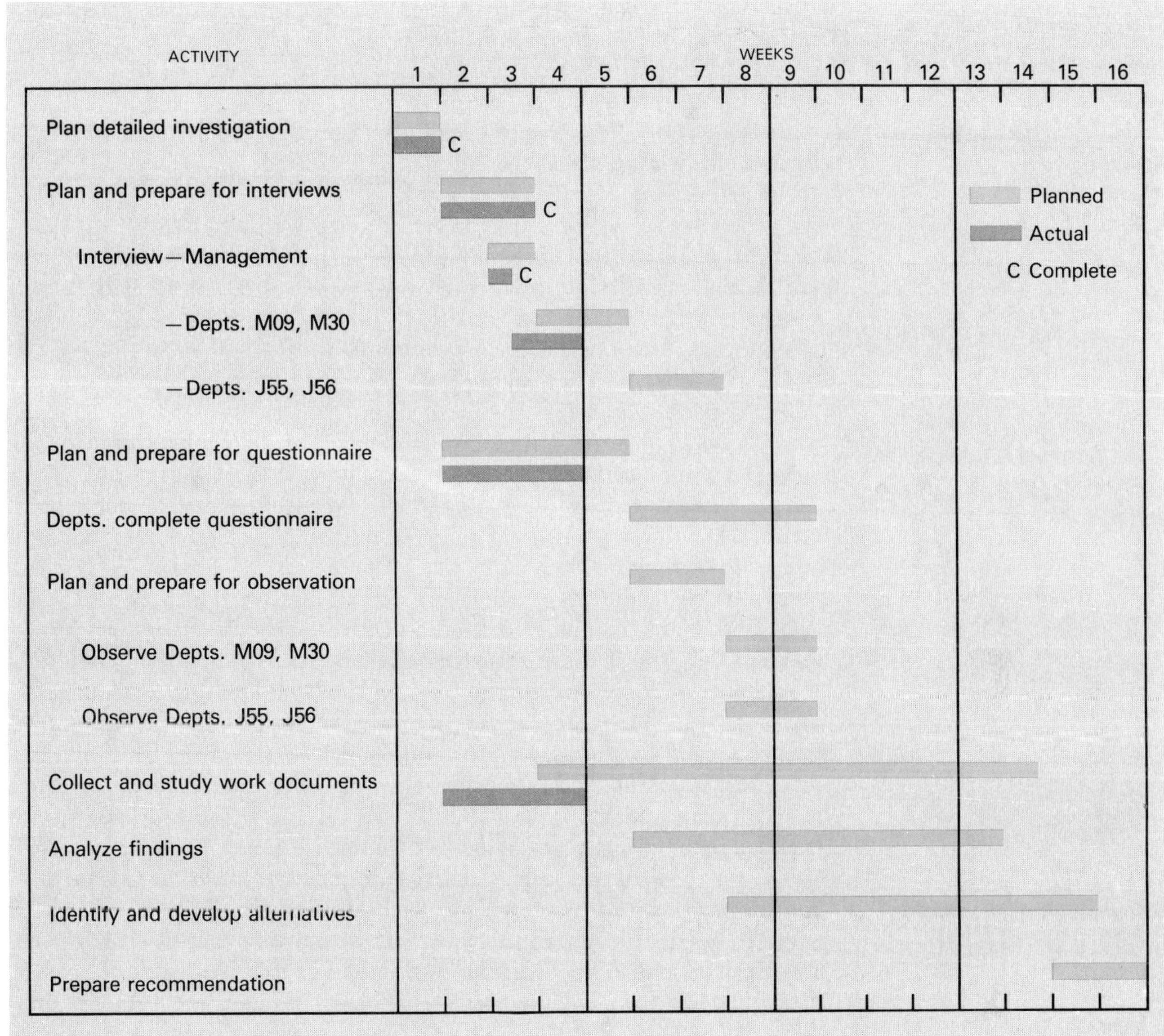
ACTIVITY
WEEKS
1 2 3 4 5 6 7 8 9 10 11 12 13 14 15 16
Plan detailed investigation
C
Plan and prepare for interviews
C
Interview—Management
C
—Depts. M09, M30
—Depts. J55, J56
Plan and prepare for questionnaire
Depts. complete questionnaire
Plan and prepare for observation
Observe Depts. M09, M30
Observe Depts. J55, J56
Collect and study work documents
Analyze findings
Identify and develop alternatives
Prepare recommendation
Planned
Actual
C Complete

Figure 8-2 **Both the planned and actual progress on tasks of a detailed investigation are shown on this Gantt chart.**

should be told in advance that it's coming. A deadline for return of the questionnaire must be stated clearly in a cover memo.

In most if not all companies, there's a difference between the formal organization (as shown on an organization chart) and the informal organization (who knows whom, who contacts whom to get work done). Differences also exist between the documented standards and procedures for work activities and how work is actually done on a day-to-day basis. Therefore, some facts can be learned only by observation. Some observations are made incidentally. For example, while waiting to interview an administration manager, an analyst may see five employees standing in line to use a single copying machine. This observation may have significance later. Some observations are intense studies of, for example, what causes a manufactured part to be classified as defective, and how defects are found (or not found) by quality-control inspectors. In general, observations are made to determine (1) the work flow, (2) who does each task and how, and (3) the physical arrangement of the work area. Users should know that observations are being made and why, even though they may not be told exactly when they will be observed.

Many of today's organizations are buried in paperwork. Analysts who attempt to review the user's written documentation may be in similar danger. Copies of existing standards, written procedures, and operating manuals should be obtained. Before studying them, the analyst should determine whether and how each is used. Factors such as the number of copies made, who receives copies, and where and how long copies are kept may be informative. Existing, completed forms used in day-to-day operations should be analyzed. (In contrast, a study of blank forms may be misleading. Some forms or portions of forms may never be used.) Finally, the day-to-day memos and other correspondence used for communication throughout the organization contain much information.

Data Analysis and Evaluation

As facts are collected, they must be recorded, organized, and evaluated. Information system personnel begin to extract, from this wealth of data, the significant factors that help them identify the user's system requirements. Increasingly, analysts are using *computer-assisted software engineering (CASE) tools* to organize and analyze data with computer help. (See below.)

Some analysts organize their findings on *data flow diagrams (DFD's).* The DFD's may be conducted manually or using a CASE tool. As Figure 8-3 indicates, a DFD is a

Increasingly, analysts are using computer-assisted software engineering (CASE) tools to organize and analyze data with computer help.

simple picture of what's occurring in a portion of the user's existing system or organization. Each box is a "source" or "sink," a point at which data enters or leaves. Each circle (also called a *bubble*) is a process performed on the data that flows into it. The numbers within the bubbles are reference numbers; they do not show the sequence of the processes. The parallel lines represent files, or collections of data retained for reference. If the process depicted by a bubble is actually made up of several subprocesses, the DFD may be "leveled." Another DFD is created to show in greater detail what is going on within that particular bubble, or process. In Figure 8-3, bubbles 8 and 9 are likely candidates for expansion.

Through creation and study of these DFD's and of related information collected during fact-finding, the analyst begins making judgments about the virtues and shortcomings of present operations. The analyst may detect task duplication, task overlap, and task inconsistencies. Workloads may be distributed unevenly, creating unnecessary delays. The user's tools and documentation may be inadequate.

Armed with the results of such analyses, the analyst is ready to develop and evaluate alternatives. At this point, the wise analyst reviews

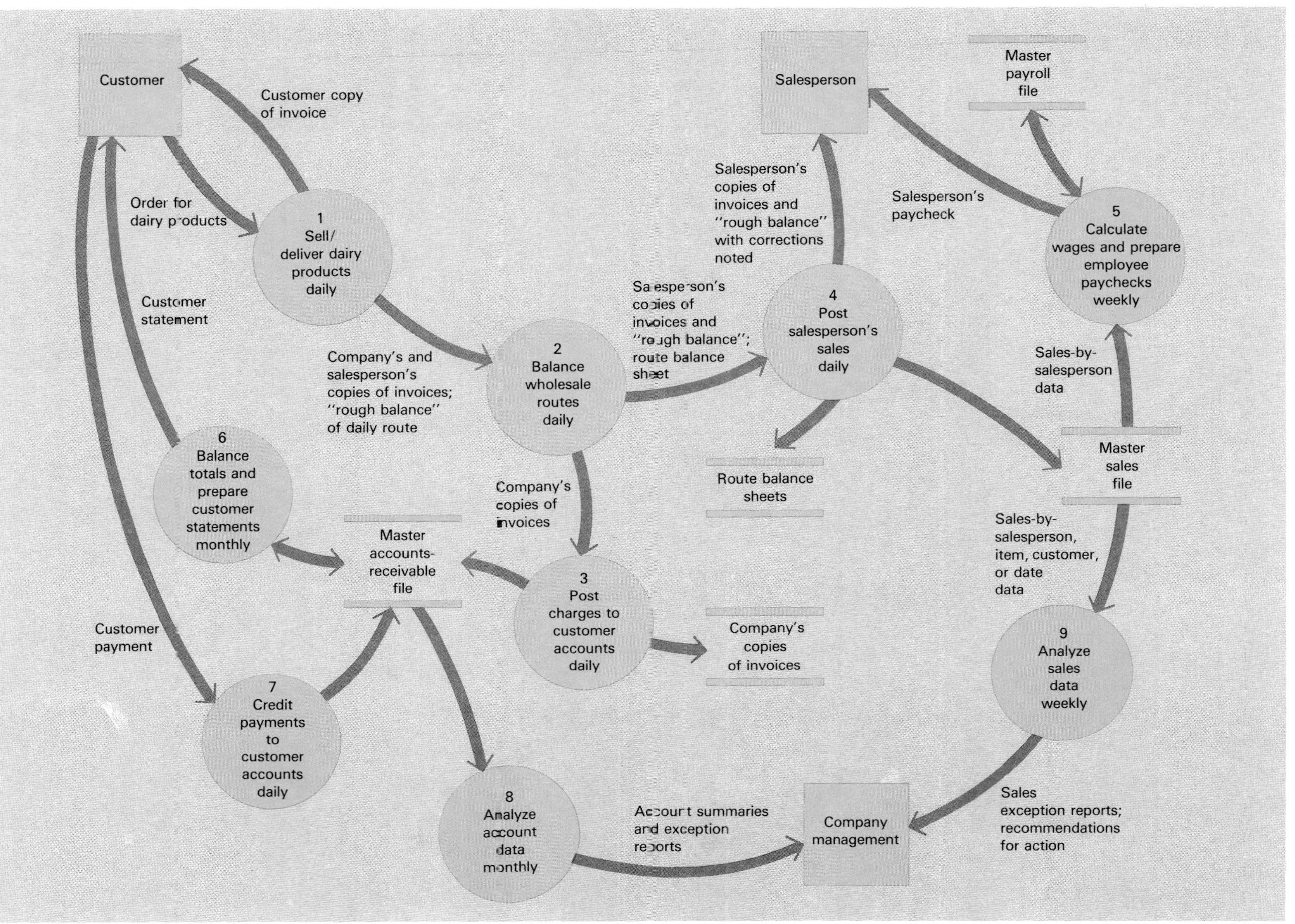
Customer
Customer copy of invoice
Order for dairy products
1 Sell/ deliver dairy products daily
Customer statement
Company's and salesperson's copies of invoices; "rough balance" of daily route
2 Balance wholesale routes daily
Salesperson's copies of invoices and "rough balance"; route balance sheet
Salesperson
Salesperson's copies of invoices and "rough balance" with corrections noted
4 Post salesperson's sales daily
Salesperson's paycheck
Master payroll file
5 Calculate wages and prepare employee paychecks weekly
Sales-by-salesperson data
Master sales file
Route balance sheets
6 Balance totals and prepare customer statements monthly
Master accounts-receivable file
Company's copies of invoices
3 Post charges to customer accounts daily
Company's copies of invoices
Sales-by-salesperson, item, customer, or date data
9 Analyze sales data weekly
Customer payment
7 Credit payments to customer accounts daily
8 Analyze account data monthly
Account summaries and exception reports
Company management
Sales exception reports; recommendations for action

Figure 8-3 Dairy deliveries to customers lead to the processes documented on this data flow diagram for wholesale-routes account processing.

Determining How Much

Many users learn the hard way that a basic problem with project estimates is that they are always too low. Why? Often, the estimates are made at too high a level: (1) The person doing the estimate is a manager without full insight into all the work items that must be done to complete the task; and (2) the estimate is calculated as a single number for the task as a whole without first estimating the time and effort required for each work item.

the agreed-upon objectives for the system development activity. The analyst must also review all constraints. Any recommended changes in staffing, operational (noncomputer-related) tools and facilities, and/or EDP-system components must be in line with the user's budgets or ability to acquire additional funds. The time available for development may be limited. For example, application programs to comply with new government reporting requirements may have to be ready by January 1.

The scope of this evaluation-of-alternatives step varies widely. If the user has no computer system, and at least one of the proposed alternatives is computer-based, equipment vendors may have to be contacted. This step also applies if significant changes or additions to an existing computer system are required. The workload of the existing system and of each proposed system should be projected three to five years into the future. Expandability should be an important criterion.

Details of system design should be left to the system design phase, but major architectural directions must be decided upon—for example, whether sequential processing or direct processing of transactions is warranted and what data entry or data processing should be done at remote locations. These system characteristics are stated as part of the initial programming functional specification (IPFS) for the project.

The possibility that the needed software already exists in package form should be investigated. The use of such packages offers many advantages: fewer in-house development resources are needed, the costs and time needed for development are easier to estimate and control, and so on. Where existing user programs can be used, or can be adapted to the user's newly recognized or changed needs, they should be. There's no merit in "starting over" just to start over. (If you're a microcomputer user, would you choose to write another program like the Lotus 1-2-3 electronic spreadsheet program, just because you didn't initially write it?)

The possibility that the needed software already exists in package form should be investigated.

If a new system is to be implemented, the user will almost certainly be confronted with the task of converting existing data to an acceptable form. For each alternative, the project team must weigh any technical difficulties in this conversion, whether or not data conversion aids can be obtained, and the cost and time required for the conversion.

Whether a data-processing system is manual or automated, users follow certain procedures in preparing input, providing that input to processing, and using output. Users who come in direct contact with the system will have to be trained to use it. Users who indirectly provide input to or receive output from the system will need to be informed of the new or changed system's capabilities.

Estimating Costs and Benefits

Before presenting a system proposal to user management, the project team must assess the costs and benefits of each alternative. Both costs and benefits can be categorized in

HOW SOON DO YOU WANT YOUR PIZZA?

On a typical Saturday night, at a typical Domino's Pizza franchise, from 4000 to 5000 calls for pizza delivery are received. All Domino's franchises promise to make each delivery within 30 minutes of receiving the call or the order is free. Clearly, to accomplish this objective, efficiently running systems are required.

Consider Tidewater Pizza in Norfolk, Virginia, as an example. In the mid-1980s, its 20 or more outlets were run much like other Domino's franchises. Each outlet had a bank of phone lines. Potential customers had trouble locating the outlets that served their particular areas. Each outlet had to staff additional help at peak times to handle the calls. Together the outlets were losing up to 20,000 orders a month. They were also losing customers.

As one step to improve its performance, Tidewater Pizza management authorized the development of a new pizza order receiving and entry system. The major design goals of the system were speed and reliability. By mid-1988 the system was operational. It's known as the Purchase Order Processing System, or POPS. POPS encompasses a centralized phone switching network and custom-designed application software running on a large computer.

Instead of having a separate bank of phone lines for each outlet, Tidewater Pizza now has one toll-free number that's used by all customers. All calls are routed through a Telcom switch that can handle up to 96 calls at a time. The switch can be programmed to vary the call load to match the skills of operators—for example, by routing more calls to faster, experienced operators. It tracks call completion times.

Each operator keys orders as they are received into an order-entry terminal. Each order is routed automatically to the appropriate Tidewater Pizza outlet. Statistics show that most customers get their pizzas within from 20 to 22 minutes. Tidewater Pizza is losing few, if any, sales due to phone line foul-ups.

Furthermore, the system handles more than order entry. It assists Tidewater Pizza management in market and sales analyses. It tracks food costs. The current on-hand inventory of raw materials (peppers, olives, sausages . . .) at an outlet can be determined at any time. *(Photos courtesy Tidewater Pizza, Inc.)*

various ways. A first major cost distinction is between *one-time,* nonrecurring costs associated with the remaining phases of system development and *ongoing* operational costs. At the end of the detailed design step, experienced analysts can estimate the costs for the system design phase with reasonable confidence. However, estimates of costs for the subsequent phases of system development and for day-to-day operations of the resultant system are educated guesses at best. They must be recognized as such and estimated again later when more is known about the project.

Some costs and benefits are *tangible;* they can be identified and measured easily. Others are *intangible;* their value is hard to quantify in dollars and cents. From another point of view, some costs and benefits are *direct;* they are readily attributable to a specific individual, group, or department. Others are *indirect;* they are not incurred as a direct result of user activity. Instead, they are allocated to users on a prorated basis. (See Figure 8-4.)

Figure 8-4 **The costs and benefits of a proposed system alternative may be classified as either tangible or intangible, and as either direct or indirect.**

COSTS/BENEFITS CLASSIFICATION	EDP RESOURCE	EXAMPLES OF NATURE OF COST OR BENEFIT
Tangible, direct	Processor, memory, I/O devices, secondary-storage devices	Purchase, lease, or rental fees, hardware maintenance contracts
	System software, application packages	Permanent license (one-time fee), periodic license (monthly charge), software maintenance contracts
	Tapes, diskettes, paper, other supplies	Purchase ($10–$15 per tape, $2–$7 per diskette, 1¢ per sheet, etc.)
	In-house staff, consultants, contractors, part-time help	Salaries, benefits, recruiting, hiring fees, hourly rates, taxes
Tangible, indirect	The computer system as an entity	Faster billing cycle (bills out 2 days earlier, e.g.), better control of inventory (only a 2-week supply), better control of cash (maximum use of cash discounts at minimum cost)
	In-house training programs, EDP general and administrative (G & A) costs and benefits, other cost-center costs (security, cleaning, etc.) and benefits (environmental control)	Allocated charges based on square feet, number of employees, number of departments, direct expense
Intangible, direct	Equipment availability (uptime), durability, expandability, flexibility (e.g., stock paper and preprinted forms)	Mean time between failures (MTBF), time to repair, field upgradability, latest technology
	Software ease of use, flexibility, corrections, extendibility	Mean time between failures (MTBF), hard-copy and online soft-copy documentation, languages supported, internal design
Intangible, indirect	The computer system as an entity Other cost-center costs and benefits, G & A costs and benefits	Corporate image derived from application of latest technology, opportunity costs and benefits (direct consumer to system interface, access to industry data banks, etc.)

■

A. Calculating the payback period, on the basis of costs

Investment recovered: −$58,000 outweighed by +$74,000

	YEAR 1	2	3	4	5	6
Current system cost	$30,000	33,000	35,000	45,000	47,000	51,000
Proposed system cost	$70,000	43,000	43,000	32,000	20,000	17,000
Investment (−)/Return (+)	−$40,000	−10,000	−8,000	+13,000	+27,000	+34,000

B. Calculating the payback period, considering costs and benefits

	YEAR 1	2	3	4	5	6
Current system cost	$30,000	33,000	35,000	45,000	47,000	51,000
Proposed system cost	$70,000	43,000	43,000	32,000	20,000	17,000
Investment (−)/Return (+)	−$40,000	−10,000	−8,000	+13,000	+27,000	+34,000
Savings through reduction in inventory	$12,000	12,000	12,000	12,000	12,000	12,000
	−$28,000	+2,000	+4,000	+25,000	+39,000	+46,000

Investment recovered: −$28,000 outweighed by +$31,000

Figure 8-5 **The payback period for a proposed system may be calculated on the basis of costs alone (A). If significant benefits are anticipated, both costs and benefits should be taken into account (B).**

Obviously, detailed cost data could consume many pages of a system proposal or many charts of a presentation. Techniques for "netting out" the estimated costs and benefits can be used to provide meaningful summary information. One of these is calculation of the *payback period,* an indicator of when the user's initial investment for the proposed system will be recovered as a result of its greater economy.

The system's payback period can be calculated in any of several ways. Two examples are shown in Figure 8-5. In Figure 8-5A, major costs are considered but benefits are ignored. The costs of the proposed system are subtracted from the costs of the user's existing system on a yearly basis. When the difference between these costs becomes a positive value (during the fourth year, in our example), the user has begun to receive a return. When the total of the positive difference values outweighs the total of the negative difference values, the user has recovered the initial investment.

Figure 8-5B shows how the payback period is calculated, taking into account a major benefit expected from the proposed system: $1000 per month, or $12,000 per year, through improved inventory control. By the end of the fourth year, the user will have recovered the initial investment and be $3000 "to the good." When a major benefit is expected from a proposed system, this way of calculating the payback period may provide better information than a way that looks only at costs. It presents a more complete picture of the situation.

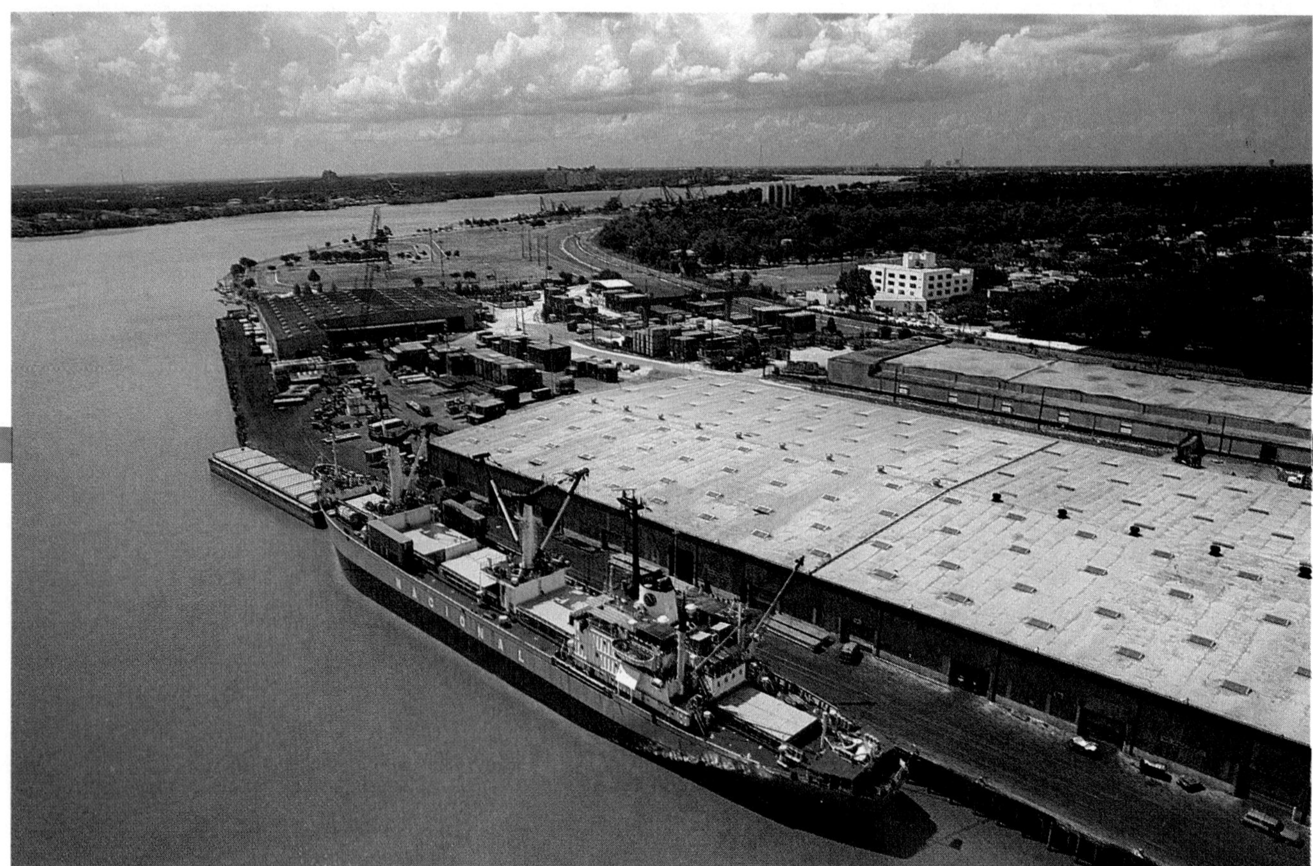

KEEP THE CARGO MOVING

The Port of New Orleans is strategically located at the point of intersection of the Mississippi River and the Gulf Intercoastal Waterway. It is linked to every corner of the United States by six major railroads, 14,500 miles of navigable inland waterways, and the U.S. interstate highway system. About 4000 ships dock at the port each year. Shippers use the port as the hub of a network to distribute cargo nationwide.

In distributing cargo, the saying "time is money" applies. The sooner freight moves on and off the dock, the faster merchants awaiting that freight can receive and distribute it to their customers, and the faster the port gets paid. To speed cargo turnaround, the port authorized the implementation of a system that would both (1) facilitate shipment schedule and billing and (2) speed the government inspection and approval process required in releasing cargo. The McDonnell Douglas Information Systems Group was contracted to serve as the systems integrator.

By mid-1989, major portions of the system, known as Crescent, were operational. A steamship line can dial into the system and electronically submit manifests (detailed lists of onboard cargo) prior to its ship's arrival at port. The Port of New Orleans can then transmit that data to the government agency that must approve the cargo's release—say, the U.S. Customs Service, U.S. Department of Agriculture, or U.S. Food and Drug Administration. Authorities from the agency can be standing by to inspect the cargo immediately upon its arrival. If the agency chooses to forgo an inspection, the agency can grant release of the cargo electronically before the ship even docks at port.

By cutting the time that cargo sits in port, the Port of New Orleans hopes not only to satisfy the needs of its current customer base (shippers) but also to attract additional shippers its way. The efficiencies achieved with Crescent enable it to handle ever-increasing shipment volumes. *(Photo courtesy Port of New Orleans.)*

CASE in Practice

Ramada Inc. is using CASE tools to improve its computerized reservations, international sales, and property management systems. Applications are being developed in two-thirds of the time and with half as many resources as were required before the tools were utilized.

System Proposal

Having done its homework well, the project team now presents the results of its findings in a *system proposal.* In a sense, what the feasibility report is to the preliminary investigation, the system proposal is to the detailed investigation. However, the system proposal is a more formal document. If and when the system proposal is accepted, it becomes a contractual agreement between the information system staff and the user for the remaining phases of the system development cycle.

A system proposal has no standard format. Generally, it begins with a brief summary of the problem or opportunity that initiated the system development activity. The system alternative that the project team prefers is presented in detail. Its estimated costs and benefits, an outline of work, and a schedule for completion are included. Other alternatives that warrant management attention are presented also. The proposal concludes with a clear recommendation to management as to how to proceed.

Before we leave this topic, it's appropriate to point out once again that the steps of the system development cycle do not apply exclusively to large organizations or large-system users. A doctor, lawyer, tax accountant, small business owner, educator, student, or family may recognize a problem or an opportunity that perhaps can be addressed with computer help. Such users (or potential users) need to understand their requirements just as large-system users do. Whether or not a computer-based solution is appropriate can only be determined by investigation. Our discussion here can serve as a general guideline. The "project team" may be the user, or the user with help obtained as the investigation proceeds, or the user and one or more specialists (system analysts) employed to lead the effort.

Using CASE Tools

As we noted when discussing computer use in manufacturing in Chapter 1, business managers facing spiraling labor costs and increasing competition have focused on increasing *productivity* (the rate of finished output per unit of labor input). Initially, tasks on the assembly line, in packaging and shipping, and in inventory control were automated or done in part with computer help. The speed and efficiency with which office tasks such as billing and accounts receivable could be accomplished were enhanced through automation as well. Managers soon realized that the speed and efficiency with which the new or improved data-processing systems needed for automation could be developed (or, rather, the lack thereof) were barriers to additional productivity increases. Not surprisingly, new questions were raised: Can some or all of the steps of system development be automated? Can a computer that helps us design and produce shoes, automobiles, and even other computers also help us design and produce its own programs?

The term *computer-assisted software engineering,* or *CASE,* has been coined to refer to the automation of tools, methods, and procedures used in system development. The products that accomplish the automation are computer programs, referred to collectively as *CASE tools.* They're grouped within two broad categories:

- *Front-end CASE tools* assist in the analysis of user requirements, description of data elements, description of operations (e.g., page sizes and numbers of copies for report printing), and high-level system design (output, input, and file formats, high-level internal program structures, and so on).
- *Back-end CASE tools* convert specifications into machine-executable code, assist in debugging and testing, and/or restructure existing databases and programs (e.g., poorly written COBOL).

Index Technology's Excelerator, Cadre's Teamwork, and Pacbase from CGI Systems are among the better-known front-end CASE tools. Fourth-generation languages such as Focus and RAMIS and application generators such as Telon and Transform Logic—which we discuss briefly in Chapter 10—are examples of back-end CASE tools. By increasing your awareness of all of the steps of system development, you are positioning yourself to make effective use of such tools if they are made available to you in your education or job environment.

Two industry trends have accelerated the development of CASE tools: (1) the increasing use of microcomputers as workstations for software developers, and (2) the increasing use of relational database management systems (DBMS's), which facilitate the development of new application systems. In general, however, the acceptance of CASE has been slower than many of the vendors of CASE tools anticipated. Why? Because so few of the tools work well together as yet, and no one vendor or product provides a comprehensive answer to all of the developers' needs. Furthermore, many user organizations must make fundamental changes to the way they develop systems before they can take full advantage of the productivity, quality, and project control benefits of CASE. As in other areas inside and outside of the business world, such changes are not always welcome. CASE vendors are establishing alliances with other CASE vendors to make their products work together, integrating their products through use of a common dictionary, and documenting their product interfaces so that other tools can access them.

System Design

An artist sketches an office building to be constructed; an architect creates a blueprint; and bricklayers, carpenters, electricians, and others skilled in trades "make it all happen." Similarly, system analysts set the direction for system development; system designers lay out a detailed plan; and programmers, testers, technical writers, and other support personnel implement the plan. An electrician cannot (and should not) work from an artist's rendition. A programmer cannot (and should not) code from the initial programming functional specification or the system proposal. Putting it simply: *a system must be designed.*

How Important Is Good Design?

Doing a poor job on design is like borrowing time at compound interest rates—from the future of your own development organization and from that of the end user. If the end user is doing application development, "organization" and "user" are one and the same.

The Chief Programmer Team

Some or all members of the project team should work on the project during the system design phase. The term *chief programmer team* is often used to refer to the group of information system specialists who carry out the remaining phases of the system development cycle.

The nucleus of a chief programmer team consists of a chief programmer, a backup programmer, and a programming librarian. (See Figure 8-6.) Additional designers, programmers, and technicians are added to the team as needed. Many of them may be specialists. For example, one designer may know the operating-system interfaces to be used by the system under development. Another may be an expert on input and output devices. Generally, a team of from 5 to 9 members is advisable.

The chief programmer may be a lead system analyst, system designer, or programmer. He or she is also the technical manager to whom all team members report. He or she designs the mainline, or control, portion of the system and defines the portions to be designed by other team members. The chief programmer also reviews the work of other team members, oversees the development and integration of all parts of the system, and keeps management informed of the project status.

The backup programmer is involved in every aspect of the system and participates in all important decision making. He or she may carry out special assignments (for example, investigating approaches to recovery of the system), thereby allowing the chief programmer to concentrate on the main line of development.

The programming librarian maintains the records of the project in a *development support library (DSL).* These records are kept in both an internal (machine-readable) form and an external (human-readable) form. Examples of internal records are the job-control statements needed to execute the portions of the system under development, the machine-readable versions of all programs, and test data. Examples of external records are current program listings, historical journals (archives) of all replaced listings, and results of all test runs. As these examples indi-

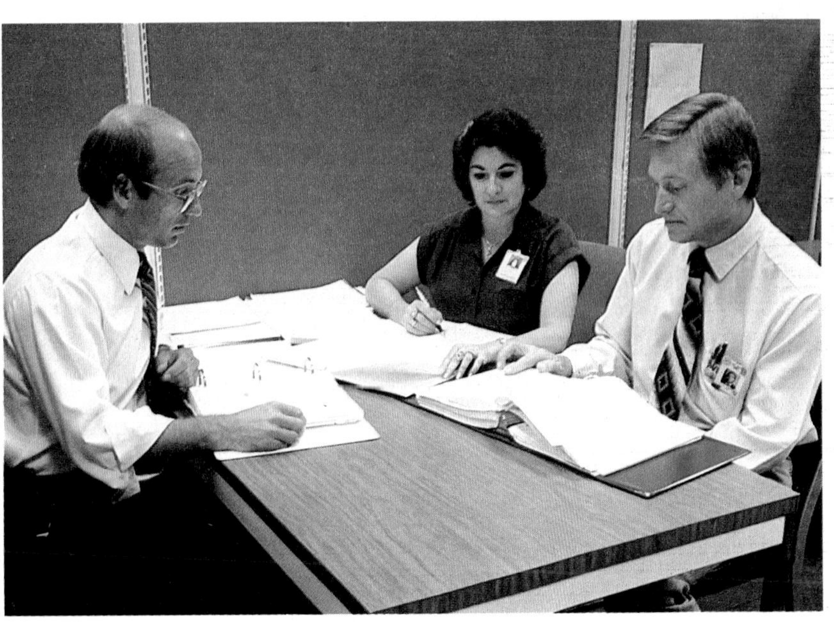

Figure 8-6 To help insure that the system being designed will meet the users' requirements and does not contain errors, the members of a chief programmer team work together to plan and carry out system design activities. (Courtesy Bell Helicopter)

cate, the DSL is established at this point in system development (in some cases, even sooner) and expanded throughout the cycle.

System Flowcharting

Still working from the point of view of the user's requirements, the chief programmer team focuses its initial attention on three basic elements:

- The output that must be provided by the system
- The input that the user will provide to the system
- The processing needed to produce the output, given the input

Notice that these are the three basic elements of any data-processing system, as we first saw in Chapter 2.

A common method of depicting these system elements is to construct one or more *system flowcharts.* Each system flowchart is a graphic representation of the procedures involved in converting data from input media to data in output form. The emphasis is on the media used and the processing or data flow. Little is shown about how the processing will be accomplished. A complete program that will later be designed in detail is often represented by one symbol on a system flowchart.

A typical system flowchart is shown in Figure 8-7. This flowchart describes an online transaction-processing system that automates certain banking functions. Each *process symbol* (▭) represents a computer program. Each *display symbol* (⬭) represents an online printer-keyboard or visual-display unit. In this example, the online units are teller terminals that are part of user workstations at bank locations. The *magnetic-disk symbol* (⌸))represents online magnetic-disk storage. Each *document symbol* (▭) represents a printer. Its operation is initiated by the user and controlled by a program executed by the microprocessor in the user workstation to which it is attached. The *annotation symbol* (⊐) is used to provide comments. The *flowlines* (—) indicate direction of flow. The *communication symbols* (⌁) indicate that some of the user workstations are at branch bank locations, connected to the host computer at the main bank via communication facilities.

Notice that three application programs are included in the system. A bank officer (i.e., user) at a teller terminal can select a stored display-screen format—for opening a checking account or acquiring a money market certificate, for example. The officer can complete the transaction by filling in blanks on the screen under direction of the Complete Customer Transaction program executed by the microprocessor, without even involving the host computer. The officer can print copies of all transactions on the nearby printer if desired.

The Create Format program is also loaded into the internal storage unit of a user workstation and executed by its microprocessor at the request of a bank officer. It allows the officer to create new display-screen or printer formats and to test them interactively before forwarding them to the central computer for inclusion in a shared format library. The texts for preformatted letters—for example, reminders of maturing savings certificates—can be created and stored, customized for a particular usage via a display-screen format, and then printed for mailing.

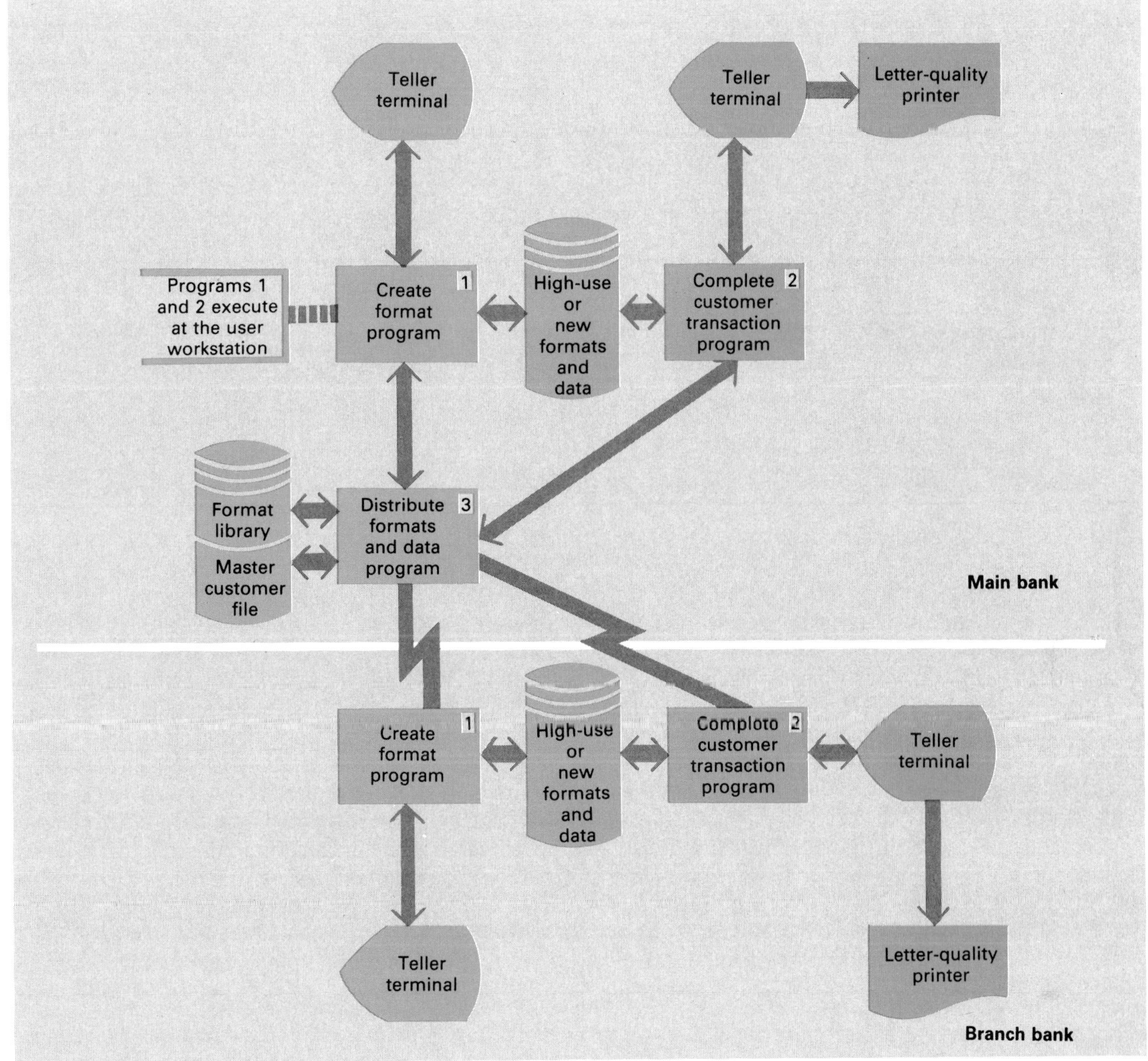

Teller terminal
Teller terminal
Letter-quality printer
Programs 1 and 2 execute at the user workstation
Create format program 1
High-use or new formats and data
Complete customer transaction program 2
Format library
Master customer file
Distribute formats and data program 3
Main bank
Create format program 1
High-use or new formats and data
Complete customer transaction program 2
Teller terminal
Teller terminal
Letter-quality printer
Branch bank

Figure 8-7 Teller terminals (some of which have letter-quality printers attached) are used to enter banking transactions in the system described by this system flowchart.

A large library of stored formats and relatively permanent data about existing customers (that may be useful in completing forms) is kept on high-speed disk storage devices at the host computer location. The Distribute Formats and Data program is executed by the host computer to receive, store, retrieve, and/or send formats and data to/from user workstations, on request. Thus, the bulk of the formats and data within the system are kept at the main bank's central computer facility.

Output, Input, File Design

To insure the user's requirements are satisfied, attention must be given during the system design phase to the

CG&E

CG&E

FOCUSING ON SERVICE

In October 1986, Cincinnati Gas & Electric Co. (CG&E) vowed to make customer service its top priority. As part of the effort, CG&E undertook a comprehensive multimillion dollar overhaul of its customer information system. A new Customer Systems department was formed. Customer surveys were conducted to determine how CG&E service activities should be expanded or changed to better meet customer needs.

Personnel within the Customer Systems department spent a full year in analysis and design before any coding was begun. The group agreed to use Teamwork, a multiuser CASE tool from Cadre Technology, Inc., as an aid in applying structured design techniques. The scope of the project was estimated at 180 person years. Coding on selected modules of the system was started in the summer of 1988. Completion of the project was targeted for 1990.

The new system is designed to handle up to 1.5 million customer records stored in relational databases managed with the help of DB2, IBM's relational database management system for use on large mainframes. Customer inquiry, billing, accounts-receivable, and other traditional business data-processing functions are handled within the system. The system also extends automation into new areas of service. For example, all service vehicles are being equipped with personal computers that can be used to communicate directly with software running on a large mainframe. If a customer calls to request service, the request can be transmitted immediately to an appropriate service request vehicle. Through such means, CG&E's goal of providing top-quality service to its customers can become a reality. *(Photos courtesy Cincinnati Gas & Electric Co.)*

contents and formats of all system outputs. Exactly what printed reports are needed, how often, and what should be on them? Should a particular report be sequenced by due date or person responsible? If an interactive system is being designed, display-screen formats must be created and tested. Designers can use any of several CASE tools to create mockups, called *prototypes,* for user review as early as possible.

Each data item provided as input and each item of information produced as output is a data element. During the system design phase, a *data element dictionary* should be set up in a machine-readable form (again, CASE tools can help). Whenever a designer identifies a new data item to be provided as input or produced as output, the name and description of the item should be added to the dictionary. Keeping the dictionary current helps to insure that the same data item isn't unknowingly handled by several programs with a different name or definition each time. It also helps to insure that when the output of one program is to be provided as input to another program, the designers of both programs define the data correctly.

Designers can use any of several CASE tools to create mockups, called *prototypes,* for user review as early as possible.

Once the data element dictionary is set up, the internal files and/or databases within the system can be designed. The formats of user data records within the system's transaction and master files should be described. Designing sequential files that will meet the needs of several application programs is a challenge. Designing files that can be accessed directly in ways that provide fast responses to user inquiries, or designing user databases, is an even bigger challenge. (We'll say more about these tasks in Chapter 12.)

If the decision has been made to purchase or lease the software (rather than develop it in-house), acquisition processes for the software must be initiated now, just as for the hardware. Contracts may have to be worked out and approved. In these cases, detailed program design, coding, and testing are not necessary. But system design still is.

Take, for example, our banking system discussed above. Let's assume that up to 10 user workstations and 3 application programs (plus any required system software) are to be purchased and installed as the first part of what may some day be quite a comprehensive banking system. General-purpose display-screen and printer formats are provided by the vendor as a starter set for the format library. Do the display-screen formats allow bank officers to enter all the data this particular bank needs when opening new accounts? If not, can the formats be modified? If not, then additional formats must be designed (and created) before the system becomes operational. Other parts of the system that must be designed include the physical layouts of the workstation areas, user training sessions, formats and contents of any user documentation needed by bank officers or by in-house personnel who will support the system, and backup and security procedures for all system components.

The system flowchart, the descriptions of the formats and contents of the system inputs and outputs and of related files, and other user-oriented (external, or functional) characteristics of the system are collected in a final programming functional specification (FPFS) for the project.

Top-Down Design

The chief-programmer-team method of organization is implemented most effectively when another system development methodology is also practiced: top-down development. In its broadest sense, *top-down development* is an all-inclusive term. It cov-

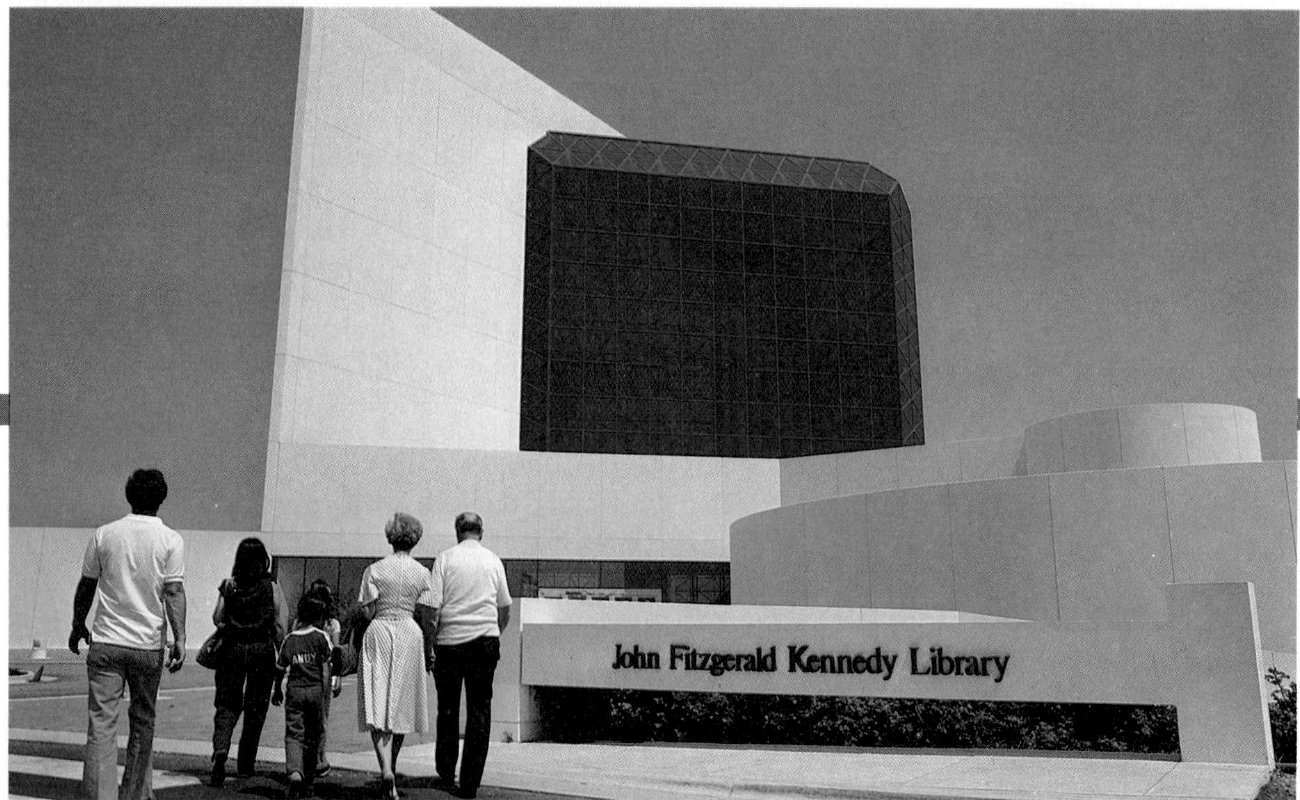
John Fitzgerald Kennedy Library

AUTOMATING THE PRESIDENTIAL LIBRARIES

What do Herbert J. Hoover, Franklin D. Roosevelt, Harry S. Truman, Dwight D. Eisenhower, John F. Kennedy, Lyndon B. Johnson, and Gerald R. Ford have in common? Each has served as President of the United States. Each is the focal point of a presidential library that is being automated.

To understand the scope of this task, consider that the presidential library system now houses more than 200 million pages of written records. The libraries have acquired hundreds of thousands of still photographs, millions of feet of motion picture film, and an ever-growing collection of audiotapes and disks. Some, like the John F. Kennedy Library in Boston, have actively sought oral interviews with people who can reflect upon their own experiences with the presidents, their times, and the historical events of their years in public life. All of these must be transcribed, screened, and processed before they are opened to research.

Each of the presidential libraries is installing a Datapoint minicomputer system. Initially, the systems will be used for administrative work—office automation. Datapoint's Vista package for word processing and Microsoft's Multiplan for electronic spreadsheet analysis are a part of each library's basic software. The systems will initially have 512K bytes of primary storage and from 20 to 40 megabytes of hard-disk secondary storage. Datapoint terminals and printers will also be installed.

Perhaps the most unique aspect of this library automation project is the top-down analysis and design effort that's going into it. It's been described as "the first top-down analysis and design ever done for a major archival institution." Previous attempts at automation involved trying to fit software developed for other libraries to the needs of an archive system that has a different cataloging system and no circulation.

The libraries' primary clients are history scholars who research broad topics for doctoral dissertations, master's theses, and books. Today, most of their needs are met through manual searching. Estimates are that 25 to 30 percent of the library staff's time is spent responding to research requests. The second part of the presidential library automation project will allow the libraries' vast collections of information to be stored in computerized databases and/or accessed via online searches of computerized indexes. Improved responsiveness to research requests and significant cost savings are expected benefits. *(Photo courtesy Miro Vintoniv/Stock, Boston)* ers top-down design, top-down programming, and top-down testing. The top-down design approach applies to the system as a whole as well as to individual programs within the system. Therefore, top-down design begins at the system design phase of the system development cycle.

Top-down design is sometimes referred to by other names—structured design, composite design, and so on. We can also describe it as "functional decomposition." When doing top-down design, we look first at the major function to be accomplished by the system. Next we look at the subfunctions of that major function. Then we look at their subfunctions, and so on. At each level of the design, only the issues relevant to that level are considered, and those issues are formulated precisely. We continue in this way until we are satisfied that we fully understand both the scope and the details of our problem-solving method.

When doing top-down design, we look first at the major function to be accomplished by the system.

Suppose, for example, that we are to design a system to automate weekly payroll processing at a construction firm. We can't accomplish this task just by finding out what has to be on an employee paycheck. It's not that simple.

Think, for example, of the "relatively permanent" employee payroll data that needs to be stored and kept current—name, department, job code, pay rate, number of dependents, United Way deduction, and so on. Think about the monthly budget-versus-actual reports that have to reflect what's being paid out in salaries. Think about government reporting requirements (quarterly employee withholding, W-2 forms, and more). Think about the necessity of providing an audit trail and of printing the weekly paychecks. Some firms establish arrangements with local banks whereby employees' net earnings can be credited directly to their bank accounts each week (without intermediate paper shuffling). Perhaps this capability is to be provided in the system we are designing.

The data flow diagrams constructed during the detailed investigation step of system analysis can be referred to at this time, to help insure that all functions and subfunctions of weekly payroll processing are provided for. If the system we are designing differs significantly from the user's existing system, we may decide to construct data flow diagrams to describe the new system as well. The diagrams will be useful to us in design and can serve as system documentation later, when other information system personnel and users need to be told about the new system.

Structure Charts

We've already seen that system flowcharts are a way of describing the input/output media and work flow of a system. They deal with the hardware, software, and data components of the system in a very general fashion. To concentrate in more detail on the internal, logical relationships within the software, manually or using CASE tools, we construct one or more *tree diagrams,* or *structure charts.* A first, high-level structure chart might show only one software component—say, Compute Weekly

Payroll. As designers understand more about the system they are designing, additional levels are added to the structure chart. (See, for example, Figure 8-8.)

As the example shows, a structure chart consists of blocks and of lines connecting those blocks. The top block of the treelike structure represents the over-all function of the system as an entity. The lower levels of the tree represent finer breakdowns of that function. A structure chart has no required or minimum number of levels. In fact, one branch of the structure may have several more levels than others. The blocks at the lowest level of each branch may be broken down further on succeeding structure charts. The Create required reports block in Figure 8-8 is a likely candidate for expansion.

A major advantage of structure charts is that they help designers to create a well-structured plan for a system. Eventually, each block on the set of structure charts becomes the basis for a program module. Each module is a relatively small, highly independent segment of coding that performs one or a very small number of functions. It is called into execution by the module above it on the structure chart. After it is finished executing, it returns control of the computer system to the module that called it. When this approach is used, systems and programs are not "bowls of spaghetti" as they are likely to be when the design task is approached without a well-thought-out methodology. The logical structure of the system practically jumps off the structure chart pages.

Figure 8-8 Up to four function levels are documented on this structure chart for a weekly payroll system.

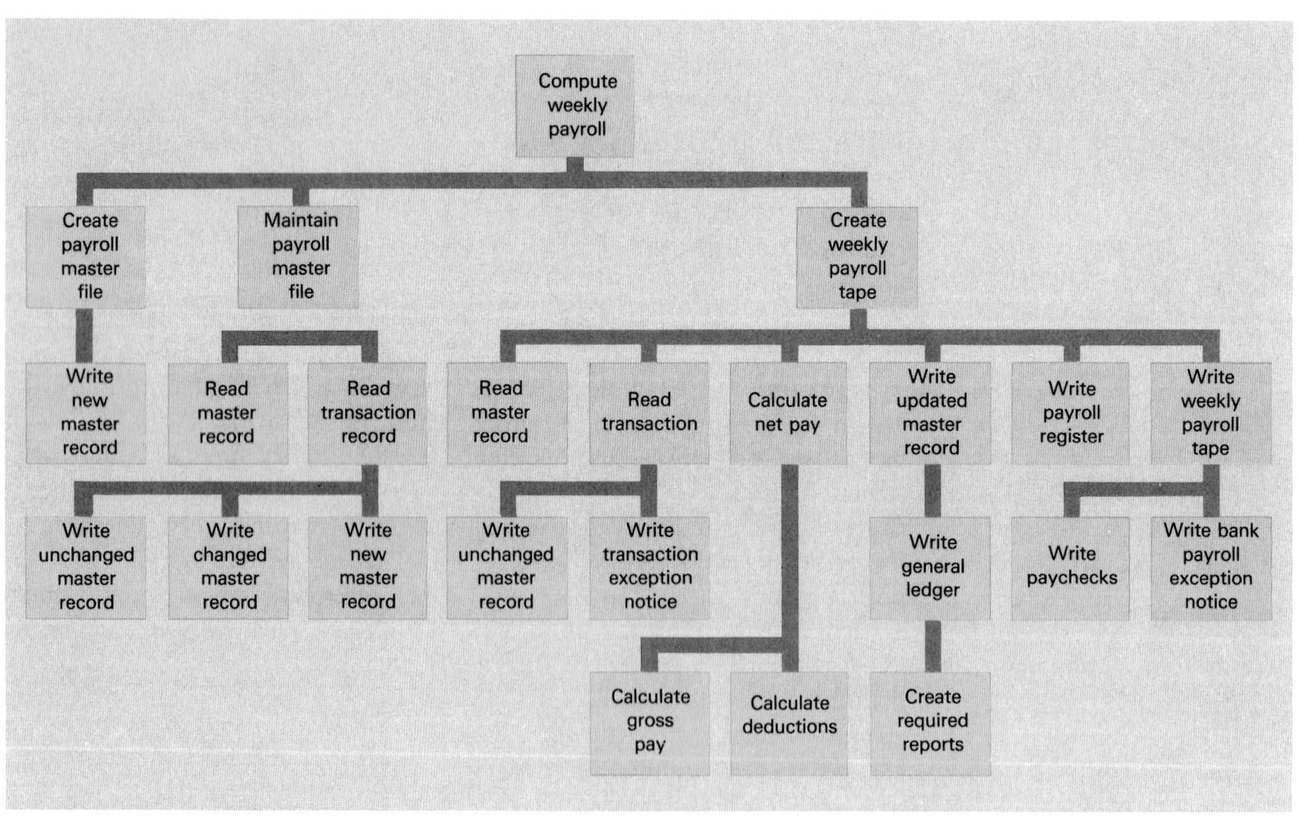

Compute weekly payroll
Create payroll master file
Maintain payroll master file
Create weekly payroll tape
Write new master record
Read master record
Read transaction record
Read master record
Read transaction
Calculate net pay
Write updated master record
Write payroll register
Write weekly payroll tape
Write unchanged master record
Write changed master record
Write new master record
Write unchanged master record
Write transaction exception notice
Write general ledger
Write paychecks
Write bank payroll exception notice
Calculate gross pay
Calculate deductions
Create required reports

The First "Bug"

One day in the 1940s, Harvard's famed Mark I—a precursor of today's computers—failed. When members of the development team looked inside the machine, they found a moth lodged in the circuitry. They removed the moth with tweezers. From then on, whenever there was a problem with the Mark I, the team said they were looking for a bug. Through the years, with respect to both hardware and software, this use of the term *bug* has stuck. *(Photo courtesy Paul Shambroom/Photo Researchers)*

Design Review

Not uncommonly, system developers and users alike share certain major concerns: the all-too-often high frequency of errors, or bugs, in system components; the difficulty in isolating, identifying, and correcting those bugs; and the care required to avoid creating new bugs when correcting existing ones. The more programs a software supplier or user installation develops, for example, the greater the resources required to maintain and correct them—that is, to support the programs in actual use. System development appears to be an error-prone activity.

Though such concerns seem to be valid, some computer professionals and users are asking why. Isn't it better to write a program correctly the first time than to patch it later? Certainly it's much less expensive in terms of both time and money to keep errors out of a system than to redo it later. The emphasis on well-thought-out design reflects efforts to do just that. To further insure that analysis, design, and implementation are error-free, techniques have been developed to detect and remove, as early as possible, any defects that do creep in.

As discussed earlier, system verification begins at the problem-definition step. The detailed investigation does not proceed until both users and information system personnel review and accept the description of the problem as stated in the feasibility report. System design does not begin until the system proposal is reviewed and accepted. After these steps have been accomplished, it's time to verify the final programming functional specification and the high-level internal software design reflected on the structure charts.

Under one approach to verification, the design documentation is distributed to selected reviewers. Each reviewer is asked to study the design and respond within an established time period, noting any changes, additions, or deletions required. This approach is known as an *informal design review.*

Under a more formal approach, the design documentation and problem-log forms are made available to from three to six people who serve as members of a review team. After a preparation period, these reviewers meet with the chief programmer or a lead designer and a moderator to conduct one type of *structured walkthrough* known as a *formal design review.*

Each reviewer is expected to have studied the design documentation. A reader (usually the designer) "walks" the group through each part of the documentation, covering any points raised by the review team. The moderator controls the session, making sure that reviewers are heard, clarifying points where necessary, focusing on error detection rather than error correction, preventing reviewers from getting bogged down on any particular topic, and so on. The moderator is responsible for the documentation of the session and of the errors encountered. The moderator's summary report is an action plan for the designer and a communication vehicle for the team. Not until all points of concern noted on the summary report are resolved is the system design step considered complete.

Project Review

Completion of the system design and resolution of any problems raised during the design review are prerequisites to a system design checkpoint review of the project with both user and information system management.

User management must formally agree that the system that's been designed will meet the user's needs. Both user and information system management must re-evaluate an updated costs-versus-benefits analysis. Information system management must verify that system implementation plans and schedules are in place and reasonable.

Regardless of whether the system development activity involves a large chief programmer team or is a one-person project, both the system design review and this project review are mandatory. For example, a small business owner who contracts the development of an accounts-receivable system to a software firm should insure that both reviews are called for in the contractual agreement and that they are carried out. Otherwise, the system that is developed may be a technological masterpiece but fail to meet the owner's needs.

Given the go-ahead at the project review, system implementation can begin. The activities that occur during system implementation and evaluation are described in the next chapter.

CHAPTER SUMMARY

1. A system is a group of interrelated elements that work together to perform a specific task or function.

2. The system development cycle provides a general framework within which phases and checkpoints can be established and tracked to achieve project control.

3. Both user and information system personnel must participate in system development. Outside groups and in-house system support groups may need to be involved as work proceeds.

4. A brief feasibility study may be initiated to decide whether or not an identified problem or opportunity warrants further investigation.

5. If a decision is made to proceed with system development, a project team is formed to do a detailed investigation. This work involves fact-finding, data analysis and evaluation, estimating costs and benefits, and preparation of a system proposal.

6. Data flow diagrams are a simple way of showing what's occurring in a user's existing system or organization. They may also be used to describe a new system that's being developed.

7. The costs and benefits of a proposed system alternative may be classified as either intangible or tangible, and as either direct or indirect. Techniques such as calculation of the payback period can be used in estimating such costs and benefits.

8. Computer-assisted software engineering (CASE) tools help to automate the tools, methods, and procedures used in system development and thereby increase developers' productivity.

9. System design is often the responsibility of a chief programmer team. The records of the project are kept in a development support library accessible to all team members.

10. System flowcharts, a data element dictionary, and structure charts are other system design tools. The latter are especially useful when a top-down approach to design is used.

11. To help insure that system analysis, design, and implementation are error-free, formalized techniques to detect and remove defects are applied throughout the system development cycle. Either informal or formal reviews of the design documentation may be carried out at this point in the cycle.

12. At the completion of system design, user and information system management conduct a project review to determine whether or not system implementation should proceed.

DISCUSSION QUESTIONS

1. (a) What is a system?
(b) Choose a system that does not involve computers. Show how it fits the definition you just gave above.
(c) Choose a computer-based system. Show how it fits the definition.

2. What is the system development cycle?

3. Support or refute this statement: "It should not be necessary to return to a preceding phase of development once that phase has been completed."

4. Distinguish between system evaluation, system analysis, system implementation, and system design.

5. Assume you are a system analyst with responsibility for conducting a feasibility study with respect to the following problem statement: "We need to know, on a week-to-week basis, how each salesperson is doing against plan." How would you go about conducting the study?

6. Discuss the advantages and disadvantages of various fact-finding techniques. Suggest situations where each is appropriate.

7. Discuss the contents and use of data flow diagrams.

8. Assume you are trying to decide whether or not to buy a computer to help you with record keeping and tax reporting. What tangible and intangible costs and benefits might you consider? Which of them are direct? Which are indirect? Which are hardest to quantify?

9. Discuss the purpose and contents of a system proposal.

10. What are some of the potential benefits of using CASE tools? Why are these benefits important in today's business environment?

11. Distinguish between system flowcharts and structure charts with respect to contents and use.

12. Support or refute the following statement: "A detailed plan and checkpoints are more necessary in a large development effort than in a small one."

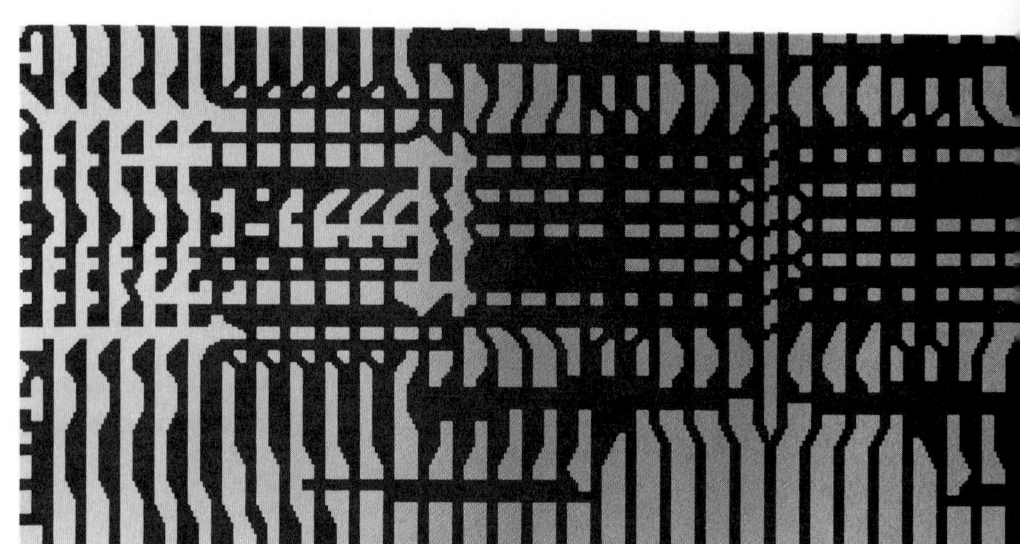

9 Developing Programs

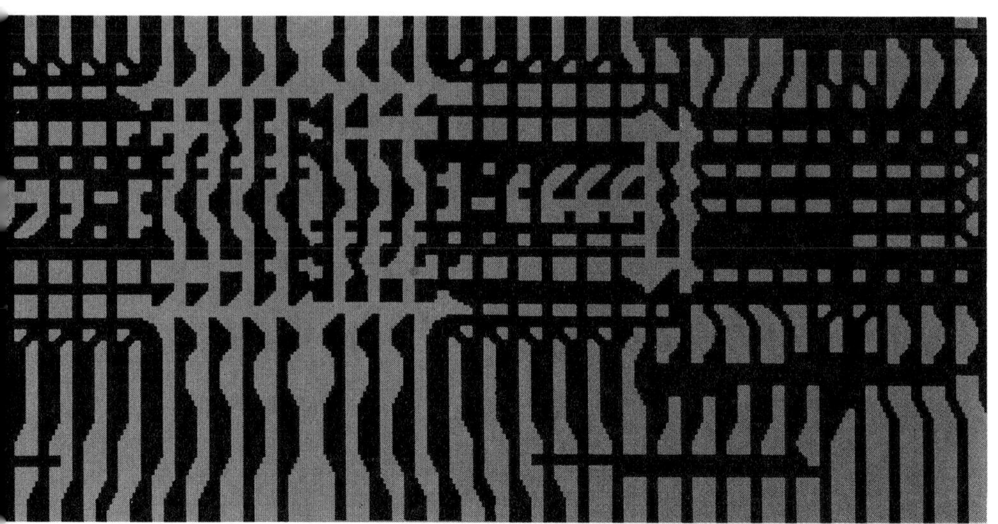

IN THIS CHAPTER

A First Problem
More About Flowcharting
Coding the Solution
Top-Down Programming
Structured Programming
Pseudocode
Checking Out the Program
Top-Down Testing
Product Certification
Documentation
System Evaluation

In this chapter, we continue our study of how to use the computer as a tool in problem solving. The computer may be a pocket computer purchased for $100 from a mail-order house or retailer. It may be a $4 billion supercomputer capable of doing 800 million operations per second. It may be a more conventional computer somewhere between these two extremes in both cost and capabilities. As we've said before, the same general approach to problem solving applies in all cases.

Let's review the phases of system development as defined in Chapter 8:

- *System analysis*—understand the user's requirements; identify ways of responding to those requirements; select the alternative that's best for this situation.
- *System design*—define in detail the output that must be provided by the system and the input that will be provided to the system; plan for the hardware, software, data conversion (if any), procedures, training, and documentation.
- *System implementation*—acquire and install any hardware that is needed; acquire or develop the needed software; create user data files and/or databases; institute required procedures; train personnel who will use the system, its input, or its output; complete the system documentation.
- *System evaluation*—review the system after it is implemented to assess whether or not it meets the user's requirements; develop plans to follow up on problems.

In Chapter 8, we directed our attention to techniques of system analysis and design. In this chapter, we discuss system implementation and evaluation.

A First Problem

Let's start with a simple problem—one we can follow all the way to completion. In doing so, we'll get a better understanding of the steps in system development. Then we'll be ready to look more closely at the tools and techniques used in system implementation.

System Analysis and Design

How many times have you read in a newspaper that a nearby furniture store is offering 30 to 80 percent discounts on all merchandise in a going-out-of-business sale, and wished you had a handy way of calculating what certain items would cost? What will your (or your daughter's) school supplies cost if you take advantage of a back-to-school sale, with discounts ranging from 10 to 50 percent? If you buy a set of tires while Sears is offering its 10-percent-off sale, what will the tires really cost?

A close look at these questions shows that they have common elements. We could solve each problem individually, but it's to our advantage to develop a general-purpose solution plan, or *algorithm,* that can be used to solve all of them. We now restate the questions in a general-purpose fashion as a problem to be solved:

> Given the original price and the discount for each of one or more items, determine the total cost of the group of items.

We can solve this problem in any of several ways. Among them are: (1) ask a salesclerk to figure the total cost for us; (2) use a pencil and paper and our knowledge of arithmetic to determine the cost ourselves; (3) use a calculator; (4) use a pocket computer we take with us to the store; or (5) get the prices for the items we're considering from the newspaper, sales catalog, a visit to the store, or a phone call, and direct the computer on our desk at home to calculate the total cost for us.

Given these choices, it is not likely we'll decide to purchase the hardware needed for alternative 3, 4, or 5 just to solve this problem. Let's assume a desktop computer with appropriate system software is available to us. Then, let's select alternative 5.

The output that must be provided by our system is the total cost of the items considered for purchase. The inputs to the system are the original price and discount for each item. Since we may decide to buy several items of the same type, let's say that the desired quantity of each item should also be entered as input. (Otherwise, if we want to buy four tires, for example, we'll have to key in the price and discount for the tires four times.) The system must accept the input values as they are keyed in from the keyboard. It must display the output on the visual-display screen.

If we shopped at a nearby computer store, we could probably find a software package that accepts keyed data values for quantity, price, and discount as input and displays a computed total cost as output. In fact, any applicable package we found would probably do much more. Since our problem is relatively simple, let's decide to develop the solution in-house instead; that is, let's design, code, test, and document the software ourselves. The system flowchart for the system is very straightforward. (See Figure 9-1.) As in Chapter 8, we use the display symbol to represent an online visual-display

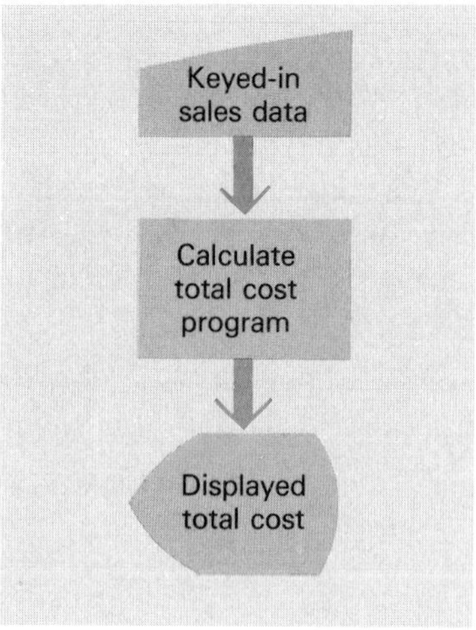

Keyed-in sales data

Calculate total cost program

Displayed total cost

Figure 9-1 Sales data is entered as input from an online keyboard and total cost is displayed as output in the Compute Total Cost system described on this system flowchart.

unit. We use the *manual-input symbol* (⏢) to emphasize that input data values are keyed in from an online keyboard. Given our desktop computer and the system software already installed on it, we need only design, code, test, and document one application program.

System Implementation

Believe it or not, we've just completed the system analysis and design for the system we're developing. We're ready to tackle the first step of system implementation. That means we're ready to plan the detailed logic within the application program. Realizing again that one picture is worth a thousand words, we construct a *program flowchart* to show the processing that's required. (See Figure 9-2.)

The oval-shaped symbols (⬭) in Figure 9-2 are called *terminal symbols;* they mark the beginning and end of the program flowchart. The *preparation symbol* (⬡) represents an initialization step. In this case, we're directing the computer to set to 0 the primary-storage location to be used to accumulate total cost.

Then we tell the computer to execute the statements within a *program loop.* The parallelogram-shaped *input/output symbol* (▱) represents an input operation; the computer reads the quantity, original price, and discount for one type of item. The rectangular-shaped *process symbols* (▭) represent internal processing operations. The computer subtracts quantity times discount from quantity times price to determine the cost for this part of the purchase. It then adds that cost to the accumulation of total cost.

The diamond-shaped *decision symbol* (◇) documents a decision-making step. If all items have not yet been processed, the computer follows the *No* path back to the start of the program loop. The program loop is re-executed until there are no more items. Then the computer follows the *Yes* path. A sales tax of 6 percent is computed and added to the accumulated total cost. The result of this addition—the final calculation of total cost—is written as output. Processing is then terminated.

To meet a key system development objective stated in Chapter 8—namely, to detect and remove as soon as possible any errors (bugs) that creep in—it's appropriate at this time to check our solution algorithm as depicted on the program flowchart. Perhaps the best way to do this is to:

1. Create a set of test data to be entered as input
2. Figure out what output the computer should provide, given the set of test data as input
3. Manually step through the program logic shown on the flowchart, assuming the test data is provided as input

For example, assuming the test data shown in Figure 9-3A is provided as input, the total cost calcu-

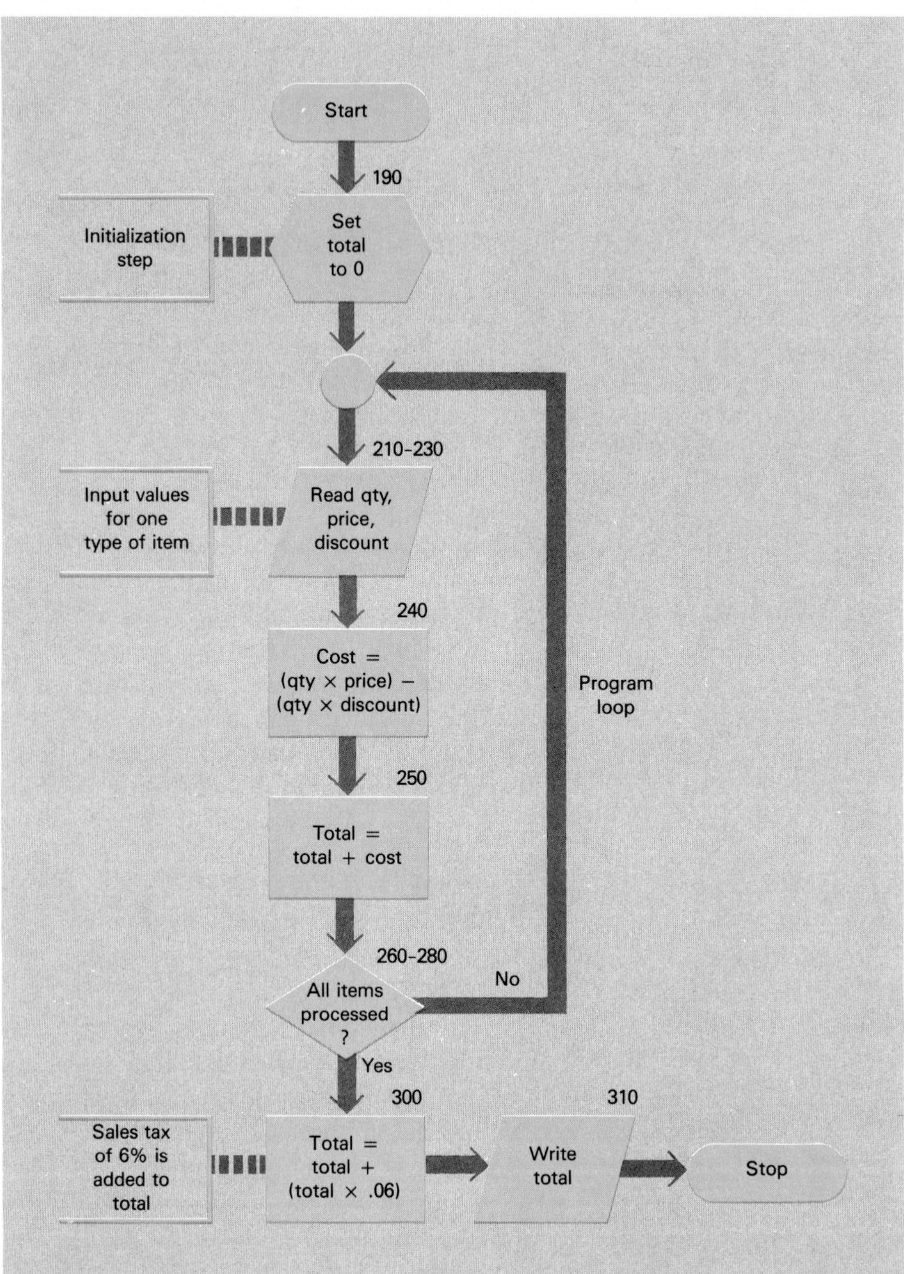
Start
190
Initialization step
Set total to 0
210-230
Input values for one type of item
Read qty, price, discount
240
Cost = (qty × price) − (qty × discount)
Program loop
250
Total = total + cost
260-280
No
All items processed ?
Yes
300
310
Sales tax of 6% is added to total
Total = total + (total × .06)
Write total
Stop

Figure 9-2 **A program loop to read sales data and compute total cost is executed repeatedly within the Calculate Total Cost program described by this program flowchart.**

lated in Figure 9-3B should be provided as output.

This approach to program checkout is called *simulation* or *desk checking*. In effect, we simulate, or pretend to be, the computer. If the output of the simulation matches the output we figure out beforehand, we can proceed with the next step of system implementation. That is, we can express the solution algorithm in a programming language. If the outputs do not match, we must find all errors, correct them, and repeat the simulation. We create other sets of test data and expected results, and continue in this manner until we're confident our solution algorithm is error-free. You may wonder why we place so much emphasis on program

A. Test data

```
3, 41.00, .10
N
1, 19.99, .20
N
10, 1.00, .15
Y
```

B. Expected results

```
 110.70    135.20 Subtotal
+ 16.00   + 8.11 Tax
   8.50    143.31 Total Cost
 135.20
X  .06
 8.1120
```

Figure 9-3 Both the data to be provided as input (A) and the expected results of processing (B) should be planned in advance when checking out a program.

quality at this point. The reason is simple: No amount of good coding can repair the damage done by poor design.

No amount of good coding can repair the damage done by poor design.

Many application programs used with desktop computers were initially written in BASIC. As we saw in Chapter 2, BASIC is an easy-to-use programming language. It's an appropriate choice here, whether we consider ourselves programmers or users who are writing an application program. A BASIC program that corresponds to the flowchart in Figure 9-2 is given in Figure 9-4. Each line in the program begins with a line number. The lines that contain the letters *REM* are remark statements. These statements provide documentation about the program for us and for others who look at the program. They have no effect whatsoever on the processing carried out by the computer during program execution. Thus, the REM statements have no corresponding symbols on the program flowchart.

Since we have already discussed the program logic, and the program is well documented, you can probably read and understand the other BASIC statements without any trouble. As an aid to understanding, most programmers place the line numbers of statements represented by the symbols on a program flowchart at the upper right of the symbols. (Look again at Figure 9-2.) The line numbers serve as *cross-references* between the flowchart and the program. By adding cross-references to the flowchart, we make it easier for others (and for ourselves, later) to follow the logic of the program.

As shown by this example, there is no need for a 1-to-1 correspondence between the symbols on a flowchart and the statements in a program. The level of detail required on a flowchart is determined by several factors. Among them are:

1. How much the programmer needs to chart to come up with the program logic or to provide a guide that can be used during coding and testing
2. How difficult the program logic is, and therefore how much help others may need to understand the program

Now we are ready to key in the program. When we're done keying,

```
100 REM TOTCOST. CALCULATE TOTAL COST
110 REM SALES TAX OF 6% (.06) IS ASSUMED (LINE 300)
120 REM T IS COMPUTED TOTAL COST OF ALL ITEMS
130 REM Q IS QUANTITY FOR AN ITEM
140 REM P IS ORIGINAL PRICE FOR AN ITEM
150 REM D IS DISCOUNT FOR AN ITEM
160 REM C IS COMPUTED COST FOR DESIRED QTY OF AN ITEM
170 REM R$ IS USER'S RESPONSE, Y OR N
180 REM INITIALIZATION
190 LET T = 0.00
200 REM BEGIN PROGRAM LOOP
210 PRINT "ENTER QUANTITY, PRICE (XX.XX), AND "
220 PRINT "DISCOUNT (.XX) FOR AN ITEM"
230 INPUT Q, P, D
240 LET C = (Q * P) - (Q * D)
250 LET T = T + C
260 PRINT "ALL ITEMS PROCESSED? ENTER Y OR N"
270 INPUT R$
280 IF R$ = "N" THEN 210
290 REM END PROGRAM LOOP
300 LET T = T + (T * .06)
310 PRINT "TOTAL COST IS $"; T
320 END
```

Figure 9-4 **The Calculate Total Cost program initially expressed in flowchart form can be written in BASIC to direct the computer.**

we desk-check what we've entered, just as we desk-checked the logic on the program flowchart. Then we tell the computer to execute the program. When the prompt

ENTER QUANTITY, PRICE (XX.XX), AND
DISCOUNT (.XX) FOR AN ITEM

appears on the display screen, we key in our first three test data values: 3, 41.00, .10. In response to the next prompt, we key in N. Hopefully, processing continues much like the simulated processing we've just completed. After we key in Y, we should receive the following output:

TOTAL COST IS $ 143.31

If this output doesn't appear on the display screen, there's a problem somewhere. We must find out what's causing the problem and correct it. If we decide to change the program logic, we must go back to the detailed planning step. If appropriate, we must change the program flowchart. Then we must change the program.

Since the program we've developed is a general-purpose one, it can handle a wide variety of data as input. As a reminder to ourselves, and for the benefit of others who want to use the program, we've noted on line 110 that .06 is used as the sales tax on line 300. This technique is a good one—it helps to insure that if a sales tax value other than .06 applies, we'll remember to change line 300 accordingly. After we're confident that the program is error-free, we key in a system command to save it under the name TOTCOST, which we've also noted in a comment (see line 100). This causes the program to be saved in secondary storage (most likely, a $3\frac{1}{2}$- or $5\frac{1}{4}$-inch disk). We can load it back into primary storage from the disk whenever we want to reuse it.

The program flowchart, the test data and expected results, and the REM statements in the program itself serve as the system/program documentation. As we've just noted, the program is kept in secondary storage. The test data and expected results may be kept there also. The flowchart and any other pertinent information about the program should be filed in a hard-copy library.

Learning the mechanics of programming—how to write instructions to the computer, or how to enter them into computer storage—is no more difficult than learning to use any other tool. The challenging part is understanding the problem to be solved so thoroughly that we can teach an extremely simple, literally minded servant (the computer) to solve it. Programmers are sometimes described as part authors, part tinkerers. When you've completed this chapter you won't be a programmer, but you'll have a good idea of what programming is all about.

More about Flowcharting

By now, you should be aware that there are two kinds of flowcharts. A *system flowchart* shows the flow of data through all parts of a system. A *program flowchart* shows what takes place within one particular program. A system flowchart is usually constructed by a system analyst or system designer during the detailed investigation step of system analysis. Program flowcharts are usually constructed by the programmers responsible for system implementation.*

To encourage uniformity in system and program flowcharting, the American National Standards Institute (ANSI) and its international counterpart, the International Standards Organization (ISO), have approved flowcharting standards. The symbols shown in Figure 9-5 comply with these standards. By using a standardized set of flowcharting symbols, we make it easier for others to understand our flowcharts.

Since standards for flowcharting exist, a logical next step is for some person or group to develop tools that make it easy for system designers and programmers to follow the standards. Several firms have done exactly that. Few programmers would be without a *flowcharting template.* The template is a plastic or metallic card containing cutout system and program flowcharting symbols as patterns. The symbols can readily be drawn on flowcharts. As a guide in positioning the symbols, the programmer uses *flowcharting worksheets.* Each 11″ × $16\frac{1}{2}$″ worksheet provides an arrangement of 50 blocks with alphabetic and numeric coordinates. The coordinates serve as identifiers (for example, A1 or D2) that can be referred to within *connector symbols* ((A1)→, →(D2)). They are especially useful when a flowchart extends over several worksheets.

* A complete explanation of how to use flowcharting techniques to construct well-structured programs is given in *Tools for Structured Design,* 2nd ed, by Bohl and Rynn (Chicago: Science Research Associates, Inc., 1989).

PROGRAM FLOWCHART SYMBOLS

SYMBOL	REPRESENTS
	PROCESS One or more instructions that perform a processing function.
	INPUT/OUTPUT Any input/output function (making data available for processing, recording information, tape positioning, etc.)
	DECISION A decision-making step; used to document a point in the program where a branch to an alternate path is possible.
	PREPARATION An instruction or group of instructions that changes the program for initialization, control, or cleanup.
	PREDEFINED PROCESS One or more operations not detailed on the particular set of flowcharts.
	TERMINAL The beginning, end, or a point of interruption in a program.
	CONNECTOR An entry from, or an exit to, a point on the program flowchart.
	OFFPAGE CONNECTOR A connector used instead of the connector symbol to designate entry to or exit from a page.
< > V Λ	FLOW DIRECTION The direction of processing or data flow.

SUPPLEMENTARY SYMBOL FOR SYSTEM AND PROGRAM FLOWCHARTS

SYMBOL	REPRESENTS
	ANNOTATION Additional explanation or comments.

SYSTEM FLOWCHART SYMBOLS

SYMBOL	REPRESENTS	SYMBOL	REPRESENTS
	PROCESS A major processing function.		INPUT/OUTPUT Any type of medium or data.
	PUNCHED CARD All varieties of punched cards.		PUNCHED TAPE Any type of punched continuous medium.
	DOCUMENT Hard-copy documents and reports of all varieties.		DISPLAY Any kind of transitory data not in hard-copy form or intermediate output data used to control processing; usually output displayed by means of online printer-keyboards, visual-display units, etc.
	OFFLINE STORAGE		ONLINE STORAGE
	MAGNETIC TAPE		MAGNETIC DISK
	MANUAL INPUT Data entered manually by means of an online device.		KEYING OPERATION An operation using a key-driven device.
	MANUAL OPERATION A process performed manually or using equipment that operates at the speed of a user.		AUXILIARY OPERATION A process using equipment not under direct control of the main computer and not limited to the speed of a user.
< > V Λ	FLOW The direction of processing or data flow.		COMMUNICATION LINK The transmission of data from one location to another via a communication medium such as wires, cables, or satellites.

Figure 9-5 Standardized sets of symbols exist (and should be used) for both system and program flowcharting.

The normal direction of flow on a flowcharting worksheet is from top to bottom and from left to right. If the direction of flow of any flowline is not normal, an arrowhead must be used on the flowline (←, ↑). If the direction of flow is normal, arrowheads are optional.

When a top-down approach to design is used, either of two flowcharting techniques may be used advantageously. One involves use of the *predefined-process symbol* (◫). The other involves placing a stripe across certain flowcharting symbols. (See Figures 9-6 and 9-7.)

Even when a flowcharting template and flowcharting worksheets are used, a programmer's "first cut" at a program flowchart is not likely to be the final version of the flowchart. That's why CASE tools that allow designers and programmers to create machine-readable versions of flowcharts and then modify them easily with computer help come in handy. The pictorial representation of program logic is a valuable guide not only during coding but also during testing. The design reflected on the flowchart can be reviewed and interpreted by other information system personnel and by users. When the system or program is released for production use, the flowchart becomes a key part of the documentation package. It can be referred to later if program modifications are needed. It must be kept up-to-date so that it is an accurate representation of the program logic at all times.

Coding the Solution

Once the programmer is satisfied that all processing steps have been identified and all alternatives and exceptions provided for, he or she codes the program. If the programming language to be used was not selected earlier, it must be selected now. So far, we've used BASIC, but there are literally hundreds of languages and application development tools to choose from. Some that are widely used are discussed in Chapter 10.

If the program design is well thought out and reviewed before coding begins, the coding task

Figure 9-6 (below left) The Validate input routine depicted on this predefined-process symbol is described in detail elsewhere, but not on this set of flowcharts. It may be a general-purpose routine in an online program library that is loaded into primary storage and executed at this point in execution of the program described on this flowchart.

Figure 9-7 (far right) Details of the Read master routine identified on this striped Input/output symbol can be found beginning at block A3 on page 4 of this set of flowcharts. Use of the *striping convention* here establishes this step as a point where the routine is invoked and tells where the routine is documented.

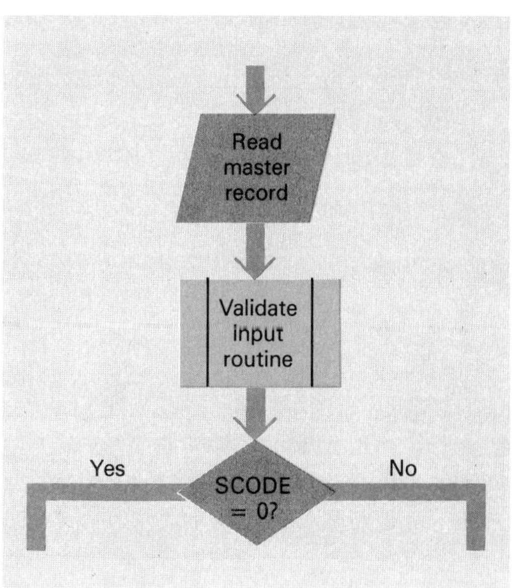
Read master record
Validate input routine
Yes
SCODE = 0?
No

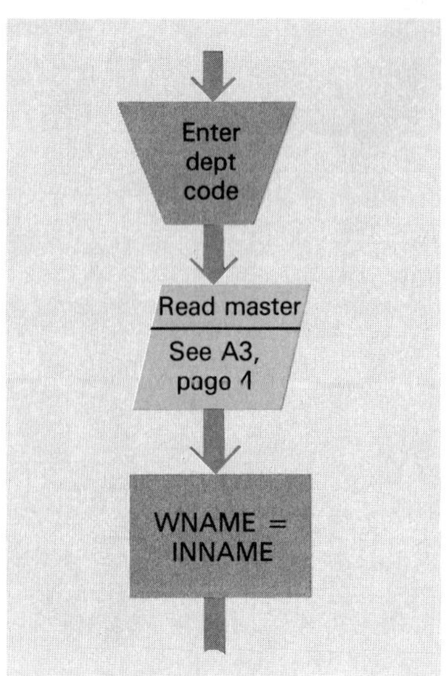
Enter dept code
Read master
See A3, page 4
WNAME = INNAME

DO COMPUTERS AND RELIGION MIX?

"Yes!" say a growing number of Sunday Schoolers, Bible students, committee chairpersons, church secretaries, and lay people. "Yes!" say priests, ministers, and rabbis who are using computers to prepare their sermons or who see computers being used for religion-related purposes.

Of course, nobody is sure how many people use computers for religious purposes. Most churches have limited budgets. Programs are likely to be written as volunteer efforts to satisfy local needs. Once written, they are likely to be shared as public domain software with similar religious groups who find them useful.

Nevertheless, several dozen companies are marketing church management software. Packages for accounting, word processing, mailings, and membership tracking are readily available. Some of these companies also market computer-readable copies of the Bible on diskettes. They have developed programs that allow users to enter specific words or phrases of interest to them. The users' systems then display Bible passages containing the words or phrases. Some programs allow users to display pas-

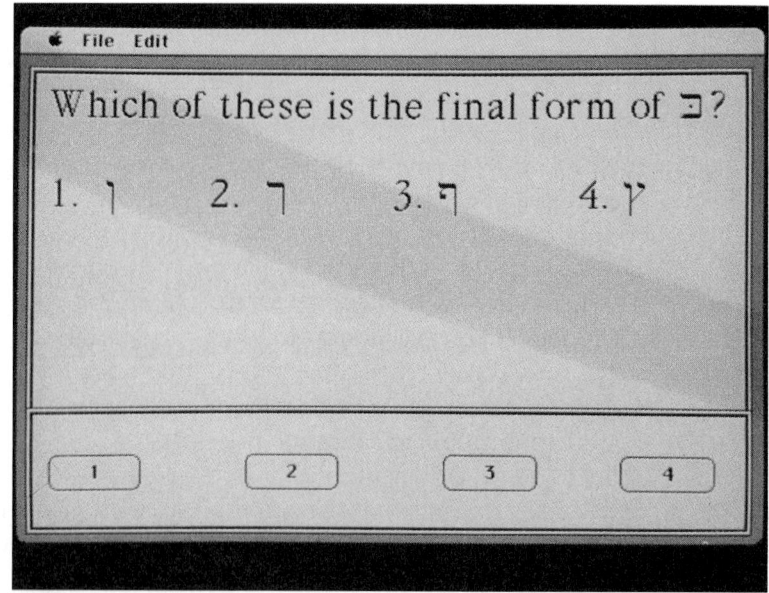
File Edit
Which of these is the final form of
1.
2.
3.
4.
1
2
3
4

File Edit
ראשון
Show/Hide Vowels
first
Show/Hide Translation
ri-SHON
Show/Hide Transliteration
Speak the Word
Previous Word
Change Unit
Next Word
Unit: SET.1.mac
Word #: 3 / 50
OK

sages from different parts of the Bible—say, the Christmas story as detailed in Matthew and in Luke—side by side on the screen, simultaneously.

Within the Bible, the New Testament was initially written in Greek; the Old Testament was initially written in Hebrew. Students of Jewish descent may desire to read other writings in Hebrew as well. For them, Davka Corporation of Chicago offers the Learning to Read Hebrew program. The Creative Hebrew Quizzer, Dynamic Hebrew Dictionary, and Hebrew Writer are also available.

If you want to use a personal computer to control the sound effects for a Mother's Day presentation by Sunday Schoolers, you may have to write the necessary program yourself (or have it written for you). If you want to use a computer to control the lighting for a "living Christmas tree" of carolers, you may decide to undertake program development. You may need technical help if you do so. For many religious activities, both software and hardware to simplify and speed required tasks are available from neighboring congregations, Christian bookstores, or mail order catalogs. *(Photos courtesy of Davka Corp.)*

should be straightforward. Nonetheless, it's a very detailed, meticulous job. Whatever the programming language, certain coding rules must be followed exactly. Otherwise, the program will not work as intended. If you've tried your hand at coding, you already know this. That's why special care in design and coding is not a "nice to have"—it's a requirement.

If the program design is well thought out and reviewed before coding begins, the coding task should be straightforward. Nonetheless, it's a very detailed, meticulous job.

If a one-program system is being implemented, a programmer may work independently with little attention, help, or hindrance from others. Contract programmers, employees of small organizations, and users who are writing programs for their own use may form one-person teams. There are significant opportunities for individuals who can develop applications for businesses they know—say, fast-food restaurants, hardware stores, or pharmacies. Independent, or free-lance, programmers operate much like authors, selling their software to publishers in return for a percentage of the sales. Some of today's best-known software—for example, dBASE and Lotus 1-2-3—got started as one-person efforts. However, caution is warranted: Many authors are finding it's easier to develop a program than to find a means to market, sell, and distribute it effectively.

With some exceptions, even much of the latest personal-computer software (let alone mainframe software) is too complicated to be designed and implemented by one individual. Not just conventional mainframe software developers such as IBM and Computer Associates but also personal-computer software firms such as Ashton-Tate and Microsoft employ hundreds of programmers. Therefore, teamwork in programming is becoming increasingly important. Today detailed design and coding are often done by a chief programmer team in a top-down development environment.

Top-Down Programming

Top-down programming involves implementing a system or program in accordance with the top-down design specified for it. As we saw in Chapter 8, that design is commonly reflected on one or more structure charts. Each programmer assumes responsibility for specific modules.

Most computer professionals acknowledge that there is no one correct way to do top-down programming. Under one approach, the code for the top module is written, then the code for the next lower level, then for the next lower level after that, and so forth. (See Figure 9-8A.) An alternative approach suggests that the paths on a structure chart should be implemented from top to bottom. (See Figure 9-8B.) For example, we may write all modules related to input functions first. Doing so permits all other modules that process the input data to operate on actual problem-related data, even in a test environment. It also permits us to take advantage of prototyping; we can more easily show users what their system will look like as it evolves and obtain their feedback at a time when changes can still be made.

When a modular approach is used, another question often arises: How big (or how small) should a module be? There are no absolute guidelines. In some cases, several very simple functions may be included in one module. For example, short segments of coding for functions at a low level may be incorporated in the module at the next higher level. If a module consists of more than 100 lines of coding, there is a good possibility that subfunctions should be identified. The most important point to be understood here is that size is no guarantee of modularity. The size of a program module should be determined by its function.

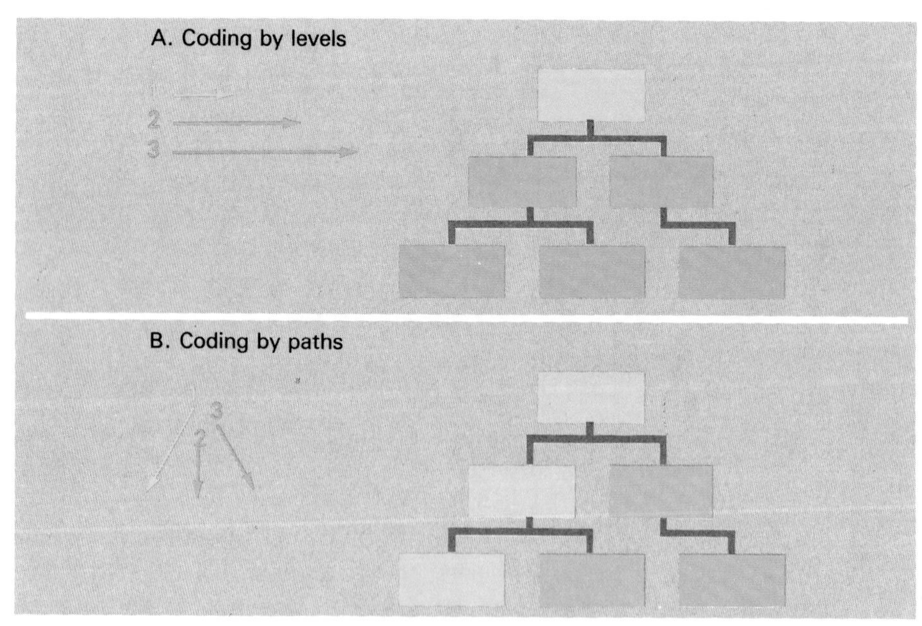

A. Coding by levels
1
2
3
B. Coding by paths
1
2
3

Figure 9-8 Under one approach to top-down programming (A), all modules at a given level are coded and tested before any modules at a lower level; under another approach (B), all modules in a particular path are coded and tested in a level-by-level fashion, then all the modules in another path, and so on.

Structured Programming

A top-down, modular approach to system development is carried to its ultimate level in *structured programming.* Structured-programming techniques can be viewed as the pulling together, or synthesizing, of ideas of top-down design and modularity and the concrete representation of them in the program code. Like these other techniques, structured programming is a direct result of attempts to achieve certain objectives:

- Emphasize the importance of well-thought-out program design
- Increase the productivity of programmers
- Reduce program complexity
- Facilitate program debugging and maintenance
- Encourage error-free coding

No one person "invented" structured programming. As early as 1965, Professor E. W. Dijkstra of The Netherlands suggested that the GOTO (or GO TO) construct could be eliminated from programming languages. In 1968, in his now-famous "GOTO letter," he tried to show that programs written using a definite structuring technique were easier to write, read, and debug, and were more likely to be correct.* The theoretical framework for structured programming is usually traced to a paper by C. Bohm and G. Jacopini.† Their "structure theorem" is a mathematical proof that any solution algorithm can be expressed using only three basic building blocks: a process box; a binary decision mechanism, usually referred to as an if-then-else; and a loop mechanism. (See Figure 9-9.)

Note that each of the structures in Figure 9-9 is characterized by a single point of entrance and a single point of exit. The process box may be thought of as a single statement or as a properly combined sequence of statements having only one entry and one exit. The if-then-else mechanism indicates that a test is made during execution and the outcome determines which of two alternative paths is followed. The loop mechanism indicates that a test is made and, depending on the outcome, either an immediate exit from the loop occurs or a set of one or more statements is executed and then the test is made again. The fact that the constructs in Figures 9-9B and 9-9C have only one entry and one exit is significant: They can themselves be thought of as process boxes.

From this framework, the basic patterns of structured programming have evolved:

- *SIMPLE SEQUENCE.* Statements are executed in the order in which they appear, with control passing unconditionally from one statement to the next. This pattern is so simple that it hardly needs mentioning, but it is necessary for the construction of a program. A problem is solved by executing certain steps in a certain order—an algorithm in program form.
- *IFTHENELSE: IF p THEN a ELSE b.* The condition p is tested. If p is true, statement a

* E. W. Dijkstra, "GOTO Statement Considered Harmful," Letter to the Editor, *Communications of the ACM* 11,3 (March 1968), pp. 147–48.

† C. Bohm and G. Jacopini, "Flow Diagrams, Turing Machines and Languages with Only Two Formation Rules," *Communications of the ACM* 9,5 (May 1966), pp. 366–71.

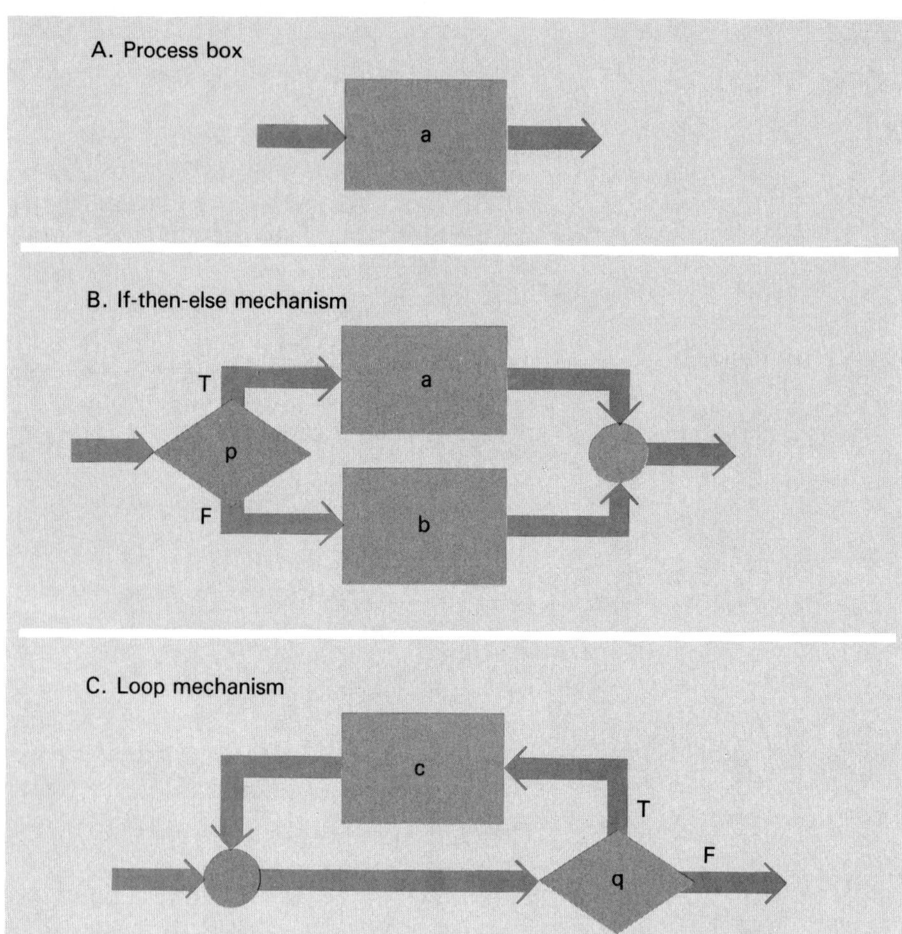
A. Process box
a
B. If-then-else mechanism
T
a
p
F
b
C. Loop mechanism
c
T
F
q

Figure 9-9 The three basic patterns of structured programming are all that's needed to plan the solution to any problem that the computer can be used to solve.

is executed and statement b is skipped. If p is false, statement a is skipped but statement b is executed. Control passes to the next statement. This is, of course, the if-then-else mechanism of Figure 9-9B. Note that each "statement" may be a single statement. It may also be a sequence of statements combined in some fashion to form a basic pattern that can be treated as a single statement. The connector symbol is used as a collector in Figure 9-9B to emphasize that the IFTHENELSE pattern has only one entry and one exit. When used as a collector, this symbol always has two flowlines entering and one flowline exiting.

- *DOWHILE: DO c WHILE q.* The condition q is tested. If q is true, the statement c is executed and control returns to the test of q. If q is false, then c is skipped and control passes to the next statement. This is the loop mechanism of Figure 9-9C. We have here a leading-decision loop: The test occurs immediately upon entering the loop. What follows is executed only if the tested condition is true. Therefore, the complete loop may never be executed. If the test condition is false, an exit from the loop occurs immediately following the test.

To avoid possible confusion, we should consider another control structure at this point—a loop that must be executed at least once. This control structure is really a combination of SIMPLE SEQUENCE and DOWHILE. It is known as the *DOUNTIL control structure.* (See Figure 9-10.)

Figure 9-10A shows the logic we want to set up. It says: "Do d once, then test for the condition *not q* (indicated by q with a line over it, or $\overline{q}$). Continue to DO d WHILE the condition $\overline{q}$ is true." Notice that when the condition $\overline{q}$ is false, we have not $\overline{q}$—and, therefore, q! If you find this negative logic confusing, don't be discouraged. That's why programmers often abandon the logic in Figure 9-10A in favor of the equivalent DOUNTIL control structure in Figure 9-10B. It says: "DO d UNTIL the condition q is true."

Note that the test in a DOUNTIL control structure occurs at the end of the loop—that is, after all other processing within the loop has occurred. Therefore, DOUNTIL can be described as a trailing-decision loop. Here, then, is the fundamental difference between DOUNTIL and DOWHILE. To reinforce your understanding of these concepts, look back at the program logic flowcharted in Figure 9-2. What kind of program loop do you see? The test for loop termination occurs at the end of the loop. The loop is reexecuted if the tested-for condition does not exist, that is, until the tested-for condition does exist. This is the logic of DOUNTIL.

Another common control structure is the *CASE control structure.* CASE is really a generalization of the IFTHENELSE pattern, extending it from a two-valued to a multivalued operation. The logic shown in Figure 9-11A is equivalent to that in Figure 9-11B. The ELSE "statement" of the

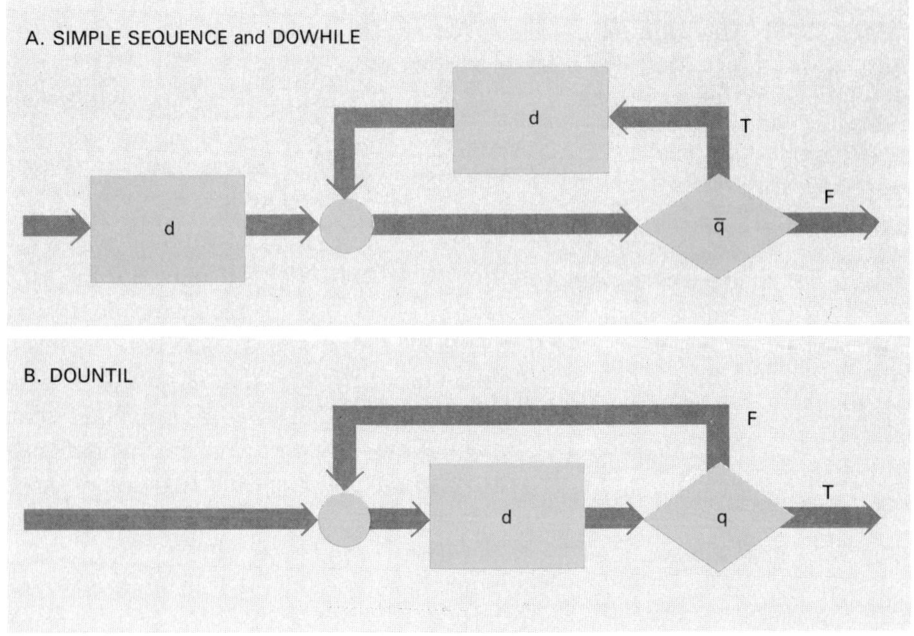

A. SIMPLE SEQUENCE and DOWHILE
d
T
d
F
q̄
B. DOUNTIL
F
T
d
q

Figure 9-10 **The logic of a SIMPLE SEQUENCE and a DOWHILE that tests for the negative of a condition (A) can be expressed by an equivalent DOUNTIL control structure (B).**

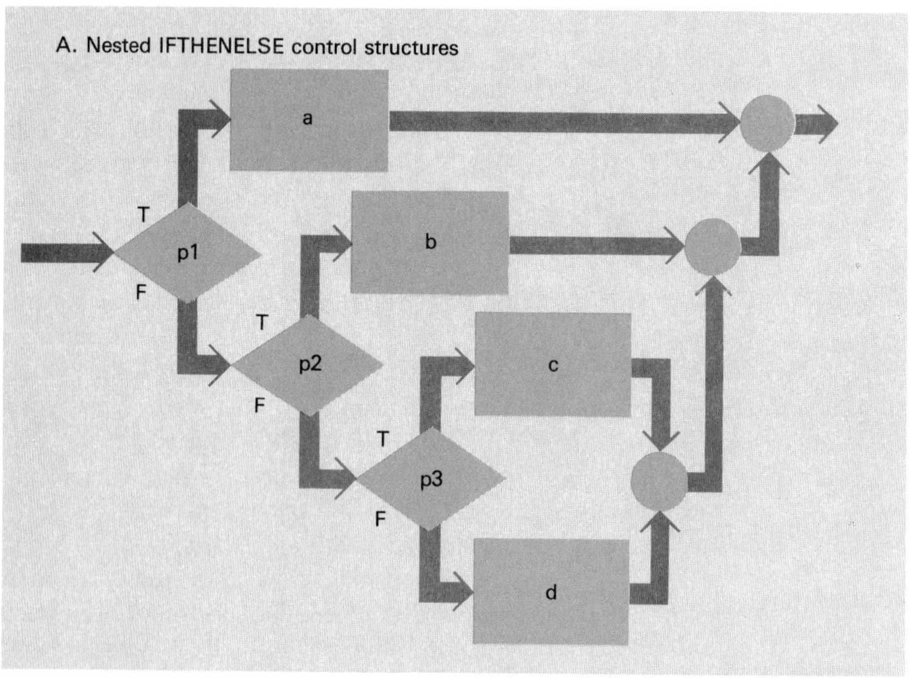
A. Nested IFTHENELSE control structures
a
T
p1
F
b
T
p2
F
c
T
p3
F
d

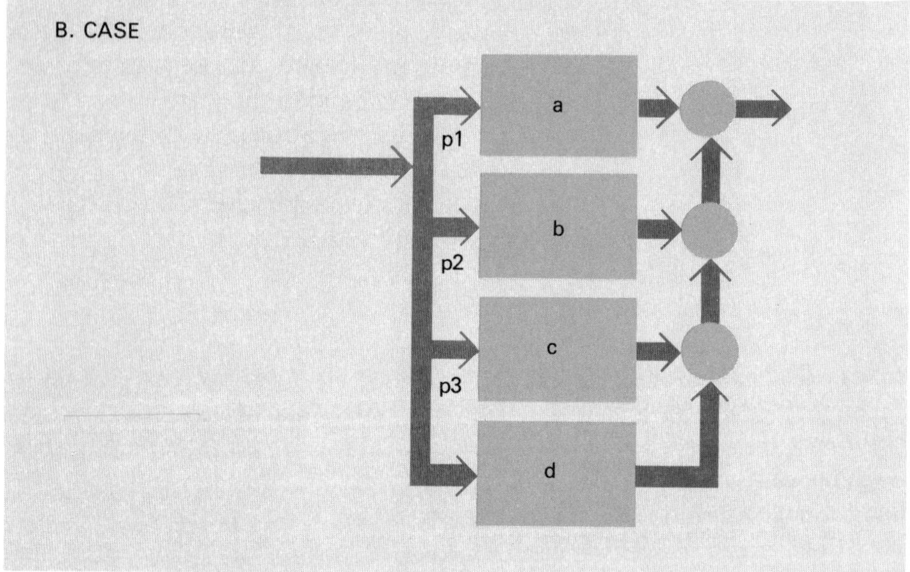
B. CASE
a
p1
b
p2
c
p3
d

Figure 9-11 **The logic of a sequence of a nested IF-THENELSE patterns (A) can be expressed by an equivalent CASE control structure (B).**

leftmost IFTHENELSE pattern in Figure 9-11A is, in fact, another IFTHENELSE pattern, which contains another IFTHENELSE. We say that the IFTHENELSE patterns are *nested.* Note, however, that the overall construct still has only one entry point and one exit point. So does its equivalent construct—the CASE control structure shown in Figure 9-11B.

The concept of nested control structures can be applied repetitively to build one inclusive control structure—a complete program. In other words, a program that is itself composed of only the basic patterns of structure programming, when combined in ways such as we have seen here, can be thought of as a single structure. A program having only one entry point and one exit point,

Structural Programming in Demand

Estimates by various trade journals indicate that at least 80 percent of the information system organizations in the United States are using structured programming for some or all development efforts.

and having a path from entry to exit for every contained control structure, is called a *proper program.*

The reverse of this building-block concept is also possible. We start with a single process box and break that box into a lower level of structures. Next we break some or all of these structures into a still lower level of structures, and so on. We continue until we have reached the level of *atomic* (basic building block) structures: single statements, if-then-else mechanisms, and leading-decision loops—our SIMPLE SEQUENCE, IFTHENELSE, and DOWHILE. This is precisely the top-down approach that we discussed above.

Not all programmers today are using structured-programming techniques. Those who do may not use them 100 percent of the time. Nevertheless, some computer professionals claim that these techniques can help to establish programming as a science instead of a craft. Hardware designers have known for years that logic circuits can be made from a few basic building blocks (resistors, capacitors, and so on). Programs can be made from basic building blocks of code in a similar fashion. This concept is carried to its ultimate when object-oriented programming techniques are employed. We discuss them briefly in Chapter 10.

Pseudocode

Figure 9-12 shows the logic for a basic read-and-print program. It reads individual records as input and writes them, unchanged, as output. Such a program often comes in handy. For example, data recorded on employee time cards may be copied to magnetic tape in a read-and-print run before the main computer run in which calculations are done. Since the data can be read from tape much faster than it can be read from cards, this approach minimizes the time needed (in one stretch) for the main computer run. The tape also provides more compact storage of the data for backup and recovery or for archiving purposes.

We can easily follow this program flowchart. The logic assumes that a *dummy record* containing only 9s has been placed as the last record in the input file. When the dummy record is encountered, program execution is terminated.

The program in Figure 9-12 meets the structured-programming criterion of containing only basic control structures. You should be able to detect several examples of SIMPLE SEQUENCE and one DOWHILE. The "statement" within the DOWHILE program loop comprises a SIMPLE SEQUENCE of two processing steps: write and read. Since the program contains only one entry point and one exit point, it is a proper program.

Notice the correspondence between the program flowchart and the paragraph of text at the right in Figure 9-12. The text is an informal method of expressing program logic, usually known as *pseudocode.* The pseudocode presents the logic in an easy-to-read, top-to-bottom fashion.

The pseudocode presents the logic in an easy-to-read, top-to-bottom fashion.

For emphasis and clarity, the keywords of the DOWHILE pattern (DOWHILE and ENDDO) are writ-

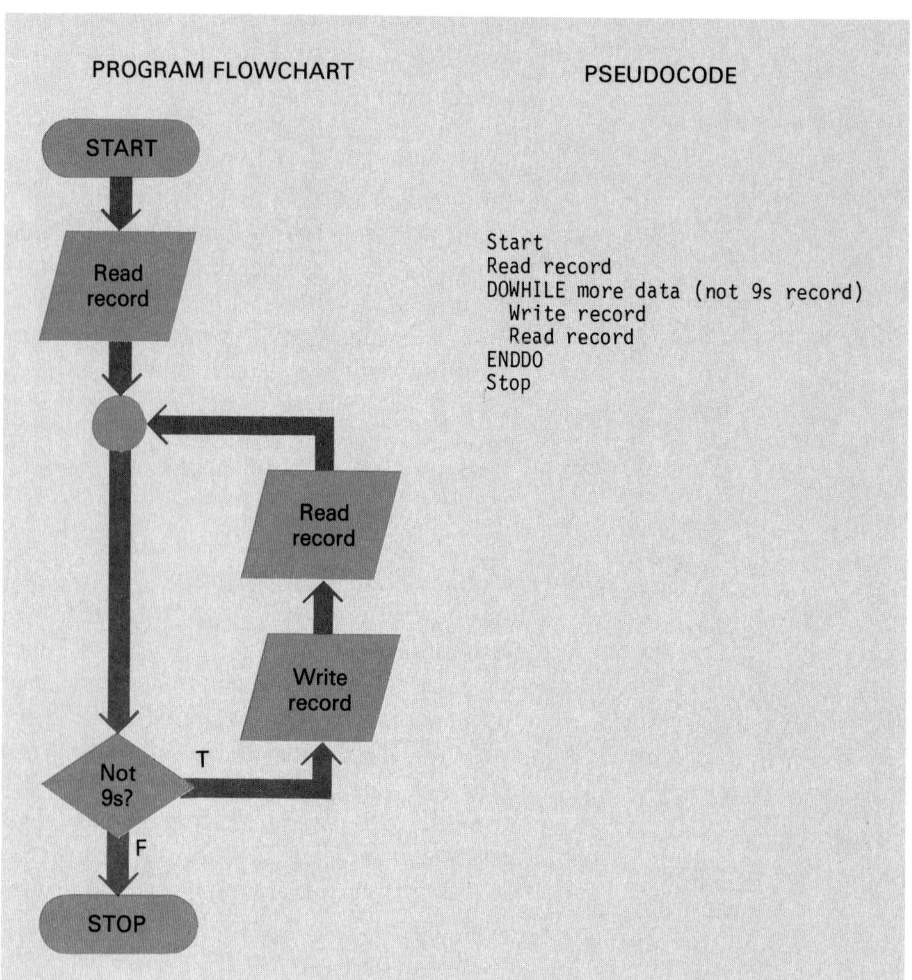
PROGRAM FLOWCHART
PSEUDOCODE
START
Read record
Read record
Write record
Not 9s?
T
F
STOP
Start
Read record
DOWHILE more data (not 9s record)
  Write record
  Read record
ENDDO
Stop

Figure 9-12 The logic of a well-structured read-and-print program can be expressed on a program flowchart or in pseudocode.

ten in uppercase letters. The letters describing functions within the DOWHILE pattern are indented two spaces to point out that they are within the DOWHILE.

Pseudocode is an especially convenient tool when designing structured programs. For example, a programmer can draw a flowchart for a program that is structured or for one that isn't. When the flowchart is finished, the programmer may have a difficult time trying to verify whether the resultant program will be structured or not! Not so with pseudocode. A programmer who writes pseudocode either uses or does not use the patterns of structured programming in the pseudocode.

The logic of the basic patterns of structured programming, and within DOUNTIL and CASE, is expressed in pseudocode in Figure 9-13. The indentions shown in these forms are a recommendation, not a requirement. (Remember, pseudocode is an informal language, not a programming language. An important advantage of pseudocode over programming languages is that it does not enforce coding rules as programming languages do. Because of its similarity to many commonly used programming languages, however, the transition from the design stage to the coding stage is straightforward.)

Another important advantage of pseudocode is that it can be entered readily into the computer from a typewriterlike keyboard. If the pseudocode is included as comments in program coding or retained on a separate but accessible computer file, it can be updated easily with computer help whenever the program logic is changed. Many CASE tools support creating and changing pseudocode.

Checking Out the Program

Whether we like it or not, a program seldom executes successfully the first time it is run. Even the simplest programs contain errors, and even experienced programmers make mistakes. It is said that a program that runs correctly the first time is as rare as a hole-in-one on the golf course! As programs become increasingly complex, more of the programmer's time

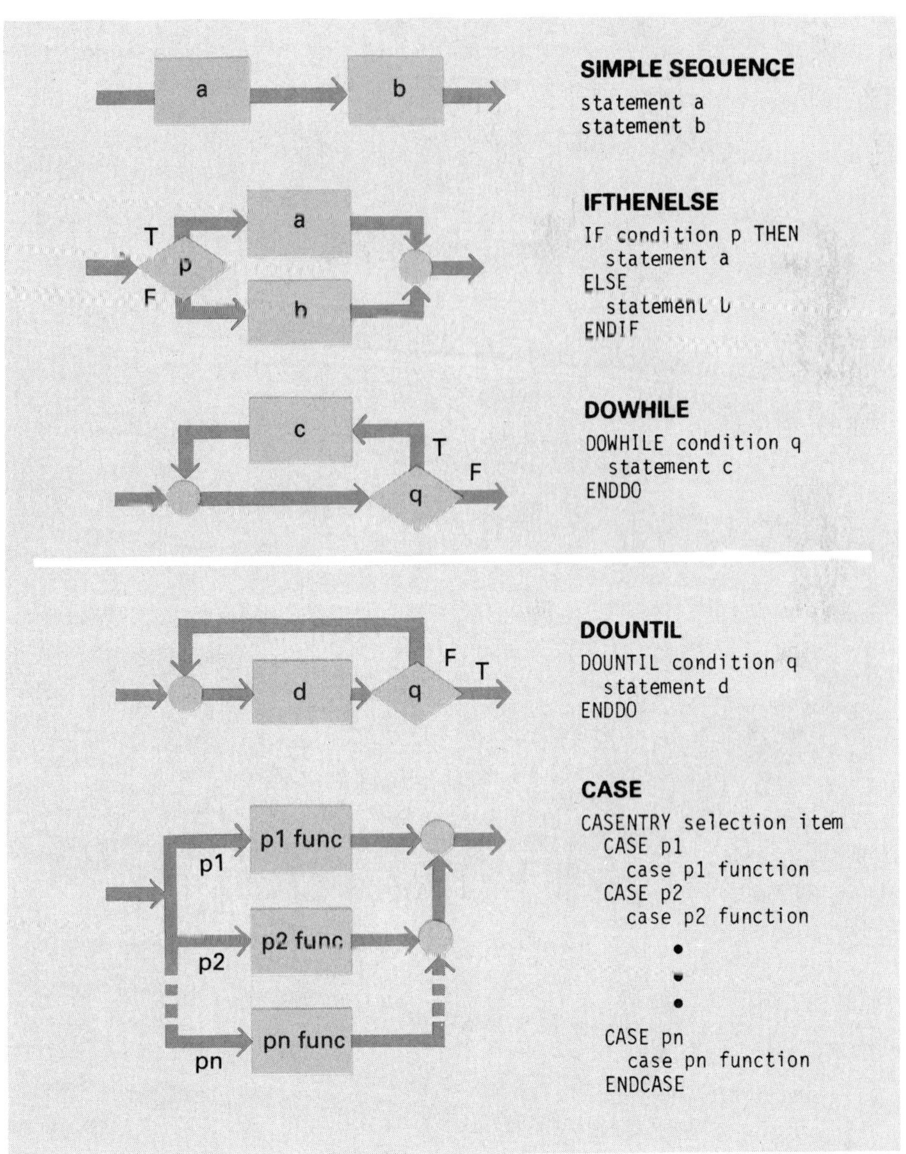
a
b
SIMPLE SEQUENCE
statement a
statement b
T
F
p
a
b
IFTHENELSE
IF condition p THEN
statement a
ELSE
statement b
ENDIF
c
T
F
q
DOWHILE
DOWHILE condition q
statement c
ENDDO
d
F
T
q
DOUNTIL
DOUNTIL condition q
statement d
ENDDO
p1
p1 func
p2
p2 func
pn
pn func
CASE
CASENTRY selection item
CASE p1
case p1 function
CASE p2
case p2 function
CASE pn
case pn function
ENDCASE

Figure 9-13 Programmers may elect to use either flowcharting or pseudocode when planning the logic of a well-structured program.

TRANSPORTING FREIGHT TO MARKET

If you've read Chapters 1 through 8 of this book, you're conditioned to think of a *terminal* as a visual-display unit, an automated teller machine, or any one of many similar input/output devices—a point at which data enters and/or information leaves a computer system. However, the word *terminal* has other meanings as well. Think now of a *terminal* as a point where ships enter or leave a land base. Matson Navigation Company's Sand Island terminal, completed in 1981, handles all of the company's Honolulu cargo operations (top). It is one of the world's finest and most efficient ocean terminals.

Like many other companies engaged in the transportation of goods, Matson Navigation Company and its subsidiaries depend on computers. The firm spent more than $30 million to develop and install its Matson Automated Terminal System, now in operation on Terminal Island in the Port of Los Angeles (bottom). Under computer control, four massive yard cranes move freight containers overhead around the yard and to and from shipside loading cranes. Container conveyors actually transfer the containers between the yard cranes and the shipyard loading cranes. The conveyers also operate under computer control. The objectives of this highly automated system are to make container handling more efficient, increase terminal capacity, reduce container and cargo damage, and provide a safer environment for workers in the terminal.

In support of vessel operations, a seaman's payroll system runs on desktop computers aboard each vessel. A consolidation and reporting system for the seaman's payroll runs on a mainframe at headquarters in San Francisco. Systems that perform vessel

Matson
MORGAN
Matson

overtime analysis, calculate voyage food expense, and analyze vessel performance also run as batch applications at headquarters.

Matson's freight documentation system generates customer bills, vessel discharge planning reports, notices of arrival, commodity statistics, and sales information. A special subsystem provides online access to customer cargo information in Honolulu. In both Oakland and Los Angeles, an online container equipment control system supports inventory control, terminal management, and vessel planning activities. The facilities and maintenance shops use small business computer systems for parts control, shop cost accounting, data input for shop employees, and billing to outside accounts.

Standard accounting applications implemented at Matson include accounts payable, accounts receivable, general ledger, capital assets accounting, and employee benefits administration. The insurance department is supported by a reporting system for cargo claims and an open claims listing system for personal injury claims. Many applications on these systems involve a great deal of batch processing and reporting. Some of the systems were developed in-house. Others were purchased as application packages and installed at the headquarters location. *(Photos courtesy of Matson Navigation Company)*

A Costly Bug

American Airlines has determined that a bug in its passenger reservations system may have cost the company as much as $50 million in lost ticket revenue during the second quarter of 1988. The system indicated that planes were sold out of discount fares when, in fact, such seats were available. Passengers requesting inexpensive fares were referred to competitors.

is spent in program checkout—debugging and testing each new or modified program. *Debugging* is the task of finding program errors (bugs) and correcting them so that the program runs properly. *Testing* consists of running the program with input data that simulates, or is a representative sample of, the actual data that will be processed. The care exercised in debugging and testing (or the lack of care) affects the success of the development effort.

Errors in programming may be either clerical or logical. Most *clerical errors* occur in the coding and keying stages of program development. A programmer may spell a key word incorrectly or use a name that has not been defined. The programmer or a data-entry operator may key in the wrong character or omit part of a statement. *Logical errors* are often harder to detect. They occur because a programmer does not understand a phase of the problem to be solved, fails to account for certain situations that may (and do) arise during processing, misinterprets some steps in the problem-solving method to be coded, and so on. Both clerical and logical errors must be detected and eliminated from the program.

Earlier in this chapter, we discussed desk checking as a means of detecting errors in the program logic reflected on a program flowchart and in the program coding. A few hours of programmer time spent in this manner can prevent needless waste of both programmer and computer time later. If the program logic won't work on paper, it won't work in the computer.

Going beyond individual effort, some programmers prefer to work in teams, checking their own programs and the programs of others in *informal code inspections.* A programmer who is familiar with a program may unconsciously read into it logic that is not there. Often a fresh viewpoint is more objective. In a chief-programmer environment, structured walkthroughs, which in this case are *formal code inspections,* may be carried out. Program listings and problem-report forms are distributed

Software Quality

While there is no universally accepted definition of what constitutes a high-quality program, most users agree that the following characteristics are important.

Correctness: Extent to which a program satisfies its specifications and meets the user's needs

Reliability: Extent to which a program performs its intended function without error

Robustness: Extent to which a program accommodates and handles unacceptable input and/or user operational errors

Usability: Effort required to operate, prepare input for, and understand output of a program

Testability: Effort required to test a program to insure it performs its intended function

Maintainability: Effort required to locate and fix an error in a program

Extensibility: Effort required to modify a program to change or enhance its function

Efficiency: Amount of computing resources required to use a program

Portability: Effort required to transfer a program from one hardware and/or software environment to another one

Reusability: Extent to which a program can be used in other related applications

to selected inspectors in much the same way as for the structured walkthroughs of system design. A reader (usually the programmer) leads the inspectors through the code. It is checked not only for errors in what the programmer intended to do, but also against the design documentation.

As mentioned earlier, a program may be written in any of several programming languages. It must be translated into machine language (1s and 0s, remember) before it can control computer operations. The *language-processor program* that does the translation examines the program statements to verify they have been coded correctly. It assists the programmer by finding some kinds of mistakes. For example, a language-processor program can detect an attempt to perform arithmetic on alphabetic data, or a missing left or right parenthesis. If errors are detected during translation, error messages, or *diagnostics,* are produced. After the errors have been corrected, the program or statement is again read into the computer to be translated. If errors persist, further corrections must be made. This procedure continues until an error-free run is achieved. Even then the programmer cannot assume that the program is error-free. (It may contain logical errors that are not detectable by the language-processor program.) Additional checkout is required.

Top-Down Testing

Top-down programming facilitates top-down testing. In effect, design, coding, and testing (or simply coding and testing, if the design is completed first) proceed in parallel. The purest approach to top-down development suggests that testing of the top module should begin as soon as it is coded. In practice, programmers usually find that at least one or two modules at a lower level must be designed and coded before any nontrivial testing can be done.

Implementation of top-down testing requires that dummy routines, called *program stubs,* be created for modules that are referred to by name in modules under test but are not yet coded. Each program stub is a substitute for a module. As such, it does not perform the actual functions of the module. It does provide sufficiently similar behavior to make the module that references it believe that it does. In most cases, a program stub also provides a *program trace.* For example, it may be advisable to include a statement causing CALLED NET PAY MODULE to be printed as output in a dummy routine. Such a printout can be very helpful in debugging.

Each program stub is eventually replaced by the module for which it serves as a placeholder. Through a staged integration procedure, the requirement for test time is distributed throughout system development. Errors are easier to detect because the suspect areas of code are more readily identifiable. There is no need to undertake the awesome task of trying to mold many separately coded and tested modules into a workable system at the end of the development effort.

Product Certification

A question that should be posed at the beginning of testing is: How will we know when we're done? The purpose of testing is to verify that a program consistently produces correct

THE COMPUTERIZATION OF COWS

Have you visited a dairy farm in recent years? Here, too, impacts of the Computer Age are likely to be evident. Today's average cow gives almost twice as much milk as the average cow of 20 years ago—12,216 pounds versus 7029 pounds. Much of this gain can be attributed to electronic technology.

A tiny transmitter housed in a plastic case is attached to the collar of each cow. When a cow enters the barn and sticks her head into a computerized feed stall, her 4-digit identification number is beeped to a minicomputer. The minicomputer scans a machine-readable file to find the cow's programmed feed allotment. It determines the proper quantity to be served and the type of feed best for the cow, based on where she is in her lactation cycle.

A small electronic box, a milker unit, and a stainless steel or tempered glass weigh jar sufficient to hold a cow's entire milk production are included in each stall. Activating the computerized milking system usually involves keying the cow's identification number into the box. A green light signals milking go-ahead; a red light indicates the cow is on medication and her milk must be discarded.

A flow sensor within the milker unit accurately monitors the milk flow and shifts vacuum levels and pulsation rates between stimulation, milking, and postmilking to give each cow the individual attention she needs. The colored indicator lights allow continued visual monitoring of the milking process. The weight of the milk, in pounds, is displayed. If the final weight of a cow's milk is substantially less than that of her previous milking, the red light is activated. The cow may be in heat or may have contracted a sudden illness. Because milk from a cow with an inflamed udder has different electrical conductivity properties than milk from a healthy cow, disease can be spotted and treated immediately.

Behind the scenes, the pipeline milking system that is basic to these operations is monitored, controlled, and cleaned with computer help. In addition, the minicomputer accumulates statistics for each cow and for the farm operation as a whole. As many as 80 data items—milk production, amount of milk fat, reproduction cycle, number of calves birthed, disposition, cash value, and so on—may be tracked per cow. Both detail and summary reports can be displayed or printed periodically and on a management-by-exception basis. *(Photo courtesy Sid Spahr, Dept. of Dairy Science, University of Illinois)* or expected results. To test all conditions that could arise during processing may be unrealistic or impossible. However, careful construction of a *test matrix* can help to increase the effectiveness of the testing process.

A question that should be posed at the beginning of testing is: How will we know when we're done?

Along the top of the matrix (column headings) the programmer or test personnel list all the functions the program can perform. On the left side of the matrix (row headings) are listed the test cases required. (See Figure 9-14.) Each test case should test only one or a very few functions. They are identified by placing check marks or X's in the matrix. If additional conditions to be tested are identified during testing, they should be added to the test matrix. If the matrix is in a computer-readable form, it can be modified easily.

Some back-end CASE tools provide *source-level debugging* capabilities. Such tools help to isolate the cause of an error by identifying the statement written by the programmer that corresponds directly to the point where the error occurred. When selecting a back-end CASE tool, information system personnel should look closely at what automated testing help each tool they're considering provides.

The extent of testing may depend on the amount of testing time

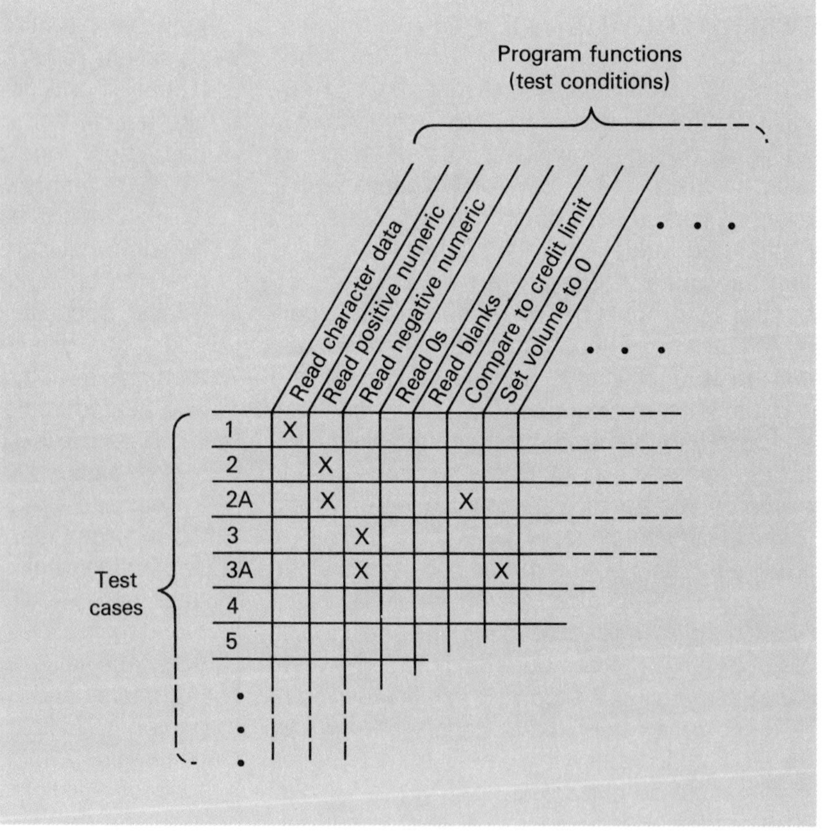
Program functions
(test conditions)
Read character data
Read positive numeric
Read negative numeric
Read 0s
Read blanks
Compare to credit limit
Set volume to 0
Test
cases
1
X
2
X
2A
X
X
3
X
3A
X
X
4
5

Figure 9-14 This test matrix provides a concise summary of the program functions to be exercised by test cases 1, 2, 2A, and so on, during program checkout.

available. A predetermined schedule and a promised system-availability date may have to be maintained. The recipient of information to be produced by the system may be willing to forgo complete testing because the information is desperately needed. In addition, little money may be available for testing. Often, the degree of testing is determined by balancing its cost against the penalties of acting on incorrect information.

Even a microcomputer user need not and should not accept a new system or program "on faith." Whether the system or program was developed under contract to the user or purchased as an off-the-shelf item, the user should test it. Remember, bugs can be either clerical or logical. Does the system or program *really* do what the documentation says it will? Does the system or program *really* do what the user wants and expects it to do?

Can we afford to test systems thoroughly? We can't afford not to.

Unfortunately, many user organizations and software development firms have learned the hard way that the consequences of inadequate testing may be very severe. It's one thing not to receive on time an expected report of last week's sales in region 2. It's another thing to have to shut down an entire production line or distribution center because a computer can't produce the required production schedule or shipping orders. Computer manufacturers and software development firms are being sued for hundreds of thousands of dollars because of clients' claims that systems were not ready for production use in reasonable time frames, did not perform as specified in contractual agreements, or failed during critical business periods. Can we afford to test systems thoroughly? We can't afford not to.

Documentation

Documentation is a term with at least two meanings:

1. The act of recording evidence about an activity
2. The recorded evidence of what has been done, is being done, or is going to be done on a project

Complete, accurate, and timely documentation of a program or system is as essential to effective use of the program or system as the actual coding itself. The long-range success (or failure) of the system development effort depends on it.

When the steps of system development are carried out as they should be, documentation is *not* an unwelcome burden imposed as a project nears completion. Instead documentation is an integral part of the system development cycle. Documentation standards should be established early and procedures enforced to insure continuous maintenance and updating. The availability of computerized or hard-copy forms helps to minimize the time required to prepare documentation. Readily usable forms help to insure complete coverage of the project.

In most development efforts, documentation must be developed for the system as a whole *and* for each program within it. As suggested earlier, a development support library should be set up. It serves as a receptacle and a retrieval mechanism for all project documentation. Trained personnel can assist system analysts and programmers both in creating high-quality documentation and in distributing or retrieving it at appropriate times.

To discuss the content and format of all the documentation that may be created during system development is far beyond the scope of this book. Figure 9-15 provides an overview of the types of documentation usually required. Some of the types of documentation are familiar to us. In Chapter 8, we mentioned the need for functional specifications outlining the system requirements. These specifications tell *what* the system under development is supposed to accomplish. They also help to insure the system will solve the problem it is supposed to solve.

The functional specifications are supported by lower-level, more technical specifications that tell *how* a system or program will perform the functions identified for it. Structure, charts, program flowcharts, and pseudocode are commonly used for this purpose. These types of documentation are the basis for communication among developers. They are essential when changes must be made to the system at a later time.

Still other types of documentation must be created for the operator who will monitor the system during execution. If users at terminals, personal computers, or workstations will interact with the system, some documentation may have to be tailored to their special needs. The complete documentation package provides a visible, understandable trail for management personnel with over-all responsibility for the project. It can also be used by auditors to verify that company policies and procedures are being carried out. To protect a company's assets, to prevent disruption of critical business operations when the unexpected occurs, to satisfy demands for government reporting, and so on, high-quality documentation is an absolute requirement.

System Evaluation

Whether or not system evaluation tasks are included in the plan for system development, system evaluation occurs. A data-entry operator may find the data-entry procedures cumbersome when large volumes of data must be keyed. The sales manager for petrochemicals may become frustrated because, although sales-by-item totals are interesting, sales-by-territory totals would give him a better fix on what he suspects is the real sales problem. A computer sort run expected to complete within an hour may actually be taking longer—so much longer that the overnight batch jobs are not getting done until 8 or 9 in the morning. Two months after a personal computer user acquires a software package to help with estimating the costs of remodeling the kitchen and family room, the package may be sitting on the shelf rather than producing output.

Because system implementation is such a major undertaking, most organizations convert to a new system gradually.

Because system implementation is such a major undertaking, most organizations convert to a new system gradually. For example, the inventory-control programs may be implemented first, then the program

Figure 9-15 The documentation created throughout system development should be kept in a development support library where it is available to all who need it.

Feasibility Report

System Proposal

Functional Specifications
- System flowchart
- Input/output descriptions
  - (printer spacing charts, display-screen layouts, etc.)
- File descriptions
  - (record layouts, etc.)

Samples of inputs and outputs

Data Element Dictionary

Logic Specifications
- Structure charts
- Program flowcharts
- Pseudocode
- HIPO diagrams
- Nassi-Schneiderman charts
- Warnier-Orr diagrams
- Decision tables
- Decision trees

Program Listings

Documentation of Structured Walkthroughs
- For formal design reviews
  - (participants' problem logs, moderator's summary report)
- For formal code inspections
  - (participants' problem reports, moderator's summary report)

Computer-Assisted Testing Information
- Test plan
- Test matrices
- Test case descriptions
- Test data and expected results
- Actual results of test runs

Operational Information
- Keying instructions
- Job-control statements
- Run instructions
- Output distribution instructions
- Backup and recovery procedures

User Documentation
- System narrative
  - (general information, user's guides, reference manuals)
- Input specifications and instructions
- Output descriptions and distribution
- Education and training materials

Maintenance Information
- Design change requests (DCR's)
- Program change log

Technical References
- Hardware specifications
- Specifications for vendor-supplied software
- Other vendor-supplied documentation

GAMBLING AND COMPUTERS

The walls are lined with mirrors and closed-circuit television screens. Thousands of people enter and leave 'round the clock. No one seems to notice or care whether it's morning or evening, daylight or dark. Yes, this is the world of slot machines and tables—the gambling casino.

With literally millions of dollars changing hands each day, running a casino is clearly big business. Not surprisingly, the operators of such casinos have turned to computers for help.

At some sites, a microcomputer is installed inside each slot machine. The microcomputer counts the number of coins entered, the number of times the machine handle is pulled, how much is paid out, and the amount of time in which all this is happening. Data is forwarded to a central minicomputer or mainframe that accumulates over-all totals and prints daily reports of slot-machine usage.

The microcomputer within a slot machine can detect tampering with the machine. It reports such events to the central computer immediately. The central computer, in turn, alerts security and surveillance personnel. The microcomputer can also detect equipment malfunctions within the machine. The types of malfunctions that may occur are identified by unique exception codes. A lead mechanic or maintenance manager receives daily reports showing the number of exception codes of each type experienced at each machine. Preventive and corrective maintenance are scheduled accordingly.

Obviously, the activities at a casino revolve around money. The money, whether cash or credit, takes the form of casino chips of various denominations. Chips may be supplied at a table or at the casino's central bank. Gamblers requesting chips on credit must have an established credit rating with the casino. That rating must be verified and the amount of money that can yet be loaned to the requestor (in lieu of his or her current account situation) determined, before the request is granted. At the bank, gamblers

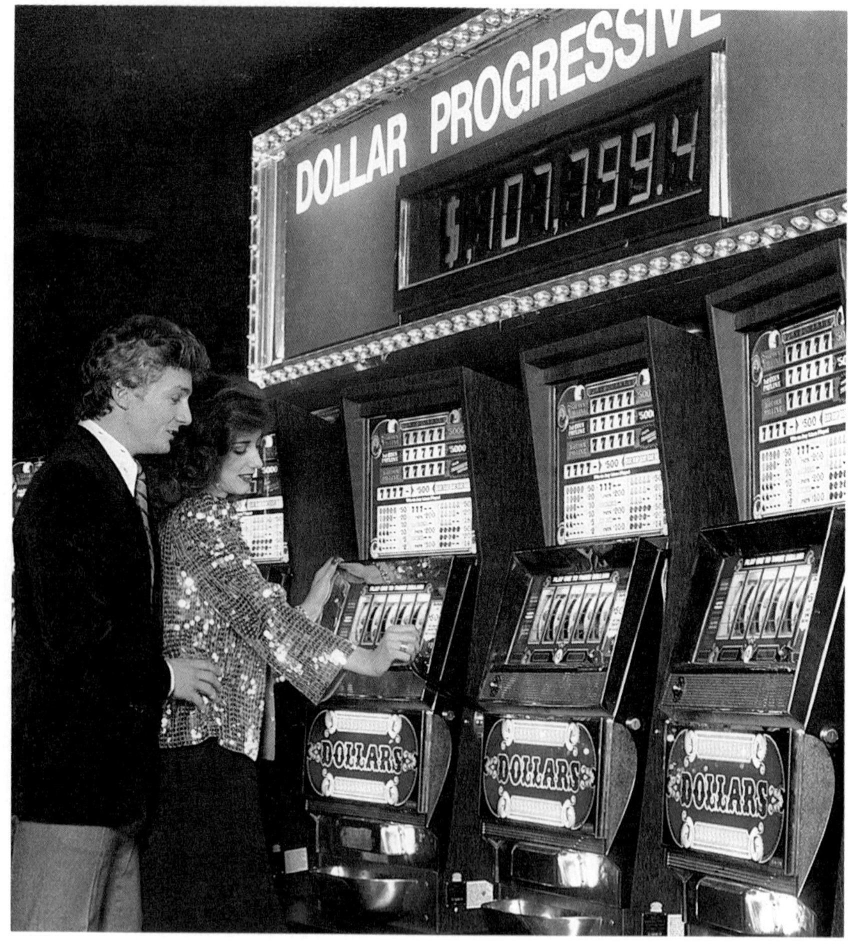
DOLLAR PROGRESSIVE
$107,799.4
DOLLARS
DOLLARS
DOLLARS

can turn in their chips for money. Bettors with big bankrolls can make deposits at the casino's bank and withdraw funds as needed. Most if not all of these financial transactions are now handled by computers.

Security is very important in the casino environment. Typically, each employee must check out a badge at the beginning of a shift and return it at the end of the work day. For a task such as opening or filling a slot machine or opening a cash box, checks of the badge, user logon ID, and user password are made by the central computer before the task is allowed to occur. The computer determines and reports how much money should be in each cash box. The amount of money actually brought to the count room is compared with the computed amount so that discrepancies are known immediately and can be resolved.

Since a casino's use of computers is so extensive, most casino operators choose to automate in stages—say, first the bank, then the site security, then individual cash drawers, and so on. To insure that their systems are always available, some operators install a second computer as backup to the central minicomputer or mainframe. If the central computer fails, the backup computer takes over immediately. On the floor, uninterrupted, gambling proceeds. *(Photo courtesy Sands Hotel & Casino, Las Vegas)*

to generate purchase orders when stock is depleted, and so on. In another approach, the petrochemicals group may get aboard the system first; then the fabrics and finishes group; then the paints and resins group; and so on. When a staged approach to implementation is employed, planned system evaluation tasks can be carried out while the use of the system is still somewhat limited.

The most rigid system evaluation is a well-defined user acceptance test. This test is an extension of the system testing we discussed earlier, but now users performing their routine job responsibilities are directly involved. The system will not be declared ready for production use until the user (client) and the contractor (in-house information system personnel or an outside development firm) agree that it is performing according to specifications and/or that satisfactory plans are in place for all discrepancies. Acquired software packages should undergo acceptance testing just as in-house-developed software does.

Formal machine-based user acceptance testing can and should be complemented by user discussions of their perceptions of the system in operation. Systematic observations of how the system is performing, whether or not the outputs of the system are being used, and so on, should be made. The over-all objective of these efforts is to determine whether or not the system is meeting the user needs it's supposed to satisfy. A second consideration is whether or not it operates within stated budget and performance limits. The findings of system evaluation should be reported to the users and to information system management. Plans should be put in place to follow up on problems.

If a program that is error-free on its first run is rare, a system that is all-things-to-all-users when first implemented is even rarer. (To attempt to achieve such an objective is unrealistic and likely to be fatal—system implementation may never occur.) Ongoing support of an installed system is a necessity from both operational and development points of view. While some refer to ongoing development support as *system maintenance,* others argue that this work should be viewed and carried out as *system development.* Certainly, care in system analysis, design, and implementation is no less critical when making changes to a system on which an organization's business depends than when initially developing it.

If the system was implemented by in-house staff, the changes will be made by in-house staff. If major portions of the system were purchased and/or implemented by another firm, either in-house staff must learn the system or ongoing support must be provided under a service contract.

CHAPTER SUMMARY

1. The steps of system development can be grouped within four phases: system analysis, system design, system implementation, and system evaluation.

2. System implementation often begins with program flowcharting, a pictorial method of planning the detailed logic within an application program. The logic shown on the flowchart should be desk-checked to detect and remove any errors as soon as possible.

3. The program flowchart serves as a guide during program coding. The line numbers of program statements can be placed by the flowcharting symbols to serve as cross-references between the flowchart and the program.

4. Structured programming is the application of ideas of top-down design and modularity at the coding level; only three basic patterns—SIMPLE SEQUENCE, IFTHENELSE, and DOWHILE—are used in a well-structured program.

5. Two commonly used combinations of basic patterns are the DOUNTIL and CASE control structures. DOUNTIL is the same as a SIMPLE SEQUENCE followed by a DOWHILE; CASE is the same as a sequence of nested IFTHENELSE's.

6. Pseudocode is an informal method of expressing program logic in an easy-to-read, top-to-bottom fashion that is especially convenient when designing structured programs.

7. Errors in a program may be either clerical or logical. Desk checking, informal code inspections, and formal code inspections can be carried out to detect and remove these errors as soon as possible.

8. The language-processor program that translates the program statements into machine language can assist the programmer by finding some kinds of errors. If errors are detected during the translation, error messages, or diagnostics, are provided as output.

9. Top-down modular programming facilitates top-down testing. Program stubs are created as substitutes for modules that are not yet coded, then replaced by the modules when they are coded and ready for testing in the system environment.

10. Complete, accurate, and timely documentation of a program or system is as essential to effective use of the program or system as the actual coding itself. When system development is carried out properly, documentation is an integral part of the system development cycle.

11. System evaluation should be planned for. Well-defined user acceptance testing should be complemented by user discussions and systematic observations of how the system is performing.

DISCUSSION QUESTIONS

1. (a) Name two types of flowcharts.
(b) Compare the two types, noting similarities and differences.

2. Construct a system flowchart for the following problem:

There are 26 students in a class. Each student is identified by a student number. His or her name, number, and term grade are to be printed on individual grade cards.

The computer is to be used to calculate each student's term grade. Eight test and classroom-assignment scores are to be used for this purpose. The scores (ranging from 0 through 100), plus the number and name of each student, are to be keyed as input from an online visual-display unit during processing. If a student's term grade is above 90, the name and number are also to be printed on an Honors List. This list is to be written on magnetic tape and transcribed later to a printed report. Processing is to be completed when all student data has been processed.

3. Repeat Question 2, but now construct a program flowchart showing the logic needed to solve the problem. In doing so, be sure to plan a well-structured program.

4. Explain desk checking—what, why, when, how, and by whom it is used.

5. Show how top-down programming and program modularity relate to one another.

6. Give five arguments for the use of structured programming.

7. How does DOWHILE differ from DOUNTIL?

8. (a) What is pseudocode?
(b) When, how, and why is it used?

9. Discuss the characteristics you think a high-quality program should have.

10. How does a language-processor program help the programmer?

11. (a) List the types of documentation needed during the various stages of system development.
(b) By whom is each type of documentation created?
(c) By whom is it used?

12. Why should system evaluation be planned for, since it will occur anyway?

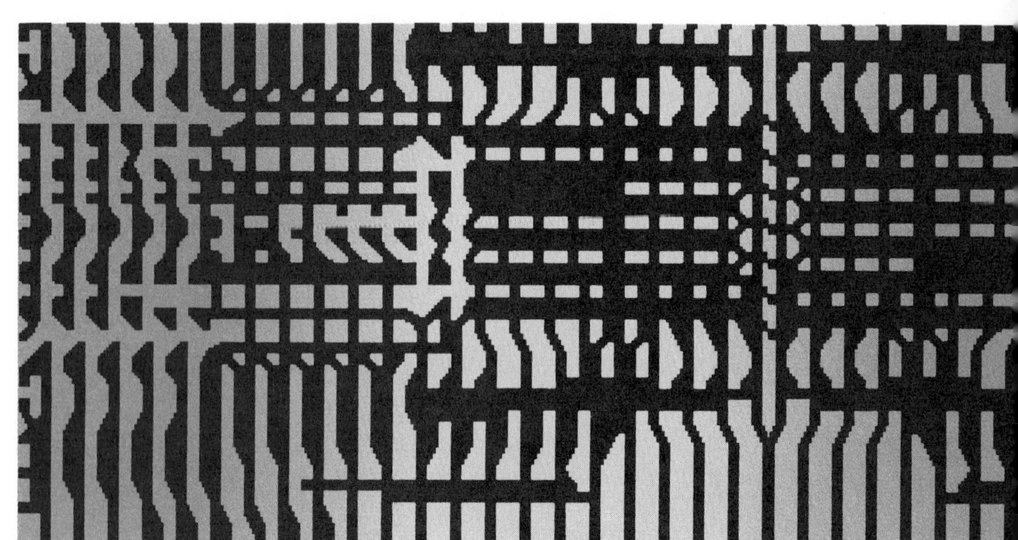

10 Programming Languages and Application Development Tools

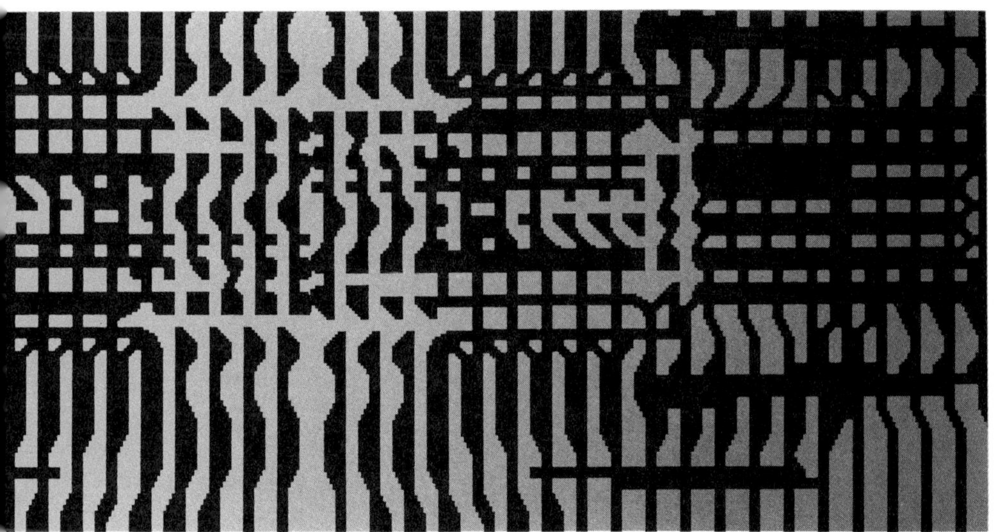

IN THIS CHAPTER

Machine Language
Assembler Languages
High-Level Programming Languages
FORTRAN
COBOL
PL/I
BASIC
Pascal
C
RPG
Fourth-Generation Languages
Natural Languages
Object-Oriented Languages
Selecting a Language

We marvel today at what computers can do. Even in the 1950s, they solved complex equations and got weekly paychecks out on time. By the 1960s they reserved seats on airline flights and managed inventories. In the 1970s they designed airplanes, bridges, and highways, and controlled manned space flights. In the 1980s they optimized gasoline usage in our automobiles and directed life-maintaining equipment in our hospitals. Truly, their abilities are limited only by our imagination.

We know, however, that a computer by itself has no power at all. Whether it is big enough to fill a room or small enough to fit in your pocket, it can do nothing unless it's directed step by step. The power that directs the computer lies in a program.

We learned earlier that a stored program is a sequence of machine-language instructions in the computer's internal storage unit that guides it in carrying out basic operations. The basic operations are simple actions such as adding, subtracting, moving, comparing, reading, and writing. In fact, these "simple" operations are even more basic—they are flows of electronic pulses between the capacitors, resistors, and other binary-state components that make up the computer.

In somewhat the same way as a computer responds to electronic pulses, our muscles respond to nerve pulses. Imagine how difficult it would be if, to move an arm or leg, we had to think through and express that movement in terms of nerve pulses. Suppose that our friends could only accompany us to the latest movie if we spelled out, in terms of nerve impulses, the actions they needed to take to get there. Fortunately, we can just say something like, "Take the Camden Avenue turnoff," or, "Wait where you are—we'll pick you up." Once again, there's more than one way to solve the problem. The way need only be communicated and then carried out.

A similar communication capability exists in programming. To fully appreciate this capability, we look first at what it takes to communicate with a computer in its own machine language—the language that directly affects the flow, presence, or absence of electronic pulses. Then we look at the next level of programming languages, those commonly known as *assembler languages.*

You'll see that it's convenient to communicate with a computer by means of languages at still higher levels. The languages at these levels are called *third-generation languages* and *fourth-generation languages,* or *4GL's.* User-oriented visual-display support is often provided with these languages to help user-programmers write programs by responding to simple prompts on the screen. In some cases the user-programmers may not even realize that they are programming!

Strictly speaking, a programming language is not software. The language is a set of carefully chosen symbols with well-defined meanings, plus a set of rules that users must follow when writing programs in that language. The software is the language-processor program that translates programming-language statements into machine-language form. Fourth-generation language translators and other application development tools are software with broader ranges of capabilities. In general, they provide more environmental and operational support for user-programmers.

You may be surprised to learn that more than 300 programming languages have been developed. There are several thousand application development tools. An obvious question is: Why so many? An analogy here is: Why are there so many kinds of shoes? Few of us would care to wear 3-inch heels to go hiking, or cowboy boots to go on a job interview, or open-toed sandals to walk across a college campus when it's 10 degrees below zero. Each kind of shoe meets a particular need. So it is with programming languages and application development tools. In this chapter, we look first at machine and assembler languages. Then we direct our attention to third-generation programming languages used on a wide range of computers: COBOL, FORTRAN, PL/I, BASIC, Pascal, C, and RPG. Then we look at 4GL's, natural languages, and object-oriented languages. Our emphasis is not on language rules. Rather, we explore the major characteristics of the languages and the applications for which they are best suited. You need this information to understand why a particular language is chosen for an application or to make such a choice yourself.

In the Beginning

In the beginning, there was but one kind of computer language. The language was called *machine language.* System designers, programmers, scientists, and mathematicians, who were the only users of computers in those days, looked upon the language and decided it was not good.

Machine Language

To review what a computer's machine language is, let's assume first that we must communicate with a computer using its machine language. We saw in Chapter 6 that a computer with a 32-bit architecture may be directed by instructions that are 32 bits in length. To cause such a computer to add two values we might write:

BINARY
010110000001000001011000000101010
010110100010000010110000000110010
010100000001000001011000000110110

In the first instruction above, we tell the computer to load a particular data item into a particular register. In the second, we tell it to add another data item to that value. In the third, we tell it to store the result. When writing these instructions, we must know exactly where the two data items will be located in storage and where to store the result. We must know the bit patterns (op codes) for the load, add, and store operations needed. Assuming we know this information, we must write it and key it into storage correctly.

Obviously, creating a complete program in this machine language would be both tedious and time-consuming. After a time, all the strings of 1s and 0s would look alike. We would almost certainly write or key in some 1s where there should be 0s and some 0s where there should be 1s.

Some of you may be thinking that writing machine-language instructions for an 8 bit microcomputer might not be so bad. Let's see. In the next column, at the left, are the instructions needed to direct an 8-bit 6502 microprocessor (as used in an early Apple II microcomputer, for example) to add two numbers and store the result.

BINARY	HEXADECIMAL
10101001	A9
00110000	30
00011000	18
01101001	69
00100010	22
10001101	8D
00000010	02
01100000	50

The patterns above are only 8 bits in length, but there are 8 patterns (not 3, as you may have expected). It's not obvious that writing a correct program in this machine language would be much easier than writing one in the first machine language we discussed.

It's only fair to note that some computers can convert values written in hexadecimal notation to equivalent binary numbers. This means that we could write instructions in hexadecimal as on the right in our example above. Hard-wired circuitry or a machine-language program in the computer's read-only memory would convert the hexadecimal digits to binary for us. An incorrect digit would be easier to detect, and keying the program into storage would be less tedious and error-prone. However, we would still have to know the exact op codes for operations and the exact storage locations for data.

There are other considerations, too. Since machine-language instructions contain the exact bit patterns (op codes) for machine operations, they can be used only on computers whose operations are defined in exactly that way. That is, A9 may mean Load to one computer but Compare to another. We cannot simply write a program for whatever computer is available and expect it to run with little or no change on another computer. Since the instructions contain exact storage addresses, we have to understand how the internal storage unit of our particular computer is organized and accessed. How would you like to modify a machine-language program initially written by someone else to, say, cause the computer to read employee addresses as well as employee names as input? How long would it take you to find a bug in 300 or more lines of 1s and 0s in a machine-language accounts-receivable program? Clearly, machine-language programming is not the key to increased productivity in the use of computers.

Clearly, machine-language programming is not the key to increased productivity in the use of computers.

Assembler Languages

Because of the obvious difficulties involved in writing, keying in, and testing machine-language programs, symbolic programming languages have been developed. These languages permit the programmer to use convenient symbols, or *mnemonics* (memory aids), when writing a program. Op codes written as mnemonics are easier to remember and interpret than op codes written as binary or hexadecimal digits. A can stand for Add, L for Load, B for Branch, and so on.

Furthermore, a programmer who codes in a symbolic language need not know the exact storage locations of data and instructions. He or she can simply select a name, or *label,* for an instruction or a data item, and then use that label to refer to the instruction or data item. For example, NAME can stand for employee name, PARTNO for part number, and RATE for hourly wage. The labels for data items are commonly called *variables* because the values of the data items may be changed many times during processing.

The first commonly used symbolic languages were called *assembler languages.* Like a machine language, an assembler language is a relatively low-level, machine-oriented language. The programmer does not have to write instructions in binary or hexadecimal, but he or she must still be very conscious of the architecture of the computer that will execute the instructions. To understand why, consider the instructions below. They tell the computer to add two values and store the result, as did our machine-language instructions above.

```
ADDROUT   L    2,DATA1
          A    2,DATA2
          ST   2,SCORE
          .
          .
          .
DATA1     DS   F
DATA2     DS   F
SCORE     DS   F
```

The current contents of the primary-storage locations reserved for variable DATA1 are loaded into register 2 by means of the Load (L) instruction. The current contents of DATA2 are added to this value by means of the Add (A) instruction. Their sum is stored in SCORE by means of the store (ST) instruction.

In order to write just these few instructions, the programmer had to know certain facts:

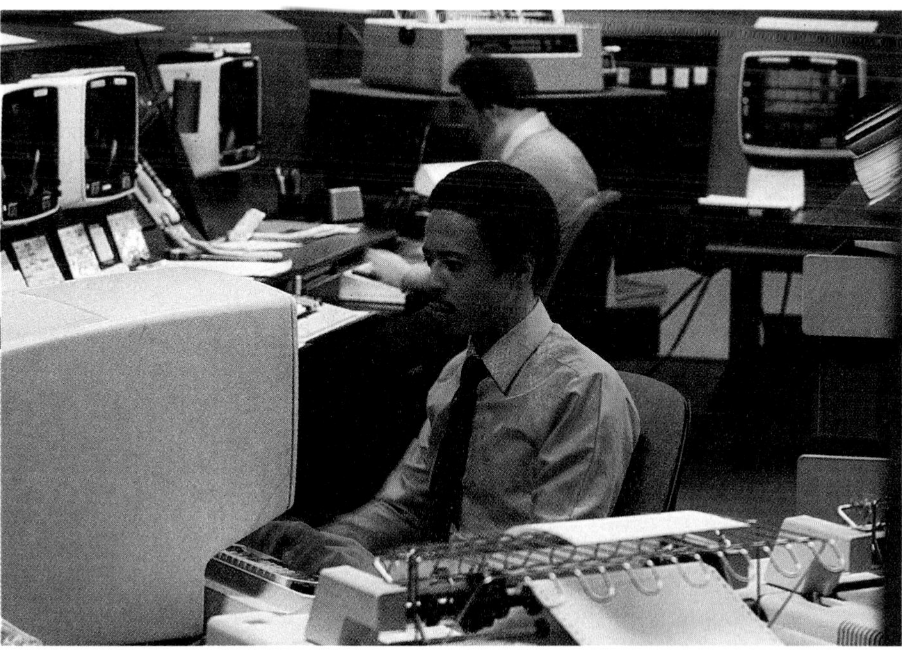

SYSTEM PROGRAMMING

Programmers employed by major computer manufacturers often develop system software for the manufacturers' machines. For such system programming, the assembler language developed for the machines in the particular product family may be an appropriate choice. It can be used to express all the operations that the machines are capable of performing. *(Photo courtesy SBS)*

- The computer has a register that can be used in addition operations and that can be referred to by the numeral 2.
- A value can be placed in a register by means of a load operation.
- The result of an add operation involving a register is placed back into the same register.
- The result in a register can be saved (before the register is reused) by storing it in another primary-storage location.

This example also shows that an assembler-language programmer cannot use labels without first defining them. The label for an instruction is defined by placing it in the label field (the leftmost positions) of the instruction that it is to identify. The labels for data items are really the labels for primary-storage locations reserved for the data items. The programmer must tell the computer to set aside certain primary-storage locations for all the data items used in a program. Furthermore, the programmer must tell what type of data each item is and how much storage should be reserved for it. In our example, the programmer used three Define Storage (DS) instructions. Each one contained F as an operand. The F tells the computer to reserve one full word of storage for a numeric value to be stored as a binary number. The programmer had to determine beforehand that one full word would hold the binary equivalent of any value that might be read as input for

DATA1 or DATA2, and of any value that might be computed as their sum. He or she had to be sure that the mnemonics L, A, and ST represent operations that can be performed on full-word binary values.

In general, each type of computer has its own assembler language. Assembler-language programming is possible with a computer only if a language-processor program known as an *assembler program* (*assembler,* for short) has been developed and is available for the computer. The steps necessary from time of problem analysis to time of output are summarized in Figure 10-1.

First, the problem is analyzed in terms of the user's needs. Then it is analyzed in terms of the computer's capabilities. The programmer expresses the needed operations in assembler language, thereby creating a *source program.* The source program is then keyed onto cards, tape, or disk for later use, or keyed directly into the primary storage of the computer to be used in processing.

An assembler program designed to operate on assembler-language programs is then loaded into primary storage. It serves as the stored program during an *assembly run.* The source program is the input data for the run. Assembler-language instructions are translated into machine-language instructions.

The assembly run produces two outputs. One output is an *object program.* It comprises the machine-language instructions. The second output is an *assembly listing.* It shows both the assembler-language coding and the machine-language instructions created from that coding. Most assembler programs can detect certain types of coding and keying errors, generally classified as clerical errors (recall "Checking Out the Program" in Chapter 9). All errors must be corrected. Then the source program can again be provided as input to an assembly run, with hope that no new errors will be found.

After an error-free assembly run has been achieved, the object program is loaded into primary storage. It serves as the stored program during a *production run.* As noted in Chapter 9, the programmer cannot assume that a successfully translated program is correct. The assembler program can detect errors in *syntax* (that is, in the way instructions are coded). It may not detect errors in logic. For this reason, test data should be processed before the actual production data is provided as input. The output results should be compared against predetermined, valid results. Not until the output of test runs appears satisfactory to the programmer and has been confirmed by the user should the program be released for production use.

High-Level Programming Languages

Another significant step in the development of programming languages was the design of high-level programming languages and language-processor programs (also referred to as *language translators, compilers,* and *interpreters*). Whereas assembler languages are machine-oriented languages, high-level languages are procedure- or problem-oriented languages. Both the user and the programmer (they may be one person—a *user-programmer*) direct their attention to the problem at hand. The programmer does not have to know how the computer will perform required operations. The term *high-level programming language* is appro-

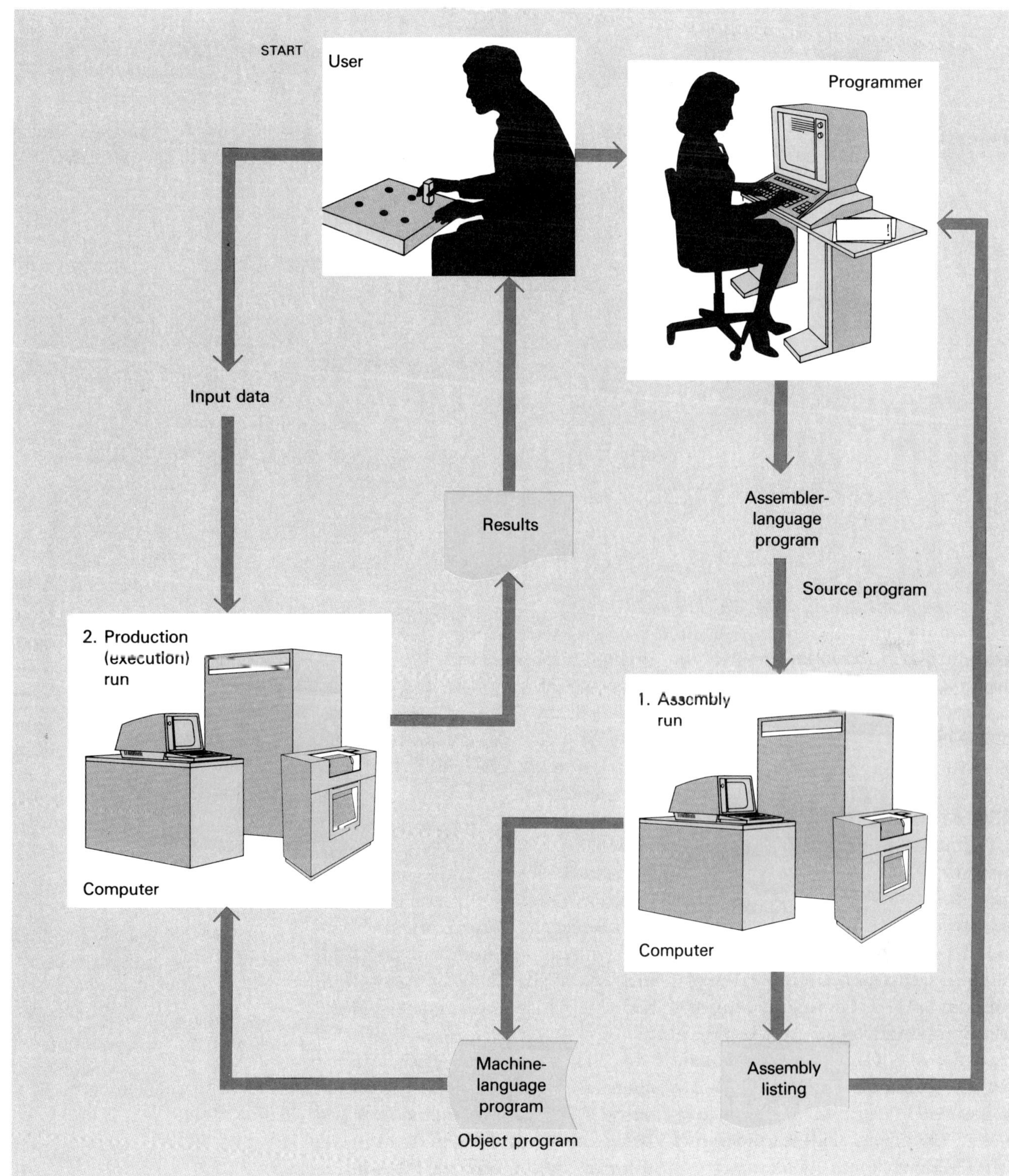
START
User
Programmer
Input data
Results
Assembler-
language
program
Source program
2. Production
(execution)
run
Computer
1. Assembly
run
Computer
Machine-
language
program
Object program
Assembly
listing

Figure 10-1 Creating, assembling, and executing an assembler-language program is a multistep process that begins with user requirements and ends with user-oriented results that satisfy those requirements.

BASIC NECESSITIES

Like many public utilities, Pacific Gas and Electric Company, headquartered in San Francisco, depends heavily on its installed computer systems. They're being used here for materials tracking (top left), customer service (top right), power systems control (center left), weather-related studies (center right), gas systems control (bottom left), and printing of bills (bottom right). As customers, we likewise depend on the computers of utility firms for basic essentials—our gas and electricity. *(Photos courtesy Pacific Gas & Electric)* priate because the programmer is removed a considerable distance from concerns related to the machine.

One statement in a high-level programming language is often used to create several machine-language instructions. For example, consider the following statement written in FORTRAN, a widely used high-level language:

```
AVCST = TOTPR/QTY
```

This one simple statement causes the computer to divide total price (TOTPR) by quantity (QTY) to determine the average cost and then store this result in AVCST. In contrast, several machine-language or assembler-language instructions would be needed to designate the same operations. The total price would have to be loaded into a particular primary-storage location or register; the quantity would have to be positioned properly; division would have to be performed; and the result would have to be stored.

The fact that one high-level-language statement corresponds to several machine-language instructions is important for at least two reasons. First, it reduces the time and effort needed for programming because fewer lines of coding are needed to designate a sequence of processing steps. Second, it cuts down on the likelihood of errors. The sequences of instructions inserted to replace high-level-language statements are pretested, correct routines. Some of these sequences are so complex that the programmer would be apt to make errors if he or she attempted to code them. However, when the programmer uses high-level-language statements, he or she need only check to make sure that the statements are written correctly. Then it can be assumed that the inserted sequences are error-free.

High-level programming languages are less rigid than low-level programming languages; the programmer has much more freedom in writing a program. Such a language is said to be *free-form*. Generally, the source-program statements do not have to be written in exactly prescribed positions on coding lines and can be keyed quite easily when using a terminal, workstation, or microcomputer.

High-level programming languages are less rigid than low-level programming languages; the programmer has much more freedom in writing a program.

A high-level language is to a large extent *machine-independent*. To appreciate this characteristic, suppose that you are the manager of an organization or of an information system department. Because of an increased workload, or because a system development effort now under way requires capabilities that your present computer system does not have, a new system has been selected. The new system is completely different and will not accept the machine-language programs that run on the old system.

If the programs were written initially in an assembler language, they will probably have to be rewritten. If, however, the programs were written in a high-level language, your staff may be able to take those programs, in their source-program form, and submit them as input to a language-processor program designed for the

Do I Really Need to Learn a Programming Language?

If you're a microcomputer user, you've probably acquired a word-processing program, an electronic spreadsheet program, and other software packages. If the packages meet all your needs, or if you can count on your company's information center support staff (or a friend) to help you, you may "get by." Failing that, you're likely to need at least a working knowledge of one programming language. Today, BASIC is the common choice.

new system. This program will develop, for each source program, an object program in the new system's machine language. It is only fair to note that some modifications to the source programs may be necessary. Such modifications will be much less than the work that would be required to rewrite them.

As this example suggests, a high-level-language program must be translated to a machine-language form before it can be executed. The language-processor program that performs the translation may be either a compiler or an interpreter.

A *compiler program* is like an assembler in that it translates each statement of a source program into equivalent machine-language instructions. It creates an object module or a complete object program in primary storage, which can then be executed immediately or saved in secondary storage for execution at a later time. (See Figure 10-2.)

In some environments, the compile step, a *link step* that combines the object module with other object modules or routines needed during execution, and the execution step are all invoked by a single keystroke. If the compile and link steps are error-free, execution occurs.

A second, optional output of most *compilation runs* is a *source-program listing*. It shows the programmer's source statements as they were provided as input to the compiler. Unlike an assembly listing, however, a source-program listing does not contain the machine-language instructions of the object program. Since a high-level-language programmer does not direct the computer in machine-oriented terms, the machine-language instructions would be of little interest or value. The programmer may have the listing printed in hard-copy form or simply view it on a visual-display screen.

An *interpreter program* reads the statements of a source program on a statement-by-statement basis. It determines the operations required to carry out each statement and causes the computer to perform those operations immediately. The interpreter does not create a sequence of machine-language instructions that can be saved and executed again at a later time. To reuse a program, the programmer must save it in source-program form and then cause it to be translated as well as executed again whenever reuse is required.

In many environments, an interpreter program is a valuable tool during program development. It allows direct interaction with the computer system as translation and execution of a program occur. If the interpreter detects an error in a source statement, the programmer is alerted to the error immediately. The programmer can correct the error and then cause translation and execution of the program to continue at that point. There is no need to resubmit the entire program for translation as there is when an assembler or a compiler is used.

Compiler programs have been developed for all common high-level programming languages. Interpreter programs are available for those most often used in interactive environments. If you are a microcomputer user, you may find that both a BASIC compiler and a BASIC interpreter are available for use on your system.

Language Standards

Since the 1960s, organizations such as the American National Standards Institute (ANSI) and the International Standards Organization (ISO) have worked to develop standards for high-level programming languages. These efforts have resulted in very detailed guidelines, or language definitions, that language-processor designers are encouraged to follow. The major objectives of standardization are to create greater uniformity in implementation of a particular language and to determine what modifications or extensions to the language are required. Ease of programmer training and interchangeability of programs are direct user benefits that can be achieved through standardization.

FORTRAN

FORTRAN is the oldest high-level programming language. A group was organized in the mid-1950s to develop the language. Programs written

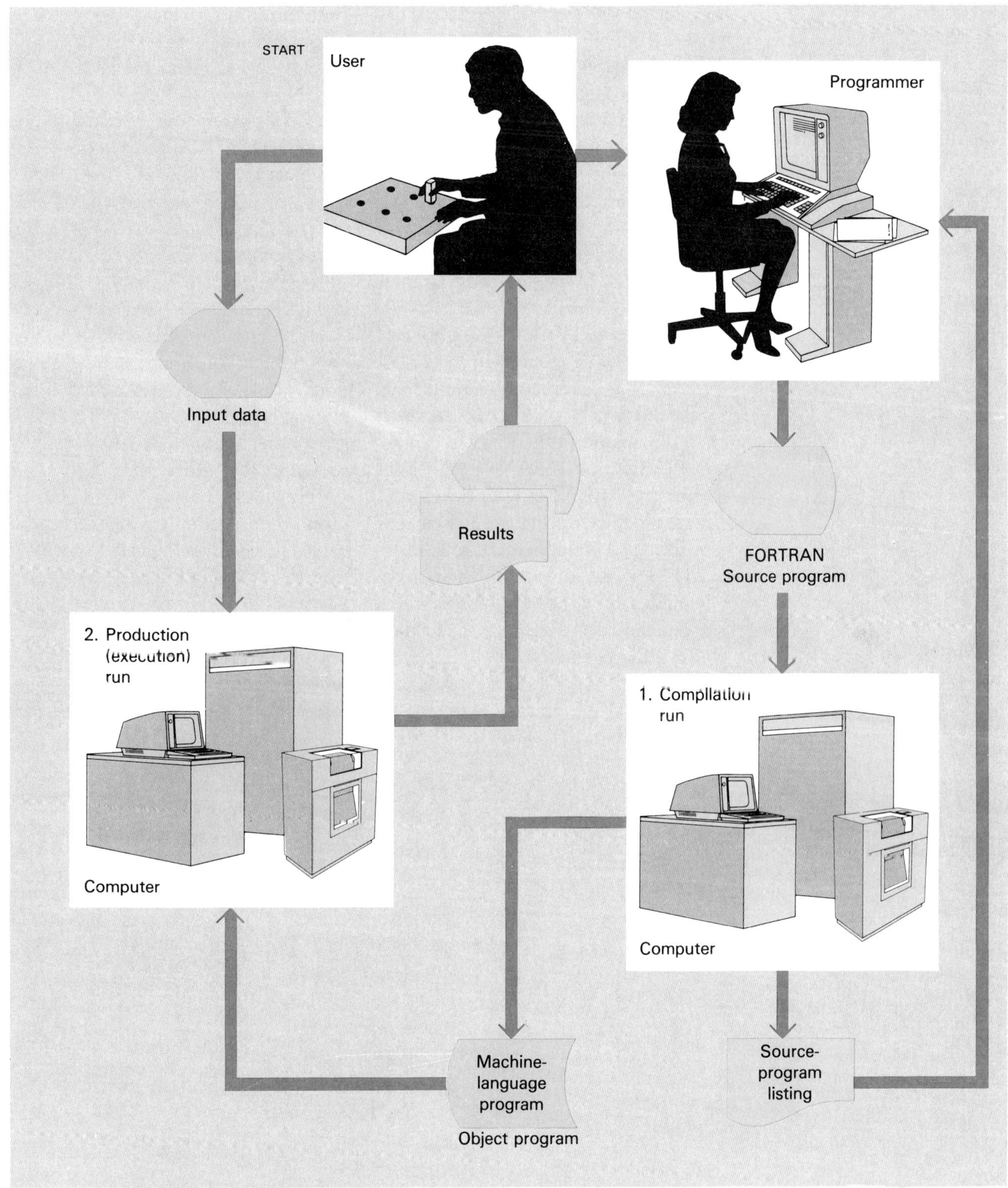
START
User
Programmer
Input data
Results
FORTRAN
Source program
2. Production
(execution)
run
1. Compilation
run
Computer
Computer
Machine-
language
program
Object program
Source-
program
listing

Figure 10-2 A high-level-language program must be translated from its initial source-program form to a machine-language form before it can direct the computer. The translation may occur during a compilation run, as shown here, or be done on a statement-by-statement basis.

FORTRAN

Today's public and private sector research centers use FORTRAN for everything from small, ad hoc calculating programs to 100,000-line application systems. Some industry-watchers estimate that as much as 25 percent of the world's available computing cycles are directed by code generated by FORTRAN compilers.

in FORTRAN were first compiled successfully in 1957. In fact, the high quality of the machine-language instructions generated by the early FORTRAN compilers proved to many skeptics that compilers were feasible—the early FORTRAN's didn't compete against other languages but against programmers. The most obvious plus of early programs was a savings in programming time. Programmers were able to run and test FORTRAN programs written in a single afternoon at a time when comparable assembler-language programs took weeks to write.

The name *FORTRAN* is derived from FORmula TRANslator. At the time the language was developed, most computer users were engineers, scientists, and mathematicians. FORTRAN was created with their needs in mind. It works well for research and analytical problems in science, engineering, and business. It is simple enough to be used by other than professional programmers to express problem solutions in a programming-language form.

The basic element in a FORTRAN program is the *statement.* The types of statements commonly included in a FORTRAN program are summarized in Figure 10-3. There are many ways these and other kinds of statements can be used. For many user applications, however, relatively simple statements of the types shown in Figure 10-3 are sufficient.

The language of FORTRAN consists largely of mathematical notation. The rules for forming mathematical expressions in FORTRAN are similar to those for forming expressions in algebra. (See Figure 10-4.) However, there are some exceptions. For example, to cause the value stored in location A to be multiplied by the value stored in location B, the FORTRAN programmer cannot write AB; the multiply operator must be specified explicitly so A*B is required. Exponents cannot be represented by writing numerals half a

Figure 10-3 A few basic types of statements are included in most FORTRAN programs.

CLASSIFICATION	EXAMPLE	PURPOSE
Assignment	PAY = HOURS * RATE RESULT = 1.5 * (BASE/3.) LOGVAR = LAST.GT.FIRST	To perform some arithmetic or logical operation, storing a result in a location identified by a variable name
Input/Output	READ (5,100) A, B, C WRITE (6,250) SUM, PROD	To read data from an input device or write information to an output device
Specification	100 FORMAT (2F3.1,F4.2) 250 FORMAT (I6,F5.2)	To describe the data being transferred to or from an input/output device
Control	GO TO 300 IF (LIM.NE.20) GO TO 60 STOP	To direct the flow of control during processing

ALGEBRAIC EXPRESSION	FORTRAN EQUIVALENT
$X = A + \frac{B}{C} - D$	X = A + B/C − D
$X = \frac{A + B}{C - D}$	X = (A + B)/(C − D)
$C = X \times Y^Z$ or XY^Z	C = X*Y**Z
$C = (X \times Y)^Z$ or $(XY)^Z$	C = (X*Y)**Z
$C = \frac{L}{M} \times N$	C = L/M*N
$C = \frac{L}{MN}$	C = L/(M*N)

Figure 10-4 The FORTRAN language is similar to common mathematics, with minimal changes that allow all values to be written on the coding line. One-letter symbols are used here to show similarities between FORTRAN and common mathematics. Today's FORTRAN compilers provide support for more meaningful names.

line above base numbers (3^5); they must be written with the exponentiation operator (3**5). Generally, parentheses are used more often in FORTRAN than in common mathematics.

Because certain I/O operations and certain operations on nonnumeric data cannot be expressed in FORTRAN, it is not well suited for problems involving file maintenance, editing of data, or production of documents. Not surprisingly, therefore, its broad user base does not come primarily from business application programming. Today—more than 30 years after its birth—FORTRAN is the dominant high-level language in supercomputing and remains the practical standard for scientific and engineering work. Whether or not FORTRAN should be selected as the programming language for a particular program should be determined largely by the kinds of operations required. When numerous complex arithmetic calculations are necessary, FORTRAN is generally appropriate.

COBOL

Seventy percent of the world's business application programming was done in COBOL 15 years ago, and it still is. By some estimates, businesses today have 80 billion lines of COBOL code. A lot of "saviors from COBOL" have come and gone, but COBOL lives on.

COBOL

The initial direction for the development of a COmmon Business-Oriented Language (COBOL) was set in May 1959 in a meeting at the Pentagon. Attending the meeting were representatives of the federal government, computer manufacturers, and the user community. The meeting participants agreed that a language developed independently for use on many manufacturers' computers was required. As the name COBOL implies, it was to be a common language designed primarily for writing business application programs.

A primary objective of the designers of COBOL was that it should be meaningful to even the casual reader. In fact, the structure of a COBOL program is comparable to that of a book. The most basic element is the *sentence* (the COBOL counterpart to the statement in FORTRAN). The next level in the structural hierarchy is the *paragraph*. Paragraphs are followed by *sections* and *divisions,* in order as named.

There are four divisions in a COBOL program: Identification, Environment, Data, and Procedure. The *Identification division* identifies the program. At a minimum, the program must be assigned a name. Information such as the writer of the program, the date it was written, and the date it was compiled can also be included.

The *Environment division* describes the type of computer that will compile the program and the type that will execute it. It relates files to be used by the program to specific I/O devices. In effect, it is the link between the machine-independent divisions of the program and the equipment used. If a COBOL program initially written for one computer is to be compiled and executed on a different computer, the Environment division will have to be changed.

The *Data division* describes all data to be processed by the program. This includes not only input and output files and data items within the files but also data items developed and processed internally. Important features of COBOL are the abilities to process alphabetic or alphanumeric as well as numeric data, and to perform a wide variety of I/O operations on user data files.

The *Procedure division* contains the program logic. It tells the processing steps to be performed during program execution and the order in which the computer is to perform them. Figure 10-5 shows the Procedure division of a COBOL program that controls processing within a common business application: print-

Figure 10-5 The Procedure division of this COBOL program directs the computer to read customer records and use the data they contain to write customer bills.

```
PROCEDURE DIVISION.
MAIN-PRINT-CUSTOMER-BILL.
    OPEN INPUT BILLING-FILE,
        OUTPUT CUSTOMER-BILL-FILE.
    PERFORM INITIALIZE-VARIABLES.
    PERFORM READ-AND-CHECK-RECORD.
    PERFORM PROCESS-BILL-RECORD
        UNTIL WS-END-OF-FILE-SW IS EQUAL TO 'YES'.
    CLOSE BILLING-FILE,
        CUSTOMER-BILL-FILE.
    STOP RUN.

INITIALIZE-VARIABLES.
    MOVE 'NO ' TO WS-END-OF-FILE-SW.
READ-AND-CHECK-RECORD.
    READ BILLING-FILE
        AT END MOVE 'YES' TO WS-END-OF-FILE-SW.
    IF NUMBER-OF-TRANS IN THIS-MONTH IS EQUAL TO ZERO OR
        CURRENT-BALANCE IS NEGATIVE, GO TO READ-AND-CHECK-RECORD.
PROCESS-BILL-RECORD.
    MOVE SPACES TO BILL-LINE-1.
    MOVE BALANCE-FORWARD TO OLD-BALANCE.
    MOVE CURRENT-BALANCE TO NEW-BALANCE.
    MOVE AMOUNT-OF-PURCHASES IN THIS-MONTH TO PURCHASES IN BILL-LINE-1.
    MOVE AMOUNT-OF-PAYMENTS IN THIS-MONTH TO PAYMENTS IN BILL-LINE-1.
    MOVE AMOUNT-OF-CREDITS IN THIS-MONTH TO CREDITS IN BILL-LINE-1.
    MOVE ACCOUNT-NUMBER OF BILL-RECORD TO ACCOUNT-NUMBER IN BILL-LINE-1.
    MOVE BILLING-DATE OF THIS-MONTH TO BILLING-DATE IN BILL-LINE-1.
    WRITE BILL-LINE-1 AFTER ADVANCING TWO LINES.
    PERFORM READ-AND-CHECK RECORD.
```

Procedure name and header for main-line paragraph

Lower-level procedure names/ paragraph headers

US
12347
US12347

THE ART AND SCIENCE OF SAILMAKING

To many, sailing about the bay or lake with a friend is lots of fun. To others, there's nothing quite as exciting as sailboat racing. Still others make their living in sailing-related activities. Racing sail manufacturers are in this category.

An experienced sailmaker knows basically what shape he wants a sail to have. The challenge is to design the sail so that it will hold that shape yet weigh as little as possible. Sailmakers are now using computers to help them achieve this objective.

A typical sail design program performs finite load analyses on alternative prototype sail designs. The program divides a proposed sail into several sections. It applies forces representing variations in wind pressure to the sections. In a stiff wind, for example, the pressure may reach 10,000 pounds per square foot on some parts of a sail. The program simulates this situation.

The results of the finite load analyses are used by sailmakers to determine how much a given sailcloth will be stretched under different sailing conditions and, therefore, what materials to use. A typical mainsail on a 12-meter racing sailboat may have over 100 pieces of sailcloth and up to 4 different types of cloth. With computer help, the sailmaker is able to tell precisely where heavy, unstretchable cloth is needed and where lighter cloths will suffice.

The results of this blend of art and science are better sails and, ultimately, faster sailboats and ever more exciting sailboat races. *(Photo courtesy Christopher G. Knight/Photo Researchers)*

ing customer bills. COBOL PERFORM verbs in the main-line, or control, paragraph (MAIN-PRINT-CUSTOMER-BILL) cause control to be transferred to (and then returned from) lower-level processing paragraphs. Thus, we see that COBOL is well suited to top-down, modular program development. Each paragraph can, in many respects, be treated as a program module. The basic patterns of structured programming are easy to code within these modules. The advantages of structured programming are important when writing large business application programs—programs that are likely to be used for several years and that will have to be changed to meet users' changing requirements.

Other important advantages of COBOL are that it employs the vocabulary of the business world and that it tends to be self-documenting. Few explanatory comments are needed. However, COBOL is not designed for the inexperienced user. It assumes an understanding of processing concepts and imposes some rather inflexible coding disciplines. Few programmers attempt to write COBOL programs without the aid of COBOL coding forms that provide positioning guidelines (A margin, B margin, and so on, as defined in COBOL).

The objective of making COBOL as English-like as possible has led to some disadvantages. COBOL programs tend to be long and wordy. (We showed only one page of a program in Figure 10-5. If we had shown all divisions of the program, Figure 10-5 would have been much longer. Not uncommonly, the source-program listing of a COBOL program extends for 20 or more pages.) A large COBOL compiler program is needed to handle all the COBOL source statements with many options and in various formats that can be provided as input. Large amounts of primary storage are required for the COBOL compiler instructions and data areas. As a result, COBOL compilers are not as readily available for workstations and personal computers as they are for large machines. Nevertheless, COBOL is the favored language for business applications.

PL/I

As noted above, FORTRAN was designed primarily for scientific problem solving. COBOL was developed for business, or commercial, programming. For a while, this distinction was valid. A similar distinction existed in hardware. Now, however, computer systems are designed and used for a broad range of activities. The business programmer may be confronted by long series of computations in statistical forecasting, operations research, and so on. The scientific programmer needs a language to simplify the task of submitting problems and to sort and edit data that provides solutions to these problems.

For these reasons, Programming Language I (PL/I) was conceived. PL/I was to be a general-purpose programming language used by programmers at all levels for all types of tasks. IBM released the first generally available PL/I compiler in 1966. It was designed for IBM's System/360 computers.

Some general characteristics and features of PL/I are shown in Figure 10-6A. This mortgage-processing program is only eight lines in length, yet it directs the computer in performing many operations. The same mortgage-processing program is written on only two coding lines in Figure 10-6B. For ease of reading and maintenance, this style of coding is not generally advisable. However, it shows the free-form coding flexibility available to PL/I users.

You can probably understand the program in Figure 10-6 with little difficulty. Values for mortgage number, old balance, current payment, and interest rate for a customer (mortgagee) are read into primary storage. The interest due is calcu-

A. A well-formatted PL/I mortgage-processing program

```
MORTGAGE: PROCEDURE OPTIONS (MAIN);
NEXTCARD: GET DATA (MORNO, OBAL, PAYM, RATE);
          CHARGE = OBAL * RATE / 12;
          PRINPAID = PAYM - CHARGE;
          BALANCE = OBAL - PRINPAID;
          PUT DATA (MORNO, OBAL, CHARGE, PRINPAID, BALANCE);
          GO TO NEXTCARD;
END MORTGAGE;
```

B. An alternate free-form coding style available to PL/I users

```
MORT:PROCEDURE OPTIONS(MAIN);S:GET DATA(M,Z,B,Y);X=Z*Y/12;A=B-X;
C=Z-A;PUT DATA(M,Z,X,A,C);GO TO S;END MORT;
```

Figure 10-6 A program to compute the current interest charge, current payment, and remaining balance on a loan can be written in PL/I using either a formatted (A) or free-form (B) style of coding.

lated by multiplying old balance by interest rate, and then dividing by 12 because monthly payments are being made. The result, or interest, is subtracted from the current payment to see how much is being repaid against the principal. This amount is subtracted from the old balance to determine the new balance of the loan. The mortgage number, old balance, and calculated amounts are provided as output. Then control is transferred back to the beginning of the program to do the same calculations for another mortgagee. When all customer data has been processed, implementation-defined end-of-file processing occurs.

The basic element of a PL/I program is the *statement*. Statements are combined into larger elements called *groups* and *blocks*. A group is headed by a DO statement. A block may be either a begin block or a procedure (headed by a BEGIN or PROCEDURE statement, respectively). Use of the block concept permits symbolic names to be known in only certain parts of a program, or to have one meaning in one part of a program and another meaning in other parts of the program. Storage can be reserved for a variable when control is transferred to a block. It can be freed when control is passed from the block. This support of the block concept helps to make PL/I especially suitable for structured programming.

Because PL/I is designed as a general-purpose language to meet all programming needs, it is both extensive and sophisticated. Beginners need to learn only the language features that satisfy their immediate programming requirements. Experienced programmers can use advanced features of the language to solve complex problems. PL/I has never achieved a level of acceptance even close to that of FORTRAN or COBOL. PL/I remains primarily an IBM-sponsored language. Like COBOL compilers, PL/I compilers tend to be large and sophisticated; they require lots of primary storage.

Therefore, the full PL/I language is not generally available on small computer systems or on microcomputers.

BASIC

BASIC was originally created in the 1960s for use with the computer system at Dartmouth College. As its name (from Beginners' All-purpose Symbolic Instruction Code) implies, it was intended to be an easy-to-learn programming language that students could use to solve simple problems in many subject areas. At that time, the system at Dartmouth was unique in that it offered a capability now often taken for granted: Users at geographically distributed terminals could interact with the computer at what appeared to be the same time. (The system was based on the concept of time sharing, which we'll learn about in Chapter 11.) BASIC was designed primarily for use in interactive (conversational) computing.

As the availability and use of systems with interactive capabilities increased, so did that of BASIC. When microcomputers such as the TRS-80, Apple II, and IBM PC arrived on the scene, the potential for increased use of BASIC arrived also. It's safe to say that this potential has been realized.

Figure 10-7 shows a BASIC program to convert temperatures recorded in Fahrenheit to Celsius. Since we've seen BASIC programs before (in Chapters 2 and 9), you can probably follow it easily.

The PRINT "FAHRENHEIT"; statement (statement 110) causes the word "FAHRENHEIT" to be printed as output. The INPUT F statement causes the computer to print out a question mark and then pause until a value for F is entered by the user. The LET statement indi-

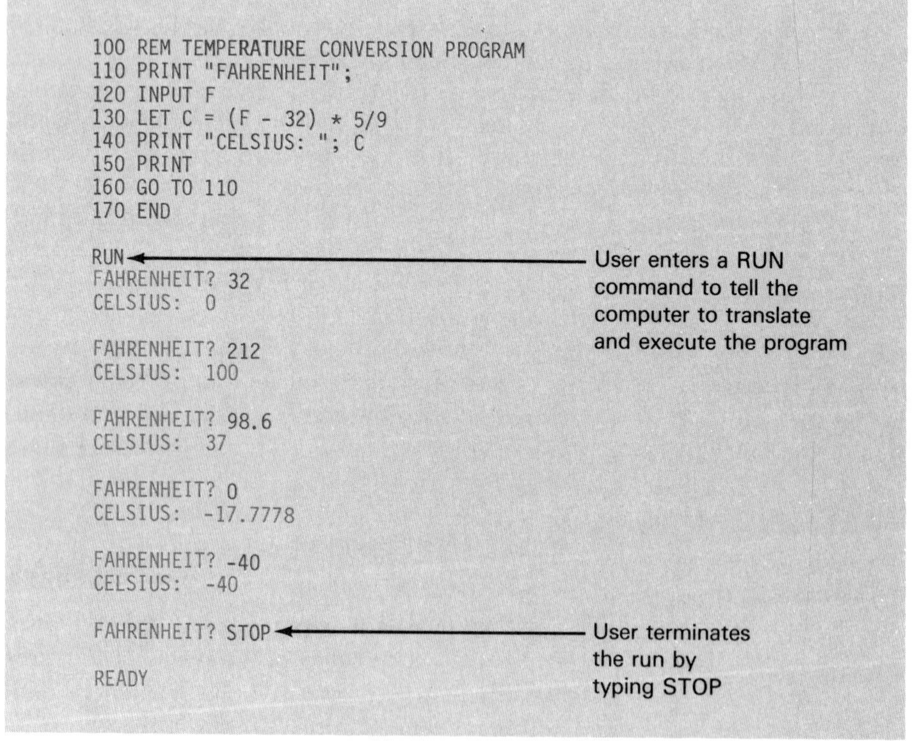

```
100 REM TEMPERATURE CONVERSION PROGRAM
110 PRINT "FAHRENHEIT";
120 INPUT F
130 LET C = (F - 32) * 5/9
140 PRINT "CELSIUS: "; C
150 PRINT
160 GO TO 110
170 END

RUN
FAHRENHEIT? 32
CELSIUS:  0

FAHRENHEIT? 212
CELSIUS:  100

FAHRENHEIT? 98.6
CELSIUS:  37

FAHRENHEIT? 0
CELSIUS:  -17.7778

FAHRENHEIT? -40
CELSIUS:  -40

FAHRENHEIT? STOP

READY
```

User enters a RUN command to tell the computer to translate and execute the program
User terminates the run by typing STOP

Figure 10-7 This BASIC program directs the computer to stop and wait until a user provides a Fahrenheit value as input, then provide the corresponding Celsius value as output.

cates that a symbol written on the left side of an equal sign (in this case, C) is to be given the value represented by the expression on the right (here $(F - 32) * \frac{5}{9}$). The word "CELSIUS," followed by a colon, and the computed value for C are printed by the second PRINT statement. The effect of the statement containing only the key word PRINT is to skip one print line. The GO TO statement causes an unconditional branch to statement 110. This sequence of processing steps is repeated as long as input is provided. Since there is no provision for stopping program execution in the program itself, the user must terminate the run. In this example, the user did so by keying in STOP.

As we saw earlier, the REM statement is used to provide remarks for documentation purposes. The END statement tells the BASIC language-processor program that this is the last statement coded by the user-programmer.

On some systems, BASIC programs can be submitted for translation and execution just like FORTRAN, COBOL, or PL/I programs (review Figure 10 2) or entered interactively. Of course, programs to be run without user interaction should not contain INPUT statements. LET statements and READ statements that access data items listed in DATA statements are alternative ways of providing data to be processed. Many BASIC implementations include statements that provide file-processing capabilities. With these, BASIC programs can be written to create, read, and update user data files.

A BASIC standard covering a minimal subset of the BASIC language (X3.60) was approved by ANSI in 1978. Unfortunately, the standard was somewhat late in coming and included only a small subset of the language supported by most BASIC language processors. The popularity of the language and user demands for additional features led to a patchwork quilt of manufacturer-dependent BASIC's, extended BASIC's, business BASIC's, and so on. An individual user or software development firm that wants a program to be usable on numerous computer systems (i.e., to be portable) is well advised to check whether or not certain language features are common across BASIC language processors before taking advantage of them. A new BASIC standard (ANSI X3.113-1987) was approved in 1987 but widespread conformance will be a while in coming.

Pascal

As with BASIC, the initial impetus for the development of Pascal came from the educational community. Professor Niklaus Wirth of Zurich, Switzerland, undertook the design of Pascal in the late 1960s with two principal objectives in mind:

- To create a language suitable to teach programming as a systematic discipline (not a hit-and-miss art) based on fundamental concepts clearly and naturally reflected by the language
- To provide for implementations of the language that are both reliable and efficient on available computers

Though many other programming languages already existed, Wirth argued that their features and concepts too often could not be explained logically. He named his new language Pascal in honor of Blaise

COMPUTERS HELP DEERE PLOW FORWARD

To farmers throughout the United States and elsewhere, the color green means well-watered, new fields of corn, beans, alfalfa, and the like. It also means tractors and other farm equipment from John Deere, Inc. Since Deere began during the U.S. industrial revolution in 1837, it has been supplying plowshares and harvesters to the world's farmers.

The information model adhered to by Deere management is one of centralized computing but decentralized decision making. In 1968 Deere established its mainframe computing site in Moline, Illinois—a centralized IBM mainframe resource for use by distributed business centers. Today, the site houses several of IBM's largest computers. Remote sites use Digital Equipment Corporation VAX machines in their factories and Tandem Computers, Inc., computers to track inventory and orders.

In the early 1980s, when inflation rates forced the demand for farm equipment down 70 percent, Deere's annual revenues decreased by millions of dollars. Deere management determined to use information systems technology to restore profitability. It applied computer-integrated manufacturing (CIM) techniques to increase the efficiency of its manufacturing operations. It installed a backbone network adhering to the manufacturing automation protocol (MAP) emerging at the time to improve communications on its factory floors.

Now a central staff of about 200 operations, software, and communications personnel run Deere's $50-million-plus information systems operations. Deere places as much emphasis on human issues as on equipment. Its goal is not necessarily to use the latest state-of-the-art technology but rather to use the *right* technology to meet its needs, whether that be old or new, or, as is often the case, some combination of both. *(Photos courtesy John Deere, Inc.)*

Pascal, a brilliant French philosopher and mathematician of the 17th century. A first Pascal compiler was operational in 1970. It ran on Control Data Corporation's CDC 6000-series computers.

Kenneth Bowles, an instructor at the University of California at San Diego (UCSD), recognized that one factor needed for increased use of Pascal was the ability to run Pascal programs on many different computers. Since microcomputers were cheapest and readily obtainable, Pascal implementations for microcomputers seemed desirable.

Bowles and his students developed a "pseudocompiler" that generated a form of pseudocode *(P-code)* rather than machine-language instructions (native code, or *N-code*). This P-code could not be executed directly by any computer. Creating a P-code machine simulator, or interpreter, that ran on a real computer for the purpose of analyzing the P-code and triggering the right actions by that computer was a relatively simple task, however. Perhaps the most significant event in microcomputer Pascal occurred in 1983 when Borland International released Turbo Pascal—a compiler noted for its lightning compilation speed, compact code, integrated editing environment, and low price. The product gained widespread acceptance and is largely responsible for the continued popularity of Pascal. Pascal is also available on a wide variety of larger systems.

The capabilities of the language are such that Pascal programs may be run as batch jobs or keyed in and run interactively by users. Figure 10-8 shows a program that determines whether or not an integer value entered as input by a user is a prime number, divisible only by itself and 1. Like all Pascal programs, this program has a heading and a body, or block. The first part of the body contains a declaration of every user-chosen symbolic name. Here, N (the name for the value entered as input) and TRIALDIV (a trial divisor value computed during execution) are declared to be integers. NODIV (no divisor) is declared to be a Boolean value; it can take on either of two values: TRUE or FALSE.

Within the statement part of the program body, a FOR statement sets up a counter-controlled program loop. An IF statement within the loop causes a test to be made. To understand this test, you need to know that Pascal provides two operators especially for integer division operations: DIV and MOD. DIV returns the quotient of integer division, and MOD returns the remainder, if there is any. In this particular test, if the value entered for N by the user can be divided evenly by some trial divisor, the value of N MOD TRIALDIV is equal to 0. This causes the value of the trial divisor to be written

Figure 10-8 Whether or not an integer value is a prime number can be determined easily with the help of a computer and this Pascal program.

```
PROGRAM PRIME (INPUT, OUTPUT); <------- Program heading
{DETERMINE IF A VALUE IS A PRIME NUMBER}

VAR
  N,
  TRIALDIV:     INTEGER;          } Declarations part
  NODIV:        BOOLEAN;

BEGIN
  {INITIALIZE VARIABLES}
  WRITELN ('ENTER INTEGER TO BE DIVIDED');
  READLN (N);
  NODIV := TRUE;
  {WRITE HEADING LINE}
  WRITELN ('LIST OF DIVISORS (IF ANY)');
  FOR TRIALDIV := 2 TO N-1 DO
     IF (N MOD TRIALDIV) = 0 THEN
        BEGIN
        WRITELN (TRIALDIV:12);
        NODIV :=FALSE
        END;                    {THEN CLAUSE & FOR}
  IF NODIV THEN
     WRITELN (N:6, ' IS A PRIME NUMBER')
END.
```

Statement part (BEGIN … END.); Program body (VAR … END.)

as output and NODIV to be set to FALSE. If there is no trial divisor that divides N evenly, NODIV is never set to FALSE. The IF statement following the program loop causes NODIV to be tested for a value of TRUE. If NODIV has a value of TRUE, the user receives a message saying the value entered as input is a prime number.

Pascal's suitability for application programming— as opposed to system programming and education— remains in dispute by some. They argue that Pascal's I/O capabilities are inconvenient to use and inadequate for the extensive I/O requirements of business applications. Popular Pascal implementations include language extensions, but programs that include extensions are not readily portable to other environments.

C

The C language was initially developed and implemented at AT&T's Bell Laboratories in the late 1960s. The UNIX operating system (also developed at Bell Laboratories) was itself rewritten in C in 1970. A C compiler was provided as part of the UNIX operating system to universities and then to commercial users in the 1970s. Initially, C was known only to the UNIX community. The movement toward C use on microcomputers did not really begin until the mid-1980s, but then it seemed to skyrocket. Today, C is the high-level language of choice among professional programmers writing system and application software for use on microcomputer systems. C compilers are also available for both UNIX-controlled and non-UNIX-controlled large computers.

What is C and why is it popular? The language is a lower-level language than Pascal, with which it is often compared. C programmers can write statements to direct computer operations at a level that is close enough to the hardware to insure fast performance of the machine code that will be generated from those statements. (As programmers say, they can flip bits and manipulate memory if they have to.) Yet C also includes higher-level constructs such as IF THEN ELSE and WHILE that lead to clean, maintainable, well-structured programs.

Perhaps the biggest advantage of C is its portability. The simple basic syntax of the language is extended through a common function library. A program written for one environment can be ported easily to other environments if the functions that the program uses are included in the common function libraries available in those environments. If any required functions are not available in a particular library, adding them to the library is likely to be more straightforward than making program modifications. Once there, the functions are also available to other C programs.

Whereas Pascal includes many features that protect programmers from themselves, C does not. For example, Pascal requires all data items to be defined very precisely and enforces strict control on how those data items are used in a program. If a function is designed to expect an integer data item, and the programmer includes logic that presents a character string to it, an error message is generated. C does not always provide such safety nets. It offers flexibility and assumes programmers know what they're doing.

Software developers can write C programs that are fast and yet require minimal amounts of memory to exe-

C

If a program for widespread use is written in Pascal, chances are that its development was undertaken in the 1970s. A similar effort undertaken today is likely to include C as the language of choice.

cute. Because C is powerful enough to handle tasks of nearly any complexity and yet is highly portable, its popularity is ever increasing. A C program *can* be written today for use on both micros and large computers.

RPG

The Report Program Generator (RPG) language was initially designed by IBM in the middle and late 1960s to duplicate the logic of punched-card equipment. Thus, minicomputers and small computer systems that used punched-card input, or that were initially acquired as replacements for punched-card data-processing systems, were often controlled primarily by programs coded in RPG.

As its name implies, the RPG language was originally designed to generate programs that produce business-oriented, printed reports as output. Initially, all reports were provided in hard-copy form. Today some RPG compilers also support the interactive design of display-screen formats for soft-copy output.

RPG is also used for operations other than report writing. Company records stored as data in EDP-system master files must be updated frequently. New data must be added or old data deleted to keep such files current. These operations are called *file maintenance.* RPG can readily be used to perform them. Today, some of the most common uses of RPG are file updating for accounts receivable, accounts payable, general ledger, and inventory control.

A programmer coding an RPG program does not write statements that represent sequential steps to be followed during processing. Instead, the programmer completes a series of descriptions, known as *specifications.* Examples of two of them are shown, in part, in Figure 10-9. As you can see, specific entries must be written in specific columns. RPG does not provide free-form coding, but English-like names and operators can be used.

Today RPG compilers are offered for many manufacturers' computers. All RPG implementations are similar, but the language is not standardized. This means that RPG programs written for one computer system may not run on others. The language is especially valuable for small computer systems because RPG compilers do not impose large storage requirements. Many small businesses rely heavily on information produced as RPG output.

Fourth-Generation Languages

If you read weekly or monthly trade publications in the computing field, you're likely to notice references to *fourth-generation languages,* or *4GL's.* Persons who use this term generally consider machine, assembler, and high-level programming languages to be first-, second-, and third-generation languages respectively. However, there is no general agreement as to what 4GL's are.

In broadest terms, a 4GL is a software tool that enhances the productivity of its users. Depending on the tool, its data-processing users may be highly trained professionals, user-programmers, or end users of computers (who do not consider themselves to be programmers). Some relatively well-known software products were developed and marketed as 4GL's before CASE tools were introduced as productivity aids.

REPORT PROGRAM GENERATOR INPUT SPECIFICATIONS

Line	Form Type	Filename	Sequence	Number (1-N)	Option (O)	Resulting Indicator	Record Identification Codes	Stacker Select	Packed (P)	Field Location From	Field Location To	Decimal Positions	Field Name	Control Level (L1-L9)	Matching Fields or Chaining Fields	Field-Record Relation	Field Indicators Plus	Minus	Zero or Blank	Sterling Sign Position
0 1	I	TIMECARD	AA																	
0 2	I									1	20		NAME							
0 3	I									78	80	1	HOURS							
0 4	I																			

REPORT PROGRAM GENERATOR CALCULATION SPECIFICATIONS

Line	Form Type	Control Level (L0-L9, LR)	Indicators (Not, And Not, And Not)	Factor 1	Operation	Factor 2	Result Field	Field Length	Decimal Positions	Half Adjust (H)	Resulting Indicators Plus (High 1 > 2)	Minus (Low 1 < 2)	Zero or Blank (Equal 1 = 2)	Comments
0 1	C			HOURS	SUB	40	OVRTME	3	1		01			
0 2	C													
0 3	C													
0 4	C													

Figure 10-9 RPG Input and Calculation specifications forms assist the user by showing what information needs to be provided to the computer.

Today the suppliers of these products are trying to extend their usefulness by emphasizing coexistence and integration with other CASE tools. Some industry watchers argue that 4GL's attack only the coding phase of software development, at most 40 percent of the total programming task. A 4GL integrated with other application development tools can help improve productivity throughout the system development cycle.

Today the use of 4GL's is increasing. We can group available products within two broad categories for discussion purposes. Perhaps best known are the products that provide end-user query and report facilities. The "end users" may be nonprogrammers or professional software developers, either of whom must be trained to use a particular tool by the tool supplier or in-house information center staff. Generally, these 4GL tools incorporate an English-like proprietary programming language, prompted queries, or menu-driven selection techniques that guide end users in obtaining information. The tools themselves are designed to interact with underlying database management systems (DBMS's) or file systems (discussed in Chapter 12). Some provide "screen painting" facilities whereby users describe input and output formats. PC versions of many of these products are being offered.

4GL's and Productivity

Most 4GL's routinely yield a 10:1 improvement in productivity relative to COBOL for business applications of medium complexity. Improvements of 3:1 are typical for complex applications requiring extensive procedural logic.

Examples of this category of 4GL's are Focus from Information Builders, RAMIS from On-Line Software International, and Nomad 2 from Must Software. Decision support systems, which are used to extract and analyze data, have much in common with these information-center products. (We discuss them in greater detail in Chapter 12.)

Application systems that formerly could be developed only by an organization's in-house programming staff or with outside programming help are now being developed successfully by users of these information-center 4GL's. They're used for everything from employee skills tracking to sales analysis to distribution planning. However, the performance characteristics of the systems generally limit their usefulness for large strategic systems. An application that will have to process 10 or more transactions per second is not a likely candidate for development using these tools.

The second category of 4GL's, programmer-oriented application generators, are effective in attacking problems of medium complexity—say, those involving 10–20,000 transactions per day, or serving up to 200 simultaneously active users, or accessing multiple-gigabyte databases concurrently. As the term *application generator* implies, the output of one of these 4GL's is an application program. With some, such as Ideal from Applied Data Research (now part of Computer Associates), Mantis from Cincom Systems, and Natural from Software Ag, the application program is in an interpretive form that can be executed immediately. Others such as Transform from Transform Logic and Telon from Pansophic Systems actually produce COBOL, PL/I, or other high-level programming language source statements as output. Such outputs are then compiled and linked to form executable programs. The generated source statements can be saved in secondary storage and modified in that form if necessary—just like other in-house-developed COBOL or PL/I source programs.

The success of application generators is based on the concept that about 50 percent of a typical application program has already been written, somewhere, as part of another application program. If a programmer has access to a library containing reusable already-coded routines, application programs that he or she may be asked to write are already half complete.

Though the validity of using thousands of lines of code (KLOC) as a measure of programmer productivity is often debated, the need to get programs up and running correctly as fast as possible is a common, well-understood objective. Advocates of application generators insist that even experienced programmers can generate code much more quickly with an application generator than when using traditional programming methods. A single generator language statement may cause several reusable routines to be inserted in a program that is being constructed. Why write 400 COBOL statements when four generator-language statements will do the job? In most cases, the program is also portable; it can be used on various manufacturers' computers.

When 4GL's are used, an organization's highly experienced developers are freed to spend their time on system analysis and design, and on coding and checkout of user-unique, nonstandard routines. Users who are not highly trained programmers can interact with computers directly to get many of their jobs done. Several human communication steps—each providing opportunities for misinterpretation of requirements—are eliminated. 4GL's are not substitutes for system analysis and design. They are, however, easy-to-use tools that shorten the time needed for detailed program design and coding. Automated office environments may arrive faster, for example, in organizations where office personnel have access to 4GL's they can use to tell computers directly about office work that needs to be done.

Natural Languages

For some users, *natural-language* software represents a level of ease of use beyond 4GL's. This software is designed to allow users to communicate with computers in their own human language—English, French, German, or whatever. The user needs only the ability to ask questions. Correct grammar is optional.

The capabilities of natural-language software are based on about 30 years of intensive research at artificial intelligence (AI) laboratories at such places as Stanford and MIT. Some systems can "remember" preceding queries, staying within the context of a line of questioning much as we humans do. For example:

What states border the Atlantic Ocean?

Which of the states have state lotteries?

Which have major statewide elections this year?

The underlying software infers from the user's queries where the required data can be found, accesses the data, manipulates it as necessary, and returns the desired result.

Typically, an experienced data-processing professional sets up an initial user dictionary, known as a *lexicon,* before users are allowed to access the system. Words and phrases that users are likely to use in referring to required data are entered into the dictionary. From there, the natural-language interface evolves through a continuing dialog with users. Contrast the "natural language" of a lawyer with that of a retail salesclerk with that of a biologist. Not surprisingly, the ease of use actually experienced by users depends to a significant extent on the care with which the lexicon is established and the ability of the system to "learn" as it goes.

Artificial Intelligence's Intellect and Natural Language from Natural Language, Inc., are examples of natural-language products that can be used with any of several DBMS's. These products and others are still evolving. One of the major objectives of ongoing AI research is to enhance the computer's natural-language capabilities. (We discuss AI further in Chapter 14.)

Object-Oriented Languages

Perhaps the greatest potential for productivity improvements in the use of computing resources stems from yet another evolving area of technology: object-oriented programming. Like application generators, *object-oriented languages* are based on the concept of reusability. However, the building blocks being reused here are not simply technical functions; they are independently developed and debugged modules, implementing *objects* used in programming. Users begin by creating *data classes* and

WHY NOT USE ENGLISH?

According to recent estimates, pharmaceutical corporations now spend about $70 million dollars and 10 years of calendar time and effort to develop and gain governmental approval to market a new drug. Clinical trials are an important part of the testing process undertaken to gain the approval. In the trials, the new drug is used with both healthy patients and diseased patients to determine whether the drug is safe and effective. Throughout the trials, recordings of each patient's vital signs and laboratory test results are stored in computerized files and databases. Natural Language software provides an English-language interface that clinical investigators use for accessing and analyzing the data to determine the drug's efficacy and to screen for possible problems of toxicity or undesired side effects.

Before Natural Language was developed, obtaining access to clinical results was a multiple-step process for the investigators. System designers and programmers had to be told of the investigators' report requirements. Programs had to be designed, coded, tested, and released to production. The programs had to be run to produce the results, which were then provided to the investigators. Weeks and even months of delay often occurred. With Natural Language, physicians and scientists can access and analyze clinical data by simply keying English-language questions into the computer system. A question such as "What is the average pulse rate by drug?" can be submitted by an investigator without assistance from information system personnel.

The ability to have immediate access to clinical data provides many benefits to the investigators. Based on initial review of the data, investigators may decide to pursue certain questions in greater depth. Investigators can formulate questions that provide results which are meaningful to them; they are not constrained to interpreting predetermined, voluminous, fixed-format reports. With the assistance of Natural Language, pharmaceutical corporations are shortening the drug approval cycle and lowering the expenses incurred in bringing new products to market. *(Photo courtesy Natural Language, Inc.)*

Which One?

In system development, one size doesn't fit all. Choosing the right programming language is as important to the user-programmer as choosing the right wood-working tool is to the carpenter. A wrong choice means that the programming task will be much harder. The end result is not likely to be a high-quality product.

defining *methods* whereby data in each of the classes responds to messages received. For example, the writer of a graphic program might create pixels (picture elements) as a data class and then define a method using pixels to plot a point on a visual-display screen. The plotting object thus formed can be used and reused, and linked together easily with other objects, even by novice programmers (who need know nothing of how the plotting is accomplished).

Today, the best-known object-oriented languages are Smalltalk V, Objective C, and C++. Smalltalk V has evolved from the initial version of Smalltalk created by Alan Kay at the Xerox Development Center in the 1970s. Objective C and C++ are extended versions of the C programming language we discussed earlier. Developers of relational DBMS's, such as Oracle and Relational Technology, are adding object-oriented capabilities to their tool sets and to their DBMS's.

Engineering design and industrial applications that are complex, performance-sensitive, and have unusual data type needs are likely candidates for object-oriented programming at this time. Business applications with similar characteristics at financial services and brokerage firms are also. As users gain experience with object-oriented capabilities, additional application areas will be identified.

Selecting a Language

How does one choose, from among the myriad of programming languages, the language that's most appropriate for a particular system development effort?

Let's back up a bit. The first phase of the system development cycle is system analysis. The second phase is system design. In most cases, after the user requirements are understood, alternative solutions can be identified. Today, most if not all user organizations are confronted by resource constraints. The programming talent, time, and money needed for in-house system development are likely to be in short supply. Therefore, if application software packages that meet or nearly meet user requirements are available, they should be considered. Perhaps a nearly-meets-requirements package can be customized to do the job. As we've said, there's no merit in writing a new program if an acceptable one already exists. However, if detailed program design, coding, and checkout are to be done, then the selection and use of one or more programming languages is required.

Usually, one assembler program is provided for each particular family of computers. Programs can be written for the computers in the assembler language that the assembler program is designed to translate. Theoretically, any number of high-level-language processors can be written for any computer. It follows that any computer can be controlled by programs initially coded in any of several high-level programming languages, depending on the language processors available.

In deciding which programming language to use, then, some specific questions should be asked. Which programming languages are available? What knowledge do you or the assigned programmers or user-programmers have of those languages? What types of problems are the various languages designed for? These and other language selection

- Language availability
- Language knowledge of assigned programmers or user-programmers
- Suitability of the language to the particular problem or application
- Ease of learning the language
- Ease of language use for coding and for debugging; over-all program development time
- Understandability of the language and of source programs; self-documentation; ease of program maintenance
- Language standardization; program portability
- Speed of source-program translation by the language processor; language-processor storage requirements
- Efficiency of resultant object programs in terms of number of instructions, execution speed, and storage requirements

Figure 10-10 Many factors must be considered when choosing the language that's most appropriate for a system development effort.

considerations are summarized in Figure 10-10. The relative importance of the selection criteria varies, depending on the situation.

For many end-user business applications, a 4GL may be the appropriate choice.

As we have seen, FORTRAN is well suited for problems that involve mathematical computations. COBOL was designed with business applications in mind. BASIC was designed to provide immediate, straightforward answers to simple problems. For many end-user business applications, a 4GL may be the appropriate choice.

The assembler language of a computer can be used to express all the operations the computer is capable of performing. If fast execution and/or minimal use of storage by the resultant object program are of primary importance, use of an assembler language may be advisable. Some 4GL tools allow assembler-language routines to be embedded in 4GL applications to perform time-critical functions.

CHAPTER SUMMARY

1. Machine-language instructions are strings of 1s and 0s containing the bit patterns for machine operations and the storage addresses of locations where data values are (or will be) stored.

2. Assembler languages allow the use of mnemonics such as A, L, and B as op codes and of labels such as NAME to refer to instructions and data items.

3. An assembler program translates assembler-language statements (a source program) into machine-language instructions (an object program) during an assembly run. The object program can then be loaded into primary storage to serve as the stored program during a production run.

4. High-level programming languages are procedure-oriented or problem-oriented languages. A language-processor program (compiler or interpreter) translates the high-level-language statements into machine-language form.

5. FORTRAN, the oldest high-level programming language, is well suited for research and analytical problems in science, engineering, and business.

6. COBOL was developed in the late 1950s and 1960s as a common language for writing business application programs usable on many manufacturers' computers.

7. PL/I was created as a general-purpose language to be used by programmers at all levels for all types of tasks.

8. BASIC was created at Dartmouth College as an easy-to-learn programming language that students could use to solve simple problems in many subject areas. It is well suited to interactive (conversational) use.

9. Pascal was developed as a tool for teaching programming as a systematic discipline and is well suited to modular, structured programming.

10. C is a powerful, highly portable programming language offered initially as part of the UNIX operating system. It is increasingly popular in both UNIX and non-UNIX microcomputer and large computer environments.

11. An RPG user completes specifications, which are then used to direct the computer in producing business-oriented printed reports.

12. 4GL's, natural languages, and object-oriented languages are designed primarily to offer ease of use and productivity to users.

13. The language that's appropriate for a particular system development effort must be chosen on the basis of carefully established criteria. The importance of the criteria varies, depending on the user situation.

DISCUSSION QUESTIONS

1. Give reasons why few programmers today are writing machine-language programs.

2. (a) Explain the terms *low-level programming languages* and *high-level programming languages.*
(b) Give examples of each.

3. Distinguish between the following: (a) source program, (b) compiler program, (c) assembler program, (d) object program, and (e) interpreter program.

4. Discuss some general characteristics of high-level programming languages.

5. (a) Why is FORTRAN an appropriate name for that programming language?
(b) For what types of applications is FORTRAN generally preferred?

6. COBOL provides for four different areas of programmer coding responsibility. Name the divisions of a COBOL program that reflect these areas and describe the function of each division.

7. (a) What happens when an INPUT statement in a BASIC program is executed?
(b) What does your response to part (a) indicate about the typical BASIC programming environment?

8. Why is a language such as PL/I useful?

9. (a) What is the function of the Pascal program in Figure 10-8?
(b) Explain how each variable in the program is used.
(c) Check your understanding of the program by creating a program flowchart or writing pseudocode to explain the program logic.
(d) Verify the correctness of the algorithm you created in response to (c) by desk-checking it. Given the data value 29 as input, what information should be provided as output? Is it? If not, where are the errors?
(e) Repeat (d), but use 117 as input; then use 61. Which of the data values you've processed are prime numbers?

10. Describe at least two types of applications that can be coded as RPG programs.

11. How can 4GL's help to improve user productivity?

12. Discuss factors that you and/or other users of computers should consider when selecting the programming language to be used for a particular business application—say, financial record keeping for a church or school in your vicinity.

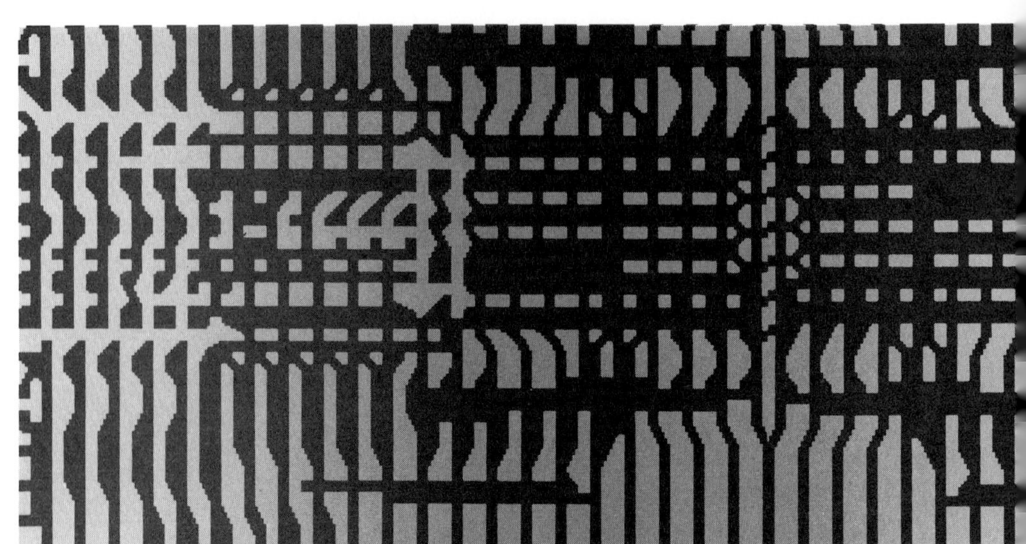

11 Application and System Software

IN THIS CHAPTER

System Software
Application Software
The Demand for Software
Early History of Software
Online Direct-Access Systems
Multitasking, or Multiprogramming
Integration and Windowing
Multiprocessing
Real-Time Systems
Time Sharing
Virtual Storage
Virtual Machines
Portable Operating Systems

Software—the part of a computer system that makes a computer different from other machines; software—the component of a computer system whereby the system can be directed to do useful work; software—where the action is in today's computing environments.

As we've seen again and again throughout this book, the capabilities of computers are expanding at fantastic rates. The importance of these capabilities to us and to others depends on the use that is made of them. The "applying" (that is, use and control) of a computer system is achieved primarily through software. We saw in Chapter 2 that the software may be either of two types: system programs and application programs. In this chapter, we look at both of these categories in greater detail. As you are probably beginning to realize, a wide variety of programs is available.

To appreciate where we are today, it's helpful to know where we've been. Therefore, after the brief overview of both system and application software, we discuss how and why operating systems came about. Because operating system software is such an integral part of any computing environment (even that of a micro), every computer user needs some understanding of it. Then we trace the evolution of major system capabilities: batch processing, online direct-access processing, multitasking, multiprocessing, real-time processing, virtual storage, and virtual machines. To help you relate the discussions of system capabilities to computer systems in current use, specific operating systems are mentioned as examples. You'll see clearly that the capabilities of typical personal computers today far exceed those of even the largest mainframes just 20 years ago.

What Counts

A computer without software is like a camera without film or a stereo system without records.

System Software

System software directs the computer in performing tasks that are basic to proper functioning of the system or commonly needed by system users. It serves as a "middleman" between the computer hardware and application programs. Suppose you want the computer to calculate new spreadsheet values under the direction of your Lotus 1-2-3 application program. You key in the appropriate commands to tell the system software (MS-DOS or PC DOS operating system) installed on your computer to read 1-2-3 into the computer's random-access memory. After you've keyed in the spreadsheet input, the operating system determines how best to manage the hardware resources of the computer system as instructions within 1-2-3, and operating-system functions that it uses are executed to calculate the new spreadsheet values. It's as if your parents told you to get an A in English I but left it up to you to figure out how to do it.

Not surprisingly, then, all systems have system software. However, some systems have much more system software than others. And the system software of some systems provides far more capabilities than that of others. The system software of one computer system may differ in many ways from that of another.

For discussion purposes, we can group system programs within three broad categories. Some or all of the programs may be available on the computer systems to which you have access. (See Figure 11-1.)

Figure 11-1 A diverse set of system software and both cross-industry and industry-specific application programs are needed to tell the computer how to convert data into useful information.

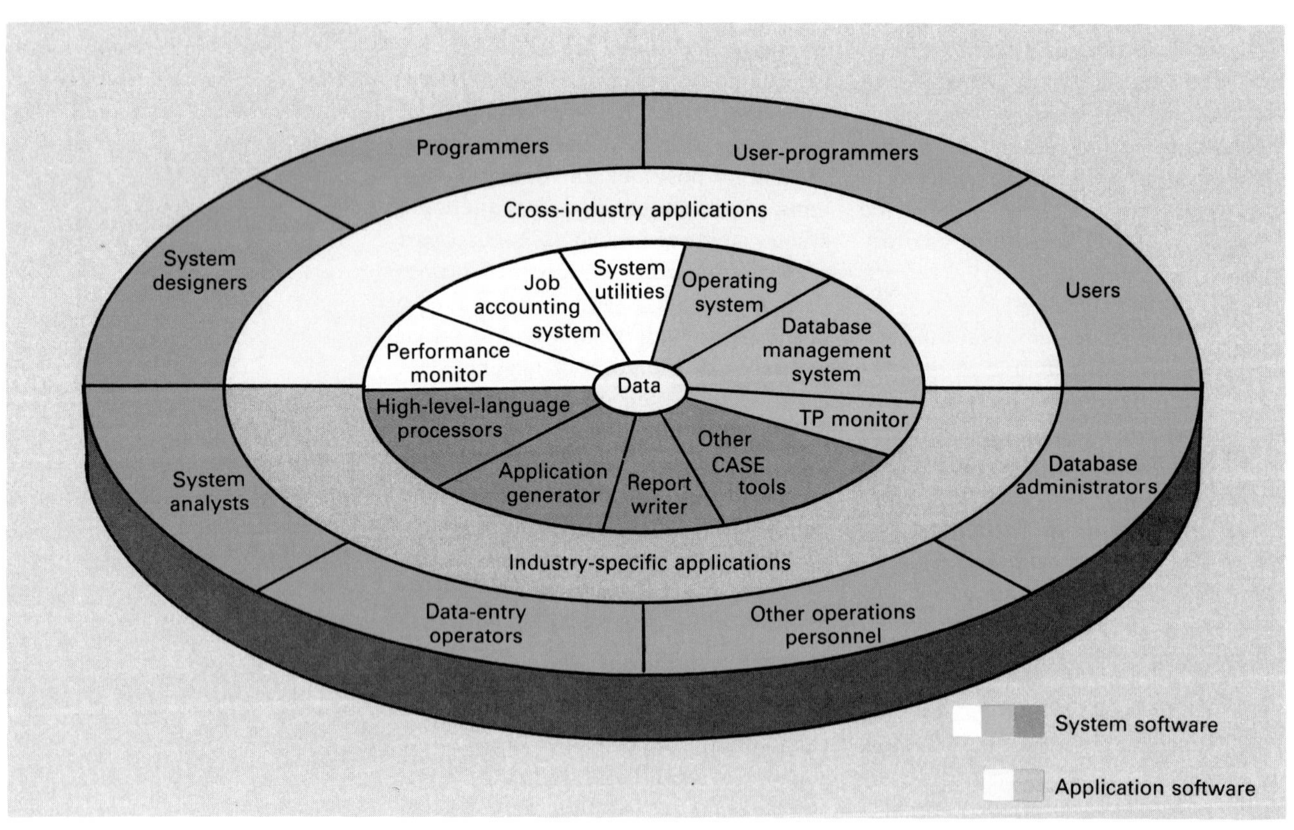
Programmers
User-programmers
Cross-industry applications
System designers
Users
System utilities
Job accounting system
Operating system
Database management system
Performance monitor
Data
High-level-language processors
TP monitor
Other CASE tools
Application generator
Report writer
System analysts
Database administrators
Industry-specific applications
Data-entry operators
Other operations personnel
System software
Application software

- *System operation*—software that manages the resources of a computer system during program execution. Examples are operating systems, database management systems, and communication (also called *teleprocessing* or *TP*) monitors.
- *System utilization*—software that manages or assists users in managing the system operation. Examples are utility programs that copy or sort data files, job accounting systems, and performance monitors.
- *System implementation*—software that assists users in preparing programs for execution. Examples are assemblers, high-level-language processors, application generators, report writers, source-level debuggers, and other CASE tools.

Traditionally, system programs have been written in low-level programming languages. A detailed knowledge of the EDP-system hardware is needed to write such programs. Therefore, neither personal computer users nor even experienced DP personnel at user installations normally attempt to write them. Instead, most system programs are obtained from external sources such as (1) the computer manufacturer, (2) a software development firm that specializes in writing system programs, (3) a service company that develops or markets programs for multiple use, or (4) any combination of these sources. Some system programs are now being written in high-level languages, but that does not mean that users are now commonly writing their own system software. The system design expertise and development resources needed for such efforts are still beyond those normally available.

Application Software

Application software directs the computer in performing specific user-related data-processing tasks. The *application* exists independently of the computer; it's simply a job to be done—administering employee benefits, keeping track of investment portfolios, or whatever.

Application software directs the computer in performing specific user-related data-processing tasks.

For discussion purposes, we can group application programs into two broad classes. Most individual users and most user installations have some programs in each class.

- *Cross-industry*—programs that perform tasks common to many industries, organizations, or user groups. Examples are general ledger, financial planning (modeling), word processing, and graphic packages.
- *Industry-specific*—programs that perform tasks unique to a particular industry, organization, or user group. Some examples are bill-of-materials processing (discrete hard-goods manufacturing), claims management (insurance), and mortgage loan accounting (banking and finance).

To help you understand the meaning of the term *industry* as it is used here, some representative examples of industrial systems are shown in Figure 11-2. That transpor-

MANN FILTER
EYC 478
nsa Cargo

Figure 11-2 Users in many industries are being helped by computers under the direction of specialized, industry-specific application programs. (Courtesy [clockwise starting at top right] Texas Instruments; Alvis Upitis/The Image Bank; IBM Corporation; Margot Granitsas/Photo Researchers; Monsanto Company (center); Apple Computer, Inc.)

tation, distribution, and retailing are industry classifications may come as no surprise to you. That medicine and health care, entertainment, and services can be treated as industries is not as obvious. Many application programs have been developed for each of these industries. Some of the programs are known only to the user organizations that developed them. Others are marketed widely as application packages.

The most popular application programs are used by individuals to improve the speed and quality of their work. That's how Lotus 1-2-3 and other spreadsheet programs gained users' attention. Another common example is word-processing software that allows a user to create, correct, and change a memo or manuscript without needless retyping. Products for business uses, like financial planning and accounting, are second in sales. (See Figure 11-3.) Programs for entertainment and educational uses follow.

The Demand for Software

User demands for both system and application software have increased significantly over the past 10 years. The most obvious reason for this increased demand is the overwhelming increase in the number of computer users. The EDP-system user base now includes multinational corporations, one-person households, and everything in between.

Substantial improvements in hardware price/performance ratios have lowered users' entry-level costs. They have also opened new application areas. Examples are automated tracking of sales contacts and follow

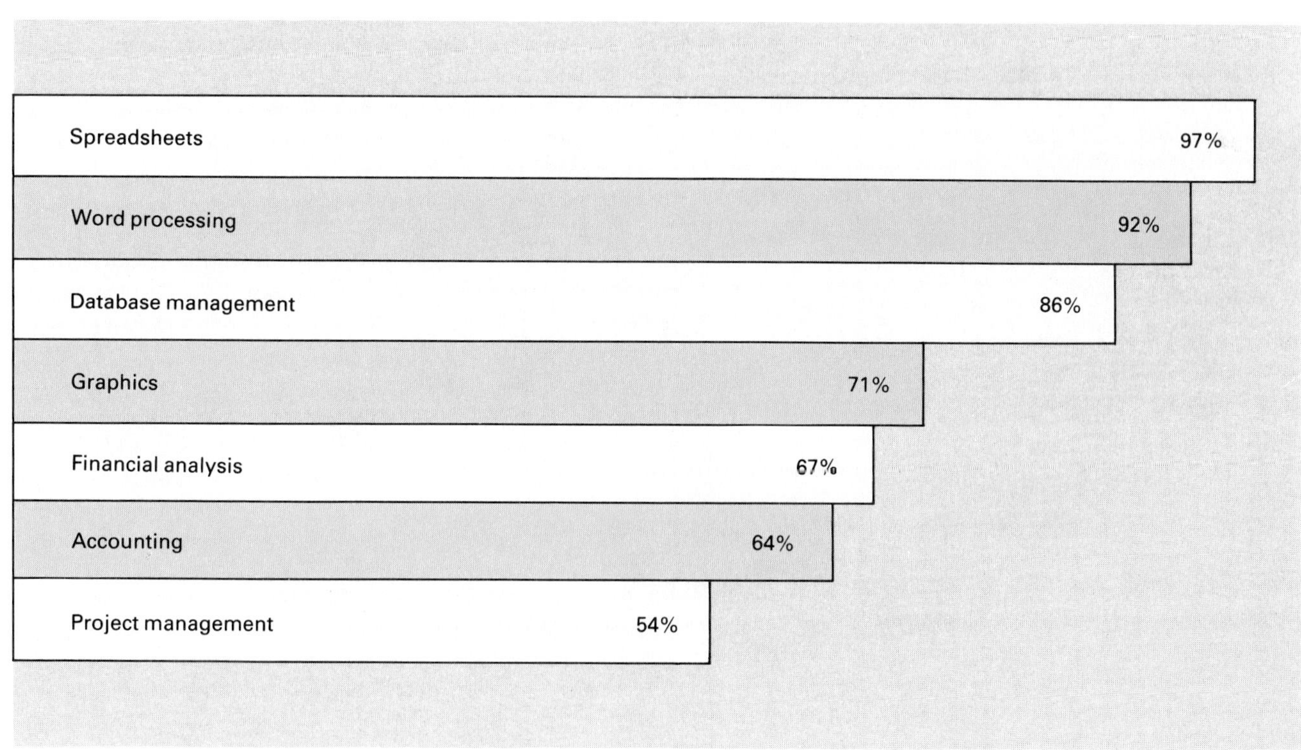

Spreadsheets 97%
Word processing 92%
Database management 86%
Graphics 71%
Financial analysis 67%
Accounting 64%
Project management 54%

Figure 11-3 A 1988 survey of application software usage among large U.S. companies shows spreadsheets and word-processing programs used almost everywhere. (Source: International Data Corporation. *Computerworld*, October 3, 1988.)

Train a Child . . .

Today's students are tomorrow's corporate users of computers. Statistics show that when given a choice, employees ask for the operating systems they used in college.

Adapted from Jon Littman, "Exploring the Options" *PC WEEK*, September 4, 1984.

up, automated project management, and electronic mail.

As an example, more than 2 million users have bought Lotus 1-2-3 and millions more are familiar with it. About 450 companies now sell products that add into Lotus 1-2-3 everything from word processing to better graphics. In the United States alone, about 20,000 companies are developing software for use by others; more than 60,000 software products have been produced. Even as existing software companies are acquired, merge with other companies, or fail, new companies spring up. The worldwide software market (annual sales revenue) is said to be about $30 billion at this time. Software industry growth rates of about 20 percent per year are predicted.

A new generation of business managers is (by both education and training) more aware of the types of applications that can be addressed with computer help. Confronted by determined competitors and unfavorable economic climates, these managers are eager to capitalize on the advantages that computers offer. Families and individuals who have acquired computers are similarly eager to make the most of their investments. Fewer and fewer users are attempting to write their own software. (See Figure 11-4.) Yet we all need software to tell computers what to do.

Early History of Software

Computer hardware has evolved through several generations characterized by the successive use of vacuum tubes, transistors, integrated

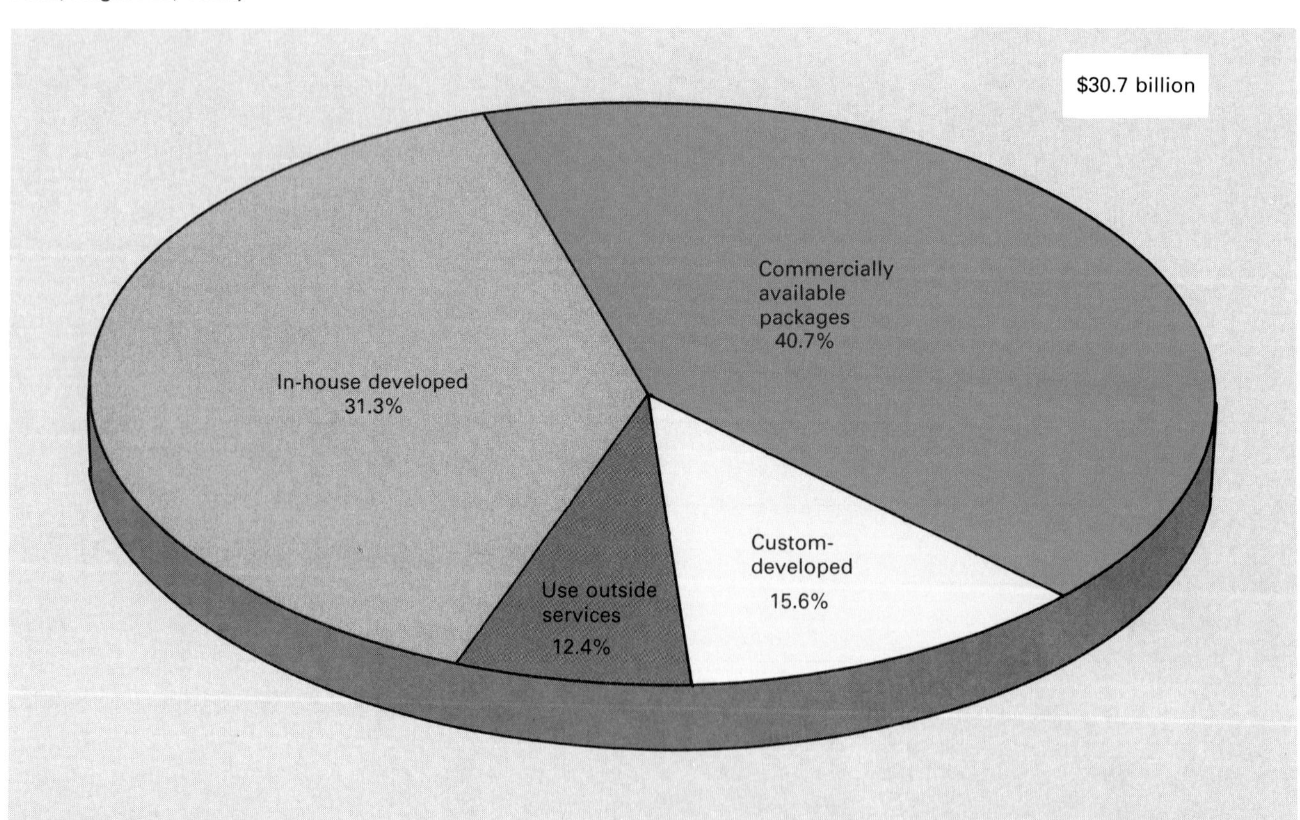
$30.7 billion
Commercially
available
packages
40.7%
In-house developed
31.3%
Custom-
developed
15.6%
Use outside
services
12.4%

Figure 11-4 Worldwide software expenditures in 1988 were estimated to exceed $30 billion, with less than one-third of that total accounted for by in-house development. (Source: Newton-Evans Research Co. *Computerworld,* August 22, 1988.)

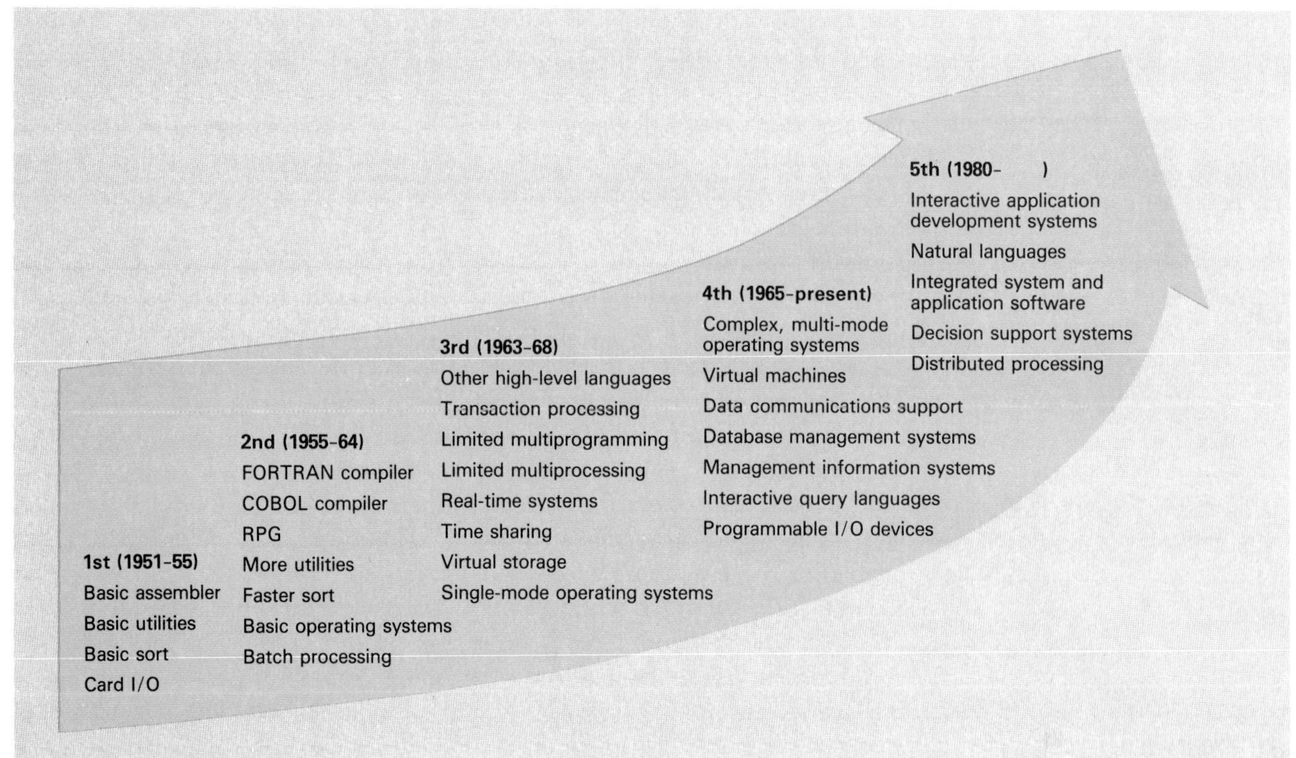
5th (1980-)
Interactive application development systems
Natural languages
Integrated system and application software
Decision support systems
Distributed processing
4th (1965-present)
Complex, multi-mode operating systems
Virtual machines
Data communications support
Database management systems
Management information systems
Interactive query languages
Programmable I/O devices
3rd (1963-68)
Other high-level languages
Transaction processing
Limited multiprogramming
Limited multiprocessing
Real-time systems
Time sharing
Virtual storage
Single-mode operating systems
2nd (1955-64)
FORTRAN compiler
COBOL compiler
RPG
More utilities
Faster sort
Basic operating systems
Batch processing
1st (1951-55)
Basic assembler
Basic utilities
Basic sort
Card I/O

Figure 11-5 System software for large computer systems has evolved through several generations, each having greater capabilities than the ones before it; personal-computer software is now evolving in a similar manner.

circuits, and very-large-scale integration (VLSI) techniques. As suggested in Chapter 10, software has also evolved. (See Figure 11-5.) We cannot say that the beginnings and endings of software generations are clear-cut, or that one generation must end before the next generation can begin. Some people assert that personal-computer software is evolving through generations similar to those of mainframe software; this evolution started slowly in the late 1970s but it is accelerating at a fast pace.

The early computers were controlled by stored programs, but they had no operating systems. Only one program occupied primary storage at a time. The computer operator loaded that program into storage, readied input and output devices, and started the processor by pressing a START button on the system console. Both setup time and breakdown time were required between jobs. Each job was a standalone application.

Computers of the mid-1950s were supported by a richer array of system software. All programs ready for execution were assigned identification numbers, or program ID's. They were stored in object-program form on magnetic tape. A small control program known as a *monitor* was loaded into primary storage. It accepted as input a single card containing one program ID. The monitor searched the magnetic tape for a matching program ID. Then it read (loaded) the corresponding object program into storage. The loaded program was then executed.

Eventually, more sophisticated monitors and more automated load procedures were developed. The operator still had to perform many tasks: putting cards into the card reader, mounting tapes, making sure the printer had paper, and so on. Programmers began to include messages to operators in their programs. During execution, these messages were printed out on a printer or on the system console. PAUSE instructions were included to make the computer "wait" until necessary tasks had been completed. Then the operator restarted the system by pressing a button on the console. Still, too much operator intervention (and too much nonproductive time) was required.

The earliest operating systems were developed to alleviate this problem. These systems could handle transitions from job to job. While one job was running, an operator could mount magnetic tapes, or position cards in the card reader, or whatever, as needed for the next job. With proper scheduling, there was no need to stop the computer between jobs. The operating system checked to see whether or not the I/O devices needed by a program were ready. If they were, execution proceeded immediately. (Note the words *operator* and *operating*—now we have some insight into why the term *operating system* came into use.)

From the user's point of view, an operating system was, and is today, an integrated set of system programs whose major function is the control of EDP-system resources. By allocating specific resources to specific, independent jobs, the operating system helps to insure that the EDP system as a whole operates efficiently and effectively. The amount of useful work that can be done in a given amount of time (i.e., the system throughput) is determined accordingly. (See Figure 11-6.)

When an operating system is installed, a human operator no longer acts as intermediary between the user and the computer system. Another means of communication between the user and the computer is required. The user has to be able to tell the computer what kind of work (jobs and job steps) is to be done. *Job-control languages (JCL's)* were developed to serve this purpose. The job-control statements needed to define a job were placed one behind another on the system input device to form a stack, or batch, of jobs. (See Figure 11-7.) An operating-system job-control program read the statements and caused the jobs to be carried out with minimal operator intervention. This was the beginning of what we know today as *stacked-job processing, batched-job processing,* or, more commonly, *batch processing.*

Many microcomputer users today are using systems that run under control of the MS-DOS operating system (or, in the case of IBM PC users, PC DOS). Why do I need an operating system, some ask. In fact, these users enter DOS *system commands* to invoke operating-system functions, much as job-control statements were used. MS-DOS consists of routines to format, compare, and copy diskettes; to compare, copy, display, erase, and rename files; to load and execute programs; to set printer and screen options; and so on. Few users could or would write their own system programs to do all of these functions.

Many microcomputer users today are using systems that run under control of the MS-DOS operating system . . .

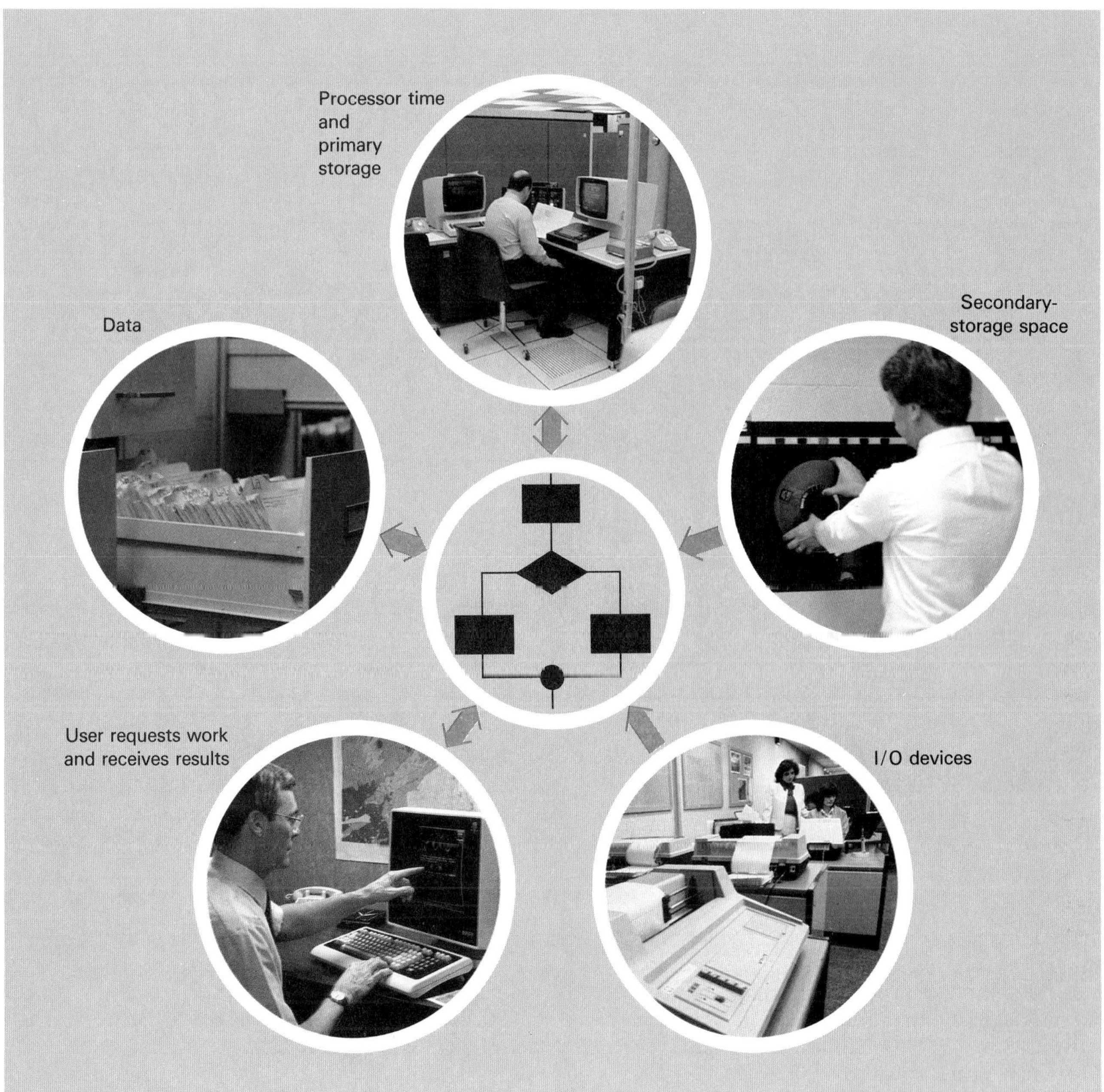
Processor time
and
primary
storage
Data
Secondary-
storage space
User requests work
and receives results
I/O devices

Figure 11-6 Operating-system software performs a control function, allocating EDP-system resources to specific jobs during processing. (Photos courtesy [clockwise] Eastman Kodak Company; Graham Magnetics Incorporated; Eastman Kodak Company; Control Data Corporation; Richard Hutchings/Photo Researchers)

Online Direct-Access Systems

In the late 1950s and early 1960s small computers such as the IBM 1401 took over tasks formerly done by users at punched-card machines in many businesses. Much larger computers from IBM, Burroughs, RCA, General Electric, and Univac were installed by universities, government agencies, and large businesses.

The batch-processing techniques we just discussed worked well where large volumes of input data were involved—say, the weekly time cards for all employees. They did not work well for small amounts of input generated randomly or for individual

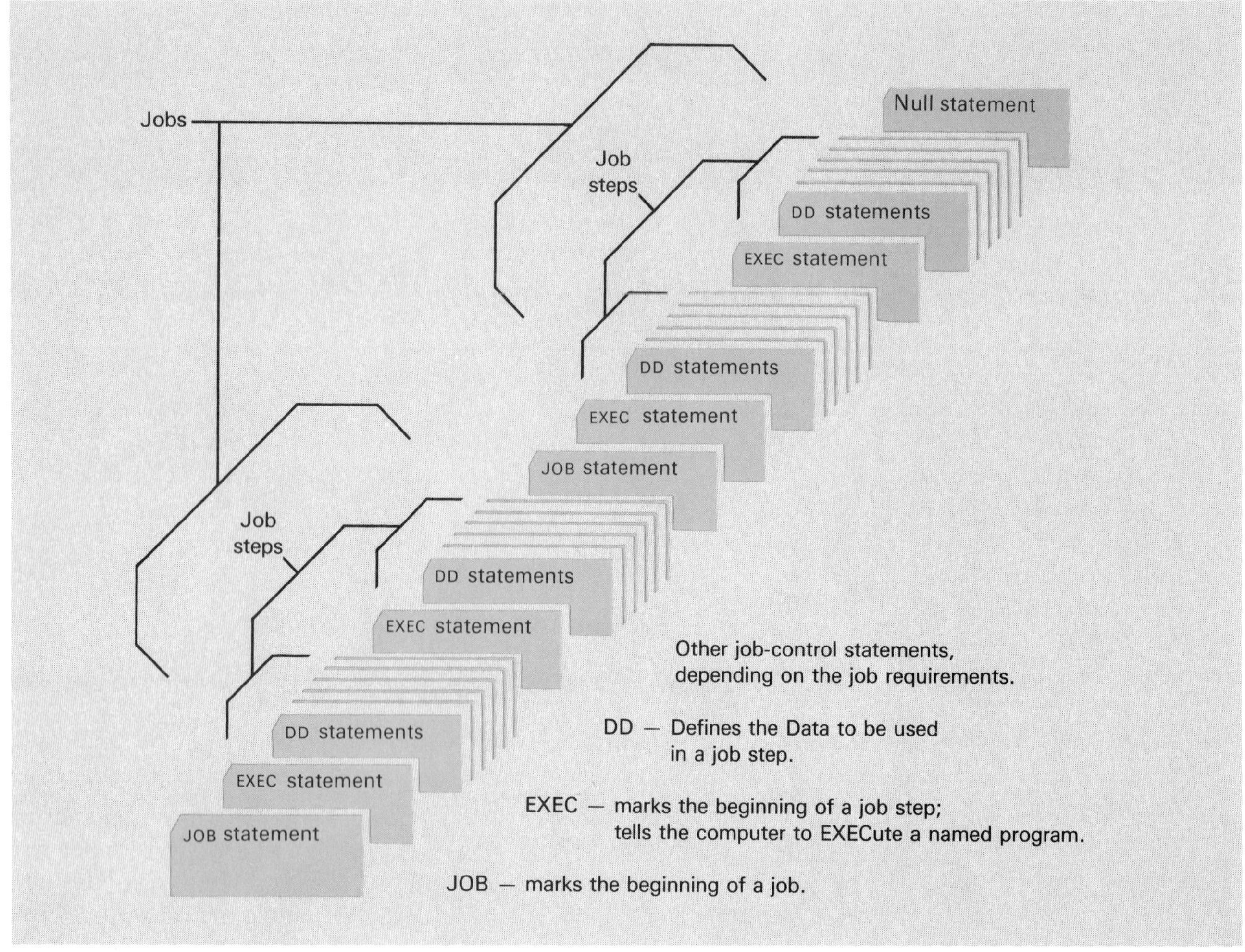
Jobs
Job steps
Null statement
DD statements
EXEC statement
DD statements
EXEC statement
JOB statement
Job steps
DD statements
EXEC statement
Other job-control statements, depending on the job requirements.
DD statements
DD — Defines the Data to be used in a job step.
EXEC statement
EXEC — marks the beginning of a job step; tells the computer to EXECute a named program.
JOB statement
JOB — marks the beginning of a job.

Figure 11-7 In the 1960s and 1970s, users placed job-control statements, punched into cards, in a job input stream to be read by an operating-system job-control program. The computer performed batch processing.

problem solving. Computer manufacturers addressed these needs by developing online direct-access systems.

In an online direct-access application, the computer communicates directly with both the source and the destination of the data it processes. The data can be sent to and received from local I/O devices, or to and from I/O devices at remote locations by way of communication channels. Input transactions can be processed as they are received. Master files can be read to produce up-to-date output information in the form of status reports, invoices, and so on. As we learned earlier, this approach is called *transaction processing.* Because queries about master-file data are received in random order, the files are generally stored on direct-access storage devices.

The first online direct-access systems were typified by the early airline reservations systems. Perhaps best known of these was the Semi-Automatic Business Research Environment (SABRE) system developed jointly by IBM and American Airlines. Planning for the system was initiated by American in 1954; it became fully operational 10 years later—the first prominent commercial example of shared computing. Ticket and sales offices in 60 U.S. cities were equipped with I/O devices, known as *agent sets,* designed especially for airline use. Master files containing seat inventory records for hundreds of scheduled flights were placed in secondary storage. Crew assignments, maintenance requirements, and fuel and catering requirements were also stored and processed within the SABRE system. Sales data, cost data, return on investment (ROI) information, and inventory control figures were maintained for airline management.

The first online direct-access systems were typified by the early airline reservations systems.

These early online direct-access systems met many user needs, but they were far from perfect. Because the systems had to respond quickly to many individual transactions, it was neither possible nor desirable to collect the transactions into batches and then process the batches to query or update master files. Instead, the master files had to be updated continuously. Otherwise, for example, a ticket agent at one location might sell airline space already sold by an agent at another location.

Furthermore, different types of transactions, say inquiries, sales, and cancellations, required different programs to process them. These programs had to be kept in secondary storage and brought into primary storage when needed. Much time was spent in locating and gaining access to data and programs, rather than in processing transactions.

To add to the problem, transactions occurred irregularly. During peak periods, hundreds of thousands of transactions had to be processed within minutes. At other times, the systems were relatively idle. It became apparent that to use EDP-system resources as efficiently and effectively as possible, new techniques had to be developed.

Multitasking, or Multiprogramming

Fortunately, during this same time period, system software and hardware developments were occurring elsewhere. In 1963, the Burroughs Corporation released its Master Control Program, or MCP, for use with Burroughs B5000 computer systems. MCP assumed greater control over system resources than its predecessors had. Input and output devices were activated by MCP rather than by application programs. This centralized control was possible because hardware interrupt conditions signaled to MCP when control of the EDP system should be passed to a special-purpose routine for I/O processing.

MCP could also assign memory areas to programs, determine the optimum sequence and mix of jobs, determine program priorities and system requirements, and provide for rescheduling if new jobs were introduced or job priorities changed. More than one user application program could be resident in primary storage at a time. Since the processor could execute only one instruction at a time, simultaneous execution of instructions from different programs was not possible. The processor could, however, execute instructions from one program, then instructions

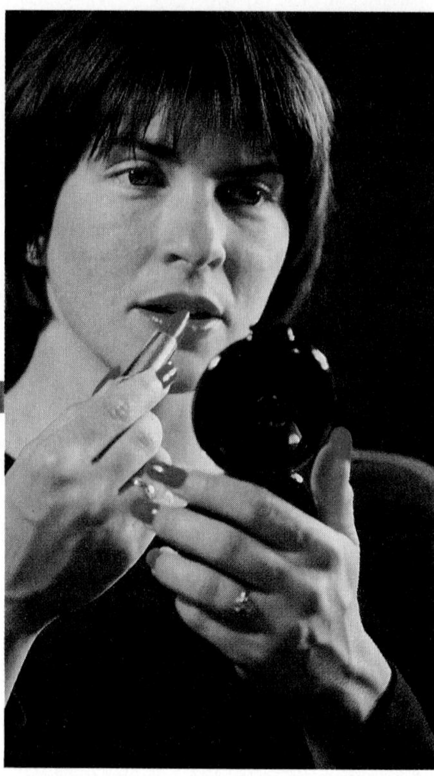

TIMELINESS IN MANUFACTURING

Risdon Corporation, headquartered in Naugatuck, Connecticut, is one of the world's leading manufacturers of cosmetic and toiletry containers. Its products range from lipstick tubes, mascara, and compact cases for Elizabeth Arden, Avon, Max Factor, and Revlon, to deodorant sticks for Procter & Gamble.

To strengthen its position as a world-class manufacturer, Risdon installed MANMAN, an MRP II (manufacturing resource planning) system from ASK Computer Systems, headquartered in Mountain View, California. Risdon is using ASK's MANMAN/REPETITIVE™, for example, to address its high-volume, low-inventory, fast-paced production requirements. Cosmetic company orders for as many as 2 million items may require from weeks to months to manufacture; with MANMAN/REPETITIVE, Risdon can manage all types of production cycles. Since implementing MANMAN, Risdon has improved on-time deliveries to its customers by 26 percent, reduced inventories by 15 percent, and increased shop delivery performance. Because the firm can plan and schedule its production more efficiently, it can give suppliers more accurate forecasts of its needs. As a result, Risdon has also experienced a 30 percent improvement in on-time deliveries of materials to Risdon from its suppliers. *(Photo courtesy Mark McKenna; MANMAN/REPETITIVE is a trademark of ASK Computer Systems.)*

from another program, then instructions from the first program again, and so on. This type of processing is called *concurrent processing*. Program logic within MCP determined which system software routine or application program had control of the B5000 processor at any given time. Today, a system that provides these capabilities is said to support *multitasking*, or *multiprogramming*.

Concurrent execution of programs is desirable because I/O operations are much slower than internal processing operations. Fortunately, the design of modern computer systems permits overlapping of I/O and processing operations (recall "Synchronous and Asynchronous Operations" in Chapter 6). Even so, if only one program is resident in primary storage and executing, chances are the processor is idle much of the time.

In 1964, IBM introduced its major third-generation operating system, OS/360, for use with IBM System/360 computers. A System/360 user could select the version of OS/360 that included a control program called *Multiprogramming with a Fixed Number of Tasks (MFT)*. Each task was simply an independent unit of work, such as a program or subroutine, that needed system resources. As its name implies, OS/MFT could operate on a fixed number of tasks concurrently. Actually, it could read jobs from as many as three job input streams, handle up to 15 job steps, and record up to 36 streams of output concurrently.

A System/360 user with extensive data-processing requirements could select another alternative: a version of OS/360 that included a control program called *Multiprogramming with a Variable Number of Tasks (MVT)*. As its name implies, OS/MVT could control a variable number of tasks concurrently. It could change the number, size, and location of reserved storage areas to meet the data-processing requirements at any given time. Like OS/MFT, OS/MVT could handle as many as 15 job steps concurrently. Moreover, once a job step was initiated by OS/MVT, that job step could, in turn, initiate the processing of other tasks. There was not a 1-to-1 relationship between job steps and tasks (as existed under OS/MFT).

OS/MVT was used only on the very largest mainframes of the late 1960s. These big mainframes sometimes had as much as 1 megabyte of primary storage! A big application program was one that needed 256K!

The Burroughs B1700, announced in 1972, was the first small computer with an operating system that supported multitasking. Today, there are microcomputer systems with equivalent or greater capabilities. MS-DOS is a *single-user, single-tasking* operating system. OS/2 is a *single-user, multitasking* operating system. It can interact with only one user, but that user may initiate the concurrent execution of two or more programs. UNIX is a *multiuser, multitasking* operating system. It can communicate at what appears to be the same time with two or more interactive users and can perform concurrent processing.

Of course, IBM and other vendors have also continued to evolve their mainframe operating systems, as we'll see below.

OS/2

OS/2 is the single-user, multitasking operating system developed by IBM and Microsoft for IBM PS/2 and PS/2-compatible microcomputers. It can simulate MS-DOS and run one MS-DOS application at a time in a foreground partition if user application needs dictate. New programs are being written, and existing ones modified, to take advantage of OS/2's multitasking and 16-megabyte addressing capabilities.

Integration and Windowing

Before 1970, EDP systems were developed and marketed as all-inclusive packages that encompassed hard-

CAN YOU NAME THE "BIG 5" FUNCTIONS OF INTEGRATED BUSINESS SOFTWARE?

The functions are database management, electronic spreadsheet analysis, graphics, word processing, and communications.

ware, software, education, and maintenance services. Then most computer manufacturers adopted a policy of *separate pricing.* The major system control program and some basic system utility programs were supplied with the main processor. Other software components had to be purchased or secured under a contractual agreement (license) from the computer manufacturer or a software vendor, or they had to be developed in-house by the user installation. Other hardware components (magnetic-tape units, disk storage units, and so on), education, and maintenance services were obtained in a similar manner. The total cost of the system was the sum of the costs of all these items.

When microcomputer systems first arrived on the scene, some vendors packaged their systems as all-in-one, or self-contained, units, hardware-wise. Other vendors marketed numerous, separate hardware components: each user could include or not include a printer, a monochrome or color display, joysticks, a first or second floppy disk drive, and so on, in his or her system. Likewise, some vendors supplied at least one system control program and a BASIC language processor in ROM as part of the basic system. Other vendors treated all programs as separately orderable items. Users could "mix and match" programs from the computer manufacturer and other software vendors as they became available.

Now user demands for an integrated, system view of the EDP-system capabilities at their disposal are emerging. A terminal or microcomputer user does not want to learn a different user interface to every program that runs on a system. "Computers for the rest of us" (quoting Apple Computer) have to be easy to use, or they won't be used. Data that has been entered as input to one application should not have to be entered again to use it in another application. Results computed under the direction of an electronic spreadsheet program should be includable within a document produced with the help of word-processing software. And so on. Vendors are responding to these demands with various approaches to integration and with windowing techniques.

Under one approach, a vendor packages programs as separate entities but emphasizes that the programs are part of a planned series of software components. Software Publishing's PFS series (PFS:File, PFS:Write, etc.) are a prominent example. Alternatively, some vendors are offering integrated application software packages that perform numerous functions. Lotus' Symphony is a popular example. The Apple Macintosh interface, Microsoft Windows, and Digital Research's GEM provide graphical environments within which user application program input and output operations occur. The outputs of several jobs can be viewed simultaneously via windowing techniques. (See Figure 11-8.)

Windows are simply designated areas on a visual-display screen, portholes to user applications. They also act as conduits between applications. For example, a user may "cut" numbers from a spreadsheet output and "paste" the numbers into word-processing output. Icons, pull-down or pop-up menus, and pointer-activated controls for scrolling and zooming are common features. A DOS shell program provided as part of MS-DOS 4.0 offers a graphic-based user interface with menus and

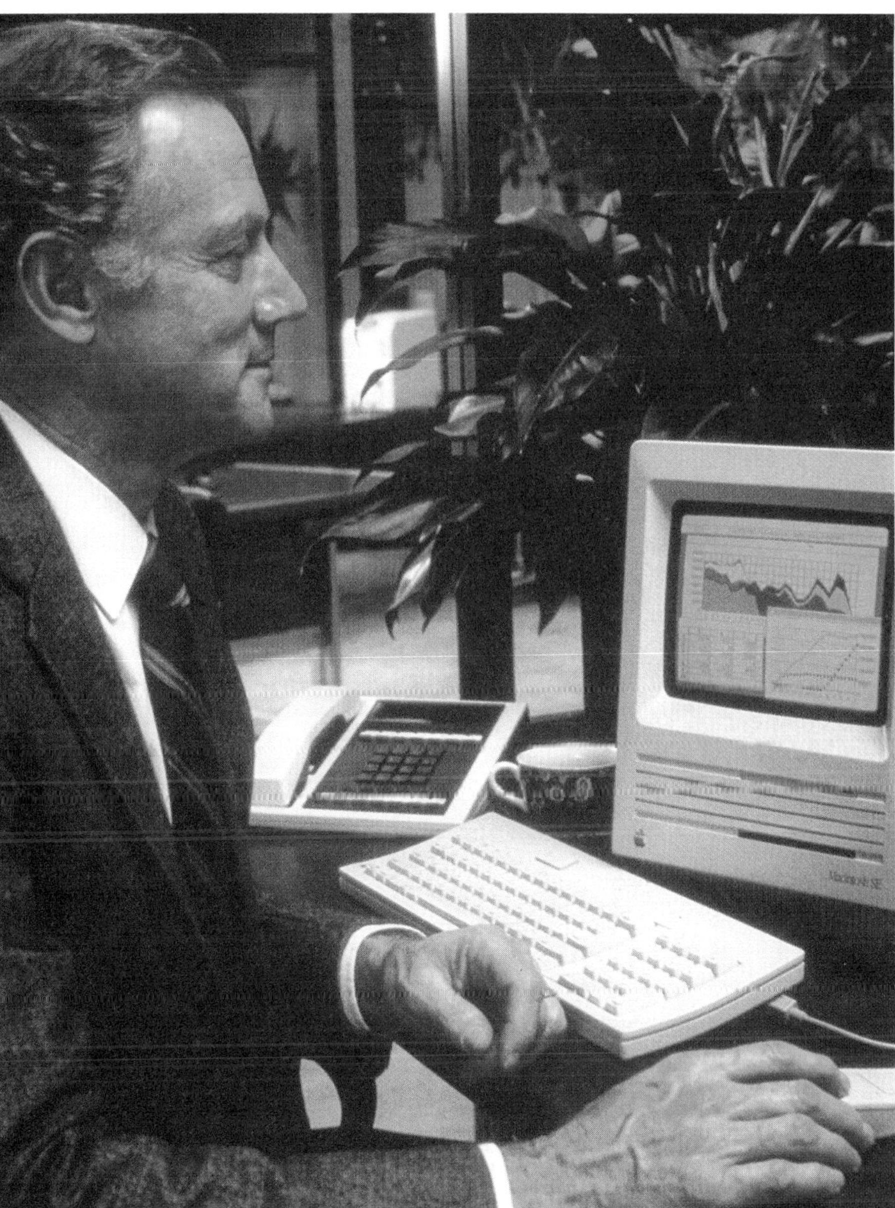

Figure 11-8 Among the ease-of-use features of Apple Computer's microcomputer systems are windowing capabilities. The output of several jobs can be viewed simultaneously through overlapping windows. Data can be moved from one window environment to another with the aid of a movable pointer, commonly referred to as a *mouse.* (Courtesy Apple Computer, Inc.)

mouse support. The interface is designed to provide user-friendliness for users who otherwise must respond to single command-line displays such as the C > prompt.

Multiprocessing

Let's pause a moment to clarify some concepts and to relate some things we've learned. Like *multiprogramming* and *multitasking,* the terms *multiprogramming* and *multiprocessing* are sometimes used interchangeably, but they do not mean the same thing. Multitasking involves concurrent execution of instructions from two or more programs sharing one processor and controlled by one major operating-system control program. In multiprocessing, instructions are executed *simultaneously* (at the same time, in parallel) on two or more processors; the processors can execute different instructions from the same program or from different programs at a given time. (We initially mentioned this capability under "Serial and Parallel Operations" in Chapter 6.)

In today's most basic multiprocessing systems, one main processor handles all major processing functions. Other co-processors handle "housekeeping" chores such as opening and closing files, input validation and editing, and file maintenance or perform complex mathematical functions. The more sophisticated multiprocessing systems involve several main processors. There is no single "computer," but rather a "computer system" that consists of several processors linked together for purposes of communication and cooperation during processing. (See Figure 11-9.)

Multiprocessing is not limited to mainframe environments. For example, the IBM PS/2 Model 70 computers introduced in late 1988 have a 32-bit Intel 80386 main processor and, optionally, an Intel 80387 math co-processor. Apple's Macintosh SE/30 announced in January 1989 has a 32-bit Motorola 68030 main processor and a Motorola 68882 floating-point (math) co-processor.

Multiprocessing is not limited to mainframe environments.

In general, multiprocessing support involves enhancements to both hardware and software otherwise used in a uniprocessor mode. Multiprocessing systems are more complex and more costly than uniprocessor systems. However, some user needs can be satisfied only when such support is provided. System availability and system reliability are vital considerations (some installations must provide for 24 hours of uninterrupted processing daily). A multiprocessing system can be designed so that at least some work can continue even if one processor is down. Many of the problems now being addressed with computer help involve lots of data and lots of very fast computation and feedback—for example, monitoring and/or controlling the many variables that must be taken

Figure 11-9 Tandem Computers' multiprocessing systems provide support for high-volume, online transaction-processing applications with many terminals, communication lines, and files that users access continuously. These applications include bank deposits and withdrawals, funds transfer, hotel or airline reservations, order processing, retail sales, credit verification, inventory control, job flow control, stock trading, and medical records. (Photo provided by Tandem Computers Incorporated)

into account when journeys into space are initiated. With multiple processors, parallel work on different problems or on the same problem is possible.

Through advances in microelectronics, hardware costs are declining rapidly. Much progress has been made in understanding the problems of processor-to-processor communication, resource contention, processor scheduling, the avoidance, detection, and resolution of deadlocks, and so on. Many of these problems can be handled by system software without involving users or user application programs. Perhaps the biggest challenge that remains is to understand more fully the parallelism that can exist in solution algorithms. To exploit this parallelism, we need to think about solution steps in ways other than sequentially. Some progress has been made in providing features to support parallelism in programming languages (most notably, Pascal and Ada). Techniques are being pursued that will enable the computer itself to detect opportunities for parallelism.

Real-Time Systems

As mentioned earlier in this chapter, an online direct-access system can accept input transactions as they are generated. A system that can also provide output fast enough to satisfy any user requirement can be further classified as a *real-time system*. Such a system makes output available quickly enough to control (not simply react to) real-life activity.

The concept of real time is closely related to immediacy. It is seen as *response time,* which we now define somewhat formally to be the interval of time between completion of input and start of output from an EDP system.

In actual operation, real time is a matter of degree, depending upon the application at hand. The customer-service representative of an insurance firm may be willing to wait from 3 to 10 seconds for details about the coverage of a policyholder. In a military defense system, responses within microseconds may be required. Variations in response time are due to differences in the system workload, internal processing requirements, frequency and type of access to computer files and/or databases, and so on. Both the hardware and the software must be capable of fast performance. In addition, the system must be tuned by system support personnel to fit the requirements imposed on it. For example, system characteristics such as the number and size of I/O areas, or *buffers,* may be set at system startup time.

Although basic business applications such as order writing, inventory control, and payroll can be implemented as real-time systems, they are not likely to be. Increasing the costs of software, hardware, development, and ongoing support is more likely to be justified for specialized applications in industries such as transportation, manufacturing, banking, and distribution. Computer-controlled robotic systems on assembly lines, automated teller machines at banks, and point-of-sale terminals at retail department stores are components of real-time systems. In hospitals, patients' vital signs are monitored by real-time systems at bedside. Mobile police units gain access to vehicle registration data, missing person files, and case data via handheld ter-

REAL-TIME AIR TRAFFIC CONTROL SYSTEM

Air traffic control is an example of a computer-assisted task that requires a constant, "real-time" flow of information. Planes carrying passengers and cargo arrive and depart in a seemingly continuous stream. Many planes in the air mean much data to manage. Yet, air traffic controllers must know the locations of all air traffic at all times. Computers help the controllers by predicting where each plane will be at any given moment. They alert the controllers to potential problems so that actions can be taken to prevent the problems from occurring. *(Photo courtesy Tom Stack & Associates)*

minals that are part of national and even international real-time computer networks.

Time Sharing

Time sharing is a technique that allows several users of an online real-time system to use that system on what *appears* to be a simultaneous basis. The speed at which the system components—both hardware and software—operate allows the system to switch from one active user to another, doing all or part of each job until all work is completed. The speed may be so great that each user believes that he or she is the only one using the system. The purpose for which one person uses the system may be totally unrelated to that of others. The system resources are shared by all.

Since the user is more concerned with the solution to a problem than with the techniques used to solve it, ease of use is an essential characteristic of any time-sharing system. In effect, the user's terminal or work station (and therefore the computer system) becomes a personal computing tool; it is used in much the same way that the slide rule, adding machine, and calculator have been used for years. In just a few hours, a manager, financial analyst, engineer, or student can learn a conversational (interactive) programming language

Since the user is more concerned with the solution to a problem than with the techniques used to solve it, ease of use is an essential characteristic of any time-sharing system.

such as BASIC or a query language. Then he or she can submit questions or problems directly to the computer and receive immediate responses. The primary function of time sharing is to make more computing power available to more users through interactive processing—rapid, repeated alternation of user input and system response.

The capability of relatively fast two-way communication with the computer system is also valuable to data-processing professionals. A beginning programmer can request that a program be translated and executed, correct any errors detected during the translation, and then rerun the program immediately. An experienced programmer can test one or several programs without waiting for the output of complete processing runs, as is normally required in a batch-processing environment. Programs developed in this manner can be used in the time-sharing environment or become part of an integrated business application. Studies have shown that the most important factor in increasing the productivity of programmers is the availability of online interactive debugging and testing facilities.

Types of Time-Sharing Systems

The earliest time-sharing systems were developed in the late 1950s and early 1960s at Carnegie Institute of Technology, Stanford University, and MIT. Of major concern to all were the difficulties often experienced in programming.

Under a $300,000 grant from the National Science Foundation, two Dartmouth professors, John G. Kemeny and Thomas E. Kurtz, pioneered development of time-sharing languages, applications, and teaching methods suitable for college students. Especially noteworthy are their efforts pertaining to BASIC, the widely used interactive programming language developed with support from General Electric. (We surveyed the major features of BASIC in Chapter 10.)

IBM/American Airlines' SABRE system, discussed earlier, can be described as a special-purpose time-sharing system. Before SABRE was fully operational, both Delta and Pan American had ordered similar systems from IBM. Today, more than 30 major airlines use such systems. Smaller airlines connect into many of them.

There are three kinds of time-sharing systems in use today:

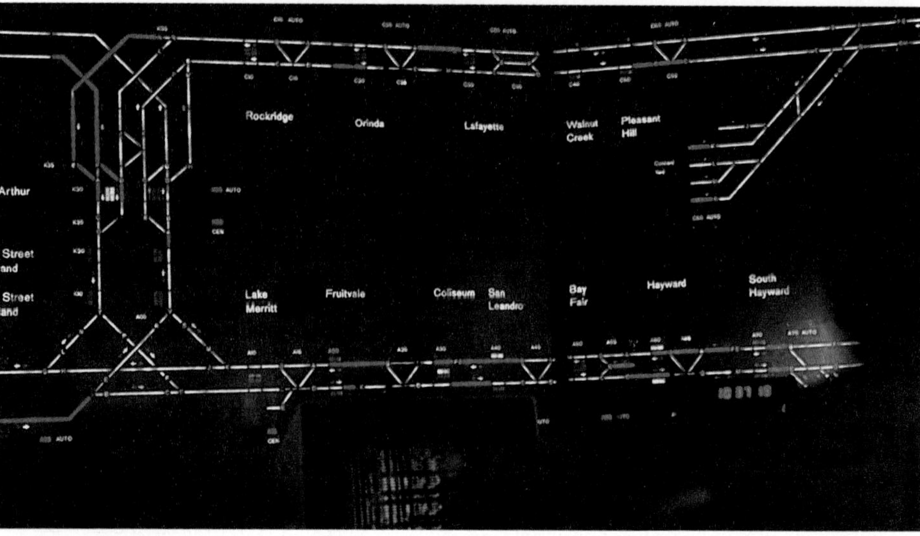
Rockridge
Orinda
Lafayette
Walnut Creek
Pleasant Hill
Arthur
Street
Street
Lake Merritt
Fruitvale
Coliseum
San Leandro
Bay Fair
Hayward
South Hayward

COMPUTERS WILL GET YOU THERE

B-A-R-T. BART. If you're a football fan, you may know of a famous quarterback by that name. Perhaps a friend or relative comes to mind. To thousands of Californians, BART means Bay Area Rapid Transit, their means of getting to and from work each day.

At the left above, we see an operator in the cab of a BART train at a test location. At the right, we see a closeup of part of the central control display board.

By the mid-1980s, more than 200,000 passengers were using BART daily. A daily ridership of 270,000 was anticipated. BART trains were being controlled by computers, but not more than 49 trains could be used within the system. BART authorities knew they had to select a new computer system that would perform reliably and handle their expanding needs.

After evaluating computer systems from ten companies, BART authorities signed an agreement to use six Data General 32-bit minicomputers, or "superminis." The six superminis were to be installed at the central control site in Oakland. They were to serve as the base for an Integrated Control System to schedule and monitor the operations of up to 115 trains. BART authorities emphasized that the Data General Eclipse software as well as its hardware was a key factor in their decision. *(Photos courtesy of Bay Area Rapid Transit)*

- General-purpose systems, which support several programming languages and allow users to create and run their own programs
- Systems in which a wide variety of programs are available for execution but cannot be modified by users
- Systems in which all programs are related to one major application, and users merely provide input and request output

In practice, a time-sharing system may be a combination of these, with the major application having first priority. The distinguishing characteristic among the three systems is the degree of user independence provided.

Approaches to Time Sharing

There are two basic approaches to the use of time-sharing facilities. One is internal to the user organization. The other involves dependencies on an external (outside) firm. An organization may use one or the other, or both.

In the first case, the user organization acquires both hardware and software for its own use (as did American Airlines). Such a system is called an *in-house time-sharing system.* It enables several departments or locations within a company to share one system. Real-time applications such as management inquiry, interactive problem solving, and engineering design are readily handled by this kind of system. Often, batch-processing applications such as accounts receivable or payroll are handled as *background programs* while time-sharing programs are executed as *foreground programs* in storage partitions assigned higher priority.

In the second approach to time-sharing, computing service is purchased from another firm, which may be called a *computer service company,* a *service bureau,* or an *information utility.* (See Figure 11-10.) The user organization pays for the computing service in much the same way that it

Figure 11-10 Many users at widely separated locations can interact with a computer at what appears to be the same time when time-sharing capabilities are available. Computer service companies such as Tymshare offer such capabilities to user organizations on a national or even an international basis. (Courtesy McDonnell Douglas Corp.)

VISA

pays for telephone service. An installation charge, basic monthly rental charges (for example, for terminals or workstations and communication equipment), and variable charges per transaction may be involved. The variable charges are based on the amount of time a particular terminal is connected to the computer, the amount of processor time actually used by each program executed from that terminal, and so on. Charges are frequently lower for evening and weekend use. Some service companies "bundle" charges into fixed fees for use of specific programs.

Most certainly, cost is one factor a user organization considers when determining whether to establish its own time-sharing system or purchase time-sharing services. An organization that needs the power of a large computer on an infrequent basis, or that requires a limited amount of computer resources on a regular basis, is a likely candidate for the second approach. New clients are sought at the $1000 to $2000 per month data-processing expenditure level. Established EDP users (including departments or functional units of large organizations with centralized computer facilities) that spend up to $7000 per month for data processing are also viewed as potential customers.

From the user organization's point of view, there are additional factors to consider. Upper-level management may decide not to take on the headaches of an internal EDP installation. Managers of business operations may be reluctant to build a data-processing staff. The space and special environmental facilities needed may be serious obstacles. For multilocation organizations, facilities for data communication as well as for data processing must be taken into account.

Virtual Storage

The desire to maximize the amount of useful work that an EDP system can do, which stimulated the development of both multiprogramming and multiprocessing, also stimulated the development of *virtual storage* (also referred to as *virtual memory*). Through virtual-storage techniques, the high costs of primary-storage components and the constraints imposed by absolute limits of primary-storage capacity are eased or eliminated. The concept was not new when IBM announced virtual-storage operating systems for its System/370 computers in 1972, but never before had the concept received such publicity. Many users first became aware of the potential benefits of virtual storage at this time.

The word *virtual* means "not in actual fact." It follows that *virtual memory* means memory that does not in actual fact exist. Fundamentally, virtual-storage capabilities give the user the illusion of a primary storage with characteristics different from those of the underlying physical storage. Usually, the significant difference is that the virtual storage is much larger. Each instruction of a program must be in primary storage (which we shall call *real storage* here, in contrast to virtual) before it can be executed, but not all parts of a program have to be in real storage at any given time. An operating-system control program keeps some portion of each executing program in real storage. Other unused portions of the program may be in virtual storage only. Such portions are loaded into real storage when (or if) the instructions or data they contain are referred to by other instructions executed within the program. Because only a portion of a program has to be in primary storage during its execution, a greater number of programs can be running at any given time.

Virtual-storage capabilities are implemented in various ways. The two principal methods are called *segmentation* and *paging*. Generally, both software and hardware are involved. In some systems, this memory management is transparent to application software. As we saw in Chapter 5, however, in some systems, application programmers have to write their programs in ways designed to take advantage of virtual-storage capabilities.

Under segmentation, each program's address space (range of storage locations referenced by the program) is split into variable-size blocks, or segments. Each segment is a logically separable unit. For example, one segment may be an I/O routine; another may be a data area. If a program being executed tries to reference a segment that is not in real storage, the system intervenes and brings the segment into real storage.

Under paging, the physical-memory space is divided into fixed-size physical blocks, or page frames. Programs and data are divided into blocks (pages) of the same size. The length of the pages is determined by the characteristics of the machine hardware rather than by program logic. The page size may be very small, say space for 256 characters, or very large, say 4K bytes. One page of information can be loaded into one page frame.

A segmentation and paging system attempts to combine the best features of both segmentation and paging. Programs are first broken into logical segments by the operating system. Each segment that exceeds the uniform page size is in turn broken into pages for loading and execution on the computer. Dynamic address translation (DAT) facilities are used to convert segment, page within segment, and displacement within page addresses to absolute addresses during program execution. (See Figure 11-11.)

When a segment (or page, depending on the implementation) not in real storage is referenced during program execution, a *missing-item fault* occurs. Some paging systems attempt to minimize the number of faults by *prepaging* techniques. When one page is loaded into real storage, certain other pages are loaded as well, with the expectation that they are likely to be referenced. Only one *page-in operation* is needed for the entire group. Other systems use *demand paging* techniques. Each page is loaded into real storage only when it is called for. There may be more page-in operations, and the system may operate more slowly because of them, but no pages are brought into real storage unnecessarily.

Virtual storage cannot, of course, provide the user with an actual super-large real storage. If all portions of real storage are in use when another segment or page is referenced, a replacement operation is necessary. Numerous replacement policies have been proposed. In IBM System/370 systems, for example, the least recently used (LRU) page in real storage is replaced. If that page was not modified while occupying real storage, it can simply be overlaid by the needed page. If the page was modified, however, a *page-out operation* must occur before replacement, to insure that a valid copy of the page will be available on virtual storage the next time it is referenced.

There is no concise, well-established rule for determining the amount of real storage that must be available to support a certain amount of virtual-storage space. We cannot say, for example, that there must be

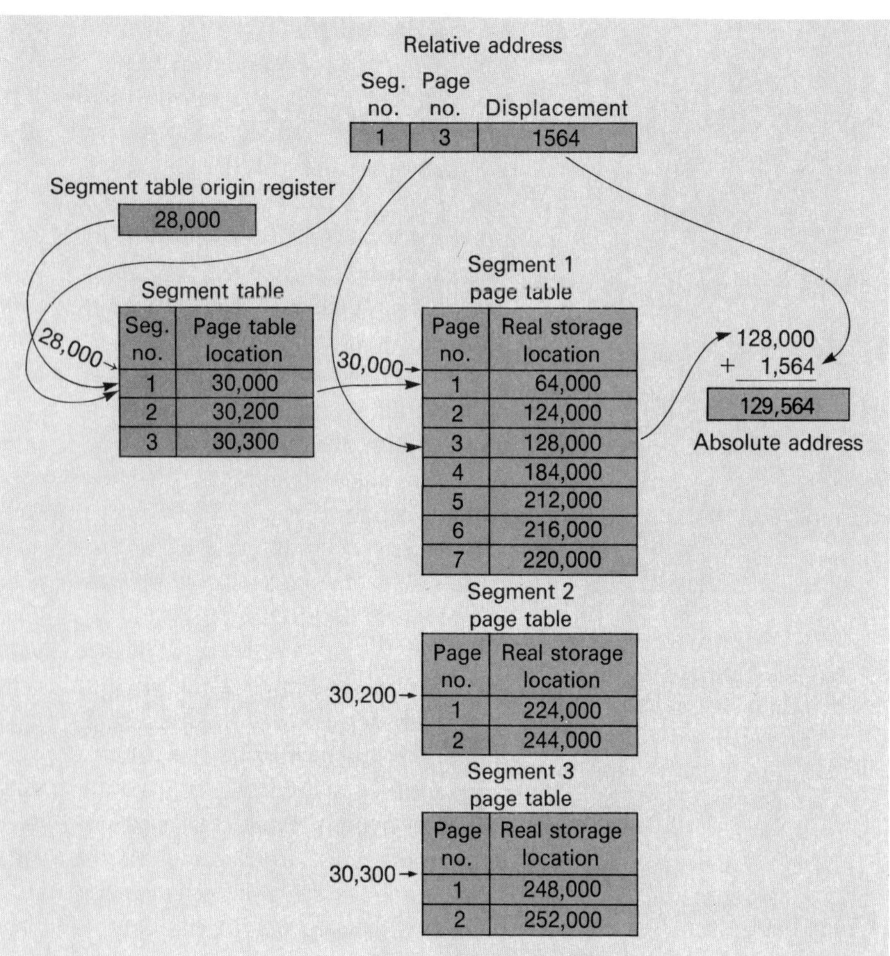
Relative address
Seg. no.
Page no.
Displacement
1
3
1564
Segment table origin register
28,000
Segment table
Seg. no.
Page table location
28,000
1
30,000
2
30,200
3
30,300
Segment 1 page table
30,000
Page no.
Real storage location
1
64,000
2
124,000
3
128,000
4
184,000
5
212,000
6
216,000
7
220,000
128,000
+ 1,564
129,564
Absolute address
Segment 2 page table
30,200
Page no.
Real storage location
1
224,000
2
244,000
Segment 3 page table
30,300
Page no.
Real storage location
1
248,000
2
252,000

Figure 11-11 A segmentation and paging system uses both a segment table and page tables to keep track of where program pages are loaded into real storage during processing.

1K of real storage for every 10K, 100K, or 1000K of virtual storage. We do know that if a program is not allocated enough real storage, many of the references to addresses within it are likely to generate missing-item faults. If a similar situation exists for numerous programs, the system is forced to spend most or all of its time moving segments or pages between virtual and real storage—a phenomenon known as *thrashing.* When thrashing occurs, the system has little time to perform useful work.

Virtual Machines

Some computer manufacturers have gone a step beyond the concept of virtual storage by offering an even more powerful capability: a *virtual-machine* environment. In a virtual-storage environment, each user is able to take advantage of internal storage that does not actually exist, but seems to. In a virtual-machine environment, each user is able to use a total computer system—both hardware and software—that does not actually exist, but seems to. The operating-system software and special hardware manage the real EDP-system resources (processor time, primary storage, I/O devices, and so on) and allocate them to active users.

The NCR Criterion series of computers are known for their support of the virtual-machine concept.

Virtual machines are "constructed" through tailorable firmware (loadable control storage on flexible disks). Users are able to perform specific tasks more economically, to operate in a selected system environment more efficiently, and to exactly duplicate the processing characteristics of another, different computer. Such capabilities are particularly attractive to existing NCR computer users who want to upgrade to the NCR Criterion series without having to rewrite all their existing application programs.

IBM supports the virtual-machine concept in its VM operating systems for medium and large computers. Each virtual machine has, by definition, a certain amount of virtual storage, a virtual processor, and a virtual system console. Other resources needed for a particular virtual machine are specified in its VM directory entry. When a user signs on to the EDP system from a terminal, personal computer, or workstation (his or her virtual console), a virtual machine is created based upon that user's entry in the directory.

Another operating system is needed to manage the resources and work flow within each virtual machine. For example, a user who is moving from a System/370 computer running under IBM's DOS/VSE operating system to an IBM 3083 computer running under VM/370 may choose to define a DOS/VSE virtual machine to run programs initially written to run under DOS/VSE.

As another example, a user installation may choose to define an MVS virtual machine. On this machine, fully checked-out business application programs (for example, general ledger) can be run on a regularly scheduled production basis—just as though they were running on an actual EDP system controlled by MVS. On other virtual machines, programmers can be writing new programs or making changes to other copies of the general-ledger programs without affecting the MVS production environment.

The conversational monitor system (CMS) is an IBM operating system that runs only under VM. It provides a user-oriented terminal environment suitable for interactive problem solving and program development. Several CMS virtual machines may be up and running under VM at any one time. (See Figure 11-12.)

Portable Operating Systems

With the decreasing costs of hardware and the exploding use of microcomputers in the early 1980s came another demand from users and vendors alike—the demand for operating-system portability. In broad terms, a *portable operating system* is one that can easily be adapted to run on any computer having a particular architecture. From the common viewpoint of microcomputer users and vendors, a portable operating system is one that can easily be adapted to run on any computer based on a particular microprocessor. Functionally, a portable operating system is not very different from an operating system designed for a particular computer (referred to as a *proprietary operating system,* for purposes of distinction). Architecturally, the machine-dependent components of the operating system are well separated from the machine-independent components. This separation allows a user or vendor to (1) write a minimal

Figure 11-12 Execution of many unrelated, independent jobs can be happening in separate virtual machines when an operating system with virtual-machine capabilities controls processing. Here, one virtual machine is doing production work—batch jobs running under the DOS/VSE operating system. A second is executing programs under a preceding release of DOS/VSE. The other three virtual machines are running under CMS. We can assume that problem solvers and software developers are interacting directly with the computer via online terminals in these environments.

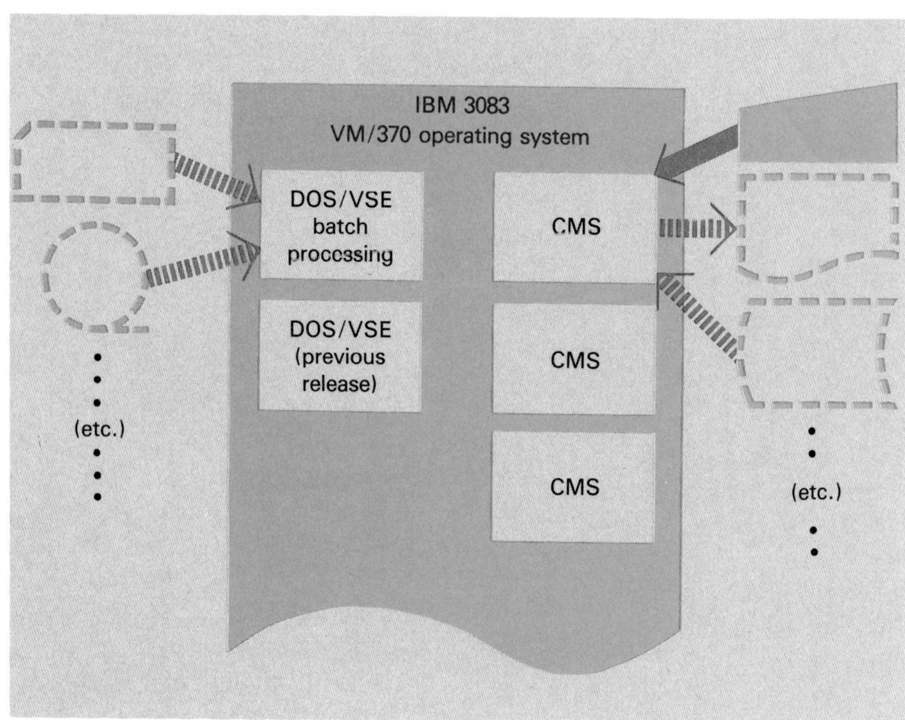
IBM 3083
VM/370 operating system
DOS/VSE
batch
processing
DOS/VSE
(previous
release)
CMS
CMS
CMS
(etc.)
(etc.)

UNIX

After years of just "getting by," UNIX is now getting attention. Industry analysts are predicting that UNIX shipments in the United States alone will grow from 204,500 units in 1987 to 846,000 units in 1992. In the personal computer arena, UNIX is expected to garner a substantial portion of the high-end commercial personal computer business; most of the other business will go to DOS, OS/2, and Macintosh.

amount of software that is unique to a particular computer system, and (2) take advantage of the machine-independent components of the portable operating system for most system functions.

In 1980, Microsoft, then a small startup firm in Redmond, Washington, responded to IBM's search for an operating system for its soon-to-be-announced IBM Personal Computer by acquiring software from a small Seattle firm and adapting it to meet IBM's needs. IBM calls the product PC DOS. Fortunately for Microsoft, the operating system was designed to be portable. Microsoft's founder, Bill Gates, retained the right to market the operating system as MS-DOS to makers of IBM-PC-compatible computers. More than 10 million copies of the operating system have been sold.

UNIX is a portable operating system that is gaining in popularity on micros, minicomputers, and mainframes. This multiuser, multitasking system was initially developed at Bell Labs. It was made available for internal use by the developers of application programs required at AT&T in the early 1970s. From there, it spread to colleges and universities working with Bell on various projects. Commercial organizations could obtain a nonsupported copy of the UNIX system on tape for a license fee of $20,000.

UNIX is unique in several ways. All system objects—including magnetic-tape units, disk drives, and terminals—look like files to both system and application programs. Thus, a high degree of device independence is achieved. Communication between the system and its users is achieved by means of a command language interpreter called the *shell.* The interpreter accepts single command lines typed by a user or sequences of commands stored within files as input. Software vendors com-

AVOIDING "HURRY UP AND WAIT"

If you're a busy traveler attending a meeting tomorrow in Chicago, or an excited vacationer looking forward to a week in Hawaii, you don't want to be told that your airplane flight has been delayed. If you're returning home after a long trip, you don't want to hear that the plane on which you're traveling has reached your destination but it can't land because of congestion on the ground.

When the airways were regulated, airplanes simply flew direct routes from one city to another. Since the early 1980s, however, American Airlines and other carriers have adopted a hub-and-spokes routing system. At certain times during the day, called *banks,* hundreds of aircraft converge on a hub airport, passengers switch planes, and the aircraft take off again carrying passengers to their destinations. By funneling flights to the hub airport, the airline can increase its passenger load per aircraft and thus reduce its cost per passenger mile.

But unless managed properly, the hub-and-spokes approach can also mean countless delays for passengers.

To avoid such delays, improve its on-time performance, and plan expansions to its existing schedule, American Airlines is using an air-traffic model called Simmod. The model runs on a microcomputer. The airspace portion of the model was developed in the late 1970s by ATAC, Inc., a research group in Mountain View, California, as a tool for optimizing air routes to conserve fuel. In the mid-1980s, American Airlines offered to design enhancements to the model to simulate ground operations as well and to actually field-test the model in its day-to-day operations. Factors such as incoming airspaces, speeds of taxiing and takeoff, numbers of gates and runways, and so forth, at the Dallas/Fort Worth airport and other nodes have been entered into the system. Even the speeds of human movements through airports have been taken into account.

Officially, the Simmod project is still in development, under the auspices of the Federal Aviation Administration (FAA). However, Simmod has already proven to be so effective at spotting potential bottlenecks — both in the air and on the ground — that American Airlines executives make few scheduling or long-term expansion decisions without first consulting it.

Upon completion, Simmod will be available as public-domain software, free of charge, from the FAA. The fact that it runs on a microcomputer will facilitate its acceptance. Additional airlines and additional passengers will benefit. *(Photo courtesy Dallas/Fort Worth International Airport)* monly incorporate customized shells to make interaction with their systems easier for users who are not skilled programmers.

Each program starts out with a standard input unit (normally the console keyboard), a standard output unit (the console screen or printer), and a standard error output unit (the console screen or printer). The user can redirect any of these to any other file at program execution time. The standard output of one program can be directed to the standard input of another program without use of an intermediate file. The programs form a *pipeline,* or *pipe.* A program whose normal mode of operation is to accept input only from its standard input, to perform some operation on it, and to provide output only to its standard output is called a *filter.* (See Figure 11-13.)

Several versions of UNIX have been developed by Bell Laboratories over the years. In addition, several UNIX-like operating systems and several UNIX-based operating systems exist. Vendors offering the former have developed software patterned after UNIX, but are not marketing the code actually written at Bell. Vendors offering the latter have acquired Bell's UNIX code through contractual agreements with AT&T. Most of them add features such as more high-level-language support, greater error detection and recovery capabilities, and ease-of-use characteristics. Microsoft entered into an agreement with Santa Cruz Operations to produce Xenix, a version of UNIX for personal computers. AT&T itself actively markets UNIX System V, declared to be the "standard" base for all subsequent releases. Vendors are forming consortiums to define and promote their own "standard offerings."

A computer vendor whose system can be run under the control of a portable operating system can point to existing third-party-developed application software available to users of the system. An independent software vendor (i.e., third party) can afford to spend the time, talent, and other resources needed to develop high-quality application software when the potential customer set for

Figure 11-13 **The UNIX operating system initially developed at Bell Labs is used on many manufacturers' computer systems. UNIX's internal pipeline structure helps to provide the machine independence needed for portability.**

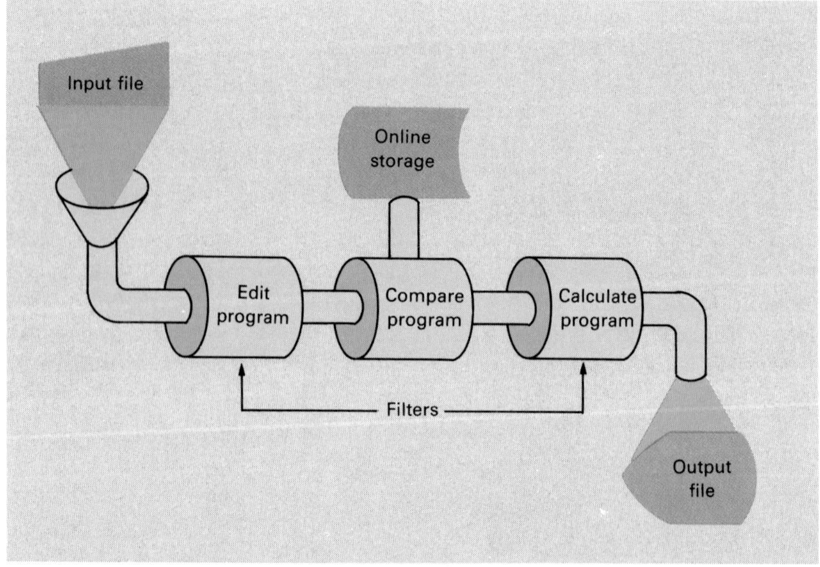
Input file
Online storage
Edit program
Compare program
Calculate program
Filters
Output file

the software includes users of many vendors' computers. A potential user who recognizes the importance of software and the lead time and resources needed to develop it is likely to choose a system for which portable operating system support is available.

USING COMPUTERS IN FLOOD CONTROL

Nobody wants a flood. Nobody wants a drought. Fruit growers, wheat farmers, and other agriculturists need the right amounts of water at the right times for their crops. Computers are helping the U.S. Army Corps of Engineers in Sacramento perform a delicate balancing act. That balancing act is the monitoring and control of reservoir operations affecting a diverse, widespread area. Other Corps groups across the United States have similar flood control responsibilities.

The key input devices to the Corps' system are microprocessor-based sensors installed in basins where water collects at 11 manned reservoirs. Data on weather and water conditions is collected every hour and sent periodically to the Corps' Sacramento office. Local data on precipitation, evaporation, and the amount of outflow from the reservoirs is also input. Data on stream flow and pool levels is collected from four unmanned reservoirs, or dams, as well. (Whereas manned reservoirs can be controlled by opening gates and letting water out, unmanned reservoirs cannot.) This data is also sent to Sacramento.

At Sacramento, a computer modeling system operates on the data to predict what will happen to water levels at specific reservoirs under various conditions. The system responds to "what-if" questions such as "What if we get one-half inch more rain?" or "What if we get no rain at all and temperatures in the 90° to 100° range for the next three months?" Corps personnel decide, for example, how much water should be released from a particular reservoir accordingly.

The Corps also makes its database available free of charge to other individuals and organizations that have need of it. Engineering-consulting firms, private landholders, and water district personnel are interested in anticipated water flows and reservoir levels, for example. The National Weather Service, the Bureau of Reclamation, and the California State Department of Water Resources are other users of the database. *(Photo courtesy U.S. Army Corps of Engineers, Sacramento District, California)*

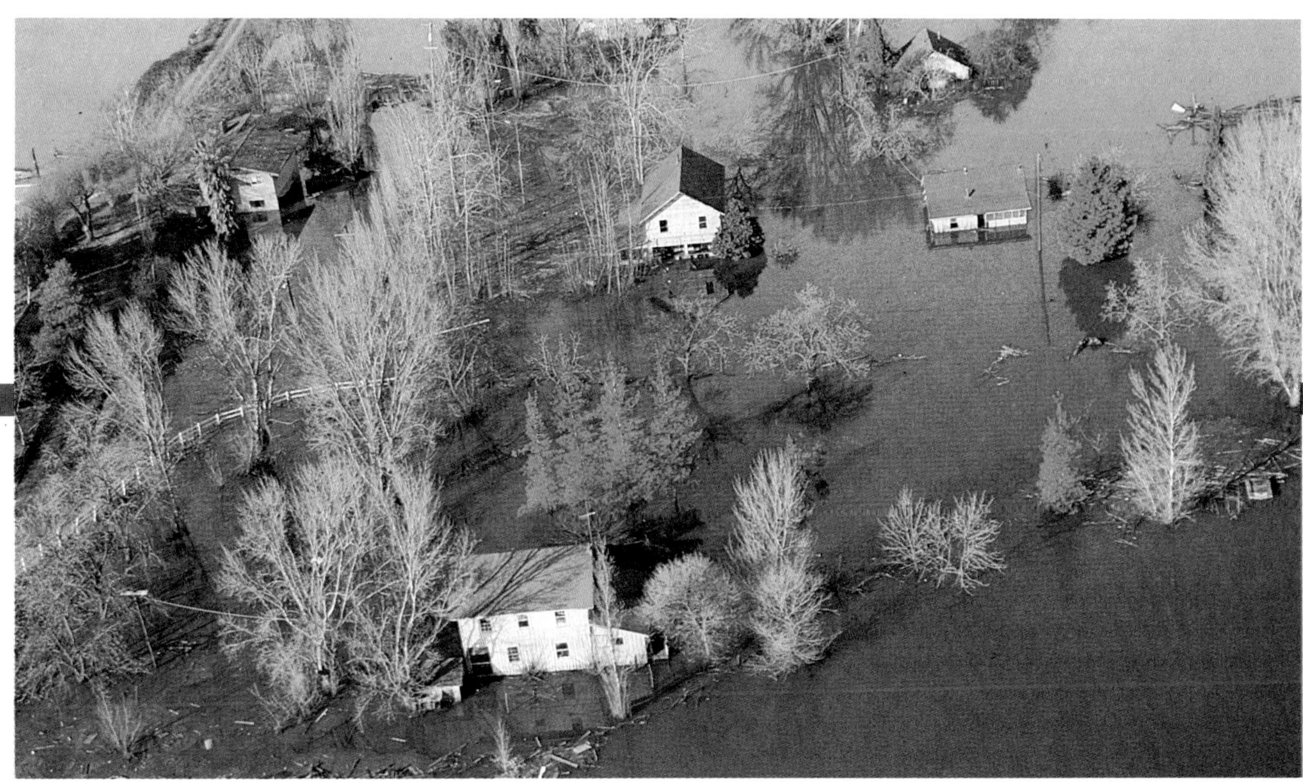

CHAPTER SUMMARY

1. Effective application of computers is heavily dependent on software. Both system programs and application programs are required.

2. Software has evolved through distinct generations just as hardware has. Initially, a small control program called a *monitor* took over the program load function formerly initiated by a human operator.

3. More sophisticated monitors and operating systems that could handle job-to-job transitions were developed. Job-control statements were used to tell the computer what to do next in batch, or stacked-job, processing.

4. Online direct-access systems were developed to process input transactions in random order as they were received and to assist individual users in problem solving.

5. In a multitasking system, more than one program resides in primary storage at a time. The processor executes instructions from one program, then instructions from another program, and so on. Keeping the processor busy in this fashion helps to maximize the amount of useful work that can be accomplished.

6. Vendors are promoting ease of use by offering planned series of software components, integrated application software packages, and windowing capabilities that allow users to view simultaneously the outputs of several jobs and to exchange data among them.

7. In a multiprocessing system, instructions from the same program or from different programs are executed simultaneously on two or more processors. Today's personal computer systems as well as large system configurations may have multiprocessing capabilities.

8. A real-time system provides output fast enough to satisfy any user requirements. It can be used to control real-life activity.

9. Time sharing allows several users to interact with a system on what appears to be a simultaneous basis. The system resources are shared among them.

10. Virtual-storage capabilities allow a system to be used as though more primary storage exists than is actually present. A greater number of programs can be running at a time than would be possible otherwise.

11. In a virtual-machine environment, each user is able to use a total computer system—both hardware and software—that does not actually exist, but seems to. Many unrelated virtual machines running different jobs can be active on the system at a time.

12. A portable operating system can easily be adapted to run on any computer having a particular architecture. MS-DOS and UNIX are examples.

DISCUSSION QUESTIONS

1. (a) List and discuss three broad categories of system software.
(b) Give examples of programs in each category, based on a system available to you.

2. Choose any one of the industry categories illustrated in Figure 11-2. Suggest application programs for that industry that might be developed and marketed to users on a national or international basis.

3. Explain why operating systems are needed on today's computers.

4. Explain stacked-job processing.

5. Distinguish between an online system and a real-time system.

6. Distinguish between multitasking and multiprocessing.

7. Describe a user application for which windowing capabilities are likely to be especially useful.

8. Give examples of applications that can be computerized only if the system available can perform real-time processing.

9. Assume you are a member of a business firm that has decided to take advantage of time-sharing capabilities.
(a) Suggest two approaches by which you can do so.
(b) What are the advantages of each approach?

10. Distinguish between a virtual-storage environment and a virtual-machine environment. In doing so, emphasize the user's point of view.

11. Assume you are a computer manufacturer, an independent software vendor, or a user. From your chosen point of view, argue for or against operating-system portability.

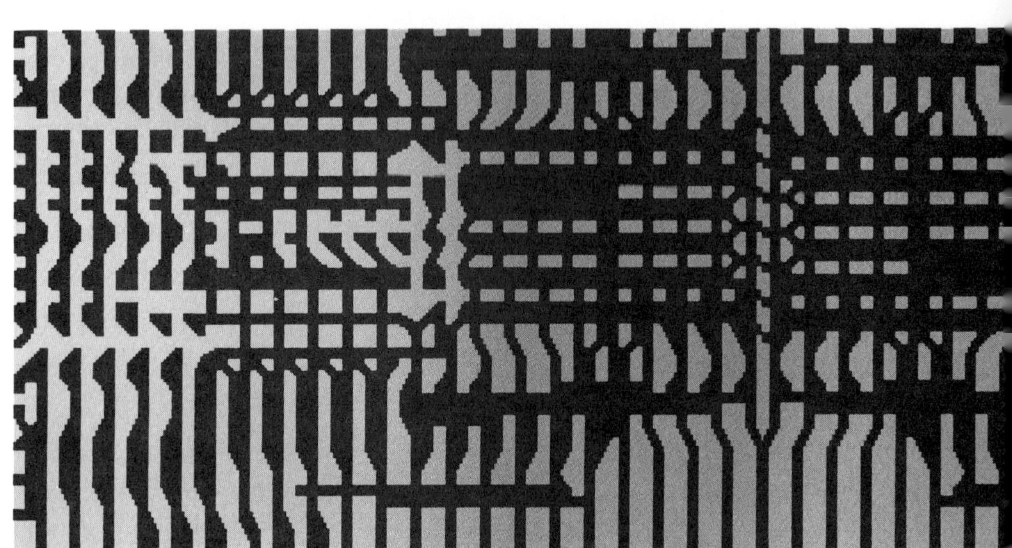

12 Managing Data

IN THIS CHAPTER

File Systems
Data Management Systems
The Database Approach
Database Design
Logical Data Structures
DBMS
SQL
Management Information Systems
Decision Support Systems
Remote Databases
Distributed Databases

There's an often-quoted saying that many of us have heard and even said ourselves. It goes like this:

> "Water, water everywhere,
> but not a drop to drink."

In many business environments today, a similar saying applies:

> "Data, data everywhere, but
> where's the information?"

Putting this thought another way, within many organizations, managers and non-managers alike are searching for the information they need to do their jobs. Ironically, many of them are drowning in data while doing so. The organizations of which these people are a part may or may not be computer-using organizations.

We mentioned earlier that information is useful if it is accurate, timely, complete, concise, relevant, and available. A sales manager can't determine whether the sales in his district are increasing or decreasing on the basis of the total sales for only one month. You can't tell how much you spent last month by looking at a 2-page listing of the checks you wrote. You need to know the total sum of the values on the checks. You also need to know about the items you paid for with cash or credit cards. How much did all of those items cost?

From our studies thus far, we understand that data to be processed with computer help must first be entered into a computer system. Not uncommonly, the data is stored on tape or disk, and then loaded into primary storage as it's needed during processing.

In Chapter 5, we looked in some detail at both tape and disk devices. We learned that records can be written to and read from tape sequentially. With disk, either sequential or direct processing can be used. That may sound simple, but it isn't. How do we know where to write a record on a disk? How can we be sure there isn't another record already there? How can we find a particular record written on a disk previously by our program or by another program? What will our program do if it tries to write to (or read from) a disk, but the disk isn't there?

If every microcomputer user had to know the number of tracks on a particular disk, how many records of a particular length can be fit on one track, what I/O operations must occur to "close" a file, and so on, chances are there would be fewer users of microcomputers!

Business application programs for payroll, accounts receivable, and inventory control have one characteristic in common: They involve a great deal of I/O activity. The activity includes not only accepting input and providing output but also creating, processing, and maintaining data in computerized files. If a user-programmer had to write all the coding necessary for I/O operations, he or she would be likely to spend 40 percent of the programming time on these operations alone. Clearly, both the producitivity of the computer system and the productivity of user-programmers are directly related to the I/O programming required.

Fortunately, a number of programming aids have been developed by computer manufacturers and software development firms. Among them are file systems, data management systems, and database management systems. Such aids are available on micros as well as on mainframes. We discuss them in this chapter. We learn more about file organization and file access. Then we study the database approach. We learn about SQL.

Finally, we discuss managers' information needs. We see how management information systems and decision support systems can be implemented to provide for these needs. We learn about remote databases that can be accessed using online electronic information services. Systems with distributed database processing capabilities allow users to access data at one site or at several sites without having to know where the data is located.

File Systems

In the 1950s, when business data processing with computer help began, programs were relatively simple. In most cases, each program and the data it processed were conceptually locked together. The data was, in effect, an extension of the program. For convenience, the data was usually grouped into records and files, kept on punched cards or on tape. Each file "belonged to" one program.

Many microcomputer users today are developing or acquiring programs that function in a similar manner. For example, consider your own financial record keeping again. You may develop or purchase a checkbook program that accepts transaction data reflecting the checks you write and the deposits you make as input. That same program may update your checking account file on a diskette or hard disk. Your microcomputer needs access to the checking account file whenever you run the checkbook program.

As early users' business application programs became more comprehensive, they dealt with data in more than one file. The relationships between files were maintained within the program that processed them. In many cases, the file descriptions were also.

Another layer of complexity was added when two or more programs were written to process the same data, but in different ways. Special sorting and merging steps were introduced to rearrange the data records as required for each program. (Could the data in the checking account file above be used by an income tax reporting program?)

Soon, multiple copies of user data records were made, and yet additional files containing some or all of the same data were created. Perhaps the system analyst, designer, or programmer was not aware that the data was already being collected elsewhere. Perhaps the data was known to be available, but the format of the data records was not suitable for the processing to be done by a new program. For example, a hospital might carry the name, address, and date of entry for each patient in an accounts-receivable master file, a patient master file, and a bed master file. The telephone number of the phone beside the patient's bed was likely to be in both the patient and bed master files, and so on. (See Figure 12-1.) This duplication of data led to the need for multiple updating (often overlooked) and the storage and processing of inconsistent data.

Both users and information system personnel looked for a different approach. Programs that dealt with the same data began to be implemented as integrated application sys

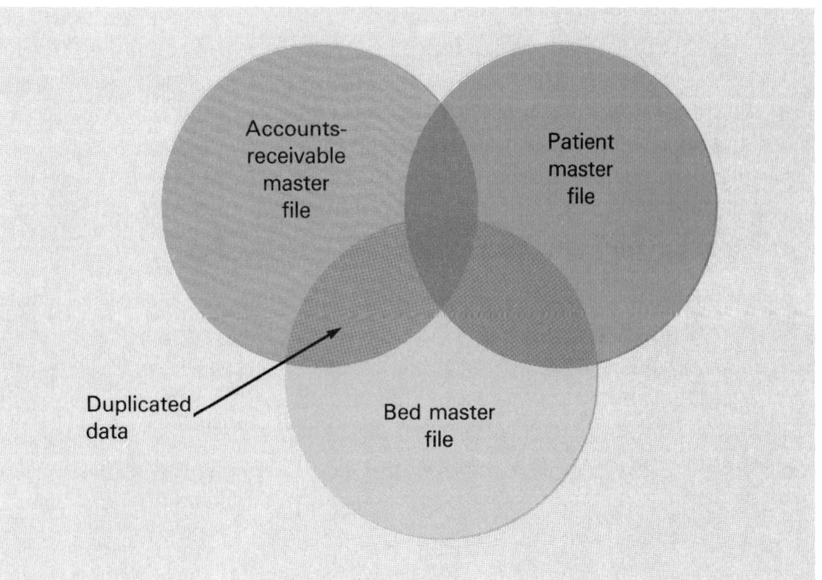
Accounts-
receivable
master
file
Patient
master
file
Duplicated
data
Bed master
file

Figure 12-1 When master files are maintained for specific applications, user data is often duplicated in two or more files.

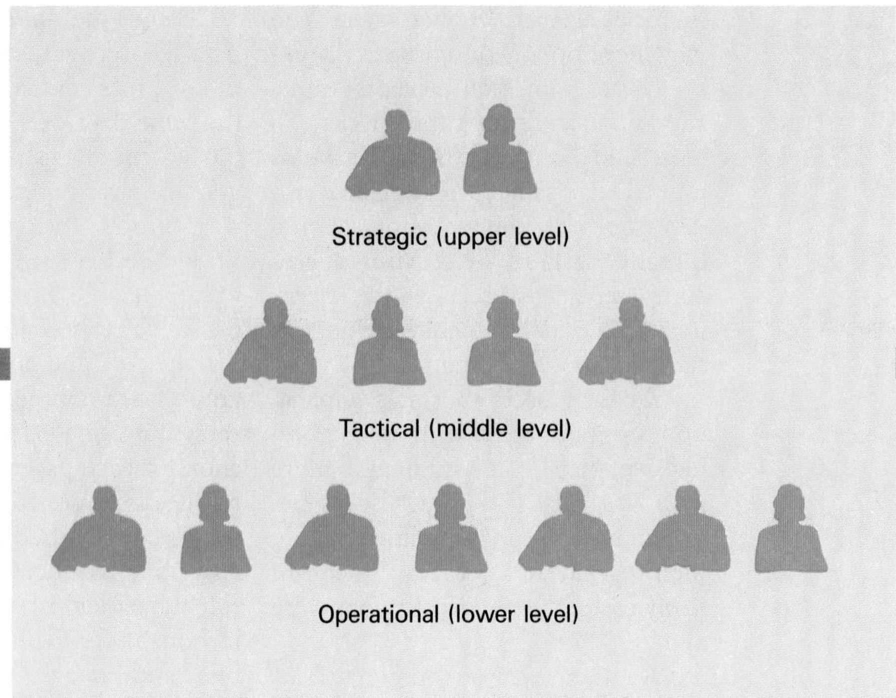
Strategic (upper level)
Tactical (middle level)
Operational (lower level)

THE BUSINESS OF MANAGEMENT

The term **management** includes both a process and the people who perform that process. As a process, the functions generally attributed to management are planning, organizing, staffing, directing, and controlling. First, a **plan** for what is to be done must be put in place. Then, an **organization** structure must be put in place to facilitate implementation of that plan. Next, the planned activity must be **staffed** with necessary personnel and they must be **directed** in the performance of the planned activity. Over-all **control** must be exercised so that the objectives of the plan are realized.

In terms of people, management is said to exist at three levels: strategic, tactical, and operational. Examples of **strategic managers** are the chairman of the board, the company president, and the heads of major divisions within the company. **Tactical managers** include directors of laboratories, plant managers, and regional managers. Supervisors and managers of administrative support groups are **operational managers.**

The managerial functions identified above are performed at all management levels, but the managers at the top level of an organization have responsibilities different from those at the middle level. Similarly, middle-level managers have responsibilities different from those at the lower level. For example, top-level managers plan the organization's activities for five years or more into the future. Tactical managers plan what their area of responsibility will do within the next year or two. Operational managers put plans in place to achieve immediate goals. Strategic managers determine the over-all business organization—its divisions or regions, overseas network, subsidiaries, and so on. Tactical managers set up the organization within their particular manufacturing plant, sales terri-

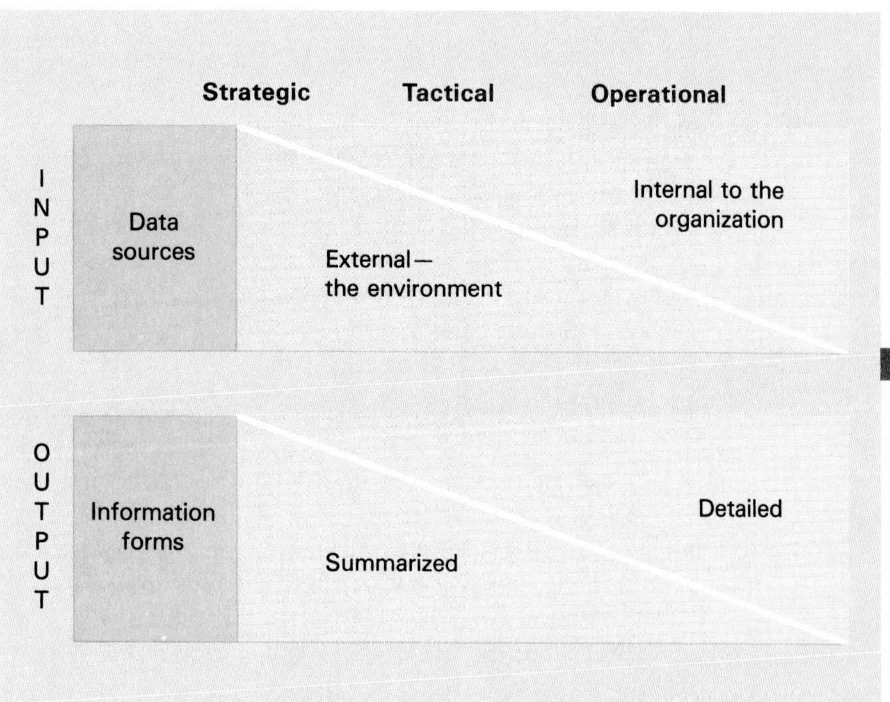
Strategic
Tactical
Operational
INPUT
Data sources
Internal to the organization
External— the environment
OUTPUT
Information forms
Detailed
Summarized

tory, or the like. An operational manager has responsibility for the organization of a given department or group.

A successful management information system must respond to the information needs of each level of management. This means that:

- Input, or raw data, must be obtained from widely varying sources.
- Output, or information, must be presented in many forms.

Strategic managers depend heavily on data sources external to the organization—from its environment. Examples of external data sources are government legislation, economic forecasts, and information about competitors available from annual reports, product announcements, and public statements by company representatives. In contrast, operational managers depend heavily on internal data—how many trucks are available, what stock must be reordered, which employees can be freed to operate a particular machine, and so on.

Similarly, strategic managers need to see production data summarized by quarter or perhaps even by year. Tactical managers need reports that enable them to spot trends, to identify underutilized or overutilized resources, and so on. Operational managers need to determine planned performance versus actuals for a particular day, perhaps for a department, or perhaps for a single employee. These management needs impose varying influences on the input and output of computer-based information systems accordingly.

tems rather than as independent entities. The need for more care in file design and for recognizing the relationships between data within files was recognized. To support this application system development, numerous vendors developed and/or marketed *file systems* as part of the system software for computers. Most file systems were able to support direct processing as well as sequential processing of user data records. The file systems were also able to:

- Assist the user in creating, changing, and deleting files
- Provide a mapping from the symbolic names known in an application program to the physical addresses needed to access the files required
- Manage the allocation of physical space on tape or disk
- Keep account of the date of creation, size, and security characteristics of each file
- Move portions of files (that is, blocks of records) to and from primary storage
- Perform other I/O functions needed by programs in execution

In today's file systems, a distinction is made between the way a file is organized and how it is accessed. *File organization* is concerned with the techniques used in arranging the records in a file on the physical storage medium. *File access* is concerned with the manner in which the records in a file are written or read. We have

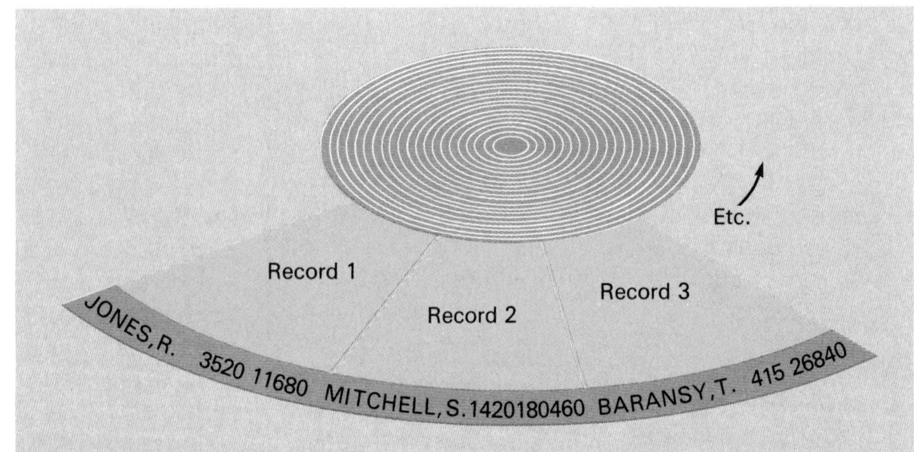
Etc.
Record 1
Record 2
Record 3
JONES,R. 3520 11680 MITCHELL,S.1420180460 BARANSY,T. 415 26840

Figure 12-2 When sequential file organization is used, user data records are positioned in successive locations on the storage medium.

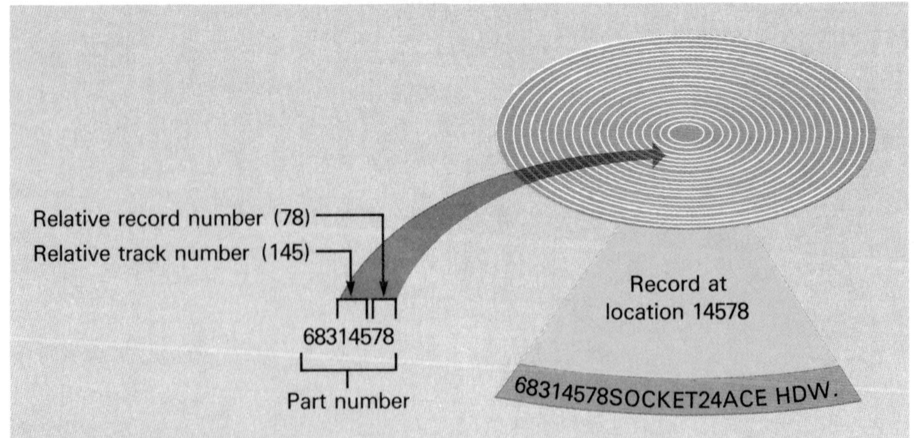
Relative record number (78)
Relative track number (145)
68314578
Part number
Record at location 14578
68314578SOCKET24ACE HDW.

Figure 12-3 When direct file organization is used, user data records are positioned and accessed on the basis of their record keys; an 8-digit part number serves as the record key in this example.

discussed two types of reading and writing operations: sequential and direct. User data files to be *accessed* using either of these approaches may be *organized* in any one of several ways. Three common file organizations are shown in Figures 12-2 through 12-4. They are sequential, direct, and indexed sequential.

In today's file systems, a distinction is made between the way a file is organized and how it is accessed.

Sequential

Records are organized solely on the basis of their successive physical locations in the file. The "next" record is the record that physically follows the current one. (See Figure 12-2.) The records are usually sequenced according to a user-selected key that exists in all records. For example, the records in a student master file may be stored in student-number order. The 100th record in the file can be read only after reading the 99 records that precede it. Therefore, for practical purposes, a sequential file can only be processed sequentially. It is not reasonable to read 99 records to get the 100th one, or 145 records to get the 146th one, and so on. A sequential file may be stored on cards, tape, or disk (or on paper, as a simple list).

Direct

Records are positioned in the file on the basis of an established relationship between the key of a record and the physical address of the location where the record should be stored. This relationship is established by logic within application programs. For example, suppose an 8-digit part-number field is the key field for records in an inventory master file. Further suppose the five rightmost digits of each key are used as the address for the record containing the key. (See Figure 12-3.) The first three of these digits are the relative track number; the remaining two digits are a relative record number on that track. Unfortunately, this means that sensitivity to these device characteristics is built into application programs. If new high-speed disk storage devices are acquired and the inventory master file is moved to the new devices, a new method of calculating physical addresses will be needed. All programs using the five rightmost digits as a physical address will have to be changed. An offsetting advantage of this approach is that, once the address of a desired record has been determined, direct processing can be used immediately to write the record as output (or read the record as input). In our example, this means that the records for parts in inventory can be processed in any order whenever the inventory changes. A direct file must be stored on a direct-access storage device.

Indexed Sequential

Records are positioned in a file in ascending or descending sequence on the basis of their record keys. In addition, one or more levels of indexes are maintained for the file. Each index entry contains the key of a record and an address that points to the location where the record is stored. (See Figure 12-4.) In a system

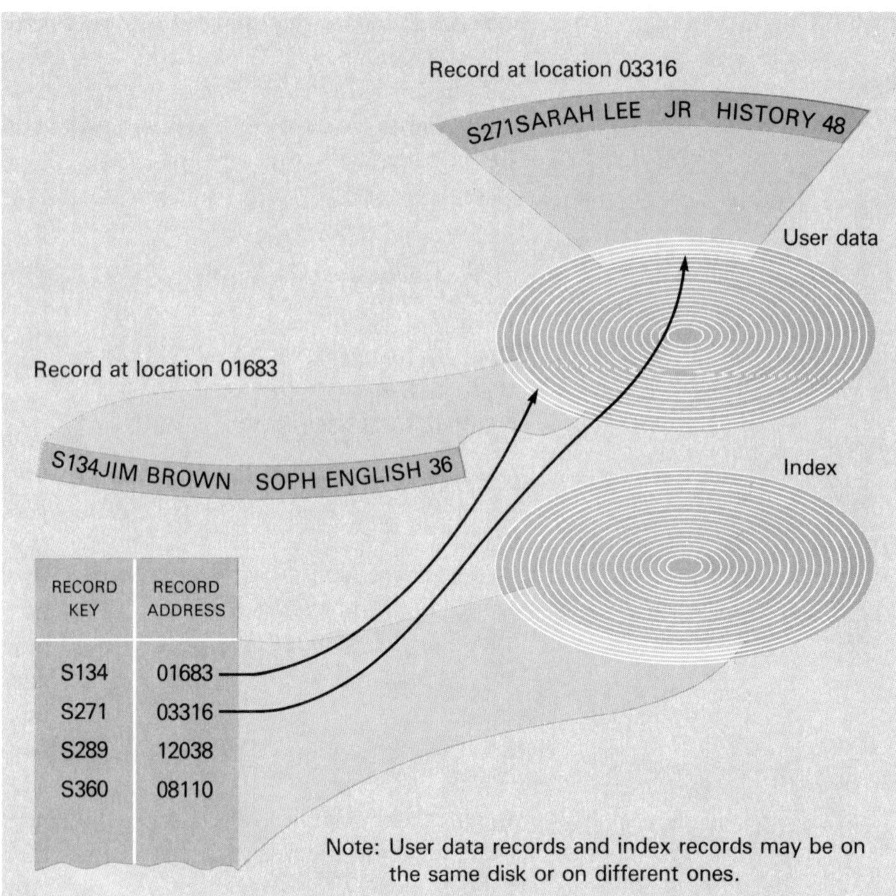
Record at location 03316
S271SARAH LEE JR HISTORY 48
User data
Record at location 01683
S134JIM BROWN SOPH ENGLISH 36
Index
RECORD KEY
RECORD ADDRESS
S134 01683
S271 03316
S289 12038
S360 08110
Note: User data records and index records may be on the same disk or on different ones.

Figure 12-4 When indexed sequential file organization is used, user data records are positioned and accessed on the basis of their record keys, and entries in a system-maintained index point to them.

that supports indexed sequential organization, the indexes are maintained by system software; they do not have to be created or updated by application programs. Even more important, user data records in the file can be accessed sequentially or directly. In sequential processing, the records are simply retrieved in record-key order. In direct processing, the system software searches the index (or indexes) to find the index entry containing a key that matches or is the nearest key beyond the key of a desired record. Upon finding the entry, the system software then determines the location of the record. Next, it retrieves the record. A law firm's accounts-receivable records may be stored in an indexed sequential file, for example. Sequential processing can be used to read all the records in sequence and print monthly statements. Direct processing can be used to access individual records in response to customers' inquiries about their accounts.

Data Management Systems

In the late 1960s users with computerized data began to insist that the costs of file storage and maintenance be reduced and the duplication of data be eliminated. They wanted to be able to store their data once, in such a way that it could be accessed, retrieved, and manipulated in a variety of ways, by any of several programs, to meet constantly changing and ever-expanding information needs. *Data management systems* were developed to provide the functions normally found in file systems and functions that permitted users to describe hierarchies of data and to name and use relationships between data items. Access-method routines were stored in online system libraries and invoked by application programs to perform I/O operations during processing.

Today such software is available for microcomputers as well as for larger computer systems. The term *file management* seems to be more common than *data management*—perhaps because it is less likely to be confused with yet another term, *database management* (discussed below). If you hear microcomputer users talking about an FMS program, for example, chances are that *FMS* stands for *f*ile *m*anagement *s*ystem. Few users can manage their data resources without this kind of software to help them.

Ways of Organizing

A *database* is a file organization concept, not a file volume concept. The complexity of the user's data relationships, not a count of the records, should determine whether or not a database approach is used.

The Database Approach

Even after users saw the need to design and implement programs as integrated application systems, separate files were often set up for each application. The employee master file was processed by the application programs that kept company personnel records; the payroll master file was used by the programs that prepared employee payrolls; the skills-inventory master file was maintained by the programs that kept track of in-house education rosters; and so on. This approach still led to several files with duplicate data. If, for example, an employee changed jobs within the company or moved to a new home, every file that contained data pertaining to job status or home address had to be changed. The separate-file approach also made it difficult to extract data that was scattered throughout various files. For example, although the payroll master file contained the current pay rate of each employee, there was no easy way to extract the current pay rates of all employees hired after a particular date, or the average wage of all employees between the ages of 50 and 65.

To meet such information needs, the concept of a *database* was developed. Under this approach, a file is not treated as a separate entity. Master files are not set up for just one application. Instead, a system or database designer works with the current or prospective users of a system to identify (1) the information needs of those users, and (2) the data that must be stored and processed to satisfy them. The designer determines whether or not the data is already being collected and stored as part of the organization's data resource. The designer works to insure that the data is organized in such a way that it can be accessed by all applications that use it.

Although we could say, for purposes of simplification, that a database is a lot of data, there's more to creating a database than just collecting data. In fact, certain characteristics are essential to a well-designed database:

- It is an organized, integrated collection of data.
- It can be referred to by all relevant applications with relative ease and with no (or, in practice, limited) duplication of data.
- It is a model of the natural relationships of the data in the user's real-world environment.

To say that data is contained in a database does not imply that files no longer exist. They do, but application programs and users may not be aware of them. System designers do not direct their attention to collecting data for use by a particular program and in ways dictated by hardware. Instead, they provide for collecting, organizing, and accessing data in ways that are natural and meaningful to users.

Database Design

Much software is being developed and marketed to support the database approach. A user organization cannot assume, however, that choosing appropriate software is all that it takes to establish database capabilities. The task of database design is prerequisite to successful database implementation. It must be done by the user organization. System or database designers study, interview, and investigate to determine what data ought to be included in the database, what interrelationships among the data exist, what kinds of inquiries will be made against the database, and so on. This is a time-consuming, difficult task, but it is an essential one. It occurs during the system analysis phase of the system development cycle.

A simple example may give us some insight into the considerations involved. Assume a company's inventory data is organized by item number, as shown in Figure 12-5. Each type of item is identified by a unique item number. If all data entered into the database is associated with these item numbers, obtaining or changing data about a particular item will be fairly straightforward.

But questions arise: Will a sales representative be able to determine how many items of a particular item class, say S1, are in stock? Will an accountant be able to determine what the current value of all in-stock items of another item class is? What if a product manager wants to know which items are obtained from supplier Z Company, whether orders for the items have been issued to that supplier, and whether it is possible to obtain the identified items from ei-

Figure 12-5 Typical users have lots of data that must be collected, organized, and entered into online databases before database processing can occur.

Item Number	Description	Quantity onhand	Quantity onorder	Reorder point	Unit cost	Item class	Bin location	Supplier 1	Supplier 2	Other data
78600	No. 2 pencils	780	—	100	4.00	P2	W9	R. Stone	Reed	
10624	Sander 1	13	200	40	32.50	S1	W5	Johnston	Lowe	
10625	Sander 2	400	—	220	16.00	S2	W1	A.W. Faber	Johnston	
40310	Wrench set	16	400	100	9.75	WR	W3	Park Sherman	WTP	
24890	Shovel	250	—	40	15.00	SH	A4	Z Company	—	
84[illegible]	Sander 1	160	—	[illegible]	30.00	S1	W6	Z Company	Lowe	

DATABASE ADMINISTRATION

Most large and medium-size organizations that opt for the database approach set up a *database administration (DBA)* group within their information system staff. DBA personnel assist users in defining data elements, designing databases, estimating DASD requirements, and the like. If file names and characteristics, underlying DASD device types, and other physical characteristics of the system must be specified at system installation or startup, the DBA group provides them. Negotiating and enforcing data-handling standards, establishing database recovery procedures, and monitoring system performance may also be DBA tasks. Many of these tasks are required even in a small organization that uses the database approach. In a microcomputer environment, a user may have to assume the DBA role. The tasks of database administration cannot simply be left undone or ignored. *(Photo courtesy IBM Corporation)*

ther of two other suppliers who are offering discounts?

To answer such questions, either (1) all data that may be needed for each item must be stored together with the item number, or (2) there must be additional data about, say, orders or suppliers, elsewhere in the database, and there must be multiple ways of getting at that data. The care (or lack of care) exercised in database design affects the success (or failure) of the database approach and of the applications that depend on it.

Logical Data Structures

During database design, a distinction is made between the way data is stored on a data-recording medium (the *physical view* of data) and the way data is seen by users or application programs (the *logical view*). Various types of logical data structures are used to model real-world data relationships. The structures are called *data models.*

At the very simplest level, all units of data are independent and logically of equal significance. They may be either ordered or unordered. If ordered, they form a linear data structure. You may hear this type of structure called a *flat file.* (Look back at Figure 12-2.)

Next in terms of complexity is the *inverted file.* Here data is modeled as one or more lists. Each list contains user data records with identical formats. Access to the lists is achieved through an index, or inversion. Each index entry contains a key value and pointers to records that contain that key value. If you're thinking that this type of data structure is similar to an indexed sequential file, you're right. (Look again at Figure 12-4.)

Since, in the real world, the user's data is often interrelated in many ways, there often exists a need for a more complex data model. When a *hierarchical model* is used, each data record is broken into logically related segments by system software. The segments are connected by logical pointers in a treelike arrangement. (See Figure 12-6.) The user's data is mapped onto this model when it is stored in the database.

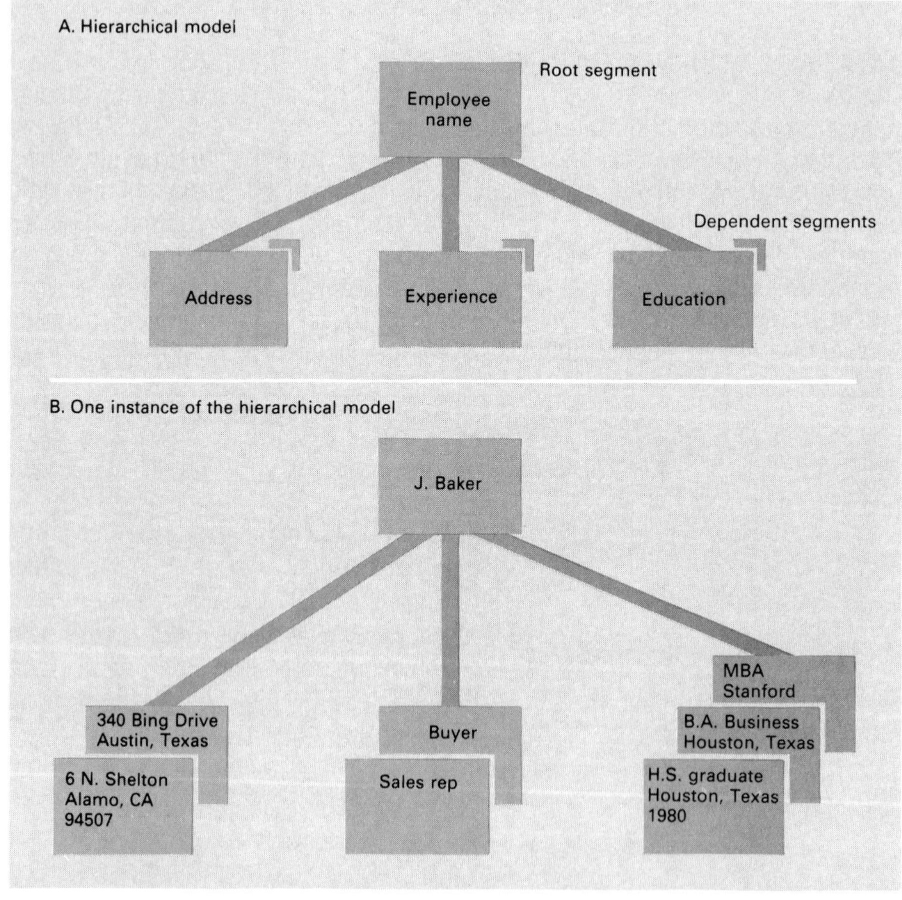
A. Hierarchical model
Root segment
Employee name
Dependent segments
Address
Experience
Education
B. One instance of the hierarchical model
J. Baker
340 Bing Drive
Austin, Texas
6 N. Shelton
Alamo, CA
94507
Buyer
Sales rep
MBA
Stanford
B.A. Business
Houston, Texas
H.S. graduate
Houston, Texas
1980

Figure 12-6 **Data about employees can be mapped onto a hierarchical data structure that models the real-world relationships of employee data items.**

WHERE QUALITY IS A MUST

Whether we realize it or not, many of us use daily the products of Corning Glass Works. Founded in 1853, the 28,000-employee company is a leading producer of consumer, scientific, and specialty glass. It also makes ceramics, fiber optics, and medical products. The company has earned its reputation for quality by continually refining its manufacturing processes. Its computer-integrated manufacturing (CIM) systems are models for others in the industry. Corning management insists that the quality of the information produced by these systems be as high as the quality of the Steuben crystal and other manufactured products they're designed to provide.

To collect, transmit, and analyze its manufacturing data, Corning relies on hundreds of Digital Equipment Corporation (DEC) VAX computers and thousands of terminals, personal computers, and workstations installed in many of its more than 50 plants worldwide. Much of the data is stored in large files written and read with the help of the DEC VMS operating system. Other data is stored in tables within INGRES databases. INGRES, a relational database management system together with supporting end-user and application development tools, has been installed in numerous Corning plants since 1986. Major INGRES applications are up and running, and additional INGRES applications are being prototyped or developed.

At one of Corning's plants, for example, nearly a million records containing data collected from machines on the plant floor are stored in an INGRES database. Operators on the floor can access the data, request analyses, and take corrective action, if necessary, to improve the quality of a manufactured part during the product manufacturing cycle.

In another application, the current values of up to 4000 data variables are collected by sensors, gauges, and other measurement devices on the plant floor. The data is stored initially in VMS files on small DEC MicroVAXes. From there, it's moved to INGRES relational databases, which provide the flexibility needed for ad-hoc query processing. Corning technicians can query tables within the databases in various ways to increase their understanding of what's happening during production. If, for example, they want to locate the possible cause of a defect, they can compare the current values of pertinent data variables and come up with a correlation in a couple of hours. Prior to implementation of the relational database management system, up to four months of traditional software development time would have been required to create, test, and release the application programs needed to obtain similar results.

Corning looks to increased use of INGRES as a vital step in meeting its four corporate goals: to simplify its processes, to design for manufacturing, to bring its processes under statistical control, and to continuously improve its products and services. *(Photo courtesy Corning Glass Works)*

As an example, assume the hierarchical data structure in Figure 12-6A is used to map data in an employee database. As with any hierarchical model, there is one root segment at the top level in the hierarchy. In this case, it's an employee-name segment. The root segment points to any number of dependent segments. In this case, each employee-name segment may point to several address segments, several experience segments, and several education segments for a particular employee.

The result of a data mapping—one *instance* of the hierarchical model in Figure 12-6A—is shown in Figure 12-6B. When applying for a job, J. Baker listed his current address and his immediately prior address; this data is stored in two address segments. Since J. Baker has held positions as a sales representative and as a buyer, the database contains two experience segments for him. The three education segments reflect the formal education he has completed before or since taking the job.

Notice that, in Figure 12-6A, only one level of dependent segments exists below the top, or root, level in the model. There could be several levels. However, each dependent segment can be pointed to (owned) by one and only one segment in a level above it. We say that a parent segment can point to (own) any number of child segments, but each child segment can have only one parent segment.

Of course, there are real-world situations where this single-owner relationship of data elements does not apply. In such situations, a *network model* may provide a better representation. (See Figure 12-7.) The general rules for the network model are that a parent segment may have any number of child segments, and a child segment may have any number of parent segments. Let's use Figure 12-7 to think this through.

In this example, a particular network model is applied to map the data collected by a community college. Notice that there are two types of segments at the top level in the model. There could be several. Notice also that each class segment at the second level in this model may be owned by one or more segments of either of two types: student-name segments and instructor-name segments. This reflects the real-world situation where a class may be taught by one or more instructors and may be attended by one or more students. In the particular data instance in Figure 12-7B, we see that instructor J. Turner teaches English I and English II, that he was an assistant professor at Luther College from 1984 through 1986, and that he has no publications to his credit. In Figure 12-7C, we see that student M. Ross, from Marble Rock, Iowa, is currently taking five classes. One of the classes is English II. There is no need to store the data about the class English II in the database twice, because it can be accessed using either the instructor-name/class relationship or the student-name/class relationship provided for by the network model.

If you think from our discussions so far that designing a database is not an easy task, you're right.

If you think from our discussions so far that designing a database is not an easy task, you're right. It's not, but recent developments have helped

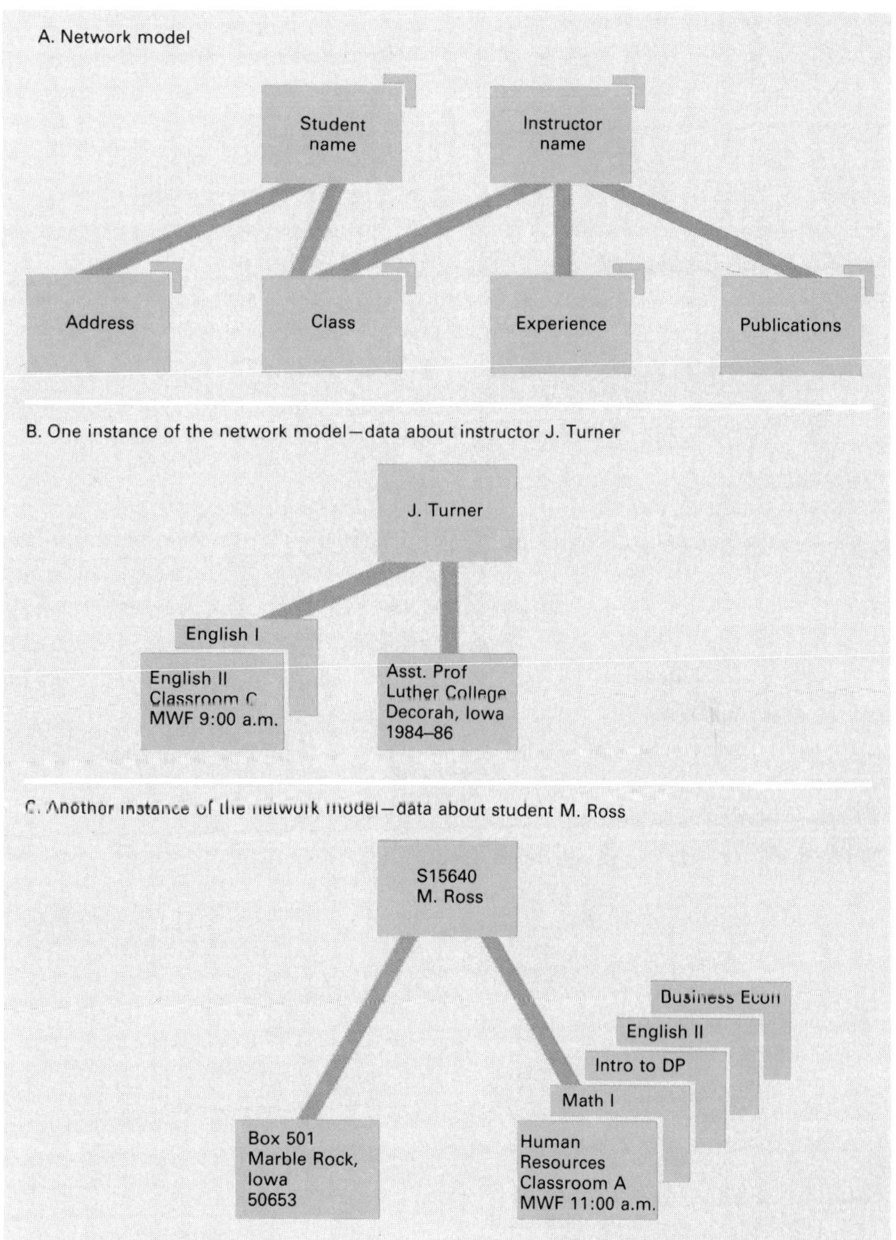
A. Network model
Student name
Instructor name
Address
Class
Experience
Publications
B. One instance of the network model—data about instructor J. Turner
J. Turner
English I
English II
Classroom C
MWF 9:00 a.m.
Asst. Prof
Luther College
Decorah, Iowa
1984–86
C. Another instance of the network model—data about student M. Ross
S15640
M. Ross
Business Econ
English II
Intro to DP
Math I
Box 501
Marble Rock,
Iowa
50653
Human
Resources
Classroom A
MWF 11:00 a.m.

Figure 12-7 A college's data may be mapped onto a network model (A) so that the classes taught by a particular professor (B) or attended by a particular student (C) can be determined easily without storing the class data several times.

to simplify the task, at least for some applications. At the heart of these developments is the *relational model.* The most significant aspect of this data model is its simplicity. When the relational model is used, all data within a database is viewed as being in relations, or tables. (See Figure 12-8.) Each table is a model of real-world data relationships. At the same time, it is a logical data structure that we as users can understand. After all, we deal with tables daily.

Figure 12-8A shows the general structure of the relational model. Figure 12-8B shows instances of 2-, 3-, and 4-column relational models as they might occur in an inventory database. Relation SN shows the numbers and names of all suppliers.

A. The general structure of the relational model

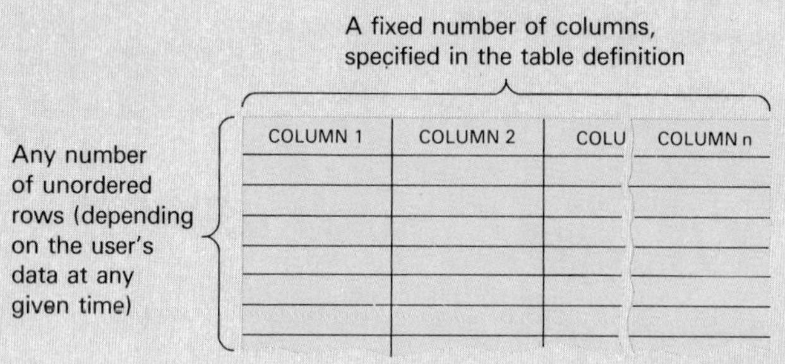

A fixed number of columns, specified in the table definition

Any number of unordered rows (depending on the user's data at any given time)

COLUMN 1	COLUMN 2	COLU	COLUMN n

B. Data instances mapped onto 2-, 3-, and 4-column relational models

Relation SN

SUPPLIER NUMBER	SUPPLIER NAME
CIA3	A.W. FABER
E240	LOWE
FL71	JOHNSTON
M549	Z COMPANY
P7A3	WTP
P894	R. STONE

Relation SI

SUPPLIER NUMBER	ITEM NUMBER	DEL. LEAD TIME (DAYS)
CIA3	10624	14
CIA3	23819	14
CIA3	34892	14
E240	17430	5
FL71	10624	7
FL71	10625	9
M549	34891	3
M549	34892	14
M549	34893	21
M549	34894	30
P7A3	59840	7
P7A3	94016	7

Relation IQ

ITEM NUMBER	ITEM NAME	QTY. ON HAND	REORDER POINT
10624	SANDER 1	200	40
10625	SANDER 2	400	220
23819	WRENCH SET	38	100
34891	SHOVEL	250	40
34892	SOCKET SET	80	200

C. The response to a user query—the number, name, quantity on hand, and reorder point for each item that supplier CIA3 provides:

SUPPLIER NUMBER	ITEM NUMBER	ITEM NAME	QTY. ON HAND	REORDER POINT
CIA3	10624	SANDER 1	200	40
CIA3	23819	WRENCH SET	38	100
CIA3	34892	SOCKET SET	80	200

Figure 12-8 **Inventory data can be stored in tables and retrieved from a number of those tables under system control when relational data-base processing capabilities are available.**

Relation SI shows the items supplied by each supplier and the delivery lead times for those items. Relation IQ contains data about each item.

Assume supplier CIA3, A. W. Faber, goes out of business. We may want to know immediately not only the number but also the name, quantity on hand, and reorder point for each item that supplier CIA3 provided. A system that supports the relational model can perform well-defined mathematical operations on the SI and IQ tables to obtain that information for us. The response to our query—also a relation—is shown in Figure 12-8C.

DBMS

In simplest terms, a *database management system (DBMS)* is system software that supports a database. It may be an integral part of the operating system for a particular computer or family of computers. More often, it

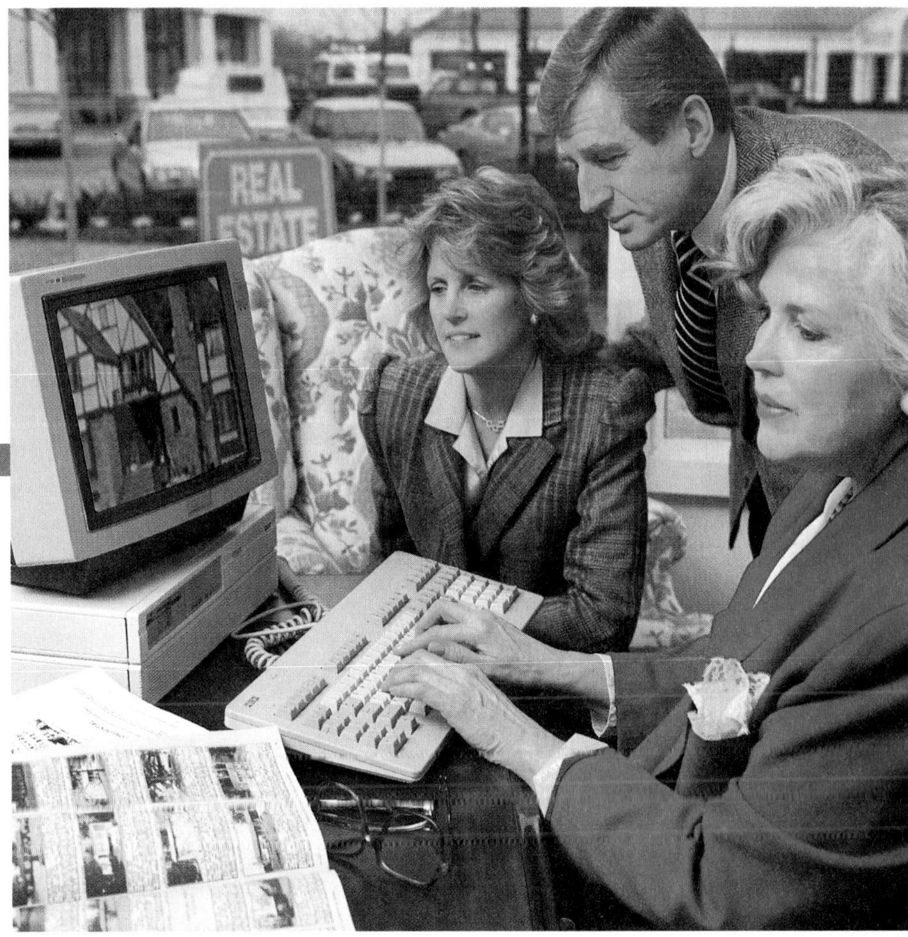
REAL
ESTATE

COMPUTER-ASSISTED REAL ESTATE SHOPPING

Have you ever trudged from apartment to apartment, house to house, or lot to lot, searching endlessly for the one that's right for you? If so, you know such searching is a tough job.

If you or one of your friends or family is active in real estate, chances are you've heard of STELLAR 2000. STELLAR 2000 is Planning Research Corporation's premier computerized multiple-listing services (MLS) system. It's designed for and marketed to real estate boards. The system encompasses all of the functions a real estate agent may want to perform in helping you to select a home.

A local real estate board that purchases STELLAR 2000 installs the system on a small, compact computer or workstation at a central location. Real estate agents access the system by means of visual-display units or personal computers. The agents can qualify clients, search local property databases (i.e., multiple listings), perform rent vs. buy analyses, access mortgage market information, and compute estimated closing costs and depreciation schedules. A feature called MLS Mail lets agents send and receive electronic messages through their MLS terminals. Broker reports provide inventories of office listings with their expiration dates, rosters of office members, and lists of prospects. Board/MLS reports detail homes sold by members, current inventories, and listings created during the past year. StellarVision allows agents to store up to 1000 photographs in their personal computers.

You can preview properties—both inside and out—on a computer screen and make well-informed decisions about the properties you want to visit. Schools, shopping centers, and other homes near any properties you are considering may be available in the system and viewed as well. You can decide "on the spot" which property you want, or use the visual tour as a preview to narrow your initial list of possibilities to those you want to visit personally. *(Photo courtesy Emhart Corp.)*

interfaces with the operating system, the database, and users or application programs.

Perhaps the best way to understand the value of a DBMS is to identify the major facilities that many of them provide. Some of the facilities have been mentioned earlier. Not all the facilities are available in all DBMS's. By thinking about why the items listed in Figure 12-9 are important, however, we may get a clearer picture of the kind of database support that's provided.

A file system or a data management system and a DBMS are not mutually exclusive system components. DBMS modules may invoke access-method routines for I/O processing just like application programs do for other than database processing. Because the DBMS does the interfacing with these file-oriented and, in many cases, device-oriented routines, users and application programs do not need to be concerned with them.

Users may interact with a DBMS in various ways. The DBMS may allow SQL (Structured Query Language) INSERT, UPDATE, SELECT, and DELETE statements to be embedded in host-language (usually, COBOL or C) application programs. The DBMS may also allow SQL or other query-language statements to be keyed directly into the system by users. In this case, no user application program is required.

Some organizations are acquiring software that enables users to transfer (*download*) data from mainframe files and/or databases to attached microcomputers. The software and related hardware (if any) is commonly referred to as a *micro-to-mainframe link.* Engineers, accountants, strategic planners, managers, and others involved in business decision making can use electronic spreadsheets, graphic packages, and other software on the microcomputers to manipulate and display the downloaded data in their work environments.

Some organizations are acquiring software that enables users to transfer (download) data from mainframe files and/or databases to attached microcomputers.

Early DBMS's for micros were little more than "electronic shoe boxes." Nevertheless, they met many users' data storage and retrieval needs. Today some micro-based DBMS's offer data-manipulation capabilities that mimic or rival those of mainframe products. Some are single-user systems. Of these, Ashton-Tate's single-user dBASE products are best known but DataEase, PC/Focus, and others are also popular. Other DBMS's allow multiple users to access data. *Database servers* are getting much attention. Here, the DBMS runs as a server on one node in a network. User application programs run on other (client) nodes. The application programs provide for user interactions with the system via visual-

Today some micro-based DBMS's offer data-manipulation capabilities that mimic or rival those of mainframe products.

- **Storage capability:** ability to store large volumes of data—enough to meet all user needs
- **Data integration:** a unified, common data storage designed to eliminate inefficiencies and inconsistencies stemming from duplicate data
- **Data independence:** separation of physical data storage characteristics from logical (user) views of the data, so that changes can be made to the database structure or underlying physical storage without causing widespread effects on application programs
- **Data security:** protection mechanisms that prevent unauthorized or accidental disclosure, modification, or destruction of stored data; privacy controls that can be applied on a data-item basis where social and legal issues are potentially involved
- **Data integrity:** protection mechanisms to insure that security controls cannot be bypassed and to prevent corruption of stored data to the degree necessary to complement storage-protection features available in hardware, and standards and procedures within the user's operational environment
- **Physical data protection:** backup and recovery mechanisms that permit restoration of missing or corrupt data if a hardware or software failure occurs
- **Ease of use:** end-user query and reporting tools; application development tools; system and data administration aids; complete, accurate, and understandable documentation
- **SQL:** support for SQL (Structured Query Language), allowing interactive users to access data by entering SQL statements and programmers to include SQL statements in application programs
- **Multiple-user:** support for concurrent use of the database by a number of users, none of whom need be aware of others; locking mechanisms and deadlock detection and resolution mechanisms that function automatically (without users or application programs having to invoke them)
- **Performance:** acceptable response times achievable under the expected user workload; can be tuned to adjust to changes in the workload over time
- **Portability:** can be run on a range of computers within a particular manufacturer's product line, or across several manufacturers' machines; runs under UNIX, MS-DOS, OS/2, . . . ; runs on 80286, 80386, MC68020, . . . microprocessors
- **Support:** ongoing support committed and readily available when questions or problems arise; product updates and enhancements provided

Figure 12-9 Managing user data is a major undertaking; a database management system can assist users by providing some or all of the facilities needed to do so.

display screens and send requests for data access to the server as needed during processing. Ease of learning, ease of use, robust error-handling, performance, and flexibility to meet ever-expanding and ever-changing user needs are emphasized.

SQL

Structured Query Language, or *SQL* (pronounced es′-que-el), is a database sublanguage used to define, manipulate, and control access to data in relational databases. Users can submit SQL commands interactively from their terminals, personal computers, or workstations. Alternatively, SQL statements can be embedded in application programs.

To define the data to be stored in an airline flight table at Denver, for example, a database administrator may enter an SQL CREATE TABLE statement:

```
CREATE TABLE      FLIGHT
  ( FNUM          CHAR(6),
    DEST          CHAR(12),
    DEPARTD       DATE,
    DEPARTT       TIME)
```

Data may be entered into the table by means of SQL INSERT statements or using a Load utility. Then, to select the numbers of all flights to Memphis, for example, an airline attendant may enter an SQL SELECT statement:

```
SELECT FNUM
FROM FLIGHT
WHERE DEST = 'MEMPHIS'
```

An SQL statement may refer to one table (as above) or to several statements. The search condition stated in a WHERE clause may be simple or very complex. For ease of use, some vendors have developed end-user query and reporter-writing tools that allow users to choose table names, column names, and search conditions from menus on visual-display screens. The SQL statements needed to retrieve the data are then generated by the tools, forwarded to the relational DBMS, and executed without any further action on the users' part.

Management Information Systems

It is sometimes claimed that every organization, whether or not it uses computers, has a *management information system (MIS).* If the implication here is that any person in a position of authority or responsibility has a way of finding out at least something about what is going on in an organization, this claim is valid. However, to increase our understanding of how computers can best be used, we must explore the MIS concept further.

We've learned that computers were not initially designed for business use. When business personnel were first exposed to computers, however, they quickly recognized their data-processing value. Basic business applications such as payroll, accounts receivable, and billing were computerized. Gradually management began to recognize the computer's potential for generating information that could be used in decision making. In this context, an MIS can be defined as a computer-based system that is capable of both:

- Processing business transactions reflecting the day-to-day operations of an organization, and
- Providing to management useful information within the time frame necessary to assist in decision making

The Makeup of an MIS

From a user's point of view, an MIS is only as good as its output, and the output is only as good as its underlying database. In a very real sense, a comprehensive online database is the foundation of an MIS. (See Figure 12-10.) Generally, the database is accessed with the help of a database management system such as we have discussed.

Even after implementation, an MIS is not a physical entity that can be processed or manipulated. Generally, it is not even a set of specially created programs, packaged and documented as an MIS. Rather, a successful MIS is a fully integrated part of the user organization. It has both computerized and noncomputerized parts. An organization cannot simply buy an MIS and install it.

Figure 12-10 An organization's online databases and functional-area information systems are integral parts of its MIS.

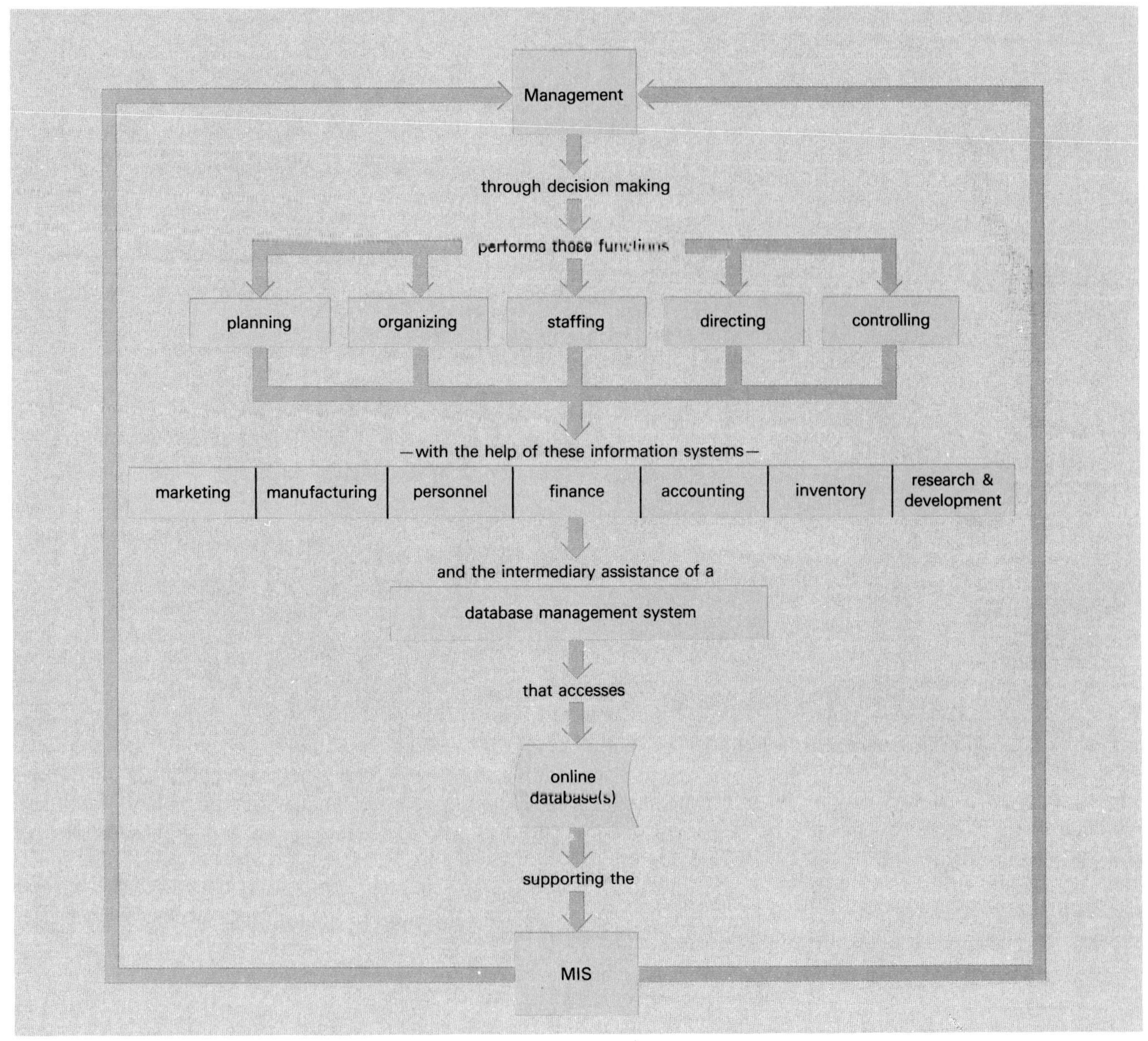
Management
through decision making
performs these functions
planning
organizing
staffing
directing
controlling
—with the help of these information systems—
marketing
manufacturing
personnel
finance
accounting
inventory
research & development
and the intermediary assistance of a
database management system
that accesses
online database(s)
supporting the
MIS

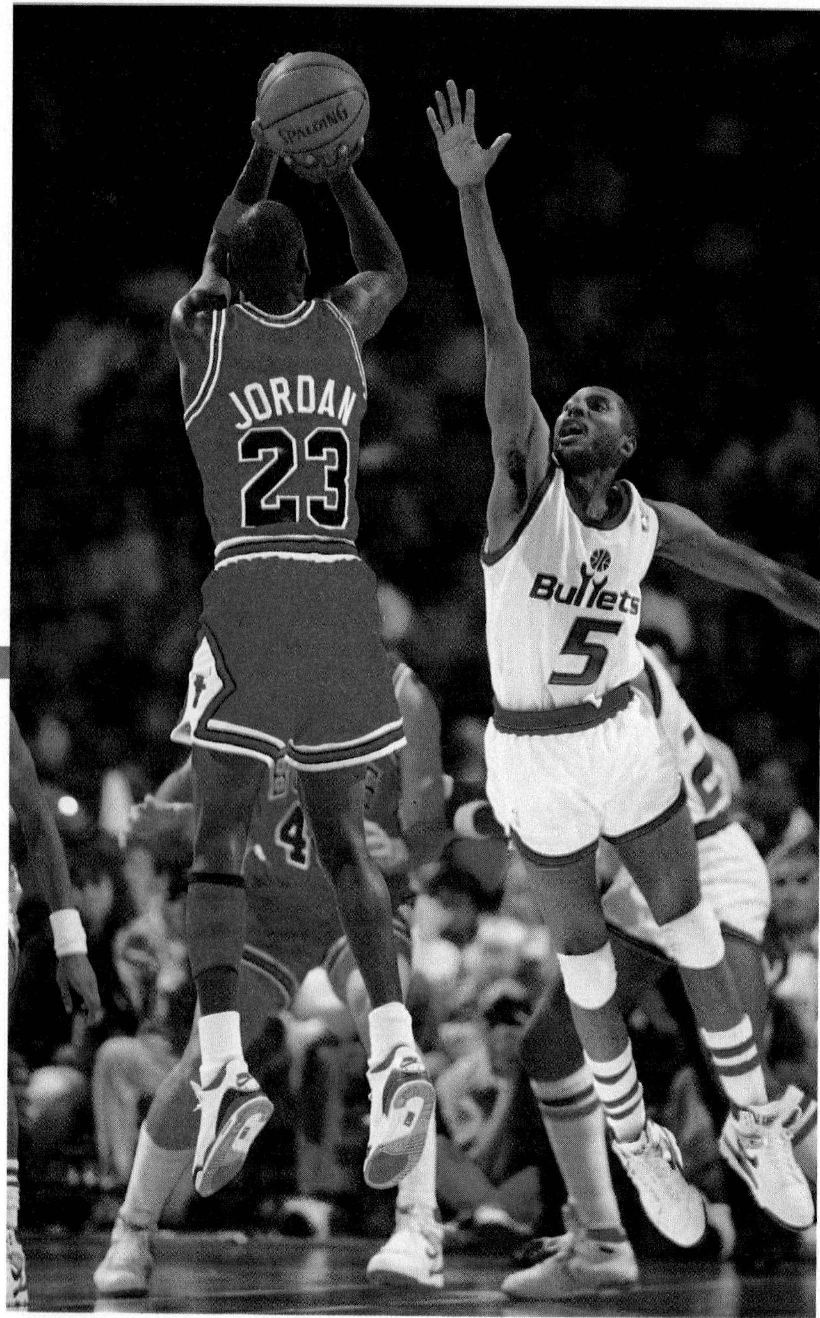
SPALDING
JORDAN
23
Bullets
5

THE NBA COMPUTERIZES

Teams, players, and fans of the National Basketball Association (NBA) are benefitting from the NBA's use of computers. Initially, the teams opted to automate their accounting and financial systems. Now they're tracking college prospects who may fit their playing style, coping with salary caps imposed under bargaining agreements, and analyzing game statistics with computer help. Team terminals linked to a mainframe at NBA's New York headquarters facilitate information sharing. Similar systems from Qantel, a subsidiary of Mohawk Data Sciences, are used by professional and collegiate football, baseball, hockey, and soccer teams worldwide as well. *(Photo courtesy Focus on Sports)*

Perhaps the best way to view an MIS is as a federation of information systems. It comprises a marketing information system, a manufacturing information system, and so on. (Look again at Figure 12-10.) These information systems are, in fact, subsystems of the MIS. Each information system has a functional identity. Within it are the bread-and-butter applications essential to normal business activities. The MIS also meets the information needs of the managers of these functional areas. It draws upon and integrates information from the functional-area information systems to provide a unified body of knowledge for use in decision making.

Let's consider the personnel information system as an example. Employee paychecks are produced within this system. (It's hard to imagine a more bread-and-butter application than that!) This information system also provides for legislated reporting requirements such as Social Security payments, equal employment opportunity statistics, occupational safety and health items, and employee retirement security amounts. Inquiries such as how many employees have at least 15 years of service and which employees earn more than $40,000 per year can also be handled within the personnel information system. Managers simply request the information they need to carry out their responsibilities.

MIS Implementation

The actual implementation of an MIS extends over a long period of time. Some information systems of the types shown in Figure 12-10 may exist prior to an organizational decision to establish an MIS. A staged development and implementation plan can be established for the others.

Certain factors are key to the successful implementation of the MIS. Foremost among these is top-level management support. This support must go beyond allocation of resources. Top-level managers must help to establish objectives and define their own information needs. Other user personnel must be aware of their direct involvement in the MIS activity.

Communication about the MIS project is needed at all levels of the organization. Both those who will prepare inputs to the MIS and those who will receive outputs from it must be helped to understand it.

The information system staff with technical responsibility for the MIS project must be trained to handle their responsibilities. They must understand the importance of user involvement in both development and implementation. They should also advise users of the 80/20 rule: Usually, 80 percent of the information that users think they need can be obtained with only 20 percent of the effort that would be required to obtain all of it. (See Figure 12-11.) Spending *five times* the effort required to attend to the top 80 percent of the users' needs is seldom warranted at the outset. As users gain experience with the MIS, they'll learn more about what information they really need. Follow-on MIS development can be planned accordingly.

No matter how sophisticated the MIS design is or how well the MIS operates, there is only one ultimate measure of success: Each user must accept the MIS as "his" or "hers" and use the information it can provide. Today, the manager with the greatest access to accurate, timely

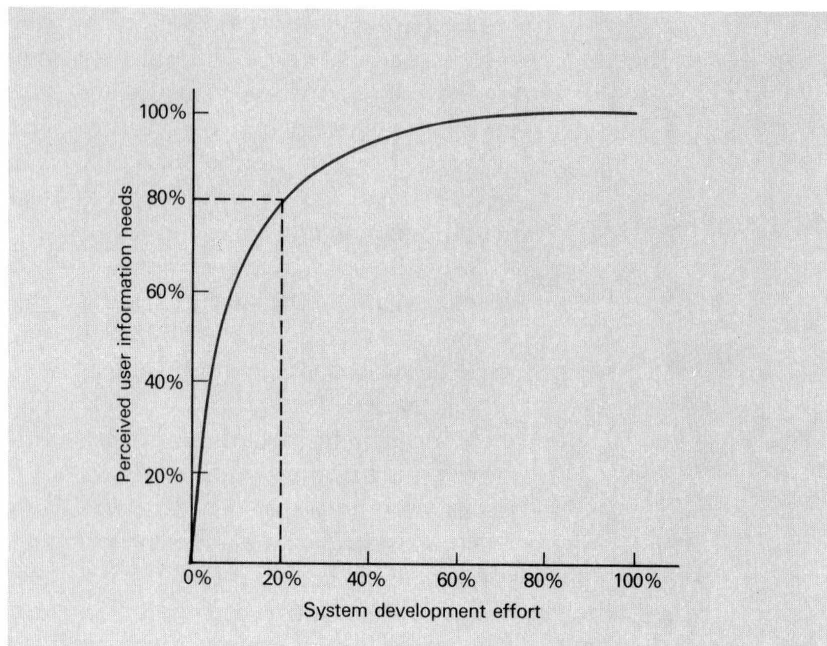
100%
80%
60%
40%
20%
Perceived user information needs
0%
20%
40%
60%
80%
100%
System development effort

Figure 12-11 Eighty percent of the information that users think they need may be obtainable with only 20 percent of the system development effort that would be required to obtain all of it.

information has the greatest competitive advantage in the business world. Knowing how to put information to work has become critical to success, and perhaps even to survival.

Today, the manager with the greatest access to accurate, timely information has the greatest competitive advantage in the business world.

Decision Support Systems

Today, users and user organizations, are being encouraged to complement their MIS, or go a step beyond it, by implementing a *decision support system,* or *DSS.* An MIS provides information for managers, but much of that information is historical; it tells managers what has happened but not what may happen. The emphasis of a DSS is to provide "what-if" help directly to managers and other professionals. Such information can be used in shaping the future.

A word of caution applies here as well as with a DBMS or an MIS: A user or user organization cannot simply buy a DSS and install it. Applications must be designed; the data required for those applications must be identified and collected; users must learn how to interact with the system; and so on. Nevertheless, hundreds of decision-support tools are being marketed. Some run only on mainframes, but many run on micros. Their prices range from $200 to $300,000.

Many DSS's have evolved from either financial modeling systems or database management systems. In this process, the financial modeling systems have acquired database capabilities; the DBMS's have acquired statistical manipulation and modeling power. A full-scale DSS must have both. In addition, because users interact directly with the DSS to ob-

Focusing

Especially at senior levels, managers are continually trying to find information in the midst of a data deluge. A well-designed decision support system can help them to separate the wheat from the chaff.

Using Data as a Resource

Today, many businesses are turning to electronic services to perform industry and market analyses. As a result, the electronic information industry, as measured by the number of available databases, has grown at a rate of 28 percent per year. In 1979 there were 400 databases. Today there are 4000. Most are available from one or more of about 350 online sources. Electronic services marketed as videotex to home subscribers have not received widespread acceptance, but business demands for online up-to-date information are accelerating.

tain information, user-oriented display facilities are usually required.

Many people are frequent users of Lotus 1-2-3, Excel, Multiplan, SuperCalc, or any of several hundred other electronic spreadsheet programs available for micros. If you haven't used at least one of them, you should try one. You may also have access to more comprehensive, integrated application software packages that provide decision support functions.

The major application areas for these micro packages include break-even analysis, return on investment (ROI) calculation, pricing strategy, loan amortization, cash flow analysis, merger and acquisition analysis, resource allocation, budget planning and control, financial statements, and intracompany, stockholder, and governmental record keeping and reporting. By experimenting with such packages, you'll get some feel for how full-scale DSS's can serve as analytical tools. You'll also see that DSS's do not make decisions. A good DSS does provide high-quality information, in a user-oriented way, so that managers of large corporations or of households can make wise decisions.

Remote Databases

Not all the data needed to manage a business is generated within that business. Whether the "business" is a multinational conglomerate such as International Telephone and Telegraph or a single-family home in Omaha, Nebraska, this statement applies. Decreasing communication costs and increasing user demands for information have made it economically feasible to distribute many kinds of data via communication networks to users at widely separated locations. Telephones, TV sets, visual-display units, and microcomputers in home and business environments serve as terminals.

Organizations such as CompuServe of Columbus, Ohio, The Source of McLean, Virginia (purchased by CompuServe), Dow Jones News/Retrieval of Princeton, New Jersey, and Dialog Information Services of Palo Alto, California, are known for their remote database services. To sign up for CompuServe, for example, all you need are a computer, telephone, modem, and basic communication software. For a one-time fee of about $40 you'll receive lifetime membership and a subscription kit that contains your identification number, your password, and the local-access phone number for your area. You simply dial the number, and prompts and menus appear on your computer screen to guide you in using the system and choosing from among the databases available. You pay only the local phone charges and CompuServe basic connect charges of from $6.00 to $12.50 per hour for most services.

As another example, more than 300 databases are accessible via Dialog Information Services. *Books in Print* details currently published, forthcoming, and recently out-of-print books in the United States; *Patlaw* summarizes intellectual property decisions covering patents, trademarks, and copyrights in both U.S. federal and state courts; *Pharmaceutical News Index* contains drug and cosmetic industry information; *Standard and Poor's News* offers late-breaking financial news on U.S. public companies; and so on. The Dialog system provides online access about 120 hours a week to professionals in law, medicine, engineering, chemistry, research, education, and business management.

Distributed Databases

In Chapter 13, we discuss data communications. We see how data-processing and data-communication technologies are being applied jointly to prove again that the whole of something—in this case, the user's total information system—can be bigger than the sum of its parts. Users who've begun to appreciate the benefits of distributed data processing (discussed in Chapter 13) are also asking for distributed databases. Inventory-control personnel at St. Louis are best equipped to maintain the parts database for stock held at a St. Louis warehouse. Similar personnel at Memphis are best equipped to maintain parts data for stock at a warehouse there. Yet corporate management in Columbus or a sales representative seeking an expedited shipment of parts to a major customer in New York may need data and summaries of data from both locations.

As the term *distributed databases* implies, the data in a system with such capabilities is not all in one place. Authorized users and programs at any site in the network may need to access data at any other site. They should be able to do so. Furthermore, they should not have to know where the data is or what DBMS is controlling it; that is, the system should provide both *location transparency* and *DBMS transparency.* (See Figure 12-12.)

Information about the users, programs, and data within a distributed database system must be kept within the system itself. It must be updated whenever conditions within the system change. Furthermore, this system information must be distributed. Why? Because the system software at each site providing the distributed database capabilities must have access to the information so that it knows where the data is and how to get it.

There should be no one single point of failure in a distributed database system—no one site that must be available in order for any of the system to function. In data-processing terminology, we say that the system must provide *site autonomy.* Each DBMS should be able to perform database processing operations on the data at its site (that is, on data that is *local* to it) even if one or several other components of the distributed system are down.

Sound easy? The best minds in the computer field will tell you it's not. The system capabilities required to support database processing in such environments are extensive. Should the system ship each transaction (user request) as a message to wherever the necessary data is? If the data is at multiple sites, should the system ship functions, and yet bundle those functions somehow as a logical unit of work that either all completes or is all backed out (thereby restoring all data to a prior consistent state)? Alternatively, should the system ship the necessary data to wherever the transaction invoking the functions is? What if a communication link is down or (worse yet) goes down during transmission? What if an entire system fails? How can the system know the current state of each and every resource within that system at the time of failure? How can the system absolutely guarantee to users that all data within the system will be restored to a consistent state, no matter what or

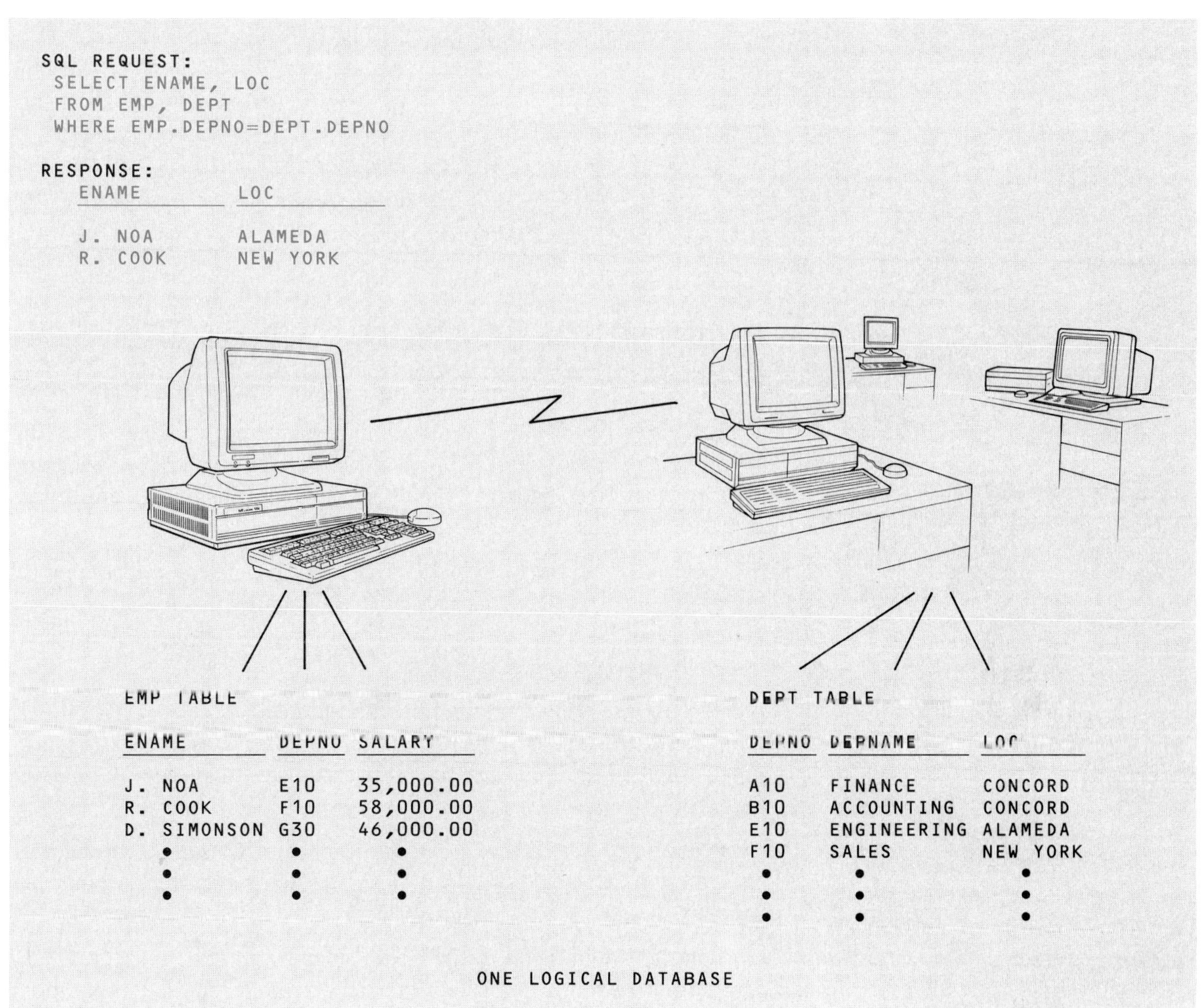
SQL REQUEST:
SELECT ENAME, LOC
FROM EMP, DEPT
WHERE EMP.DEPNO=DEPT.DEPNO
RESPONSE:
ENAME LOC
J. NOA ALAMEDA
R. COOK NEW YORK
EMP TABLE
ENAME DEPNO SALARY
J. NOA E10 35,000.00
R. COOK F10 58,000.00
D. SIMONSON G30 46,000.00
DEPT TABLE
DEPNO DEPNAME LOC
A10 FINANCE CONCORD
B10 ACCOUNTING CONCORD
E10 ENGINEERING ALAMEDA
F10 SALES NEW YORK
ONE LOGICAL DATABASE

Figure 12-12 Users can access data without having to know where the data is located when using a system with distributed database processing capabilities.

when user errors, program errors, or system failures occur?

Relational Technology was the market leader in providing distributed database capabilities when it announced INGRES/STAR, the distributed version of its relational DBMS, in 1986. Data could be retrieved from one site or from several sites in response to a single query request. In response to a single insert, update, or delete request, data from one site (but not more than one) could be inserted, deleted, or updated. There are many applications for which such capabilities are useful. For example, suppose a nationwide retailer's employee database is distributed. Employee information can be accessed from the local sites or from corporate headquarters. However, only the site that has responsibility for (owns) an employee's personal data can change it.

Research and development efforts to extend the capabilities of distributed database systems are continuing. Users who want to take advantage of such capabilities must do some preparatory work within their organizations also. Database design and administration capabilities must be dealt with. What data is or should be stored in personal computer databases? What data is or should be stored only in corporate mainframe databases? Which users should have access to which data and for what purposes? Such questions cannot be answered by DBMS vendors; they must be answered by user organizations.

CHAPTER SUMMARY

1. Managers are responsible for planning, organizing, staffing, directing, and controlling the activities of a business or other organization. Strategic, tactical, and operational managers have different responsibilities and different information needs.

2. File organization is concerned with the techniques used in arranging the records in a file; file access is concerned with the manner in which the records are written or read. Three common methods of organization are sequential, indexed sequential, and direct.

3. Under a database approach, the information needs of users are analyzed. The data that must be stored and processed to satisfy those needs is identified. Well-thought-out database design is prerequisite to successful database implementation.

4. Logical data structures known as *data models* are used to model real-world data relationships. The simplest data structure is a flat file. An inverted file supports indexed access to user data records.

5. More complex data relationships can be represented by mapping the user's data onto a hierarchical or network data model. The relational model, which deals with data in tables, is noted for its simplicity.

6. A DBMS provides many of the facilities needed to support the database approach. It interfaces with other system software, the database, and users or application programs.

7. Structured Query Language, or SQL, is a database sublanguage used to define, manipulate, and control access to data in relational databases.

8. A computer-based management information system (MIS) processes business transactions reflecting the day-to-day operations of an organization and provides management information for making decisions.

9. A decision support system (DSS) provides "what-if" help directly to managers and other professionals. Such information can be used in shaping the future.

10. Access to remote databases containing data on a wide variety of subjects is now marketed by many companies. The latest news, weather, sports, travel, publishing, legal, pharmaceutical, and investment information are examples of common offerings.

11. The data in a distributed database system is not all in one place. Users and application programs can access data at any sites in the system without having to know where the data is stored or what DBMS is controlling it. Information within the system is used by system software to determine where the data is and how to get it.

DISCUSSION QUESTIONS

1. (a) List the five functions generally attributed to management.
   (b) Show, by example, how an operational-level manager in a business organization of your choice performs each of these functions.

2. Show, by example, how the organizational level at which a manager operates affects his or her need for information.

3. Explain why a file system is often needed by users. In doing so, point out functions that it is likely to perform.

4. Describe how a file system, a data management system, and a DBMS are related. In doing so, explain how they are alike and how they differ.

5. What is a database?

6. Explain, by example, what it means to "model the relationships of data in the real world."

7. Are you aware of any computer files or databases in which personal data about you is stored? If so, name one and tell what you know about its contents and use.

8. (a) Describe a real-world situation in which multiple ways of getting at a particular data item are required.
   (b) How might a database containing the data item be set up to provide for this requirement?

9. (a) What is a DBMS?
   (b) What are some of the functions it can be expected to perform?

10. What is SQL and why is it useful?

11. What is an MIS?

12. Why is user involvement from the outset critical to the success of an MIS?

13. Discuss some of the capabilities a DSS is likely to provide.

14. (a) Distinguish between remote databases and distributed databases.
    (b) Suggest situations where these kinds of databases are likely to be especially useful.

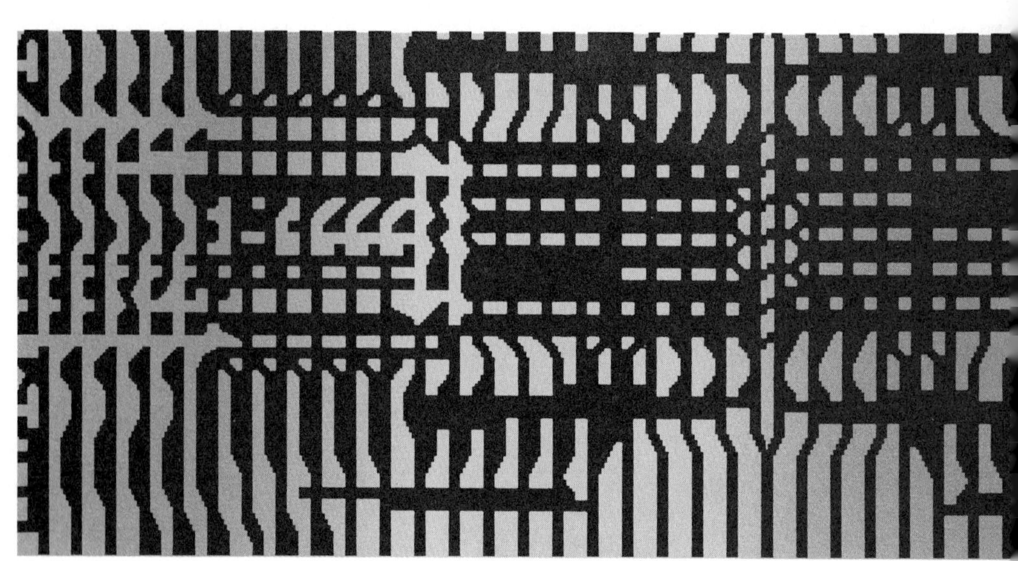

13 Data Communications and Office Automation

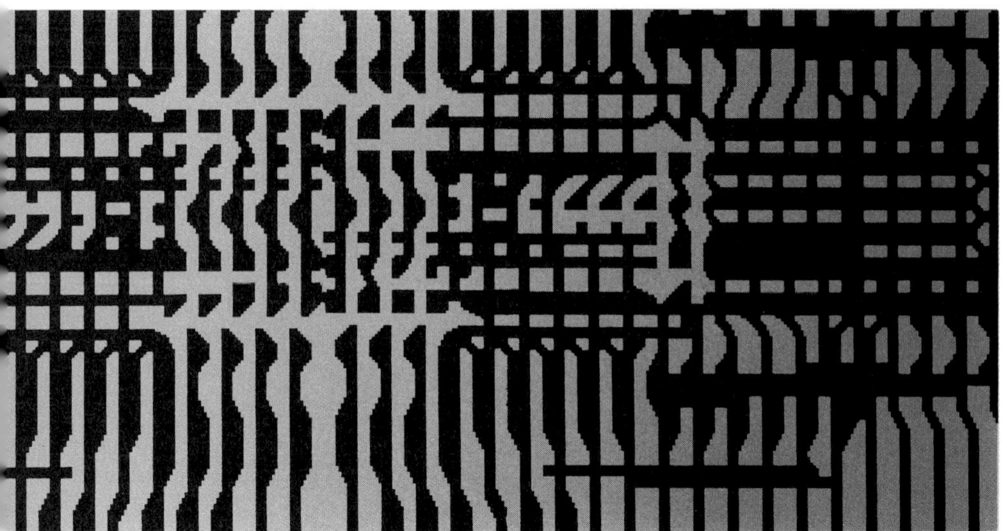

IN THIS CHAPTER

What It Takes to Communicate
Data Transmissions Options
Communication Service Offerings
A Changing Telecommunications Industry
Distributed Processing; Cooperative Processing
Automating Office Functions
Workgroup Communications
Electronic Data Interchange
Teleconferencing
Computing Services

The managers of today's complex and diversified businesses must have up-to-date knowledge of company operations in order to serve their customers and control their business activities. This need calls for rapid collection, processing, and distribution of large amounts of business data. Efficient, dependable data-collection and data-distribution capabilities are particularly important in cases where geographically separated facilities are controlled from one central facility, or where operations at one facility have a direct bearing on operations at another. For example, the corporate offices of a large grocery chain may maintain up-to-the-minute records of available inventory at all its supermarkets and provide direction and control to its fleet of trucks on a nationwide or even international basis. As another example, the orders for parts received at remote warehouses may have a direct effect on the number of parts that must be produced at central production facilities.

With the increased recognition of the potential of electronic data processing, more and more business applications have been computerized. Because data collection or distribution by mail, courier (runner or messenger), or carrier (motor freight line, bus company, or the like) is slow and subject to both traffic and weather conditions, other types of data transmission are needed. Initially, attention was directed to telephone and telegraph facilities. The latter provided printed copies of whatever was transmitted.

Greater transmission speed was obtained through use of punched paper tape. Administrative correspondence was recorded on paper tape, transmitted in coded form over telegraph lines, then rerecorded on paper tape at the receiving location. Later, data from the field (orders, production costs, and so on) was punched into paper tape, transmitted over telegraph lines to the central computer site, and converted to a form usable as direct input to a computer there. The next step was the development of equipment that could transmit data directly from punched cards or magnetic tape, thus eliminating the initial paper-tape-conversion step as well. Finally, online direct-access systems came into use. We looked at capabilities of such systems in Chapter 11.

For purposes of emphasis and clarity, let us define *communications* to be the transmission of information between points of origin and destination without altering the content or sequence of the information. We refer to communication over long distances as *telecommunications.* Telephone, radio, and television are examples. *Teleprocessing* is a word formed by combining *telecommunications* and *data processing.* As we might expect, a *teleprocessing system* makes it possible to collect data at one or more points of origin, transmit that data to a designated location for processing, and distribute the results of processing to one or more points of use. In common practice, the term *data communication* refers to the transmission of data from one location to another, and a teleprocessing system is also called a *data-communication system.*

In this chapter, we look first at the basic components of a data-communication system and at the data-transmission options available. Since telecommunications (and data communication as one form of telecommunications) are subject to governmental regulations, we discuss the roles of the Federal Communications Commission and state agencies in doing this regulating. You'll understand what common carriers are and why events like the breakup of AT&T come about.

Distributed processing makes it possible for users to enter data, process it, and receive results where they are, yet also access programs and data elsewhere if desired. Word processing done with the help of computers, desktop publishing, and electronic storage and retrieval capabilities are all facets of *office automation.* Electronic mail and voice mail are meeting users' day-to-day communication needs. *Electronic data interchange,* or *EDI,* allows purchase orders, invoices, and other business forms to be exchanged electronically between trading partners. Some organizations are turning to *teleconferencing* when remote group communications are required.

We conclude the chapter by summarizing the vast range of data-processing/data-communication capabilities that are currently available from computer service companies.

What Is Office Automation?

Office automation is the use of technology to increase productivity and achieve goals in the office environment.

What It Takes to Communicate

Suppose you chat with a friend in the hallway or call your dad via phone. What happens? Look at Figure 13-1A. Any communication, in its most basic form, involves at least four parts:

1. Sender, or data source
2. Message
3. Communication channel
4. Receiver of the transmitted data

When information (feedback) is transmitted to tell the sender that the message has been received, or when the receiver initiates communication with the sender, the roles of sender and receiver are reversed. (See Figure 13-1B.) The same communication channel or a different one may be used.

The primary elements of a data-communication system can be viewed within this same general framework. Source data is converted into electrical signals (encoded) by a sending terminal. These signals are the message, in a transmission-code form. Usually, a transmitter, or modulator, impresses the signals on a communication channel (for example, a telephone line) to send the message to its destination. When it arrives there, a demodulator "undoes" the work of the modulator by reconstructing the signals for a receiving terminal.

In an online direct-access system, there is no receiving terminal recognizable as a separate unit. A special *communication control unit* connected to the computer (or sometimes integrated within it) converts data in the transmission code used by the telecommunications equipment to a form acceptable as computer input. It then forwards the converted data to primary storage. Similarly, information written out from pri-

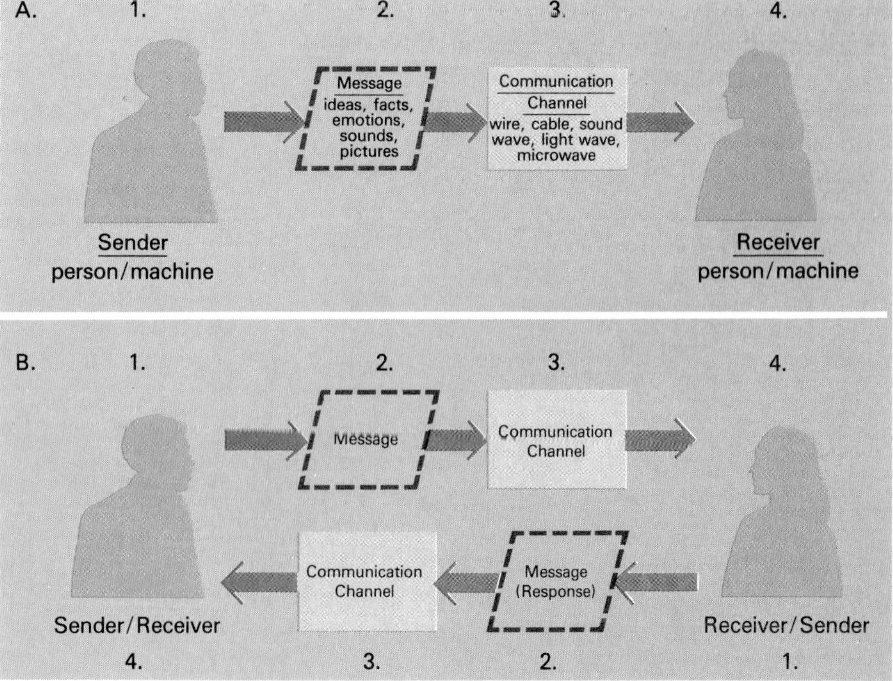
A.
1.
2.
3.
4.
Message
ideas, facts, emotions, sounds, pictures
Communication Channel
wire, cable, sound wave, light wave, microwave
Sender
person/machine
Receiver
person/machine
B.
1.
2.
3.
4.
Message
Communication Channel
Communication Channel
Message (Response)
Sender/Receiver
Receiver/Sender
4.
3.
2.
1.

Figure 13-1 In any communication, a sender, message, communication channel, and receiver are involved (A). When the receiver sends a response, the roles of sender and receiver are reversed (B).

DUMB, SMART, OR INTELLIGENT?

If you are selecting, or assisting users in the selection of, remote terminals, you must first decide whether your, or the users', application needs are best served by a terminal that is dumb, smart, or intelligent. A *dumb terminal* is totally dependent on the computer to which it is connected. It provides for online data entry or information output, but that's all. A *smart terminal* has certain editing capabilities as well. For example, a stored data definition may specify that only numeric values are acceptable as input for number of units sold and price per unit. The data keyed in by the terminal user is checked by hard-wired circuits to insure that only digits are entered. Some smart terminals have small storage areas (buffers) where data can be stored and modified before it goes to the central computer. This means that the terminal user can check to be sure the data is correct (and fix it if it isn't). An *intelligent terminal* is user-programmable. It contains not only a storage area but also a microprocessor. The terminal can be programmed to communicate with and instruct the user who is entering data. It can also do some processing of the data (sorting, summarizing, checking both input and computed values for reasonableness, and so on). In some systems, personal computers and workstations are being used as intelligent terminals. *(Photo courtesy IBM Corporation)*

mary storage may be converted by such a control unit to a form suitable for transmission over telecommunications facilities.

Some vendors have developed sophisticated control units that can perform other functions besides code conversion, such as error detection and recovery when signals are lost or distorted during transmission, adding or deleting message headers or other control information used in routing, and so on. A special computer, known as a *communications,* or *front-end, processor,* may serve as a communication control unit in a system that must support many users and/or heavy traffic on the data-communication network.

In a data-communication system, any I/O device at the end of a communication channel is called a *termi-*

nal. More specifically, since the device is located at a point other than where the main computer is, it is called a *remote terminal.* In practice, almost any I/O device found in a main computer room can be taken out of that room and attached to a communication channel. Usually, however, a remote terminal is a user-oriented device designed to meet specific input/output needs in the user's ordinary environment. Many such devices were described in Chapters 3 and 4.

Data Transmission Options

An organization that decides to take advantage of data-communication capabilities has many options. To determine what's best, a system analyst looks first at the organization's needs. Must data be transmitted between locations, or simply between points at a single location? Is speed of transmission important—say, to provide immediate responses to customers' inquiries about accounts? Is the volume of traffic fairly constant, or does it vary widely during the working day? Perhaps some data is to be batched and transmitted to the home office at night. The analyst evaluates available communication options against the identified requirements. We need to be aware of some of the options in order to understand the data-processing/data-communication systems that are in use today.

Analog or Digital Transmission

Source data can be transmitted over a communication channel in either of two forms: analog or digital. Initially, users' ordinary telephone lines served as communication channels in the vast majority of systems. *Analog transmission* was the major (if not the only) type of transmission available. When this type of transmission is used, the signals that constitute a message exhibit a continuous-wave form. (See Figure 13-2A.) At any point, the wave form has three major characteristics:

- *Amplitude*—the height of the wave, which is a reflection of the strength of the signal
- *Phase*—the duration in time of one complete cycle of the wave form
- *Frequency*—the number of times the wave form is repeated during a specified interval

Changing any one of these three characteristics beyond specified limits changes the signal that is sent. For example, we can let the normal amplitude of the wave represent a 1 bit. We can alter it to represent a 0 bit. (See Figure 13-2B.) This way of impressing signals on a wave is called *amplitude modulation,* or *AM.* Alternatively, we can let the normal frequency of the wave represent a 1 bit. We can alter it to represent a 0 bit. (See Figure 13-2C.) This way of impressing signals is called *frequency modulation,* or *FM.*

Are the terms *AM* and *FM* familiar to you? Yes, they identify techniques used to transmit the audible tones we hear on radio. We have just described how the techniques can be used to transmit data. Converting signals from a binary-digit pattern (pulse form) to a continuous-wave form is called *modulation.* The reverse—converting from wave form to pulse form, thereby reconstructing the signal—is called *demodulation.*

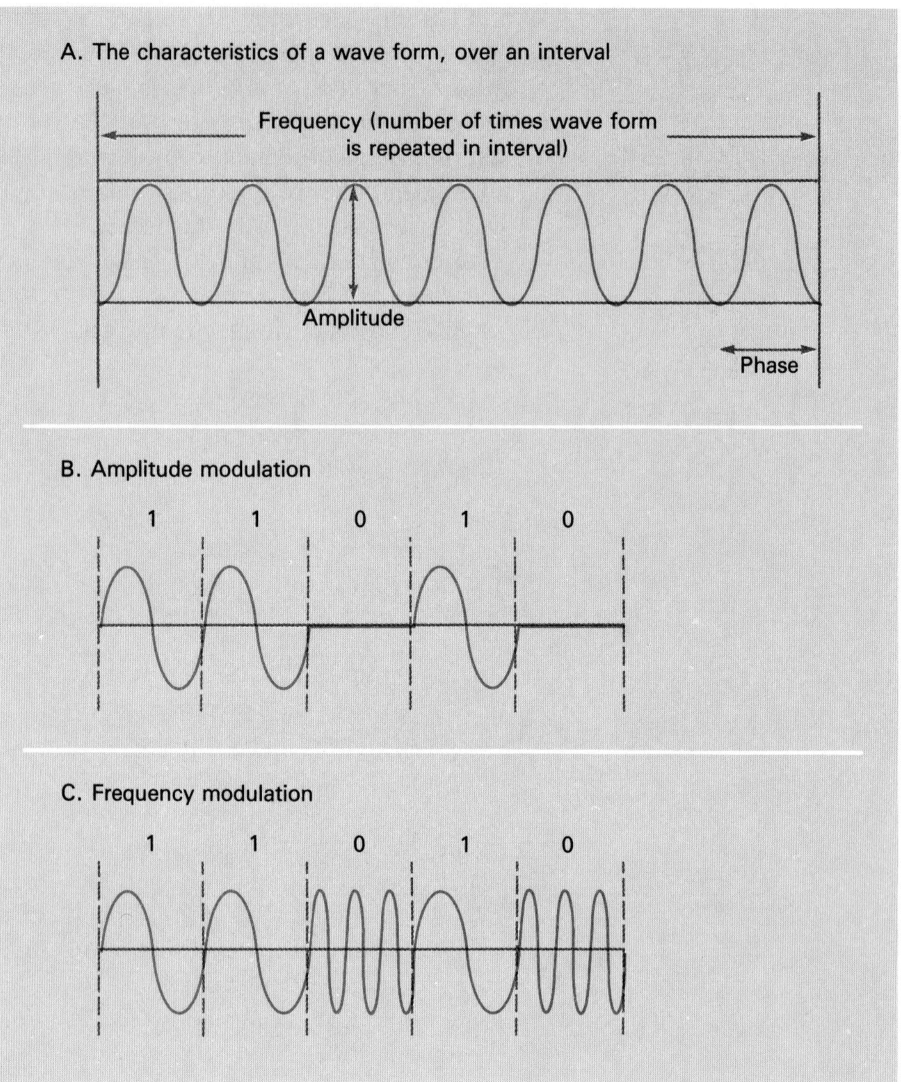
A. The characteristics of a wave form, over an interval
Frequency (number of times wave form is repeated in interval)
Amplitude
Phase
B. Amplitude modulation
1 1 0 1 0
C. Frequency modulation
1 1 0 1 0

Figure 13-2 **Either amplitude modulation (B) or frequency modulation (C) may be used to impress the signals of a message onto a continuous-wave form for analog transmission.**

When analog transmission is used, both are required.

In common practice, the *mo*dulation-*dem*odulation device is called a *modem.* If you own a personal computer and you want to use it for communication purposes—say, to access remote databases or in home banking—you'll probably need to acquire one. An *acoustical modem* (also called an *acoustic coupler*) allows you to connect to the system by placing the handset of an ordinary telephone into a receptical on the modem. A *direct-connect modem* is electrically connected to the telephone line.

With *digital transmission,* source data is not transmitted in wave form. Instead, it is transmitted as distinct

Digital transmission offers a substantially lower error rate and significantly better response time than analog transmission.

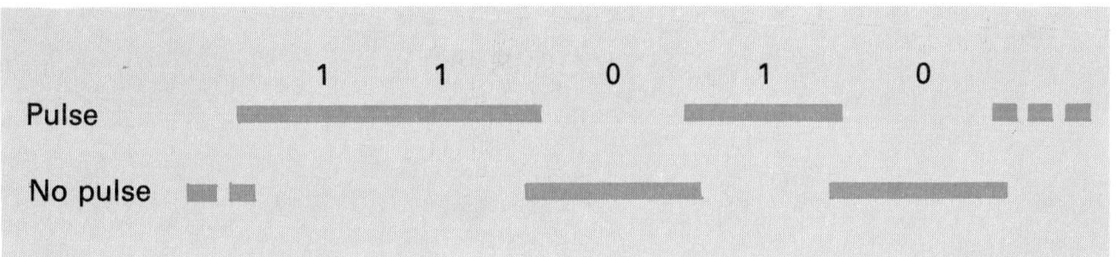
1
1
0
1
0
Pulse
No pulse

Figure 13-3 Message signals are transmitted as distinct pulses when digital transmission is used.

pulses (on/off) in much the same way that it travels in the computer. (See Figure 13-3.) Hence, modulation and demodulation need not occur. The elimination of these steps means less transmission time, less telecommunications equipment, and so on.

Digital transmission offers a substantially lower error rate and significantly better response time than analog transmission. The lower error rate (about 100 times lower) means users can transmit large amounts of data, even complete files, more reliably. The faster response time means better performance for the same amount of work, or the ability to handle more users or a larger volume of work and yet stay within existing response-time standards. Fortunately for users, digital transmission services are becoming increasingly available.

Start/Stop (Asynchronous) or Synchronous Transmission

When electrical signals are sent over a communication channel by a transmitting unit, the receiving unit must be in synchronization with that unit. If the receiving unit does not start at the proper point, or does not maintain the same interval as the transmitting unit, it cannot interpret the transmitted signals correctly. Two techniques commonly used to keep sending and receiving units in step are start/stop synchronization and synchronous transmission.

When the *start/stop method* of synchronization is used, a start signal is transmitted at the beginning of a group of data bits (say, a character). A stop signal is transmitted at the end of the group. (See Figure 13-4A.) Upon receiving the start signal, the receiving unit sets up a timing mech-

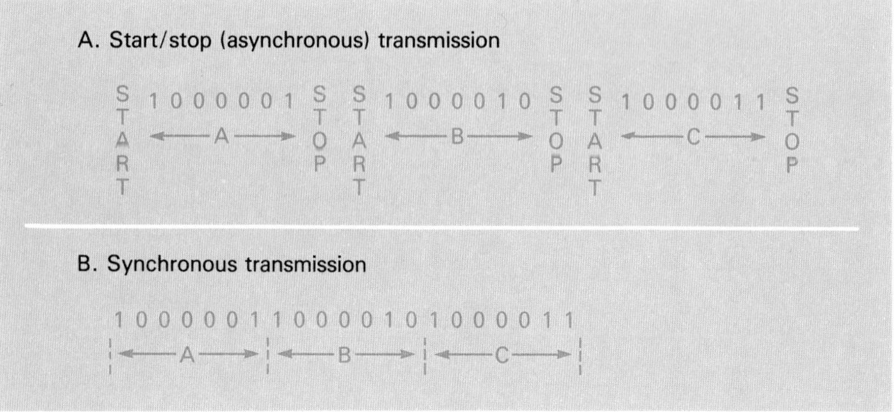
A. Start/stop (asynchronous) transmission
START 1000001 STOP START 1000010 STOP START 1000011 STOP
A
B
C
B. Synchronous transmission
100000110000101000011
A
B
C

Figure 13-4 Either start/stop (asynchronous) transmission (A) or synchronous transmission (B) may be used to keep sending and receiving units in step during communication. Asynchronous transmission is dependent on the start and stop signals that bound every character. Synchronous transmission is dependent on timing circuitry within the network.

anism to time the arrival of the bits in the group. The stop signal brings the receiving mechanism to rest. In effect, the sender and receiver are synchronized for the transmission of each character as an independent, single unit. Hence, the start/stop transmission mode is sometimes called *asynchronous transmission.*

Figure 13-4B shows what is known as *synchronous transmission.* The bits of one character are followed immediately by the bits of the next character. No start and stop signals are needed because the group of communication channels, or *circuit,* is sampled at regular intervals to receive and record data bits.

The terminal equipment for a synchronous system is more complex and more costly than that required for start/stop transmission. From the user's point of view, the potential for gains in both speed and efficiency may justify the costs. More data can be transmitted over a circuit per unit of time because no insertion, transmission, or reception of start and stop signals is necessary. During transmission, the receiving unit is kept in step with the sending unit by special timing circuitry.

Simplex, Half-Duplex, or Full-Duplex Transmission

Yet another way to characterize communication is by allowable direction of transmission. If communication can occur in only one direction, the transmission is said to be *simplex.* A terminal that communicates via such a channel can either send or receive, but cannot do both. The involved user or program normally needs a return path for control information or error signals, even if data has to be transmitted in only one direction. Therefore, simplex transmission is rarely used in an EDP environment.

If communication can occur in only one direction at a time, but that direction can change, the transmission is said to be *half-duplex.* (See Figure 13-5, top.) This type of transmission is used for most telephone service and for data transmitted via existing telephone networks. For example, source data can be keyed in by the user. *After* an entry has been received by the computer, a program in the computer can send an acknowledgment back to the user. *After* that acknowledgment has been received, the user can enter more data.

If communication can occur in both directions at the same time, the transmission is said to be *full-duplex.* (See Figure 13-5, bottom.) In systems that support computer-to-computer communication, full-duplex capabilities are usually established. Without them, undesirable delays or bottlenecks are likely to occur.

Communication Service Offerings

When you talk to a friend on the telephone, your communication passes through one or more *public exchanges,* or *switching facilities.* We now know that our ordinary telephone lines, sometimes referred to as *switched,* or *dial-up, lines,* can also carry data. The lines belong to firms known as *common carriers.* Under conventional public exchange service, a connection to a destination is made when a user at a terminal places a call to that destination. When data is to be transmitted, the user dials or presses the number of the destination (either a central computer facility or another user loca-

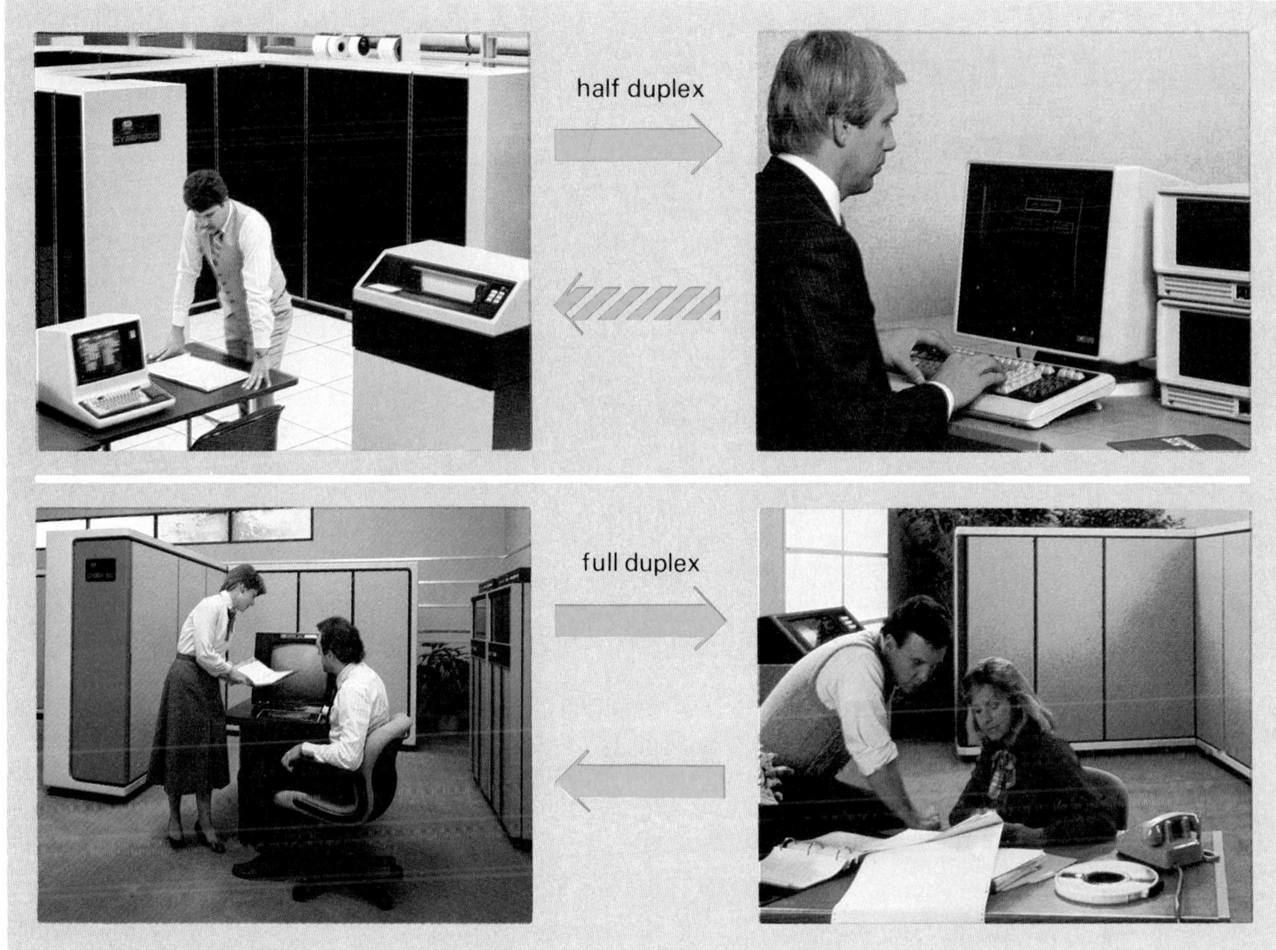
half duplex
full duplex

Figure 13-5 Half-duplex transmission allows data to be transmitted in either of two directions at one time (top). A system supporting computer-to-computer communication usually has simultaneous, two-way, full-duplex transmission capabilities (bottom). (Photos courtesy Control Data Corporation)

tion), just as for an ordinary telephone call. The user must compete with other users for an available line. A busy signal may be encountered. The user or user organization is charged for the time used, with rates depending on the time of day, day of week, and distance traveled (plus a monthly service charge for right of access to the system). Switching facilities are often connected via *trunk lines* that can transmit many communications simultaneously. However, only half-duplex transmission is possible.

When you talk to a friend on the telephone, your communication passes through one or more *public exchanges,* or *switching facilities.*

Alternatively, a user organization can acquire access to a *non-switched line* on a full-time basis. Since the line is available at any time, dialing is not required to make a connection. The non-switched line may be either leased or private. *Leased lines* are usually telephone or telegraph lines acquired via a fixed-term rental agreement from a common carrier. *Private lines* are privately owned and operated—by a user organization, a firm offering data-transmission facili-

ONLINE ORDER PROCESSING FOR PERISHABLE ITEMS

No one wants to buy, send, or receive a wilted plant. A "sad-looking bouquet" is seldom a bargain.

Hines Wholesale Nurseries, for example, has nurseries in Houston, Texas, and Santa Ana and Vacaville, California. It grows well over 20 million plants each year—about 800 varieties.

To insure that every order is processed within 24 hours or less, Hines has installed an online order processing and billing system. The three nurseries are connected via dedicated communication lines to a single computer running integrated financial application software. Sales representatives use portable terminals to submit orders from locations throughout the United States.

When an order is received, it undergoes a credit check and is either put on hold or cleared for shipment. A shipping manager is notified of a cleared order by the system itself and advised as to the nursery or nurseries at which it can be filled. The shipping manager keys into the system the number of the truckload in which the order will be shipped.

The system calculates the size, weight, and shipping charges of the order. It also factors in special charges such as boxing costs. Then it assigns a dock number for loading. Picking labels are printed, detailing required loading information. Tractors traverse the nursery fields to fill the order. Quality assurance personnel visually inspect the plants and make any required changes or include any required explanations prior to shipment. Finally, a bill of lading is printed to accompany the shipment.

The major benefits of this online order processing and billing system are faster order processing, better control and turnover of inventories, more efficient use of the nurseries' harvesting, loading, and distribution resources, and more effective financial management in numerous areas of the business. *(Photo courtesy Eunice Harris/Photo Researchers)* ties to subscribers, or a telecommunications equipment manufacturer. Full-duplex transmission may be provided. In common usage, the terms *leased* and *private* are used interchangeably to mean "other than public."

Leased or private lines can be connected through switching facilities to provide a private version of an exchange service. You'll hear such facilities referred to as a *private branch exchange,* or *PBX.* Telephone calls can be routed from callers to callees over any or all of the leased or private lines under control of the switching facilities. Calls can also be routed to outside lines for local or long-distance transmission. The leased or private lines can also be connected to a central computer facility for data-transmission purposes. Networks that handle voice as well as data traffic in digital form are controlled by computer-based PBX's, or *CBX's,* at various points. User costs generally consist of flat monthly rental charges based on length and type of lines. *Tie lines* are leased trunk connections acquired by a large user organization to connect its locations.

Leased lines generally provide faster response and better-quality transmission than dial-up lines because of various techniques used to "condition" the lines. Privacy is more easily maintained with leased lines. Dial-up services provide greater access to the user's external environment because extensive interconnections are available through the public exchange facilities.

In general, a user's choice between leasing a line and using public dial-up facilities is based on an analysis of over-all costs, message volume, and service requirements. The breakeven point is a function of distance, average call time, and urgency. Low message volume favors dial-up; heavy message volume favors leased facilities.

Few users today depend entirely on either leased lines or dial-up facilities. As suggested above, even users who lease lines often want to interconnect those lines to public networks. An organization dependent on communication between locations for its basic business operations may acquire leased lines to speed that communication but also maintain dial-up facilities as backup.

A Changing Telecommunications Industry

A telephone is a telephone. A computer is a computer. We wouldn't use a telephone to do what we need a computer to do. We wouldn't use a computer to do what we need a telephone to do. Well, maybe. In some systems that exist today it's difficult to determine where use of telephone facilities ends and use of computer facilities begins. Some systems allow voice and data calls to be made simultaneously. So what, you may be thinking. Who cares? Well, historically, *data communication* has been subject to governmental regulation. *Data processing* has been open to free enterprise. Let's start by understanding why.

In some systems that exist today it's difficult to determine where use of telephone facilities ends and use of computer facilities begins.

Recall that, when communication occurs, signals travel in wave or pulse form in a certain frequency domain within the electromagnetic spectrum in our universe. No two communications can use the same part of the electromagnetic spectrum at the same time without interfering with each other. Specific portions of the spectrum must be allocated to specific users to prevent such interference. In the United States, the *Federal Communications Commission* (*FCC*) performs this allocation function. The seven-member FCC is an independent agency established by Congress through the Communications Act of 1934 to regulate communication facilities originating in the United States. Any organization intending to construct, operate, or acquire communication facilities must file a schedule, or *tariff,* giving details of the intended service, charges to users, and so on. The FCC may grant the organization a *license,* thereby authorizing it to offer the service. The standard governing the granting of a license is "public interest, convenience, or necessity."

In most countries, the government owns and administers a nationwide telephone system. Often that system is allied with both postal and telegraphic services. In countries where the telephone system is provided by an organization independent of the government, as in Canada, a monopoly is usually granted to the organization. This approach avoids costly duplication of resources and insures coverage for the entire population. The monopoly is allowed and protected because it is deemed to be a public necessity.

The practice in the United States differs from this pattern. A number of companies offer telephone services. All are licensed to do so. The scope of "communication facilities" under the jurisdiction of the FCC includes terrestrial (land) lines as well as the electromagnetic spectrum. The FCC licenses and regulates radio, television, telephone, telegraph, facsimile (fax, or digitized imaging), and other transmission by wire, cable, and microwave. It also licenses communication services that use satellites as relay stations for microwave signals. In addition, each state has a *public utilities commission* (*PUC*) that regulates intrastate communication.

In most instances, the FCC and the PUC's act as complementary agencies. Together, they grant (or refuse to grant) and enforce monopoly rights in specific communication areas. They also regulate the prices charged for communication services in order to allow the providing organizations a fair rate of return on their investments and yet protect users from excessive rates.

Common carriers are organizations authorized by the FCC and/or state agencies to provide communication services to the public. Typically, the organizations are investor-owned and privately operated. Today there are about 3000 common carriers. American Telephone and Telegraph (AT&T), Western Union, and GTE Corporation are examples. (See Figure 13-6.) Through the first three quarters of this century, AT&T grew to become (1) the parent company of the Bell System—a vast communication network—and of Bell Laboratories; (2) the owner of Western Electric, a subsidiary that produced equipment to meet needs of the Bell System; and (3) the owner of all or part of the stock of 22 independent telephone companies often referred to as the Bell operating companies or BOC's.

JKL
5
MNO
6
PRS
7
OPER
0
*

Figure 13-6 **Today AT&T's Network Operations Center in Bedminster, New Jersey, uses its advanced computer systems to manage more than 19.5 million interstate calls on a typical business day (left). At the same time, researchers at Bell Laboratories are placing more and more circuitry on smaller and smaller chips for use in many system components (right).** (Courtesy of AT&T Bell Labs)

Initially, computer-using organizations that wanted to acquire data-communication capabilities turned to the common carriers for support. Over time, other options have opened to them.

The "winds of change" started in 1968 when the FCC, by its Carterfone decision, opened the public switched telephone network to independent (other than AT&T Bell System) equipment. Prior to that time, only AT&T's equipment was allowed to be directly attached to the network. The transmission of data was dependent on Teletypes, which are inherently slow, or on remote batch terminals whose throughput was constrained by the lack of high-speed modems. The FCC's decision prompted the development of high-speed modems. It sparked American ingenuity to pursue new business opportunities in telecommunications.

In 1971, the FCC allowed firms other than the authorized monopoly common carriers to construct and offer terrestrial communication services. In 1972, it permitted the launching of communication satellites by new common carriers intending to offer services that could compete directly with terrestrial communication systems. Known as the "open skies policy," this decision encouraged organizations to compete in applying satellite technology to a wide variety of domestic private-line services.

Specialized common carriers are firms other than the authorized (albeit regulated) monopoly common carriers that have approval from the FCC or state agencies to offer communication services. Among the leaders are MCI Telecommunications and U.S. Sprint. Both are authorized to offer terrestrial private-line services for voice and data transmission. Both are meeting AT&T head-on in an area where AT&T is strong—namely, long-distance phone service—and doing it successfully. You may be an MCI or U.S. Sprint subscriber.

GTE's Telenet and McDonnell Douglas Corporation's Tymnet are examples of *value-added networks,* or *VAN's.* These firms and other *value-*

EDUCATION VIA SATELLITE

To offer high-quality technical education to its employees and customers, IBM has implemented an Interactive Satellite Education Network (ISEN). Instructors at studios in New York, Chicago, and Los Angeles interact with students at 11 IBM education centers across the country. Digital video pictures of an instructor and of the slides or foils he/she is using are transmitted via a satellite orbiting 22,300 miles above the earth. To ask a question of the instructor, a student simply presses a button on one of the student response units located in a classroom. The instructor activates the microphone within that response unit. All students hear the question and the instructor's answer. *(Photo courtesy IBM Corporation)*

added carriers are not competing directly with the established common carriers. Instead, they improve (add value to) common-carrier offerings. In doing so, they use leased common-carrier communication channels—typically, those underutilized at all but peak hours or overutilized during peak hours (and therefore not capable of handling the workload). VAN switching facilities provide economical, low-error, fast-response communication services to meet the needs of computer users. An organization whose terminals and computers communicate through a VAN pays only for data transmitted and not for idle, unused capacity. The network handles daily and seasonal fluctuations without degradation and can absorb long-term growth in traffic.

The era of commercial use of satellites for telecommunications began when the Communications Satellite Corporation, or COMSAT, was set up by Congress in 1962, not as a government agency, but as a shareholder corporation. It was to be the "carrier's carrier," responsible for the launching and operation of communication satellites to serve as relay stations in worldwide communication networks.

As mentioned above, in the early 1970s the FCC ruled that essentially any qualified firm could own and operate domestic communication satellites. AT&T, American Satellite Company, ITT, RCA Americom, and Western Union are among today's *satellite carriers.*

In a typical satellite system, microwave signals are transmitted from an antenna on the ground to a satellite orbiting 22,300 miles above the earth. At that distance, the circular speed of the satellite exactly matches the speed of rotation of the earth, and the satellite appears to be stationary overhead. The satellite can "see" and be seen from about one-third of the earth; theoretically, signals broadcast from the satellite can be picked up by any antennas and receivers in that area. For example, Home Box Office (HBO) uses satellite transmission to distribute movies to cable television companies that then make the movies available for viewing to their subscribers. The U.S. space program has been financed in part by satellite carriers who pay to have their communication satellites launched as a part of U.S. space missions.

Not surprisingly, AT&T determined that it wanted to move into data-processing areas just as other firms were moving into communications. Until 1980, an AT&T vs. the U.S. Justice Department antitrust settlement (the 1956 consent decree) prohibited it from doing so. AT&T could enter no business that was not regulated by the FCC. In December 1980, the FCC ruled that AT&T could expand into new areas, provided that it did so through a separate subsidiary. AT&T complied by implementing a *divestiture plan* whereby the 22 BOC's were grouped within seven regional holding companies. (See Figure 13-7.) Each of the regional holding companies is publicly held. Even at the start, each had about 90,000 employees and was among the top 50 in *Fortune* magazine's ranking of the top 500 companies, as measured by their assets.

Not surprisingly, AT&T determined that it wanted to move into data-processing areas just as other firms were moving into communications.

In practice, the regional holding companies conduct day-to-day local telephone operations through the BOC's assigned to them. As a part of the divestiture, 165 *local access and transport areas,* or *LATA's,* were defined within the United States. The BOC's and other independent carriers can provide telephone service within LATA's, but inter-LATA traffic must be handled by an authorized long-distance carrier such as AT&T, MCI, or U.S. Sprint. If you're paying phone bills within the United States, you're probably aware of this differentiation.

The regional holding companies are also aggressively pursuing other business opportunities. Most of them have set up subsidiaries to handle unregulated products and services. For example, NYNEX markets computers and computer-related products through many retail outlets. PACTEL provides mobile cellular telephone and radio paging services in several U.S. locations.

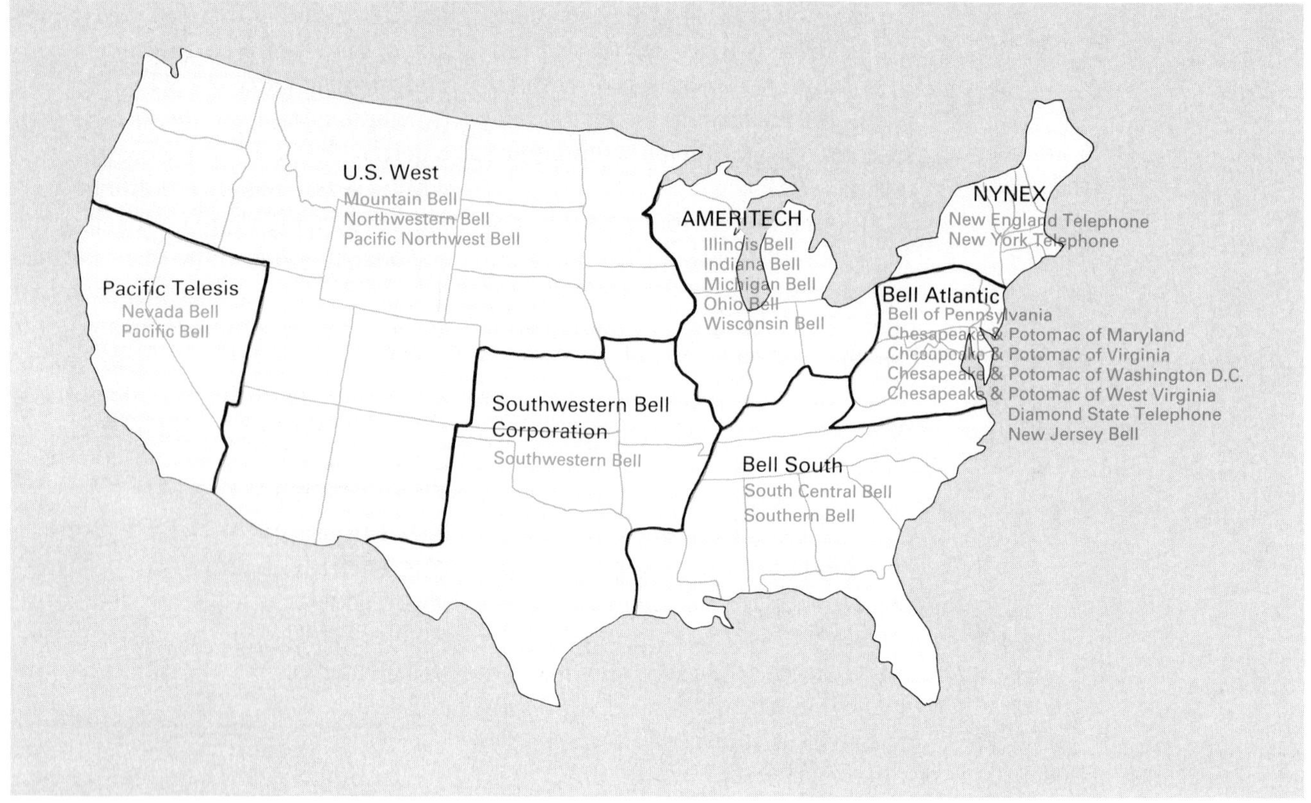
U.S. West
Mountain Bell
Northwestern Bell
Pacific Northwest Bell
Pacific Telesis
Nevada Bell
Pacific Bell
AMERITECH
Illinois Bell
Indiana Bell
Michigan Bell
Ohio Bell
Wisconsin Bell
NYNEX
New England Telephone
New York Telephone
Bell Atlantic
Bell of Pennsylvania
Chesapeake & Potomac of Maryland
Chesapeake & Potomac of Virginia
Chesapeake & Potomac of Washington D.C.
Chesapeake & Potomac of West Virginia
Diamond State Telephone
New Jersey Bell
Southwestern Bell
Corporation
Southwestern Bell
Bell South
South Central Bell
Southern Bell

Figure 13-7 Seven regional holding companies were formed as part of the divestiture plan that positioned AT&T to enter nonregulated business areas. Each company is publicly held and offers a variety of services.

Even after the divestiture AT&T is still the largest common carrier in the United States. It retained about 20 percent of the Bell System assets and more than 300,000 employees. Its nationwide long-distance network is awesome. Bell Laboratories continues to be a research leader. Western Electric is now known as AT&T Technologies, Inc. AT&T participates in both free enterprise and regulated activities.

Distributed Processing; Cooperative Processing

For almost three decades following its introduction, the business computer system occupied an "inner sanctum" of corporate America. Giant mainframes crunched on numbers in air-conditioned, glass-walled isolation. That's changing, as we've seen throughout this book. Yes, there are still mainframes. Yes, there are still tasks that can only be accomplished with the help of mainframes. On the other hand, you're likely to find a computer at work wherever you find (or expect to find) a desk, a typewriter, or a telephone.

In recent years, many geographically dispersed, nationwide, and even multinational organizations have evolved. Initially, management of these organizations saw a need for tight-fisted, centralized control, particularly with respect to profit and loss accountability. Large, fast, centralized computer systems served as important tools in achieving this control.

Yet, counter to this move toward centralization, management techniques favoring decentralization of control have also evolved. Profit centers have been created at various organizational levels. Managers of geograhical locations and/or functional areas are being given opportunities to control their own destinies. They, in turn, are demanding control of the organizational resources for which they are accountable. They are also demanding better information, so they can exercise control effectively.

There may have been a time when organizations were forced to centralize their EDP-system resources to achieve economy of operation at low cost. That time has passed for most organizations. The declining costs of medium-sized computers, personal computers, and workstations are forcing organizations to take another look at their approach to EDP. Organizations that have considered EDP capabilities beyond their reach are also taking another look. Technological advancements are paving the way for *distributed processing.*

What is distributed processing? There is no universally accepted definition. Perhaps its one basic characteristic is a dispersion of the processing power, or intelligence, within an EDP system among geographically separated locations. The functional groups or site locations within an organization can do most of their data processing locally. In addition, an executive may dial the large central computer, or *host,* at the beginning of the business day (to get the latest corporate-wide directives or management information). At the end of the day, a shop supervisor may dial the central computer to get the totals of production activities at a particular plant.

Cooperative processing implies capabilities beyond simply the ability to process data at multiple locations. In a cooperative-processing environment, application programs at two or more locations work together to accomplish a specific task. Personal computers and/or workstations not only take over display functions but also perform some computational and decision-making tasks.

Cooperative processing implies capabilities beyond simply the ability to process data at multiple locations.

Consider an order processing application as an example. Assume sales personnel may submit orders from workstations at their branch offices. Further assume that both customer data and inventory data are stored in relational databases managed with the help of a database management system that runs on a mainframe at corporate headquarters. (See Figure 13-8.)

The workstations are known as *clients;* the mainframe acts as a *server.* Examples of functions likely to be done at the workstations are: reading the order data as input; performing data validation; providing online HELP information if the user requests it; and formatting results to be displayed as output. Examples of functions likely to be done on the mainframe are: accessing the customer database to obtain customer data; accessing the inventory database to confirm quantity on hand exceeds quantity ordered and decreasing quantity on hand by quantity ordered for each item ordered; returning status information to the user at the workstation; and preparing packing slips and shipping orders for subsequent processing.

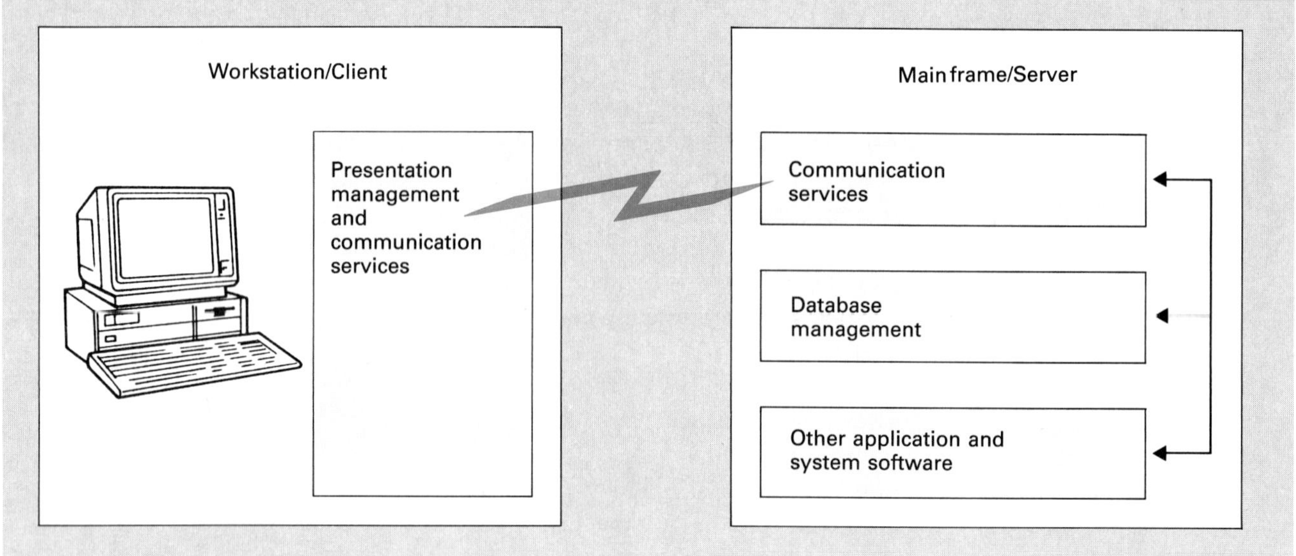

Workstation/Client
Presentation management and communication services
Mainframe/Server
Communication services
Database management
Other application and system software

Figure 13-8 Application programs running on clients and servers work together to accomplish a specific task in a cooperative-processing environment.

Because less data is transmitted to and from the central computer in a distributed processing environment than in an environment where all processing is centralized, communication costs are lower. Since the mainframe workload is reduced, expensive large-computer upgrades may be postponed or avoided. Users whose data is processed locally experience faster job turnaround. Routine business documents can often be produced where they are needed as byproducts of ongoing activities. In our order-processing application above, for example, customer invoices may be generated as the sales-order data is entered at the various offices and processed successfully.

System availability may be improved in a distributed-processing environment. Even if a central computer or some or all of the data-communication facilities are inoperable, a local data-processing system may be able to function independently. Applications that access only local data can be run successfully.

An organization that elects to move to EDP using a distributed-processing approach can do so gradually at its own pace. In effect, the user can do top-down planning but bottom-up implementation by, for example, first establishing a computer-controlled production system at a manufacturing facility, then an inventory control system at each of several warehouses, and so on. The marriage of word processing or desktop publishing and data processing is perhaps most readily achieved within an over-all framework of distributed processing.

A Direct Approach

The most reliable method of determining whether or not your office staff is comfortable in their automated office environment is to ask them.

Automating Office Functions

Why all the interest in word processing? Just what is it anyway? In simplest terms, the basic appeal of word processing can be understood by anyone who's had to use White Out to correct a mistake on a letter, retype several pages of a report because somebody wants to add one paragraph, or type a zillion copies of a form letter just so that every recipient of the letter gets "an original."

In Chapter 1, we learned that *data* is raw material—facts and figures generated from one or more sources. *Data processing* is the manipulation of data to achieve a desired result. The finished product of data processing is *information. Word processing* is a term coined to emphasize the manipulation of certain types of data—characters combined to form words, sentences, paragraphs, memos, letters, reports. The term *text processing* is often used interchangeably with *word processing.* A system that can handle long, multiple-page documents is said to perform *document processing.*

The initial impetus to develop word-processing equipment arose from a desire to automate certain office functions. The ultimate goal was to raise office productivity. Consider a simple example. In a conventional office, a secretary receives a handwritten or dictated piece of correspondence. He or she types a rough draft; returns it to the writer for approval, changes, or corrections; and corrects the revised draft until the writer is satisfied. Each revision usually means a complete retyping of one or more pages of the document. While typing, the secretary is interrupted frequently—to answer the phone, find a memo, escort a visitor from the lobby, schedule a conference room for an afternoon meeting, and so on. Finally, a retyped version of the document is accepted as satisfactory. The secretary makes as many copies as needed, using a photocopying machine. Each copy is readied for mailing.

Suppose a microcomputer system with Microsoft Word, WordStar, Word Perfect, or other popular word-processing software is available. Initially, someone types paragraphs of text or uses a scanner to enter existing pages of text as input. As the person types, the characters are displayed on a visual-display screen. Text can be centered on a line or on a page; margins can be changed; lines can be justified on the right (as well as on the left); words, sentences, and paragraphs can be moved from one part of a page to another, even from one page to another; and so forth. Corrections can be made to the stored form of the document.

Most word-processing packages allow paragraphs of text to be stored for quick insertion into standard documents such as contracts. Form letters can be merged with names and addresses, then printed to produce any number of personalized originals. Only when a document is exactly right need it be committed to a final, hard-copy form.

In 1984, the document-processing capabilities available to users were extended further with the introduction of *desktop publishing*—the ability to manipulate graphics as well as text with computer help, and to combine text and graphics on a single page, to create high-quality documents. Aldus' PageMaker desktop publishing software for Apple Macintosh microcomputers was introduced and gained widespread acceptance. Its leading competitor, Xerox Corporation's Ventura Publisher, was introduced in 1986. Within the same time frame, Apple Computer released its LaserWriter printer for the Macintosh, and Hewlett-Packard introduced its inexpensive LaserJet printer. Together, these products made individual-user microcomputer-based publishing possible. (See Figure 13-9.)

Today, individuals and companies are producing memos, newsletters, technical manuals, brochures,

Figure 13-9 Desktop publishing packages such as Xerox Corporation's Ventura Publisher allow users to integrate text from word-processing programs and artwork from graphics programs within a single page or document. (Courtesy Xerox Corporation)

business forms, mail-order catalogs, posters, annual reports, and even restaurant menus with the aid of personal computers at a fraction of the price and time that would be required using traditional publishing procedures and methods. *W*hat *y*ou *s*ee *i*s *w*hat *y*ou *g*et, or *WYSIWYG* (pronounced "wizzywig"), capabilities allow users to view on a display screen an exact or very close representation of what will appear as output on a printed page. Even art directors of national publications are flocking to desktop publishing. The *Wall Street Journal* Dow Jones Average charts are done on a Macintosh. The "Insider" section of *TV Guide* is laid out with personal computer help. Indeed, entire books are being created and produced, start to finish, through desktop publishing. (Recall also our brief discussions of desktop publishing, WYSIWYG, and page description languages in Chapter 4.)

According to recent surveys, U.S. businesses now deal with more than 300 billion documents. That number is increasing by billions annually. Some documents are "one-time shots," but even routine intracompany memos are often retained for reference or as proof of commitments that have been made. Electronic storage and retrieval capabilities are allowing business professionals and administrative staffs to deal with electronic copies of documents when they choose to. Electronic-mail facilities (discussed below) can be used together with these capabilities to facilitate communication.

Workgroup Communications

Remember the last time you tried repeatedly, and unsuccessfully, to phone a friend or business associate? Chances are you finally resorted to leaving a message. Likewise, chances

About Communications

The typical office worker wastes 20 minutes each day trying to contact others within the organization. The wasted time constitutes two weeks of missed work per employee per year. About $3\frac{1}{2}$ calls are required to make a desired contact. Only 1 out of 4 calls is successful on a first attempt. Over half of all calls are for one-way transfer of information. Seventy percent of all calls are less important than the work they interrupt, and 76 percent of the calls don't require an immediate response. What's the impact? Decisions are delayed. Unnecessary costs are incurred. Revenue is late in coming or lost to the company.

are you were out when the other person returned your call.

Remember the business, church, or school meeting notice you received the day *after* the meeting? The package you had to go after because the delivery person wouldn't leave it when you were out? The letter or report that somehow got lost in transit and never did arrive?

Eliminating problems like these in today's business environments is what *electronic mail* is all about. It is the delivery, by electronic means, of messages that otherwise would be transmitted physically through intracompany mailrooms or external postal systems, or verbally via telephones. Each message may be a short one-liner, a copy of one page of text, or a several-hundred-page document.

Electronic mail offers the speed and convenience of a phone call without the frustration of "telephone tag" and with the option of communicating simultaneously with a number of persons.

Studies show that the most intensive and time-critical communications in business today take place at the workgroup level. Typically, a workgroup includes from 50 to 500 people. In a small company, the workgroup may encompass the entire firm. In a large company that's organized along functional lines, the workgroup may be engineering, the accounting department, customer service, or marketing. In a company that's organized on a product or project basis, the workgroup may include everyone who's working to make a June 30 deadline for finished product.

Studies show that the most intensive and time-critical communications in business today take place at the workgroup level.

Strictly speaking, electronic mail is not new. The telegraph and Morse code, Western Union's TWX/Telex and Mailgram services, and low-cost, low-speed Teletypes and similar machines have been around for some time. *Facsimile (fax) equipment* can provide a hard-copy duplicate at the receiving end of an original message that exists in hard-copy form at the sending end. Signatures and line drawings or other graphics as well as text can be transmitted. For most purposes, a fax machine functions as a copier at the end of a telephone line. In the middle 1970s, electronic mail became synonymous with computer-based message systems. Electronic document distribution became a practical reality.

For our purposes in this book (and in practice), the electronic-mail facilities we're discussing are used primarily for intracompany and intraworkgroup communications. Numerous vendors have developed hardware and software that allows managers and other communicators to create their own correspondence, change it, send it to one or more colleagues, file it, and destroy it at their convenience. (See Figure 13-10.) Of course, managers can't become skilled typists overnight, and some are reluctant to use keyboards. To appeal to them, vendors are continuing to emphasize user-friendliness. Some systems simulate the in-basket, pending, and out-basket functions with which managers are familiar. Many provide full-screen menus. Managers simply move a mouse to position the cursor and press one key

TUNED FOR PERFORMANCE

There are few experiences today that demonstrate mastery of one's discipline, talented experts working together, and dedication to excellence as does an on-stage performance of a renowned symphony orchestra.

Before, during, and after the performance, many behind-the-scene activities occur that help to make the performance possible. In many of the activities, computers are involved.

For example, the volunteers and administrative staff supporting a symphony orchestra often use computers for word-processing functions. Chances are the symphony relies heavily on individual and corporate donations for revenue. Thousands of donor names may be kept in a computerized mailing list. A standard word-processing or desktop publishing package can be used to prepare and print personalized solicitation letters and other correspondence to all names on the list or to specially selected subsets of them. Subsets may be selected on the basis of historical data on donor activity or geographic data about the donors, kept in other computerized databases. Access to this kind of data is often the key to success in a fund-raising effort.

Ticket sales are another source of revenue. Some symphony attendees buy tickets for specific performances. Others are season ticket holders. A complex web of telephone orders, renewals, seating charts, seating upgrades, group events, credit authorizations, and the like must be processed and managed. Tickets must be designed, printed, and readied for distribution—again, word processing or desktop publishing. Season brochures, press releases, and other marketing publications are also prepared and printed with computer help.

The symphony functions like a business in many respects. Budgets are prepared. Costs are tracked. Actual costs are compared with budgeted costs to determine where and why variations from budgets have occurred. Traditional business applications such as general ledger, accounts payable, accounts receivable, and fixed-assets accounting are also handled with computer help.

Some symphony groups use computers for applications that are less traditional. Performance repertoires—the scores and arrangements included within each concert—are assembled, modified if necessary as a season nears or progresses, and then filed for historical reference in planning subsequent concerts. Guest artists and conductors, musician audition his-

tory, and current orchestra personnel data is organized and accessed with computer assistance. A symphony's entire music library may be cataloged and managed in a similar fashion. The library may consist not only of hard-copy documents but also of audio tapes of past performances. Guest artists and conductors may "get a feel for" the orchestra, concert environment, and listener expectations by reviewing the library materials. *(Photo courtesy Milton Feinberg/ Stock, Boston)*

or touch one area on a screen to choose from a variety of message-handling alternatives.

The personal computers and workstations used in an electronic-mail system may be connected via communication lines to a medium-sized computer or mainframe that receives all messages from senders and performs routing functions. Alternatively, the users' machines may be interconnected within a *local area network*, or *LAN*. The term *local* is appropriate here because such a network is designed to service users within a relatively small area—say, the same room, building, or group of buildings. In addition to electronic mail, the LAN may provide other capabilities. Examples are: the ability to share an expensive system resource such as a large disk or a letter-quality printer; the ability to share program files (for example, if the members of the workgroup are doing software development or need to use

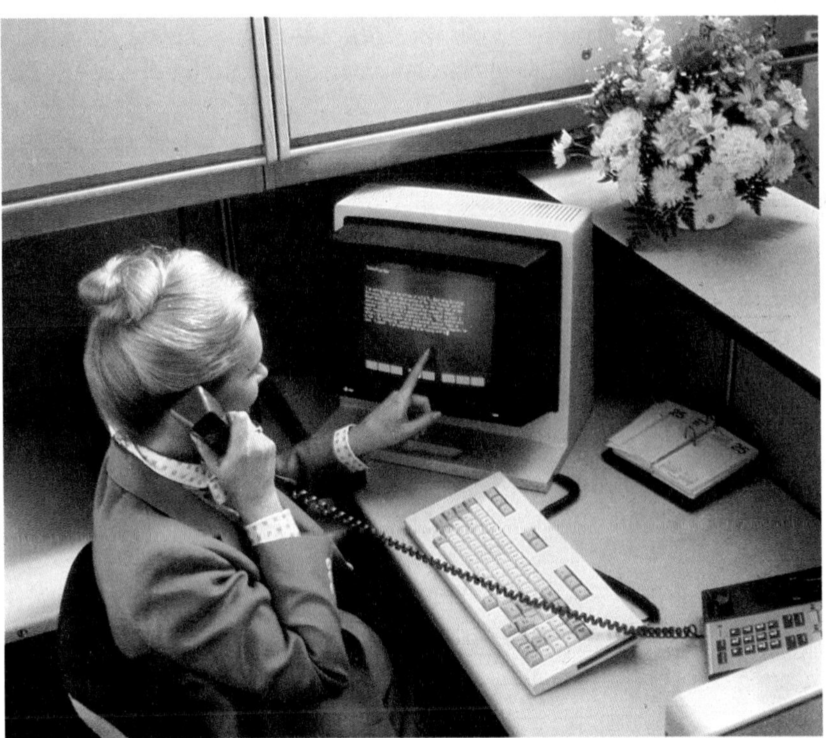

Figure 13-10 Telephones are appropriate for some office-to-office communications, but many managers and other business professionals are turning increasingly to desktop computer systems with electronic-mail capabilities. (Courtesy of AT&T Information Systems)

When Should an Executive Consider Putting Office Automation Technology to Work in the Inner Suite?

Part of the hesitation has been that a machine on the executive's desk would receive little use. But this point may not take into account the size of the executive's salary (and the value of his or her time). Expecting 100 percent utilization of a personal computer or workstation is no more valid than insisting that a telephone be used every minute of every workday.

the same accounting program); and the ability to share data, which helps to insure that all users have access to the latest information.

If user needs dictate, a LAN may be interconnected with public transmission facilities through a small computer known as a *gateway processor.* For example, an insurance firm that has LAN's in five major cities may interconnect the LAN's to a public value-added network such as Telenet or Tymnet for office-to-office communications.

In addition to (or instead of) electronic-mail facilities, some firms are installing *voice-mail systems.* Generally, a firm's voice-mail system is linked to its ordinary phone system via one or more lines. A caller becomes aware of the system when the person he or she is calling fails to answer a phone call. After a few rings, the caller hears a recorded voice message from the person he or she is calling. The caller may in turn leave a recorded message in that persons' mailbox, to be heard by the person when he or she returns to the desk or work location.

Like electronic-mail systems, voice-mail systems are based on the electronic storage and retrieval of data. The data consists of voice messages spoken by system users. The messages (audio data) are converted to a digital form and stored on disks within the system. Most systems permit users to dial into the network to retrieve and erase messages stored in their mailboxes. Such calls can be made locally or from phones at geographically distant locations to which the voice-mail system is not linked directly. Accesses to mailboxes are controlled by unique mailbox numbers and user passwords in such environments.

Recently, integrated systems that offer both electronic-mail and voice-mail capabilities are emerging. Such systems allow users to transfer numeric data and text as well as voice messages in a single communication. When using such a system, you might send a complete document to a co-worker and annotate it with a voice message advising your co-worker to look first at a particular illustration or section of the document.

Electronic Data Interchange

Electronic data interchange, or *EDI,* is the transfer of structured business data from the computer system of one organization to the computer system of another. The data routinely recorded on purchase orders, invoices, remittance/payment notices, and other business forms is exchanged electronically in a machine-readable format between trading partners. EDI transactions go from application to application between buyers and sellers without human intervention. EDI advantages include: reduced paper handling, fewer data errors because rekeying is eliminated, reduced personnel costs, improved inventory management, and faster transaction turnaround times. Organizations are using EDI to strengthen their trading relationships with key business partners and to enhance their competitive positions in the marketplace.

***Electronic data interchange,* or *EDI,* is the transfer of structured business data from the computer system of one organization to the computer system of anoter.**

EDI and the Consumer

General Motors' two major areas of EDI use are in the material-release and ship-notice functions, informing suppliers of the number and type of car parts to send. EDI supports General Motors' just-in-time (JIT) manufacturing operations, controlling part inventories so that supplies are on hand only when needed. The firm estimates that EDI can, over time, save the consumer at least $200 on the price of an automobile.

Just as humans who want to communicate must understand a common language, so trading partners must agree on the contents and formats of business documents to be exchanged electronically. As long ago as 1978, the American National Standards Institute (ANSI) formed a committee to develop cross-industry standards for business forms and computer protocols. By 1983, it had approved an initial ANS X12 Business Data Interchange Standard. In 1986, it extended standards coverage to additional forms and capabilities. During the same time frame, ad hoc groups were working to define standard ways of representing information in electronic messages passed between partners in international trade. Eventually, a group was commissioned to merge their efforts with the ANS X12 standards. Its work led to the international standard commonly known as UN/EDIFACT (United Nations/Electronic Data Interchange for Administration, Commerce, and Transport).

Because these standards deal with the contents and formats of messages but not with communication protocols, EDI documents can be sent using a variety of communication mechanisms. Trading partners must decide whether data will be sent via public telephone networks; via one partner's private communication network; through a value-added network (VAN) provided by an organization such as General Electric Information Services (GEISCO), IBM Information Network, GTE, or McDonnell Douglas; or by a combination of these. Intercompany electronic-mail and bulk file transfer capabilities may be acquired through purchase of special software or as part of complete service offerings.

To date, EDI has been used most widely in transaction-intensive industries such as automobile manufacturing, retailing, transportation, and distribution. General Motors demanded long ago that suppliers who wanted to remain on its selected-supplier roster establish facilities to trade electronically. Kmart, J. C. Penney, Mervyn's, and Levi Strauss are among leading retailers who communicate electronically with hundreds of suppliers. Navistar International Transportation Corporation (formerly named International Harvester) claims it reduced inventory carrying costs by $167 million within 18 months after adopting EDI. Hewlett-Packard reports that its 2000 buyers are saving 10 percent of their time each week due to EDI. Digital Equipment Corporation has used EDI to trim administrative cycle times from five weeks to three days. Texas Instruments' EDI system now handles 70 percent of the company's freight bills, processes 40 percent of its purchase orders, and is used with about 500 suppliers and 300 customers. In the minds of some leading executives, EDI is no longer a novel idea; it's a necessity.

Teleconferencing

Teleconferencing is group communication achieved in spite of the fact that the source of a message and the recipients of that message are at geographically distant locations. The participants in a teleconference communicate with those presenting information through two-way audio, one-way video, or two-way video. In most cases, the viewers can see and hear the presenters but are not on camera themselves, though their questions and comments may be heard. The viewing screen may present moving pictures (full motion) or

A COMPETITIVE ADVANTAGE

Mervyn's, a large retail clothing chain headquartered in Hayward, California, is a major user of electronic data interchange, or EDI. The use of EDI was advocated by Mervyn's Information Services department in 1986 and quickly embraced by upper management as a strategic imperative. Initially, Mervyn's purchase orders were converted to EDI. They're processed using in-house-developed software that runs on an IBM 3090 mainframe. For communications with its suppliers, Mervyn's uses EDI *Express, a communication package and network services provided by General Electric Information Services Co. (GEISCO) of Rockville, Maryland. By year-end 1988, several hundred suppliers were enrolled as trading partners. Invoices, freight bills, shipping notes, and sales and inventory data are being converted to EDI using off-the-shelf software in subsequent steps.

According to Mervyn's management, the use of EDI enables the firm to reduce lead times and minimize inventory because it can order from its suppliers intermittently and in small quantities. EDI allows quick responsiveness and streamlines the logistics of getting merchandise from vendors to customers—a major focus of Mervyn's and other retailers. *(Photo courtesy Mervyn's, Dublin, California, store)*

static images (freeze-frame or slow-scan television). Color and high-resolution graphics may be offered as options. Screen sizes vary widely.

Satellite carriers and licensed vendors of communication services using satellites as relay stations are marketing teleconferencing as a means of eliminating travel time and travel expense, improving and personalizing communications, and increasing productivity. Suggested uses of teleconferencing include company stockholder, sales, and product information meetings; personnel training; continuing education programs; corporate staff communications with regional counterparts; and joint planning, consultation, and decision making in ongoing business activities.

User experiences to date indicate that teleconferencing is most likely to be successful in cases where a group of people at geographically distant locations must meet frequently—so frequently that travel is either burdensome or out of the question. The acceptance of teleconferencing by large organizations such as Sears, J. C. Penney, Chrysler, and IBM has raised its visibility and convinced other potential users that teleconferencing is a communication method worth considering.

Hewlett-Packard rented equipment to hold its first teleconference in 1981. The firm has since invested millions of dollars in equipment and satellites to produce, transmit, and receive teleconferences. Apple Computer uses one-way video to enable employees at numerous locations to see and hear its annual company stockholder meeting activities. Tandem Corporation has developed a company meeting format called "Tandem Talk" in which key executives talk about company developments and respond to employee questions. Though two-way video is most expensive, numerous organizations have established their own two-way video teleconferencing facilities.

Western Union and AT&T are among several carriers now offering teleconferencing services. Holiday Inn was the first hotel chain to offer teleconferencing. Its subsidiary, Holiday Inn Video Network (Hi-Net), held its first teleconference for TRW on June 4, 1980. Marriott, Hilton, Sheraton, and several large independent hotels offer teleconferencing at selected locations. The extent to which these offerings are used will help to determine the future of this technology. (See Figure 13-11.)

Computing Services

The data-processing/data-communication alternatives available to users include vendor offerings referred to collectively as *computing services.* Through these offerings, the computing power of large mainframes is made available to, and shared by, many of them. Personal computers and workstations often play vital roles as both remote terminals and processors. Vendors direct their attention to the tasks that users want to accomplish, as well as to the tools needed to accomplish them. (See Figure 13-12.)

Generally, the basic offering of a computer service company is the capability to handle *remote batch* work. Here, an organization submits its data for batch processing via remote batch terminals linked in a communication network with the vendor's service center. Each terminal must have a storage area, or

Figure 13-11 User organizations with occasional remote group communication needs may be able to use teleconferencing facilities at leading hotels in their areas. (Courtesy of AT&T Information Systems)

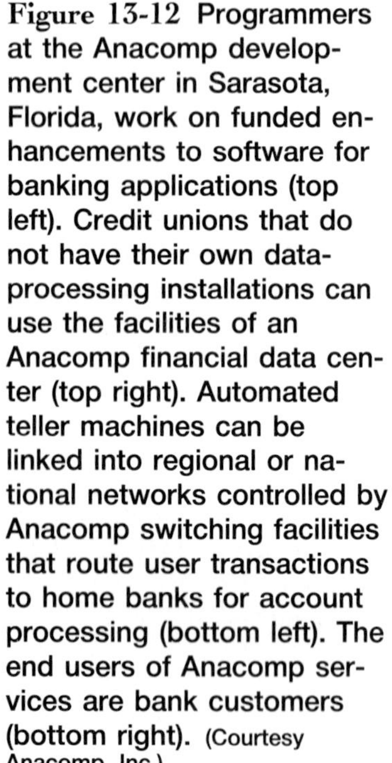

Figure 13-12 Programmers at the Anacomp development center in Sarasota, Florida, work on funded enhancements to software for banking applications (top left). Credit unions that do not have their own data-processing installations can use the facilities of an Anacomp financial data center (top right). Automated teller machines can be linked into regional or national networks controlled by Anacomp switching facilities that route user transactions to home banks for account processing (bottom left). The end users of Anacomp services are bank customers (bottom right). (Courtesy Anacomp, Inc.)

buffer, where the data can be collected prior to transmission. The buffer can be high-speed (semiconductor memory) or low-speed (magnetic-tape cassette or flexible disk). Some vendors accept batched data transported to their centers via regular mail or courier facilities.

To understand the magnitude of such processing, consider Automatic Data Processing, headquartered in Roseland, New Jersey, as an exam-

HELP

The simplest way to get work done may be to have someone else do it.

ple. This firm, commonly known as ADP, performs computerized payroll processing for more than 6000 companies and prepares paychecks for one of every 12 people in the country. On a cost-comparison basis, manual preparation of payroll, including record keeping and filing quarterly reports with the government, costs about $3 per check. A company can process its own payroll with computer help at about $1.20 per check. ADP can do it for about 42¢ per check. Computer service companies can handle applications such as payroll processing more cheaply because they have enough work to keep their computers busy full time and because the cost of software updating and maintenance can be spread over a huge customer base.

Remote job entry (*RJE*) capabilities are a step beyond remote batch. Here, a terminal can be used to initiate the execution of an application program as well as to supply input to it. In effect, the remote location is job-oriented rather than data-oriented. The user's terminal serves much like a remote system console. It may be part of an RJE station that also includes a printer and a disk unit providing local data-storage capabilities. A complete microcomputer system may function as an RJE station.

As explained in Chapter 11, users may acquire interactive problem-solving capabilities through access to an outside (vendor-supplied) time-sharing system. Because the marketing of time-sharing systems is highly competitive, many vendors offer application packages consisting of programs specialized for an industry (e.g., electric power) or a discipline (e.g., accounting). Graphic packages that run on everything from Apple IIs to Unisys multiprocessing systems and that do everything from business charts to 35-mm slides are prevalent here as elsewhere.

In addition to data-processing services, many vendors now offer consulting services. GEISCO may develop an application system under contract in far less time (and with far less impact on users' resources) than would be required if the system were developed in-house. Boeing Computer Services offers development assistance and remote computing services to the Boeing Company and to other organizations worldwide.

As another feature, many vendors are establishing large databases, or *data banks,* for commercial use. Examples of the kinds of data available are (1) lists, updated daily, of stolen or lost credit cards issued by membership firms; and (2) regularly updated reports on stocks, bonds, commodities, futures, options, gold and other precious metals, money markets, mutual funds, foreign exchange, and Treasury rates. In Chapters 1 and 12, we discussed CompuServe and other leading suppliers of remote databases on a seemingly unlimited variety of subjects.

Plummeting hardware costs, increasingly powerful micros, and stable or rising communication costs have made in-house systems formidable alternatives to remote service offerings. In response, some vendors are marketing *turnkey systems.* Both system and application software are optimized to run on a particular computer configuration and provide a complete solution to specific user needs. One of the largest users of such services is the federal government. In some cases, users are told *what* to do as well as *how* to do it. Such offerings are a recognition of the fact that users want help in solving their total business problems—not just a convenient way of electronically processing data.

CHAPTER SUMMARY

1. A data-communication system provides for the transfer of information from one location to another without altering the content or sequence of the information.

2. When analog transmission is used, the signals that constitute a message are transmitted in wave form. In digital transmission, the signals are transmitted as distinct pulses in much the same way that data travels in the computer.

3. Modems are needed to convert digital data in pulse form to wave form prior to analog transmission, and to reconvert the data to pulse form at its destination.

4. Sending and receiving units are kept in step during the communication process through either start/stop synchronization or synchronous transmission facilities.

5. When a user places a call to send voice or data traffic over a switched, or dial-up, line, a connection to the call destination is established through one or more public exchanges, or switching facilities.

6. A user organization with heavy message volume may acquire leased or private lines and connect them through a PBX or CBX for better-quality transmission and flexibility.

7. Common carriers are organizations authorized by the Federal Communications Commission (FCC) and/or state public utilities commissions (PUC's) to offer communication services. MCI Telecommunications and U.S Sprint are prominent specialized common carriers. GTE's Telenet and McDonnell Douglas Corp.'s Tymnet are examples of value-added networks.

8. Satellite carriers operate communication satellites that serve as relay stations for microwave signals. Each satellite can "see" and be seen from about one-third of the earth.

9. AT&T gained the right to participate in free enterprise as well as regulated communication activities through implementation of a divestiture plan. Seven regional holding companies were established. Its 22 Bell operating companies were grouped within the holding companies to handle local telephone operations and pursue other business opportunities.

10. Distributed processing is characterized by a dispersion of the processing power, or intelligence, within an EDP system among geographically separated locations. In a cooperative-processing environment, application programs at two or more locations work together to accomplish a specific task.

11. Word processing is the manipulation of character data to form words, sentences, paragraphs, memos, letters, and reports. Desktop publishing is the ability to manipulate graphics as well as text with computer help, and to combine text and graphics to create high-quality documents.

12. Studies show that the most intensive and time-critical communications in business today take place at the workgroup level. Electronic-mail and voice-mail systems are being installed in organizations to meet workgroup and other users' communication needs.

13. Business trading partners are using electronic data interchange to transfer data usually recorded on purchase orders, invoices, remittance/payment notices, and other business forms from the computer system of one of the partners to the computer system of the other.

14. Teleconferencing provides for group communications between persons at geographically distant locations. Satellite carriers, vendors of services using satellites, and large hotel chains are marketing teleconferencing as a means of eliminating travel time and expense, improving and personalizing communications, and increasing productivity.

15. Computer service companies offer remote batch, remote job entry, time sharing, application packages, consulting services, access to data banks, and turnkey systems—all tailored to user needs.

DISCUSSION QUESTIONS

1. Show, by example, the difference between data processing and data communication.

2. List and explain the basic elements of a data-communication system, giving the primary functions of each.

3. List three sets of characteristics of data transmission from which a user organization must select options to meet its needs.

4. Assume you are the president of a tri-state trucking firm, specializing in long hauls of perishable goods. What telecommunication needs might your firm have and how might they be met?

5. What is the role of the FCC in telecommunications?

6. (a) Why and how did the breakup of AT&T occur?
   (b) Discuss how it is affecting users of computers and communication facilities.

7. Suggest advantages and disadvantages of distributed processing from the point of view of a large brokerage firm such as Dean Witter or E. F. Hutton.

8. Show how word processing and data processing are alike, and how they differ.

9. Distinguish between word processing and desktop publishing.

10. Discuss electronic mail systems. In doing so, point out the capabilities they have that are not available with conventional mail or telephone services.

11. In what ways might the use of electronic data interchange by Levi Strauss, J. C. Penney, or Mervyn's benefit you as a consumer?

12. Describe user situations where teleconferencing may be appropriate.

13. Show how a savings and loan, real-estate agency, or community college might take advantage of remote computing services.

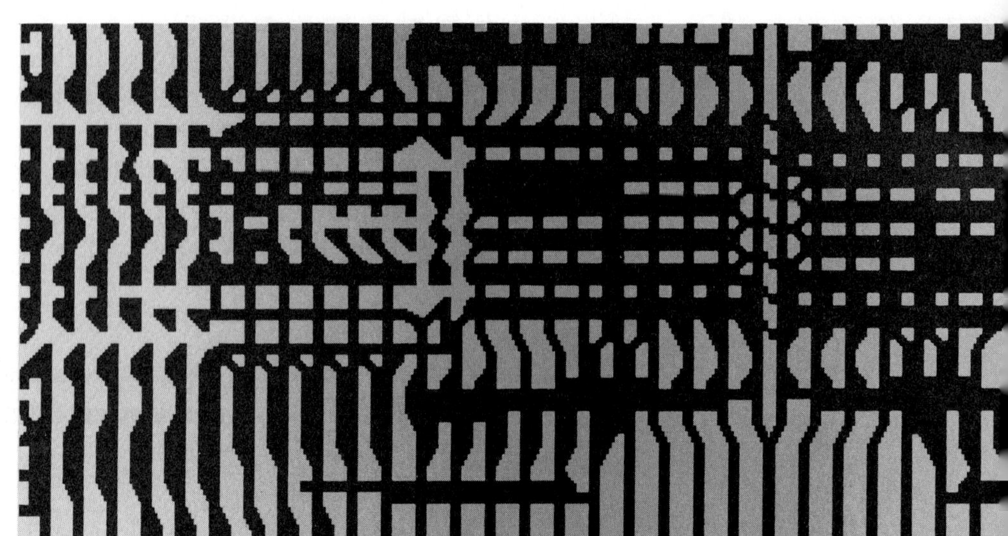

14 Computing Issues and Impacts

IN THIS CHAPTER

Computing and Organizations
Computing and Jobs
Telecommuting
Robotic Systems
Artificial Intelligence
Individualism and the Right of Privacy
Computer Crime
Organizational Protection Mechanisms
Legal Protection Mechanisms
Social Dependency and Vulnerability
Environmental Protection Mechanisms
A Perspective

Was our calendar year 1984, bounded by January 1 and December 31, *the* 1984 described by George Orwell in his now-famous novel *1984*? Has Orwell's vision of totalitarianism based on the control of access to information come to pass? Perhaps not. But 1984 was the year when party goers, cabdrivers, and church secretaries joined your discussions of personal computers by telling you about their personal computers and what they're doing with them. Few if any persons among us would dispute the fact that computers affect each and every one of us daily. Few if any would debate the claim that the Computer Age is here.

Since computers are so powerful and so prevalent, it's appropriate for us to step back a moment as we study them. What effects are these machines having on organizations, and on us as members of those organizations? On society, and on us as members of society? On each of us as individuals? What do those effects imply and what, if anything, should we be doing about them? In the years ahead, you can expect to face such questions, and they will not be easy to answer. The purpose of this chapter is to help you think about computers from several perspectives. The need to do so is increasingly urgent.

In this chapter we look first at the impact of computing on organizations. Then we look more closely at the impact of mechanization, automation, and computers on jobs, and we discuss job attitudes. Both current and potential applications of two rapidly emerging technologies—robotic systems and artificial intelligence—are described.

Much has been said about the computer's ability to destroy our individualism and to invade our privacy, so we examine the dangers and safeguards in these

areas. The threats of computer crime and other natural and man-made disasters are with us daily. We look at the extent of our exposure to such threats and suggest some security mechanisms. We also look at how legal protection mechanisms such as copyrights and patents apply.

When you have completed this chapter, you will not know all there is to know about the use of computers in our society. New technologies and new uses are evolving daily. You will have acquired a background that positions you to deal with the challenges and opportunities computers provide.

Computing and Organizations

Computers are impacting organizations, first and foremost, because computers are used by organizations. In the 1960s and 1970s, the typical business computer was a large mainframe, enclosed in a special environment-controlled room at a central site. Data was transported to that site; processing was done there; and a centralized DP group did whatever needed to be done computerwise. Some persons argue that the centralized DP function simply mirrored the corporate structure of user organizations of the time. Other persons suggest that the centralized nature of these computing systems not only supported but also fostered large, centralized organizations.

Today, that picture has changed. To be sure, there are still large mainframes and there are still large organizations. There are many more small computer systems, however. They are appearing in organizations of all types and sizes—from elementary schools to research labs; from "mom and pop" grocery stores to Fortune 500 companies. As we've noted throughout this book, computing power is migrating from mainframe-based data centers to manufacturing floors, offices, and briefcases. "Keeping up with the Joneses" doesn't mean having faster, bigger (or smaller), more expensive (or less costly) computers than other organizations in the same industry segment, sales territory, or service area. It does mean having the computing tools needed to be competitive and successful.

An obvious impact of computing on organizations is the direct economic impact. Computers cost money; computer programs cost money; computer talent is expensive; and so on. Conversely, computers save money—the carrying costs of inventory are lower because stock levels better match demands; customer payments are received sooner because bills are generated and mailed sooner; fewer employees are needed in the payroll department because the computer can do many of the routine, repetitive tasks of payroll preparation; and so on.

Computers also have an indirect economic impact on organizations. For example, they can compute and display trends in customer buying habits. A firm that anticipates and responds to customer wants in a timely fashion is positioned to outsell competitors who have not had access to trend data. As another example, a computer can produce reports showing actual schedules and costs of product development versus planned schedules and costs. On the basis of these reports, the responsible managers can initiate corrective action immediately instead of discovering too late that schedule and cost overruns have occurred.

Computers may also impact organizational structure and individual behavior. The management and control of an organization may be centralized. Alternatively, a geographically or functionally diverse organization may be managed as several independent business units. Each unit can be supported by computing systems that meet its particular needs. The units can stand alone, just as their systems can stand alone, for some purposes. The units can interact or communicate, just as their systems can communicate, when it's appropriate to do so. There is no conclusive empirical proof that computers cause centralization or decentralization; we can see that computers facilitate either. They also support a management style in which policies and directives are set at a corporate level, but authority and accountability for day-to-day operations rest with lower-level line managers.

If knowledge is power, and if information is a source of knowledge, then we can assume that information is also a source of power. The individual or department that controls an organization's computing systems—or even one of its several computing systems—controls at the very least a potential source of power. The individual or department determines not only its own use of the organization's information resource, but also who else has access to the information and with what priority. The individual may be the president of the organization, the head of MIS, or whatever. The department may be a central DP department, an information system staff, or one of several user divisions or departments.

If knowledge is power, and if information is a source of knowledge, then we can assume that information is also a source of power.

An individual or department with information power may view the proposed acquisition of 15, 100, or even 1000 microcomputer systems as a threat to that power. Persons knowledgeable in the computing field are quick to advise cooperation rather than resistance to such a proposal. In most organizations, the backlog of unmet user requirements is large. Information system staffs commonly point to three years' worth of application development work ahead of them. Multiple approaches to such backlogs are warranted.

Over time, many organizations have established *information centers.* The centers are in-house departments staffed with a few skilled information system personnel, chartered to support and promote end-user computing. In practice, they've had mixed reviews. Usually, information center personnel work with users to help them understand what their information requirements are and how the requirements can be satisfied. A few key software packages and/or complete systems are installed at the center for demonstration, hands-on experience, and training purposes. Product information, application design assistance, and timely responses to users' questions are provided.

Some organizations have also established the role of *CIO,* or *chief information officer.* The CIO is charged with knowing information needs throughout the company and working to insure the needs are satisfied.

Computing and Jobs

The *mechanization* of work is not new. It's been going on for centuries. Stated simply, it's the use of a machine or group of machines to carry out a process under the direction of a human operator. *Automation* is not new either. It's the performance of a specific combination of actions by a machine or group of machines "automatically"—without the aid of a human operator. Most of us tend to think of automation as something that's happening in manufacturing plants and warehouses, but it's not limited to that. The processing of our tax returns, of the checks we write, and of the letters we send is highly automated. These are but a few of the many ongoing examples of office automation.

In 1940, white-collar workers, blue-collar workers, and service-industry workers (narrowly defined to include just those workers who provide services primarily to consumers) constituted 31, 57, and 12 percent, respectively, of the U.S. labor force. Forty years later, they constituted 54, 34, and 12 percent. (See Figure 14-1.) The impressive growth in white-collar workers occurred primarily in two U.S. Bureau of Labor groupings: (1) professional, scientific, and technical workers, and (2) managerial and administrative workers.

Consider General Electric Company as an example. The firm manufactures thousands of different items, from night lights to huge turbine engines. Yet not more than 40 percent of its employees are directly engaged in production; the rest work in in-house producer services, ranging from planning to personnel to marketing.

Most of us tend to think of automation as something that's happening in manufacturing plants and warehouses, but it's not limited to that.

In a major way, computers have facilitated this redistribution of labor. More often than not, a machine or group of machines not under the direction of a human operator is under the direction of a computer. In many cases, the machine is a computer. Although computers have not *caused* mechanization or automation, they have increased the rate at which firms are automating and the extent of that automation.

In 1850, farmers made up 64 percent of the U.S. labor force. Today

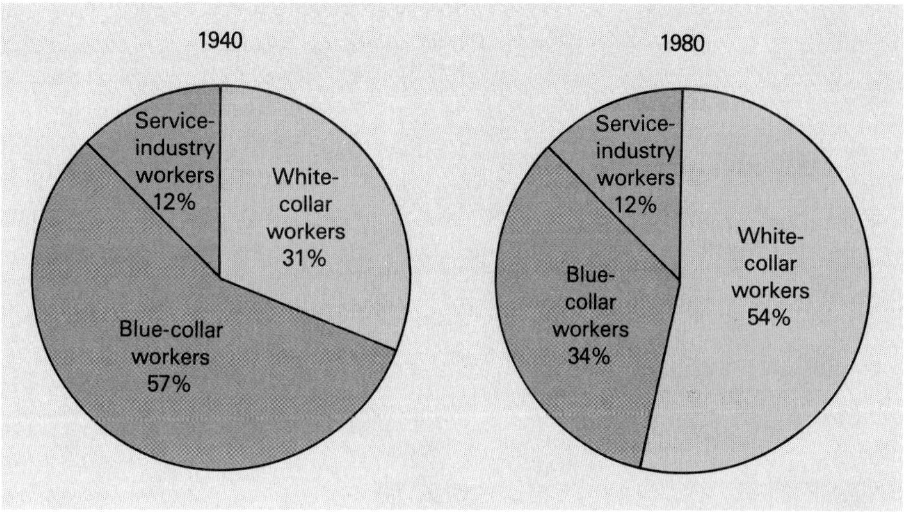

Figure 14-1 The ever-increasing use of automation has led to a significant redistribution of labor within the U.S. labor force. By 1980, more than half of U.S. workers were primarily engaged in white-collar, information-related activities.

$ $ $

In the 1980–90 time frame, the capital investment for the average information (white-collar) worker equaled that for the average factory worker on the assembly line. Comparable statistics in the 1940–50 time frame showed only $2000 invested per information worker and $25,000 invested per factory worker—a 1.0 to 12.5 ratio.

only 3.1 percent of American workers are engaged in agriculture. Some persons are concerned that computers may cause a shift in the American workplace as fundamental as our move from an agricultural to an industrial economy. If there are fewer jobs, what happens in a society in which a job not only defines a person (he's a dentist, she's a housewife . . .) but also provides much of the person's meaning in life? Where is the "social cement," or togetherness, that work has long provided?

In response to such concerns, other experts point out that the traditional work ethic is changing. Many Americans do not need a job classification to have an identity. "Success" is not measured in terms of the size of one's annual income or one's position on the corporate ladder. For the most part, American workers have had a positive attitude toward technological advancements; they view such advancements as making jobs less tedious and easier, rather than as threats to their livelihood. Data-entry operators in industries such as banking may feel under more time pressure and more closely supervised because their rates of keystroking can be monitored by computers and reported to management. Financial analysts who like to work with numbers may get bored if the computer does all the "tough stuff." Obviously, computers have had a more direct effect on lower-level jobs than on higher ones. However, there is no conclusive research showing that this effect has led to a more negative attitude on the part of workers in those lower-level jobs. Here, as elsewhere, individuals react differently.

For the most part, American workers have had a positive attitude toward technological advancements; . . .

In any case, persons studying this problem point out that the time for contemplating whether or not computers should be allowed to enter the workplace has long since passed. We've grown too accustomed to the benefits of having them there—more goods to choose from, lower prices than would be possible otherwise, and so on. Furthermore, as we've

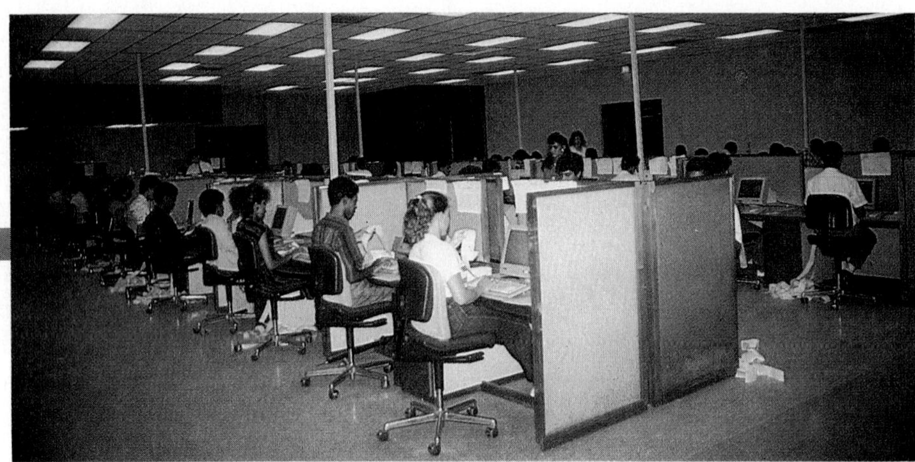

ENTIRE OFFICES MAY TELECOMMUTE

Initially, telecommuting meant allowing a few employees to work out of their homes or neighborhood work centers. Today, entire departments may "set up shop" thousands of miles from their home offices. One firm with such departments is AMR/Caribbean Data Services, a subsidiary of American Airlines.

In 1986, AMR/Caribbean moved its data-entry function from Tulsa, Oklahoma, to two offshore facilities it owns in the Caribbean. An average of 225,000 used American Airlines tickets are gathered in New York and flown to its Barbados facility daily. About 400 workers key data from the tickets into a computer. Within 24 hours, the keyed data is transmitted to Tulsa, where it's used to reconcile accounts.

At AMR/Caribbean's second facility, in the Dominican Republic, 650 employees process some used tickets plus insurance claims, market surveys, canceled checks, and the like for about 25 corporations that have contracted with AMR/Caribbean for data-entry services. Most of the companies receive machine-readable versions of their data, on magnetic tapes, within four days. The data is then used by the corporations in subsequent business data processing. *(Photo courtesy AMR Information Services)*

seen throughout this book, computers are creating new jobs even as they're taking over old ones. They are even creating new industries—semiconductors, software publishing, home information, and space exploration, to name a few. Our approach, then, should be to understand just what computers can and can't do, and to capitalize on this knowledge. There are no easy, wand-waving solutions to fill the vacuum created when vast numbers of jobs for which the current labor force has been trained disappear. Perhaps a computer can help these workers decide what other jobs (or nonjob activities) they'd like to do. Perhaps it can retrain them. By looking directly at the challenges presented in this Computer Age, we can better equip ourselves, our organizations, and our society to deal with them.

TELECOMMUTING

If you've biked, driven, or ridden in an overcrowded bus, subway, or commuter train morning and night, five days a week during rush hours, chances are you've thought: "There's *got* to be a better way." As long ago as 1970, in his book *The Third Wave,* writer Alvin Toffler prophesied there would be. Envisioning once-busy factories and office towers standing half empty, Toffler wrote of *electronic cottages*—our homes, the workplaces of a radically changed society.

Today, millions of commuters struggle daily to survive rush hours. However, there are thousands of others for whom telecommuting is a viable option. The term *telecommuting* means working at home or in a neighborhood work center, using a microcomputer or a terminal that is linked electronically or via diskettes transported physically to an employer's host computing facility. In most instances, electronic linkages are achieved via low-cost modems and ordinary telephone lines. (See Figure 14-2.)

An employee who works at home saves on fuel and other transportation costs and on traveling time. Home workers also tend to spend less on clothing and child care. Other advantages cited by telecommuters are: less office-related stress; the ability to work at one's own pace; and the opportunity to stop work when children or other family members need attention and then resume work after they are in bed or busy with their own studies.

From an employer's point of view, when employees are telecommuting, savings on office and parking space are likely. More importantly, research studies have shown that worker productivity increases of from 20 to 40 percent are typical. Telecommuters tend to spend more time working. Since there are likely to be fewer interruptions, the work day can be more intensive as well. Telecommuters can interact with their employer's host computing system during off-hours. They experience shorter system response times. The over-all load on the host system is better distributed—a potential benefit to all of the firm's employees.

No one knows for sure how many U.S. workers are telecommuting. Industry estimates of the num-

Figure 14-2 Telecommuters who are free to select their own dress codes, work hours, and work surroundings tend to be highly productive and have high levels of job satisfaction. (Courtesy Apple Computer, Inc.)

ber of full- or part-time corporate telecommuters range from 1 to 5 million. As many as 15 million corporate employees may be working out of their homes or work centers by the mid-1990s.

Telecommuting seems to be most suitable for people who do "information work." Employees whose jobs involve individualized, creative thinking or whose jobs are "in the machine" are likely candidates. So are those who have well-defined tasks needing little or no interaction with others and little or no supervision. People who rely on personal computers or workstations as integral parts of their jobs tend to be less dependent on memos, files, and other hard-copy materials scattered throughout their offices.

J. C. Penney spent the early 1980s testing the concept of telecommuting out of its Milwaukee telemarketing center. Today, about 50 home-based telemarketing telecommuters (out of a Milwaukee work force of 800) equipped with company-owned computers take incoming calls on catalog orders. The telecommuting approach has helped the giant retailer with both employee recruitment and employee retention. It intends to have from 25 to 50 employees from each of its 15 telemarketing centers working out of their homes in the near future.

Employees at Pacific Bell in Los Angeles began working at home during the 1984 Olympics. Telecommuting seemed like a viable way to avoid otherwise inevitable traffic problems. In 1985, the company began a formal work-at-home program for some 100 engineers, analysts, public relations personnel, and others at management levels. Today, about 600 employees work at home from one to four days a week and about 400 more work at home roughly once a month.

Setting up the facilities for telecommuting is rarely a technical challenge today. A company can expect to spend from $4000 to $6000 to equip a telecommuter with the necessary furniture, computer system, and phone lines. Questions of an employee's right of privacy in his or her home, the security of an employer's confidential resources, and how to manage people who telecommute are more difficult to deal with. Labor unions have expressed concerns that work-at-home programs may invite worker exploitation and curtail union organizing. Some experts warn that telecommuters are less likely to receive promotions than their office-based counterparts.

Nonetheless, employees who are telecommuting tend to be strong advocates of telecommuting. It may evolve as a transitional work style, used by employees periodically to fulfill family obligations or to enhance their quality of life. Since increased productivity on the part of employees may be reflected in lower product and service costs, and less commuter traffic may mean fewer traffic snarls and less pollution, all of us may benefit.

ROBOTIC SYSTEMS

According to the Robot Institute of America (a Michigan-based association of suppliers and users of robotic equipment), a *robot* is "a reprogrammable multifunctional manipulator designed to move materials, parts, tools, or specialized devices through variable programmed motions for the performance of a variety of tasks." Stated simply, a robot is a general-purpose programmable machine that can do any of several tasks under stored-program control.

Stated simply, a robot is a general-purpose programmable machine that can do any of several tasks under stored-program control.

The early 1980s are sometimes referred to as "the heyday of the robotics industry." At that time, industrial robotic systems seemed to be undergoing a virtual population explosion. Their numbers increased from about 200 in 1970, to 3500 in 1980, to 8000 in 1983. The leading users of robotic systems were the large automotive manufacturers. (See Figure 14-3.) Firms in the steel, aerospace, and equipment-manufacturing industries also installed them. Expected benefits such as high product quality, product uniformity, and increased production efficiencies were being realized. Robotic industry revenues peaked in 1985 at $595 million.

What happened? The slowdown in the automotive industry directly impacted the robotic industry. General Motors alone canceled millions of dollars of orders as part of its cost-cutting measures. Robotic sales were also hurt by the downturn in the semiconductor industry, where specialized clean-room robots were being used to improve manufacturing yields. Though robotic systems offered significant advantages, significant challenges confronted users who wanted to install them—providing high capital outlay, modifying the workplace to make room for them, figuring out how to integrate the robotic systems with existing equipment, and so on.

Today, there's a sense of cautious optimism among robotic system manufacturers. The "old guard"

Figure 14-3 Chrysler Corporations' Robogate and other robotic systems lock the two body sides and the underbody assembly of a car into position and weld them into a car body (left). Other large industrial robots apply uniform base coats to cars with high transfer efficiency and minimal waste (right). (Courtesy Chrysler Corporation)

robot makers such as GMF Robotics (Auburn Hills, Michigan), ABB Robotics (New Berlin, Wisconsin), and Cincinnati Milacron (Cincinnati, Ohio) continue to make large industrial robots for heavy manufacturing. Many of these systems look like giant cranes; cables run along their mechanical arms to computers that transmit instructions as pulses to their clamps and claws. These firms and newer, aggressive firms such as Adept Technology (San Jose, California) and Intelledex (Corvallis, Oregon) are also producing lighter-weight machines designed for pick-and-place jobs—assembling small parts from a position above the workplace.

Assembly applications fall into two broad categories: electronic assembly, or populating printed circuit boards; and mechanical assembly, or putting together structural or moving parts. (See Figure 14-4.) To populate printed circuit boards, a robot may have to handle up to 400 different components. It may have to build hundreds of different board configurations, in small lot sizes. Because the robotic system can be reprogrammed, it has the flexibility needed. Similar systems may be used by other companies to assemble

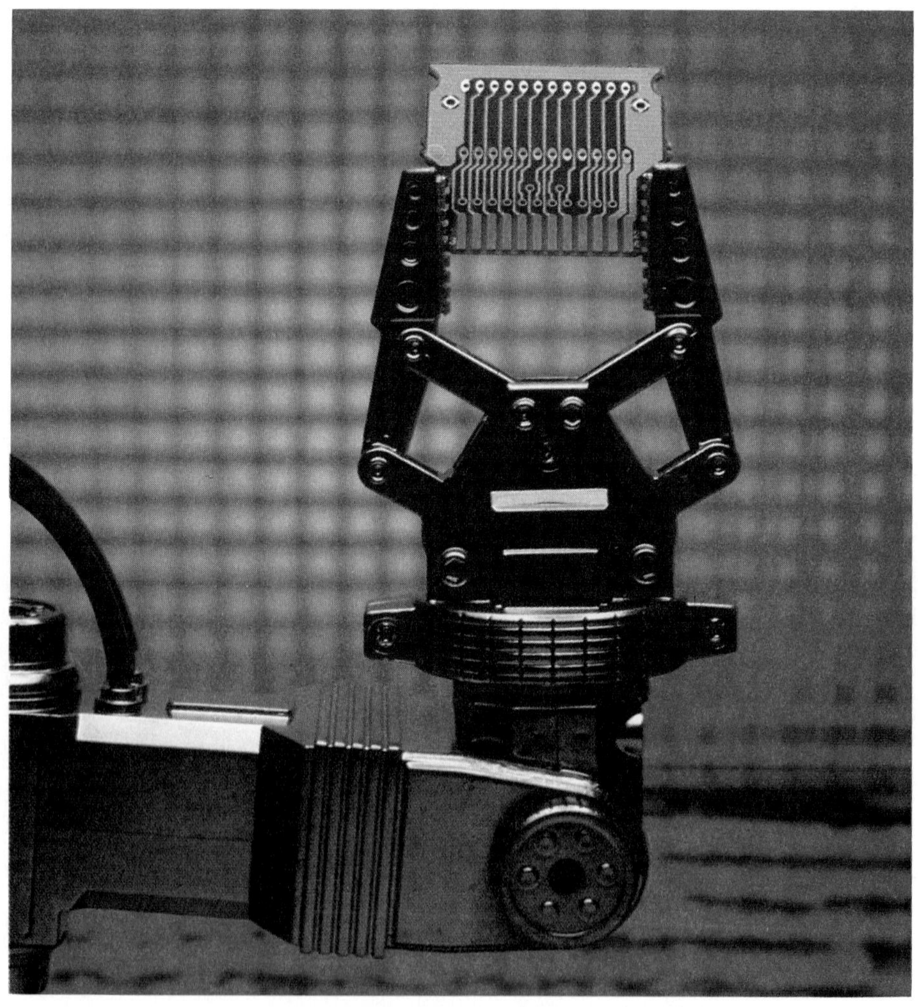

Figure 14-4 Robotic systems work with consistent precision (say, ±.00032 inch) to build high-quality products for our use. (Courtesy Antonio Rosario/The Image Bank)

"The choice that confronts American industry is to automate, emigrate, or evaporate."

James Baker, Executive Vice President, General Electric Company, (*U.S. News & World Report,* January 16, 1984)

wristwatches, music boxes, small appliances, electric motors, computers, and even parts of automobiles.

The most advanced robotic systems have feedback mechanisms—touch sensors and optical scanners that enable them to adapt to changing conditions. For example, if a parts-feeder tray is empty, a robotic system may bypass it and go on to the next tray. If a part is mispositioned, the system may jiggle it into place. Some systems perform quality inspections, checking that all parts are present and positioned properly. Defective work is discarded. A robotic system works untiringly, first, second, and third shifts, without complaining. It can work near blast furnaces, radioactive materials, or noxious fumes. Robotics enthusiasts argue that robotic systems improve the quality of worklife by reducing the number of dull, dirty, and dangerous tasks that must be performed by humans.

Moreover, since the systems are computer-based, they can generate data for management reports and for diagnostic purposes. Indeed, *before* we automate, we should recognize that manufacturing information automation is as vital as equipment automation. If we automate a machine tool, but we don't have the right marketing or engineering information about what the machine tool should be making, we may be automating the production of scrap.

Without doubt, some workers—autoworkers in spot welding and body painting, for example—feel that robotic systems have taken away their jobs. Many of these workers have been retrained, but the total number of employees needed within their companies is likely to be lower than it would be without the robotic systems. Nevertheless, we should realize that industries that are unable to modernize, or companies that are unable to meet or exceed the productivity levels of their competitors, may fail entirely. In that event, there would be no jobs at all.

Artificial Intelligence

As humans, we perceive the world around us. Through our senses, we distinguish or "make sense" of the barrage of signals confronting us. We set goals and strive to attain them. We fail, and we learn from our failures. We make and break habits. We build up a background of experiences. We view old and new things in light of those experiences. We adapt to our surroundings. In doing so, we communicate with one another in our natural language (English, French, Spanish, or whatever). We both produce and understand utterances in that language. We reason. We draw conclusions on the basis of our findings.

These capabilities are said to make us different from other creatures. We don't understand very well *how* we think, but we know we *do* think. Since the 1950s, a few leading artificial intelligence (AI) researchers have been trying to develop computers that do likewise.

Early successes—machines that could beat humans at checkers, prove mathematical theorems, and make logical deductions—led to optimistic predictions of accomplishments to come. Leading corporations set up AI labs, only to back off in the 1960s when the task of building machines that could think proved to be more difficult than many had anticipated.

Let's first look at why we might want machines to think. Your first

GATE SCHEDULING BY EXPERTS

Throughout the highly competitive airline industry, delayed flights and missing luggage translate into unhappy travelers, bad publicity, and lost revenues to responsible carriers. To reduce or eliminate such annoyances, several carriers are applying expert systems. Over a 10-month period, for example, Texas Instruments engineers met with members of United Airlines' gate operation team to create the knowledge base for an expert system called GADS (Gate Assignment Display System). The system takes many factors into account in scheduling gate assignments: arriving and departing flights; unoccupied gates; gates that can only accommodate certain planes; inoperative equipment on certain planes or at certain gates; weather conditions; and so on. The system has been operational at both Stapleton Airport in Denver and O'Hare Airport in Chicago since July 1987. At Houston Intercontinental Airport, System One Gatekeeper, a similar expert system developed by Ascent Technology, is helping Texas Air subsidiary Continental Airlines to avoid thousands of instances of misconnected passengers and luggage. By connecting the expert systems to airports' flight-display systems, the airlines can inform their own personnel and passengers of gate changes as they occur. *(Photo courtesy Ascent Technology)*

reaction may be that we don't. Letting computers do manual labor for us is one thing. Letting them do our thinking for us is another. The following are positive examples of machine-thinking applications.

- *Expert systems:* Knowledge-based systems, in which the computer sorts through masses of data (knowledge) obtained from one or more experts in a particular field to detect patterns; determines which inference (if-then) rules apply on the basis of its findings; applies them to generate new data and identify new patterns; and so on—thereby bringing "intelligence" to bear on fuzzy, nonnumerical problems. In medicine, for example, Caduceus helps doctors at the University of Pittsburgh diagnose any of a wide variety of adult illnesses. In mining, SRI International's Prospector helps locate mineral deposits. At Schlumberger Ltd., Dipmeter Advisor interprets down-hole data collected from an oil-drilling site and advises whether to continue drilling or write off the operation as a dry hole. At Digital Equipment Corporation, XCon configures most computer systems. Expert systems that design circuit chips, diagnose problems in airplanes and automobiles, screen credit authorization requests, give financial advice, and determine how fabric designs can be woven are benefiting many in our society.

- *Vision systems:* The "eyes" of straightforward product-inspection systems and of robotic systems, enabling them to digitize images, compare the images to stored patterns, and determine whether they are "seeing" what they're supposed to see. Some can recognize silhouettes. Others can determine surface quality—say, of sheet metal or of composite body panes used in vehicles. Still others can distinguish among three-dimensional objects. The most advanced vision systems can provide complete graphic representations of objects on a display screen, even when not all parts of the objects are within the observing machine's view.
- *Natural-language query systems:* Programs that allow English-speaking people to use ordinary English (not just an English-like query language) to submit questions about data stored in a database. For example, Natural Language (mentioned in Chapter 10), Artificial Intelligence Corporation's Intellect, and Microrim's Clout can accept and respond to typed questions such as "How many employees are paid weekly?" and "Who works in Accounting?" Today, programs that interface directly with users and are marketed internationally must support several human (natural) languages. The natural language of French-speaking Canadians, for example, differs significantly from the natural language of Italians.
- *Continuous speech recognition:* Programs that accept and understand ordinary conversational speech unpunctuated by deliberate silences, such as are required by conventional voice-input units. (For review, see Chapter 3.) With truly continuous speech recognition, widespread direct use of computers by busy executives, computer-based training (CBT) on almost any subject, and verbal programming by many of us may become realities.

AI computers that play games continue to be popular. These expert systems have progressed from checkers to backgammon and chess. (See Figure 14-5.) A computerized backgammon program developed by Hans Berliner, a computer scientist at Carnegie-Mellon, has been beating human backgammon grand masters since 1979. A $100,000 Fredkin Foundation grant was earmarked by Edward Fredkin of MIT in 1980 to go to the first person designing an unbeatable chess program. In September 1988, a chess-playing machine called Hitech—the result of a student project at Carnegie-Mellon

HANDroid

Figure 14-5 AI-based chess-playing machines that take on human opponents do not suffer from distractions such as hunger, fatigue, or lack of interest. Some rank in the top 0.5 percent of all chess players. (Courtesy Dan McCoy/Rainbow)

University (CMU) in Pittsburgh—beat a grand master chess player (the highest rank in the chess world). Today, Hitech is said to defeat players with a ranking of expert or below 100 percent of the time and to defeat players ranked within the top 50 about 12 percent of the time.

Why, you might ask, are the best minds at Duke, Northwestern, Bell Labs, and elsewhere trying to develop unbeatable chess programs? Well, $100,000 sounds good, but they were trying before the $100,000 was offered. In attempting to teach computers to think, these researchers are understanding more about how we think. When selecting a chess move, for example, a human player does not identify every possible move and then plow through those moves in a brute-force trial-and-error fashion until he or she finds one that's acceptable. Rather, most chess players try to control the center of the board—an elementary rule of thumb—and focus their attention accordingly. When AI designers began taking advantage of similar, seemingly acquired learning (that is, began using *heuristics*), they started to achieve success in game playing and theorem proving. Some AI researchers will tell you that mimicking the way an expert thinks about a topic is easy; figuring out how or why a child reacts to certain stimuli is something else.

The goal of AI researchers is not to develop machines that *think* for us, but rather machines that *help* us. Some of these AI machines are doing or will do work formerly done by humans. However, many researchers caution that people in business may again be expecting too much too soon. Furthermore, attention must be directed to the potential impact of AI technology. What work can justly be done by machines? What work should be done by people? If 900 persons are doing a particular kind of job, and 100 other persons who also can do the job are looking for work,

AI HELPS THE HANDICAPPED

Computer research in artificial intelligence (AI) is leading to systems that can be used effectively by persons who are handicapped. For example, a telesensory system in which a probe scans text on a display screen and converts the text to braille can be used as an input/output unit on a computer system; blind persons can use the system to do work at their jobs or to obtain information for personal use that might not be available to them otherwise. Workstations that allow handicapped users to drive computer keyboards by means of voice commands have been developed. Similar capabilities are the basis for voice-driven telephone keypads. Here, as in many instances, computers and AI research are not taking away jobs. They're helping people to do jobs and to lead busy, useful lives. *(Photo courtesy Dan McCoy/Rainbow)*

should the work be shared among them? Or should the pay? Should overtime be eliminated? Suppose a 4-day workweek, or even a 3-day one, becomes a widespread reality! The technical questions to be resolved are perhaps not the most difficult ones.

The goal of AI (artificial intelligence) researchers is not to develop machines that *think* for us, but rather machines that *help* us.

Individualism and the Right of Privacy

Computers work primarily with numbers. The numbers are data. Much of the data is about us. When we're at school, the computer keeps records of courses taken, grades obtained, fees due, and so forth. When we've got a job, the computer keeps records of rate of pay, taxes withheld, vacation, and lots more. The computer must track separately each person's data. (Joe's travel expense check mustn't go to Mary.) That means each person's data must be identifiable. Names won't do as identifiers; there may be several J. P. Halls. An alternative is to make sure that each person the computer keeps data on is assigned a unique number.

Following this line of reasoning, as computer use spread, many people began to worry about *depersonalization:* Soon we would no longer need to have names; we would be known by numbers.

That hasn't happened. We *do* have student numbers, employee numbers, credit-card numbers, trip numbers, course numbers, even numbers for numbers. We *do* get mad when the computer sends us the same bill three months in a row, even after it's been paid (there's been a program or data mixup.) We *do* become frustrated when a customer service representative fails to address our problem and instead (1) says that a computer is at fault, or (2) challenges us to prove the computer is wrong before action will be initiated. On the other hand, computers *can* deal with letters as well as numbers. Our bills still are addressed to us by name. Our paychecks are made out to us by name. We give our names when applying for jobs. We sign our names on the checks we write.

As employees of a computer-using firm understand more how to communicate with computers and with the information system staff, they are less prone to hide behind them. As computer hardware and data-communication costs come down, workstations, personal computers, and terminals seem to be everywhere. Sometimes we're expected to interact with them to do business. We may get the computer's attention more quickly than we can get that of a teller or salesclerk. On the other hand, we may feel that a computer-generated telephone response is too impersonal. We all bear the responsibility to help determine where person-to-person communication is needed, and where a computer interface is acceptable.

We all bear the responsibility to help determine where person-to-person communication is needed, and where a computer interface is acceptable.

Another concern related to the computer's use of numbers as identifiers is the fear that some day all the data about each of us may be related by a unique universal identifier. Our Social Security numbers—which by definition must be unique, with or without computers—are pointed to as likely candidates. The real concern here is our individual right of privacy and whether or not that right is endangered because of computers.

As used here, the term *privacy* refers to the rights of each individual regarding the collection, processing, storage, release, and use of data concerning the individual. In this context, privacy is therefore a social and legal issue. It involves questions such as how and what data will be collected, how and by whom it will be used, and how and by whom it can be changed. Such questions are not new. The issue of how much control individuals should have over data about themselves is not new. It is rooted in a basic dilemma of social organization: Individuals rightly desire to withhold certain personal information from others, yet numerous public and private organizations need (or think they need) certain personal information to carry out their agreed-to social or business responsibilities.

The first large, centralized data banks were started by the federal government. As long ago as 1980, it had about 7000 data banks, containing an average of 18 files for every American. The Internal Revenue Service, Social Security Administration, Veterans Administration, Secret Service, FBI, Department of Labor, Department of Justice, Department of Transportation, Department of Housing and Urban Development, and Department of Health and Human Services are among groups using them. State and local governments maintain data banks for a variety of uses also. These include tax collection, welfare programs, motor vehicle registration, law enforcement, and criminal justice. Both the number and the size of government-controlled data banks are still growing. (See Figure 14-6.)

Private business has not lagged far behind government. To see this, we need only discuss a couple of examples.

Today, the personal data collected by private organizations is manipulated within a vast information network. At the switchboard of this network are a few nationwide credit bureaus. Each credit bureau relies primarily on credit-card companies, financial institutions, department stores, and local governments for data. For example, TRW's Information Services Division in Orange, California, the leading supplier of credit reports, has files on about 138 million Americans. It processes about 400,000 inquiries daily from merchants and other credit bureaus. With the aid of high-speed data-communication facilities and computers, these "information brokers" provide information to financial institutions, department stores, employers, landlords, lawyers, academic researchers, mailing-list companies, insurance companies, government

ENTER
HERE

Figure 14-6 State-owned or state-authorized computer systems collect and maintain personal data about hundreds of thousands of licensed drivers and motor vehicle registrants. These expanding databases are used for many purposes. (Courtesy Mark McKenna)

agencies, credit-card companies, and other credit bureaus.

Suppose you live in Omaha, Nebraska. Concerned because of increasing family responsibilities, you decide to apply for life insurance. You are doing business, not with one company in Omaha, but with the whole life insurance industry. About 700 life insurance companies—accounting for more than 90 percent of the life insurance coverage in the United States—exchange personal medical information via a computerized data bank in Boston called the *Medical Information Bureau.* This bureau holds the health histories of 11 million individuals.

Fortunately, out of concern comes action—albeit sometimes slowly. The first federal legislation aimed directly at computerized personal data collection was the Fair Credit Reporting Act, passed in 1971. It pertains to credit-reporting systems and the extensive information network mentioned above. The act insures to you the right of access to credit information collected about yourself. You can also find out the sources of that information. If you dispute the information, the credit bureau with whom you are dealing must either verify it or delete it.

Few Americans have not heard of the Nixon Administration and Watergate. A very unfortunate incident, some say. Others say Watergate was good for us. It alerted us anew to the dangers of wiretapping, snooping, and surveillance. Out of the resultant political climate came amendments to the Freedom of Information Act (initially passed in 1970) and the Privacy Act of 1974. Under these acts you can write for copies of personal records about yourself that have been collected by federal agencies. You can correct inaccuracies in those records. You can, to a great extent, control the disclosure of those records to other agencies. Unfair practices (i.e., invasions of privacy) are subject to criminal and civil penalties.

The Privacy Act also established a Privacy Protection Study Commission. Its charter was to study the effects of the act and to recommend to the President the extent to which provisions and principles of the act should be applied to the private sector. The Commission's final report* was presented to President Carter and Congress on July 12, 1977. Its general thrust was toward openness and fairness in record keeping. When a person establishes a relationship with a private organization, he or she is to be told what data will be collected, what records will be kept, what role the records will have in decisions about him or her, with what organizations the records will be shared, his or her right to see, copy, and correct the records, and by what organizations the records or portions thereof will be verified.

Even while the final report was being prepared, additional privacy legislation was being discussed in Congress. The Right to Financial Privacy Act was passed in 1978. This act spells out the procedures that federal authorities must follow to obtain records of an individual or small-partnership customer of financial institutions (such as banks, savings and loan institutions, and credit unions). If you are such a customer and the government wants to obtain records about you, it must notify you. It must also outline your right to block the

* *Personal Privacy in an Information Society,* U.S. Government Printing Office (Superintendent of Documents, Washington, D.C. 20402), July 1977, Stock No. 052-003-00395.

action. Access may be authorized by you, or under administrative or judicial subpoena, search warrant, or formal written request. Any records obtained under this procedure cannot be transferred to another government agency or department unless related "to a legitimate law enforcement inquiry."

Also passed in 1978 was the Electronic Funds Transfer Act. This act requires financial institutions to make available written documentation of each transfer of funds (even though such transfer can be accomplished without it). The act protects your resources as a consumer by limiting your liability for unauthorized transfers to $50 per transfer and to $500 for multiple transfers. It protects your privacy by requiring financial institutions to notify you if any data about you or your transactions is released to a third party.

The Electronic Communications Privacy Act of 1986 extends protection from eavesdropping on mail and telephone communications to include digital data communications such as electronic mail and remote computing. It protects data at off-site locations from unauthorized access by government officials or employees of computing service companies.

Lest we become complacent, it's appropriate to pause a minute. In 1935, President Roosevelt pledged confidentiality of the Social Security Administration records. Yet in 1982 the Selective Service System persuaded Congress to allow it to use data obtained through Social Security applications to identify American men who had not yet registered for the draft. The list of names so obtained was to be matched against Department of Defense and Department of Transportation files to delete the names of those currently serving in the military services and the Coast Guard. The culled list was then to be matched against IRS files to find the current addresses of these persons. (About 525,000, or 7 percent, of all draft-age men were claimed to be still unaccounted for.)

In the late 1970s and early 1980s, computer matching of files was used by the federal government to search for welfare recipients who were also on federal or District of Columbia payrolls. The Reagan Administration initiated computer matching of files to check veterans with loans and other benefits, food stamp recipients, Medicare users, students with federal loans, housing beneficiaries, and others. The justification given for these computerized searches was an all-out war against waste and fraud.

We should ask ourselves several questions: Do ends justify means? For what purposes might other, more extensive searches be used? The focus of what we've discussed thus far has been on massive databases and the dangers associated with them. These dangers still exist. However, the technical emphasis in many cases has shifted to widely distributed databases, electronic mail, home information systems, and interactive computing. Many American households are wired for cable TV. Most of us have telephones. Computers and terminals selling for less than $100 apiece are readily available. Both cable TV and telephone-based systems are being used to test-market a wide array of two-way communication (videotex) services to consumers. Our homes are data sources. We are not only information receivers but also data generators. Since these interactive systems operate in real time, eavesdroppers can learn about our actions as they occur, not simply after the fact. The difference can be

"Who Done It?"

Trust is often the victim in computer crimes. Studies show that employees at all levels in an organization do most of the thieving.

compared to learning from your credit records that you traveled to Chicago last month versus learning that you are in Chicago attempting to make a purchase right now. Such information may be useful for many purposes.

In 1981, Illinois became the first state to enact legislation to protect individuals from invasions of privacy in the operation of cable TV systems. Its Cable Television Privacy Act prohibits the installation of equipment that can be used to monitor a subscriber's set or viewing habits except for service purposes. In October 1981, Warner Amex, operator of the Qube system in Columbus, Ohio, published its own voluntary code of privacy. This was the first such code to be promulgated by an operator of an interactive consumer service offering. At this writing, several states have created state cable commissions, but statewide subscriber privacy rules are yet to be formed in most instances.

The core of the privacy issue is each individual's right to choose what he or she reveals to others.

Free-market advocates argue that decisions about secondary uses of personal data should be left to individuals, not dictated by privacy advocates. The core of the privacy issue is each individual's right to choose what he or she reveals to others.

Computer Crime

The subject of privacy, and more specifically, the computer-assisted invasion of privacy, leads us to a broader issue of computing. That issue is computer crime. Here, too, there are many questions without tidy textbook answers. What is computer crime? What causes it? How can we as individuals, organizations, or society prevent it? How can we detect it? Are there computer criminals and, if so, how should they be punished? Are computers causing us to think differently about what is right and what is wrong? Are they changing the moral behavior of our society?

At this writing, there is no widely accepted definition of the term *computer crime.* To prod our thinking, Jay Bloombecker, as Director of the National Center for Computer Crime Data (NCCCD), Los Angeles, proposed several scenarios. (See Figure 14-7.) Rather than use the official labels associated with some types of crimes, he used names that provoke mental pictures and thus serve as memory joggers. The second scenario on the list points out that any of us may unknowingly assist others in committing computer crimes if we're careless in the way we handle information.

The term *virus* has also taken on a new meaning associated with computer abuse. In this context, a virus is a self-replicating block of code that enters a system via diskette or tape, over communication lines, or keyed in manually. Like its biological namesake, the virus "infects" other programs and systems as it comes in contact with them. The virus may modify or destroy data or program files, reformat a disk, flash a message on the screen of each system it enters, and eventually bring down a system or even a large communication network as the replicated copies consume all available storage space or jam the communication lines. Even seem-

The Playpen: An act is committed as the result of an experiment, out of mischief, by a person or persons knowledgeable about computers—e.g., a student finds and accesses files containing course grades.

Fantasyland: A person unknowingly assists others in committing a crime, not realizing the consequences of his or her actions—e.g., an employee discards company-confidential computer output into a waste bin that can be searched by others during off-hours.

The Cookie Jar: Someone who is in need of money (or thinks so) has access to a computer system handling financial accounts and uses that access for personal gain.

The Land of Opportunity: Even when there is no financial need, someone knowledgeable about computers or computer-related procedures is tempted by the ease with which he or she can obtain funds by accessing the computer for personal gain.

The Toolbox: The computer serves as a tool in carrying out noncomputer-related illegal operations—e.g., a sophisticated crime syndicate uses a computer as a means to more efficient and less easily detectable law breaking, as in interstate gambling or drug traffic.

The Soapbox: A person or group desiring the attention of an individual, organization, or society at large uses the computer as a means of getting that attention—e.g., a terrorist organization sabotages a computer installation.

The War Zone: The computer serves as a tool of revenge—e.g., a disgruntled employee modifies a program so that it lowers customer account balances in a firm's accounts-receivable master file.

Figure 14-7 Computer crimes of many kinds are being committed daily. These scenarios show common examples of such crimes, for which prevention and detection procedures are now being developed.

ingly harmless message viruses are grim reminders that unauthorized users may be able to gain access to program and data files we do not intend them to see if they choose to do so.

The term *virus* has also taken on a new meaning associated with computer abuse.

With the increasing accessibility of computers and the spreading knowledge of how to use them, the opportunities to commit computer crimes and the likelihood of such crimes are increasing also. (See Figure 14-8.) NCCCD studies show that former and current employees are by far the most serious threat to the security of an organization's computer systems. Many suspected computer crimes are grouped within the category of "white-collar crimes" by law enforcement agencies such as the Federal Bureau of Investigation (FBI). Let's see why.

The possibilities for theft, or *larceny*, in an EDP-system environment are limited only by the imaginations of all who directly or indirectly come in contact with the system. Diskettes, semiconductor chips, and even complete computer systems may be taken from inventory. Software—say, the backup copy of a program that does

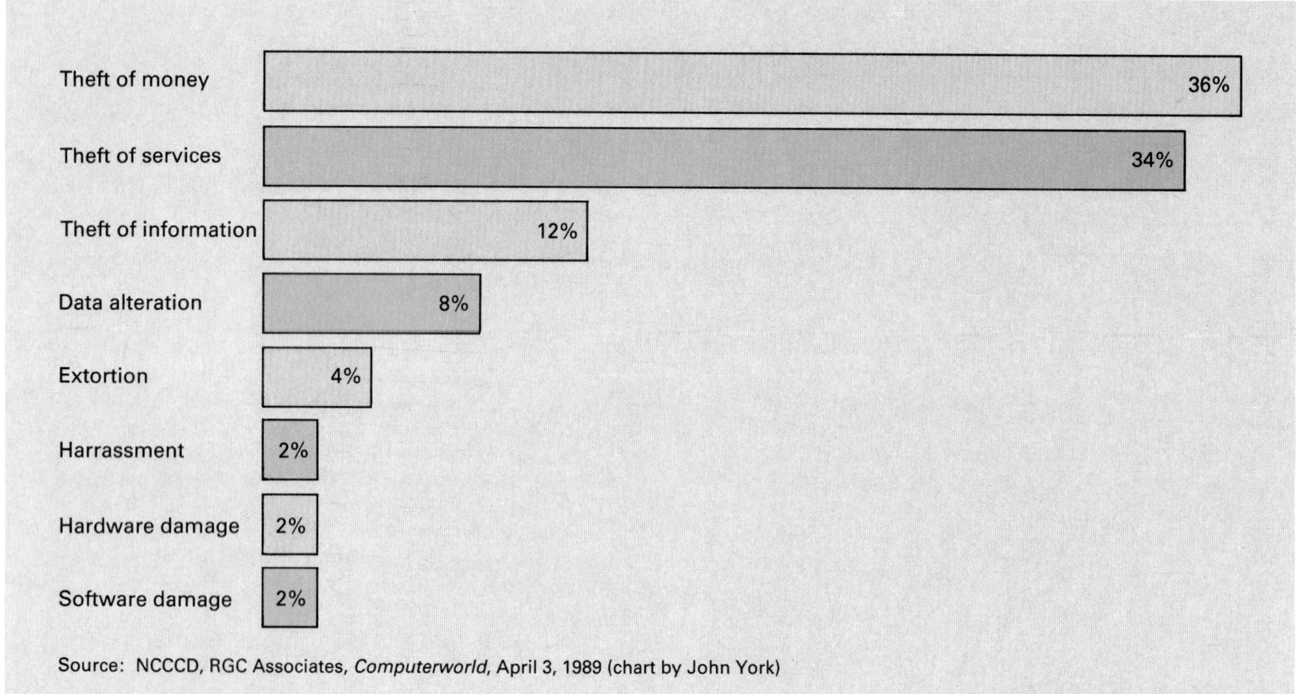
Theft of money
36%
Theft of services
34%
Theft of information
12%
Data alteration
8%
Extortion
4%
Harrassment
2%
Hardware damage
2%
Software damage
2%
Source: NCCCD, RGC Associates, *Computerworld*, April 3, 1989 (chart by John York)

Figure 14-8 Thefts of money and services account for 70 percent of prosecuted computer crimes, as tracked by a National Center for Computer Crime Data (NCCCD) study released in 1989.

marketing analysis—may be removed from a library. In 1982, in California's Silicon Valley, many loyal Apple users were stunned to learn that an in-house theft ring had diverted scores of Apple II and Apple III computers from the company's shipping and receiving department for illicit sale on the open market. Publicized thefts continuing to this date show that Apple has not yet curbed this problem.

Fraud is, in legal terms, intentional deception to cause another to give up property or some lawful right. In an EDP-system environment, it is reflected most often as data manipulation or program modification. For example, in an order-processing application, an employee may favor one supplier by keying larger orders to that supplier for a "cut of the take." Fraud may also occur as unauthorized access to computer-controlled funds. For example, one member of a household may use another member's Versateller card to withdraw cash without authorization to do so.

Embezzlement is the theft or fraudulent appropriation of money or other substance entrusted to one's care. It is a crime that has existed since the practice of having someone else do work began. A trusted employee may write or modify a program to calculate compound interest amounts, truncate them to the nearest dollar, and keep track of the truncated amounts. Over a large computer run, the accumulated sum of the truncated amounts can be sizable—a tidy nest egg to be routed to the account of a cooperating friend or relative.

Computer files containing proprietary (company-owned) data, programs, product designs or specifications, and marketing plans can be copied, and the copies sold to a competitor, all with the help of the rightful owner's computer. Yet the original files may remain in place. If the competitor uses the files discreetly, no one may be the wiser.

An organization may purchase or lease a software product, then make copies of that software to run on computers in several departments. School kids make copies of copyrighted games stored on diskettes, trading for opportunities to do so among themselves with the same casualness they exhibit when trading baseball cards. Let's face it—there are few managers and employees, few instructors and students, who could *not* be aware of the rabbit-like multiplication of copies of copyrighted software packages that's occurring in their environments. Yet such acts are thefts, known as *software piracy*. Where is the concern for right and wrong?

An instructor or student may use computer time and storage space available on campus or via a timesharing network for non-school-related purposes. Similarly, an employee may use a firm's computer system to write and debug programs, then sell those programs to small businesses via a software publishing firm. These persons may see computer time as an intangible asset, something that cannot be stolen physically, and therefore something that cannot be a proven loss to the computer system's owner. If other instructors, students, or employees ignore and therefore seemingly condone the usage, are they not also involved?

Estimates of the costs of reported computer crimes range from one hundred to several hundred million dollars per year. In 1989, the NCCCD released figures showing that the costs of computer crime the previous year exceeded $555 million. Some experts who've been studying this issue argue that even these costs are but the tip of the iceberg—say from 5 to 15 percent of the computer crimes that occur. The victims of computer crimes often knowingly absorb the losses, perhaps fearing even greater losses because of bad publicity if the crimes were known. Are you and I likely to buy stock in a firm whose Vice President of Development has just been charged with siphoning more than $300,000 (the *average* payoff in a white-collar computer crime) from the firm's operating funds to a bogus vendor account? Are we likely to use a bank's ATM's if we are fully aware that fraud losses involving the ATM's are doubling or tripling each year? By law, banks now have to report when their computer systems have been compromised, but they are not likely to publicize it. Other businesses are not bound by such a requirement.

In the early 1980s, about 20 states passed laws dealing with computer crime. At this writing, only two states—West Virginia and Vermont—have no legislation on the subject.

In 1984, the U.S. Congress passed the Computer Fraud and Abuse Act of 1984, a federal computer crime bill designed to prevent unauthorized access to computers used by the federal government and federally insured financial institutions. A maximum penalty of 10 years in prison and/or a $10,000 fine could be imposed on convicted offenders.

The Computer Fraud and Abuse Act of 1986 expanded federal jurisdiction to cover interstate computer crimes in the public sector. This legislation makes it a federal misdemeanor to traffic in stolen passwords with intent to defraud or to intentionally trespass in a "federal interest computer" to observe or obtain data. Accessing such a computer for a theft-by-computer scheme or to alter or destroy computer data without authorization—if the victim suffers a loss of at least $1000 or if the files are medical records—is a felony. Conviction under the legislation could result in a federal jail sentence of up to 5 years for the first offense and up to 10 years for a second one.

The Computer Security Act of 1987 is designed to further protect the security and privacy of data stored in federal computer systems. It establishes a central authority for developing guidelines for protecting unclassified but sensitive information stored in government computers. Each agency must formulate its own security plan based on the guidelines but tailored to its circumstances. Periodic computer security training for the operators of such systems is mandatory.

While some persons laud these measures, critics point out that such legislation tends to be reactive in nature. Little or no protection is given to data in private organizations' computer systems. Through societal pressures, persons who use and manage computers in private organizations are being asked to take on greater legal responsibility for the safety of their organizations' data and computer services. Some organizational protection mechanisms are discussed below.

Organizational Protection Mechanisms

Since many computer crimes go undetected or do not surface until much harm has been done, preventing computer crimes *before* they occur is the best approach. When we recognize that trusted employees are still the biggest threat to an organization's computer systems, the need for all computer-using organizations to take preventive, protective measures is obvious. According to Don Parker of SRI International, a 20-year leader in computer security research, *data diddling*—changing data before or as it goes into the computer system—is especially common. Fortunately, many basic steps can be taken at the organizational level. Most of them are just good business practices. They include:

- Carefully screening all job applicants and making sure all employees are aware of and follow organizational procedures and policies.
- Separation of functions so that, for example, the same employee is not writing a program, running it during normal production use, and retrieving its output; restricting access to programs and data on a "need-to-use" basis.
- Caution in the use of new software, acquiring it only from known, reputable sources and reviewing it carefully on a standalone computer system before installing it on other systems for normal use.
- Physical security mechanisms, such as cardkey locks that control parking lot entrances and exits, doors, and the use of equipment such as copy machines; closed-circuit television (CCTV) systems; and premise alarms that can be activated during off-hours. (See Figure 14-9.)
- Programmed controls, invoked within computer systems, such as user identification and password verification; input edit routines that check values for consistency or reasonableness; record counts and other control totals that are balanced from run to run; and software locks designed to prevent users from copying programs and data files.

Figure 14-9 Electronic security systems that include closed-circuit television (CCTV) monitors are being used nationwide to protect people and property. (Courtesy The Picture Cube)

- Encryption of proprietary and sensitive data, programs, and other computer-related information.
- Systematic and complete auditing procedures, conducted by both internal and external auditors, around, through, and with the help of the computer. For example, both normal and exception-handling procedures for data-entry operators, data center librarians, and other information system staff must be documented, understood, and followed at all times. The contents of changed master-file records can be compared with activity logs at periodic intervals manually or with computer help to verify complete and accurate processing.

The increasing use of distributed-processing systems and techniques encompasses the transfer of data over communication lines and the input of data and distribution of information at points far removed from any central computer facility. The use of encryption/decryption is increasing in such systems. At a minimum, the use of passwords is supplemented by: (1) requiring each user to enter a cardkey bearing his/her unique password as well as key in his/her assigned user identification number; (2) callback techniques that verify each user password is entered from a designated work location of the user to whom the password is assigned; or (3) password generation systems whereby the user enters a system-returned random number into a handheld password device that generates a password which must match the password generated by the system for that number.

Biometric security mechanisms based on fingerprint or handprint identification, speech verification, or scanning of the retina of the eye are being applied in governmental and military systems involving top-secret data. As such mechanisms become easier to implement and less costly, their use will spread.

McDonald's
AT&T
AVIS
QUAKER
Registered trademark of McDonald's Corporation

Registered trademark of American Telephone and Telegraph Company

Registered trademark of Avis Rent A Car Systems, Inc.

Registered trademark of SAS Institute Inc.

Registered trademark of General Electric Company

Registered trademark of International Business Machines Corporation

Registered trademark of The Quaker Oats Company

Legal Protection Mechanisms

Individuals, organizations, and society at large can also employ legal mechanisms to protect computer-related and computer-controlled assets. Among the mechanisms that organizations and individuals are using are trade secrets, trademarks, copyrights, and patents. In addition, almost all vendors use licensing agreements—specific terms and conditions regarding the use of data, software, hardware, or systems agreed to by all parties involved. The law of contracts encompasses such licensing agreements and thus applies to them.

Trade Secrets

A trade secret gives to its owner the exclusive rights to use a particular technology, so long as the technology remains secret. The holder of the trade secret must go all out to keep the proprietary information secret. If the holder attempts to recover damages for the use of that information by another—say, in a competitive process or product—the holder must be able to prove in court that all reasonable and prudent precautions were taken to protect the information.

Common law and state legislation provide the basis for using the concept of trade secret as a legal protection in the computing industry. In recent years, it has become an issue when a skilled, knowledgable employee has resigned from one company and joined a competitor. What is the proper balance between (a) protection of the former employer's commercial information not generally known to the public from actual or threatened misappropriation, and (b) protection of the right of the employee to earn a livelihood and the right of the new employer to compete in the marketplace? When you are applying for a job, be sure to read carefully all papers you are asked to sign. Chances are they deal with your rights both while you are an employee of the company and if or when you leave it.

Trademarks

Organizations and individuals who are using trademarks are doing so primarily to protect selected names as unique identifiers. For example, MS-DOS is a registered trademark of Microsoft Corporation; PostScript is a registered trademark of Adobe Systems, Inc.; and UNIX is a registered trademark of AT&T. Especially in mass-market areas, brand names like these may be significant factors when users are making product selections. "If it's . . . , it's got to be good."

Copyrights

Basically, copyrighting gives the owner of a copyright the right to prevent others from making copies of more than insubstantial portions of the copyrighted work; from making modifications, translations, and other derivatives of the work that are substantially similar; and from displaying the work without the owner's permission. A work is copyrighted *automatically* when it is first fixed in a tangible medium of expression. The copyright does not apply to the idea that is being expressed; rather, it applies to (and hence protects) the expression of the idea. The burden of proof of infringement is left to the owner of the copyright, who must show that copying has occurred.

Electronic Copies?

Even an electronic representation in a computer's random-access memory (RAM) can be considered a *copy* of a printed document, program, or other copyrighted material.

We tend to think of copyrighting as a way of protecting printed documents. The fact that copyrights are also being used to protect other forms of expression makes them especially interesting to the computer-using community.

The basic law of copyrighting in the United States is set forth in the Copyright Act of 1976, which took effect on January 1, 1978. It was a major overhaul of U.S. copyright law, which had not been updated since 1909. The law was clarified with respect to computer programs by the Computer Software Copyright Act of 1980. There are two instances in which someone legally may make a copy of a copyrighted program:

- To create a backup copy of the program as a means of asset protection.
- If making a copy of the program is an essential step in using it.

When a computer program is created by an employee as a part of his or her job, the employer owns the copyright. A program created by a consultant belongs to the consultant, however, not to the client. The employer or the consultant may, of course, sign over the ownership of the copyright to another organization or individual. The program or other copyrighted work may be either unpublished (kept close to the vest through restrictive licensing) or published (marked with a prescribed form of copyright notice and distributed widely). Where the owner is not a single individual, the copyright is effective for 75 years in the case of published works, and for 100 years in the case of unpublished works. Where the owner is a single individual, the copyright is effective for the life of that individual plus 50 years.

In recent years, issues relative to what copyright protection for software really means have been contested hotly within the U.S. judicial systems. Indeed, directly conflicting rulings about what is protectable by copyrights have been made. That both the source-language and machine-language (object code) versions of a program are copyrightable is now accepted widely. So are the structure, sequence, and organization of all or a "quantitatively important" (not necessarily quantitatively large) segment of a program, according to some rulings. So is an individual screen display, not as an audiovisual work, but as a compilation.

It's in the latter two kinds of situations that the concepts of "look and feel" come into play. At this writing, numerous "look and feel" lawsuits are pending. Is the use of specific icons within specific areas on a display screen to represent specific operations a copyrightable expression, for instance?

Proponents of "look and feel" protection claim that such protection rewards inventors for their creativity, protects their investments, and thus encourages further investments.

Proponents of "look and feel" protection claim that such protection rewards inventors for their creativity, protects their investments, and thus encourages further investments. Opponents argue that such protection forces software developers to design programs, screens, and work sequences that are complex, counterintuitive, and confusing—thus inhibiting widespread use of computers. Conflict exists throughout the industry. It's likely that additional legal rulings will be needed to provide the over-all directional framework required.

Patents

Patenting is an attractive protective measure to many because it provides such broad protection: a government-granted monopoly. The owner of a patent may prevent all others from making, using, or selling the invention covered by the patent during the 17 years of the life of the patent. These rights apply even if another inventor comes up with the same invention *independently* of the patented work after the date of the initial invention.

To qualify for patenting, an invention must pass at least three tests: (1) it must be novel, meaning original; (2) it must be nonobvious; and (3) it must be useful. By law, a patent holder must fully disclose his or her invention, thus contributing to the advancement of knowledge. The patent holder may choose to license to others the right to use or implement the invention—for example, Intel can allow other firms to manufacture 80386 microprocessors. However, the inventor is not forced to do so.

Patents have been used to protect the creative works of scientists, engineers, and other designers for some time. Now patenting is also being used to protect creative work embodied in software.

Many software developers favor patent protection for software. As with copyrights above, opposing groups argue that allowing such protection forces programmers to "reinvent the wheel" rather than build on technological progress and impedes the spread of computer use.

The U.S. Supreme Court has taken various positions on software patentability. Initially, programs were seen to be unpatentable on the grounds that they were implementations of mathematical algorithms. However, a 1981 ruling indicated that inventions using software or firmware cannot be denied patents solely because they contain such software or firmware. Since that ruling, numerous software patents have been granted. Literally thousands of additional applications for software patents have been filed and are awaiting action by the U.S. Patent and Trademark Office.

Social Dependency and Vulnerability

In this section we examine the broad concerns of how computing affects certain aspects of our lives, namely, our *social dependency* on technology and our *social vulnerability* as a result of that dependency. We know that more and more individuals, businesses, governments, and other organizations are directly and indirectly using computers. More and more kinds of activities are being done or controlled by computers. In terms of the actual volume of work accomplished, computer use is increasing at a phenomenal rate. Do we realize the scope of these computer-related activities? Let's consider some examples.

It's obvious that a hospital patient whose respiratory system functions as a result of computer-directed, life-sustaining equipment is dependent on that equipment. In a similar fashion, the "life" of the hospital as an organization is likely to

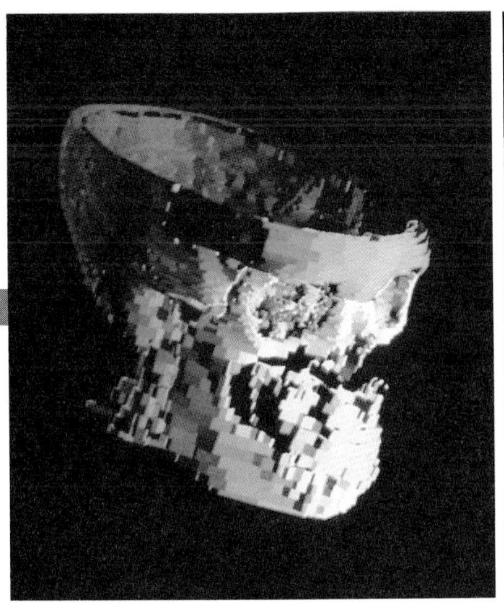

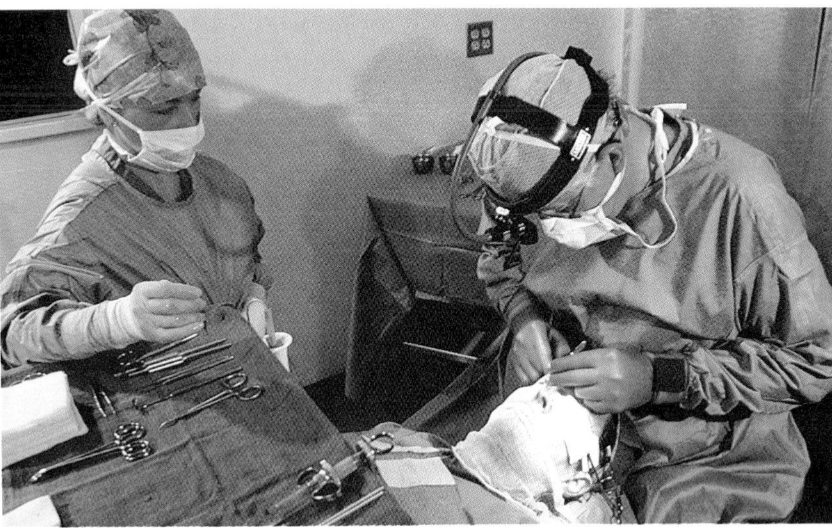

GUIDING A SURE HAND

Plastic surgery—the thought of such an operation being performed makes all but the staunchest of us pause for a while. Yet plastic surgery is one of the fastest-growing medical specialities in America. In 1984 alone, certified surgeons performed more than 1.3 million reconstructive surgeries such as burn treatments and rebuilding of breasts after mastectomies. Another .5 million esthetic surgeries were performed—optional procedures to make essentially normal, healthy people look better.

Plastic surgery is no longer a skill that goes only skin deep. In addition to doing skin grafts, surgeons work with underlying fat, muscle, and even bone. Computer imaging techniques are being used by many of these surgeons to anticipate problems that might otherwise be encountered by surprise in the operating room. For example, a surgeon may prepare to deal with a patient who suffers from Crouzon's disease, a failure of the middle of the face to grow forward during fetal development. First, the patient's specific facial contours taken from CAT scans are supplied as input to a computer system. Then the surgeon simulates the operation step by step, watching the results of his (or her) work evolve on a visual-display screen. If a step proves to be inadvisable, that step can be undone and an alternative approach taken instead. The surgeon enters the operating room later with much greater confidence that he knows what he's up against. That feeling of confidence can be shared with the patient and others involved. *(Photos courtesy [left] James D. Wilson/Newsweek; [right] Bernard Gottfryd/Newsweek)*

depend on computer systems. Furthermore, each person who lives in the vicinity of the hospital lives with the expectation that if he or she needs a service provided by the hospital, the service will be available.

A leading banking executive once said: "If our computer installation is down for an hour, our bottom line is directly impacted. If we're down for 24 hours, the state's business revenue is impacted. If we're down for 48 hours or more, the GNP [gross national product] of our nation suffers."

To the extent that computer crimes prevent or impede the correct functioning of an EDP system, they are a major threat to that system. For example, acts of sabotage and vandalism are man-made disasters to which a computer system, hence an organization, and hence society, may be vulnerable.

Fires, floods, rainstorms and lightning, spillage of industrial chemicals or gases, and explosions are environmental disasters that can and do destroy computer systems. Perhaps because fire is often an aftereffect of other types of disasters, such as earthquakes, tornadoes, hurricanes, strikes, or riots, fire is the most widely feared threat, and also the most common one. The tons of paper and other materials stored near computers are highly combustible. Moreover, once a fire starts, heat, smoke, and toxic fumes as well as flames may cause extensive damage. (See Figure 14-10.)

Only the small, battery-operated computers are immune to electrical power failures. What air is to humans, electricity is to most computers. As noted earlier, a loss of power may do more damage than simply stopping opertions. In a system with storage components that are volatile, a loss of power is a loss of stored data and instructions. Furthermore, power surges can be as damaging to some types of equipment as power failures. Mainframe systems commonly require special air-conditioning facilities. If the air conditioning fails, serious damage to system components may occur. Even systems that do not require special facilities may bc damaged by excessive heat, humidity, dirt, dust, and other contaminants.

The most common software losses are attributable to program errors, or bugs. The greatest danger here is the program that appears to work but doesn't—the output that is "almost right." Designers, programmers, and/or testers may be at fault. Another consideration here is that the software may not have been developed in-house. Errors in acquired software may be hard to detect, isolate, and report (or correct), espe-

Figure 14-10 Fires can cause extensive damage to computer systems. Fire-damaged equipment may be repairable, but users must plan backup and recovery procedures *beforehand* to avoid extensive downtime or loss of programs and data. (Courtesy Peter Arnold, Inc.)

cially if in-house personnel are not familiar with the software or do not have access to related documentation.

Computer operators can damage equipment by, for example, dropping or mishandling disk packs or diskettes. They may also mount the wrong input tapes, or mount the right tapes on the wrong drives and thus cause valuable data to be destroyed. The hazard of accidental modification of data is perhaps best exemplified by such everyday occurrences as keying errors made by users or data-entry personnel. We all make mistakes. Are such mistakes likely to be serious? A prominent security analyst puts it this way: "The crooks will never catch up with the incompetents."

Environmental Protection Mechanisms

Whether an organization's EDP system consists of six IBM 3090s housed in a central computer facility, a nationwide network of DEC VAX machines in office environments, or one Compaq microcomputer, computer security should be a part of the organization's over-all security program. Management should consider: What assets do we want to protect? What are the risks and hazards to which the assets are exposed? What is the potential cost and the likelihood of each hazard's occurring? For each asset, management may decide to (1) do nothing, (2) lower the dollar impact in case an identified problem does occur, or (3) lower the probability or possibility of the problem's occurring.

EDP-system components housed in a main computer room can be safeguarded by a number of environmental protection mechanisms:

- Automatic smoke, heat, and fire detection systems
- Carbon dioxide or halon fire prevention systems
- Automatic sprinkler systems
- Raised flooring; structured floors with positive drainage
- Switch for choice among public utility, standby power generator, or uninterruptible power system (UPS)
- Premise alarm
- CCTV to guard station
- Identification card reader or electronic security check

An organization's environmental protection mechanisms must be complemented by well-designed security procedures. The procedures must be well understood and adhered to by all system users. Just as application programs must be tested, an organization's security mechanisms and procedures should be tested regularly. All too often, for example, personnel who work in an output distribution center do not know where the handheld fire extinguishers are, much less how to use them. Document classifications such as INTERNAL USE ONLY or CONFIDENTIAL—RESTRICTED are ignored. (See Figure 14-11.)

Whether distributing computing power throughout an organization lessens or increases that organization's security exposure is a topic that can be debated from several viewpoints. Since system components are positioned at various locations rather than at a central site, a single environmental disaster should be less devastating, at least from an equipment-cost point of view. On the other hand, office personnel may

How Important Is Data Security?

Suppose a company's accounts-receivable master file was destroyed by a water leakage in the computer room or as a result of programmer or operator error. Further suppose there was no backup copy. Picture an ad in the surrounding area newspapers: "All Individuals or Companies Owing Money to Janus Furniture—Please Let Us Know How Much."

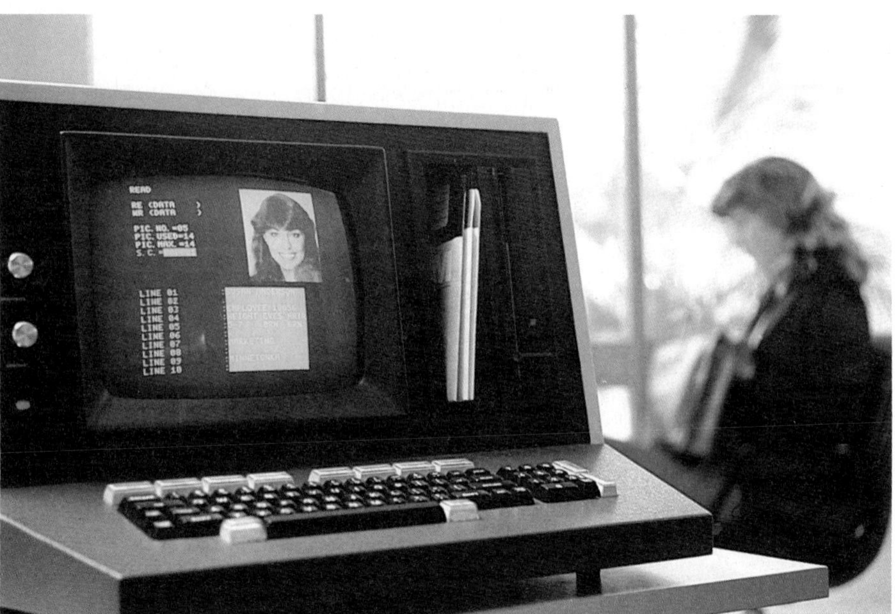
READ
RE CDATA)
WR CDATA)
PIC. NO. =05
PIC. USED=14
PIC. MAX. =14
S. C. =
LINE 01
LINE 02
LINE 03
LINE 04
LINE 05
LINE 06
LINE 07
LINE 08
LINE 09
LINE 10

Figure 14-11 Computer facilities can be safeguarded by a variety of protection mechanisms. The computer itself may play a key role, verifying the authorization of employees who attempt to enter the facilities. (Courtesy Alvis Upitis/The Image Bank)

not realize that a wealth of proprietary information can be accessed by means of the terminals or microcomputers at their disposal. Their lack of awareness may prove to be costly. Security analysts point out that messages sent over public communication lines may be read en route by unauthorized network penetrators. In any case, the security of a computer system is as strong as its weakest link, but no stronger.

Because not all security problems and disasters will be prevented, an organization's approach to security must include provisons for *backup,* that is, a means to recover when a problem or disaster occurs. Even a microcomputer user learns early to make duplicate copies of important programs and data files. To fail to do so is to learn the hard way, when a diskette becomes unreadable or a file stored on a hard disk is written over by mistake. In like manner, the information system staff of a large organization may make daily or weekly backup copies of master files, accumulate log data sets reflecting all changes made to the master files between copy runs, and then re-apply the changes to a particular master file if it becomes necessary to do so. For greatest security, the backup files must be kept off-premises. Consider for a moment the vast databases of the Social Security Administration, the IRS, or the FBI. The contents of these databases are irreplaceable; many day-to-day functions of society depend on them. Plainly, there is no room for error in designing, implementing, and adhering to backup and recovery procedures for these files.

Site evacuation, damage assessment, emergency processing, salvage operations, permanent-site restoration, and methods of keeping system users and perhaps stockholders and the general public informed about developments are considerations that must be addressed as a part of contingency planning. An organization with similar processing facilities at multiple locations may have an easier time planning for emergencies than an organization that has one large

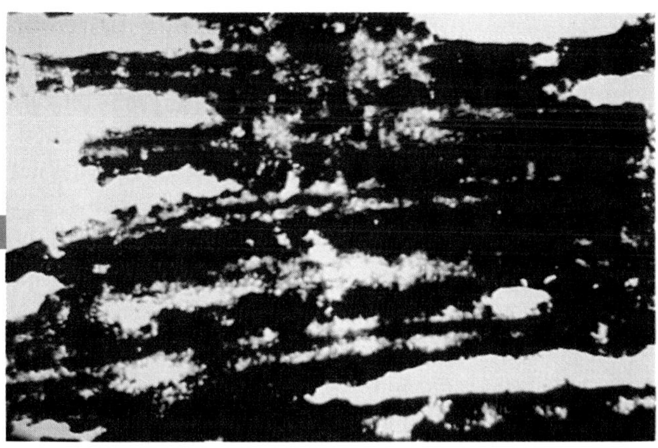

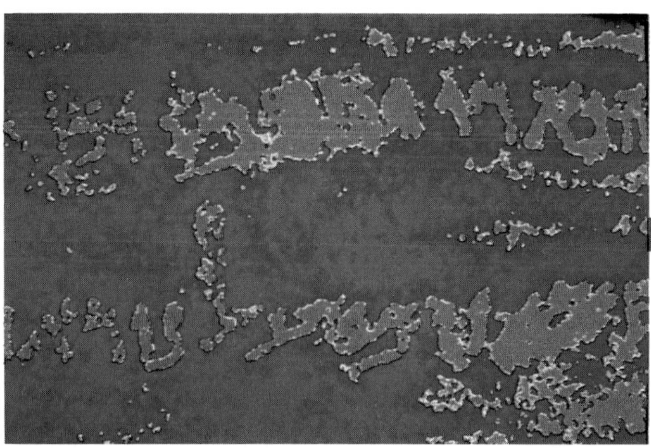

READING THE UNREADABLE

When found, portions of ancient writings known as the Dead Sea Scrolls (left) were largely unreadable. Their black ink and dark brown parchment had both eroded over the centuries. Through a process called pseudocolor, the edges of letters whose boundaries are blurred shades of gray are highlighted in distinct colors with computer help. The writings are magnified and enhanced through many processing steps. The resultant output (right) can be read by an expert in ancient languages. Without computer assistance, the contents of the Scrolls may have remained forever a mystery. *(Photos courtesy Philip Borden/PhotoEdit)*

centralized data center. Reciprocal emergency-processing agreements and group mutual aid pacts agreed to by multiple organizations are other alternatives. Some service companies offer backup processing facilities. Of course, an order-entry system that normally runs on an IBM AS/400 can't be moved to a Hewlett-Packard 9000 merely because that happens to be the nearest computer system on which processing time and storage space are available! Here again, preplanning is required.

A Perspective

Social dependency becomes social vulnerability when the technologies that we are dependent on are in themselves dependent on conditions that we cannot control, or cannot control without massive disruption to the normal functioning of our society. The computer is not one large machine that provides for all the needs of a utopian society, but many socially important things depend on computing—military systems, airlines, banks, telephones, to name a few. Concerns about such dependencies are not based on the assumption that all these computer-assisted activities will fail at once. A sizable failure in any one of them can cause major problems. To what extent is it reasonable and safe to depend on highly automated, complex computer sys-

Social dependency becomes social vulnerability when the technologies that we are dependent on are in themselves dependent on conditions that we cannot control . . .

tems for management and monitoring of critical functions?

The impacts of computers have raised many questions that have not yet been answered. For some questions, there may be no answers in the foreseeable future. For others, the answers may be set before we face the questions. The point at issue may really be whether computing is under human control. Most of us tend to believe that it should be.

In support of this belief and to keep pace with the spread of computer technology, we must continue to develop system safeguards to protect the privacy of our personal affairs, the integrity of our organizations, and the foundations of our society. We must keep abreast of advancements in technology and of their social implications. In doing so, we help to insure that 1984 continues to be just what it was—simply a calendar year. It will *not* become an Orwellian-postulated life-style reality.

CHAPTER SUMMARY

1. Computers are having both direct and indirect economic impacts on organizations.

2. Computers may also impact organizational structure (for example, by facilitating centralization or decentralization, or a blend of both). The individual or department that controls an organization's computing systems controls a source of power within the organization.

3. Automation is the performance of a specific combination of actions by a machine or group of machines "automatically"—without human intervention. Computers are increasing both the rate at which firms are automating and the extent of that automation.

4. A robot is a general-purpose programmable machine that can do any of several tasks under stored-program control.

5. Artificial intelligence researchers are trying to understand how we think and, accordingly, to develop machines that help us in thinking-machine applications. Expert systems, vision systems, natural-language query systems, and continuous speech recognition are leading application areas.

6. Concerns about depersonalization—even to the extent of replacing our names with numbers—have not materialized. Each of us has a responsibility to help determine what kind of, and where, a computer interface is acceptable to us.

7. Privacy is a social and legal issue involving questions such as how and what data will be collected about each of us, how and by whom it will be used, and how and by whom it can be changed. Both federal and state laws have been passed to help protect our rights in this area.

8. Computer crimes involving larceny, fraud, embezzlement, software piracy, and so on are prevalent, costly, hard to detect, and often go unreported (even when detected). Some laws dealing specifically with computer crime have been passed. Good business practices can help to prevent computer crimes from occurring.

9. To protect their computer-related assets, individuals and organizations are using trademarks, trade secrets, copyrights, patents, and licensing agreements. Each of these legal protection mechanisms serves a unique purpose that can be applied to computing.

10. As more organizations use computers, as more kinds of activities are done or controlled by computers, and as the volume of work done by computers increases, our social dependency on computers increases also.

11. The threats to EDP systems include sabotage, vandalism, fires, floods, rainstorms and lightning, industrial chemicals and gases, explosions, electrical power failures or surges, and human errors reflected as operational mistakes or program bugs.

12. EDP systems can be protected by environmental protection mechanisms and well-designed security procedures. Backup and recovery procedures for system resources must be designed, implemented, and adhered to before disasters occur.

13. Social dependency becomes social vulnerability when the technologies that we are dependent on are in themselves dependent on conditions that we cannot control, or cannot control without massive disruption to the normal functioning of our society. Each of us must keep abreast of advancements in technology and of their social implications.

DISCUSSION QUESTIONS

1. (a) Show, by example, key differences between centralized and decentralized organizations in the way tasks are accomplished.
(b) Point out how computers can support either method of organizational structure.

2. Discuss the implications of the following statement: "If knowledge is power, and if information is a source of knowledge, then we can assume that information is also a source of power."

3. Show, by specific examples, how computers are changing the nature of jobs.

4. (a) What is a robotic system?
(b) Why might robotic systems be viewed unfavorably by American workers?
(c) How might workers benefit from them?

5. Describe some current practical applications of artificial intelligence.

6. (a) Suggest some concerns that might lead an individual, organization, or society to decide against further research or application of artificial intelligence.
   (b) How might these concerns be dealt with?

7. What constitutes invasion of privacy?

8. Using specific examples, argue for or against federal or state government use of data initially collected for one purpose, for other purposes also.

9. Choose any one of the computer crime scenarios in Figure 14-7.
   (a) Give specific examples of that scenario as they might occur in your home or business environment.
   (b) How can each crime that you named in part (a) be detected?
   (c) How might it be prevented from occurring in the first place?

10. (a) Show, by specific examples, what software piracy is.
    (b) What preventive or punitive actions do you think are warranted for these examples of piracy?

11. Compare copyrights and patents as legal protection mechanisms for software.

12. Distinguish between social dependency and social vulnerability with respect to computers.

13. How are you addressing the issues and impacts of computing in your ongoing activities?

BASIC Appendix

Using the Computer in Problem Solving

Getting Started
Signing On
Using System Commands
A First Problem
More about BASIC
BASIC Statements and Line Numbers
BASIC Data Types
Variables
The LET Statement
The REM Statement
The END Statement
The INPUT Statement
The PRINT Statement
The DATA, READ, and RESTORE Statements
File Input/Output
Program Control Flow
The GO TO Statement
The IF . . . THEN Statement
The DO Statement
Selection, or Choosing between Alternatives
Looping
The FOR and NEXT Statements
Nested Control Structures
Implementation-Supplied Functions
Using Functions in a BASIC Program
Summary

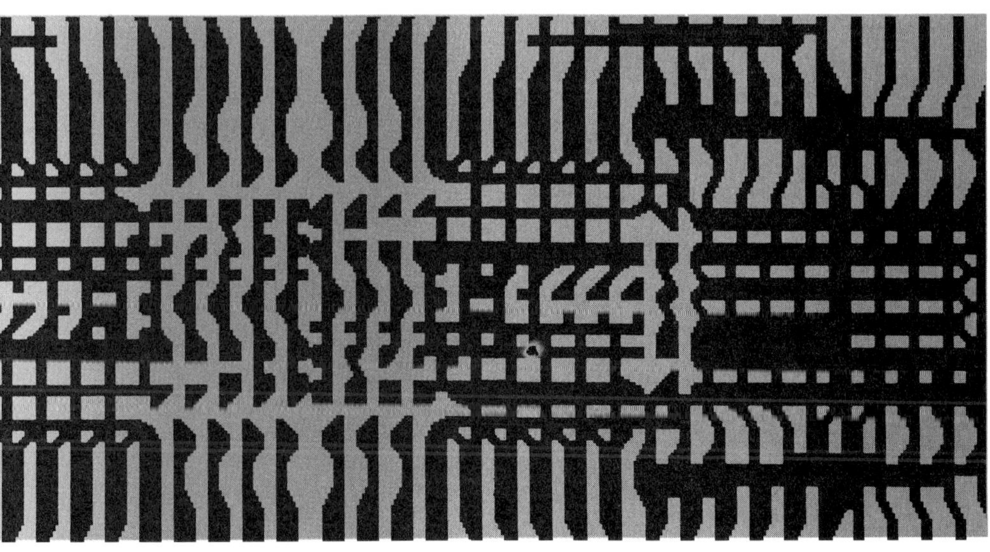

There are several ways to learn about computers. One way is to talk with people who use them—say, your neighbor who works as a programmer at Hewlett-Packard or Safeway Stores; your accountant who uses a small business computer to produce tax returns, quarterly reports, and so on; or your co-worker or fellow student who has purchased an Apple Macintosh microcomputer for personal use.

Another way to learn about computers is to visit a computer installation in your area. Once there, you can see what data is entered into computers, and what results are provided by them. In this way, you may get some feel for what computers can do.

Still another approach is to read about computers in daily newspapers, monthly trade journals, computer manufacturers' literature, and books such as this one, intended for self-study or classroom use.

Perhaps the best way to understand what computers are all about is to use one yourself. The purpose of this appendix is to guide you in doing just that. When you have completed this appendix, you will know quite a lot about how to use the computer as a tool in problem solving.

In Chapter 9 of this book, problem solving is broken down into the following tasks:

1. Defining the problem
2. Planning a solution to the problem
3. Coding the solution (that is, writing a program)
4. Checking the program
5. Providing documentation

In this appendix, we'll direct our attention to several relatively straightforward problems. You'll learn how to develop solutions to such problems and how to express problem solutions in the BASIC programming language. In other words, you'll learn how to write BASIC programs.

It is not the purpose of this appendix to turn you into a BASIC programmer. Do not expect to be one when you finish. You will, however, gain some understanding of how a computer is used, and you will have some experience in problem solving.

Getting Started

To use a computer in problem solving, you must have access to the computer. Today, there are two common modes of operation:

Batch mode. Program statements are written on coding forms. The coding forms are submitted to a data-entry group for keying into punched cards or directly into the computer. The program statements and the data to be processed by the computer as directed by those statements are submitted to the computer for processing. Some time later, the results of the processing are distributed as output.

Interactive mode. Program statements or responses to menus or forms on display screens that cause program statements to be generated are entered directly into the computer by the user. The data to be processed is also provided as input at that time. The program is executed and the results are provided as output to the user.

The BASIC programming language can be used in either batch or interactive mode. It is especially well suited for interactive use. In fact, BASIC was initially designed as an easy-to-learn programming language that students could use in interactive problem solving. This appendix assumes (but does not require) that such an environment is available.

In general, an interactive programming session comprises two phases. In the first phase, the user establishes contact with the computer and "signs on" to the system. In the second phase, the user communicates with the computer through system commands and program statements.

Signing On

The sign-on procedure used to establish contact with a computer varies considerably from one computer system to another. On some systems, terminals are permanently connected to the computer. To begin, a user need only turn on such a terminal and press the ENTER key (or its equivalent) on the keyboard once. Microcomputers are like that. On other systems, terminals are connected to the computer through dial-up facilities. A user must call the computer via a telephonelike device (acoustic coupler or other modem). Knowledge of the computer's telephone number is required to gain access to it. If a high-pitched tone is received over the telephone line, the computer is ready to receive input. The user places the telephone handset firmly into the acoustic coupler. This connection links the terminal to the computer through the telephone line. As above, the user then presses the ENTER key once to begin. If the high-pitched tone is not received or the connection is not completed successfully, the user must hang up the handset and try again.

After the user has established contact with a microcomputer or through a terminal, the computer usually displays on a televisionlike screen a greeting and a message asking the user to enter his or her assigned unique user number. For example:

```
ON AT 10:16 MONDAY, DECEMBER 18, 1989
USER NUMBER, PASSWORD—
```

The user number uniquely identifies the user to the system. Only persons who enter valid user numbers are accepted as authorized users and allowed to proceed. On many systems, a password mechanism provides a second level of security. It helps to protect the user's program and data files from other users. Whereas user numbers are relatively permanent, passwords are changed frequently, say at least once every two to four months. At any given time, the user must enter a combination of user number and password that is known to the system before he or she is allowed to interact further with the computer.

In preparation for your work with BASIC, you should obtain a valid user number from your instructor, lab assistant, supervisor, or computer center operations staff. If passwords are required on the system available to you, you will also need to establish a password. After both items have been made known to the computer, you need only enter them at the beginning of an interactive session to be recognized as an official, authorized user of the computer's problem-solving capabilities.

Using System Commands

Once the computer accepts a user number and password entered from a keyboard as valid, it may type out or display a simple response message, or prompt. For example:

```
READY
```

During the interactive session that follows, the user communicates with the computer by means of system commands known to the system.

To indicate that a BASIC program is to be written and/or executed, the user may type:

```
ENTER BASIC
```

and press the ENTER key. The computer may in turn respond:

```
OLD OR NEW-
```

By entering OLD, the user tells the computer that an existing BASIC program is to be used during the interactive session. By entering NEW, the user indicates he/she intends to enter statements of a new BASIC program. In either case, the user presses the ENTER key. Once again, the computer may respond:

```
READY
```

As above, the READY message signals the user to proceed.

Like the sign-on procedure, the system commands available to users vary considerably from one computer system to another. Many of the functions that users need are similar, however, irrespective of the system environment. All users need to be able to enter program statements. They need to signal the computer when their programs are complete and ready to be executed. Most if not all users need to be able to save programs they've written for reuse later, in their original or slightly modified forms. To avoid having to re-enter the program statements, the programs should be saved in storage. Users who have saved several programs may want the computer to display the names of those programs, to help them recall what's been stored.

Figure A-1 shows the forms and meanings of system commands commonly used on some computer systems. In preparation for your work, you should find out what system commands are available on the computer system you will be using. A user's manual or operator's guide for the system will supply this information.

A First Problem

Now that we've taken care of some of the "mechanics," we're ready to look at a problem to be solved. Let's suppose that quizzes have been administered daily in a basic math class you've taken. It's late Friday, and you'd like to know your total score for the week.

DEFINE THE PROBLEM. Given five daily test scores achieved by a student as input, determine the total number of points earned.

PLAN THE SOLUTION. Let M, T, W, H, F = the individual test scores for Monday, Tuesday, Wednesday, Thursday, and Friday, respectively.

Then S = M + T + W + H + F.

We can use the computer to carry out this solution plan. In doing so, we first make sure the daily test scores are available to the computer. Next we tell it to add the scores. When the addition is completed, we want the computer to provide the result as output. We state this plan in the form of a sequence of simple action steps, or *algorithm,* as follows:

System command	Meaning
ENTER BASIC	The user intends to write, modify, or execute a BASIC program.
OLD	The program to be used already exists in the user's program library within the computer.
NEW	A new program is to be created during this session.
SAVE	The program currently being used is to be stored in the user's program library within the computer for later use.
UNSAVE program	The specified program is to be deleted from the user's program library.
RENAME program-name	Change the name of the program currently being used to the program-name specified.
LIST	Display the program statements of the program currently being used, on a televisionlike screen or on a printer.
CATALOG	Display the names of the programs in the user's library.
RENUMBER	Renumber the statements of the program currently in use, beginning with 100 and continuing with successive numbers in increments of 10 (100, 110, 120, . . .).
RUN	Execute the program currently being worked on by the user.
STOP	Stop program execution at once. (This command can be entered while the computer is executing the program. On many systems, a key on the keyboard can be pressed to achieve the same effect.)
OFF	Terminate this interactive session.

Figure A-1 **Some typical system commands for interactive programming**

- Read in five test scores.
- Add the scores to determine the total number of points.
- Print the total number of points as output.

WRITE THE PROGRAM. At this point, we look again at the problem to be solved and at the solution plan. Will the plan we've developed solve the problem? Assuming we decide that our plan is correct, we're ready to express it in the BASIC language. (See Figure A-2.)

Notice that each statement in the program begins with a *line number.* The line numbers are important, because they determine the order in which the required operations will be carried out by the computer. We could have used any numbers in the range from 1 through 9999 as line numbers.* Beginning with 100 and using increments of 10 between numbers are wise programming practices, however. If statements need to be added to the program later,

* As we'll discuss later, some features of BASIC differ slightly from one computer system to another. Some systems allow line numbers as high as 9999, but others allow line numbers up to 65529 or even as high as 99999. We've used the lower value here, thereby insuring that our highest line number is acceptable in all environments.

```
100 INPUT M, T, W, H, F
110 LET S = M + T + W + H + F
120 PRINT S
130 END
```

Figure A-2 A BASIC program to compute total points

there's room to insert them without renumbering existing lines. For example, up to nine statements (numbers 101, 102, . . . , 109) could be inserted between lines 100 and 110 in this program.

Line 100 is an *INPUT statement.* It will be recognized as such because of the *keyword* INPUT. The letters M, T, W, H, and F are *numeric variables.* Each variable is associated with a storage location within the computer where a numeric data item can be stored. In an INPUT statement, the variables are separated by commas as shown in Figure A-2. Each variable used in a BASIC program must be unique. Since we used T for Tuesday, we could not use T for Thursday; we chose H, the second letter of Thursday, instead.

As we'll discuss later, some BASIC implementations allow numeric variables to be up to 31 characters in length. Choosing meaningful names for variables helps to insure that programs are understandable to human readers. Therefore, if longer variables are allowed on the system available to you, you may want to use them. To insure the programs shown in this appendix are usable on all BASIC implementations, we'll use 1- or 2-character variables but we'll explain the values they represent.

When the computer encounters an INPUT statement (or, more precisely, the machine-language equivalent of an INPUT statement) during program execution, it prints a question mark on the terminal or microcomputer display screen, pauses, and waits for the user to enter a value for each variable named in the INPUT statement.

Line 110 is a *LET statement,* also called an *assignment statement.* It directs the computer to evaluate the expression to the right side of the equal sign and assign the result of the evaluation to the variable named to the left of the equal sign. Each + is an *arithmetic operator,* telling the computer to perform an addition operation. The computer completes the addition operations and stores the result in the computer storage location represented by the variable S. In a LET statement, the symbol = does not mean "is equal to." Rather, = is used as an *assignment symbol,* telling the computer to evaluate the expression at its right and assign the result to the variable at its left, as we've just described.

Line 120 is a *PRINT statement.* When the computer encounters this statement during program execution, it will provide the current value of the variable S as output.

The last statement in every BASIC program must be an *END statement.* It must have the highest line number in the program. For this reason, some users adopt the programming practice of always using 9999 or 99999 as the END statement number. There can be one and only one END statement in a program. Its purpose is twofold. First, when the BASIC program is being translated from the BASIC language to machine-language instructions, the END statement indicates that there are no more statements to be translated.

Second, if encountered during program execution, it causes execution to be terminated.

TEST THE PROGRAM. Now it's time to be sure the program really directs the computer as it's supposed to do. First, we need to make sure that we've written the BASIC statements correctly (that is, that the *program syntax* is correct). Next, we need to make sure that the *program logic* is correct. Is our solution plan really a good one? An effective way to tell is: Try out the program on the computer!

When we execute the program on the computer, we need to provide a set of *test data* as input. A wise approach is to use simple test data initially. We must also figure out beforehand what the result of the *test run* should be. Otherwise, we may be too willing to agree with the computer.

For an initial test run, let's use the values, 1, 2, 3, 4, and 5 as daily test scores. Since 1 + 2 + 3 + 4 + 5 = 15, the value 15 should be printed as output.

To get ready to enter a BASIC program, use the sign-on procedure and system commands on the system available to you. Then type in the statements of Figure A-2. Type RUN (or its equivalent). If the computer pauses and prints a question mark on the screen, all's well so far. You need only type in (on the same line) the test scores, separated by commas. Then press the ENTER key. If the program you've entered is correct, you should see something like this:

```
? 1,2,3,4,5
15
```

If your interaction with the computer doesn't occur more or less as we've described, you may have made a mistake—say, procedurally, or in typing. The computer may have printed a message to you describing the error. You should check again the actions you've taken and/or the system documentation available. Correct your mistake and try again. Next, choose another set of test data, calculate what the result of the test run should be, and rerun the program. Does the computer's result agree with yours? If not, you must find the error, correct it, and try again.

When you are satisfied that the program you have entered is correct, use the system commands available to you to save the program for later use. Give the program a meaningful name, such as POINTS, by which you can refer to it at that time.

PROVIDE DOCUMENTATION. Since you helped to develop the program in Figure A-2, you know what its function is. When the computer paused and printed a question mark during program execution, you knew what it expected you to do. You also understood the value provided as output. Will you remember all these facts when you attempt to use the program later? What if someone other than you were to run the program? To insure that the program will be useful later, we need to provide documentation of it.

```
10 REM POINTS. COMPUTE TOTAL NUMBER OF POINTS EARNED.
20 REM M, T, W, H, F ARE TEST SCORES FOR MONDAY THRU FRIDAY.
90 PRINT "ENTER FIVE DAILY TEST SCORES"
100 INPUT M, T, W, H, F
110 LET S = M + T + W + H + F
120 PRINT "THE TOTAL NUMBER OF POINTS IS", S
130 END
```

Figure A-3 A documented BASIC program

There are features of the BASIC language that allow us to document a program, its inputs, and its outputs. An improved version of the program, including such documentation, is shown in Figure A-3.

Lines 10 and 20 are *REM statements,* or *remarks.* Line 10 tells the name of the program and its function. Line 20 tells what the input variables M, T, W, H, and F stand for. REM statements have no effect on program execution. They are intended to be read by humans who want to understand the program.

Line 90, a PRINT statement, immediately precedes the INPUT statement. The PRINT statement contains the *character-string constant* ENTER FIVE DAILY TEST SCORES. In BASIC, a character-string constant can contain letters, digits, and special characters such as $ and #. If the constant is specified in a PRINT statement, it must be enclosed in quotation marks.

When lines 90 and 100 are executed, the computer will print the following prompt on the screen and then wait for data to be entered:

```
ENTER FIVE DAILY TEST SCORES
?
```

See how the PRINT statement assists the user. It provides documentation of the input data values required. Including a PRINT statement for this purpose before each INPUT statement is good programming practice.

Line 120 is also a PRINT statement, as in our initial version of the program, but the PRINT statement has been modified. When the computer encounters this statement during program execution, it will print out the character-string constant THE TOTAL NUMBER OF POINTS IS (without the quotation marks) and the current value of the variable S.

TEST THE PROGRAM (AGAIN). Since we've developed a modified version of our initial program, we need to repeat the test step of program development. As before, use the sign-on procedure and system commands available to you. Retrieve the initial program that you saved. Modify it as we have done. Use 1, 2, 3, 4, and 5 as the daily test scores in a test run. Verify that 15 is provided as output. You may wonder about the spacing of the values in the output line. It may seem unusual, but do not assume that you have made an error. We'll learn more about the PRINT statement later. There are capabilities you can use to further control the spacing of output if desired.

DO IT NOW
SET A

A1. What are the five tasks of program development?

A2. Discuss what it's like to use a computer in interactive mode.

A3. Explain what will happen when the following BASIC program is executed:

```
100 REM TEMP. H AND L ARE THE HIGH AND LOW TEMPERATURE
110 REM READINGS FOR THE DAY, RESPECTIVELY
200 PRINT "ENTER THE HIGH AND LOW TEMPERATURE READINGS"
300 INPUT H, L
400 LET R = H - L
500 PRINT H, L, R
600 END
```

A4. Check your response to Exercise A3 by entering the program shown there into the computer, and then running it. Use 60 as the low temperature and 83 as the high temperature for your initial test run. What values should be provided as output? What values are? (If you and the computer don't agree, find where the error has occurred.)

A5. The following statements contain errors; rewrite them correctly.
- (a) 100 LET B – C = A.
- (b) 255 REMARK. ACCNTS. DETERMINE AMOUNT DUE
- (c) INPUT A, D
- (d) 200 PRINT "MY NAME IS," N
- (e) 9999 END MYPROG

A6. Plan, write, test, and document a program that accepts the total daily sales for each of seven days at a local bakery as input. It should print the total sales for the week as output.

More about BASIC

If you've followed the suggestions given so far in this appendix, you've already learned how to interact with the computer. In fact, you've already used the computer to solve simple problems. The BASIC language has lived up to its name: **B**eginners' **A**ll-purpose **S**ymbolic **I**nstruction **C**ode. BASIC has many additional capabilities. You need only learn a few of them to be able to solve a wide variety of problems. There are also some simple rules you need to be aware of when using BASIC. Otherwise, you are apt to make errors unknowingly.

Many computer manufacturers and software development firms have developed BASIC language processors, known as *BASIC compilers* or *BASIC interpreters*. These language processors are programs that translate the BASIC statements of a user's program into machine-language code that can be executed by a particular computer. An American National Standard for Minimal BASIC (X3.60-1978) was formally approved by the American National Standards Institute in January 1978. The American National Standard for BASIC (X3.113-1987) published in August 1987 superseded this standard. It contains major changes, improvements, and additions to BASIC. The intent in this appendix is to look primarily at BASIC capabilities that are alike across implementations. Where minor variations are known to exist, they are pointed out.

BASIC Statements and Line Numbers

BASIC is a line-oriented language. It is also a statement-oriented language. Normally, one statement occupies one line. The line number serves as a label for the statement contained in the line. Generally, each statement can be as long as the line length on the terminal or microcomputer from which the statement is entered. Today that's generally from 40 to 120 characters.* Spaces cannot appear at the beginning of a line or within line numbers, keywords, numeric constants, or variables. Each keyword in a program must be preceded by at least one space and must be followed by at least one space if it is not at the end of a line.

As mentioned earlier, line numbers may range from 1 to 9999 or higher. (The 1987 ANS BASIC standard allows line numbers up to 50000.) Leading zeros have no effect. Lines need not be entered in ascending line-number sequence. That is, you may type in line 700 and then type in line 670, for example. The BASIC language processor arranges the lines in ascending line-number order prior to program execution.

BASIC Data Types

Data processed by a BASIC program may be of two types: numeric and character.

NUMERIC VALUES. BASIC accepts and displays numeric values in three formats: *integer, decimal,* and *exponential.* (See Figure A-4.) In the integer and decimal forms, the values are expressed as we usually write them (but without any commas). The decimal form includes a decimal point. A plus sign may precede a positive value. If a value is negative, it must be preceded immediately by a minus sign. The maximum number of digits in both integer and decimal formats varies with the implementation. In some, if a numeric value to be printed has more than six digits, the exponential format is used.

In the exponential form, an integer or a decimal number is followed by the character E, which is in turn followed by a signed or an unsigned 1- or 2-digit integer. The number following the E indicates what power of 10 the number preceding the E should be multiplied by to get the actual numeric value. Thus, 14.3E5 means 14.3×10^5, or $14.3 \times 100{,}000$, which is 1,430,000. Similarly, 124.5E-2 means 124.5×10^{-2}, or $124.5 \times .01$, which is 1.245.

* The 1987 ANS BASIC standard and some BASIC language processors support certain characters (&, for example) as continuation characters (thus allowing a statement to extend over multiple lines). Some support certain characters as separator characters (thus allowing multiple statements per line). However, to avoid implementation dependence, it's wise programming practice *not* to take advantage of these capabilities.

Form	Example	Value
Integer	6 +389 −2478	As expressed
Decimal	6.7 +389.41 .0052 −13.6 −.89	As expressed
Exponential	13E2 −157.3E2 2154E−3 2.1E−5 −.2978E+3	1300 −15730 2.154 .000021 −297.8

Figure A-4 Numeric values in BASIC

To think of exponential form another way, positive E notation says that the decimal point (assumed to be just before the E if there is none) should be moved to the right the number of places specified. Negative E notation says that the decimal point should be moved to the left the number of places specified. Another name for this notation is *floating-point notation,* since the point can be moved (floated) and the integer following the E adjusted accordingly. The notation allows for handling very large or very small values. It is commonly used in scientific problem solving but is seldom needed for business applications.

When a numeric value is used in a BASIC statement, like the numeric value 5 in

```
300 LET A = B + 5
```

the value is called a *numeric constant.* It's called a constant because it won't change during program execution. Whenever this LET statement is executed, the numeric value of 5 will always be 5.

CHARACTER DATA. In BASIC, character data exists as a string of characters (i.e., *character string*). The character string may consist of any of the 26 letters of the alphabet, the digits 0 through 9, and special characters (question marks, dollar signs, commas, periods, and so on). When a character string is specified in a BASIC statement, the string is called a *character string constant* (as mentioned earlier). For instance, the value TOTAL AMOUNT DUE IS is a constant in

```
800 PRINT "TOTAL AMOUNT DUE IS", T
```

When a character-string constant is used in a BASIC statement, it must be enclosed in double quotation marks as shown here.* Some BASIC imple-

* Some BASIC implementations accept single quotation marks as delimiters. With such support, 'TOTAL AMOUNT DUE IS' is recognized as a valid character-string constant. Some implementations accept both single and double quotes. However, it's generally wise programming practice to follow the recommended standard—in this case, double quotation marks.

mentations allow the quotation marks to be omitted under certain conditions when character-string values are provided as input. However, to avoid implementation dependence or errors of omission (in situations where quotation marks are needed), it's wise to include them. It's never an error to use the enclosing quotation marks.

Like numeric constants, character-string constants cannot be changed during program execution.

The length of a character-string constant is the number of characters in the string, not counting the delimiting quotation marks. Everything between the delimiters—even blanks, or spaces—must be counted. The maximum number of characters that can be included in a character-string constant varies among BASIC implementations. Usually, the limit is far more than you need. According to the 1987 ANS BASIC standard, the default limit must be at least 132; it is defined as the maximum number of characters that will fit on one input or output line.

Here are some examples of character-string constants and their lengths:

Constant	Length
"ABCD"	4
"MY NAME IS"	11
"A ""SMASH"" HIT"	13
"123"	3

Notice that when the character-string constant contains quotation marks, they must be represented by pairs of quotation marks. However, each pair counts as one character. Notice also that a character string consisting of only digits is still character data. The character-string constant 123 cannot be used in arithmetic operations.

VARIABLES

We've just observed that in the BASIC statement

```
300 LET A = B + 5
```

the 5 is a numeric constant; its value is 5 throughout program execution. In contrast, the B in this statement is not a constant; furthermore, its value is not B. Rather, the B is a *numeric variable.* At any given time, it represents, or stands for, a single numeric value. As the term *variable* indicates, the value represented by B can be changed many times during program execution. In fact, the numeric variable B is associated with a certain location (or locations) in computer storage. At one time during program execution, the location(s) may contain the numeric value 156; at another time, the location(s) may contain 68; and so on. Thus, the numeric variable B represents different values at different times. BASIC implementations that adhere to the 1987 ANS BASIC standard allow a numeric variable to consist of up to 31 characters.

In like manner, a *string variable* represents a string of characters. Standard-conforming BASIC implementations allow a string variable to consist of up to 30 characters followed by a dollar sign. Thus, at one time during program execution, CITY$ may represent the string value SAN FRANCISCO, CA. At another time, CITY$ may represent PITTSBURGH, PA. N$ and CAN$ are other examples of valid string variables.

Just as a character-string constant has a length associated with it, a character string represented by a string variable has a length associated with it, too. According to the 1987 ANS BASIC standard, the length of the string may vary during program execution; the length is simply the number of characters stored in locations reserved for the string variable at any given time. It may range from zero characters (specifying the null or empty string) to the maximum allowed for the string variable. For example, assume the character string J. MARVIN is assigned to the variable NAME$; its associated length is 9. Assume that later the character string R. B. GARCIA is assigned to NAME$; its associated length is 12.* The current length of the string determines the number of spaces the value represented by the variable will occupy if it is written on an output line.

DO IT NOW
SET B

B1. Express the value three hundred eighty-five:
(a) In integer form __________
(b) In decimal form __________
(c) In exponential form __________
(d) As a character-string constant __________

B2. Express the following values in integer or decimal form:
(a) 1.456E + 02 __________
(b) −3.7891E + 03 __________
(c) 2.1783E − 03 __________
(d) −6.734E + 06 __________

B3. Explain the difference between constants and variables.

B4. What distinguishes a string variable from a numeric variable?

B5. Plan, write, test, and document a program that accepts a customer account number, customer name, and customer address as input. The program should print out four lines to be used as a mailing label. The first line should contain the account number; the second line should contain the name; the third line, the street address; and the fourth line, the city, state, and zip code.

* In some BASIC implementations, the length associated with a string variable is fixed throughout program execution. It does not vary according to the number of characters in the string assigned to it. For example, unless the user specifies otherwise, a length of 132 may be associated with each string variable throughout program execution. In such implementations, a DIM (dimension) statement can be used to assign a different length (say, up to a maximum of 255) to specific string variables if desired. The fixed length associated with a string variable determines the number of characters that can be stored in the computer storage locations reserved for it. A disadvantage of this approach is that the output generated by PRINT statements may contain extraneous spaces (the contents of reserved storage locations that contain only blanks).

B6. Plan, write, test, and document a program that accepts a length expressed in yards as input. The program should compute the total number of feet and the total number of inches corresponding to the input value. The length expressed in yards, in feet, and in inches (each labeled appropriately) should be printed as output. (*Hint:* In BASIC, a multiplication operation is specified by the arithmetic operator * .)

THE LET STATEMENT

The LET, or assignment, statement is a data manipulation statement. The general form of this statement is:

```
line no. LET variable = expression
```

In some BASIC implementations, the keyword LET is optional. However, to avoid implementation dependence or errors of omission, it's wise to include LET. (BASIC language processors that adhere fully to the 1987 ANS BASIC standard require it.) The LET statement tells the computer to evaluate the *expression* at the right of the assignment symbol and assign the result to the receiving *variable* named at the left of the assignment symbol. If the receiving variable is a string variable, the expression can be a character-string constant or the current value of a string variable. If the receiving variable is a numeric variable, the expression can be a numeric constant, the current value of a numeric variable, or a combination of numeric constants, numeric variables, and arithmetic operators.

You can use the LET statement to move, or copy, data. You can also use it to perform arithmetic operations. Let's look at some move operations first:

```
100 LET D$ = "DEPT. 64"
200 LET C = X
```

As these examples show, BASIC allows both arithmetic and character-string assignments. When line 100 is executed, the character-string constant DEPT. 64 is assigned to the string variable D$. Whatever was in D$ before the start of the operation is overlaid by the moved constant. Line 200 causes the current value of the numeric variable X to be copied into the computer storage locations reserved for the numeric variable C. Whatever was in C before is overlaid by the current value of X. The current value of X in its original storage locations is unchanged. (That's why, in fact, a "move" from one area of the computer's internal storage unit to another is what we might usually perceive as a copy operation.)

To direct the computer to perform arithmetic operations by means of a LET statement, you specify a numeric expression containing one or more BASIC arithmetic operators and one or more numeric constants and/or variables used as operands. There are five BASIC arithmetic operators. (See Figure A-5.)

Some straightforward LET statement numeric expressions containing these operators are:

```
200 LET D = R * T
210 LET H = M / 60
```

Operation	BASIC symbol*	BASIC numeric expression	Arithmetic example
Exponentiation	^	X^2 244^.5	X^2 $244^{1/2}$
Multiplication	*	X*Y 60 * S	XY 60 x S
Division	/	N/3 D / T	$\frac{N}{3}$ D ÷ T
Addition	+	B+C V + 15	B+C V + 15
Subtraction	−	X−Y S − 1.05	X−Y S − 1.05

*The circumflex symbol ^ shown here is the ANS recommended symbol for exponentiation. Use of the symbol ** or ↑ for exponentiation is also common in BASIC implementations.

Figure A-5 BASIC arithmetic operations

The spaces preceding and following the assignment symbols and arithmetic operators help to make the statements readable to us, but they are not required.

If you want to specify more than one arithmetic operation within one LET statement, you need to know the order in which these operations will be carried out by the computer. Consider the following statement as an example:

```
300 LET V = 2 + 3 * 10
```

Will the computer first add 2 to 3, to get 5, and then multiply 5 by 10, thus determining a final result of 50? Or will the computer first multiply 3 by 10, to get 30, and then add 2, thus determining a final result of 32? Obviously, the order in which the + and * operations are carried out makes a difference!

If you are familiar with the rules of common mathematics, you'll find the BASIC rules that determine the order of arithmetic operations easy to follow:

1. Exponentiation is done first.
2. Multiplication and division are done second.
3. Addition and subtraction are done third.
4. If two or more operations at the same level of precedence are specified (say, one division and two multiplications), the operations are done from left to right.

Looking back at our example, we conclude that the computer will first multiply 3 by 10, and then add 2. (Since there are no exponentiations, rule 2 is applied, and then rule 3.)

Here are two more examples:

```
400 LET A = 4 * T * R^2
410 LET B = R / 3 - S * T
```

Assume R has a value of 3, S has a value of 4, and T has a value of 5 when these statements are executed. Line 400 causes the computer to first raise R (i.e., 3) to the power of 2, giving 9; then 4 is multiplied by T, giving 20; then 20 is multiplied by 9, giving 180; this result is assigned to the receiving variable A. Line 410 tells the computer to first divide R by 3 (to get 1); next multiply S by T (to get 20); and then subtract 20 from 1 (to get −19); this result is assigned to the receiving variable B.

Parentheses can be used to clarify (for persons who may read the statements in a BASIC program) or to override (during program execution) the normal rules of precedence stated above. To appreciate the importance of this capability, suppose the temperature readings at the same time on three successive days are 31°C, 44°C, and 48°C. Further suppose we write the following BASIC statement to direct the computer to find the average temperature for this three-day period:

```
500 LET A = 31 + 44 + 48 / 3
```

When this statement is encountered, the computer will first divide 48 by 3, to get 16 (rule 2); then add 31 and 44, to get 75 (rules 3 and 4); then add 75 and 16, to get 91 (rules 3 and 4 again); and finally assign the result 91 to A. The average of 31, 44, and 48, however, is obviously not 91! (Compute the average temperature manually. You should determine that the correct result is 41.)

How do we fix this situation? We need a way to tell the computer that, in this particular situation, the addition operations are to be done *before* the division operation. To do so, we rewrite the BASIC statement, enclosing the addition operations in parentheses:

```
500 LET A = (31 + 44 + 48) / 3
```

Now, the computer will add 31 and 44, to get 75; then add 75 and 48, to get 123; then divide 123 by 3, to get 41; and finally assign the result 41 to A. This result is as it should be.

As this example shows, parentheses are used in BASIC just as in common mathematics to control the order of expression evaluation. All operations within a set of parentheses are done before operations outside the parentheses. If there are parentheses within parentheses, the computer performs the operations in the innermost set of parentheses first. If there are multiple operations within a set of parentheses, the normal rules of precedence are applied to determine the order of operations within the set. Here are two more examples:

```
600 LET R = (5+A)*(3*B)
610 LET T = ((5+A)*B)^2
```

Assume A has a value of 1 and B has a value of 2 when these statements are executed. Line 600 causes the computer to first add 5 and A (i.e., 1), to get 6; then multiply 3 by 2, to get 6; then multiply 6 by 6, to get 36; this result is assigned to the receiving variable R. Line 610 tells the computer to first add 5 and 1, to get 6; then multiply 6 by 2, to get 12; then raise 12 to the power 2, to get 144; this result is assigned to the receiving variable T.

It's wise programming practice to include parentheses within any numeric expression involving several arithmetic operations. Doing so is a way of insuring we are really telling the computer to do what we think we are telling it to do. In some cases, the parentheses are needed to change the order of expression evaluation as described above. In others, they're needed to separate operators that would be consecutive otherwise. For example,

```
620 LET U = A^(-2)
```

Unnecessary but correctly placed parentheses reflecting the order in which operations occur can serve as valuable program documentation. The computer is not bothered by extraneous parentheses, telling it to do what it would do otherwise anyway.

Before ending this discussion of the LET statement, we need to look at one more use of its capabilities:

```
700 LET C = C + 1
```

As this example shows, a variable that appears to the right of the assignment symbol in a LET statement can also appear as the receiving variable in the statement. Here, the current value of the variable C is increased by 1, and the result of the addition operation is stored back into the computer storage locations reserved for the variable C. This technique is often used in programming to increase or decrease by a fixed amount the value of a variable used as a counter. When we add 1 each time, we are, of course, counting by 1s. We might do so to keep track of the number of input values processed for control purposes.

The REM Statement

As the problems that you solve with computer assistance increase in complexity, the use of REM statements, or remarks, to document your solution algorithms becomes increasingly important also. The general form of the REM statement is:

```
line no. REM comment
```

You may include REM statements to explain the over-all function of a BASIC program and/or of specific parts of the program. As we saw earlier, REM statements can also be used to explain the data represented by variables. If the length of a comment exceeds the space available on a line, the comment can be continued on subsequent lines. A line number and the keyword REM must appear on these lines, just as on the first line.

The REM statement is a *nonexecutable statement.* That is, it is not translated into machine-language code by the BASIC language processor, and it has no effect on the execution of the program. Rather, it is simply printed out together with the other program statements in response to a LIST command (or its equivalent), as an aid to persons who want to read and understand the program. As with other BASIC statements, the line numbers of REM statements determine their order on the program listing. Since REM statements are nonexecutable, they can be included wherever they are needed in the program.

Some BASIC implementations provide an additional documentation capability—support for the inclusion of comments on the same lines as *execut-*

able statements (LET, PRINT, etc.). Where such support is provided, the use of such a comment is usually signaled by a special character, say, an exclamation point, immediately preceding the comment. For example:

```
100 LET P = P * 1.065 !COMPUTE SIMPLE INTEREST, 6 1/2%
```

Some implementations also allow comment-only lines introduced by special characters. Such statements are called *null statements.* An example is:

```
200 ! EXECUTION TERMINATES WHEN A ZERO VALUE IS ENCOUNTERED
```

To determine whether these documentation capabilities are available on your system, you should consult the system documentation.

THE END STATEMENT

Every program must have one and only one END statement. It must be the last statement in the program and therefore must have the highest line number in the program. The general form of the END statement is:

```
line no. END
```

This statement tells the BASIC language processor where the BASIC program ends. When encountered during program execution, it causes program execution to stop. As mentioned earlier, the use of all 9s as the line number for the END statement is a common programming practice. Use of this practice may help you to remember to include the END statement and to insure that it's positioned properly.

DO IT NOW
SET C

C1. Distinguish between executable and nonexecutable statements. In doing so, give one or more examples of each.

C2. Assume the variables A, B, and C have been assigned the values 12, 6, and 2, respectively. Determine what value will be assigned to R, as a result of executing each LET statement below.

(a) LET R = A + B − C
(b) LET R = A + (B − C)
(c) LET R = A + B / C
(d) LET R = (B + C)^2
(e) LET R = (A / (B − 4)) / (B − A)
(f) LET R = (A/3)^.5
(g) LET R = ((C^2) + (A/C) / (5 − B)

C3. Express the following arithmetic operations using BASIC LET statements to direct the computer to perform the operations specified and assign the result to R.

(a) $\frac{1}{2}bh$
(b) $b^2 - 4ac$
(c) $P(r + 1)^n$
(d) $2\pi r$ (use 3.1416 as a value for π)
(e) πr^2 (use 3.1416 as a value for π)
(f) $\frac{A^2 + B^2}{C(B - A)}$
(g) $\frac{(A + B)^N}{CD^{.5}}$

C4. Look at your response to Exercise C3(d) above. You've expressed the formula for finding the circumference of a circle as a BASIC LET statement. Use that statement in developing a BASIC program that accepts the radius of a circle as input, computes the circumference of the circle, and provides both the radius and the circumference as output. The program should accept the radius value in whatever unit of measure the user wants, but it should ask the user what unit is to be used, and include that information as part of the output documentation.

Use the following sets of data as input for test runs of your program. Remember to determine manually what the results of the test runs should be beforehand. To verify that the computer's results are correct, you may need to read and understand exponential format. You should learn to convert readily between exponential and decimal or integer forms.

Radius	Unit used
2	Meters
2.2468	Inches

C5. Look at your responses to Exercise C3(e) above. You've expressed the formula for finding the area of a circle as a BASIC LET statement. Use that statement in developing an enhanced version of the program that you developed in response to Exercise C4. It should accept the radius of a circle as input, compute both the circumference and the area of the circle, and provide the radius, circumference, and area as output. The unit of measure should be documented as above. Again, determine what results should be provided as output before making your test runs. If the actual results do not agree with your expected results, find your error (or errors), correct them, and rerun the program.

C6. Each salesperson at a local brokerage firm is paid a monthly commission, based on his or her total sales for the month (S) and a particular commission rate (R) that applies. Plan, write, test, and document a BASIC program to compute a salesperson's commission, given his or her name, total sales, and commission rate as input. Use the following data as the basis for input to the first and second test runs of your program.

Employee	Total sales	Commission rate
J. Sonya	$ 5,024.00	8.0%
M. L. Riley	$13,800.00	8.5%

The INPUT Statement

As we saw earlier, the unique, very important function of the INPUT statement is to allow the user to provide input data to a program while the program is being executed. The general form of this statement is:

```
line no. INPUT variable, variable, . . ., variable
```

When this statement is encountered, the computer prints a question mark or similar prompt on the display screen and waits for the user to key in values, separated by commas, and then press the ENTER key (or its equivalent). The first data value entered is paired with the first variable; the second one is paired with the second variable; and so on. Both numeric variables and string variables can appear in a single INPUT statement. The type of each data item must be the same as the type of the variable to which it is assigned. That is, numeric data in integer, decimal, or exponential format must be supplied as input for numeric variables; character-string data must be supplied as input for string variables.

After the ENTER key (or its equivalent) has been pressed, the computer verifies that the number of data values entered, the type of each value, and the range of each value are acceptable for the variables named in the INPUT statement. If the input is accepted as valid, the entered data values are assigned to the variables. If the user has made a data-entry error, a message asking for re-input is displayed.

Whereas the ANS Standard for Minimal BASIC required that all values be validated before any assignment of values occurred, the 1987 ANS BASIC standard does not. An input-response of 9, 2, X in response to INPUT HIGH, LOW, MEDIAN may cause the values of HIGH and LOW to be changed even though the value the user entered for MEDIAN will not be accepted as valid. You should experiment by entering various sets of values in response to INPUT statements to determine how validation is implemented on the system available to you.

The program in Figure A-6 computes the inventory cost and sales value of an item in stock, based on the unit cost paid for the item and the current unit price of the item. Notice that the program contains two INPUT statements. Why might it be good programming practice to structure the request for input to this program in this fashion? What does the use of a string variable rather than a numeric variable to represent the item number allow for?

As Exercise D1 (below) suggests, use the sign-on procedure, system commands, and keyboard available to you to enter this program into the computer. Given the representative data values for the input variables, determine what the resultant output should be. Then run the program. Check the re-

Figure A-6 Computing inventory cost and sales values

```
100 REM STOCK.  COMPUTE INVENTORY COST AND SALES VALUE
110 REM OF ITEM IN STOCK.
120 REM I$ IS ITEM NUMBER.
125 REM Q IS QUANTITY ON HAND.
130 REM C IS UNIT COST.
135 REM P IS UNIT PRICE.
140 PRINT "ENTER ITEM NUMBER"
150 INPUT I$
160 PRINT "ENTER QUANTITY, UNIT COST, UNIT PRICE"
170 INPUT Q, C, P
180 REM I IS INVENTORY COST (PAID OUT FOR ITEM).
190 LET I = Q * C
200 REM S IS SALES VALUE (AT CURRENT MARKET PRICE).
210 LET S = Q * P
220 PRINT "ITEM NO.", "QTY", "INV. COST", "SALES VALUE"
230 PRINT I$, Q, I, S
240 END
```

sults against your expected results. Do they agree? If not, you should find the error, correct it, and rerun the program.

The PRINT Statement

In a very real sense, a BASIC program is of value to us because the result of processing accomplished during program execution can be printed or displayed as output. The PRINT statement performs this function. The general form of this statement is:

```
line no. PRINT list
```

To skip a line on output, the simplest kind of PRINT statement is used. It consists of only a line number and the keyword PRINT. For example:

```
300 PRINT
```

When this statement is encountered, it causes an end-of-print character to be generated within the system. In common usage, the user perceives a blank line on the printed or displayed output. (We might think of this as "double spacing.") To skip two lines (i.e., provide "triple spacing"), we use two blank PRINT statements. For example:

```
300 PRINT
310 PRINT
```

The *list* specified in a PRINT statement may consist of one or more variables, numeric expressions, and/or character-string constants separated by commas or semicolons. It may also contain one or more invocations of the TAB (tabulation) function. As we shall continue to see, the PRINT statement is designed to provide simple, documented output or volume output in a consistent tabular form.

In general, the PRINT statement as discussed here causes the output of program execution to be returned to the user at the device from which the program and/or RUN command (or its equivalent) are entered. Increasingly, the output medium is a display screen—say, a visual-display unit attached to a large computer, or a microcomputer such as a Compaq Deskpro 386 or an IBM Personal System/2. As explained in this book, such output is often referred to as "soft-copy" output. Special action on your part may be needed to create printed, paper ("hard-copy") output. For example, some BASIC implementations require the use of PRINT to cause output to be directed to a display screen, and of LPRINT to create hard-copy output. In other systems, whether the output of a BASIC program goes to a display screen, or to the printer, or to both, is determined by user-specified system commands, independent of BASIC language facilities. For your work here, you need only find out how various forms of output are produced on the system available to you, and plan your work accordingly.

PRINTING NUMERIC VALUES. A numeric value to be printed can be specified as a numeric variable, a numeric constant, or a numeric expression containing a combination of numeric variables, numeric constants, and arithmetic operators. The rules the computer applies in evaluating a numeric expression in a PRINT statement are the same as those it applies in evaluating a numeric expression to the right of the assignment symbol in a LET statement. The result of the evaluation is printed as output.

A numeric value in its printable form consists of a leading space if the number is positive or a leading minus sign if the number is negative, followed by the decimal representation of the absolute value of the number and a trailing space. Usually, numeric values consisting of six or fewer digits are printed in integer or decimal format. Extremely large or extremely small values are printed in exponential format.

To cause multiple values to be printed on a single line of output, we can specify multiple values in a single PRINT statement. We control the spacing of the values on the output line by means of the *print separator character* we specify in the PRINT statement. In the BASIC programs developed so far, we've used the *comma* as a print separator. Use of the comma causes each output line to be divided into a fixed number of *print zones*. The number of zones and the width of the zones are not specified within the 1987 ANS BASIC standard. Flexibility was recognized as desirable, to accommodate a variety of output devices. In general, the number and width of zones depend on the length of the output line. All print zones except possibly the last one must be the same length. Assume the line is divided into five equal-size print zones, beginning in columns 1, 16, 31, 46, and 61. For example:

```
Col. 1         Col. 16        Col. 31        Col. 46        Col. 61
↓              ↓              ↓              ↓              ↓
 345           -432            14            -4455.1         28
```

This output resembles typewriter output with tab stops every 15 spaces. Can you see how multiple executions of PRINT statements using the same format can be used to generate consistent tabular output?

There are ways to further control spacing. For example, suppose we want to create centered, two-column output. We can tell the computer to skip certain print zones. In BASIC implementations that adhere to the 1987 ANS BASIC standard, we might write

```
100 LET A = -368
110 LET B = 430
120 PRINT ,A,,B
```

to cause the following output:

```
Col. 1         Col. 16        Col. 31        Col. 46        Col. 61
↓              ↓              ↓              ↓              ↓
               -368                           430
```

Normally, each PRINT statement execution causes the printing of output to begin on a new line. If a PRINT statement ends with a comma, however, the output of the next PRINT statement starts in the next available print zone. Thus, the statements

```
100 LET A = 200
110 PRINT A, 3 * A,
120 PRINT A, 5 * A
```

provide the following output:

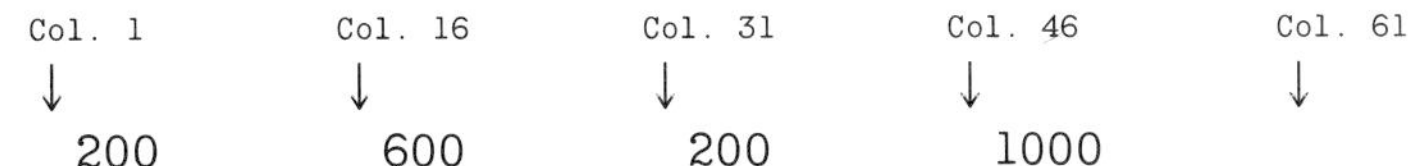

Col. 1
Col. 16
Col. 31
Col. 46
Col. 61
200
600
200
1000

Sometimes we neither want nor need the wide spacing of the fixed print zones. We can use the *semicolon* as a print separator character to cause output to be packed more closely on a line. In BASIC implementations that adhere to the 1987 ANS BASIC standard, the semicolon *does not* cause extra spacing. Therefore, between two positive values on a line there are two blank spaces: one is the trailing space of the first value; the second is the leading space of the second value. If the second value is negative, there is only one blank space between them: the trailing space of the first value. The next print position holds the leading minus sign of the second value. An example is:

```
Col. 1  6       12  15       24
↓       ↓       ↓   ↓        ↓
 345 -432  14 -4455.1  28
```

Ending a PRINT statement with a semicolon has an effect similar to that of ending with a comma: output of a subsequent PRINT statement execution may follow on the same output line. Thus, the statements

```
100 LET A = 8
110 LET B = 6
120 PRINT A; A^2;
130 PRINT B; B^2
```

are functionally equivalent to

```
100 LET A = 8
110 LET B = 6
120 PRINT A; A^2; B; B^2
```

Either group of statements provides the following output:

```
Col. 1  5  9  12
↓       ↓  ↓  ↓
 8  64  6  36
```

Both commas and semicolons can be used in a single PRINT statement if desired. For example, the statements

```
200 LET A = 6
210 PRINT A; A + 10, A; A * 10
```

provide the following output:

```
Col. 1 5            16   20
↓      ↓            ↓    ↓
 6  16               6  60
```

The BASIC program in Figure A-7 does nothing fancy or sophisticated. Nor does it solve a common business problem. Rather, it's simply designed to encourage you to experiment. Enter into your computer system some LET statements assigning numeric values to variables. As you do so, be sure to include some very big values and some very small values. Some should be positive and some should be negative. Then enter some PRINT statements referring to those variables, and containing numeric constants and expres-

```
100 REM TRYIT.  SEE WHAT PRINT STATEMENTS DO.
110 REM ASSIGN VALUES TO VARIABLES.
120 LET A = 123456
130 LET B = -963.3
140 LET C = .0123
150 LET D = .000135
160 LET E = -24680246
170 LET F = .00001122
180 REM
190 REM
200 REM PRINT OUT VALUES.
210 PRINT A
220 PRINT B, 2 * B
230 PRINT C, D
240 PRINT E, F
250 PRINT A/B, A*B, C^2
260 PRINT D + F, B * D, B / D
270 END


 123456
-963.3          -1926.6
 .0123           1.35E-04
-2.46802E+07     1.122E-05
-128.159        -1.18925E+08      1.5129E-04
 1.4622E-04     -.130046         -7.13556E+06
```

Figure A-7 Printing numeric values

sions as well. Use both commas and semicolons as print separator characters. Add an END statement, press RUN (or its equivalent), and see results provided by the program you've created. By becoming somewhat familiar now with the system available to you, you'll be better equipped to tell the computer exactly what you want it to do.

Most BASIC language processors provide one additional positioning facility we've not discussed as yet. It's called the *TAB function*. You can use this function to state the exact position on an output line at which printing is to begin. For example, the statement

```
200 PRINT TAB(10); A
```

causes the current value of the numeric variable A to be printed, beginning at the tenth print position of the output line. (That is, print position 10 will contain the leading space of a positive value, or the leading minus sign of a negative value.)

The value in parentheses following the keyword TAB is called the *function argument*. It may be specified as a numeric expression to be evaluated. For example:

```
300 PRINT A; TAB(N); B
```

When this statement is encountered, the current value of A will be printed, beginning in column 1. Then the current value of N will be determined. If the current value of N is not an integer, it will be rounded to an integral value. If there are not more than N − 1 characters on the current line, then the current value of B will be printed, beginning at position N on the current line. If there are already more than N − 1 characters on the current line, then the current value of B will be printed, beginning at position N on the next line.

Because the TAB function allows specification of a particular print position, it can be used to generate output in a consistent, tabular form. The lengths of output values do not cause relative positioning anomalies as they may do otherwise.

PRINTING CHARACTER DATA. Character data to be printed can be specified as a character-string constant or a string variable. You may want to print character data for any of several reasons. We've seen some of them. Recall the following statement from our program to compute the total number of points earned on five daily tests:

```
90 PRINT "ENTER FIVE DAILY TEST SCORES"
```

This PRINT statement contains the character-string constant ENTER FIVE DAILY TEST SCORES. The statement immediately precedes an INPUT statement. (Look back at Figure A-3.) Its function is to tell the user what input is expected when the INPUT statement causes the system to wait for data to be entered.

A second PRINT statement in the same BASIC program is:

```
120 PRINT "THE TOTAL NUMBER OF POINTS IS", S
```

Here the character data documents the computed result provided as output. Multiple values are to be printed by this single PRINT statement. We use the comma as a print separator here as we did when printing numeric values. The comma causes print zones to be established as it did above. If the length of a character string exceeds the width of one print zone, it is continued in the next print zone. If another value is printed on the same output line, it simply begins in the next print zone after that.

In this example, the constant THE TOTAL NUMBER OF POINTS IS contains 29 characters. (We do not count the enclosing quotation marks.) Assuming again that print zones are established as 15-position intervals, representative output is:

```
Col. 1         Col. 16        Col. 31
↓              ↓              ↓
THE TOTAL NUMBER OF POINTS IS   479
```

We know that position 31 contains the leading space of the positive numeric value to be printed. The character string to be printed ends at position 29 of the output line. Hence, two blank spaces separate the two values on the output line.

Let's consider another example. Assume the part number and quantity on hand for a particular item in inventory are printed out by the following statement:

```
200 PRINT "THE QUANTITY ON HAND FOR", P$, "IS", Q
```

A representative output is:

```
Col. 1         Col. 16        Col. 31        Col. 46        Col. 61
↓              ↓              ↓              ↓              ↓
THE QUANTITY ON HAND FOR      N34Q01         IS              268
```

To improve the readability of this output, we can use semicolons rather than commas as print separators in the PRINT statement. The statement

```
200 PRINT "THE QUANTITY ON HAND FOR "; P$; " IS "; Q
```

causes the same information to be printed in a much more readable form:

```
Col. 1
↓
THE QUANTITY ON HAND FOR N34Q01 IS  268
```

Recall that, in ANS BASIC, the semicolon does not cause any extra spaces to occur between printed values. Since we want a space between the word FOR and the first character of the part number, we include a trailing space after FOR in the first character-string constant to be printed. Since we want a space between the last character of the part number and the word IS, we include a leading space as part of the second character-string constant. If we could assume that the numeric value represented by Q would always be positive, we would not need to provide a trailing space as part of the second character-string constant (because positive values to be printed always have a leading space, remember). But if back orders of inventory items may cause negative values to be computed for Q, we need a trailing space after IS to provide one blank on the output line preceding the leading minus sign of a negative value on output.

Yet another reason for printing character data is to provide a heading on output in tabular form. In effect, we want to create the *title* for a printed report. Here, the TAB function is apt to be useful also. For example:

```
300 PRINT TAB(24); "WEEKLY SALES-BY-ITEM REPORT"
```

This statement causes the constant WEEKLY SALES-BY-ITEM REPORT to be printed. By invoking the TAB function, we cause the constant to begin at print position 24 rather than at the left margin (column 1) as it would otherwise.

To create *column headings* beneath this title on the report, we might write:

```
310 PRINT
320 PRINT
330 PRINT " ITEM", "      ITEM", " ", " SALES", "     SALES"
340 PRINT "NUMBER", "DESCRIPTION", " ", "THIS WEEK", "YEAR-TO-DATE"
```

These statements, and the output created by them, are shown in Figure A-8. A PRINT statement causing a subsequent *detail line* to be printed, and representative output of that statement, are also provided.

Some BASIC implementations do not support the use of consecutive commas as a means of skipping print zones as described earlier. The use of a character-string constant consisting only of blanks is an alternative means of accomplishing such skipping. Notice also that the PRINT statements as coded in Figure A-8 assume that the character string represented by the string variable D$ is at least 16 characters in length (otherwise, the value represented by S will begin printing in the third print zone, rather than the fourth one as intended). Some experience with representative sales data will show whether or not this assumption is valid. If not, this part of the program

```
.
.
.
300 PRINT TAB(24); "WEEKLY SALES-BY-ITEM REPORT"
310 PRINT
320 PRINT
330 PRINT " ITEM", "    ITEM", " ", "  SALES", "    SALES"
340 PRINT "NUMBER", "DESCRIPTION", " ", "THIS WEEK", "YEAR-TO-DATE"
.
.
.
820 PRINT
830 PRINT I$, D$, S, Y
.
.
.


                       WEEKLY SALES-BY-ITEM REPORT

 ITEM             ITEM                          SALES          SALES
NUMBER         DESCRIPTION                    THIS WEEK     YEAR-TO-DATE

AB0531         3-RING PLASTIC BINDER           143.20         447.16
   .              .                              .              .
   .              .                              .              .
   .              .                              .              .
```

Figure A-8 Printing report and column headings, and detail lines

should be changed. (The TAB function could be used in line 830, for example.) The 1987 ANS BASIC standard also includes a PRINT USING capability that allows more precise formatting of output—for example, aligning of decimal points in columns of dollars-and-cents amounts, and inclusion of leading dollar signs—if desired.

DO IT NOW SET D

D1. (a) Assume the following data is entered as input to the stock program in Figure A-6. What should the results be, and in what format?

Item number	Quantity	Unit cost	Unit price
A0B345	435	3.47	3.89

(b) Using the sign-on procedure and system commands available to you, key in the program in Figure A-6. Run the program, and compare the actual results to the results you predicted in D1(a) above. If the results do not agree, find the error and correct it. If you made changes in the program as you entered it initially, rerun the program. Continue in this manner until correct results are provided.

D2. After you are satisfied the program in Figure A-6 as you have entered it runs correctly on your system, try some experiments.

(a) Does your BASIC language processor require quotation marks around character-string data entered as input?

(b) What happens if you enter four data values in response to the input request on lines 160 and 170?

(c) What happens if you enter only two values?

(The point here is that you need to become familiar with the features supported on your system and with how the system lets you know when an error has been made. Where do you find the information you need to correct the error and continue your work?)

D3. When an amount of money, called the *principal,* or p, is invested at an annual rate of i percent compounded q times per year, for n years, the principal compounds to an amount a determined as follows:

$$a = p\left(1 + \frac{i}{q}\right)^{nq}$$

Plan, write, test, and document a BASIC program to compute the compound amount. Use the following sets of data as the basis for input to test runs of your program:

p	i	q	n
$1000	.16	4	10
$5200	.09	1	5

D4. Have you ever asked yourself the following question: How many miles can I drive on $5.00 worth of gasoline? Or $2.00 worth? Or $10.00 worth? Plan, write, test, and document a BASIC program to determine the answer to this question, given the amount you have to spend, the price per gallon, and the expected miles per gallon for the TR7, Honda, or whatever you intend to drive. Compute total mileage (i.e., do not assume a round trip). Use the following sets of data as input to test runs of your program:

Vehicle	Amount to Spend	Price/ gallon	Miles/ gallon
1989 Oldsmobile Omega	$10.00	$1.28	25.3
1981 Chevrolet Nova	$ 5.00	$1.19	16.8

The DATA, READ, and RESTORE Statements

So far, we have learned two ways of establishing values for variables:

- Assigning values to the variables by means of LET statements
- Accepting values for the variables as input from the user in response to INPUT statements that cause the computer to wait for the values to be entered

If we know the data values we want the computer to process when we write a BASIC program, why make the computer halt during processing to obtain them? We could write a LET statement to assign each value to a particular variable, but we may not want to do that either. (We might find ourselves writing "umpteen" LET statements!) Often, a wiser approach is to include the data values in one or more DATA statements as part of the program and use READ statements to cause the computer to assign the values to variables at appropriate times.

The general form of the DATA statement is:

```
line no. DATA value, value, . . ., value
```

Each *value* listed in a DATA statement is a numeric constant or a character-string constant. There can be any number of DATA statements in a program, and they can be located anywhere in the program. Before the program is executed, the BASIC language processor places all the values in all the DATA statements into one combined *data list*. The ordering of values within the list is based on two rules:

1. Those of the DATA statement with the lowest line number are first in the list, those of the DATA statement with the second-lowest line number are next, and so on.
2. Within each DATA statement, the leftmost value is first, the second leftmost value is next, and so on.

Thus, the data values from three DATA statements in a BASIC program are ordered as shown below:

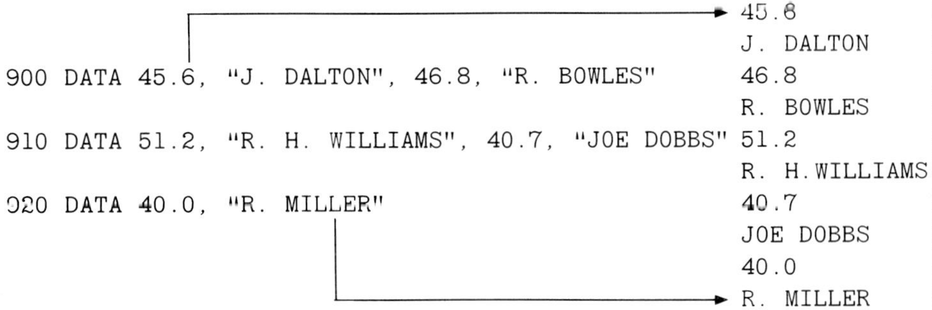
900 DATA 45.6, "J. DALTON", 46.8, "R. BOWLES"
910 DATA 51.2, "R. H. WILLIAMS", 40.7, "JOE DOBBS"
920 DATA 40.0, "R. MILLER"
45.6
J. DALTON
46.8
R. BOWLES
51.2
R. H.WILLIAMS
40.7
JOE DOBBS
40.0
R. MILLER

Conceptually, one value is at the top of the data list at any given time. After that value has been read, the next one is at the top of the list, and so on.

The general form of the READ statement is:

```
line no. READ variable, variable, . . ., variable
```

When this statement is encountered, the computer takes the appropriate number of values from the combined data list and assigns them, in order, to the *variables* in the READ statement. Conceptually, it's as though a read pointer is used to keep track of what data value is next to be assigned (i.e., is at the top of the data list) at any given time.

As an example, assume the combined data list shown above has been formed but not referenced when the following READ statement is executed:

```
200 READ H, N$
```

The numeric constant 45.6 is assigned to H. The character-string constant J. DALTON is assigned to N$.

If, later in program execution, line 200 is executed again, the numeric constant 46.8 is assigned to H (overlaying the previously assigned value). The character-string constant R. BOWLES is assigned to N$ (similarly overlaying the previous value).

Alternatively, assume the statement

```
510 READ L, U$, P, V$
```

is executed after line 200 above has been executed only once. The values 46.8, R. BOWLES, 51.2, and R. H. WILLIAMS are assigned to the variables L, U$, P, and V$, respectively.

As our examples show, a single DATA statement can contain both numeric and character data, and a single READ statement can contain both numeric and string variables. The only requirement is that the type of a data value must correspond to the type of the variable to which it is assigned. Otherwise, an error occurs. Our examples also show that the number of variables in a READ statement need not be the same as the number of values in a particular DATA statement containing data to be read by it. However, if an attempt is made to read a value from the combined data list after all values in the list have been read, an error occurs. You must be careful to arrange your DATA statements, and the values specified in them, so they'll be read in the sequence you intend. Generally, it's wise programming practice to group all the DATA statements in a program just ahead of the END statement in the program.

The program in Figure A-9 provides an "official printout" documenting one entry for a statewide Barbershop Quartet Jamboree. The program can be entered as shown and then saved in computer storage for reuse. Whenever a quartet entry is received, the program can simply be retrieved from storage and displayed on the screen. A sequential entry number can be assigned to

Figure A-9 Documenting a barbershop quartet entry

```
100 REM QENTRY. RECORD A BARBERSHOP QUARTET ENTRY.
110 REM S  IS SEQUENTIAL ENTRY NUMBER (SEE LOG FOR NEXT NUMBER)
120 REM D$ IS DATE ENTRY RECEIVED IN FORM MM/DD/YY
130 REM N$ IS QUARTET NAME; O$-R$ ARE PARTICIPANTS' NAMES
140 REM L$ IS QUARTET'S SPONSORING LOCATION
150 REM SEE DATA STATEMENTS, LINES 280 - 300
160 READ S, D$, N$, L$
170 READ O$, P$, Q$, R$
180 PRINT S, D$
190 PRINT
200 PRINT N$
210 PRINT L$
220 PRINT
230 PRINT O$
240 PRINT P$
250 PRINT Q$
260 PRINT R$
270 REM DATA VALUES MUST BE ENTERED IN ORDER SHOWN BELOW
280 DATA 33, "04/25/89"
290 DATA "THE MISTER BIG'S", "YANKSTOWN, LA"
300 DATA "ROY HART", "AL GOOD", "JOHN LOVE", "ART FULL"
310 END
```

the entry and keyed in as a replacement for the number assigned to the immediately preceding entry (33, in our case) in the DATA statement in line 280. Other data about the new quartet entry can be keyed in as modifications to the DATA statements in lines 290 and 300. Then the program can be rerun to produce the official printout for the new quartet entry. The program can be saved in storage as before. When a subsequent quartet entry is received, it can be assigned the next sequential entry number, and these steps repeated to create an official printout for it.

Sometimes, it is convenient to reuse (i.e., reread) some or all of the values in a data list. The RESTORE statement provides a capability we need to do this. The general form of the RESTORE statement is:

```
line no. RESTORE
```

When this statement is encountered, it causes the read pointer that we mentioned above to be moved from wherever it's pointing in the data list to point to the value initially at the top of the data list. In effect, we start over with the data values; the entire data list is made available for reuse.

To more fully understand this capability, look at the program in Figure A-10. This program finds the sums and differences between one value and three subsequent values.

The first READ statement (line 170) causes the four numeric values in the DATA statement at line 310 to be assigned to the numeric variables A, B, C, and D. Lines 180, 190, and 200 cause the values B, C, and D, to be added to A; the sums of the addition operations are stored back in B, C, and D, overlaying the values used in the addition. This means that before the subtraction operations in lines 250, 260, and 270 can be performed as intended, B, C, and D must once again be assigned their original values.

Lines 220 and 240 cause the read pointer to be repositioned and the values for A through D to be read again. Why do we reread a value for A,

Figure A-10 Finding sums and differences

```
100 REM SUMDIFF.  FIND SUMS AND DIFFERENCES.
110 REM A, B, C, D ARE ANY FOUR NUMERIC VALUES.
120 REM BECAUSE THE VALUES OF B, C, D ARE OVERLAYED,
130 REM THE RESTORE ON LINE 220 IS NEEDED SO THAT
140 REM THE VALUES CAN BE REASSIGNED.
150 REM FOR DATA, SEE LINE 310.
160 REM FIND AND PRINT SUMS
170 READ A, B, C, D
180 LET B = A + B
190 LET C = A + C
200 LET D = A + D
210 PRINT "SUMS ARE", B, C, D
220 RESTORE
230 REM FIND AND PRINT DIFFERENCES
240 READ A, B, C, D
250 LET B = A - B
260 LET C = A - C
270 LET D = A - D
280 PRINT
290 PRINT
300 PRINT "DIFFERENCES ARE", B, C, D
310 DATA 14000, 5680, 4200, 9800
320 END
```

since its content has not been changed? Because a RESTORE statement always causes the read pointer to be set to point to the top value in the data list (which is the value for A, in this case). We have to reread the value for A to get to the values to be assigned to B, C, and D. If line 240 were simply READ B, C, D, we'd read only three values, rightly enough, but we'd read the *first three* values. Clearly, that's not what we want to happen. (A would still be 4000; B would also be 4000; C would be 5680; and D would be 14200.) The computer would not detect our logic error, because it is not necessarily an error to have a data value in a DATA statement that is never read.

FILE INPUT/OUTPUT

As explained earlier, the BASIC programming language can be used in either batch or interactive mode. We are using BASIC interactively. The amount of data handled by our programs is relatively small. We assign values to variables by means of LET, INPUT, or READ and DATA statements.

Business application programs dealing with employee payroll, customer accounts, inventory control, and so on are usually designed to run in batch mode. Such programs must handle large volumes of input and output. As explained in Chapter 6, related data items are grouped into records; related records are grouped in files or databases; and the files or databases are placed on a secondary-storage medium, such as magnetic tape or disk. The data can be read into primary storage, by a wide variety of application programs, as needed during processing.

The BASIC programming language is being used to write such application programs. To provide the capabilities needed, additional BASIC statements supporting input/output operations on files are included in most BASIC implementations. Some examples are:

```
220 OPEN #3: NAME "ACCTS"
260 ERASE #3
680 ASK HN: KEY PNUM$
700 CLOSE #2
```

Unfortunately, the forms of these statements vary considerably among implementations. Since the programs we write will not handle large volumes of input or output, and because we want to direct our attention to BASIC capabilities that are alike across most implementations, we will not discuss BASIC statements for file input/output further in this appendix. However, you should understand that large data files do commonly exist, separate from programs, and that BASIC can be used to write programs to create and process such files.

DO IT NOW
SET E

E1. Study the program in Figure A-9. Sketch the format and contents of the output provided by it.

E2. Using the sign-on procedure and system commands available to you, key in the program in Figure A-9. Run the program, and compare the actual results to the results you predicted in E1 above. If the results do not agree, find the error and correct it. If you make changes to the program as you entered it initially, rerun the program. Continue in this manner until correct results are provided.

E3. Assume 150 chickens have an average weight of 4 pounds each.

(a) How much are all the chickens worth, at 89¢ per pound?

(b) Disregarding other expenditures, how much profit can be made if the chickens are sold at a price of $1.09 per pound? (In business terminology, this is called *gross profit.*)

(c) Handling and storage costs per chicken are 20¢. Assuming all chickens are sold, how much profit remains after these costs are deducted? (In business terminology, gross profit less expenses is called *net profit.*)

E4. Plan, write, test, and document a BASIC program that directs the computer to perform the computations you performed manually in response to Exercise E3 above. Use LET statements to perform the computations. Since you are dealing with one set of very specific data values, you can express the data values as numeric constants in the LET statements. The number of chickens, purchase cost, gross profit, and net profit (labeled appropriately) should be provided as output.

E5. Now create a generalized version of the BASIC program that you developed in response to Exercise E4. The program should read values for number of chickens, average weight, cost per pound, selling price per pound, and handling and storage costs per chicken contained in a DATA statement as input. It should provide output similar to that described above.

Use the following sets of data in creating DATA statements for test runs. Note that to change the set of data values on which your program operates, you need only change the DATA statements in the program. For each set of values, determine what the results should be before you run the program.

Number of chickens	Average weight	Cost per pound	Selling price per pound	Handling and storage costs per chicken
150	4 lb	.89	1.09	.20
400	3 lb 8 oz	.80	1.04	.18

E6. In today's business environments, various techniques are used to depreciate capital assets. Perhaps the simplest of these techniques is the straight-line depreciation method. Assuming an initial cost (C), a salvage value (V), and a useful life of N years, the depreciation (D) in year n is computed as follows:

$$D_n = \frac{C - V}{N}$$

Plan, write, test, and document a BASIC program to compute the depreciation in year n, where $1 \leq n \leq N$. The program should read the description of the asset and values for initial cost, salvage value, and expected life contained in DATA statements. These values and the computed depreciation amount, labeled appropriately, should be provided as output. Use the following data in creating DATA statements for test runs:

Description	*C*	*V*	*N*
Office printer/copier	12,000	400	5
Plating machine	150,300	20,500	20

Notice that no value for *n* is required in computing this depreciation; the depreciation amount does not vary from one year *n* to another. That's why the name "straight-line" is appropriate for this depreciation method.

Program Control Flow

Already, we've analyzed several relatively simple but nonetheless practical problems. We've developed solutions to those problems and learned enough of the BASIC language to express our solutions as computer programs. Doing so has allowed us to use the computer in problem solving.

The programs we've developed thus far are alike in certain ways. All the statements in each program are executed sequentially, in order from the lowest-line-numbered statement to the highest-line-numbered statement—the same order in which they are stored within the computer.

Sometimes, we may want the computer not to execute certain statements in a program. Suppose, for example, that we want it to execute one series of computations if an input data value is positive, but another series of computations if the input data value is negative or zero. We need a way to tell the computer to *branch* to whichever sequence of statements is appropriate.

In another problem situation, we may want the computer to re-execute certain statements. That is, we may want it to execute certain statements repetitively. For example, why write a program to calculate the average of just one set of five test scores? Why not design the program so that it can be used to process many sets of test scores? We need a way to tell the computer, after it has computed and printed the average for one set of test scores, to loop back and compute the average for another set of test scores accepted for processing.

In BASIC, various forms of the GO TO, IF . . . THEN, and DO statements provide the *branching* and *looping* capabilities we need to direct program control flow. We shall look at some general forms of the statements first. Then we shall use the statements in developing some well-structured solutions to problems.

The GO TO Statement

The GO TO statement tells the computer to branch (go) to an executable statement elsewhere in the program. The general form of this statement is:

```
line no. GO TO transfer line no.
```

If desired, the blank between the keywords GO and TO may be omitted (i.e., GOTO is permissible). The statement branched to may precede or follow the GO TO statement. Because this GO TO statement always causes the program flow to be altered, it is often called an *unconditional branch* or *unconditional GO TO statement.*

The statement

```
480 GO TO 100
```

causes program execution to continue at line 100 (which precedes this GO TO statement).

The statement

```
500 GO TO 600
```

causes program execution to continue at line 600 (which follows this GO TO statement).

The line number specified as the branch destination in a GO TO statement should be the line number of an existing executable statement in the program.

THE IF . . . THEN STATEMENT

In contrast to the GO TO statement, which causes the computer to branch unconditionally, the IF . . . THEN statement sets up a *conditional branch.* It tells the computer to branch to a specified line only if a particular condition is true. The general form of the IF . . . THEN statement is:

```
line no. IF condition THEN transfer line no.
```

The condition specified in an IF . . . THEN statement can be quite complex. It is usually a relation between two data values. The data values may be expressed as constants, variables, or combinations of constants, variables, and arithmetic operators. The relation, or condition being tested for, is represented by a *relational operator.* There are six BASIC relational operators. (See Figure A-11.) Where two symbols are used to represent an operator, they must be adjacent. That is, no spaces are allowed within <=, >=, or <>.

Figure A-11 BASIC relational operators

Relational operator	Meaning	Condition example
=	equal to	A = 0 C$ = "N"
< >	not equal to	C < > 30 F$ < > "CA"
<	less than	X − Y < 300
<=	less than or equal to	X <= (A − B)/2
>	greater than	C^2 > R
>=	greater than or equal to	(M + T + W + H + F)/5 >= 40

Some straightforward IF . . . THEN statements containing relational operators are:

```
460 IF A = 0 THEN 500
480 IF X <= (A - B) / 2 THEN 200
```

Line 460 causes the computer to branch to line 500 only if A is *equal to* zero. Otherwise, the computer does not branch. It executes the statement immediately following the IF . . . THEN statement, in ascending line-number order (as though the IF . . . THEN were not there). Program execution proceeds normally. Line 480 causes the computer to branch to line 200 only if the value of X is *less than or equal to* the value of A minus B, divided by 2.

Character-string constants and string variables can be used in IF . . . THEN statements. Some examples are:

```
500 IF A$ = "END OF DATA" THEN 200
520 IF D$ <> E$ THEN 320
```

If the data values named in an IF statement consist of only letters and blanks, the relation is evaluated just as we might arrange the values alphabetically. Thus, END OF DATA is equal to END OF DATA. DATA comes before (is less than) END OF DATA. FINAL VALUE comes after (is greater than) END OF DATA.

When character strings contain numbers and special characters, the evaluation of relations other than equal to and not equal to depends on the *collating sequence* of the computer being used. In some, numbers are greater than letters and special characters; in others, numbers are lowest; and so on. Since the equal to and not equal to relations are uniform across computers, and provide all the flexibility we need, we shall use only these relations in our work here.

The DO Statement

The DO statement is used to set up the logic needed to form a program loop. It tells the computer to execute the statement or sequence of statements within the loop. How many times the statement or sequence of statements is executed depends on the outcome(s) of condition test(s) carried out by the computer when the DO statement is encountered during processing. The general form of the DO statement we shall use here is:

```
line no. DO WHILE condition
                  :
line no. LOOP
```

The condition specified in the WHILE clause of the DO statement can be quite complex. It is usually a relation between two values. As in the IF . . . THEN statement, the relational operators shown in Figure A-11 may be used.

A simple example is:

```
680 DO WHILE A > (2 * B)
```

This statement causes the statements within the loop that follows to be executed not at all, once, or a number of times, depending on whether the value of A is greater than 2 times the value of B whenever the condition is evaluated—the first time the DO statement is encountered and after each succeeding execution of the statements within the loop (if any) during processing.

Selection, or Choosing between Alternatives

In Chapters 9 and 10 of this book, several programming techniques and languages are introduced. We've applied the program development tasks listed in Chapter 9 in the problem-solving work we've done so far. Now we're ready to try our hand at problems involving branching and looping. Since the problem-solving logic is somewhat more complicated, we'll use *flowcharts* and *pseudocode* as tools in problem solving.

Figure A-12 shows the logic required to solve a simple problem involving a selection between alternatives: Accept two data values as input, and print out the larger of those values. In both the flowchart and pseudocode representations of the solution algorithm, the data values are represented by the numeric variables A and B. The larger value is printed, and program execution is terminated.

The problem-solving logic in Figure A-12 uses two of the basic patterns of structured programming:

- SIMPLE SEQUENCE. Statements are executed in the order in which they appear, with program control passing unconditionally from one statement to the next.

Figure A-12 Printing the larger of two values

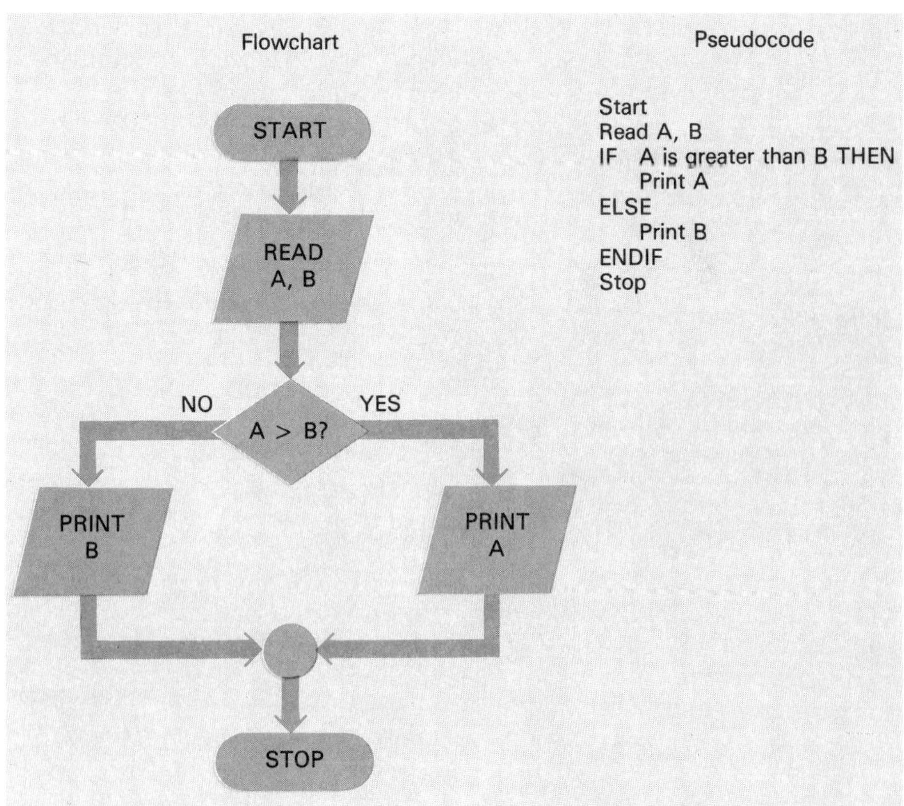
Flowchart
START
READ A, B
NO
A > B?
YES
PRINT B
PRINT A
STOP
Pseudocode
Start
Read A, B
IF A is greater than B THEN
Print A
ELSE
Print B
ENDIF
Stop

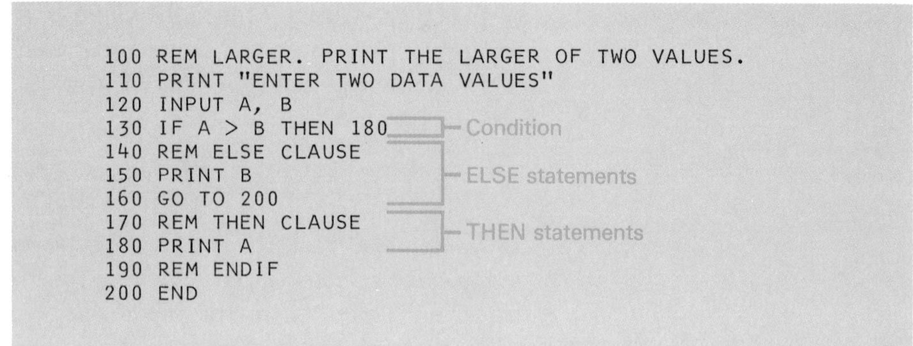

```
100 REM LARGER. PRINT THE LARGER OF TWO VALUES.
110 PRINT "ENTER TWO DATA VALUES"
120 INPUT A, B
130 IF A > B THEN 180
140 REM ELSE CLAUSE
150 PRINT B
160 GO TO 200
170 REM THEN CLAUSE
180 PRINT A
190 REM ENDIF
200 END
```

Condition
ELSE statements
THEN statements

Figure A-13 BASIC program to print the larger of two values—IF . . . THEN

- IFTHENELSE. A condition is tested. If the condition is true, one statement (or group of statements) is executed. If the condition is false, another statement (or group of statements) is executed instead.

Notice that the IFTHENELSE pattern on the flowchart begins with the diamond-shaped decision symbol. The keywords IF, THEN, ELSE, and ENDIF emphasize the selection between alternatives in the pseudocode representation.

The same problem-solving logic is expressed in BASIC in Figure A-13. REM statements are included to help you to see clearly the THEN alternative and the ELSE alternative. If A is greater than B, we tell the computer to branch to line 180 to execute the THEN alternative. Otherwise, the computer simply executes the next statement in sequence—the ELSE alternative. We use a GO TO statement at the end of the ELSE alternative to tell the computer to branch around the THEN alternative to line 200. We know that either the THEN alternative or the ELSE alternative should be executed, but not both.

The 1987 ANS BASIC standard provides for the keyword ELSE and an accompanying clause as part of the IF . . . THEN statement (in effect, it becomes an IF . . . THEN . . . ELSE statement). When this capability is available, there is no need to use GO TO statements to branch as we've described. The logic to print the larger of two values can be programmed as shown in Figure A-14. If this capability is available on your system, you should take advantage of it when a choice between alternatives is required.

Figure A-14 BASIC program to print the larger of two values—IF . . . THEN . . . ELSE

```
100 REM LARGER. PRINT THE LARGER OF TWO VALUES.
110 PRINT "ENTER TWO DATA VALUES"
120 INPUT A, B
130 IF A > B THEN
140    PRINT A
150 ELSE
160    PRINT B
170 END IF
180 END
```

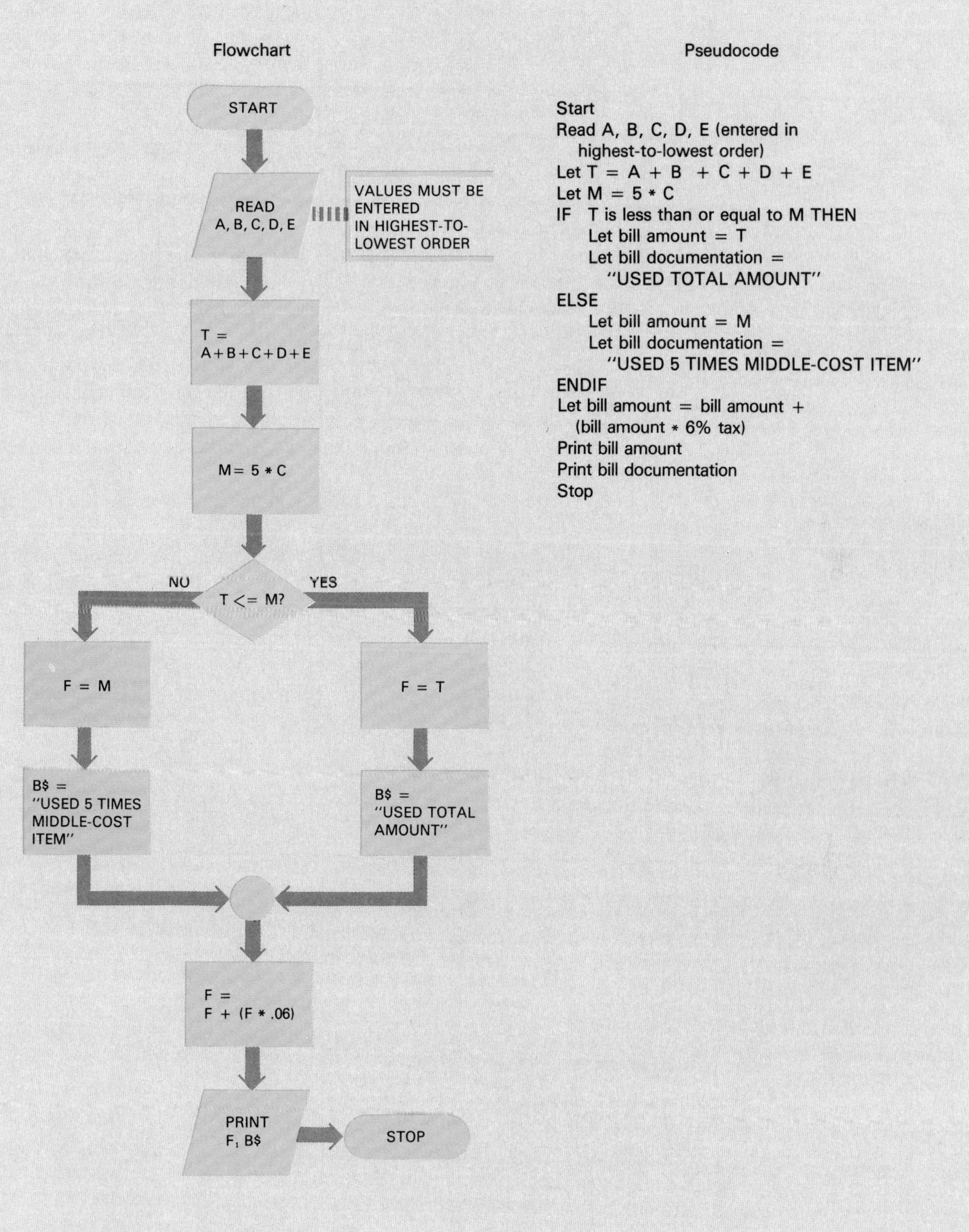

Flowchart
Pseudocode
START
READ
A, B, C, D, E
VALUES MUST BE ENTERED IN HIGHEST-TO-LOWEST ORDER
T = A+B+C+D+E
M= 5 * C
NO
YES
T <= M?
F = M
F = T
B$ = "USED 5 TIMES MIDDLE-COST ITEM"
B$ = "USED TOTAL AMOUNT"
F = F + (F * .06)
PRINT F, B$
STOP
Start
Read A, B, C, D, E (entered in highest-to-lowest order)
Let T = A + B + C + D + E
Let M = 5 * C
IF T is less than or equal to M THEN
Let bill amount = T
Let bill documentation = "USED TOTAL AMOUNT"
ELSE
Let bill amount = M
Let bill documentation = "USED 5 TIMES MIDDLE-COST ITEM"
ENDIF
Let bill amount = bill amount + (bill amount * 6% tax)
Print bill amount
Print bill documentation
Stop

Figure A-15 Computing total amount owed

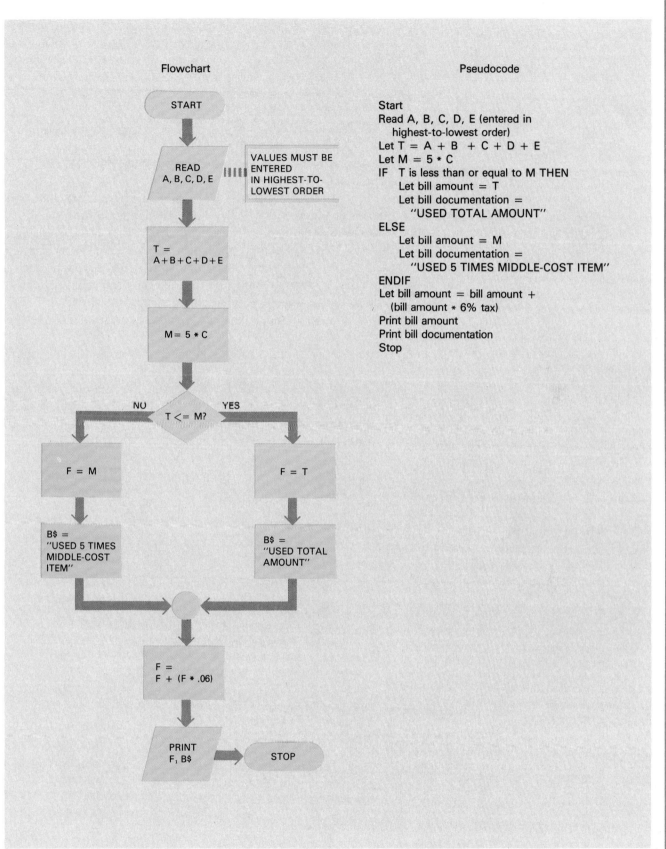

Now let's tackle another problem involving a selection between alternatives. Assume you are going on a shopping expedition. A local merchant has advertised the following "Grand Opening Special": Choose any five items. You pay *either* the total cost of those items, *or* five times the cost of the third-most-expensive item. Since you may choose the alternative you prefer, the lower of the two calculated totals can be assumed to apply. In either case, the sales tax of 6% is to be added to the calculated total, to determine the final amount of the bill. The merchant needs a BASIC program that performs the calculations required and provides the final amount, labeled appropriately, as output.

The logic needed to solve this problem is shown in both flowchart and pseudocode forms in Figure A-15. A BASIC implementation of the solution algorithm is shown in Figure A-16. Since this program is somewhat more complex than those we've developed previously, we should check it carefully to satisfy ourselves that it's correct. A wise first step is to choose representative values for the input variables and step through the program logic manually, pretending to be the computer. (We also remember to determine what the output should be beforehand, so that we are not unduly influenced by the computer.)

After you are satisfied that the program logic in Figures A-15 and A-16 is correct, use the sign-on procedure, system commands, and keyboard available to you to enter the program into the computer. Run the program, providing input upon request, and see whether the computer's result agrees with yours. If not, find out why the discrepancy occurs.

Figure A-16 BASIC program to compute total amount owed

```
100 REM BILLING. COMPUTE BILL AMOUNT.
110 REM A, B, C, D, E ARE COSTS OF FIVE ITEMS
120 REM ENTERED IN ORDER, HIGHEST TO LOWEST.
130 REM T, M ARE INTERMEDIATE RESULTS.
140 REM F IS FINAL BILL AMOUNT.
150 PRINT "ENTER COSTS OF FIVE ITEMS, IN ORDER FROM HIGHEST TO LOWEST"
160 INPUT A, B, C, D, E
170 LET T = A + B + C + D + E
180 LET M = 5 * C
190 IF T <= M THEN 260
200 REM ELSE CLAUSE
210 LET F = M
220 LET B$ = "USED 5 TIMES MIDDLE-COST ITEM"
230 GO TO 280
240 REM THEN CLAUSE
250 LET F = T
260 LET B$ = "USED TOTAL AMOUNT"
270 REM ENDIF
280 LET F = F + (F * .06)
290 PRINT
300 PRINT "AMOUNT DUE IS"; F
310 PRINT
320 PRINT B$
330 END
```

DO IT NOW SET F

F1. Use BASIC statements to express and document the problem-solving logic below.

IF quantity ordered does not exceed 100 THEN quantity shipped = quantity ordered
ELSE quantity shipped = 100 + (1/2 of quantity ordered in excess of 100)
ENDIF
Print quantity shipped

F2. Examine the following program.

```
200 READ A, B, P
210 IF B > 0 THEN 240
220 LET A = A * P
230 GO TO 250
240 LET A = (A + B) * P
250 PRINT "THE AMOUNT DUE IS $";
260 PRINT A
270 DATA 600, 150, .40
280 END
```

(a) Show the format and contents of the output provided by this program.
(b) What does the program accomplish?
(c) Express the problem-solving logic in pseudocode form.
(d) What changes must be made to the program to process the values 15000, −25, and .16 for A, B, and P, respectively?
(e) Show the format and contents of the output provided by the program as modified.
(f) By intent, this program is designed to accept an amount ordered, assumed base order quantity (if any), and price per unit as input. Any base order quantity less than or equal to zero is to be ignored for the purposes of this computation. The total order quantity is to be multiplied by the price per unit, and the resultant bill amount is to be provided as output. Increase the program's potential value to users by including REM statements as documentation where appropriate. Key in the program from your terminal or microcomputer, then run it to verify that the output looks as you expect it to look (for both F2(a) and F2(e) above).

F3. Automobiles can be rented from any of several agencies on either a daily or weekly basis. The cost for daily rental is equal to the number of days (D) times the daily rate (R) plus the number of miles driven (M) times the agency's rate per mile (A). The cost for weekly rental is equal to a base weekly charge (W) plus the cost of the gasoline for the week (G). The gasoline cost (G) is equal to the number of miles driven (M) divided by the rate of gas usage (mpg) times the cost per gallon (cpg).

Using either flowcharting or pseudocode to plan the logic of a BASIC program that computes both the daily cost and the weekly cost of anticipated rental car usage on a routine business trip. The program should obtain estimated or actual values for the required parameters from DATA statements. It should compute the rental expense for the trip under each approach and then find out which approach appears to be less expensive, and by how much. It should provide as output both costs (labeled appropriately), the difference between them, and a recommendation of how to proceed. If the costs are equal, the daily rental plan should be used.

Assume the first set of data values below is provided as input to your solution algorithm in flowchart or pseudocode form. Step through the program logic carefully. What results are provided as output? After you have fixed any errors and are satisfied the results are correct, repeat the processing steps on the second set of data values.

D	R	M	A	W	mpg	cpg
4	10.00	540	.14	48.00	18	1.24
5	8.50	752	.10	35.00	16	1.29

F4. Write, test, and document a BASIC program that directs the computer in accord with the solution algorithm that you developed in response to Exercise F3. Use the same data in test runs. Do the computer's results agree with yours? If not, find out why. Correct the error (or errors) and rerun the program.

Looping

Looping is a programming technique we use to cause the computer to re-execute a certain part of a BASIC program. Rather than write 50 LET statements to tell it to add 50 pairs of numbers, for example, we write one LET statement and tell it to re-execute the LET statement 50 times. In using this technique, we set up the third pattern of structured programming:

- DOWHILE. A condition is tested. If the condition is true, one statement (or group of statements) is executed and control returns to the test of the condition. In effect, a *program loop* is formed. If the condition is false, the statement (or group of statements) is skipped and control passes to the next statement following the program loop.

The logic of the DOWHILE pattern is shown, by example, in Figure A-17. The logic is expressed in flowchart, pseudocode, and BASIC forms.

Choose several sets of values for A and B. Walk through the DOWHILE logic manually to gain familiarity with it. Doing so now will help you to prepare to use the logic in problem solving.

Notice that the DOWHILE pattern is a *leading-decision loop:* The test of the condition occurs immediately upon entering the loop. Whether or not succeeding statements are executed depends on the outcome of the test. If the condition is false the first time it is tested, the remaining steps in the loop are not executed at all. (If you did not choose a set of values where A was initially less than B, do so now. What happens as a result of the first condition test?)

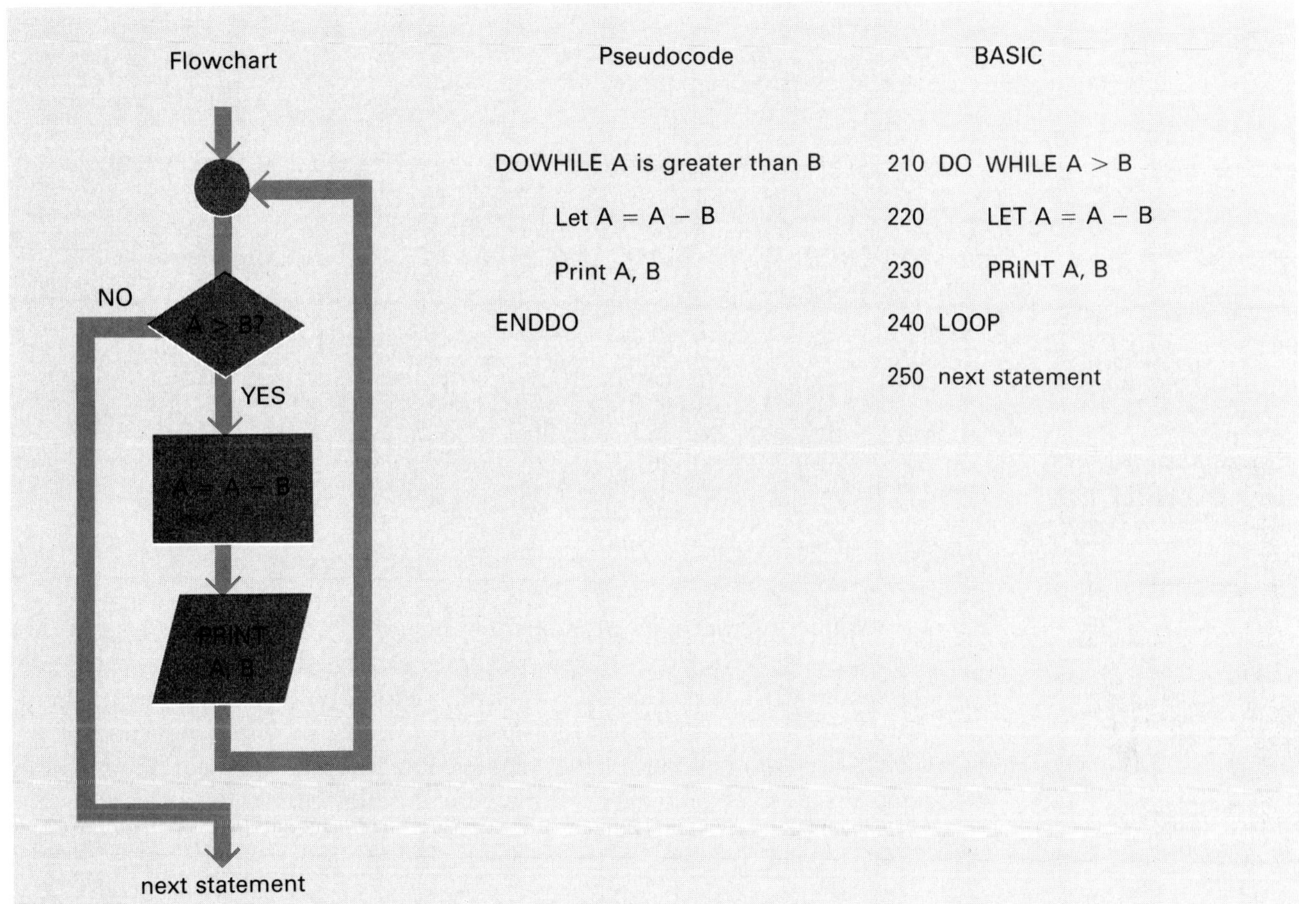
Flowchart
Pseudocode
BASIC
NO
A > B?
YES
A = A − B
PRINT A, B
next statement
DOWHILE A is greater than B
Let A = A − B
Print A, B
ENDDO
210 DO WHILE A > B
220 LET A = A − B
230 PRINT A, B
240 LOOP
250 next statement

Figure A-17 The logic of DOWHILE

A complete BASIC program including a DOWHILE pattern similar to the one we're discussing is shown in Figure A-18. The program accomplishes division by means of repeated subtraction. Both input values must be positive, or both must be negative. We've eliminated the print step shown in Figure A-17 because there's no need to print out the intermediate results of the processing. An important point to notice is that the variables A, B, C, and T must all be set to their initial values (i.e., *initialized*) before they are used in processing. Here, C and T are assigned values by means of LET statements. The initial values for A and B are entered by the user. As we've learned, READ and DATA are a third way of assigning initial values to variables.

Do you see why the temporary save area, T, is necessary? Since we intend to modify the value of A within the DOWHILE loop, but we need its original value later for printing, we must save the initial value before we store a new value over it. This saving is accomplished by line 180, the statement that initializes T to its first (and only) value.

As mentioned earlier, a common reason for looping is to accept and process multiple sets of input values. Let us use this technique as we plan, write, test, and document a program to provide a Weekly Overtime Report for upper management. For each employee who worked overtime during the past week, the following data values are to be provided as input: employee

```
100 REM DO WHILE. DIVIDE BY REPEATED SUBTRACTION (A * B > 0).
110 REM C IS A COUNT OF SUBTRACTIONS
120 REM T IS A SAVE AREA FOR A'S INITIAL VALUE
130 REM A AND B ARE THE DIVIDEND AND DIVISOR
140 REM INITIALIZE VARIABLES
150 PRINT "ENTER TWO NUMERIC VALUES, DIVIDEND AND DIVISOR"
160 PRINT "THE VALUES MUST HAVE LIKE SIGNS"
170 INPUT A, B
180 LET T = A
190 LET C = 0
200 DO WHILE A <= B
210     LET A = A - B
220     LET C = C + 1
230 LOOP
240 PRINT
250 PRINT T; "DIVIDED BY "; B; "IS "; C
260 PRINT "THE REMAINDER IS "; A
270 END
```

Figure A-18 BASIC program using DOWHILE logic

number, employee name, number of hours overtime (expressed to the nearest tenth of an hour, HH.T), and overtime earnings (expressed in dollars and cents, DDD.CC). A data value of "END OF DATA" for employee number is to be used as a signal that all input has been processed. A listing of the employee data, a count of the number of employees who worked overtime, and the total amount of overtime compensation are to be included in the Weekly Overtime Report.

Figure A-19 shows one solution to this problem, expressed in pseudocode form. A BASIC implementation of the solution algorithm is shown in Figure A-20. The correspondence between the two is straightforward. Note that both LET and READ statements are used to initialize the variables used within the DOWHILE loop before the loop is entered the first time. (See lines 230–260.) Since we want the loop to be executed *while there is more data to process,* we test for the condition E$ is not equal to "END OF DATA" in the WHILE clause that controls loop processing.

Enter this program, or write a similar program that provides the required Weekly Overtime Report. Create test input and enter it in the DATA statements. You'll need to provide dummy values for employee name, hours, and earnings as well as "END OF DATA" as the final set of input. (See line 470 in

Figure A-19 Preparing a Weekly Overtime Report (pseudocode)

```
Start
Print report title and column headings
Initialize variables
DOWHILE more data (not "END OF DATA")
        Add 1 to count of employees
        Add earnings to total overtime compensation
        Print detail line
        Read next set of input values
ENDDO
Print count of employees and total overtime compensation
Stop
```

```
100 REM OVERTIME.  PREPARE WEEKLY OVERTIME REPORT.
110 REM E$ AND N$ ARE EMPLOYEE NUMBER AND NAME
120 REM H AND E ARE OVERTIME HOURS AND EARNINGS
130 REM C IS COUNT OF EMPLOYEES WHO WORKED OVERTIME
140 REM A IS TOTAL OVERTIME COMPENSATION
150 REM PRINT REPORT HEADINGS
160 PRINT TAB(17); "WEEKLY OVERTIME REPORT"
170 PRINT
180 PRINT
190 PRINT "EMPLOYEE", "EMPLOYEE", "OVERTIME", "OVERTIME"
200 PRINT " NUMBER ", "  NAME   ", "  HOURS ", "EARNINGS"
210 PRINT
220 PRINT
230 REM INITIALIZE VARIABLES
240 LET C = 0
250 LET A = 0
260 READ E$, N$, H, E
270 REM
280 DO WHILE E$ <> "END OF DATA"
290     LET C = C + 1
300     LET A = A + E
310     PRINT E$, N$, H, E
320     READ E$, N$, H, E
330 LOOP
340 PRINT
350 PRINT "NUMBER OF EMPLOYEES WORKING OVERTIME ="; C
360 PRINT "TOTAL OVERTIME COMPENSATION = $"; A
370 PRINT
380 PRINT
390 PRINT "END OF WEEKLY OVERTIME REPORT"
400 REM
410 REM EMPLOYEE DATA FOLLOWS
420 DATA "P08972", "R. SCHNEIDER", 4.2, 40.20
430 DATA "I50431", "S. KIRK", 5.6, 42.00
440 DATA "U33055", "C. GIBSON", 8.0, 96.00
450 DATA "V01456", "L. MORGAN", 16.3, 160.30
460 DATA "A11654", "R. CAMPBELL", 8.0, 60.00
470 DATA "END OF DATA", " ", 0, 0
480 END
```

Figure A-20 Preparing a Weekly Overtime Report (BASIC program)

Figure A-20.) Otherwise, when the computer attempts to read that set of input, it is apt to tell you that you've entered an incorrect number of values. Be sure that not only the detail lines but also the count and total overtime earnings are correct on your printed report.

DO IT NOW
SET G

G1. Use BASIC statements to express and document the problem-solving logic below.

DOWHILE total is less than 1000
    Read group name, number attending
    Let total = total + number attending
    Print group name, number attending

ENDDO
Print message indicating the group currently being processed and the number of persons in that group that cannot be accommodated within the 1000 limit

G2. Examine the following program.

```
200 LET R = 0
210 LET N = 0
220 DO WHILE R <= 300
230     LET R = N * 5
240     PRINT R, N, 5
250     LET N = N + 10
260 LOOP
270 END
```

(a) Show the format and contents of the output provided by this program.
(b) What does the program accomplish?
(c) Express the problem-solving logic in pseudocode form.
(d) Increase the program's potential value to users by including REM and PRINT statements for documentation purposes as appropriate. Key in the program from your terminal or microcomputer. Then run the program to verify that the output looks as you expect it to look.

G3. Students at a local community college earn points toward their final grades in Economics 709 based upon a weighted average of their quizzes, midterm exam, final exam, and assigned projects. The weighting takes four items into account: the average of the three quizzes (q1, q2, q3) plus the midterm grade (mt) plus twice the final exam grade (fe) plus the cumulative project score (ps). The sum of these four items is then divided by 4 to determine a final point score.

Use either flowcharting or pseudocode to plan the logic of a BASIC program to compute the total points earned by students whose grades are entered as values in DATA statements. The program should provide a listing of student ID's and computed final point scores as output. A value of 000000 for student ID should be used as a signal that all grade data has been processed.

Assume the following data is provided as input to your solution algorithm in flowchart or pseudocode form. Step through the program logic carefully. What results are provided as output? After you have fixed any errors and are satisfied the results are correct, repeat the processing steps, using another set of input values. What happens if you fail to provide an end-of-file indicator (student record with 000000 for student ID)? What happens if the end-of-file indicator is the only input provided?

Student ID	q1	q2	q3	mt	fe	ps
134903	97	83	90	94	98	130
345902	85	90	83	78	84	72
444902	98	84	73	90	77	90
345780	70	79	91	90	95	110
000000	0	0	0	0	0	0

G4. Write, test, and document a BASIC program that directs the computer in accord with the solution algorithm that you developed in response to Exercise G3. Use the set of data given in Exercise G3 in test runs. Do the computer's results agree with yours? If not, find out why. Correct any error (or errors) and rerun the program.

THE FOR AND NEXT STATEMENTS

Though we've been discussing how to solve problems only a short period of time, you've learned a great deal. Incredible as it may seem, a mathematical proof exists that *any* solution algorithm can be expressed using only the SIMPLE SEQUENCE, IFTHENELSE, and DOWHILE patterns of structured programming.* Since you've been introduced to BASIC statements that can be used to implement these patterns, you now have the fundamental tools you need to express the logic of any solution algorithm as a BASIC program.

Nevertheless, it's to our benefit to proceed a step or two further. Because counter-controlled loops are needed so frequently in implementing solution algorithms, the designers of the BASIC language have provided a pair of statements—FOR and NEXT—that perform many of the counter-controlled loop functions automatically. The FOR statement appears at the beginning of the loop. The NEXT statement signals the end of the loop. The general forms of these statements are:

```
line no. FOR v = initial value TO limit [STEP increment]
                   :
line no. NEXT v
```

Here, *v* is a numeric variable. The *initial value, limit,* and *increment* can be numeric constants, numeric variables, or combinations of constants, variables, and arithmetic operators. They are used in implementating the FOR and NEXT statement logic as shown in Figure A-21.

When the FOR statement is encountered, the variable *v* is assigned the *initial value.* A test is made to insure that the *limit* has not been exceeded. If it has not, the steps within the FOR-NEXT loop are executed once. The *increment* is added to *v*, and control returns to the test at the beginning of the loop. If the *limit* has been exceeded, control passes to the statement following the NEXT statement in the BASIC program. Note that this loop is a DOWHILE, or leading-decision, loop. The steps within the loop may not be executed at all.†

* See "Structured Programming" in Chapter 10 and the references listed in the footnotes in that chapter.

† Not all BASIC implementations adhere to the 1987 ANS BASIC standard with respect to FOR and NEXT. In some, the test of the loop variable occurs at the end of the loop, so the steps within the loop are always executed at least once. In others, the loop is a leading-decision loop as described here, but the value of the variable upon normal loop exit is the last value used rather than the first value not used. Do some experimenting with the FOR and NEXT statements on the system available to you, to determine precisely the logic behind them.

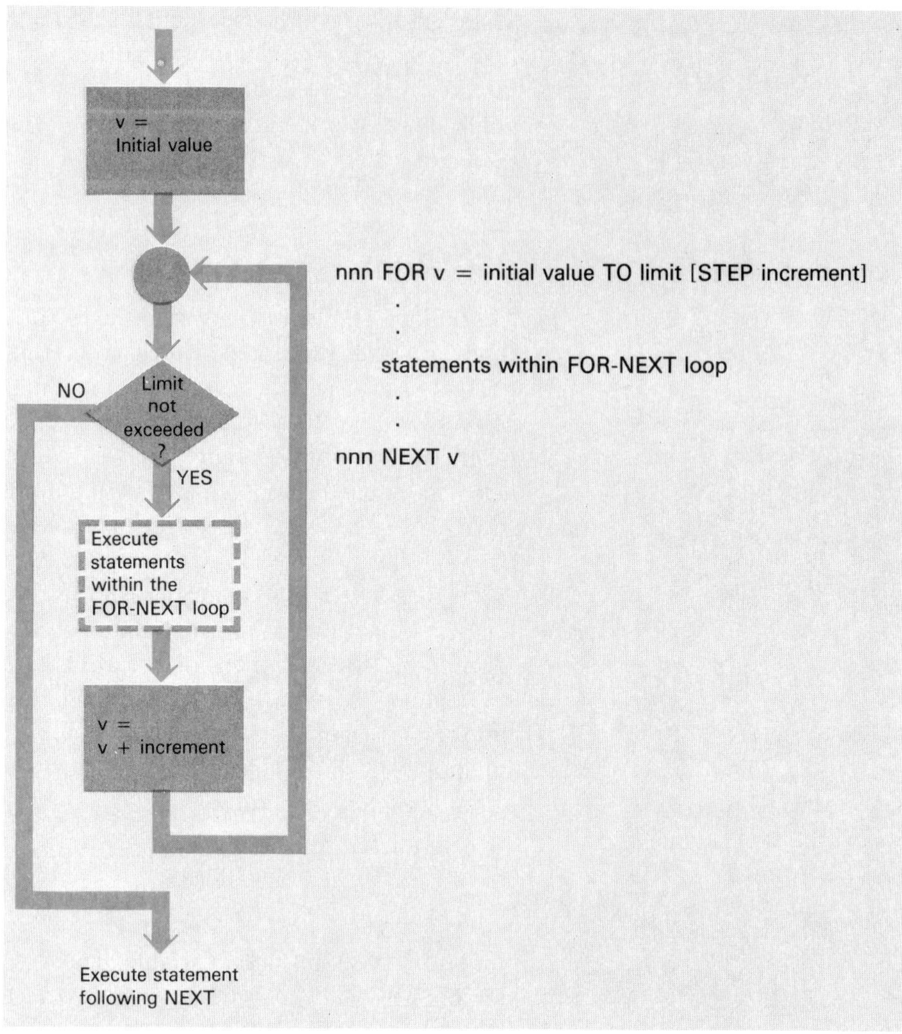
v =
Initial value
NO
Limit not exceeded ?
YES
Execute statements within the FOR-NEXT loop
v =
v + increment
Execute statement following NEXT
nnn FOR v = initial value TO limit [STEP increment]
.
.
statements within FOR-NEXT loop
.
.
nnn NEXT v

Figure A-21 The logic of FOR and NEXT

As the brackets around the STEP *increment* clause indicate, this clause is optional. If it is omitted, the BASIC language processor assumes the increment is +1. Some BASIC implementations do not require specification of the loop variable in the NEXT statement. (That is, the *v* following NEXT is optional.) To help avoid programming errors, and to make the program logic easy for others to read and understand, it's wise programming practice to specify the loop variable in the NEXT statement, whether it's required or not.

Now let's try some simple examples. Suppose we are to create a two-column table containing the numbers from 1 through 25 and their squares. Using a DO statement to set up a leading-decision loop, we might write:

```
200 REM INITIALIZE VARIABLES
210 LET X = 1
220 DO WHILE X <= 25
230    PRINT ,X,,X*X
240    LET X = X + 1
250 LOOP
```

Using FOR and NEXT to set up similar logic, we might write:

```
200 FOR X = 1 TO 25
210       PRINT ,X,,X*X
220 NEXT X
```

Are you beginning to see the convenience that the FOR and NEXT statements offer? One pair of FOR and NEXT statements is equivalent to a LET, DO, another LET, and LOOP.

To gain more experience using FOR and NEXT, let's suppose we are to create a table of numbers and their squares as above, but we need the squares of even numbers only. We can write:

```
300 FOR X = 2 TO 24 STEP 2
310       PRINT ,X,,X*X
320 NEXT X
```

If we had written

```
300 FOR X = 2 TO 25 STEP 2
310       PRINT ,X,,X*X
320 NEXT X
```

would the results have been different? Create a program containing lines 300, 310, and 320 as we wrote them initially. Run it, and see what the results are. Then modify line 300 as proposed above. Run the program again and see what results are provided.

As these examples show, the loop variable named in a FOR statement can be referenced in statements within the FOR-NEXT loop; so can the limit and increment if they are specified as variables. For example:

```
400 FOR X = M TO N STEP S
410       PRINT "HOW TO COUNT BY "; S; "FROM "; M; "TO "; N
420 PRINT X
430 NEXT X
```

However, it is not acceptable to attempt to change any of the values specified in a FOR statement within the FOR-NEXT loop. The loop control function will not work correctly if we attempt to modify (by statements we write) any of the FOR statement values after loop processing has begun.

Another important point to note is that the step increment can be a negative value. If it is, then the adding of the increment actually becomes a subtraction operation. For example, the statements

```
200 FOR I = 15 TO 1 STEP -3
        ⋮
600 NEXT I
```

cause the value of I to be decreased by 3 each time the FOR-NEXT loop beginning at line 200 is executed. The value of I on successive executions is 15, 12, 9, 6, and 3. When I has a value of 0, the condition test at the start of the loop finds that the limit (1) has been exceeded. This causes the loop to be exited.

Sometimes, we may not know, when we write a BASIC program, exactly how many times we want each FOR-NEXT loop within the program to be executed. This is commonly the case if we are using a FOR-NEXT loop to process sets of values read as input. If our program is intended for reuse, it's to our advantage to make it general-purpose—capable of handling as many sets of values as the user provides. We saw earlier that one way of signaling end of input is to have the user enter a certain value such as "END OF DATA" after all input had been entered. An alternate approach is to ask the user, at the start of execution, how many sets of values are to be entered. If we are using DATA and READ statements, we can specify the number of inputs in a DATA statement, where it's easy to find and change. We can use the specified number as the limit in the FOR statement. The execution of the loop is controlled accordingly.

As an example, assume we are to write a program to print a sales listing each week for one of the local supermarkets. The listing should give the description and sales price of each product to be placed on sale during the coming week. The number of products on sale will vary from week to week. The user entering the data will know how many sets of input he or she intends to provide.

Figure A-22 shows a solution to this problem, expressed in pseudocode form. A BASIC implementation of the solution algorithm, using FOR and NEXT statements, is shown in Figure A-23. To obtain multiple copies of the sales listing produced by the program (say, one for each checkout counter), the user may choose any of several alternatives: (1) rerun the program several times, producing one listing each time; (2) use multiple-part paper on the printer used for output; or (3) produce only one listing with computer help, but use a typical office copy machine to make multiple copies of the printed output. As mentioned earlier, you may need to use a special form of the PRINT statement provided on the BASIC system available to you, to produce hard-copy output.

There are other possible uses of a program like the one in Figure A-23 that are exciting to contemplate. Assume terminals or computers at the supermarket, and terminals or personal computers in homes, are part of a large communication network. Would you like to know what products are on sale this week at the local supermarket? Just sign-on your terminal or personal computer, and issue a system command to cause the SLIST program to be executed and the results to be returned to you. You may then decide to invoke another program that allows you to place an order for the products you desire. The products are delivered to your home by the supermarket's routine delivery service—nonstop shopping from the convenience of your kitchen or family room.

Figure A-22 Printing a sales listing (pseudocode)

```
Start
Print headings for sales listing
Initialize variables (set N to number of inputs to process)
DOWHILE more data (loop variable I <= N)
      Read product name and sales price
      Print product name and sales price
ENDDO
Print end-of-listing message
Stop
```

```
100 REM SLIST.  PRINT SALES LISTING.
110 REM N$ IS PRODUCT NAME; P IS PRODUCT SALES PRICE
120 REM N IS TOTAL NUMBER OF PRODUCTS ON SALE THIS WEEK
130 REM PRINT HEADINGS FOR LISTING
140 PRINT TAB(29); "SALES LISTING"
150 PRINT
160 PRINT
170 PRINT " ", "PRODUCT", " ", "SALES"
180 PRINT " ", " NAME   ", " ", "PRICE"
190 PRINT
200 PRINT
210 REM
220 REM INITIALIZE VARIABLES
230 READ N
240 REM BEGIN DOWHILE
250 FOR I = 1 TO N
260     READ N$, P
270     PRINT TAB(12); N$; TAB(46); "$"; P
280     PRINT
290 NEXT I
300 PRINT
310 PRINT
320 PRINT "TOTAL NUMBER OF PRODUCTS ON SALE ="; N
330 PRINT
340 PRINT
350 PRINT "END OF SALES LISTING"
360 REM
370 REM SALES DATA FOLLOWS
380 DATA 5
390 DATA "BONELESS CHUCK ROAST, LB.", 2.49
400 DATA "MJB COFFE, 2 LBS.", 4.99
410 DATA "COKE, TAB, SLICE, 2 LITER", 1.29
420 DATA "NECTARINES, 3 LBS.", 1.00
430 DATA "CHERRY TOMATOES, BASKET", .79
440 END
```

Figure A-23 Printing a sales listing (BASIC program)

To reuse this program from week to week, the responsible supermarket personnel need only save the program in computer storage, then retrieve and display it as needed. The sales data for the coming week can be keyed in as modifications to line 380 and subsequent lines. Of course, new lines can be added and existing lines deleted if required. The program can be rerun in its modified form, and then saved in storage in that form. The following week, this procedure can be repeated using the next week's sales data.

Nested Control Structures

A capability well worth mentioning at this point is the ability to nest program control structures. An IF . . . THEN . . . ELSE structure can be included within a DOWHILE loop. One DOWHILE loop can be included within another DOWHILE loop. The statements within one FOR NEXT loop can be contained entirely within one or more other DOWHILE or FOR-NEXT loops. We set up nested control structures just as we set up single (unnested) ones.

According to ANS BASIC, when FOR-NEXT loops are nested, they cannot use the same loop variable. An example of valid nesting is shown in Figure A-24A. Each time the outer loop is executed once, the inner loop is

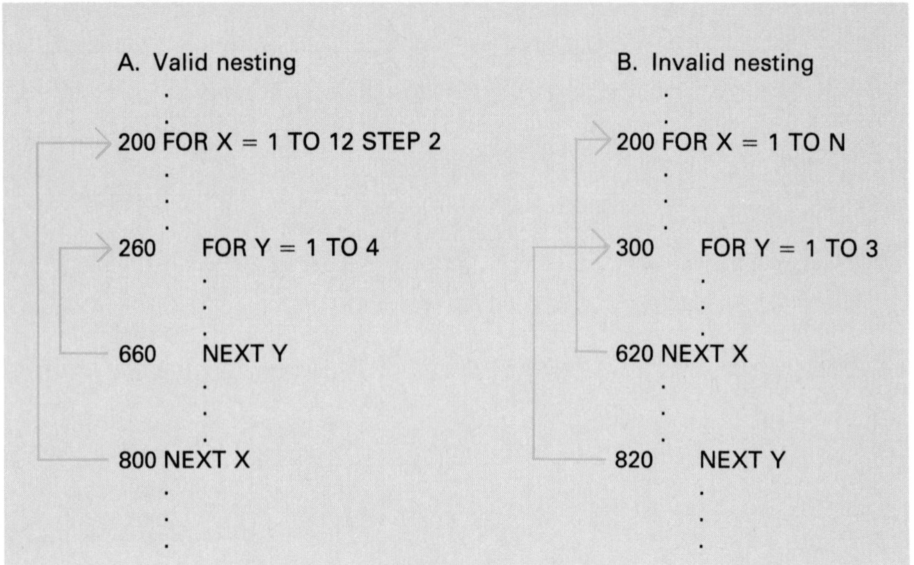
A. Valid nesting
200 FOR X = 1 TO 12 STEP 2
260 FOR Y = 1 TO 4
660 NEXT Y
800 NEXT X
B. Invalid nesting
200 FOR X = 1 TO N
300 FOR Y = 1 TO 3
620 NEXT X
820 NEXT Y

Figure A-24 Valid and invalid nesting of FOR-NEXT loops

executed N times. An example of invalid nesting is shown in Figure A-24B. The FOR X = 1 TO N statement comes *before* the FOR Y = 1 TO 3 statement, so the NEXT X statement must come *after* the NEXT Y statement. Since it does not, an error will be signaled by the BASIC language processor.

The pseudocode for a problem solution using legally nested loops is shown in Figure A-25. A BASIC program implementation of the same logic is shown in Figure A-26. The program produces a horizontal bar chart showing the trend, on a monthly basis over a full-year period, of employee absenteeism. Each bar reflects the number of employees absent more than 5% of the time during a particular accounting month. (In the business environment, accounting months comprise four or five full-week periods. Therefore, calendar months and accounting months tend to be similar but not identical. For example, the June accounting month may begin May 27.)

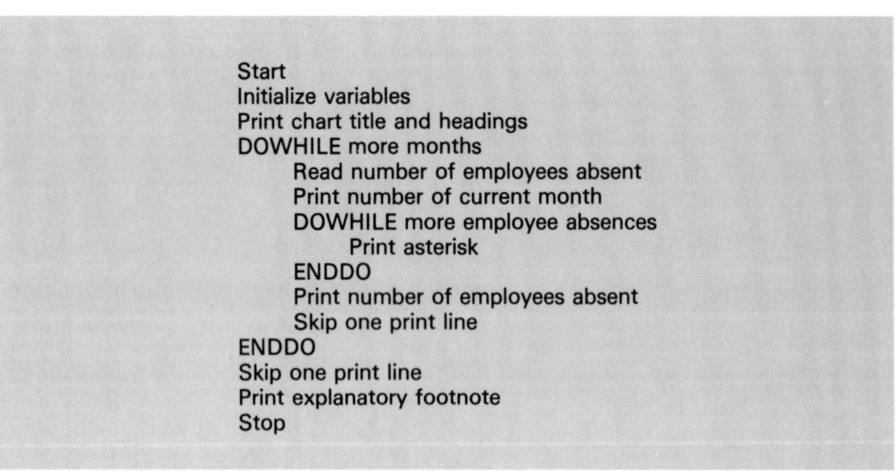
Start
Initialize variables
Print chart title and headings
DOWHILE more months
Read number of employees absent
Print number of current month
DOWHILE more employee absences
Print asterisk
ENDDO
Print number of employees absent
Skip one print line
ENDDO
Skip one print line
Print explanatory footnote
Stop

Figure A-25 Pictorial representation of employee absenteeism (pseudocode)

```
100 REM CHARTER. PRODUCE A BAR CHART SHOWING THE TREND OF
110 REM EMPLOYEE ABSENTEEISM ON A MONTHLY BASIS OVER A YEAR PERIOD.
120 REM A IS NUMBER OF EMPLOYEES ABSENT MORE THAN 5% OF MONTH.
130 REM INITIALIZE VARIABLE SHOWING YEAR BEING DESCRIBED.
140 READ Y$
150 REM
160 REM PRINT HEADINGS FOR BAR CHART
170 PRINT TAB(24); "EMPLOYEE ABSENTEEISM"
180 PRINT
190 PRINT TAB(24); "CALENDAR YEAR = "; Y$
200 PRINT
210 PRINT
220 PRINT "MONTH"; TAB(11); "NUMBER OF EMPLOYEES"
230 PRINT
240 REM BEGIN OUTER LOOP
250 FOR I = 1 TO 12
260     READ A
270     PRINT I; TAB(7);
280     REM BEGIN INNER LOOP
290         FOR J = 1 TO A
300         PRINT " * ";
310         NEXT J
320     PRINT " "; A
330     PRINT
340 NEXT I
350 PRINT
360 PRINT "NOTE: EACH ASTERISK REPRESENTS ONE EMPLOYEE ABSENT"
370 PRINT "MORE THAN 5% DURING THE MONTHLY ACCOUNTING PERIOD"
380 REM
390 REM YEAR FOR WHICH DATA RECORDED
400 DATA "1989"
410 REM NUMBER OF EMPLOYEES ABSENT MORE THAN 5% OF MONTH, BY MONTH
420 DATA 15, 10, 16, 18, 40, 45, 45
430 DATA 56, 30, 08, 20, 55
440 END
```

```
                         EMPLOYEE ABSENTEEISM

                         CALENDAR YEAR = 1989

MONTH     NUMBER OF EMPLOYEES

 1   ***************      15

 2   **********     10
 .        .
 .        .
 .        .
```

Figure A-26 Pictorial representation of employee absenteeism (BASIC program)

The outer loop (I loop) in Figures A-25 and A-26 is executed once for each accounting month of the year. The inner loop (J loop) is executed once for each employee absent more than 5% of the time during a particular month. Each execution of the inner loop causes one asterisk to be printed, thus extending the bar for a particular month. For clarity, the statements of the inner loop are indented on both the pseudocode and the BASIC program listing. To help you visualize what the program accomplishes, the first part of the results of a test run is shown beneath the program listing in Figure A-26.

DO IT NOW SET H

H1. Two formulas are commonly applied in physics to determine the speed acquired by a falling object and the distance traveled by that object. These formulas are:

$$\text{Speed} = 32T^2$$
$$\text{Distance} = 16T^2$$

In both formulas, T is the time the object spends in falling.

Using these two formulas, plan, write, test, and document a BASIC program to compute the speed and distance traveled for an object dropped from a glider if the time required for it to reach the earth varies from 50 to 200 in intervals of 10. Determine before running the program:

(a) What should the first set of results be?
(b) What should the last set of results be?
(c) How many sets of results should be provided?

H2. Among personal computer users, checkbook programs are especially popular. Assume your checking account number is 1183-3218. Your current checkbook balance is $354.83. You've written four checks, numbers 206 through 209, on 6/13, 6/13, 6/15, and 6/19/89, in the amounts of $17.41, $7.50, $106.45, and $20.16, respectively. You've made two deposits: $45.80 and $115.00, on 6/13 and 6/18/89, respectively.

Plan, write, test, and document a BASIC program to adjust your current checkbook balance based on checks written and deposits made (in chronological order). Print out a record of each check or deposit and a running balance. Finally, print out your new balance. If your account is "in the red," a warning message should be printed to help insure that you don't overlook the minus sign preceding the negative new balance. In any case, a count of the number of transactions processed should be printed as a reference for control purposes.

Although you know the exact number of transactions (checks and deposits) in this particular case, design the program in a general-purpose fashion. Use a FOR-NEXT loop with the number of transactions stored in a variable named as the limit in the FOR statement. Use an IF . . . THEN statement nested within the loop to distinguish checks from deposits. The account number, current balance, number of transactions, and transaction data should be contained in DATA statements in the program.

IMPLEMENTATION-SUPPLIED FUNCTIONS

Earlier in this appendix, we learned about the five BASIC arithmetic operators: +, −, *, /, ^. To help insure that BASIC is easy to use, the 1987 ANS BASIC standard also defines a number of *functions* as part of the BASIC language. These functions are powerful combinations of numeric constants, variables, and arithmetic operators. Because they are supplied as predefined algorithms within the BASIC language, we can direct the computer to perform a complete sequence of operations by means of a simple *function refer-*

ence (rather than plan and code the complete sequence ourselves). The general form of the function reference is:

```
function name (argument)
```

The *function name* is a unique identifier of the function. The *argument* is a numeric expression (numeric constant, numeric variable, or combination of constants, variables, and operators). To use a BASIC function, we write the function name, followed by the argument within parentheses. Some examples are: SQR(X), ABS(X − Y). There are a few functions for which no arguments need to be specified.

Figure A-27 shows some of the functions included in the 1987 ANS BASIC standard. Of these, the first four are commonly used in business application programming. Most BASIC implementations supply many additional functions as well; the functions are designed to make BASIC programming easier for users.

The *SQR (square root) function* returns the square root of a number. For example, the statement

```
100 LET W = SQR(X)
```

directs the computer to find the square root of the value represented by the variable X and assign the result to the variable W. The value of X cannot be

Figure A-27 BASIC implementation-supplied functions

Function	Function value
SQR(X)	The nonnegative square root of X; X must be positive.
ABS(X)	The absolute value of X.
SGN(X)	The algebraic sign of X: −1 if X < 0, 0 if X = 0, and 1 if X > 0.
INT(X)	The largest integer not greater than X.
RND	The next pseudorandom number in an implementation-supplied sequence of pseudorandom numbers uniformly distributed in the range 0 <= RND < 1.
EXP(X)	The exponential of X, that is, the value of the base of natural logarithms (e = 2.71828...) raised to the power X (e^X); if EXP(X) is less than the minimal value that can be represented on the computer, its value is set to zero.
LOG(X)	The natural logarithm of X ($\log_e X$); X must be greater than zero.
SIN(X)	The trigonometric sine of X, where X is in radians or degrees.*
COS(X)	The trigonometric cosine of X, where X is in radians or degrees.*
TAN(X)	The tangent of X, where X is in radians or degrees.*
ATN(X)	The arctangent of X, where X is in radians or degrees.*

*There are 2π radians in a circle. To convert a value expressed in degrees to radians, the number of degrees can be multiplied by .0174533 or divided by 57.2957795.

negative. As shown below, if X is 4 then SQR(X) is 2; if X is 144 then SQR(X) is 12; and so on.*

X	SQR(X)
4	2
144	12
29.16	5.4
2^6	8

The *ABS (absolute value) function* returns the absolute value of the argument. The returned value is always positive. That is, if X >= 0 then ABS(X) = X; if X < 0 then ABS(X) = −1 * X. Some examples are:

X	ABS(X)
16.8	16.8
0	0
−4.3	4.3
.53E−03	.53E−03

The *SGN (sign) function* determines the sign of the argument. It returns either −1, 0, or 1, depending on whether the argument is negative, zero, or positive, respectively. Some examples are:

X	SGN(X)
−62	−1
0	0
144	1
2^5 − 4 * 3	1

The *INT (integer) function* returns the largest integer that is less than or equal to the argument. Some examples are:

X	INT(X)
5.3	5
5.6 * 8	44
−3.2	−4
−165.9	−166

Notice that the INT function does not round a number to the nearest integer. In effect, digits to the right of the decimal point are truncated. If the argument is a negative value, INT returns a number that is lower than the argument value. Nevertheless, though INT doesn't round, a very useful application of the INT function is in rounding values to the nearest integer, tenth, hundredth, or other degree of precision wanted. For example, to round a value to the nearest integer, the statement

```
200 LET A = INT(X+.5)
```

* The result obtained by using the SQR function can also be obtained by raising the argument specified in the function reference to the one-half power—for example, X^.5. However, since the SQR function is incorporated in the BASIC language, execution of the function is normally faster than evaluation of the expression X^.5.

can be used. If X = 8.3 then X+.5 = 8.8 and INT(8.8) = 8. If X = 8.6 then X + .5 = 9.1 and INT(9.1) = 9.

In business programs, we often deal with dollars-and-cents values. To round a value to two decimal positions, we can write

```
300 LET A = INT ((X+.005) * 100)/100
```

If X = 60.3138 then X + .005 = 60.3188, INT(60.3188 * 100) = 6031, and 6031/100 = 60.31, which is assigned to A.

As these examples show, function references are often used in numeric expressions within LET statements. They may also be used in PRINT statements. The computer evaluates functions before any other operations on a left-to-right basis within a numeric expression. Parentheses can be used to change this normal order of evaluation, as described earlier for BASIC arithmetic operators.

To determine the functions supplied on the BASIC system available to you, you should consult the system documentation. Since use of these functions can be very convenient and often helps to avoid programming errors, it's to your benefit to become familiar with them. Many implementations include functions that operate on character data. For example LEFT$(A$,4) returns the four leftmost characters of the character string represented by A$; RIGHT$(A$,1) returns the rightmost character of the string represented by A$; and MID$(A$,5,3) returns three characters—those in the 5th, 6th, and 7th positions—of the string A$.

Using Functions in a BASIC Program

In many business organizations, the costs of inventory are a major consideration. Inventory policies are established to minimize the total costs of ordering and carrying inventory. An economic order quantity (EOQ) is calculated for each item using the formula

$$EOQ = \sqrt{\frac{24 * U * O}{C * I}}$$

where U = average number of units required per month
O = cost of placing one order
C = cost of one unit
I = inventory carrying cost expressed as a decimal fraction (a percentage based on the value of the average inventory)

The EOQ is the optimum number of units to order and at the same time minimize the organization's total inventory cost.

The BASIC program in Figure A-28 computes the economic order quantity for a particular inventory item. The values to be used in the computation are entered by the user. On line 290 the SQR function determines an initial value for E (i.e., EOQ) as in the formula above. Since it makes no sense to order part of a unit, the INT function is invoked on line 300 to round the result of the initial computation to the next-higher integral number. The value returned by the INT function, and the input values on which the computation is based, are provided as output.

```
100 REM EOQ.  COMPUTE ECONOMIC ORDER QUANTITY.
110 REM U IS AVERAGE NUMBER OF UNITS REQUIRED PER MONTH
120 REM O IS COST OF PLACING ONE ORDER
130 REM C IS COST OF ONE UNIT
140 REM I IS INVENTORY CARRYING COST EXPRESSED AS A DECIMAL FRACTION
150 REM N$ IS ITEM NUMBER
160 REM INITIALIZE VARIABLES
170 PRINT "ENTER NUMBER OF ITEM"
180 INPUT N$
190 PRINT "ENTER AVERAGE NUMBER OF UNITS USED PER MONTH"
200 INPUT U
210 PRINT "ENTER COST OF ORDERING"
220 INPUT O
230 PRINT "ENTER COST OF ONE UNIT"
240 INPUT C
250 PRINT "ENTER PERCENTAGE OF AVERAGE INVENTORY VALUE"
260 PRINT "THAT IS CARRYING COST"
270 INPUT I
280 REM COMPUTE EOQ
290 LET E = SQR((24*U*O)/(C*I))
300 LET E = INT(E+.05)
310 PRINT
320 PRINT
330 PRINT "FOR ITEM "; N$; " THE EOQ IS"; E
340 PRINT
350 PRINT "THIS RESULT IS BASED ON:"
360 PRINT "AVERAGE USAGE OF"; U
370 PRINT "ORDERING COST OF"; O
380 PRINT "UNIT COST OF"; C
390 PRINT "CARRYING COST OF"; I
400 END
```

Figure A-28 BASIC program to compute economic order quantity of inventory item

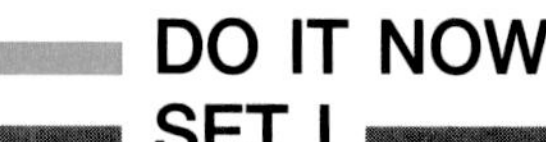

DO IT NOW

SET I

I1. A well-known formula for finding the area of a triangle is:

$$\text{Area} = \sqrt{S(S - A)(S - B)(S - C)}$$

where A, B, and C are the lengths of the sides of the triangle, and

$$S = \frac{A + B + C}{2}$$

Plan, write, test, and document a program to calculate the area of a triangle, given the lengths of its sides as input. Note that if S(S − A)(S − B)(S − C) is less than 0, a triangle cannot exist. Include a check for such a condition and print out an appropriate message if the condition occurs.

Use the following sets of data, contained in DATA statements, as input. The number of sets to be processed should also be contained in a DATA statement and used as the limit for a FOR-NEXT loop that controls repetitive processing.

A	B	C
4	6	8
5.3	6.9	11
8	12	15
4	6	12

12. The combined effect of wind and temperature on the human body is quite severe, particularly in cold climates. This effect is expressed in a relative fashion as a *wind-chill factor.* That factor can be computed as follows:

$V_1 = .447 * \text{windspeed}$
$V_2 = (10.45 + 10 * \sqrt{V_1} - V_1) * (33.0 - \text{temperature in degrees Celsius})$
$\text{Wind-chill factor} = 33.0 - (V_2/22.034)$

Plan, write, test, and document a BASIC program to calculate the windchill factor, given a location, and the windspeed and temperature in degrees Celsius at that location, as input. The program should process any number of sets of input. It should provide the location name, windspeed, temperature, and wind-chill factor for each location as output. The program should recognize the character string END OF DATA as a location value as a signal that all data has been processed. Use the following sets of data as input to test runs:

Location	Windspeed (mph)	Temperature (°C)
Waterloo, IA	15	−10
Chicago, IL	20	−5
Denver, CO	10	5
END OF DATA	0	0

SUMMARY

At the beginning of this appendix, we reviewed briefly the steps in problem solving:

- Defining the problem
- Planning a solution to the problem
- Coding the solution (writing a program)
- Checking the program
- Providing documentation

We continued our work by applying these steps to solve practical problems.

During the planning-a-solution step, we used any of several techniques to develop and express our solution algorithms. Among them are simple narrative, flowcharts, and pseudocode. The latter proved to be especially useful in developing well-structured algorithms, composed of the basic patterns of structured programming:

- SIMPLE SEQUENCE
- IFTHENELSE
- DOWHILE

After we had developed the solution to a problem, we were ready to express the solution in a programming language. Doing so enabled us to use the computer as a tool in problem solving. For our work here, we used the BASIC programming language. Because BASIC is easy to learn and easy to use, it was an apt choice. Further, it's especially well suited for interactive problem solving. You had to learn a little about the sign-on procedures and system commands on the particular computer system available to you. Having done so, you were able to write and execute BASIC programs.

Statement	Function	Example
`LET`	Computes and assigns a value to a variable.	`200 LET D = P(1 + I/100)^N` `210 LET D$ = "MONDAY"`
`REM`	Documents a program or portion thereof.	`100 REM SALES. CALCULATE SALES AMOUNT` `600 REM N IS NUMBER OF SALES`
`END`	Marks the physical end of a program and terminates program execution.	`999 END`
`INPUT`	Accepts data values as input from user during program execution.	`300 INPUT A, B` `340 INPUT D$, E$, F`
`PRINT`	Provides the results of processing as output.	`400 PRINT "THE SUM IS ", S` `410 PRINT A, (A*B)/2`
`DATA`	Contains data values to be read.	`900 DATA 300, 6, 542, .6` `910 DATA "J. BAKER", 42.8`
`READ`	Reads data values from a DATA statement data list.	`400 READ A, B, C, D` `410 READ N$, H`
`RESTORE`	Allows data values in a data list to be reread.	`600 RESTORE`
`GO TO`	Causes an unconditional branch.	`420 GO TO 800` `600 GO TO 210`
`IF...THEN`	Causes a conditional branch. Control is transferred only if a tested condition is true.	`300 IF A = N THEN 800` `400 IF C >= 3 * Y THEN 210`

`IF...THEN`
`...ELSE`
	Provides for a selection between alternatives.	`300 IF H >= 100 THEN`
		`310    PRINT H, "SELL"`
		`320 ELSE`
		`330    PRINT H, "HOLD"`
		`340 END IF`

`DO WHILE`
`.`
`.`
`.`
`LOOP`
	Controls loop processing.	`600 DO WHILE N <> 0`
		`610    LET N = N - 20`
		`620    PRINT N, N^2`
		`630 LOOP`

`FOR`
`.`
`.`
`.`
`NEXT`
	Provides counter-controlled loop processing.	`400 FOR I = 1 TO 12`
		`410     N = V * I`
		`420     PRINT N, V`
		`430 NEXT I`

Figure A-29 Summary of BASIC statements

As we continued to use BASIC to solve a variety of problems, we learned more about the language and about the data that it can be used to process. We now know about numeric constants and character-string constants. We can combine numeric constants, numeric variables, and BASIC arithmetic operators to tell the computer to perform arithmetic operations. We can use BASIC relational operators to set up decision-making steps that control branching and looping operations. We know about implementation-supplied functions and how to use them. In short, we can supply data to the computer and obtain information from it.

The BASIC statements that we've learned to use are summarized, in the order we studied them, in Figure A-29. Obviously, we have not yet learned all there is to know about the BASIC language, but we have learned enough to be able to direct the computer in problem solving.

Having completed this appendix, you have some idea of what an obedient servant the computer really is: It does exactly what you tell it to do (no more and no less). If you fail to direct it correctly, it doesn't operate correctly. If you tell it what to do, in a correct and straightforward way, using a language such as BASIC, it works with amazing speed and accuracy. In our work here, we've seen the importance of program testing—using sample data, for which expected results are determined beforehand, as input to test runs. We test to verify that our problem-solving logic directs the computer as we think it does.

Because you now have some idea of how a computer works and what it does, you are better equipped to deal with it. You may use it indirectly, such as through information system personnel in your on-the-job environment as an accountant, sales representative, or office manager. Chances are you will also deal with it directly. The computer is a powerful machine. You can put it to work for you.

Glossary and Index

A

access mechanism: the physical unit comprising the read/write heads of a direct-access storage device: 132–35

access time: the time interval between the instant when transfer of data to or from a storage device is requested and the instant when the transfer of data is completed: 116–117, 134–35

accumulator: a register that accumulates results: 151, 167

acoustic coupler: a special type of modem that performs functions required to transmit information over ordinary telephone facilities. *Also called* an acoustical modem: 47, 370, 435

Ada: a high-level programming language developed in the late 1970s and early 1980s primarily for use in implementing embedded computer systems: 319

adder: an internal computer component whose output is a representation of the sum of the quantities represented by its inputs: 153–54

address: a name or numeral that designates a particular register, storage location, or other data source or destination: 42, 116, 156–57

address register: a register that contains the address of a storage location or device. *Also called* an address buffer or a data counter: 151, 167

algorithm: a set of well-defined rules for the solution of a problem in a finite number of steps; for example, a complete statement of a procedure for computing a rate of return: 240, 436–37

alphanumeric: pertaining to a character set that includes both alphabetic characters (letters) and numeric characters (digits) and usually special characters such as punctuation marks: 150, 284

Altair 8800: MITS' microcomputer in kit form, marketed to hobbyists in 1975: 22–23

amplitude modulation (AM): 369–70

analog computer: a computer that operates on data in the form of continuously variable physical quantities such as flow, pressures, or temperatures, translated into related mechanical or electrical quantities which serve as analogs (representations) of the data. *Contrast with* digital computer.

analog transmission: the electrical transfer of a continuously variable signal or wave form. *Contrast with* digital transmission: 369–70

ANSI (American National Standards Institute): 113, 245, 280, 289, 389, 441–42

Apple Computer: 20, 71–72, 184, 191–94, 316–17

application: the specific problem or job to be accomplished by automatic data processing; for example, inventory control, payroll, information retrieval, or project management: 305–306

application generator: a computer program that accepts user-oriented generator-language statements or specifications as input and produces an application program as output: 226, 295

application software: programs that direct the computer in performing specific user-related data-processing tasks. Examples are weekly payroll programs, order-processing programs, and programs that produce sales reports: 36–37, 305–308, 330–31

application software package: specialized programs for a particular industry or discipline, marketed for widespread customer use. *Also called* "canned software": 23–24, 180, 194–95, 195–96, 220, 307, 308, 316, 400

arithmetic/logic unit: the part of a processor containing the circuits that perform arithmetic and logical operations: 41–42, 150, 167

artificial intelligence (AI): the study of how humans think and the application of that research to develop machines that appear to do likewise: 128, 296, 407–411

ASCII (American Standard Code for Information Interchange): a 7- or 8-bit code adopted as a standard to facilitate interchange of data between various machines and systems: 113–115, 129, 133

assemble: to prepare a machine-language program from a program written in an assembler language by substituting absolute operation codes for symbolic operation codes and absolute or relocatable addresses for symbolic addresses: 276–77

assembler language: a symbolic programming language similar to machine language, and which, in the usual case, exhibits a one-to-one correspondence with the instruction and data formats used in the computer on which programs written in that language will be run: 272, 274–77, 293, 298–99

assembler program: a computer program that assembles programs written in an assember language to produce machine-language programs: 276–77, 298

assembly listing: a printed output of an assembly run, showing both the source-program (assembler-language statements) and the object program (machine-language instructions) created from them, as well as other information that is useful to the programmer: 276–77

asynchronous operations: events occurring without regular time relationship. Hence, as applied to program execution, unexpected or unpredictable events with respect to instruction sequence. *Contrast with* synchronous operations: 164–65
asynchronous transmission: a method of electrical transfer of data in which the sending and receiving units are synchronized on each character, or small block of characters, usually by the use of start and stop signals. *Synonymous with* start/stop transmission. *Contrast with* synchronous transmission: 371–72
Atari: 23, 184
AT&T: 292, 328–29, 376–77, 379–80
ATM: *See* automated teller machine.
audio response: *See* voice output.
auditing: 421
automated teller machine (ATM): an unattended (self-service) banking device designed for direct use by customers. *Contrast with* teller terminal: 17, 25, 55, 75, 319, 392
automatic data processing: data processing performed largely by a machine, without intervention by a human operator; when that machine is an electronic digital computer, the sequence of operations may be referred to specifically as electronic data processing: 31
automation: the performance of a specific combination of actions by a machine or group of machines without the aid of a human operator (i.e., "automatically"). *Contrast with* mechanization: 400–402. *See also* industrial automation; office automation; robotic system.
auxiliary storage: storage that supplements primary storage. *Synonymous with* secondary storage: 43, 110

B

background program: In a multiprogramming environment, a program that can be executed whenever the facilities of the EDP system are not required by a program having higher priority. *Contrast with* foreground program: 323
backup: alternative files, equipment, or procedures available for temporary or emergency use in case of total or partial system failure: 124, 131, 132, 139, 267, 426, 428–29
band printer: 88
bar code: a machine-printed data representation consisting of lines that can be read by an optical reader: 64–65, 77–78
BASIC (Beginners' All-purpose Symbolic Instruction Code): a high-level programming language designed primarily for use in interactive problem solving by engineers, scientists, and others who may not be professional programmers: 23, 36, 47–49, 243–45, 288–89, 321, 434–93
arithmetic operators: 438, 446–49
assignment (LET) statement: 438, 446–49
branching: 466–68
character data: 440, 443–44, 457–59, 468
comma, use of: 454–55, 457–58
comment: 449–50
constant: 440, 443–44, 457–58
DATA: 460–64, 492
DO: 468–69, 476–77, 492
END: 288–89, 438–39, 450, 492
executable statement: 449–50
file I/O: 464
FOR: 479–84, 492
functions: 486–89
GO TO: 288–89, 466–67, 470–72, 492
IF . . . THEN: 467–68, 470–72, 492
INPUT: 288–89, 438, 451–53, 460, 492
keyword: 438, 442
LET: 288–89, 438, 446–49, 460–61, 492
line number: 243, 437–38, 442
looping: 466, 468–69, 474–77, 479–83
nested loops: 483–84
NEXT: 479–83, 492
nonexecutable statement: 449
null statement: 450
numeric data: 438, 442–43, 453–57
parentheses, use of: 448–49
PRINT: 288–89, 438, 440, 453–59, 492
quotation marks, use of: 440, 443–44, 457–58
READ: 460–64, 492
relational operators: 467–68
REM: 243–45, 288–89, 440, 449–50, 492
RESTORE: 460–64, 492
semicolon, use of: 455–56, 458
space, use of: 442, 444, 447, 454, 466, 467
standardization: 289, 441–42
statement length: 442
TAB function: 456–57, 458
variable: 438, 444–45
batch processing: a technique in which data to be processed or programs to be executed are collected into groups to permit convenient, efficient, serial processing. *Also called* stacked-job processing. *Contrast with* transaction processing: 54, 64, 310, 312, 434
beltbed plotter: 95
belt printer: 88
binary component: an element that can be in either of two possible conditions at any given time: 112, 117–19
binary notation: 112–13, 273
binary number system: a numeration system using the digits 0 and 1 and having a base of 2. For example, the binary numeral 1001 means $(1 \times 2^3) + (0 \times 2^2) + (0 \times 2^1) + (1 \times 2^0)$, which is equivalent to the decimal numeral 9: 153–54
binary numeral: a multidigit symbol of the binary number system: 153–54
binary state: one of two possible conditions of a component. Most digital-computer components (for example, vacuum tubes, magnetic cores, transistors, and logic gates) are essentially binary in that they have two stable states: 112, 117–19
biometric security mechanism: 421
bit: an acronym for *b*inary dig*it*; the smallest unit of data in the representation of a value in binary notation. A bit can be either a 0 or a 1: 112–13, 128, 132
bit-mapped graphics: *Also called* raster graphics: 67, 100
block: (1) a group of words, characters, or digits handled as a unit and read into or written from primary storage in one I/O operation: 129; (2) in block-structured programming languages, a section of program coding treated as a unit, largely for purposes of storage allocation and transfer of control; for example, a PL/I procedure or begin block: 287
buffer: a storage area used to collect data in order to compensate for differences in rates of data flow or times of occurrence of events when transmitting data from one device to another: 167, 319
bug: an error in a design or in program coding or an equipment fault: 49, 235, 259, 426

bus: a physical path along which data and/or control signals travel within a computer system; may be referred to specifically as a data bus, a control bus, or an I/O bus: 150–51, 162, 167–68
business graphics: 105. *See also* desktop publishing.
byte: a fixed number of adjacent bits operated on as a unit (usually shorter than a computer word in length). For example, in several modern computers, a byte is a group of eight adjacent bits and can represent one character of data: 115

C

C: a machine-independent, assemblerlike language developed as part of the UNIX operating system and used primarily for system programming: 292–93, 298
cache: high-speed memory that serves as a staging area for data and instruction transfers: 168
CAD/CAM (computer-aided design/computer-aided manufacturing): 4–10, 72, 95, 198–99
CAE (computer-aided engineering): 13
card punch: a device that punches holes in designated locations on cards to store data; these devices range from electronic punches used as online output devices of computers to manually operated punches such as the keypunch: 56–57
card reader: a device that reads, or senses, holes in punched cards, transforming the data from hole patterns to electrical pulses for input to another device, usually a digital computer: 55–57
card read-punch: a device having the capabilities of both a card reader and a card punch: 56–57
Carterfone decision: 377
CASE: *See* computer-assisted software engineering.
CASE control structure: 253–57
cathode-ray tube (CRT): an electronic vacuum tube containing a screen on which information can be stored or displayed: 95
CBX (computer-based PBX): 375
CD ROM: *See* compact disk read-only memory.
central processing unit (CPU): *See* processor.
chain printer: 87–88
channel: *See* communication channel.
character-addressable: pertaining to a computer that performs operations on variable-length words. *Contrast with* word-addressable: 162
chief information officer (CIO): 400
chief programmer team: 226–27
CISC: *See* complex instruction set computing.
client node: 352, 381–82
clone: hardware or software that is a copy of other, previously existing hardware or software: 196
COBOL (Common Business Oriented Language): a high-level programming language designed primarily for business data processing: 283–86
code inspection: 259
color output: 97, 98
COM (computer output microfilm): 103–105
Commodore: 20, 184, 187, 190
common carrier: a company that furnishes communication services to the general public under the regulation of appropriate local, state, or federal agencies; examples are American Telephone and Telegraph (AT&T) and Western Union: 372, 376
communication: the transmission of intelligence between points of origin and destination without altering the sequence or information content of such transmission: 366, 385
communication channel: a data path along which signals (messages) may flow: 367–69
communication control unit: 367–68
communication, regulation of: 376–79
communication satellite: 377–79, 390
compact disk read-only memory (CD ROM): 138
Compaq Computer: 195, 196–97
compatibility: the ability to use programs, data, and/or devices of one computer system on another computer system without change: 150, 182, 190–91, 196
compile: to prepare a machine-language program from a high-level-language program by making use of the over-all logic structure of the program to generate more than one machine-language instruction for each source-program statement, or by performing functions similar to those of an assembler, or both: 171, 280–81
compiler program: a program that compiles programs in a high-level programming language to produce machine-language programs: 171, 276, 280–81, 441
complex instruction set computing (CISC): the conventional approach to computer design. *Contrast with* RISC: 169
composite design: *See* top-down design.
CompuServe: 24, 359, 393
computer: a device capable of solving problems by accepting data, performing prescribed operations on the data, and supplying the results of these operations. In data processing, the device is usually a stored-program computer, which performs these operations without the intervention of a human operator: 1–2, 35–36, 39–42, 145–46, 177, 318. *See also* analog computer; digital computer.
computer-aided design/computer-aided manufacturing (CAD/CAM): 4–10, 72, 95, 198–99
computer-aided engineering (CAE): 13
computer-assisted software engineering (CASE): 218, 225–26, 230, 231, 233, 247, 257, 262, 293–94
computer-based PBX (CBX): 375
computer history: 40–41, 55–57, 117, 145, 180–81, 190, 191–94, 280–82, 283, 286, 288, 289–90, 292, 293, 308–315, 321, 328
computer impact: 396–430
computer input microfilm (CIM): 105
computer-integrated manufacturing (CIM): 9, 290
ComputerLand: 23, 203
computer literacy: 2
computer output microfilm (COM): 105–107
computer store: 23, 26–27, 191, 203
computer, uses of: 1–27. *Note:* In addition, application boxes throughout this book illustrate uses of computers.
computer word: a sequence of bits or characters moved, used in operations, and stored as a unit: 115, 178
COMSAT: 378–79
concurrent processing: 315
conditional branch: an instruction that may or may not cause a transfer from the normal sequence of instruction execution, depending upon the result of some operation, the content of some register, or the setting of some indicator. *Contrast with* unconditional branch: 159–60, 467–68

constant: a value that does not change during processing. *Contrast with* variable: 440, 443–44, 457–58
control field: a fixed portion of a data item or record where information for control purposes is placed; for example, account numbers used for sequencing or transaction codes used for identifying the types of operations to be performed on input data. *Also called* a key: 124, 340–42
control section: the part of a processor that effects the retrieval of instructions in proper sequence, the interpretation of each instruction, and the application of the proper signals to the arithmetic/logic unit and other parts of the computer system in accordance with this interpretation: 41–42, 148–49
control unit: a device functioning between the central processing unit and one or more I/O devices to perform code conversion, error detection and recovery, and similar functions during I/O operations. *Also called* a controller: 367–68
conventional memory: primary storage up to 640K in an MS-DOS environment. *Contrast with* expanded memory; extended memory: 120–21
conversational computing: *Synonymous with* interactive computing: 45–50, 55, 288–89, 320–24, 434
cooperative processing: 381–82
copyrighting (to protect software): 422–24
core storage: an internal storage unit consisting of magnetic cores: 117–19
cost/benefit analysis: 220–23
courseware: computer programs for instructional use: 20–22
CP/M (Control Program for Microcomputers): a well-known portable operating system especially common on early 8-bit microcomputer systems: 190
CPU: *See* central processing unit.
crime, computer: 416–20
CRT: *See* cathode-ray tube.
cursor: an indicator that shows the current position on a visual-display screen; not uncommonly, the indicator is an underscore character: 48, 71–72, 192
cycle time: the time the computer takes to get ready to process a request: 116–17
cylinder: all tracks accessible at one setting of the access mechanism of a direct-access storage device: 134

D

daisywheel printer: 87
DASD: *See* direct-access storage device.
data: any representation of a fact or an idea that can be manipulated and to which meaning can be assigned. *Related to* information: 3, 52–80, 335, 383. *See also* database.
data bank: (1) a comprehensive collection of libraries of data (in inventory control, for example, one line of an invoice constitutes an item, a complete invoice constitutes a record, the complete set of such records constitutes a file, a collection of inventory-control files forms a library, and the libraries used by an organization are known as its data bank); (2) loosely, a database: 393, 413–14
database: a comprehensive, integrated collection of data organized to avoid duplication of data, yet permit retrieval of information to satisfy a wide variety of user information needs: 343–50
database administration (DBA): 345
database management system (DBMS): software that handles the organizing, cataloging, locating, storing, retrieving, and maintaining of data in a database: 226, 307, 316, 350–54, 355
database server: 352–54, 381–82. *See also* database management system.
data-collection device: 75
data communications: the electrical transfer of data from one point to another: 366
data-communication system: *Synonymous with* teleprocessing system: 366, 367–69
data diddling: 420
data element dictionary: 231
data entry: 25, 52–80. *See also* input.
data flow diagram (DFD): a pictorial representation of what occurs in a user's existing system or in a proposed system, created for analysis purposes: 218–19, 233
data interchange: the transfer of data from one computer system to another: 129. *See also* electronic data interchange.
data management system: *Also called* a file management system: 342–43, 352
data model: *Synonymous with* logical data structure: 345–50
data processing: a systematic sequence of operations performed on data to achieve a desired result: 2–4, 383
data-processing system: the people, equipment, and procedures that perform data processing: 2–4, 33–34
data recorder: a key-to-tape device used for manual keying of data on magnetic tape: 57–58
data transfer: 124, 117, 130, 135
DBMS: *See* database management system.
DBMS transparency: 360
debugging: the task of detecting, locating, and eliminating mistakes in a program or malfunctions in equipment: 49, 235, 259–60
decision support system (DSS): a data-processing system designed to provide "what if" help directly to managers and other professionals as an aid in decision making: 358–59
demodulation: the process of retrieving the information content from a modulated carrier wave; the reverse of modulation: 367, 369–70
depersonalization: 412
design review: 235
desk checking: visually inspecting a program design or coding and tracing its logic to eliminate errors before coding or before submitting the program to the computer. *Also called* simulation: 242–43, 244, 259, 472
desktop computer: *Also called* an office computer or a workstation: 198-200. *See also* microcomputer.
desktop film recorder: 105
desktop publishing: computer-assisted preparation of documents containing both graphics and textual data: 67–68, 83, 91, 100, 194, 383–84
destructive operation: a process of reading or writing data which erases the data that is read or that was stored previously in the receiving storage location (it must be re-stored if it is to be used again). *Contrast with* nondestructive operation: 116, 129
detail file: *Synonymous with* transaction file.
development support library (DSL): 227, 265. *See also* documentation.

Dialog Information Services: 359–60
digital audio tape (DAT): 131–32
digital computer: a computer that operates on discrete, quantified data, performing arithmetic and logical operations on it. Generally, the data is expressed in a numerical form. *Contrast with* analog computer: 41. *See also* computer.
digital transmission: the electrical transfer of discrete, or discontinuous, signals whose various states are distinct intervals apart. *Contrast with* analog transmission: 370–71
digitize: to convert data to a discrete form of representation, for example, to a sequence of on-off electrical pulses acceptable as input to a computer: 67
digitizer: *Also called* a graphics tablet: 72. *See also* digitize.
direct-access storage device (DASD): 123. *See also* magnetic disk.
direct file organization: 340–42
direct processing: a technique of handling data in random order, without preliminary sorting, and utilizing files on direct-access storage devies. *Synonymous with* random processing. *Contrast with* sequential processing: 124–27
direct storage: storage media allowing access times not significantly affected either by the location of data to be read or by the location to which data is to be written (because there is no need to pass all preceding data in the file). *Synonymous with* random-access storage. *Contrast with* sequential storage: 123
disk: *See* magnetic disk.
diskette: *Synonymous with* flexible disk: 60–61, 135–36
diskette input/output unit: 61
disk pack: (1) a set of disks with surfaces on which areas can be magnetized; (2) a medium to or from which data is transferred by a read/write head of a disk drive: 133–35. *See also* magnetic disk.
distributed databases: 360–62
distributed processing: the dispersion and use of the processing power, or intelligence, within an EDP system among geographically separated locations: 366, 380–82
divestiture plan: 379
documentation: 245, 263–65, 439–40. *See also* development support library.
document processing: 383. *See also* desktop publishing; word processing.
dot-matrix character: 86
dot-matrix printer: 87–89, 97
DOUNTIL control structure: 253–57
DOWHILE basic pattern: 252–57, 474–77
Dow Jones News/Retrieval: 359
drum plotter: 95–96
drum printer: 88
DSS: *See* decision support system.
dumb terminal: an I/O device that provides for data entry and information exit when connected to a computer but has no additional capabilities. *Contrast with* intelligent terminal; smart terminal: 368
dummy record: 255–56, 476–77
duty cycle: the manufacturer-recommended usage of a printer, usually expressed as number of pages per month: 91, 92
dynamic address translation (DAT): the conversion of a virtual-storage address to a real-storage address when the instruction or data at that location is referenced during program execution: 325

E

EBCDIC (Extended Binary Coded Decimal Interchange Code): an 8-bit code used to represent specific data characters in many current computer systems: 112, 113–14, 129, 133
eighty-twenty rule: 169, 357–58
electronic bulletin board: 205
electronic data interchange (EDI): transfer of structured business data from the computer system of one organization to the computer system of another: 366, 388–89, 390
electronic data processing (EDP): data processing performed largely by electronic equipment, such as electronic digital computers, rather than by manual, mechanical, or electromechanical techniques. *Related to* automatic data processing: 31, 32–35
electronic digital computer: *See* digital computer.
electronic funds transfer: a communication between computer systems or within a computer system to transfer monetary values from one account to another electronically: 17, 415
electronic mail: automated communication through electronic transmission facilities and devices: 201, 385–88, 415
electronic security system: 420–21, 427–28
electronic spreadsheet program: software developed to aid users in break-even analysis, budget planning and control, cash flow analysis, loan amortization, and other common business applications. Examples are Lotus 1-2-3 and Excel: 24, 75, 182, 194, 198, 307, 316, 359. *See also* Lotus 1-2-3.
electrophotographic printer: *Also called* a xerographic printer: 91, 97
electrostatic plotter: 95, 97
electrostatic printer: 91
embezzlement (with computer help): 410
employee security: 420, 422, 427–28
employment (in computing): 25–27, 402–404
emulation: a process by which one device is made to function like another, in order to accept the same kind of data, execute the same instructions, and achieve the same kind of results: 93, 149
encryption: 421
ENIAC: 40–41, 166
EOS: *See* erasable optical storage.
erasable optical storage (EOS): 139
ergonomics: human engineering; the study of human factors that need to be considered when designing and implementing computer systems: 59, 70
E13B type font: 61–62
E-time (execution time): the time required to perform the operation specified by an instruction. *Contrast with* I-time: 160–61
expanded memory: in a microcomputer system, primary storage below 1 megabyte available via "windows" mapped onto a memory board. *Contrast with* conventional memory; extended memory: 120–21
expanded storage: supplementary addressable storage in an IBM 3090 mainframe environment: 121
expert system: *Also called* knowledge-based system: 128, 408–409
extended memory: primary storage above 1 megabyte in a microcomputer system. *Contrast with* conventional memory; expanded memory: 120–21
external data transfer: 124

F

facsimile equipment: digitized imaging devices often used as terminals in communication systems. *Also called* fax machines: 385
fact-finding: 216–18
feasibility report: 215
feasibility study: 215
Federal Communications Commission (FCC): 376–79
file: (1) a collection of related records (in inventory control, for example, one line of an invoice constitutes an item, a complete invoice constitutes a record, and the complete set of such records constitutes a file). *Also called* a data set: 123, 229–31, 464. *See also* master file; transaction file.
file access: 340–41
file maintenance: the process of updating master files by adding, changing, or deleting data to reflect the effects of nonperiodic changes; for example, the addition of new-product records to an inventory-control master file: 293, 464
file management system: 343. *See also* data management system.
file organization: the techniques used to arrange the records in a file on a physical storage medium: 340–42
file system: software that manages physical space allocation on storage media, the creation and manipulation of files, and similar I/O-related functions: 336–42, 352
firmware: *See* microcode.
fixed-length operation: pertaining to an operation in which operands always have the same number of bits or characters. *Contrast with* variable-length operation: 162–64
fixed-length word: 162–64
flatbed plotter: 95–96
flat file: 346
flexible disk: a single thin manipulatable disk with one or two magnetic recording surfaces. *Synonymous with* diskette; floppy disk: 60–61, 135–36
floppy disk: *Synonymous with* flexible disk.
flowchart: a pictorial representation of the types and sequence of operations within a program (program flowchart) or the data, flow of work, and workstations within a system (system flowchart): 228–29, 241–43, 245–47, 469–85. *See also* program flowchart; system flowchart.
flowcharting:
cross-referencing: 243
striping convention: 247
symbols: 245–47
template: 245
worksheet: 245
foreground program: in a multiprogramming environment, a program that has a high priority and therefore takes precedence over other programs when contention for system resources occurs. *Contrast with* background program: 323
formal code inspection: 259
formal design review: 235
FORTRAN (FORmula TRANslator): a high-level programming language designed primarily to facilitate the preparation of programs to perform mathematical computations: 279, 280–83
fourth-generation language (4GL): (1) a very-high-level programming language designed primarily to help nonprogrammers gain access to computerized data; (2) a software tool that enhances the productivity of its users; examples are generator languages, query products, report writers, and other information-center software: 226, 272, 293–95, 299
fraud (with computer help): 418, 419–20
frequency modulation (FM): 369–70
front-end processor: 368
full-duplex transmission: 372–73
fully-formed characters: 86

G

G: gigabyte; in discussion of addressable storage locations, 1G = 1024M, where 1M = 1024K, and 1K = 1024 bytes: 115
Gantt chart: 217
gateway processor: 388
general-purpose (general) register: 152–53. *See also* register.
gigabyte: (1) roughly, one billion bytes; (2) G, where 1G = 1024M, or 1024K bytes, or 1,173,741,824 individual storage locations: 115
GOTO-less programming: 251
graphics tablet: *Also called* a digitizer: 72. *See also* digitize.

H

half-duplex transmission: 372–73
handheld computer: *Also called* a pocket computer: 180–81
handheld terminal: 77–78, 319
handwritten input: 66–67
hard copy: a permanent record of machine output in human-readable form; generally, reports, listings, and other printed documents. *Contrast with* soft copy: 83, 85, 97, 453
hardware: physical equipment such as mechanical, magnetic, and electronic devices. *Contrast with* software: 37, 201
hard-wired: a characteristic of a device having a fixed set of operations established by internal wiring set up before the device is placed in operation: 37, 273
head positioning: placing a read/write head that is to read or write data when data is being read or written by a direct-access storage device: 134–35
head switching: activating the read/write head that is to read or write data when data is being read or written by a direct-access storage device: 134–35
HELP facility: 97–98, 202
heuristics: 410
hexadecimal notation: 157, 273
hexadecimal number system: a numeration system having a base of 16 and using the symbols 0, 1, 2, 3, 4, 5, 6, 7, 8, 9, A, B, C, D, E, F: 157
hierarchical data model: 346–48
high-level programming language: a problem-oriented or procedure-oriented programming language; for example, FORTRAN, COBOL, PL/I, BASIC, Pascal, or C. *Contrast with* low-level programming language: 276–80, 293
Hollerith code: a code widely used for representing data on 80-column punched cards: 55–56
home computer: 22–25, 184–88. *See also* microcomputer.
home information system: 24–25, 186–87

housekeeping: pertaining to operations in a program or system that do not contribute directly to the solution of a problem but are essential processing functions; for example, checking the labels on data files and determining whether all I/O devices are attached to a system and readied for processing: 318

I

IBM-compatible: like IBM-produced similar hardware or software with respect to interfaces and function: 150, 182, 190–91, 196
IBM PC: 38, 45–49, 150, 180, 191, 195–96, 328. *See also* microcomputer; personal computer.
IBM PS/2: 136, 166, 191, 196, 200–201, 318. *See also* personal computer; workstation.
icon: a small on-screen graphic used as a symbol for an operation or object: 71
IFTHENELSE basic pattern: 251–57, 469–72
image scanner: 66. *See also* scanner.
impact printer: 86, 87–89
indexed sequential file organization: 34–42
industrial automation: 400–402. *See also* CAD/CAM; robotic system.
informal code inspection: 259
informal design review: 235
information: the meaning that a human assigns to data by means of known conventions used in the data representation; processed, or "finished," data: 3, 82–105, 335, 383
information center: 294–95, 399–400
information utility: *Also called* a computer service company or service bureau: 323–24
ink-jet printer: 89–91, 97
input: data to be processed by a computer: 32–35, 43–45, 52–80, 229–31
input/output buffer: *See* storage register.
input/output device: a unit used to submit data to the computer or to provide information from it: 43–45, 179
instruction: a set of characters that specifies an operation to be performed and the value or location of one or more operands: 154–57
instruction counter: an internal computer component that indicates the location of the next instruction to be executed. *Also called* an instruction address register, program counter, control register, or sequence control register: 153
instruction cycle: 158
instruction execution: 158–62
instruction format: 156–58
integrated circuit (IC): a complete, complex electronic circuit, capable of performing all the functions of a conventional circuit containing numerous discrete transistors, diodes, capacitors, and/or resistors, all of whose component parts are fabricated and assembled in a single integrated process: 119
intelligent terminal: an I/O device that can be programmed to perform functions such as data editing, data conversion, sorting, summarizing, and communication with or control of other I/O devices. *Contrast with* dumb terminal; smart terminal: 368
interactive computing: a mode of processing that permits frequent interchange between the user at a terminal or microcomputer and the computer itself during the execution of a program; generally, each entry from the user elicits a response from the computer, and vice versa. *Synonymous with* conversational computing: 45–50, 55, 288–89, 320–24, 434
interblock gap (IBG): on a data-recording medium, the distance between the end of one block and the beginning of the next one: 130
internal data transfer: 117
internal storage unit: *Synonymous with* primary storage: 35, 41–42
interpreter program: a computer program that processes high-level language statements on a statement-by-statement basis, determining the operations required and causing the computer to perform those operations immediately: 94, 276, 280, 290–91, 441
interrupt: a signal, condition, or event that causes normal processing operations to be suspended temporarily. Examples are completion of an input or output operation or an attempt to write in a protected location: 164–65
inverted file: 346
ISO (International Standards Organization): 245, 280
item: an amount of data treated as a unit; thus, for example, in inventory control, one line of an invoice constitutes an item, a complete invoice constitutes a record, and the complete set of such records constitutes a file: 123
I-time (instruction time): the time required to move an instruction from primary storage to the address and operation-code registers; that is, the time required to set up circuit paths necessary for instruction execution. *Contrast with* E-time: 158–60

J

job: a unit of work to be done by an EDP system: 310–12, 315
job-control language (JCL): the programming language used to write job-control statements to tell the computer what kind of work (jobs and job steps) is to be done: 310–12
job step: the execution of a program identified explicitly on a job-control statement; a job may comprise one job step or a sequence of job steps: 310–12
just-in-time (JIT) production: 8

K

K: a value meaning 1024 bits, bytes, or words, in discussion of addressable storage locations; for example, 64K bytes usually means 64 × 1024 bytes, or 65,536 bytes; 1K = one kilobyte: 115
key: one or more characters associated with a particular item or a particular record and used to identify that item or record, especially in sorting, collating, or direct I/O operations. *Also called* a control field: 124
keypunch: a manually operated device that is used to punch data into 80-column cards. *Related to* card punch: 56–57
key-to-disk: 58–60
key-to-diskette: 60–61
key-to-tape: 57–58
keyword: (1) in programming, an identifier that, when used in the proper context, has a special language-defined or implementation-defined meaning in a program: 438, 442; (2) in design, when using pseudocode, a word that emphasizes the logical structure of the solution algorithm, or program: 255

L

label: (1) an identification assigned for control purposes to a data file or a data-recording medium such as a magnetic tape; (2) a name attached to or written near the entity it identifies; for example, a key attached to the item or record it identifies, or a name written near a statement on a coding sheet: 274–75, 442

language-processor program: a computer program that accepts programming-language statements as input and produces machine-language instructions as output. *Also called* a language translator. Examples are assemblers, compilers, and interpreters: 94, 260, 276, 441

lap-top portable computer: 180–84, 200

larceny: 418–19

laser: a pure-color light beam: 91, 103, 137–39

laser printer: 91–93

learning system: educational software (courseware) comprising a series of lessons that can be administered simultaneously to dozens of students: 20

leased line: *See* private line.

letter-quality: 86

lexicon: 296

light pen: a photosensitive device used in conjunction with a cathode-ray tube (CRT); its position on the CRT can be determined by a computer: 72

line printer: 85

local access and transport area (LATA): 379

local area network (LAN): a communication system designed to transmit data from one point to two or more other points simultaneously within a relatively small area: 201, 387–88

location transparency: 360

logical data structure: *Synonymous with* data model: 345–50

logical operations: 150

Logo: a programming language for use with microcomputers that is designed to help students learn how to perceive things, how to think: 20

look-and-feel: characteristics of the user-computer (sometimes called man-machine) interface when a user interacts with a computer: 95–97, 423–24

looping: executing a sequence of instructions repetitively, usually with modified addresses (causing different locations to be referenced) or upon different data (because the contents of referenced locations are changed): 241–42, 251–53, 255–57, 474–77, 479–83. *See also* DOUNTIL control structure; DOWHILE basic pattern.

Lotus 1-2-3: a popular electronic spreadsheet program that runs on IBM and IBM-compatible microcomputers: 24, 38, 75, 198, 307, 308

low-level programming language: a machine-oriented programming language; machine languages and assembler languages are in this category. *Contrast with* high-level programming language: 305

luggable computer: *Synonymous with* transportable computer.

M

M: megabyte; in discussion of addressable storage locations, 1M = 1024K, where 1K = one kilobyte, or 1024 bytes: 115

machine cycle: the length of time required for the computer to perform completely one machine operation: 158, 169–70

machine independence: a characteristic of some programming languages, allowing programs written in those languages to be executed on any of several computers with little or no modification; the program, in turn, is said to be machine independent or portable; 279–80

machine language: a language that can be interpreted directly by the internal circuitry of the computer: 156–57, 171, 272, 273–74, 293

machine-oriented language: a programming language in which source-program instructions correspond closely to machine instructions recognized and executed by the computer. *Contrast with* problem-oriented language; procedure-oriented language: 274, 276

Macintosh: 71, 166, 192–95, 316–18

magnetic core: a small piece of magnetic material that can be placed in a spatial relationship to current-carrying conductors and whose magnetic properties are essential to its use; a common component of primary storage in the 1960s and 1970s: 117–18

magnetic disk: a flat circular plate with magnetic surfaces on which data can be written by selective magnetization of portions of its surfaces; the disk may be either conventional (hard) or flexible (floppy). *Contrast with* optical storage: 43, 132–37

magnetic ink: an ink containing particles of a magnetic substance that can be detected by magnetic sensors and, therefore, read automatically: 61–63

magnetic-ink character recognition (MICR): the machine reading of characters printed with magnetic ink. *Contrast with* optical character recognition (OCR): 61–63.

magnetic tape: a tape with a magnetic surface on which data can be written by selective magnetization of portions of the surface: 126–32

magnetic-tape unit: 43–45, 126–32

mail-order house: 23, 203–205

mainframe: (1) the processor of a large computer system; (2) a nickname for a full-scale computer: 147, 167, 168, 177–78, 318

main storage: *Synonymous with* primary storage.

management information system (MIS): a data-processing system designed to provide primarily historical information to management as an aid in decision making: 338–39, 354–58

manufacturing resource planning (MRP II): 7, 314

Mark I: 40–41

master file: a file containing relatively permanent data used as reference, usually updated periodically. *Contrast with* transaction file: 124–27, 337

material requirements planning (MRP): 5–7

MCP (Master Control Program): an early, multitasking operating system developed by Burroughs Corporation: 313–15

mechanization: the use of a machine or group of machines to carry out a process under the direction of a human operator. *Contrast with* automation: 400

megabyte: (1) roughly, one million bytes; (2) M, where 1M = 1024K bytes, or 1,048,576 storage locations: 115

megahertz: millions of cycles per second; a measure of processor speed: 168

memory: *Synonymous with* primary storage: 35, 41

menu: a list of choices shown on a visual-display screen, from which the user selects a command or data to be entered into the computer: 71–72, 294, 316

MICR: *See* magnetic-ink character recognition.
microcode: a sequence of basic subcommands, or pseudocommands, built into the computer and executed automatically by hardware. Generally, these commands are in read-only memory (ROM). *Also called* firmware. *Related to* microprogramming: 37–39, 111, 149, 169, 327
microcomputer: a complete computer on a single miniature circuit board: 20, 42, 122, 147, 150, 176–205, 266, 316, 329, 336–37, 343. *See also* handheld computer, home computer, lap-top portable computer, office computer, personal computer, transportable computer, workstation.
microfiche: 103–105
microfilm: 103–105
micrographics: 103–105
microprocessor: a one-chip central processing unit: 1, 41, 93–94, 147–48, 166–72, 178, 318. *See also* processor.
microprogramming: controlling an EDP system by means of instructions, each of which, instead of being executed directly, causes the execution of a sequence of small, separate operational steps called microcode instructions: 37–39
microsecond: one millionth of one second: 117, 158
micro-to-mainframe link: 201, 352
millisecond: one thousandth of one second: 135, 158
minicomputer: a stored-program computer, generally having less memory and a smaller word size than larger machines, and available in a basic configuration at a purchase price of less than $50,000: 58–60, 147, 177–78, 322
MIPS: millions of instructions per second; a measure of processor speed: 168
MIS: *See* management information system.
missing-item fault: a condition that occurs in a virtual-storage system when a page or segment referred to during program execution is not present in real storage: 325
mnemonic: a symbol chosen to aid human memory; for example, an abbreviation such as L for Load or B for Branch: 274
modem: an acronym for *mo*dulator-*dem*odulator; a device that both modulates and demodulates signals transmitted over communication facilities: 370. *See also* acoustic coupler.
modular programming: an approach to programming that emphasizes the organization and coding of separable program units, usually on the basis of function: 250
modulation: the process of varying the characteristics of a wave in accordance with another wave or signal, usually to make user equipment signals compatible with communication facilities. *Contrast with* demodulation: 367, 369–70
monochrome display: 98
mouse: a handheld pointer that may be used to manipulate the cursor on the display screen of a microcomputer: 71–72, 179, 192–93, 317
MS-DOS: a popular disk-based operating system developed by Microsoft for use with microcomputer systems having 16-bit microprocessors; the IBM PC version of this operating system is known as PC DOS: 42–43, 120, 121, 182, 190–91, 195, 197, 310, 315, 316–17, 328
multiprocessing: a technique for executing two or more sequences of instructions simultaneously in a single computer system, generally by the use of more than one central processing unit: 148–49, 317–19
multiprocessor system: 148–49, 162, 317–19
multiprogramming: a technique for handling two or more independent programs at the same time by loading them into primary storage and executing their instructions concurrently. *Also called* multitasking: 313–15, 317

N

nanosecond: one billionth of one second: 117, 158
National Center for Computer Crime Data (NCCCD): 416–19
National Crime Information Center (NCIC): 16
natural language: the language a person uses daily. Examples are English and French: 296–97, 409
nested control structures: 254–57, 483–84
network data model: 348–49
nondestructive operation: a process of reading data that does not erase the data being read. *Contrast with* destructive operation: 116, 129
nonimpact printer: 86, 89–91
nonvolatile storage: 119, 179
notebook-sized portable computer: 181
numerical control (NC): 7, 57

O

object-oriented graphics: *Also called* vector graphics: 100
object-oriented language: a high-level programming language that supports user-defined constructs (objects) and operations and emphasizes reusability: 296–98
object program: a program expressed in a machine-language form that can be acted on by a particular computer. *Contrast with* source program: 276–77, 280–81
OCR: *See* optical character recognition.
OEM: *See* original equipment manufacturer.
office automation: the use of machines to do many clerical and administrative tasks formerly done by humans: 366, 382–84. *See also* desktop publishing; electronic mail; word processing.
office computer: *Also called* a desktop computer or workstation: 198–200. *See also* microcomputer.
offline: pertaining to equipment or devices that are neither in direct communication with nor controlled by the CPU. *Contrast with* online: 56–57
online: pertaining to equipment or devices that are in direct communication with or controlled by the CPU. *Contrast with* offline: 56–57
online direct-access system: a computer system that performs transaction processing by means of its direct-processing capabilities and online input/output and direct-access storage devices: 311–13
open skies policy: 377
operand: (1) a unit of data upon which an operation is performed; (2) the part of an instruction that tells where to find the data or equipment to be operated on: 156–57
operating system: an organized collection of software used to assist and in part control the operations of a computer: 36, 310–11, 327–31
operation code (op code): (1) a code used to represent a specific operation of a computer; (2) the part of an instruction that tells what operation is to be performed: 156–57
operation-code register: a register that contains the operation-code portion of a machine-language instruction during interpretation and execution of that instruction. *Also called* an instruction register: 151

optical-character recognition (OCR): the machine reading of characters or other symbols through use of light-sensitive materials or devices. *Contrast with* magnetic-ink character recognition (MICR): 63–66, 67, 77–78
optical disk: 103–104. *See also* optical storage.
optical mark: an ordinary pen or pencil mark placed on a specific area of a source document and interpreted by an optical-mark reader when provided as input to a computer: 63–64
optical scanner: 55, 64–65, 67
optical storage: disk storage units on which data is recorded using laser-beam technology; may be compact disk read-only memory (CD ROM), write once, read many (WORM), or erasable optical storage (EOS). *Contrast with* magnetic disk: 137–39
original equipment manufacturer (OEM): a firm that incorporates another firm's products (for example, microprocessor, DASD) into its own products for resale purposes: 168
OS/2: a sophisticated, disk-based operating system developed by IBM and Microsoft for use with microcomputer systems based on Intel 80286, 80386, and subsequent similar microprocessors: 121, 182, 196, 315
output: the result of processing: 32–35, 43–45, 82–105, 229–31
overflow: (1) in an arithmetic operation, the portion of a positive quantity exceeding the capacity of the register or storage area in which the result is to be stored; (2) the generation of overflow as in (1). *Contrast with* underflow: 153
overlapped processing: a technique whereby reading and internal processing, writing and internal processing, or reading, writing, and internal processing can occur simultaneously: 165, 315

P

page description language (PDL): a set of device-independent commands used to describe the characteristics of output. An example is PostScript. *Contrast with* printer control language: 93–94
page printer: 85
paging: the process of breaking data or program coding into fixed-size blocks, or pages, and loading the pages into real storage when needed during processing: 325–26
paper tape: a ribbonlike strip of paper in which a pattern of holes or cuts is used to represent data: 57
parallel adder: 154–55
parallel operation: pertaining to the simultaneous processing of individual parts of a whole, such as the bits of a character or the characters of a word, using separate facilities for the parts. *Contrast with* serial operation: 154–55, 160–62
Pascal: 289–92, 319
password: 47, 435
patenting (to protect software): 424
payback period: 223
PBX: *See* private branch exchange.
PC DOS: the operating system developed for use with IBM Personal Computers: 195, 196, 310, 328. *See also* MS-DOS.
pen plotter: 95–96, 97
personal computer: a microcomputer acquired for individual use: 31, 184–97. *See also* microcomputer.
PET: the first ready-to-use, fully assembled microcomputer marketed to consumers, by Commodore Business Machines, in 1976: 190
picosecond: one trillionth of one second: 158
pixel: picture element; a minute dot, thousands or millions of which, together, form an image: 94–95
PL/I (Programming Language I): a high-level programming language designed to facilitate the preparation of computer programs to perform both business and scientific processing: 286–88
plotter: a device that produces graphic output by automatic movements of a pencil or pen or by electrostatic means: 44, 94–97
pocket computer: *Also called* a handheld computer: 180–81
point-of-sale (POS) terminal: a cash-register-like I/O device: 73–74, 319
polling: a systematic, periodic testing of each I/O device on a system to find out whether or not it needs servicing (i.e., has I/O to do): 164
portable computer: 75. *See also* lap-top portable computer; transportable computer.
portable software: 260, 292, 295, 327–31
portable terminal: a hand-carriable I/O device that can be used to collect and transmit data to a computer from remote locations: 44, 75–76, 79
PostScript: a page description language developed by Adobe Systems for use in desktop publishing: 93–94.
preliminary investigation: *Synonymous with* feasibility study.
primary storage: the general-purpose storage of a computer, into which both data and instructions to perform operations on that data must be stored prior to processing. *Synonymous with* internal storage unit; main storage; memory; real storage: 41–42, 110–121
printer: a device capable of printing characters on paper or other media; may be a serial, line, or page printer, further characterized as impact or nonimpact, depending upon whether printing is accomplished by the action of print hammers against a surface or by thermal, electrical, ink-jet, xerographic, or similar means: 44, 84–94
printer control language (PCL): a machine-specific set of commands used to control printer output. *Contrast with* page description language: 93
privacy (and the computer): 411–16
private branch exchange (PBX): 375
private line: a communication channel and channel equipment furnished to a customer for exclusive use; also referred to as a leased line. *Contrast with* public line: 373–75
problem-oriented language: a programming language designed to facilitate solution of a particular type of problem, such as string processing, report generation, or the control of a machine tool. Examples are SNOBOL, RPG, and ADAPT. *Contrast with* procedure-oriented language; machine-oriented language. *Note:* Use of this term is sometimes extended to include procedure-oriented languages as a general group in contrast to machine-oriented languages: 276
procedure-oriented language: a programming language designed to facilitate description of data-processing or computational processes in terms of procedural or algorithmic steps. Examples are BASIC, COBOL, FORTRAN, and PL/I. *Contrast with* problem-oriented language; machine-oriented language: 276

processing: in data processing, to read, manipulate, or perform other operations in accordance with some algorithm (in electronic data processing, the algorithm is generally expressed as a computer program): 32–35, 144–72
processor: (1) the portion of an electronic data-processing system that contains the circuits which control the interpretation and execution of instructions; (2) the control section and the arithmetic/logic unit of a computer; frequently primary storage is also considered a part of the CPU. *Synonymous with* central processing unit (CPU): 41–43, 147–48, 318. *See also* microprocessor.
processor unit: the physical component of an EDP system that houses the processor (arithmetic/logic unit and control section) and, usually, the internal storage unit: 41–43, 147–49
productivity: the rate of finished output per unit of labor input: 5, 225, 294–95, 321, 336
program: a sequence of instructions that directs the computer to perform specific operations to achieve a desired result (often, the solution to a specific problem); it may consist of one or several modules or routines, each of which may be composed of several subroutines: 7, 35–37
program flowchart: a detailed pictorial representation of the steps necessary to solve a problem. *Also called* a block diagram or logic diagram. *Contrast with* system flowchart: 241–43, 245–47, 255–56, 469–85
programmed control: a security mechanism set up within the computer itself by means of stored-program instructions; examples are techniques for access management and various types of input edit routines: 420
programmer: a person who defines the solution to a problem and writes instructions to the computer to implement that solution. A programmer who also participates in system analysis and design may be called a programmer/analyst: 25–26, 36, 227, 249
programming language: a language used in writing programs to direct processing steps carried out by a computer: 270–99. *See also* high-level programming language; low-level programming language.
program stub: 260
program trace: 260
program trading: computerized buying and selling of stocks: 18
project review: 235–36
prompt: a message provided to guide the user during processing: 47–49, 244, 294, 440, 451–53
proper program: a structured program with only one entry point and one exit point, and, for every contained control structure, a path from entry to exit that includes it: 255
protected mode: 121
prototype: 230, 250
pseudocode: an informal design language that is especially suitable for planning structured programs: 255–57, 469–85
public line: a communication channel and channel equipment shared by a number of users of common-carrier facilities; often referred to as a switched or dial-up line, since line-switching techniques are used to establish paths for communication. *Contrast with* private line: 372, 375
public utilities commission (PUC): a state agency that has, as one of its tasks, communication regulation responsibilities: 376
punched cards: 55–57
punched paper tape: 57

R

RAM (random-access memory): (1) storage whose contents may be changed many times during processing. *Contrast with* ROM: 110–111, 179; (2) as commonly used, same as semiconductor storage: 119
RAMAC: 137
random-access storage: *Synonymous with* direct storage.
random processing: *Synonymous with* direct processing.
raster graphics: bit-mapped graphics: 100
read-only memory (ROM): storage whose contents cannot be changed by stored-program instructions; it generally contains nonalterable programs and data. *Contrast with* RAM: 37–39, 111, 149, 179
read/write head: a small electromagnetic component used for reading, writing, or erasing the polarized spots that represent data on magnetic tape, disk, or similar storage media: 129–31, 132–35
real mode: 121
real storage: the primary-storage space that actually exists in a computer system, from which the control section of the processor can directly obtain instructions and data, and to which it can directly return results. *Synonymous with* primary storage. *Contrast with* virtual storage: 324
real-time processing: the capability of a fast-response online system to obtain data from an activity or a physical process, perform computations, and return a response rapidly enough to affect the outcome of the activity or process: 319–20, 321
record: a group of related data items; for example, in inventory control, one line of an invoice constitutes an item, a complete invoice constitutes a record, and the complete set of records constitutes a file: 123
reduced instruction set computing (RISC): a design philosophy that favors a small set of simple instructions optimized for performance: 169–72, 199
register: an internal computer component capable of storing a specified amount of data and accepting or transferring that data very rapidly: 150–53, 167, 274–75. *See also* accumulator; address register; general-purpose register; operation-code register; storage register.
relational data model: 349–50
remote batch: 391–93
remote databases: 359–60
remote job entry (RJE): 393
remote terminal: an I/O device that is operated at a distance from the central computer facility: 72–79, 369
response time: (1) in an online system, the interval between completion of input and start of output from an EDP system: 319; (2) loosely, turnaround time.
RISC: *See* reduced instruction set computing.
Robogate: 405
robotic system: a general-purpose programmable machine that can do any of several tasks under stored-program control. *Also called* a robot: 7–9, 319, 404–407
ROM: *See* read-only memory.

rotational delay: the time required to position a particular record below an activated read/write head on a direct-access storage device. *Also called* latency: 134–35
RPG (Report Program Generator): a high-level programming language designed primarily to construct programs that perform report-writing functions: 293–94

S

SABRE (Semi-Automatic Business Research Environment): an online direct-access system developed jointly by American Airlines and IBM to provide timely processing of airlines data: 312–13, 321
satellite communications: 377, 378–79, 390
scanner: an input device that converts hard-copy data to a form acceptable to a computer through optical character recognition (OCR) or image scanning techniques: 44, 55, 64–65
secondary storage: storage that supplements primary storage. *Also called* auxiliary storage: 41, 110–111, 123–39, 179
secondary-storage device: an input/output unit used for temporary or intermediate storage of programs and data. *Also called* an auxiliary-storage device: 43, 124, 179
security (of a computer system): 419–21, 427–29
segmentation: the process of breaking a program into logically separable units, or segments, and loading the segments into real storage when needed during processing: 325–26
selection: choosing from among alternatives: 251–57, 469–72. *See also* CASE control structure; IFTHENELSE basic pattern.
semiconductor: a small two-state component having an electrical conductivity that lies between the high conductivity of metals and the conductivity of insulators; semiconductor elements include transistors and crystal diodes: 119
semiconductor storage: storage constructed of semiconductor elements that serve as binary components for purposes of data representation. *Also called* random-access memory (RAM): 119, 179
separate pricing: a policy of charging for certain hardware and software components, education, and maintenance services independently, apart from the basic EDP-system hardware and (in most cases) the major system control and some basic system utility programs: 316
sequential file organization: 340–42
sequential processing: a technique for handling data, one item or record after the other, that generally requires preliminary sorting of transaction files, which are then processed against master files on which data is also stored sequentially. Generally, sequential processing is also batch processing. *Contrast with* direct storage: 124–26, 129
sequential storage: storage media to which data is written, or from which data is read, in a serial (one-after-the-other) fashion, starting at the beginning of a file and continuing in sequence. *Contrast with* direct storage: 123
serial adder: 154–55
serial operation: pertaining to the sequential processing of individual parts of a whole, such as the bits of a character or the characters of a word, using the same facilities for successive parts. *Contrast with* parallel operation: 154–55, 160–62
serial printer: 85
server node: *See* database server.
shared processor: 58–60
sign-off procedure: 49–50
sign-on procedure: 45–47, 434–35
SIMPLE SEQUENCE basic pattern: 251–57, 469
simplex transmission: 372
simulation: (1) representation of the functioning of one system by another; for example, representing a computer or a physical system by the execution of a computer program, or a biological system by a mathematical model: 4–5, 10, 22, 46, 188, 331; (2) same as desk checking: 242–43
site autonomy: 360
small business system: 31
smart terminal: an I/O device that provides for data entry and information exit and has limited data editing capabilities. *Contrast with* dumb terminal; intelligent terminal: 368
social dependency: 424–30
social vulnerability: 424–30
soft copy: a temporary, or nonpermanent, record of machine output; for example, a CRT display. *Contrast with* hard copy: 83–84, 453
software: (1) a collection of programs, routines, and subroutines that facilitate the programming and operation of a computer; (2) as in (1), but also including documentation and operational procedures. *Contrast with* hardware: 36–37, 180, 202, 302–331
software piracy: 418–19
software publishing: 27, 249
software quality: 260, 263, 267
solid modeling: 11
source data automation: the capture of data in a machine-readable form at the place where it is generated: 54–55. *See also* magnetic-ink character recognition; optical character recognition; voice input.
source document: 54
source-level debugging: 262
source program: a program written in a programming language such as COBOL, FORTRAN, or PL/I for input to a language processor (such as an assembler or compiler). *Contrast with* object program: 276–77, 280–81
source-program listing: a printed output of a compilation, showing the source-program statements as they were provided as input and other information useful to the programmer: 280–81
specialized common carrier: a company that furnishes communication services under the regulation of local, state, or federal agencies, generally by providing enhancements or special features to tailor common-carrier communication offerings to specific user needs: 377
speech synthesizer: 100–102
SQL: *See* Structured Query Language.
stacked-job processing: *Synonymous with* batch processing.
start/stop tape drive: 130
start/stop transmission: *Synonymous with* asynchronous transmission.
storage: pertaining to a device into which data can be entered and retained, and from which data can be retrieved at a later time: 108–141. *See also* primary storage; secondary storage.
storage capacity: 114–15

storage register: a register to which an instruction is moved (from primary storage) when the instruction is to be interpreted and executed by the computer. *Also called* an input/output buffer or a data register: 151, 167
streaming tape drive: 130–31
structure chart: a pictorial representation of the logical structure of a program or system; a tree diagram: 233–34, 250
structured design: *See* top-down design.
structured programming: a top-down, modular approach to program development that emphasizes certain basic patterns and control structures, and short one-entry-point/one-exit-point modules: 251–54, 285–86, 287, 292, 469–95
Structured Query Language (SQL): a database sublanguage used to define, manipulate, and control access to data in relational databases: 352–54, 361
structured walkthrough: a formalized defect removal technique in which reviewers go step-by-step through design or code; a formal design review or formal code inspection: 235, 259
stylus: a penlike device used with a graphics tablet, or digitizer: 72
supercomputer: 177–78
synchronous operations: events occurring at regular, timed intervals. *Contrast with* asynchronous operations: 164–65
synchronous transmission: a method of electrical transfer in which a constant time interval is maintained between successive bits or characters. Equipment within the system is kept in step on the basis of this timing. *Contrast with* asynchronous transmission: 371–72
syntax: 276, 439
system: a set of interrelated elements that work together to perform a specific task or function: 210–11, 212
system analysis: the study of an existing task or function in order to understand it and to find better ways to accomplish it: 211–26, 239, 240–41
system analyst: a person who works with current or potential users of a system to understand their particular application requirements or information needs: 25, 213, 227
system commands: 48–49, 310, 435–37
system design: the creation of a detailed plan for the purpose of developing a new or improved system: 211, 226–36, 239, 240–41
system designer: a person who responds to particular user application requirements or information needs by creating a design, or plan, for a system that will satisfy them: 25, 213–14, 227
system development cycle: 211–13, 294
system evaluation: 211, 239, 264–68
system flowchart: a general, over-all diagram that shows the data flow and the operational sequence of a given system. *Contrast with* program flowchart: 228–29, 241, 245
system implementation: 211, 239, 241–45
system proposal: 225
system software: programs that direct the computer in performing tasks that are basic to proper functioning of the system or are commonly needed by system users: 36, 275, 304–305, 309

T

Tandy/Radio Shack: 20, 180, 181, 184, 190–91, 203
telecommunication: the transmission of information over long distances by telegraph, radio, or other electromagnetic means: 366
telecommuting: 402–404
teleconferencing: a specialized communication service offering designed to facilitate remote group communication: 389–91
teleprinter: 87
teleprocessing: an activity involving both data-processing and telecommunications functions: 366
teleprocessing system: a system in which data is collected at one or more points of origin, transmitted to a central location, and processed to produce results that are distributed to one or more points of use. *Synonymous with* data-communication system: 366
teller terminal: a special-purpose I/O device used by banking-industry employees to interact with their computer systems when serving customers. *Contrast with* automated teller machine: 73–74, 228–29
terminal: a point (or device) in a system or communication network at which data can enter or exit: 42–44, 368–69. *See also* remote terminal.
testing: the running of a program or system of programs against representative data to insure the adequacy of the program or system for regular use: 233, 259–60, 262–63, 267, 439–40. *See also* top-down testing.
text processing: *Synonymous with* word processing.
thermal printer: 89–90, 97
The Source: 24, 359
third-generation language: 272, 293
third party: an independent consultant, software development firm, or equipment manufacturer who markets to, or assists, a computer-using organization: 330
thrashing: the continual movement of pages or segments from virtual storage to real storage because of reference to program coding or data that is not in real storage during processing: 326
throughput: (1) the rate at which work can be handled by an EDP system; (2) the total volume of useful work performed by a system over a given period of time: 310
time sharing: a technique or system for supplying computing services to a number of users at geographically scattered terminals, providing rapid responses so that each user appears to be the only one using the system: 288, 320–24, 393
top-down design: planning a system or program by using an approach of functional decomposition—looking first at the major function, then at its subfunctions, and so on, until the scope and details of the system or program (solution algorithm) are fully understood: 231–33
top-down development: an approach to program development that encompasses top-down design, top-down programming, and top-down testing: 231–33, 285
top-down programming: coding a program in the top-down manner specified in its design: 233, 250
top-down testing: checking out a system or program, beginning with the top-level module, and continuing with lower levels of modules until all portions of the system or program have been checked out: 233, 260
touch-sensitive screen: 71–72
trace: documentation of specified events and of the sequence in which those events occur during the execution of a program: 260

track: the portion of a storage medium such as a tape or disk that is accessible to a given position of a read/write head: 128–29, 132–33
trademark: 422
trade secret: 422
train printer: 87–88
transaction: (1) in a terminal-oriented system, the system representation of a user communication with the system; (2) an input to an EDP system, causing the system to do useful work; (3) in some EDP systems, a recognizable logical unit of work, for recovery purposes: 54–55, 124–27
transaction file: a file containing relatively transient information; for example, records of individual transactions occurring during one day in an inventory-control application. *Synonymous with* detail file. *Contrast with* master file: 124–27
transaction processing: the handling of individual inputs (transactions) as they are generated, without preliminary sorting or editing and without collecting them into batches. *Contrast with* batch processing: 54–55, 64, 228–29, 312–13, 318
transportable computer: a relatively large portable computer: 181
tree diagram: *Synonymous with* structure chart.
TRS-80 microcomputer: 180, 181, 190–91. *See also* home computer; microcomputer; personal computer.
trunk line: 373
turnaround file: 124–25
turnaround time: the elapsed time between submission of a job to a computer center and receiving of output: 57, 382
turnkey system: a ready-to-go computer system installed for customer use: 393

U

unconditional branch: an instruction that always causes a transfer from the normal sequence of instruction execution; loosely, a GO TO. *Contrast with* conditional branch: 159, 466–67
underflow: (1) in an arithmetic operation, the portion of a negative quantity exceeding the capacity of the register or storage area in which the result is to be stored; (2) the generation of underflow as in (1). *Contrast with* overflow: 153
uninterruptible power system (UPS): 427
UNIVAC I: 40–41, 63
Universal Product Code (UPC): a standardized bar code that can be read by OCR devices: 64–65
UNIX: a multitasking, multiple-user (time-sharing) system developed at Bell Labs to create a favorable environment for programming research and development: 171, 182, 190, 199, 292, 315, 328–30
user-programmer: a person who is not a programmer by profession but nevertheless interacts directly with the computer to enter data and instructions, and receive results: 276
utility program: a general-purpose routine that performs some activity required in most EDP systems such as transferring files from punched cards to magnetic tape or preparing direct-access storage media for use in subsequent processing: 305

V

value-added carrier: a firm that is authorized to offer a communication service derived by enhancing (adding value to) a common-carrier offering; for example, the service may be based on leased common-carrier communication channels: 377–78
value-added network (VAN): a communication service offering based on leased common-carrier communication channels that are enhanced to improve (add value to) the service, for example, through specialized switching facilities. Examples are Telenet and Tymnet: 377–78, 389
value-added reseller (VAR): 203–205
variable: a name, or label, whose value may be changed many times, during processing. *Contrast with* constant: 274, 438, 444–45
variable-length operation: pertaining to an operation in which operands may consist of a variable number of bits or characters. *Contrast with* fixed-length operation: 162
variable-length word: 162
vector graphics: object-oriented graphics: 100
verifier: a device used to check the correctness of card-punch operations: 56
video digitizer: an input device that can capture live or recorded images and convert them to a form acceptable as input to a computer: 68
video game: 23, 184, 187
videotex: the delivery of information from computerized files and databases over cable or telephone lines for display on TV screens in homes and offices: 186–87, 359, 415
virtual machine: a computer system—both hardware and software—that does not in actual fact exist but provides functions similar to those of the system it imitates: 326–28
virtual storage: addressable space that appears to the user as real storage, provided through a combination of hardware and software techniques, generally to effect increased primary-storage capacity. *Synonymous with* virtual memory. *Contrast with* real storage: 43, 324–26
virus: 416–17
vision system: 409
visual-display unit: a televisionlike output device: 70, 95–100
voice-input unit: 68–69, 409
voice-mail system: 388
voice output: 100–102
volatile storage: 119, 179

W

wait state: 168
wand reader: a handheld OCR input device containing photoelectric cells that convert reflected light beams to machine-readable code: 44, 64, 77–78
Winchester disk drive: a direct-access storage device in which not only the disks but also the vertical shaft, access mechanism, and read/write heads are enclosed in a sealed cartridge to achieve high recording density and reliability: 136–37
window: a portion of a display screen used for computer-user interaction independently of the rest of the screen: 72, 192, 315–17
wire-matrix printer: *Also called* dot-matrix printer: 87–89

word-addressable: pertaining to a computer that performs operations on fixed-length words. *Contrast with* character-addressable: 164

word processing: the manipulation of certain types of data (characters combined to form words, sentences, paragraphs, memos, letters, reports). *Synonymous with* text processing: 24, 60–61, 66, 67, 182, 307, 316, 383

workstation: *Also called* a desktop computer or an office computer: 170–71, 191, 198–200, 226, 381–82. *See also* microcomputer.

WORM: *See* write once, read many device.

write once, read many (WORM) device: 138–39

WYSIWYG: what-you-see-is-what-you-get; the contents of the visual-display screen matches printer output: 100, 384

xerographic printer: *Also called* an electrophotographic printer: 91, 97